High Performance Compilers for Parallel Computing

High Performance Compilers for Parallel Computing

MICHAEL WOLFE

Oregon Graduate Institute of Science & Technology

Addison-Wesley Publishing Company
Redwood City, California · Menlo Park, California · Reading, Massachusetts · New York
Don Mills, · Ontario · Wokingham, U.K. · Amsterdam · Bonn · Sydney · Singapore · Tokyo
Madrid · San Juan · Paris · Seoul · Milan · Mexico City · Taipei

Sponsoring Editor: J. Carter Shanklin
Executive Editor: Dan Joraanstad
Production Editor: Ray Kanarr
Editorial Assistant: Melissa Standen
Cover Design: Cloyce Wall
Text Design: Peter Vacek, Eigentype Compositors
Composition: Electronic Technical Publishing Services
Copy Editing and Proofreading: Elizabeth Gehrman

©1996 by Addison-Wesley Publishing Company, Inc.

All rights reserved. No part of this publication may be reproduced, or stored in a database or retrieval system, or transmitted, in any form or by any means, electronic, mechanical, photocopying, recording, or otherwise, without the prior written permission of the publisher. Printed in the United States of America. Published simultaneously in Canada.

The programs and the applications presented in this book have been included for their instructional value. They have been tested with care but are not guaranteed for any particular purpose. The publisher does not offer any warranties or representations, nor does it accept any liabilities with respect to the programs or applications.

Library of Congress Cataloging-in-Publication Data
Wolfe, Michael Joseph, 1954–
    High Performance Compilers for Parallel Computing / Michael Wolfe.
      p.   cm.
    Includes bibliographic references and index.
    ISBN 0-8053-2730-4
    1. Parallel processing (Electronic computers) 2. Compilers
(Computer programs) I. Title.
QA76.58.W62 1995
005.4'53—dc20   94-24588
                                                                                           CIP

ISBN 0-8053-2730-4

1 2 3 4 5 6 7 8 9 10 – DOCR – 99 98 97 96 95

Addison-Wesley Publishing Company
390 Bridge Parkway
Redwood City, CA 94065

CONTENTS

PREFACE		**xv**
1	**HIGH PERFORMANCE SYSTEMS**	**1**
1.1	An Example Program: Matrix Multiplication	3
	1.1.1 Scalar Architecture	3
	1.1.2 Vector Architecture	8
	1.1.3 Multiprocessor Architecture	13
	1.1.4 SIMD Architecture	16
	1.1.5 Message-Passing Multicomputer Architecture	19
	1.1.6 Compound Architectures	21
1.2	Structure of a Compiler	22
	1.2.1 Preserving Program Behavior	23
	1.2.2 User Interface	24
1.3	In the Pit	25
1.4	Further Reading	26
	Exercises	26
2	**PROGRAMMING LANGUAGE FEATURES**	**31**
2.1	Languages for High Performance	31
	2.1.1 Fortran and C	31
	2.1.2 High Performance Fortran	37
	2.1.3 Declarative Languages	39
2.2	Sequential and Parallel Loops	40
2.3	Roundoff Error	44
2.4	In the Pit	45
2.5	Further Reading	46
	Exercises	47
3	**BASIC GRAPH CONCEPTS**	**49**
3.1	Sets, Tuples, Logic	49

v

3.2	Graphs		50
	3.2.1	Trees	53
	3.2.2	The Control Flow Graph	56
	3.2.3	Spanning Trees	56
	3.2.4	Finding Cycles in Directed Graphs	60
	3.2.5	Dominators	64
	3.2.6	Dominance Frontier	68
	3.2.7	Postdominators	69
3.3	Control Dependence		71
	3.3.1	Labeled Control Dependence Edges	74
	3.3.2	Data Structure for Control Dependence	74
	3.3.3	Single-Exit Control Flow Graphs	78
3.4	Further Reading		79
	Exercises		80

4 REVIEW OF LINEAR ALGEBRA — 84

4.1	Real Vectors and Matrices		84
	4.1.1	Matrices	87
4.2	Integer Matrices and Lattices		93
	4.2.1	Integer Matrices	96
	4.2.2	Hermite Normal Form	97
	4.2.3	Lattices	98
4.3	Linear System of Equations		100
4.4	System of Integer Equations		106
	4.4.1	Single Equation	106
	4.4.2	Many Unknowns	108
	4.4.3	Many Equations	114
4.5	Systems of Linear Inequalities		117
	4.5.1	Fourier-Motzkin Projection	119
	4.5.2	Solution Procedure	123
4.6	Systems of Integer Linear Inequalities		123
	4.6.1	Dark Shadows	126
	4.6.2	Solution Procedure	128
4.7	Extreme Values of Affine Functions		129
	4.7.1	Nonrectangular Regions	130
4.8	In the Pit		132
4.9	Further Reading		133
	Exercises		133

5 DATA DEPENDENCE — 137

- 5.1 Data Dependence in Loops — 139
  - 5.1.1 Iteration Space — 141
  - 5.1.2 Iteration Vectors — 141
  - 5.1.3 Dependence Distances — 142
  - 5.1.4 Direction Vectors — 144
  - 5.1.5 Loop-Carried Dependence Relations — 145
  - 5.1.6 More About Iteration Vectors — 147
  - 5.1.7 Nontightly Nested Loops — 149
- 5.2 Data Dependence with Conditionals — 153
  - 5.2.1 Conditionals in Loops — 154
- 5.3 Data Dependence in Parallel Loops — 155
  - 5.3.1 Forall Loop — 155
  - 5.3.2 Dopar Loop — 156
  - 5.3.3 Dosingle Loop — 157
  - 5.3.4 Other Constructs — 158
  - 5.3.5 Nested Loops — 159
- 5.4 Program Dependence Graph — 159
- 5.5 In the Pit — 160
- 5.6 Further Reading — 162
- Exercises — 162

6 SCALAR ANALYSIS WITH FACTORED USE-DEF CHAINS — 166

- 6.1 Constructing Factored Use-Def Chains — 169
  - 6.1.1 Join Sets — 170
  - 6.1.2 Equivalence to Iterated Dominance Frontier — 173
  - 6.1.3 ϕ-Term Placement Algorithm — 174
  - 6.1.4 FUD Chaining Algorithm — 176
- 6.2 FUD Chains for Arrays — 180
- 6.3 Finding All Reaching Definitions — 182
- 6.4 Implicit References in FUD Chains — 183
  - 6.4.1 Input/Output — 183
  - 6.4.2 Procedure Calling — 184
  - 6.4.3 Aliases — 185
- 6.5 Induction Variables Using FUD Chains — 191
  - 6.5.1 Classifying Cycles — 192
  - 6.5.2 Wrap-Around Variables — 199

		6.5.3	Trip Counts	200
		6.5.4	Nested Loops	202
	6.6	Constant Propagation with FUD Chains		204
	6.7	Data Dependence for Scalars		210
		6.7.1	Output Dependence	215
		6.7.2	Anti-Dependence	216
	6.8	In the Pit		218
	6.9	Further Reading		219
		Exercises		219
7	**DATA DEPENDENCE ANALYSIS FOR ARRAYS**			**224**
	7.1	Building the Dependence System		225
		7.1.1	Loop Limit Constraints	226
		7.1.2	Symbolic Analysis	227
		7.1.3	Other Complications	229
	7.2	Dependence System Solvers		233
		7.2.1	Single Equation	233
		7.2.2	Multiple Equations	241
		7.2.3	Linear Combinations	243
		7.2.4	Splitting a Dependence Equation	244
	7.3	General Solver		246
		7.3.1	Adding Inequality Constraints	247
	7.4	Summary of Solvers		249
	7.5	Complications		250
		7.5.1	Storage Association	250
		7.5.2	Dynamically Allocated Arrays	254
	7.6	Run-Time Dependence Testing		254
	7.7	In the Pit		255
	7.8	Further Reading		256
		Exercises		257
8	**OTHER DEPENDENCE PROBLEMS**			**260**
	8.1	Array Region Analysis		260
		8.1.1	Constructing Array Regions	262
		8.1.2	Simple Bounds	266

		8.1.3	Triplet Notation	271
		8.1.4	Array Kill Analysis	273
	8.2	Pointer Analysis		277
		8.2.1	Points-To Analysis	277
		8.2.2	Array Pointers	283
		8.2.3	Dynamic Data Structures	285
		8.2.4	Pointer Arithmetic	286
		8.2.5	Allocation Dependence	287
	8.3	I/O Dependence		288
	8.4	Procedure Calls		288
	8.5	Interprocedural Analysis		289
		8.5.1	Call Graph Construction	290
		8.5.2	Interprocedural MOD Information	292
		8.5.3	Interprocedural Constant Propagation	299
	8.6	In the Pit		303
	8.7	Further Reading		304
		Exercises		304

9 LOOP RESTRUCTURING   307

	9.1	Simple Transformations		308
		9.1.1	Statement Reordering	308
		9.1.2	Unswitching	310
		9.1.3	Loop Peeling	311
		9.1.4	Index Set Splitting	312
		9.1.5	Scalar Expansion	313
	9.2	Loop Fusion		315
		9.2.1	Array Assignments	316
		9.2.2	Complications	318
		9.2.3	Fusing Parallel Loops	320
		9.2.4	Loop Alignment	322
		9.2.5	Fusion with Scalars	322
	9.3	Loop Fission		323
		9.3.1	Fission with Conditionals	325
		9.3.2	Nested Loops	326
		9.3.3	Fission Algorithm	328
		9.3.4	Fission for Parallel Loops	329
	9.4	Loop Reversal		330

9.5	Loop Interchanging		331
	9.5.1	Tightly Nested Loops	332
	9.5.2	Interchanging with Parallel Loops	333
	9.5.3	Multiple Interchanges	334
	9.5.4	Loop Limits	335
	9.5.5	Nontightly Nested Loops	337
	9.5.6	Interactions with Other Loop Transformations	340
9.6	Loop Skewing		341
9.7	Linear Loop Transformations		344
	9.7.1	Nonunimodular Transformations	347
9.8	Strip-Mining		350
9.9	Loop Tiling		352
9.10	Other Loop Transformations		356
	9.10.1	Circular Loop Skewing	356
	9.10.2	Striping	357
	9.10.3	Loop Collapsing	358
9.11	Interprocedural Transformations		360
	9.11.1	Procedure Inlining	360
	9.11.2	Loop Embedding and Extraction	361
9.12	In the Pit		362
9.13	Further Reading		362
	Exercises		363

10 OPTIMIZING FOR LOCALITY — 367

10.1	Single Reference to Each Array		368
	10.1.1	Tiling	369
	10.1.2	Quantifying Reuse	370
	10.1.3	Other Considerations	375
10.2	Multiple References		376
	10.2.1	Reducing the Reuse Distance	378
	10.2.2	Reordering Loops for Locality	379
10.3	General Tiling		380
10.4	Fission and Fusion for Locality		381
10.5	In the Pit		382
10.6	Further Reading		382
	Exercises		383

11 CONCURRENCY ANALYSIS — 385

11.1 Code for Concurrent Loops — 385
- 11.1.1 Scheduling Policies — 387
- 11.1.2 Nested Concurrent Loops — 392
- 11.1.3 Private Variables — 392
- 11.1.4 Reductions — 392
- 11.1.5 Synchronization for Dependence — 393
- 11.1.6 Procedure Calls — 398
- 11.1.7 Strength Reduction — 399

11.2 Concurrency from Sequential Loops — 399
- 11.2.1 Handling Scalars — 400
- 11.2.2 Loop Carried Dependence Relations — 402

11.3 Concurrency from Parallel Loops — 409
- 11.3.1 Other Parallel Loops — 410

11.4 Nested Loops — 411
- 11.4.1 Synchronization — 411
- 11.4.2 Transformations — 413
- 11.4.3 Tiling — 416
- 11.4.4 Optimizing Performance — 416

11.5 Roundoff Error — 417

11.6 Exceptions and Debuggers — 418

11.7 In the Pit — 418

11.8 Further Reading — 419

Exercises — 420

12 VECTOR ANALYSIS — 422

12.1 Vector Code — 422
- 12.1.1 Conditionals — 423
- 12.1.2 Reductions — 424

12.2 Vector Code from Sequential Loops — 425
- 12.2.1 Handling Scalars — 426
- 12.2.2 Dependence Cycles — 427
- 12.2.3 Loop Fission with Temporaries — 428
- 12.2.4 Vectorization Despite Cycles — 430

12.3 Vector Code from `Forall` Loops — 438

12.4 Nested Loops — 439
- 12.4.1 Loop Interchanging — 440

12.5	Roundoff Error, Exceptions, and Debuggers	443
12.6	Multivector Computers	443
12.7	In the Pit	444
12.8	Further Reading	445
	Exercises	445

13 MESSAGE-PASSING MACHINES — 448

13.1	SIMD Machines	448
	13.1.1 SIMD Code	449
13.2	MIMD Machines	451
	13.2.1 SPDD Code	452
13.3	Data Layout	452
	13.3.1 Alignment to Templates	454
	13.3.2 Replication	456
	13.3.3 Distribution of Templates	458
	13.3.4 Local Memory Layout	458
13.4	Parallel Code for Array Assignments	462
	13.4.1 SIMD Context Computation	464
	13.4.2 Multicomputer Code	470
13.5	Remote Data Access	478
	13.5.1 Regular Communication	480
	13.5.2 Communication Optimizations	492
	13.5.3 Communication Patterns	496
	13.5.4 Irregular Communication	500
	13.5.5 Dynamic Alignments	502
13.6	Automatic Data Layout	503
13.7	Multiple Array Assignments	504
13.8	Other Topics	505
	13.8.1 Conditionals	505
	13.8.2 Reductions	506
	13.8.3 Pipelining Sequential Loops	506
	13.8.4 Multiple Templates	508

	13.9	In the Pit	509
	13.10	Further Reading	509
		Exercises	510
14	**SCALABLE SHARED-MEMORY MACHINES**		**514**
	14.1	Global Cache Coherence	515
		14.1.1 Affinity Scheduling	515
		14.1.2 Reduced Write Sharing	517
		14.1.3 Sharing Patterns	519
		14.1.4 Hierarchical Systems	520
	14.2	Local Cache Coherence	520
		14.2.1 Cache Policies	521
		14.2.2 Stale Cache Lines	522
		14.2.3 Local Cache Coherence Schemes	523
		14.2.4 Other Schemes	524
	14.3	Latency-Tolerant Machines	525
	14.4	Further Reading	526
		Exercises	527
GLOSSARY			**528**
REFERENCES			**547**
AUTHOR INDEX			**558**
INDEX			**560**

PREFACE

Techniques for constructing compilers for parallel computers have been developed in academic and commercial environments over the past 30 years. Some of these techniques are now quite mature and in common use, but there is still much active research in this area. Most of the reference material is scattered over many conference proceedings and journals. This book is intended to serve as coherent presentation of the important basic ideas used in modern compilers for parallel computer systems. It can be used as a reference or as a text for a second or third course on compilers at the senior undergraduate or graduate level.

This book differs from previous collections in that its focus is not the automatic discovery of parallelism from sequential programs, though that is also included. Instead, its focus is techniques to generate optimized parallel code, given the source program and target architecture. The optimizer in high performance compilers is organized as a deep analysis phase followed by a code generation, or synthesis, phase. This book follows that organization.

The first chapter introduces the material and takes one example program through several stages of optimization for a variety of target machines. Each target architecture is presented at a high level, and is modeled after current commercial machines.

Chapter 2 discusses programming language issues. Of particular interest are the parallel language extensions proposed for various languages, such as array assignments in Fortran 90, the `forall` statement in High Performance Fortran, and other parallel loop constructs.

Chapters 3 and 4 introduce basic analysis algorithms that are in common use in compilers. Chapter 3 focuses on algorithms for graphs, which are used in compilers to represent control flow, interprocedural calls, and dependence. Chapter 4 discusses various aspects of linear algebra, which is becoming more important in compilers, including subjects such as solving linear and integer systems of equations and inequalities.

Chapters 5 through 8 cover aspects of the analysis phase of the optimizer. Chapter 5 presents the basic ideas behind data dependence relations, as used in compilers. In order to allow the most freedom in reordering and optimizing a program, compilers find dependence relations between program statements that cannot be violated without changing the meaning of the program.

Chapter 6 discussed various aspects of scalar analysis that are important for parallel computing, such as constant propagation and precise data dependence analysis for scalars, In particular, induction variable detection is important for array analysis.

Chapter 7 shows how to use the linear algebra techniques from Chapter 4 to find data dependence relations between array references. Because the linear algebra appears separately, this chapter is somewhat shorter than such a chapter might be in other books on the subject.

Chapter 8 discusses other problems related to dependence analysis, such as summarizing array accesses across procedural boundaries, solving data dependence analysis problems in the presence of pointers and I/O, and so forth.

Chapter 9 details the techniques used in the restructuring phase of creating the optimizer, focusing on loop structuring techniques. A catalogue of loop optimizations is presented, along with examples to show effects on performance.

Chapters 10 through 14 show how to tailor the code generation for various target architectures. Chapter 10 discusses a sequential target machine in which the compiler restructures the program to take advantage of a memory hierarchy (typically one or more levels of processor cache memory).

Chapter 11 presents methods to generate code and optimize for shared-memory parallel computers, which are now becoming common even at the workstation level. Automatic discovery of parallelism is also discussed.

Chapter 12 shows how to apply similar techniques for vector instruction sets, including automatic vectorization and supervector code generation.

Chapter 13 presents code generation methods for massively parallel message-passing computer systems, of both the SIMD and MIMD variety.

Chapter 14 shows techniques for massively parallel shared-memory systems. Different methods are used for the three varieties of machines in this category, depending on whether processor cache memories are kept consistent using global information or local information, or are absent altogether.

Each chapter includes a section titled "In the Pit," which includes hints and other anecdotal material that may be of some use when applying the information covered in the chapter. A "Further Reading" section contains citations to the original material in the reference list, and the exercises can be used as assignments or to test comprehension of the material.

Additional material that has proved useful for teaching is available via anonymous FTP from the machine bc.aw.com in the directory bc/wolfe/highperform. This material includes Postscript copies of the figures, programs implementing many of the algorithms, and the Tiny loop restructuring tool. A more complete bibliography, in Bibtex format, along with citations by chapter, can also be found. There is a README file containing useful information about the rest of the directory.

Acknowledgments

This book grew out of a series of short courses that I offered over the past three years. Little of the material in this book is original or invented by the author; I owe a debt of gratitude to the many developers of the techniques used here. My introduction to this topic was working with the Parafrase group at the University of Illinois from 1976 to 1980. Many ideas now crucial in modern restructuring compilers were developed during that time. During my tenure at Kuck and Associates, Inc., I learned the important distinction between science and engineering, and that good engineering in a compiler is critically important. After joining the Oregon Graduate Institute, I have had more contacts with compiler researchers and developers around the globe; I have learned more during this period than ever before.

I especially thank the reviewers, who helped maintain consistency and made numerous important and helpful suggestions: Ron K. Cytron of Washington University, James Larus of the University of Wisconsin, Carl Offner of Digital Equipment Corp., J. (Ram) Ramanujam of Louisiana State University, David Stotts of the University of North Carolina, and Alan Sussman of the University of Maryland. Any errors contained herein are, of course, entirely my own fault. Several students at OGI reviewed selected chapters: Tito Autrey, Michael Gerlek, Priyadarshan Kolte, and Eric Stoltz. The editors and staff at The Benjamin/Cummings Publishing Co. were very encouraging, and to them I owe a great deal of gratitude.

Michael Wolfe

High Performance Compilers for Parallel Computing

1 HIGH PERFORMANCE SYSTEMS

Compiler writers must understand how to take advantage of the features of the target architecture that can enhance performance. These features include memory hierarchies, vector instruction sets, and multiple processors in various configurations. We demonstrate a set of techniques that can be used to change the structure of programs to take advantage of a wide variety of architectures. The same technology is used to optimize for memory hierarchies on a uniprocessor as to minimize communication on a massively parallel supercomputer. Because of the large performance improvements possible with this compiler technology, the interface with the programmer has become more important.

Computer designers use two means to achieve high performance: technology and architecture. Levels of integration and clock speeds have continued to improve over the past few decades, and will likely get even better for the foreseeable future. To achieve a performance advantage with a given level of technology, many designers use various architectural features aimed at a particular application market. Some of these, such as cache memories, are useful to a wide audience, while others, such vector instruction sets, are aimed at a more narrow market. In all cases, the goal is high performance at a reasonable price.

Given a level of technology, the inclusion of appropriate architectural features gives one design an advantage over others in the target market. Over the past 20 years, the most successful architectures have been designed with the capabilities and requirements of software in mind. Since most software is now written in high level languages, this means that architectural design should be done with the capabilities and requirements of compilers in mind. Similarly, the design and implementation of compilers for high performance computer systems requires a thorough understanding of the target architecture to deliver the highest level of performance.

Throughout this book, we assume that reasonably standard CPU designs are used: register files; integer, floating point, and logical functional units; and an appropriate control unit. A system may include a few or many processors, connected in various fashions.

The main memory is typically organized into a hierarchy. The whole hierarchy in a modern virtual memory system may include a rotating disk-backing store, semiconductor main memory, and one or two levels of high speed cache memory. Memory at higher levels (closer to the processor) is smaller and faster than memory at lower levels. The memory hierarchy is designed to take advantage of the memory reference behavior of typical programs. Many programs exhibit a certain amount of locality of reference; that is, if the program refers to any given word in memory, there is a high likelihood that in the near future the program will refer to the same location in memory (temporal locality) or a nearby location (spatial locality). Most memory hierarchies are intended to work transparently with respect to the program; that is, the program need not be cognizant of the presence or design of the hierarchy. Nonetheless, many programs can be rewritten to enhance their locality of reference, taking advantage of the memory hierarchy and delivering even higher performance. Some of the optimizations discussed in this book are designed to do this automatically.

Vector computer designs were the earliest high performance systems, and have historically been the most successful. The ability to take advantage of the vector functional units is an important optimization in the compiler for such a machine. The delivered performance of the vector functional unit may be four to 40 times that of nonvector (scalar) instructions on a given operation.

In a multiple processor system, programs can often be redesigned to use the parallel processors and deliver higher performance. One topic of interest is automatic detection of parallelism, which allows existing sequential programs to benefit from the presence of multiple processors. In addition, programs written in an explicitly parallel language need to be mapped onto the parallel processors in such a way as to optimize performance. Parallel programs may also need to be compiled and executed on uniprocessor systems. The optimizations discussed in this book describe automatic parallelism detection, as well as optimization of explicitly parallel programs.

Many current large-scale parallel processor systems use a message-passing paradigm, where each processor has a small amount of local memory and processors communicate by sending messages. Much current work in languages and compilers is designed to optimize programs written in a single-memory model for such a distributed memory system. Some of these systems are designed as SIMD (single instruction/multiple data) processor arrays, where there is one control unit that decodes instructions and an array of processors, each with registers and functional units, that all execute the same operation at the same time. More common are the MIMD designs (multiple instruction/multiple data), where each processor is essentially equivalent to a commodity microprocessor, complete with control unit, execution unit, and memory interface. This book discusses many optimizations for various forms of these systems. Early work in programming these systems focused on the network that interconnected the parallel processors. More recent designs allow any processor to communicate with any other processor with very little penalty for distant communication, unless there is contention for network resources.

1.1 An Example Program: Matrix Multiplication

To introduce the analysis and optimizations used in this book, we present a simple example program and show how it can be optimized for various target machine architectures. The example used is a matrix multiplication program, shown in Figure 1.1.

```
for i = 1 to n do
    for j = 1 to n do
        for k = 1 to n do
            C[i,j] = C[i,j] + A[i,k]+B[k,j]
        endfor
    endfor
endfor
```

FIGURE 1.1 Simple matrix multiplication C = A x B.

Each element of the result matrix C[i,j] is assigned the dot-product of the ith row of matrix A and the jth column of matrix B. This is not necessarily the optimal way to compute a matrix product, but it is the most obvious; we call this the ijk form of the algorithm, from the order of the loops. Pictorially, each element of the result matrix is computed as the dot product of a row of A and a column of B, as shown in Figure 1.2. To give a flavor of the types of optimizations considered in this text, we show how this simple program can be optimized for execution on a variety of architectures.

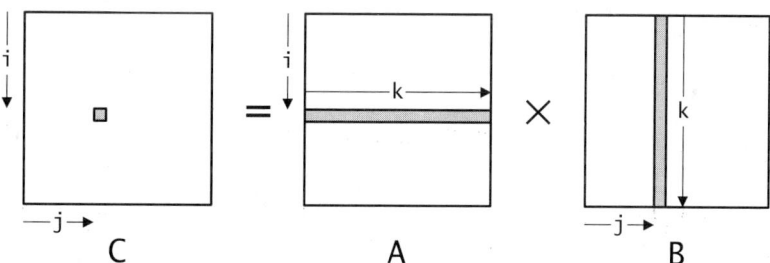

FIGURE 1.2 Computation of C[i,j] as the dot product of ith row of A and the jth column of B.

1.1.1 Scalar Architecture

For a scalar architecture, the performance of a nested loop is likely to be dominated by the performance of the code in the innermost loop. We assume a relatively modern RISC (reduced instruction set computer) architecture, with a large set of integer and floating point registers, load and store instructions to refer to memory,

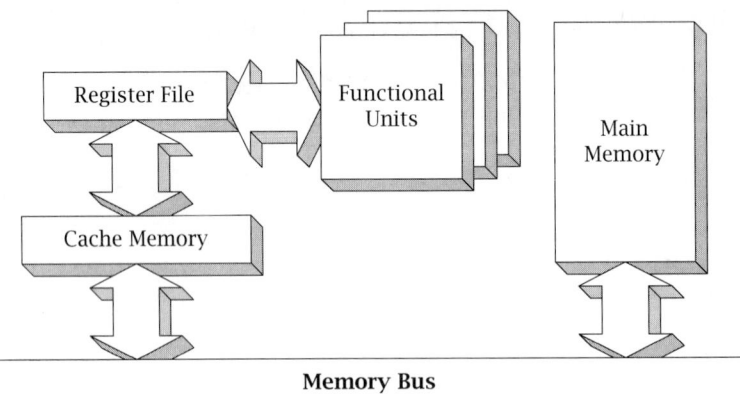

FIGURE 1.3 Data paths for a load-store architecture processor.

and the full complement of arithmetic and control instructions. Figure 1.3 shows a high level view of the data paths for a uniprocessor. The form of matrix multiply given above is already more or less optimized for scalar execution, in that the scalar code for the inner loop can be optimized down to eight (or fewer) instructions for many architectures, as shown in Figure 1.4.

```
                            ; initial state:
                            ; f1 holds value of C[i,j]
                            ; r1 holds value of n
                            ; r2 holds address of A[i,1]
                            ; r3 holds address of B[1,j]
                            ; r13 holds size of row of B
                            ; 4 is the size of an element of A
          loop:             ; loop label
    (1)   loadf f2,(r2)     ; load A[i,k]
    (2)   loadf f3,(r3)     ; load B[k,j]
    (3)   mpyf  f4,f2,f3    ; A[i,k]*B[k,j]
    (4)   addf  f1,f1,f4    ; accumulate C = C + A*B
    (5)   addi  r2,r2,#4    ; increment pointer to A[i,k+1]
    (6)   add   r3,r3,r13   ; increment pointer to B[k+1,j]
    (7)   subi  r1,r1,#1    ; decrement r1 by 1
    (8)   bnz   r1,loop:    ; branch to loop if r1 ≠ 0
```

FIGURE 1.4 Scalar inner loop of matrix multiply.

Many architectures can reduce the instruction count with instructions that perform floating point arithmetic in conjunction with memory loads, that perform floating multiply-add, or that decrement and branch in a single instruction. The advantage of the ijk formulation is that the dot product can be accumulated in a processor register, in this case in floating point register f1. In this instruction set, each iteration of the inner loop issues two memory references, two floating point arithmetic operations, two pointer updates, and two instructions to handle the loop condition.

Improving Spatial Locality

Instruction count is not the only factor that determines performance. For many systems, the delivered performance is closely related to how fast the memory can deliver the operands. To improve the average memory access time, modern computer systems use a high speed cache memory. The cache is divided into *cache lines*. When a memory fetch *hits* in the cache (i.e., that memory address is present in the cache), the cache can deliver the value without slowing down the processor. When a fetch *misses* in the cache, the fetch must be forwarded to the main memory, which is significantly slower. Usually, a cache miss causes the cache to request an entire cache line from the main memory. The intent is to keep the requested word in the cache in case it is fetched again in the near future (to satisfy temporal locality), and to keep nearby words also (to satisfy spatial locality). When the program exhibits enough locality, the cache works well and enhances performance.

Let us return to our matrix multiplication example. Suppose the matrices are laid out in memory by rows, so that adjacent words in a single row are stored in the same cache line, as shown in Figure 1.5. The inner loop has two memory fetches. One of them, the fetch of A[i,k], proceeds sequentially across the row in the inner loop, showing good spatial locality; when one word of A is fetched, there is a high probability that the entire cache line will eventually be fetched. However, the fetch for B[k,j] proceeds down a column. When one word of B is fetched, the rest of that cache line will not be needed until the whole column has been processed. If B is small enough that all the cache lines for the whole column can fit into the cache, then processing the second column should result in a high cache hit ratio, since

FIGURE 1.5 Cache lines laid out in a matrix stored by rows.

most of those elements will have been cached when loading the first column. If B is large, however, all the memory bandwidth to load cache lines may have been wasted; later fetches of elements of B will cause the cache lines saved by earlier fetches to be replaced. This loop may run with very low performance on many modern machines.

One way to improve spatial locality is to reorder the loops so that all the memory references are *stride-1*; that is, refer to consecutive memory locations in the inner loop. In this example, reordering the loops to get the ikj form will satisfy that goal:

```
for i = 1 to n do
    for k = 1 to n do
        for j = 1 to n do
            C[i,j] = C[i,j] + A[i,k]+B[k,j]
        endfor
    endfor
endfor
```

The inner loop will contain three memory references (loads of B[k,j] and C[i,j], and a store of C[i,j]), but the spatial locality may allow the memory subsystem to deliver higher overall performance. Pictorially, the inner loop is updating a row of the result matrix by adding a multiple of a row of the B matrix; see Figure 1.6.

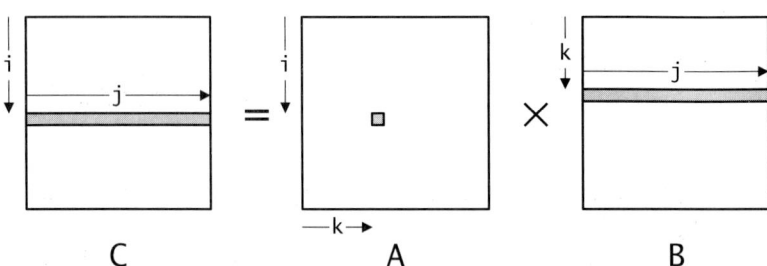

FIGURE 1.6 Computation of the ith row of C as the product of A[i,k] and the kth row of B.

Does the reordered loop compute the same results as the original loop? What other loop reorderings are possible? How does reordering the loop affect performance? In later chapters, we shall see how to determine the conditions that allow or prevent interchanging or reordering loops, as well as when reordering is beneficial.

Improving Temporal Locality

Even after reordering the loops, the program has little or no temporal locality when the matrices are large enough. The entire B matrix is fetched for each iteration of the i loop; unless the cache is large enough to hold the entire matrix, it will exhibit no temporal reuse. If the matrices are so large that the cache cannot hold a whole row of C and B, then even the references to C in the inner loop will not benefit from temporal locality. We can address this by using a submatrix-multiplication formulation. Essentially, we divide the matrices into rectangular submatrices, as shown below.

$$\begin{pmatrix} C^{11} & C^{12} & C^{13} \\ C^{21} & C^{22} & C^{23} \\ C^{31} & C^{32} & C^{33} \end{pmatrix} = \begin{pmatrix} A^{11} & A^{12} & A^{13} \\ A^{21} & A^{22} & A^{23} \\ A^{31} & A^{32} & A^{33} \end{pmatrix} \times \begin{pmatrix} B^{11} & B^{12} & B^{13} \\ B^{21} & B^{22} & B^{23} \\ B^{31} & B^{32} & B^{33} \end{pmatrix}$$

Here we have chosen a submatrix size $s = n \div 3$. The first submatrix C^{11} can be computed by submatrix multiplication:

$$C^{11} = A^{11} \times B^{11} + A^{12} \times B^{21} + A^{13} \times B^{31}$$

We reformulate the program to perform submatrix multiplication, where the $s \times s$ submatrices are small enough that all three submatrices fit into the cache memory. Since each submatrix multiplication does $2s^3$ operations and uses only $3s^2$ data elements, it will benefit from temporal locality and the cache can deliver very high performance. The program for the reformulated algorithm is shown in Figure 1.7.

```
for it = 1 to n by s do
    for kt = 1 to n by s do
        for jt = 1 to n by s do
            for i = it to min(it+s-1,n) do
                for k = kt to min(kt+s-1,n) do
                    for j = jt to min(jt+s-1,n) do
                        C[i,j] = C[i,j] + A[i,k]+B[k,j]
                    endfor
                endfor
            endfor
        endfor
    endfor
endfor
```

FIGURE 1.7 Submatrix multiplication formulation.

The outer three loops step between submatrices, while the inner three loops perform a single submatrix multiplication. Pictorially, the inner loop runs across a submatrix row of C and B, as shown in Figure 1.8.

Does the submatrix-multiplication program compute the same results? How can the submatrix-multiplication form be generated from the original program? Can

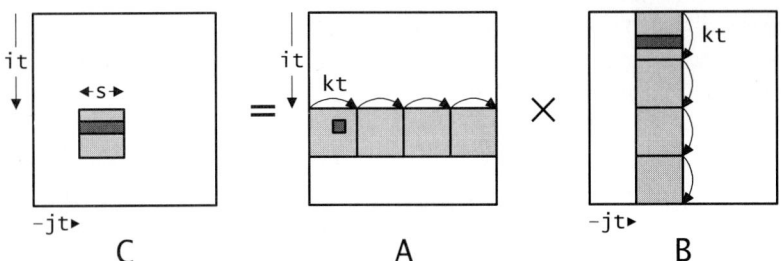

FIGURE 1.8 Computation of the ith row of a submatrix of C as the product of A[i,k] and the kth row of a submatrix of B.

the same transformation be applied to other algorithms? We shall see that the submatrix formulation gives exactly the same answers as the original program, and can be generated by a program transformation called *tiling*.

1.1.2 Vector Architecture

Many early supercomputers were vector processors. Our model of a vector computer includes a large vector register file, where each vector register comprises a number of elements (we use a vector register length of 64); the data paths for such a machine are shown in Figure 1.9. In addition to a full set of scalar instructions, the system includes vector instructions such as those shown in Figure 1.10. Taking full advantage of the vector instruction set is generally critical to the performance of programs on the machine. Sometimes, the vector instructions can produce results 10 to 40 times faster than the corresponding scalar code.

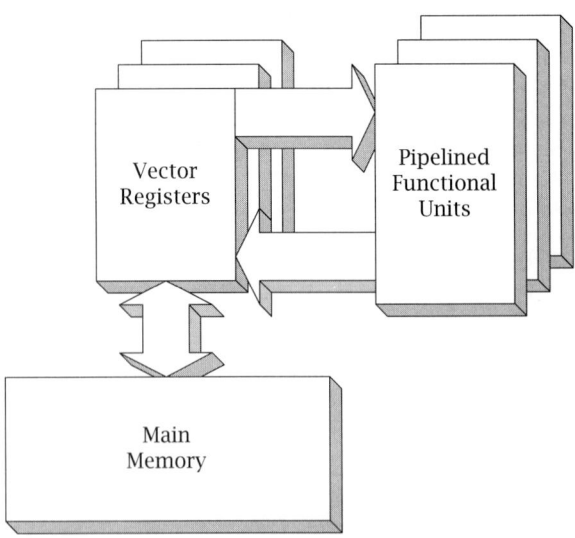

FIGURE 1.9 Data paths for a vector processor.

1.1 ■ An Example Program: Matrix Multiplication

binary arithmetic	vector := vector op vector
unary arithmetic	vector := op vector
binary arithmetic	vector := vector op scalar
memory fetch	vector := memory[start:stop:stride]
memory store	memory[start:stop:stride] := vector
indexed fetch	vector := memory[vector]
indexed store	memory[vector] := vector
compare	mask := vector op vector
merge	vector := if mask then vector else vector
conditional arithmetic	if mask then vector := vector op vector

FIGURE 1.10 Types of vector instructions.

In the matrix multiplication example, the inner loop of the ikj form can be converted to vector instructions; we represent vector operations by using *array assignments*, a la Fortran 90:

```
for i = 1 to n do
    for k = 1 to n do
        C[i,1:n] = C[i,1:n] + A[i,k]+B[k,1:n]
    endfor
endfor
```

We say the j loop executes in vector mode, or has been *vectorized*. Pictorially, the matrix product is computed just as in the row-oriented sequential code, except the inner loop is replaced by a vector operation, as shown in Figure 1.11. The actual code would be a sequence of vector instructions to load and store vector operands, and perform vector operations. We show the instructions corresponding to the inner loop in Figure 1.12.

The performance of the inner loop will be dominated by the vector instructions. There are five vector instructions: three memory operations and two arithmetic. Given the loop ordering shown, however, the store of C[i,1:n] at line 9 stores the

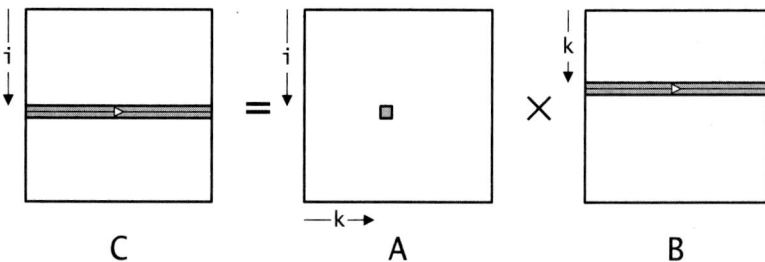

FIGURE 1.11 Vector computation of the ith row of C.

vector in one iteration of the k loop, and the load at line 7 reloads the same value in the next iteration. Thus, the load and store can be floated out of the k loop, as shown in Figure 1.13.

```
(1)     for i = 1 to n do
(2)         for k = 1 to n do
                                    ; initial state:
                                    ; r1 holds value of n
                                    ; r2 holds address of A[i,k]
                                    ; r3 holds address of B[k,1]
                                    ; r4 holds address of C[i,1]
                                    ; r13 holds row size of B and C
(3)             setvl r1            ; set vector length to 'n'
(4)             loadf f2,(r2)       ; load A[i,k]
(5)             loadv v3,(r3)       ; load B[k,1:n]
(6)             mpyvs v3,v3,f2      ; A[i,k]*B[k,1:n]
(7)             loadv v4,(r4)       ; load C[i,1:n]
(8)             addvv v4,v4,v3      ; update C[i,1:n]
(9)             storev v4,(r4)      ; store C[i,1:n]
(10)            addi r2,r2,#4       ; point to A[i,k+1]
(11)            add r3,r3,r13       ; point to B[k+1,1]
(12)        endfor
(13)        add r4,r4,r13           ; point to C[i+1,1]
(14)    endfor
```

FIGURE 1.12 Vector code for matrix multiply.

```
(1)     for i = 1 to n do
(3)         setvl r1                ; set vector length to 'n'
(7)         loadv v4,(r4)           ; load C[i,1:n]
(2)         for k = 1 to n do
(4)             loadf f2,(r2)       ; load A[i,k]
(5)             loadv v3,(r3)       ; load B[k,1:n]
(6)             mpyvs v3,v3,f2      ; A[i,k]*B[k,1:n]
(8)             addvv v4,v4,v3      ; update C[i,1:n]
(10)            addi r2,r2,#4       ; point to A[i,k+1]
(11)            add r3,r3,r13       ; point to B[k+1,1]
(12)        endfor
(9)         storev v4,(r4)          ; store C[i,1:n]
(13)        add r4,r4,r13           ; point to C[i+1,1]
(14)    endfor
```

FIGURE 1.13 Vector code after code floating.

Now the inner loop has only three vector operations, only one of which is a memory operation. Its performance will be dominated by arithmetic (as opposed to memory bandwidth).

When can a loop be converted to vector code? How can a compiler do this automatically? Does it help to have a language (like Fortran 90) that has array assignments? Later we will explain the conditions that allow vector code generation from sequential loops, and will discuss the problems of generating vector (or sequential) code from array assignments.

Strip-Mining

Unfortunately, this vector code is not very general; if n is larger than the size of a vector register, this code will not work. To handle the general case, the vector code must be *strip-mined*; that is, divided into strips where each strip is no longer than a vector register. Essentially, the vector loop is split into two loops: an outer loop to step between strips and an inner loop that corresponds to the vector operations. At the source level, the strip-mined code is as follows:

```
for i = 1 to n do
    for k = 1 to n do
        for js = 0 to n-1 by 64 do
            vl = min(n-js,64)
            C[i,js+1:js+vl] = C[i,js+1:js+vl] +
                              A[i,k]+B[k,js+1:js+vl]
        endfor
    endfor
endfor
```

Pictorially, the long vector operation in Figure 1.11 is split into short operations, as shown in Figure 1.14. At the machine level, the strip-mined vector code might look as shown in Figure 1.15. Note that one of the strips may be short, if the iteration count is not a multiple of the vector register length; this is usually either the first or (as computed here) the last strip. With this loop ordering, however, the load and store of C cannot float out of the strip loop js, because the addresses

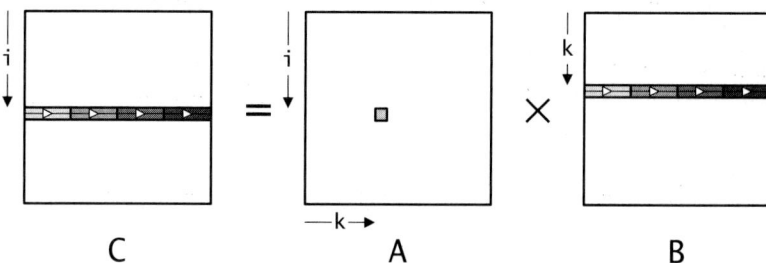

FIGURE 1.14 Strip-mined vector computation of the ith row of C.

```
(1)   for i = 1 to n do
(2)     for k = 1 to n do
                              ; initial state:
                              ; r2 holds address of A[i,k]
                              ; r3 holds address of B[k,1]
                              ; r4 holds address of C[i,1]
                              ; r13 holds row size of B and C
(3)       loadf f2,(r2)       ; load A[i,k]
(4)       for js = 0 to n-1 by 64 do
(5)         r1 = min(64,n-js)
(6)         setvl r1          ; set vector length
(7)         loadv v3,(r3)     ; load B[k,js+1:js+vl]
(8)         mpyvs v3,v3,f2    ; A[i,k]*B[k,js+1:js+vl]
(9)         loadv v4,(r4)     ; load C[i,js+1:js+vl]
(10)        addvv v4,v4,v3    ; update C[i,js+1:js+vl]
(11)        storev v4,(r4)    ; store C[i,js+1:js+vl]
(12)        shl r1,r1,#4      ; r1 = 4*vector length
(13)        addi r3,r3,r1     ; point to B[k,js+vl+1]
(14)        addi r4,r4,r1     ; point to C[k,js+vl+1]
(15)      endfor
(16)      addi r2,r2,#4       ; point to A[i,k+1]
(17)    endfor
(18)  endfor
```

FIGURE 1.15   Vector code after strip-mining.

being loaded are modified in that loop. The vector performance of the inner loop will again be dominated by the three vector memory operations.

How does this strip-mining relate to the submatrix formulation shown earlier? Does the locality at the cache level correspond to locality at the vector register level? Does optimizing for memory stride (to get sequential memory access) matter for vector processors? We will see that the submatrix formulation can be derived by strip-mining the loops, then reordering the resulting nested loops. Optimizing for locality can be done at many levels, including register, cache, and virtual memory.

Super-Vector Performance

By reordering the loops of the strip-mined code, we again achieve the benefit of moving the load and store for C out of the inner loop. We must interchange the k and js loops so that the inner loop is again the k loop. Note that the scalar load of A[i,k] must remain inside the k loop, so it will now be executed more frequently. However, the benefit of floating two vector memory operations out of the inner loop more than justifies sinking the scalar load into the loop. The resulting code is shown in Figure 1.16. Pictorially, when computing a single strip of the result, a whole column of strips of the B matrix are fetched. This program

```
        for i = 1 to n do
                                ; initial state:
                                ; r2 holds address of A[i,1]
                                ; r3 holds address of B[1,1]
                                ; r4 holds address of C[i,1]
                                ; r13 holds row size of B and C
            for js = 0 to n-1 by 64 do
                r1 = min(64,n-js)
                setvl r1            ; set vector length
                loadv v4,(r4)       ; load C[i,js+1:js+vl]
                addi r5,r3,#0       ; copy address of B to r5
                for k = 1 to n do
                    loadf f2,(r2)   ; load A[i,k]
                    loadv v3,(r5)   ; load B[k,js+1:js+vl]
                    mpyvs v3,v3,f2  ; A[i,k]*B[k,js+1:js+vl]
                    addvv v4,v4,v3  ; update C[i,js+1:js+vl]
                    addi r5,r5,r13  ; point to B[k+1,js+1]
                    addi r2,r2,#4   ; point to A[i,k+1]
                endfor
                storev v4,(r4)      ; store C[i,js+1:js+vl]
                shl r1,r1,#4        ; r1 = 4*vector length
                addi r4,r4,r1       ; point to C[1,js+vl+1]
                addi r3,r3,r1       ; point to B[1,js+vl+1]
            endfor
        endfor
```

FIGURE 1.16 Vector code after reordering for super-vector performance.

keeps the strip of C in a vector register until it is fully computed before storing it to memory. Since this generates better performance than the simple strip-mined vector code, it has been called *super-vector performance*. It is very similar in spirit to the locality optimizations used for scalar caches, except that it is optimized for locality in a vector register.

Clearly, reordering the loops has a great deal to do with the potential performance. One of the most powerful optimization tools for a high performance compiler is the ability to reorder loops. We will study in detail the techniques for doing this.

1.1.3 Multiprocessor Architecture

A common multiprocessor architecture has several processors (up to 30) sharing a single main memory. Each processor may have a private cache memory; a high cache hit rate improves average memory latency and reduces the memory bandwidth required to keep the processor busy. Usually, hardware provides coherence between the cache memories when the same memory location is accessed by multiple processors. Figure 1.17 shows a simplified view of such a machine.

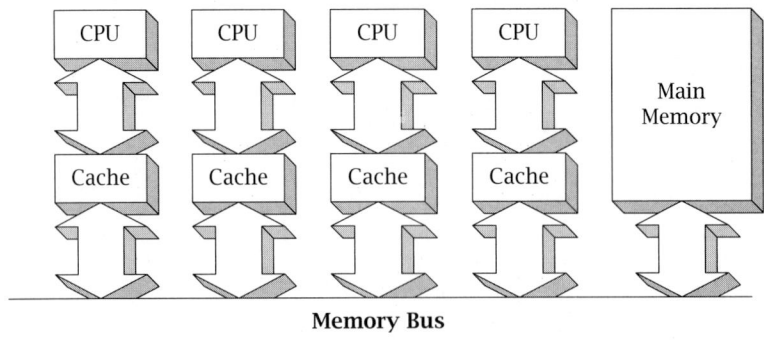

FIGURE 1.17 Simplified view of a cache-coherent multiprocessor.

To achieve high performance, a program must take advantage of the multiple processors. One way to do this is to discover when iterations of a loop can be executed in parallel, and to assign the iterations to different processors. If there is more than one iteration for each processor, the distribution, or scheduling, of iterations to processors should be done to balance the load between processors and increase locality of reference on each processor (to take advantage of the processor caches). One master processor will execute the scalar code up to the parallel loop, then will *fork* tasks that will be run on other processors to execute the parallel iterations. When each task is done, it will synchronize at a *barrier* at the end of the parallel loop. When all workers are done, the master starts executing the scalar code up to the next parallel loop. Such a scheme is often called a doall loop, since all the iterations can be done in parallel.

In the matrix multiply example, the i or j loops could be executed in parallel. One way to generate code is to execute the j inner loop in parallel, as follows:

```
for i = 1 to n do
    for k = 1 to n do
        doall j = 1 to n do
            C[i,j] = C[i,j] + A[i,k]+B[k,j]
        enddoall
    endfor
endfor
```

Figure 1.18 shows the parts of the array that will be accessed by the first four iterations of the j loop executing in parallel on four processors. This code would have a relatively high synchronization cost. For each of the n^2 iterations of the outer two loops, the tasks are forked at the doall and synchronize at the enddoall. Additionally, because of the array layout, different processors may be accessing

C[i,j] and C[i,j+1], which might lie on the same cache line, causing interprocessor cache interference.

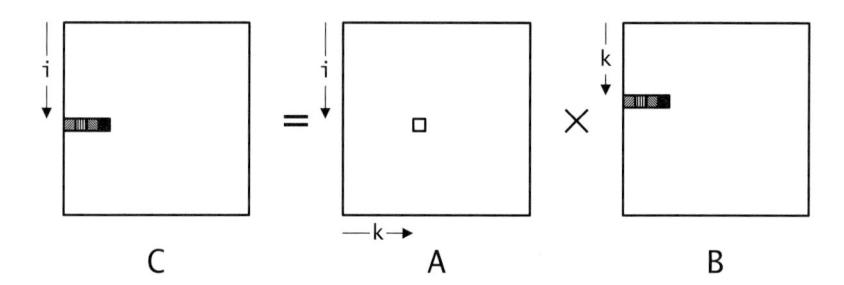

FIGURE 1.18 First four parallel iterations of the inner loop.

An alternative is to execute the outer loop in parallel:

```
doall i = 1 to n do
   for k = 1 to n do
      for j = 1 to n do
         C[i,j] = C[i,j] + A[i,k]+B[k,j]
      endfor
   endfor
enddoall
```

This program forks tasks only once; each task is a large-grain operation, comprising two inner loops. Figure 1.19 shows the first four iterations of the outer loop executing in parallel, computing the first four rows of the output matrix. Note that each parallel task will fetch the whole array B.

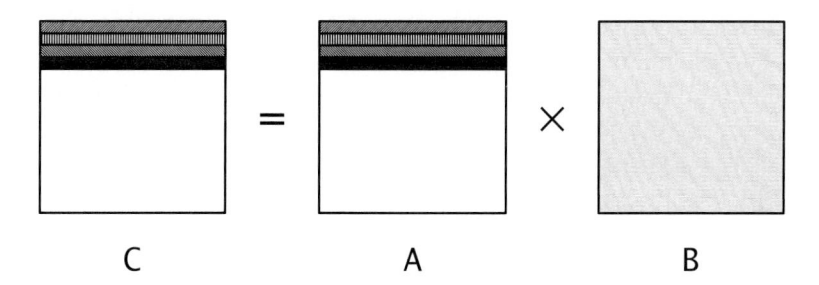

FIGURE 1.19 First four parallel iterations of the outer loop.

In this formulation, locality within each processor for access to A and C is high, since each element is used n times in each iteration of the parallel outer loops, where n is the size of the array. However, locality for B is poor; each element is used only once in each parallel iteration.

What are the exact conditions for deciding when a loop can be executed in parallel? How do these conditions relate to those for executing in vector mode? Why choose the nonstride-1 loop to execute in parallel? As we shall see, executing a loop in parallel has different restrictions than executing the loop in vector mode. Among the optimization goals of generating parallel code is to prevent any cache interference between the processors.

Locality for Multiprocessors

We can also use the submatrix multiplication formulation for multiprocessors. For instance, we can formulate the algorithm as before, but look for parallelism at the submatrix level. In the following code, each parallel task executes a series of submatrix products, where each submatrix product will have high cache locality and low interference from other submatrix products.

```
doall it = 1 to n by s do
    for kt = 1 to n by s do
        for jt = 1 to n by s do
            for i = it to min(it+s-1,n) do
                for k = kt to min(kt+s-1,n) do
                    for j = jt to min(jt+s-1,n) do
                        C[i,j] = C[i,j] + A[i,k]+B[k,j]
                    endfor
                endfor
            endfor
        endfor
    endfor
enddoall
```

If the original loop can be executed in parallel, can the corresponding submatrix loop always execute in parallel? Is there a way to support multiple nested parallel loops? How do the parallel tasks get scheduled onto the processors? We shall see that a parallel loop is still parallel after strip-mining, and that scheduling parallel iterations onto the processors can be done in a number of ways.

1.1.4 SIMD Architecture

A single instruction/multiple data (SIMD, pronounced *sim-dee*) machine has a single controller, or front-end, that issues instructions, and an ensemble of back-end processor elements (or PEs) that all execute each instruction in lock-step parallelism. Figure 1.20 shows a small part of a SIMD processor ensemble in which each processor is connected to the others by a communication network and controlled by the front-end. Harnessing this parallelism can give very high performance. This is typically done by using *data parallelism*, which executes the same operation in parallel on different parts of the data set. Early systems had limited network band-

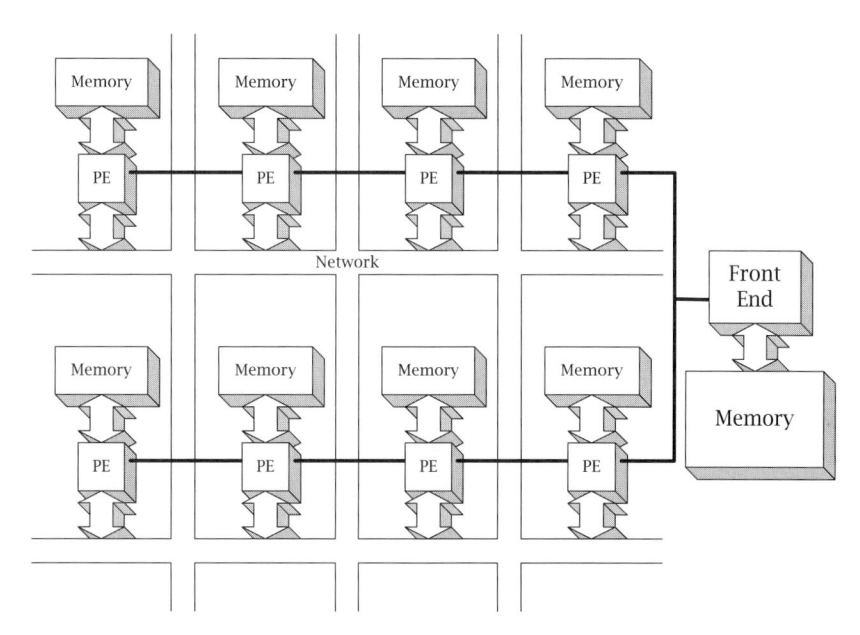

FIGURE 1.20 SIMD processor ensemble, with interconnection network and front-end processor.

width, so optimizing for the topology of the network was very important; current systems have a more flexible network. Code for a SIMD machine is divided into scalar and parallel code. The scalar code is executed on the front-end itself, as, for instance, the control operations for sequential loops. The memory of a SIMD machine is typically distributed across the back-end PEs. Each back-end PE can access its local memory directly, but messages must be used to access values from another PE's memory.

For our example, we assume the matrices are distributed across the memory of the back-end PEs such that each PE's memory has one row of each matrix. Clearly, we want to map the parallelism onto the machine to take advantage of the memory layout; this means that a loop used as a row index can be executed in parallel. In our matrix multiplication program, this is either the i index (which is used as a row index for C and A) or the k index (used in B). We choose to execute the i index in parallel, since it is used as the row index of more variables, and the left-hand side variable in particular. The generated code would look something like that shown in Figure 1.21.

The front-end processor executes the k and j loops sequentially, and broadcasts the parallel instructions to the back-end PEs. The variables lA, lB, and lC contain the corresponding rows of A, B, and C on each PE; they are the "local" parts of the matrices on each PE. The fetch operation fetches one element (lB[j]) from PE k-1, which contains the value of B[k,j], into the front-end variable Bkj; that is broadcast to all PEs in the subsequent assignment statement. The notation PE[0:n-1] means the assignment statement is executed in parallel on each PE in

```
for j = 1 to n do
    PE[0:n-1] Ctmp = 0
    for k = 1 to n do
        Bkj = fetch[k-1](1B[j])
        PE[0:n-1]: Ctmp = Ctmp + 1A[k]+Bkj
    endfor
    PE[0:n-1] 1C[j] = Ctmp
endfor
```

FIGURE 1.21   SIMD code for matrix multiply.

the index range 0 to n-1. Note that the i index is implicit in the parallel execution of the assignment statement. Each PE accesses its own memory, so PE i-1 will access row i of C and of A. Each PE accumulates a dot-product into a scalar Ctmp, which could be allocated to a PE register to reduce the number of memory accesses in the inner loop, as was done for the scalar code in Figure 1.4.

The form of the program is similar to that for vector code. How similar is writing SIMD code in general to writing vector code? Are the conditions for generating SIMD code for a loop the same as for vector code? How does the data distribution affect the parallelism and the code generation? Subsequent chapters show that SIMD is closely related to vector code generation, though the factor of improvement is often quite a bit higher.

Strip-Mining

When the number of rows is smaller than the number of PEs, the generated code must disable PEs that have no row of the matrices. On the other hand, when the number of rows is larger than the number of PEs, each PE must compute several rows of the matrix product. If each PE has several rows of each matrix, the parallel code must first compute the first row stored on each PE, then the second row, and so on. The front-end code must have a loop to sequence through the several rows owned by each PE. In general, we strip-mine the i loop of the matrix multiplication, as we did for vector execution, where one loop corresponds to stepping between PEs and will execute in parallel, and the other loop corresponds to stepping through the rows on each PE and will execute sequentially. Suppose the rows are distributed across PEs such that row i is stored on PE $(i-1)$ mod P, where P is the number of PEs. The generated code might look like that shown in Figure 1.22, where the number of rows stored on each PE is represented by nrows; we leave for subsequent chapters the issue of when the number of PEs does not evenly divide the number of rows. This code again uses a scalar temporary, Ctmp, on each PE to hold the result of the accumulation, which reduces the number of memory accesses for 1C, but there is still a fetch and broadcast of Bkj in the innermost loop.

How does strip-mining for SIMD code relate to strip-mining for vector code? We shall see that these are exactly the same transformation, though the code generation is very different.

1.1 ■ An Example Program: Matrix Multiplication

```
for is = 1 to nrows do
    for j = 1 to n do
        PE[0:P-1] Ctmp = 0
        for k = 1 to n do
            Bkj = fetch[(k-1) mod P](1B[(k-1)/P+1,j])
            PE[0:P-1]: Ctmp = Ctmp + 1A[is,k]+Bkj
        endfor
        PE[0:P-1] 1C[is,j] = Ctmp
    endfor
endfor
```

FIGURE 1.22 SIMD code when n > P.

Minimizing Messages

The broadcast for Bkj in the last version of the SIMD code may be somewhat costly. We can reduce the number of broadcasts by reordering the loops, since the value that is broadcast is independent of the i loop. Unfortunately, this eliminates the benefit of using the scalar register in the inner loop:

```
for j = 1 to n do
    for k = 1 to n do
        Bkj = fetch[(k-1) mod P](1B[(k-1)/P+1,j])
        for is = 1 to nrows do
            PE[0:P-1]: 1C[is,j] = 1C[is,j] + 1A[is,k]+Bkj
        endfor
    endfor
endfor
```

This transformation trades off less efficient code in the innermost loop for the benefits of fewer broadcasts.

How does transforming the program to minimize messages relate to optimizing for locality? As we have seen, the same techniques arise over and over: strip-mining and reordering the loops. In fact, in Chapter 9 we shall see a large number of loop restructuring techniques that a compiler can use.

1.1.5 Message-Passing Multicomputer Architecture

A message-passing multiple instruction/multiple data (MIMD, pronounced *mim-dee*) machine, here called a *multicomputer*, can be programmed using data parallelism, much like a SIMD machine. Such a machine has a global structure like a SIMD machine, as shown in Figure 1.23, but the processors are likely to be commercial microprocessors. As with SIMD systems, we ignore the network topology for the purposes of our discussion. Data is distributed over the processor nodes, and each processor executes a sequential program, communicating with the others to complete the entire computation. When each processor executes

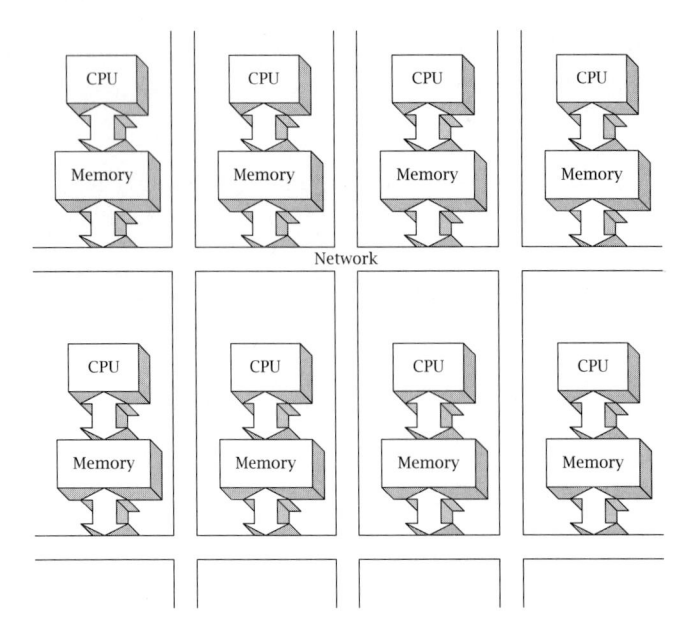

FIGURE 1.23 Multicomputer made of processor/memory pairs connected by an interconnection network.

a copy of the same program, we say the multicomputer is programmed in single program/multiple data style (SPMD, pronounced *spim-dee*); more specifically, when the program is working on a distributed data set, we call it a single program/distributed data (SPDD, pronounced *speedy*) program.

Figure 1.24 shows the SPDD program for the matrix multiplication where there is one processor for each row of each matrix. There is a direct correspondence

```
for j = 1 to n do
    Ctmp = 0
    for k = 1 to n do
        if( k-1 = Pindex )then
            Bkj = lB[j]
            broadcast( Bkj )
        else
            receive( Bkj )
        endif
        Ctmp = Ctmp + lA[k]+Bkj
    endfor
    lC[j] = Ctmp
endfor
```

FIGURE 1.24 SPDD code for matrix multiply.

between this code and the SIMD code. The broadcast operation sends the value of Bkj from the processor whose local index is Pindex to all other processors. As before, this involves n^2 broadcast operations, each of a single word. SIMD machines are optimized for broadcasts, since the instructions are broadcast from the front-end, whereas broadcasts on a multicomputer may be quite a bit less efficient.

Minimizing Broadcasts

Reordering the loops, we can reduce the number of broadcast operations by increasing the size of each message. We will organize the computation so that each processor will broadcast its row of B all at once, as shown in Figure 1.25. Now there are only n broadcast operations, each sending n elements. The code for the computation is less efficient, since a scalar cannot be used to accumulate the dot-product. Again, this trades computation efficiency for communication efficiency.

```
for k = 1 to n do
    if( k-1 = Pindex )then
        Bk[1:n] = lB[1:n]
        broadcast( Bk[1:n] )
    else
        receive( Bk[1:n] )
    endif
    for j = 1 to n do
        lC[j] = lC[j] + lA[k]+Bk[j]
    endfor
endfor
```

FIGURE 1.25   SPDD code after reducing broadcasts.

Strip-Mining

As with the SIMD code, it is likely that the number of rows exceeds the number of processors. We handle that situation in the same fashion, by strip-mining the i loop, and having each processor execute a sequential loop to step through the rows stored on that processor. We can arrange to keep the number of broadcast operations down to n by keeping the k loop outermost, as shown in Figure 1.26.

Clearly, there is a close correspondence between the SIMD and the multicomputer code. We shall see that the distributed memory model makes these machines more similar to each other than either of them are to vector machines or multiprocessors.

1.1.6   Compound Architectures

A particular machine may have features of several of these architectures. For instance, a multiprocessor may have vector instructions on each processor. A multicomputer may have multiple processors or vector processors at each node. Generating a program for such a compound architecture may involve tradeoffs between

```
for k = 1 to n do
    if( k-1 = Pindex )then
        Bk[1:n] = lB[1:n]
        broadcast( Bk[1:n] )
    else
        receive( Bk[1:n] )
    endif
    for j = 1 to n do
        for i = 1 to nrows do
            lC[i,j] = lC[i,j] + lA[i,k]+Bk[j]
        endfor
    endfor
endfor
```

FIGURE 1.26 SPDD code after strip-mining.

the levels of parallelism. In some cases, there is a clear split between the levels. For a vector multiprocessor, for instance, we want multiprocessor parallelism at outer loops and vector parallelism for inner loops. Other cases may be more difficult. To generate a program for a multiprocessor multicomputer, it may be appropriate to optimize for the large-scale parallelism of the multicomputer, then optimize the resulting node program for the multiple processors on each node.

1.2 Structure of a Compiler

This text discusses compiler optimizations for these high performance systems. The optimizations are based on an analysis of the high level structure and behavior of the program. For many classical compiler optimizations, the granularity of the optimization is at the instruction level. Here we work at a larger granularity, e.g., of a variable reference, subexpression, statement, or loop. Thus, the analysis depends on keeping or finding higher level structure in the program; in particular, a compiler front-end that immediately lowers the program into instructions or pseudo-instructions may inhibit some of the analyses or optimizations discussed here.

This is not to say that instruction-level optimizations are not equally important. In order to enjoy the maximum benefit from running parallel programs, each task must be optimized as well as the original scalar program would have been. However, low level optimizations must follow the higher level analyses and optimizations presented here. A high performance compiler has a series of high level analysis and optimization phases. This is followed by lowering the representation to one that more directly corresponds to machine instructions, and by another series of low level analyses and optimizations. The later optimizations may deal with details of the processor chip, such as the instruction pipeline, while the earlier optimizations deal with the general architecture, such as multiple processors and vector operations. Figure 1.27 shows the structure of a compiler, with possible

1.2 ■ Structure of a Compiler

program representations that feed each stage. A common high level representation of the program is an abstract syntax tree (AST); another is a statement list with an expression tree for each statement. The details of the representation may make some analyses or transformations more convenient, but others less so; no one representation has been accepted as uniformly efficient and effective.

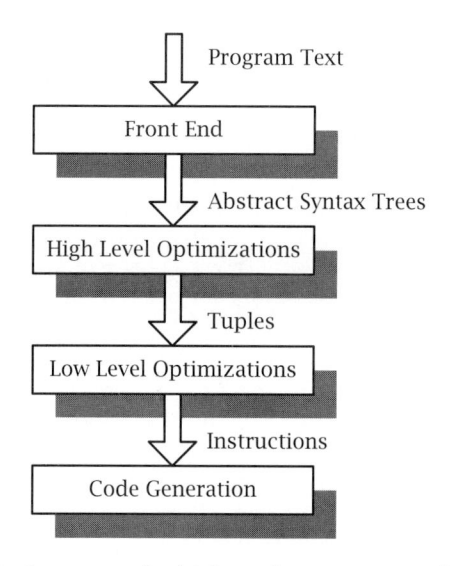

FIGURE 1.27 Structure of a high performance compiler.

1.2.1 Preserving Program Behavior

Generally, compiler optimizations should not change the behavior of the program they are compiling. It does little good to make the program run twice as fast if the answers are wrong. But we must be careful to define what behavior we must preserve. One aspect of the behavior is the execution time; the whole point of compiler optimizations is to change that aspect.

We will define an optimization as *safe*, or *correctness preserving*, if it preserves the observable behavior of a program when the program executes correctly and terminates. We assume that the compiler can identify the observable behavior of the program. This is generally taken to be any explicit input or output, calls to unknown functions or procedures, and accesses or modifications to volatile memory locations. Other characteristics of behavior, such as the order in which operations are performed, or whether a multiplication can be replaced by addition or shifting, are considered unobservable. This makes debugging optimized code quite difficult; debuggers access characteristics of the program that are considered by the compiler to be unobservable, such as the state of variables during execution and the order of the statements being executed. Debugging optimized code is another problem altogether.

This definition allows optimizations that change the behavior of programs in subtle and interesting ways. A program that terminates with an exception when compiled without optimization may terminate with a different exception when compiled with optimization, if the optimization reorders the operations. The program may even execute to completion without generating an exception, if the code that generated the exception was eliminated as dead.

Another program behavior characteristic that we hope to change by optimization is use of the target architecture. In general, we hope to take advantage of any performance enhancements offered by the architecture. Some architectural features are meant to be "invisible" to the program; cache memories are such a feature. A cache is intended to improve the performance of programs without having to change the program at all. Most programs exhibit locality, and a computer with a cache will take advantage of that locality. However, a program that is compiled and optimized to take advantage of the cache memory will achieve even higher performance.

1.2.2 User Interface

As with many architectural features, many compiler optimizations are intended to work without user intervention. Most of the low level optimizations (constant propagation, strength reduction, code floating, etc.) fall into this category. If the optimizations are safe, the behavior of the program will be the same, and there is no reason to report their results to the programmer. Most such optimizations improve the program by only a little bit; a performance improvement of a factor of two or three is quite impressive. Moreover, there is little that the programmer can do to enhance their effectiveness.

When optimizing for parallelism, however, the situation is a bit different. The performance payoff for generating optimized parallel code for a multicomputer compared to generating scalar code can be a factor of 100 or 1000. Many users are willing to do a little reprogramming to pick up large performance improvements. Feedback from the compiler can be an effective mechanism to achieve this. Evidence of this comes from early automatic vectorizing compilers in the 1970s and 1980s. For most programmers, the vectorizing compiler was the primary (and often, the only) way to generate vector code for the target machine. These compilers would generate a report in a listing for each procedure compiled, giving the status of each loop in the procedure. Loops that could not be executed with vector instructions were noted, along with very explicit reasons why vector instructions could not be used. The reason could be as simple as a nonvectorizable statement (procedure call or input/output statement) in the loop, or as detailed as a data dependence condition (sometimes called a data hazard) preventing vectorization. Programmers would identify the time-critical parts of the program, often using a profile tool, and inspect these reports to see if the performance could be improved. By removing the nonvector condition (removing the input/output statement, or perhaps manually reordering the loops) vectorization could usually succeed.

Thus, program tuning for these machines involved a dialogue between the compiler (through the report) and the programmer (through rewrites of parts of the program). This had two effects; the first was that the program being developed (or ported from another machine) would run fast. The second was that the programmer learned what program characteristics would work in the vectorizing compiler and what would not. After a while, the programmer learned the "vectorizable subset" of the language, and would program in that subset. While syntactically compatible with the full language, the vectorizable subset would generally give much better performance than a program using the full language. Moreover, the vectorizable subset had a high degree of portability across machines and compilers. A program written for a Cray would work well for a Convex or Fujitsu vector computer.

Since the compiler feedback to the user can be important, the design of compiler optimizations should take this into account. In particular, when automatic optimization is ineffective and the reason can be described briefly in terms of the source program, reporting this allows the programmer to understand the limits of the optimization technology and to learn what subset of the language to use for best performance.

To improve the interaction between the compiler and the programmer, many vendors have chosen to develop interactive programming tools. Some of these tools are little more than browsers that allow the programmer to see profile data related to the program text and perhaps how effective the compiler was at optimizing the critical parts of the program. Other tools are global programming environments, which can give more immediate feedback about the predicted behavior when constructing a program.

1.3 In the Pit

The computer architectures are presented here at a very high level. Many important details are left out both for simplicity and because there is a great deal of similarity between machines of the same class. For instance, two cache-coherent multiprocessors may use different coherence strategies, but the optimizing for parallelism and locality for the two machines will be almost identical. There are also details of the operating system that can affect the compiler, such as how resources are allocated to a running program. Many multiprocessors are used as "cycle servers," that is, mostly to increase the throughput of programs, not to reduce the execution time of single jobs. In such a multiprogramming environment, creating lots of parallel tasks that will each execute sequentially may not be worthwhile.

There are a number of loop optimizations that will not be discussed in this book. For instance, loop unrolling is often used to improve the instruction schedule, and is related to some of the transformations we will present. However, we leave instruction scheduling and other low-level optimizations for another book.

In the 1970s and 1980s, optimizations such as those presented here were aimed at only the highest performance (and highest cost) supercomputers. Even some of these vendors did not think that the cost and complexity of aggressive loop restructuring techniques were worth the effort. In the 1990s, the speed of microprocessors is approaching the supercomputer class, and microprocessors themselves incorporate a certain degree of parallelism. Moreover, memory continues to get much slower, relative to the processor. Optimizing for cache locality has become critically important for performance in the past decade. Now, every major workstation vendor in the United States delivers a compiler with loop restructuring locality optimizations similar to those presented in this book.

1.4 Further Reading

A description of commercial and research compilers aimed at high performance and parallel computer systems can be useful to understanding what people have found important and what lessons they have learned. While specific optimizations are often published, overview papers of whole compilers are rare. General compiler techniques, such as parsing, type inferencing, and creating an intermediate form, can be found in standard textbooks such as those by Fischer and LeBlanc (1988) and Aho et al. (1986). Zima and Chapman (1991) and Wolfe (1989) give reasonable overviews of techniques used in parallelizing compilers of the late 1980s; Banerjee et al. (1993) also give a much briefer summary.

The compiler research group at the University of Illinois developed the Parafrase Analyzer (Kuck et al. [1984]). A contemporaneous project at Rice University developed the PFC parallelizing compiler (Allen and Kennedy [1987]). PTRAN was developed at IBM's T. J. Watson Research Laboratory around the same time (Allen et al. [1988]). Together, these three research efforts pioneered many of the analysis methods on which modern parallel compiler research and development are based.

Current high performance and parallel computer system designs can often be found in the proceedings of various conferences, such as the annual International Conference on Parallel Processing, the International Symposium on Computer Architecture, the Supercomputing conferences, or the Compcon meetings. A summary of various parallel computer systems is given by Hwang (1993), who includes a chapter on parallel programming models, languages, and compilers. The terms SIMD and MIMD were introduced by Flynn (1972). The SPMD programming model was introduced by Darema et al. (1988) for shared-memory parallel programming.

EXERCISES

1.1 Write the matrix multiplication loop as a subroutine in C or Fortran, and compile it on a RISC machine. Compare the assembly code with optimizations on and off. See whether you can improve the code for the inner loop by hand. The Fortran code is:

```
subroutine matmul(a,b,c,n)
real a(n,n), b(n,n), c(n,n)
integer i,j,k
```

```
            do i = 1, n
               do j = 1, n
                  do k = 1, n
                     c(i,j) = c(i,j) + a(i,k)*b(k,j)
                  enddo
               enddo
            enddo
            end
```

If you have both Fortran and C compilers, write the routine in both Fortran and C and compare the generated code. If you use C, write two versions of the routine using array indexing and pointer arithmetic, and compare the generated code. Also, in C, write the routine once using global variables for the arrays and again using formal parameters for the arrays, and compare the assembly code output.

1.2 Write a driver program to initialize the A and B arrays, and call the matmul subroutine from the previous exercise. The initialization can initialize the input arrays as shown in Figure 1.28.

```
            program main
            parameter(n=100)
            real a(n,n),b(n,n),c(n,n)
            integer i,j,init
            init = 1325
            do i = 1, n
               do j = 1, n
                  init = mod(3125*init,65536)
                  a(i,j) = (init - 32768.0)/16384.0
                  init = mod(3125*init,65536)
                  b(i,j) = (init - 32768.0)/16384.0
                  c(i,j) = 0.0
               enddo
            enddo
            call matmul(a,b,c,n)
            end
```

FIGURE 1.28 Driver program for matmul subroutine.

Compare the execution time of the program with optimization on and off. Find out how to isolate the execution time for a single subroutine, and get the execution time for just the matmul subroutine. Vary the matrix size n to 50, 100, 200, 500, and 1000.

1.3 Try reordering the loops in the matmul routine and repeating the experiments in the previous assignment in the ikj form and the jki form. Compare the execution times for the various loop orderings. Write a routine to compare the results of different formulations; are the results identical? If you have both Fortran and C compilers, compare the Fortran and C timings for the ikj and jki forms. How many loop orderings are there? Do they all give identical results?

1.4 Try rewriting the program to run one or more of the loops backward. In particular, run the k loop backward, from n down. Are the computed answers identical? If they are different, are they the same to some number of digits? If the answers are different, it may be due to roundoff error from accumulating the summation in the k loop in a different order. Running a loop backward is called *loop reversal*, and is a transformation we will see in Chapter 6.

1.5 The inner loop of the ikj (or jki) form of the matrix multiplication is called a SAXPY (or DAXPY, if it is double precision), since it computes a scalar A times a vector X plus a vector Y. In simple form, the SAXPY operation is:

```
for i = 1 to n do
    y[i] = y[i] + a*x[i]
endfor
```

See if your machine has hand-optimized BLAS (basic linear algebra library) routines; if so, SAXPY is one of those routines. Replace the inner loop of the ikj or jki form of the matrix multiplication by a call to SAXPY, and compare its performance to the compiler-generated performance.

1.6 If you have access to a vectorizing compiler for a vector machine, try running your matrix multiplication program through the vectorizer with various levels of optimization. Look at the generated code and compare the performance.

1.7 If you have access to a parallelizing compiler for a multiprocessor, try running your matrix multiplication program through the parallelizer with various levels of optimization. Again, look at the generated code and compare the performance for different numbers of processors. Draw a speedup surface plot, where $S(n, p) = T(n, 1)/T(n, p)$, where $T(n, p)$ is the execution time of multiplying two $n \times n$ matrices on p processors, and $S(n, p)$ is the speedup of running on p processors compared to running on one processor.

1.8 Try multiplying very large matrices (500×500 or 1000×1000) using any of your program versions. Program a submatrix-multiplication formulation of the matrix multiplication. See if the temporal locality improvements for the submatrix-multiplication formulation affect performance at all. Try different submatrix sizes. Make sure to compare your results with the nontiled version to see if you are getting the correct answers. The submatrix formulation, sometimes called a block formulation, is an example of tiling the loops, which we will present in Chapter 9.

1.9 If a submatrix formulation of matrix multiply optimizes for cache locality, how should it be written to optimize for a two-level cache?

1.10 One common predictor of performance is the number of operations divided by the number of data elements referenced. For each of the three multiprocessor codes shown in this chapter, compute the computation to data ratio for a single parallel task.

1.11 For the simple SIMD code shown in Figure 1.21, draw a picture showing what data is accessed by each PE at iteration j and k of the sequential loops.

1.12 If you have access to a multicomputer, try writing the program shown in Figure 1.25 and executing it.

1.13 The matrix multiplication program for a multicomputer can be written to have only P broadcasts (where P is the number of processors) instead of n, but more data needs to be sent with each message. This is done by strip-mining the k loop and sending all the data from one processor to all the others in one message. Modify the program shown in Figure 1.25 to have only *P* broadcasts. If you have access to a multicomputer, try executing this program and compare the execution time.

1.14 Matrix multiplication can actually be written for a message-passing SIMD machine or multicomputer with no broadcasts whatsoever. Suppose we have one row of each matrix stored at each processor. Then, each processor can certainly start the computation with local data. Eventually, to compute the local row of the target matrix, each processor must see all the rows of the matrix B, though not all processors need to see the rows in the same order. In sequential code, the program to do this is as follows:

```
for i = 1 to n do
    for j = 1 to n do
        for k = 1 to n do
            kk = ((k-1 + i-1) mod n) + 1
            C[i,j] = C[i,j] + A[i,kk]+B[kk,j]
        endfor
    endfor
endfor
```

Write this program in Fortran or C, and see whether the answers computed are the same as for the simple matrix multiplication.

1.15 Write the program from the previous exercise for a SIMD machine or multicomputer, assuming one row is stored at each processor. Since the i loop is now parallel, the reference to i-1 must be replaced by a reference to the PE index. For 4×4 matrices, show what happens at each time-step.

The matrix multiplication program is an interesting example because the loops can be reordered in any way and still give the same answer. The following exercises use a different example program:

```
iters = 10
for k = 1 to iters do
    for i = 2 to n-1 do
        for j = 2 to n-1 do
            a[i,j] = 0.25*(a[i-1,j]+a[i,j-1]+
                           a[i+1,j]+a[i,j+1])
        endfor
    endfor
endfor
```

where the array a is initialized as follows:

```
for i = 1 to n do
    for j = 1 to n do
        a[i,j] = 0.0
    endfor
    a[i][1] = 1.0
endfor
a[1][n/2] = 50.0
```

1.16 Write this routine in C or Fortran. Compare the results of the routine as shown with the results after running the i or j loop backward. Do the results differ? If the number of iterations is increased (the value of iters), do the results get closer or not?

1.17 Try reordering the loops. Does interchanging the i and j loops make any difference in the results? Can the k loop be interchanged at all?

1.18 What kind of locality does this loop exhibit? Can you write a submatrix formulation of this loop? Will a submatrix formulation of this loop help with temporal locality?

1.19 If you have a vectoring or parallelizing compiler available, try running this routine through your compiler to see whether it can find any parallelism automatically.

1.20 The above program is sometimes called a *four-point difference solver*, because it solves a difference equation using four neighboring points. Another difference equation solver uses an eight-point formulation:

```
iters = 10
for k = 1 to iters do
    for i = 2 to n-1 do
        for j = 2 to n-1 do
            a[i,j] = 0.125*(a[i-1,j-1]+a[i-1,j]+
                            a[i-1,j+1]+a[i,j+1]+
                            a[i+1,j-1]+a[i+1,j]+
                            a[i+1,j+1]+a[i,j-1])
        endfor
    endfor
endfor
```

Code this routine in Fortran or C; compare the results before and after reordering the loops. Does reordering the loops preserve the answers? Can either the i or j loop be run backward without affecting the answer? What kinds of locality does this loop exhibit, and how can we take advantage of it?

1.21 The last example routine for this chapter is Gaussian elimination without pivoting:

```
for k = 1 to n do
    for i = k+1 to n do
        a[i,k] = a[i,k] / a[k,k]
        for j = k+1 to n do
            a[i,j] = a[i,j] - a[i,k]*a[k,j]
        endfor
    endfor
endfor
```

This is the kij form of the loop. As with matrix multiplication, there are six forms of this algorithm, depending on the loop ordering. See how many of these you can find by hand. Code your routines to insure that you get the same answers as you got for the kij form, using the same initialization as in Exercise 1.2. In Chapter 9, we will see methods to generate all the forms automatically.

2 PROGRAMMING LANGUAGE FEATURES

Though many high-level computer languages have been designed, most programs for high performance systems are written in some version of Fortran or C. Some of the details of these languages hinder advanced analysis and optimization. Various attempts have been made to add explicit parallelism to these languages; we present a simple framework for parallel loops in an imperative language.

This book concentrates on compiler issues imperative languages, such as Fortran, C, and Pascal. Most of the methods presented here are aimed at optimizing the performance of loops. While a sequential loop is essentially the same in any language, many types of parallel loops have been proposed and implemented for various machines. Several versions of Fortran have array assignments or vector loops. We will discuss the meanings of the various types of parallelism in a uniform framework. As it turns out, some constructs common to declarative languages can also be dealt with in the same framework.

A language has particular rules for data layout; we will present some language issues dealing with structures and data layout. We will also discuss how dynamic array allocation can be handled.

2.1 Languages for High Performance

For largely historical reasons, the dominant language in high performance computation is Fortran. Despite the wishes and efforts of many computer scientists to the contrary, it may well remain so for the foreseeable future. For that reason, it is a fact of life that survival in the commercial high performance marketplace requires a good Fortran implementation. Many programmers are migrating toward C as an implementation language, mainly because it has dynamic allocation and richer data structures, even though its management of arrays is quite weak. In fact, both Fortran and C have much the same model of computation, so it is not clear that such a move has more than cosmetic benefits. Both languages are evolving: C into C++, Fortran into Fortran 90 and High Performance Fortran. We concentrate on the features of C, C++, and Fortran 90.

2.1.1 Fortran and C

Fortran 90 and C have the same control structures; both have conditionals, multiway branches, several types of loops, and recursion. They have the same basic types of data (integer, real, and character), although Fortran also supports the data type *complex*. C has structures, where Fortran 90 supports user-defined types.

Fortran 90 has explicit support for multi-dimensional arrays with bounds specified by the user. Support for arrays in C is defined in terms of address arithmetic; in essence, all C arrays have a lower bound of zero.

Both C and Fortran 90 have pointers, but Fortran 90 pointers are much more restricted. Fortran 90 pointers are typed, like Pascal pointers, and there is no mechanism to defeat the typing system. In fact, there is no syntax to specify a way to access the value of the pointer itself, unlike in both C and Pascal. Any reference to the pointer name implicitly dereferences the pointer; thus there is no analog to C pointer arithmetic in Fortran 90.

The languages support dynamic allocation, C through a standard run-time library and Fortran 90 through the `allocate` statement. In C, the size of the allocated object must be calculated in terms of bytes (or address units), whereas in Fortran 90, the size is computed by the compiled code.

The languages have similar scoping rules for names, except C allows declarations to appear at the start of any statement block. Fortran 90 allows nested procedures, which potentially improve the program structure, but many C implementations allow nesting also. Fortran 90 also has Modules, a la Ada Packages, to collect related data and procedures. Native C has nothing similar, but the object model of C++ can be used to achieve the same goals, and has other significant benefits also. Both Fortran 90 and C++ allow operator overloading; C++ has a richer set of operators and the overloading rules are more flexible, whereas Fortran 90 allows the programmer to define new operators using the "dot-dot" syntax, such as `.newop.` for new operator newop. C++ allows overloading of procedure names according to the types in the argument list; Fortran 90 also has procedure name overloading, though it is a bit more tedious.

One of Fortran 90's major additions is aggregate array assignments, which allow many matrix algebra operations to be written in a natural style, rather than using loops and elemental assignments.

By many measures, Fortran 90 is a higher level language than C, in that it does a better job of abstracting the target machine from the program. Moving from C to C++ with the proper object library can provide most of the abstractions that are lacking in native C. However, the implementation must be specified by the object library programmer; it is not native to the language. This can be viewed as an advantage or disadvantage; if the goal is to provide an extensible higher level language, the object model of C++ is an advantage. If the goal is to provide high performance, the object model of C++ does not give any advantage for compiled code over native C.

Data Layout

In most cases, the relative layout of elements in an array does not affect the meaning of the program. However, modern computer systems are optimized to take advantage of the locality of a reference in memory, and array layout can affect the locality. C, like most imperative programming languages, uses row-major storage order for arrays. In row-major order, two array elements whose index differs by one in the last (rightmost) subscript position will be allocated consecutively in memory. An array in C declared as `float a[3][4]` (so the array bounds are 0:2 and 0:3) will be laid out in memory as shown on the left in Figure 2.1. Fortran, on the other hand, uses column-major storage order for arrays; in column-major order, the first (leftmost) subscript position is laid out consecutively in memory. A Fortran array declared as `real a(3,4)` (so the array bounds are 1:3 and 1:4) will be laid out in memory as shown on the right in Figure 2.1.

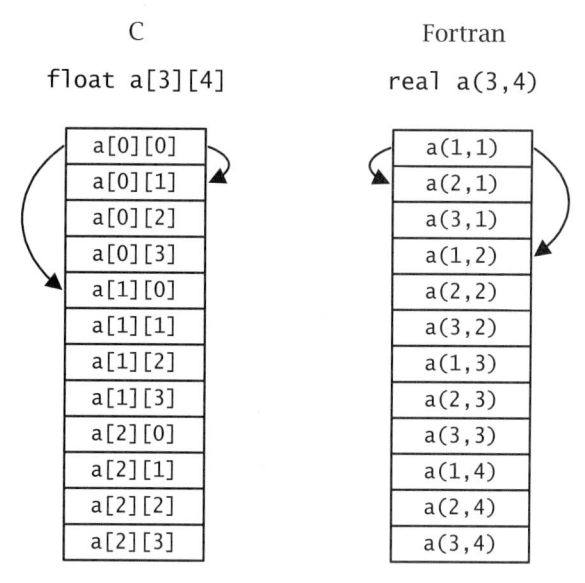

C	Fortran
`float a[3][4]`	`real a(3,4)`
a[0][0]	a(1,1)
a[0][1]	a(2,1)
a[0][2]	a(3,1)
a[0][3]	a(1,2)
a[1][0]	a(2,2)
a[1][1]	a(3,2)
a[1][2]	a(1,3)
a[1][3]	a(2,3)
a[2][0]	a(3,3)
a[2][1]	a(1,4)
a[2][2]	a(2,4)
a[2][3]	a(3,4)

FIGURE 2.1 Row-major and column-major storage order for a 3×4 array.

The *stride* of a dimension is the distance in memory words between two elements of an array whose indices differ by one in that dimension. As shown in Figure 2.1, the distance in words between `a[0][0]` and `a[1][0]` in row-major storage order is four words, so the first dimension has a stride of 4. In column-major storage order, the distance between `a(1,1)` and `a(2,1)` is one word, so the leftmost dimension of a Fortran array is the stride-1 dimension. Row-major or column-major storage order matters only when optimizing for memory locality. A compiler needs to know which dimension is the stride-1 dimension; whether it was originally leftmost or rightmost matters only to the parser.

A one-dimensional array in C can be dynamically allocated by computing the number of bytes (or address units, in general) to be allocated. The program sets a pointer to the base address of the array, and the subscripts are used as offsets from the base address. To dynamically allocate a two-dimensional array, a C program uses a one-dimensional array of pointers, each element of which points to one row of the two-dimensional array. The first subscript of the two-dimensional array reference is used as an offset into the array of pointers, retrieving the row pointer; the second subscript is used as an offset from the row pointer to get to the element. In C++, a matrix class could be used to hide these details behind a set of access functions.

In Fortran 90, multi-dimensional, dynamically allocated arrays are supported directly. An `allocate` statement specifies the lower and upper bounds for each dimension; the compiled code determines the size of the array, allocates that much memory, and saves a data structure, called a *dope vector*, to hold the array pointer and the array bounds. For instance, given the following array pointer declaration and allocation:

```
Real, Pointer :: p(:,:)
allocate p(2:n,-4:4)
```

the compiler can generate code to determine how many words are needed. The extent of the first dimension is $n - 2 + 1$, while the extent of the second dimension is $4 - (-4) + 1$; the product is $(n - 1) \times 9$. After allocating this many words, say at address *new*, assuming byte addressability and four bytes per array element, the code will set up the dope vector for p as shown in the following table.

address	A	new
lower-1	l_1	2
upper-1	u_1	n
stride-1	s_1	4
lower-2	l_2	-4
upper-2	u_2	4
stride-2	s_2	$4 \times (n - 1)$

To access element p(i,j), the generated code computes the address as $A + (i - l_1) \times s_1 + (j - l_2) \times s_2$. Some compilers optimize this access by extending the dope vector by one more value, the virtual address of the element by all zero subscripts, called the *origin*. This is easily computed as

origin	A_0	$new - l_1 \times s_1 - l_2 \times s_2$

With the virtual address of the origin, the address of any element p(i,j) can be simplified to $A_0 + i \times s_1 + j \times s_2$.

Example 2.1

Show the dope vector of a two-dimensional Fortran 90 array p allocated with bounds (2:10,-4:4) at address 1000, on a byte-addressable machine with four bytes per array element.

Solution
The dope vector would be filled in as shown in the following table.

address	A	1,000
lower-1	l_1	2
upper-1	u_1	10
stride-1	s_1	4
lower-2	l_2	-4
upper-2	u_2	4
stride-2	s_2	36
origin	A_0	1,136

For instance, the address of p(5,0) could be computed as $A + (5 - l_1) \times s_1 + (0 - l_2) \times s_2 = 1{,}000 + 3 \times 4 + 4 \times 36 = 1{,}156$, or using the origin as $A_0 + 5 \times s_1 + 0 \times s_2 = 1{,}136 + 20 = 1{,}156$.

Fortran Storage Association

Fortran `equivalence` statements allow multiple names to be used to access the same storage, to break the type-checking rules, for instance. The relation between the shared locations is determined by the storage association rules. Thus, a Fortran `real` variable must be the same size (in memory address units) as a Fortran `integer`, while a `complex` or `double precision` is twice as large. Thus, a `complex` variable can be equivalenced to two `real` variables, where the `real` variables will access the real and imaginary parts of the `complex` variable. This is defined by Fortran *storage association* rules, which define the relative sizes of typed objects. The *sequence association* rules for array layout define how two equivalenced arrays are mapped to the same locations.

Fortran `common` blocks are used to specify named global blocks of memory. Different subroutines or functions can give different declarations of the variables comprising a `common` block, again defeating the type-checking mechanism.

Within a single routine, the compiler must be aware of the aliasing that can occur between accesses through different names. Fortran `equivalence` statements can cause static aliasing between names, which can be handled easily. For intraprocedural analysis, `common` blocks may need to be treated as a single entity, with each variable mapped to its offset from the start of the block.

Argument-Passing Conventions

Fortran compilers use a call-by-reference argument-passing convention. The address of the actual argument is passed to the subroutine; this means that updating the formal argument also immediately updates the variable passed as the actual argument. If the actual argument is also visible in the subroutine, the two names are *aliases*; this is the situation for a and x in subroutine sub in Figure 2.2.

```
          common/block/ a
          a = 1
          call sub(a)
          print a
            :
          subroutine sub(x)
          common/block/ a
          x = 2
          print a
          end
```

FIGURE 2.2 Program with formal/actual aliasing in subroutine sub.

Two formal arguments can also be aliases if the same actual argument is passed to the two formals. Formal argument aliasing can seriously restrict the analysis and optimizations that a compiler can perform, unless the compiler can determine when aliasing does and does not occur. The Fortran standard allows argument aliasing, but states that whenever any formal is an alias of any other visible variable in a routine, only the formal can be accessed or updated; the original variable should not be used. A compiler or programming environment can also use interprocedural analysis to determine aliasing relationships.

The C language specifies a call-by-value parameter-passing convention for all actual arguments. To pass an array or a data structure, the calling routine must pass the address of the structure. With no prohibition on pointer aliasing, more compiler analysis is needed to determine whether an assignment to one array formal argument might update some other formal argument through aliasing. Either interprocedural analysis or procedure inlining can alleviate this problem, and the ANSI C standards committee is looking at directives to address this aliasing problem.

C++ defines call-by-value and call-by-reference parameter passing; the call-by-reference is shorthand for passing the address and dereferencing through the address in the called routine. Fortran 90 allows arbitrary subarrays to be passed to an assumed-shape array. The actual argument must be passed by dope vector, to include the bounds and strides of each dimension.

Pointer Aliasing

A compiler can treat each pointer dereference as another variable; in C, this means that *p can be treated like another variable, distinct from p, q and from *q. The compiler will still need to determine aliasing relationships between all these variables. For instance, can *p be aliased with *q, and can either of them be aliased with any other declared variable in the program? A first-order approximation of pointer aliasing is that any pointer dereference might be aliased with any other pointer dereference and with any variable whose address might have been assigned to that pointer; a global pointer might have been assigned the value of any global variable. Pointer tracking can help determine, at each dereference operator, what addresses might be in the pointer variable.

Fortran 90 pointers are more restricted, in that they can point only to objects of the same type. Moreover, only variables with the *target* attribute can have their address taken, so the alias sets for dereferenced pointers do not get so large. Fortran 90 also defines a special type of pointer variable, called an *allocatable* variable, which can be defined only by an `allocate` statement; an `allocatable` variable cannot be an alias for any other declared variable.

Fortran 90 has array pointers (different from pointer arrays) that are implemented by dope vectors. When the array pointer is assigned, either by a pointer assignment or by dynamic allocation, the dope vector base address, as well as the bounds and strides for each dimension, are filled.

C allows pointer arithmetic; in practice, this is used by programmers to get the effect of the standard strength-reduction optimization included in most compilers. Thus, rather than writing

```
for( i = 0; i < n; ++i ) a[i] = b[i] + 1;
```

a C programmer will write

```
for( ap = a, bp = b; ap < a+n; ++ap ) *ap = *bp++ + 1;
```

Compiler analysis must try to determine whether `ap` and `bp` are aliases of each other. The extra work that the programmer went through to write this loop actually obfuscates the intent of the loop to the compiler, and makes the kind of analysis required for parallel execution much more difficult.

2.1.2 High Performance Fortran

With the emphasis on highly parallel computer systems, many vendors, users, and researchers realized that current languages do not adequately support a migration path from existing programs to a data-parallel computational model. This has spawned a group called the High Performance Fortran Forum, whose goal is to design language extensions for Fortran to allow development of portable data-parallel programs.

The most important feature in High Performance Fortran (HPF) is that it allows the user to specify how to decompose and distribute the data arrays. This is done in three stages:

1. the programmer may declare one or more *templates*, or virtual processor domains;
2. the programmer aligns each distributed data array to another array or to one of the templates;

3. the programmer distributes the arrays or templates onto the actual processor ensemble.

In the simplest form, a program can simply distribute an array directly. As an example, an HPF program may start with the following declarations:

```
real x(16),y(16),z(16)
distribute x(block), y(cyclic), z(cyclic(2))
```

If this is executed on four processors, then the data will be distributed among the processors as shown in Figure 2.3. The details of more complex data layouts are covered in Chapter 13.

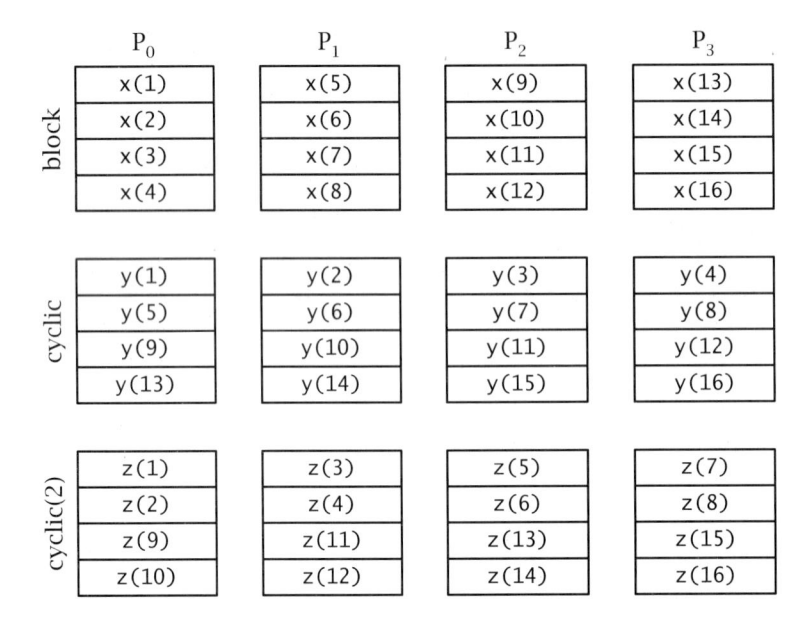

	P_0	P_1	P_2	P_3
block	x(1)	x(5)	x(9)	x(13)
	x(2)	x(6)	x(10)	x(14)
	x(3)	x(7)	x(11)	x(15)
	x(4)	x(8)	x(12)	x(16)
cyclic	y(1)	y(2)	y(3)	y(4)
	y(5)	y(6)	y(7)	y(8)
	y(9)	y(10)	y(11)	y(12)
	y(13)	y(14)	y(15)	y(16)
cyclic(2)	z(1)	z(3)	z(5)	z(7)
	z(2)	z(4)	z(6)	z(8)
	z(9)	z(11)	z(13)	z(15)
	z(10)	z(12)	z(14)	z(16)

FIGURE 2.3 Data layout for distributed arrays.

When a subroutine is called, there is a potential mismatch between the distribution of the actual argument and that of the formal. There are three ways to resolve this, and all three are supported in HPF. The first is for the compiler to generate code to redistribute the actual argument so it will match the distribution of the formal argument. Upon return, the argument must be sent back to its original distribution. This is essentially a call-by-value-result convention, except that if the actual and formal arguments have the same distribution to start with, no copying is necessary.

The second option is for the formal argument to inherit the distribution of the actual argument. This makes for an efficient call statement, but potentially generates inefficient code in the procedure, since the procedure must be able to support any possible data distribution. Interprocedural analysis may allow the compiler to find all distributions that are actually used at any call site, and only generate code to support those distributions.

The third option is for the procedure to declare a distribution and to require that the actual argument match that distribution. This essentially makes the distribution part of the type of the formal argument; the compiler may be able to check that the distribution matches at call statements just as it checks for type conflicts.

HPF also added a `forall` construct, essentially a type of parallel loop. We discuss parallel loops in general, and the HPF `forall` in particular, in Section 2.2.

Implementation of HPF requires a sophisticated compiler to determine when and where to insert interprocessor communication and use temporary variables, and to have each processor execute a portion of each parallel construct. Because of the nature of the machines on which it will run and the applications for which it is designed, any sequential bottleneck in HPF will result in drastically reduced performance. Many of these details are discussed in Chapter 13. Since the language is still somewhat experimental, many details may change over time.

2.1.3 Declarative Languages

Declarative languages try to address some of the problems of the Fortran and C family of languages. A declarative language avoids explicit parallelism in favor of implicit parallelism, extracted by the compiler, the run-time system, or the hardware. Each name in a declarative language is defined once; the definition gives the type and the value of the name. Since the values do not vary, such a language does not have variables. Since each name is defined only once, the value of any name used anywhere is naturally easy to find. SISAL, Haskell, and Crystal are examples of declarative languages designed to address some of the application domains in which Fortran and C are now used.

Compilers for these languages must perform several important optimizations to improve the quality (speed and memory usage) of the generated code. For instance, to support the single-assignment rule, a declarative program often uses many times more memory than a corresponding imperative program. Since an array name cannot be redefined, a new array must be allocated and defined, even if most of the values have not changed. A compiler can perform two important analyses to optimize this, and experience has shown that the analyses are effective:

- Build-in-place analysis determines when the memory for an expression can be preallocated (perhaps statically) and the computation converted into assignments to those memory locations. This is particularly important when looking at programs that concatenate two arrays; if the two arrays can be preallocated to be adjacent in the first place, then the concatenate operation turns into a no-op. The analysis looks for nonloop expressions (whose size can always be determined) and uniform loop expressions (in which the same number of elements are generated with each iteration of the loop).

- Update-in-place analysis determines when the computation for a new array can be replaced by assignments to elements of the old values for the array. If there are no more uses for, or instances of, the old array, the computation can always be done "in place." If there are potentially more uses for the old array value, the compiler may delay the update until the old uses are complete, and then update the array in place.

The technology for optimizing declarative languages is the same as that for imperative languages. The process of finding the parallel and sequential operations differs, but declarative language compilers use the same analysis methods and the same optimization and mapping strategies to generate code.

2.2 Sequential and Parallel Loops

Many languages used in research include some sort of parallel iterative control structure. Calling this a parallel loop is an oxymoron, since there is no "loop" in a parallel loop, but it gets the idea across. Here we explore several types of loops, or iterative constructs, and show how they relate to one another.

In our examples, we use for to mean a sequential loop. A sequential loop is defined to mean that the second iteration does not start until the first iteration is complete, and so on. In the same way, a sequential list of statements is defined to mean that the second statement does not start until the first statement is complete. As we mentioned in Chapter 1, the compiler and system really need to preserve only the observable behavior of the program; if the compiler can determine that reordering the iterations or statements is not observable, then it is legal to do so.

An array assignment, as in Fortran 90, is similar to an iterative construct. In many cases, an array assignment can be replaced by a sequential loop. For instance, the array assignment:

```
a(1:n) = b(0:n-1)*2 + c(2:n+1)
```

can be executed as the Fortran loop:

```
do i = 1, n
    a(i) = b(i-1)*2 + c(i+1)
enddo
```

as long as a is not an alias for b or c. In fact, Fortran 90 defines an array assignment as fetching all right-hand side variables, computing the right-hand side expression, and then assigning the left-hand side variable. Thus, the array assignment:

```
a(1:n) = a(0:n-1)*2 + a(2:n+1)
```

is not equivalent to the sequential Fortran loop:

```
do i = 1, n
    a(i) = a(i-1)*2 + a(i+1)
enddo
```

The array assignment will use "old" values for a(0:n-1) and a(2:n+1), whereas the loop will use old values for a(i+1), but will use newly computed values for a(i-1). For example, with n=4 and the initial values as shown, the following table gives the values computed by the array assignment and the loop above.

	initial value	after array assignment	after loop
a(0)	1		
a(1)	2	1 + 3 = 4	1 + 3 = 4
a(2)	3	2 + 4 = 6	4 + 4 = 8
a(3)	4	3 + 5 = 8	8 + 5 = 13
a(4)	5	4 + 6 = 10	13 + 6 = 19
a(5)	6		

To capture this behavior, we define a parallel loop corresponding to an array assignment, called a forall loop. A simple forall loop may contain one or more assignment statements. If a forall loop contains a single assignment, then it is executed just like an array assignment, as defined earlier. If the forall loop contains several assignments, then each statement is executed completely for all values of the index variable before the next statement is started. Strictly speaking, the forall is not defined to be parallel, but is aimed at data-parallel computations, and parallel implementations are allowed. The above array assignment could thus be written as follows:

```
forall( i = 1:n )
    a(i) = a(i-1) + a(i+1)
endforall
```

Another type of parallel loop is designed for multiprocessor execution. We call this a *dopar*, which may contain one or more assignments or other statements, or even other loops. The execution model is that each iteration of the loop is executed in parallel by a different processor; the code within each iteration is executed sequentially. Moreover, the initial state of all the data seen by each processor (or each iteration) is the initial state before the loop was initiated. That is, any variable updates done in one iteration cannot be seen by any other iteration, since the other iteration starts with a clean slate. If two different iterations change the same variable or array element, each iteration sees only its own modification. After the loop, all modified data is combined into the global state. If two iterations changed the same variable, the result is a nondeterministic merge (one of the two modified values will win). If we replaced the `forall` by a `dopar` in the short example above, the results would be the same. The results of `forall` and `dopar` execution can differ when there are multiple statements.

Example 2.2

Show the values generated by the following loop if written as a `for`, `forall`, or `dopar`.

```
loop i = 1,4
    a(i) = a(i)+1
    b(i) = a(i-1)+a(i+1)
endloop
```

Solution

The three loops in question are:

```
for i = 1,4              forall( i=1:4 )           dopar( i=1:4 )
  a(i)=a(i)+1              a(i)=a(i)+1               a(i)=a(i)+1
  b(i)=a(i-1)+a(i+1)       b(i)=a(i-1)+a(i+1)        b(i)=a(i-1)+a(i+1)
endfor                   endforall                 enddopar
```

The difference is that the assignment to b(i) in the `for` loop sees the updates to a only from *previous* iterations; the assignment in the `forall` sees the updates to a from *all* iterations, whereas the assignment in the `dopar` sees *no* updates to a except the one in that iteration, to a(i), which is not used in the assignment to b(i). The following table with the initial value of the array a shows the computed value of the array b by each loop.

	initial value		after for loop	after forall loop	after dopar loop
a(0)	1				
a(1)	2	b(1)	4	5	4
a(2)	3	b(2)	7	8	6
a(3)	4	b(3)	9	10	8
a(4)	5	b(4)	11	11	10
a(5)	6				

The name `doall` is given to a `dopar` where there are no conflicts between iterations; that is, where an element that is assigned is used on that iteration only. In such a case, executing the iterations sequentially or in parallel in any order is legal, since the result does not depend on the order. Note that a doall is a special case of a dopar, not a separate type of loop. A sequential loop that has no conflicts is also sometimes called a doall.

Some people use the term doacross to mean a loop that is executed on multiple processors by assigning different iterations to different processors, but in which values assigned in one iteration are used in another iteration. A doacross is the same as a sequential for loop; since it is not really a type of a loop, we will not use the term doacross.

The final type of loop we discuss represents single-assignment execution, called dosingle. Each variable assigned in a dosingle loop must be indexed by all the loop index variables, and each element must be assigned only once (the single-assignment rule). Any use of a variable or element must use the value assigned to that element; since each element is assigned only once, there is no ambiguity. The loops shown in Example 2.2 cannot be written as dosingle, because they define a variable in terms of itself (a(i)=a(i)+1) or they define variables in terms of each other (a(i)=a(i-1)+a(i+1)).

The following loop gives different results when it is written as a for, forall, dopar, or dosingle:

(1)   loop i = 1:4
(2)   a(i) = a(i-1)+1
(3)   b(i) = b(i+1)+a(i-1)
(4)   endloop

The four types of loop have different interpretations as to whether the old value (coming into the loop) or the new value (computed in the loop) will be used for the three array references on the right-hand side. A statement in a for sees updates from previous iterations, or from previous statements in this iteration. A statement in a forall sees all updates from previous statements, regardless of the iteration of the update. A statement in a dopar sees only updates from previous statements in the same iteration. A statement in a dosingle sees all updates, from previous or subsequent iterations and from previous or subsequent statements. For this example, the following table tells which right-hand side references would get old or new values, depending on the type of the loop.

	(2) a(i-1)	(3) a(i-1)	(3) b(i+1)
for	new	new	old
forall	old	new	old
dopar	old	old	old
dosingle	new	new	new

Suppose the initial values are:

	0	1	2	3	4	5
a	3	3	3	3	3	3
b	1	2	3	4	5	6

If the loop is replaced by one of the four loop types, the newly computed values will be as shown in Figure 2.4.

for	0	1	2	3	4	5
a	—	4	5	6	7	—
b	—	6	8	10	12	—
forall	0	1	2	3	4	5
a	—	4	4	4	4	—
b	—	6	8	9	10	—
dopar	0	1	2	3	4	5
a	—	4	4	4	4	—
b	—	6	7	8	9	—
dosingle	0	1	2	3	4	5
a	—	4	5	6	7	—
b	—	24	21	17	12	—

FIGURE 2.4 Newly computed values for arrays a and b for a simple loop; the dashes mean those elements are not changed from the previous value.

2.3 Roundoff Error

Computer floating point arithmetic has finite precision; the computational result of adding two numbers may not always be the exact arithmetic answer. If the machine has only 7 digits of accuracy, adding 1.000000 to 0.000000001 will produce 1.000000. The lost digits are called *roundoff error*. It used to be the case that different computers had different floating point representations and rounding algorithms, so that programs might get different answers depending on the host machine. Now, most computers use IEEE floating point representation, so this problem is greatly reduced. While IEEE floating point arithmetic is commutative (the result of a*b is the same as b*a) it is not necessarily associative; (a+b)+c may give a different result than a+(b+c). Reassociation of unparenthesized expressions is allowed by many languages. In fact, some languages allow the compiler to replace an expression with any computationally equivalent expression. This allows replacing division by 2 with multiplication by 1/2, for instance, or even applying the distributive rule to change b*c+b*d into b*(c+d). Note that the inverse replacement is not generally allowed, since parentheses usually cannot be violated by the compiler.

Most of the transformations presented here will preserve the behavior of the program, right down to preserving the same roundoff error. Some optimizations will change the roundoff error. It is important to note that a different answer isn't necessarily wrong. It isn't any more wrong than the original answer was; both answers suffer from roundoff error. If a difference in roundoff error accumulation causes a significant difference in the answer, perhaps the algorithm is unstable and should be replaced. This is out of the realm of compilers. In later chapters we will see that there are ways to preserve the roundoff error of optimized code. Commercial compilers have a command line switch to disable any roundoff-sensitive transformations.

2.4 In the Pit

The Fortran rules for argument passing allow the use of a call-by-value-result convention; however, all compilers use a call-by-reference mechanism. Pascal, for example, uses call-by-value for read-only scalar parameters, and call-by-reference for read-write scalars and for all arrays and structures. Call-by-value for arrays and structures would involve copying potentially large amounts of memory, so call-by-reference is more efficient; call-by-value for scalars eliminates the extra dereference through the argument pointer to get to the argument value.

Fortran programs, however, do not need to declare the intent of each argument; any argument may be read or modified. Moreover, the compiler cannot tell from the call whether the formal argument is a scalar or an array. For instance, the following call statement:

```
real a(4,4), x
call sub( a(2,2), x )
```

might be passing a(2,2) to a scalar (in which case call-by-value-result would be efficient) or it might be passing a(2,2) as the starting point of an array (in which case call-by-reference is appropriate). The mapping of the elements of a to the array in the subroutine is determined by the column-major storage layout. The result is that the calling convention for arrays and scalars must be compatible, so call-by-reference is used. Fortran 90 includes `interface` blocks, in which the type and intent of formal arguments can be declared. This may allow compilers to use an efficient call-by-value convention for read-only scalars.

The Fortran rules for formal argument aliasing actually state that when a formal is aliased to another variable and one of the aliases is updated, the result of the program is undefined. This means that the compiler may generate code that preserves the aliasing relationship or that violates it, but the nonstandard behavior need not be detected. Programs that depend on aliasing behavior may not be portable across compilers. Since most programs do not use aliases in this way, this is not a serious problem. However, some programs do depend on aliasing, so commercial compilers usually have a switch to let the programmer tell the compiler whether the program violates the aliasing rules.

Both C and Fortran allow arrays to be reshaped across a call; that is, an array declared to be $n \times m$ can be passed to a routine that declares the incoming array to be a different shape. The routine might declare it to be a single nm-long one-dimensional array, or it might declare it as a $n/2 \times 2m$ array, or some other shape. In Fortran, using storage association rules, the routine may even declare the array to be of a different type. Such practices can complicate interprocedural analysis and inlining.

Of the early vendors of massively parallel systems, few had data-parallel languages that did not expose the details of the architecture as part of their program development toolkit. Several had adopted a parallel Fortran in which the unit of parallelism was an array assignment statement. High Performance Fortran owes much of its design to experience with these languages and to research work on the Suprenum machines and the Fortran D language.

In HPF, there are actually four levels in the data decomposition and distribution strategy. The third level distributes the virtual processor domain onto what are called abstract processors; system software finally determines the mapping of abstract processors to physical CPUs.

To handle the problem of subroutines with multiple reaching distributions, the Fortran D compiler performs interprocedural reaching distributions analysis, and clones each subroutine that has more than one set of reaching distributions for its arguments.

The term `forall` was suggested as an extension to Fortran 90 as an alternative to array assignments. It was implemented in the Thinking Machines' Connection Machine Fortran compiler, and subsequently added to the HPF standard. The `dopar` model of parallel loop was supported by the hardware and operating system of the Myrias SPS parallel computer system.

2.5 Further Reading

A history of the early Fortran language and compilers is given by Backus (1981); several interesting comments are made there, including some from users who were unhappy with the speed of the compiler, and an excerpt from a November 1954 Fortran Preliminary Report stating that "...Fortran should virtually eliminate coding and debugging ..." (relative to machine language programming, of course). Fortran 90 programmers can find a description of the language by Metcalf and Reid (1990), whereas compiler writers may want the complete details by Adams et al. (1992). High Performance Fortran is fully described in the handbook by Koelbel et al. (1994). Both the "traditional" C language and ANSI standard C are described by Harbison and Steele (1991). C++ is described by in a primer by Lippman (1991). Pros and cons of using C for numerical computing are discussed by MacDonald (1991).

The general parallel loop model discussed in this chapter is presented more extensively by Li and Wolfe (1994).

Advocates of higher level programming languages have always been hampered by the relatively weak performance of these languages on numerical codes compared to sequential languages like Fortran or C with aggressive optimizing compilers. Cann (1992) shows evidence that optimized SISAL code can approach and beat the speed of Fortran code, so performance should no longer an obstacle for declarative programming languages.

EXERCISES

2.1 Simulate the execution of the following program with three parameter-passing conventions:
   (a) call-by-value;
   (b) call-by-value-result;
   (c) call-by-reference.

```
global x
x = 1
call sub( x )
print x
procedure sub( a )
global x
a = 2
print x
end sub
```

2.2 Show the values computed for the array a in the following program:

```
for i = 1 to 5 do
    a(i) = i
endfor
for i = 1 to 4 do
    a(i) = a(i+1) - 1
endfor
```

2.3 Show the values computed for the program above if the for is replaced by a forall.

2.4 Show the values computed for the program above if the for is replaced by a dopar.

2.5 Show the values computed for the program above if the for is replaced by a dosingle.

2.6 Show the values computed by the program above if the loops are run backward instead of forward.

2.7 Loop reversal (running a loop backward) can change the meaning of a sequential loop. Can it change the meaning of a `forall`, `dopar`, or `dosingle`? In each case, if so, give an example; if not, explain why not.

2.8 In Chapter 1, we mentioned that the i or j loops of the matrix multiplication routine could be written as `doall`. Verify this by showing that no element assigned in any iteration of the i (or j) loop is used by any other iteration of that loop.

2.9 Which loops of the matrix multiplication routine could be written as `forall`?

2.10 Matrix multiplication can be written with all `dosingle` loops, but the left-hand side array must be expanded with another dimension to allow each iteration to assign a different element. Rewrite matrix multiplication with `dosingle` loops, after expanding c to a three-dimensional array.

2.11 The exercises of Chapter 1 showed a routine for Gaussian elimination without pivoting. Which of the loops of that routine could be converted to a `dopar`?

2.12 Prove that a `dopar` loop containing a single statement always computes the same result as a `forall` loop with the same limits and single statement.

2.13 Prove that computer arithmetic has finite precision by computing the following sum, in the language of your choice:

```
sum = 0.0
oldsum = sum
addend = 1.0
while oldsum ≠ sum do
    oldsum = sum
    addend = addend / 2
    sum = sum + addend
endwhile
```

Print out the value of sum and addend.

2.14 Find the smallest number that can be added to 1.0 in floating point notation and still be computationally significant. This is done with the following loop:

```
epsilon = 1.0
while epsilon+1.0 ≠ 1.0 do
    epsilon = epsilon / 2
endwhile
epsilon = epsilon * 2
```

Compute the value of epsilon for single precision (Fortran `real` or C `float`) and for double precision (Fortran `double precision` or C `double`).

3 BASIC GRAPH CONCEPTS

Compilers use sets and graphs to represent various aspects of the program while doing analysis and optimization. This chapter focuses on notation and terminology that are commonly used in compilers, and introduces several important algorithms. It also provides an introduction to many basic graph concepts that are used throughout the rest of the text. A short review of terminology dealing with logic, sets, and tuples is followed by discussion of graphs, directed graphs, trees, and algorithms related to graphs. We assume familiarity with set notation and set algebra (set membership, union, intersection, difference). We close with computation of control dependence in a control flow graph. The word iff is used in the common way to mean "if and only if."

3.1 Sets, Tuples, Logic

A *set* is a collection of objects; we use capital italic letters to denote sets, such as A and B. The *cardinality* of a set is its number of elements, and is a nonnegative integer; we write $|A|$ to denote the cardinality of the set A. The cardinality of a set may be zero, in which case we say the set is *empty*; we use $\emptyset$ to denote the empty set. The cardinality of a set may be infinite, such as $|\mathbb{N}|$, since there are infinitely many natural numbers. The symbols $\mathbb{N}$, $\mathbb{Z}$, and $\mathbb{R}$ are used to represent natural numbers, integers, and real numbers. We use common notation for sets; for example, $P = \{red, blue, green\}$ denotes the set P of the three primary colors. We say that *red* is a member of the set P by writing $red \in P$. A set A is a subset of B, written $A \subseteq B$, iff every element of A is also a member of B. The set A is a proper subset of B, written $A \subset B$, iff $A \subseteq B$ but $A \neq B$.

A *tuple* is an ordered pair of objects. We write $\langle x, y \rangle$ to denote the pair x and y in that order. Note that x may be equal to y. Whereas order and duplication do not matter for sets, they do for tuples. The set $\{red, blue\} = \{blue, red\}$, but $\langle red, blue \rangle \neq \langle blue, red \rangle$. We extend the concept of ordered pair in the natural way to an ordered list of n objects and call this an n-tuple, written $\langle x_1, x_2, \ldots, x_n \rangle$.

The *cross product* of two sets A and B is the set of all tuples $\langle a, b \rangle$ such that $a \in A$ and $b \in B$. The cross product is denoted $A \times B$. A *partition* of a set A is a sequence of sets $A_1, A_2, \ldots, A_n$ such that $A_i \cap A_j = \emptyset$ whenever $i \neq j$, and $A_1 \cup A_2 \cup \cdots \cup A_n = A$.

A *proposition* is a statement that is either true or false. Thus the statement $a \in B$ is a proposition that is true if a is in the set B, and false if not. We use the logical negation operation $\neg$ or an overbar to mean "not"; if P is true, then $\neg P$ and $\overline{P}$ must be false. We can combine propositions with logical operators, such as $\wedge$ to mean "and," as in $a \in B \wedge b \in B$, and $\vee$ to mean "or," as in $a \in B \vee b \in B$. The former statement is true only if both a and b are in set B, while the latter is true if either element is a member of the set. We also use the symbol $\Rightarrow$ for implication. The statement $a \in B \Rightarrow \{a\} \subseteq B$ means that the second proposition ($\{a\} \subseteq B$) is true whenever the first proposition ($a \in B$) is true. Formally, if P and Q are propositions, the implication $P \Rightarrow Q$ is equivalent to $\neg P \vee Q$. Two propositions are equivalent, written $p_1 \equiv p_2$, when $(p_1 \Rightarrow p_2) \wedge (p_2 \Rightarrow p_1)$.

We will use the existential quantifier $\exists$, read as "there exists," and the universal quantifier $\forall$, read as "for all," to bind free variables in propositions. Thus $(\forall x \in \mathbb{Z})(\exists y \in integer)[x = 2y]$ is a proposition that states that for all integers x, there is an integer y such that $x = 2y$; this is a false proposition, because letting $x = 1$, there is no integer y such that $1 = 2y$. We can use propositions to define sets, such as the set of even integers:

$$\{y | (\exists x \in integer)[y = 2x]\}$$

3.2 Graphs

A graph G consists of a set of *nodes* (or *vertices*) V, and a set of *edges* E, where each edge $e \in E$ is an ordered pair of nodes. Formally: $G = \langle V, E \rangle$ where $E \subseteq V \times V$. A graph $G' = \langle V', E' \rangle$ is a *subgraph* of G if $V' \subseteq V$ and $E' \subseteq E$.

A graph is *undirected* if $\langle X, Y \rangle \in E \Rightarrow \langle Y, X \rangle \in E$; that is, edges are undirected if they connect nodes in both directions. If $\langle X, Y \rangle \in E$ then X and Y are *adjacent* nodes of G, or are *neighbors*. The *degree* of a node is the number of neighbors adjacent to it.

Example 3.1

What is the degree of each node in the undirected graph shown in Figure 3.1?

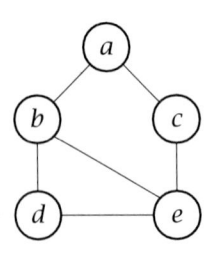

FIGURE 3.1 Sample undirected graph.

Solution

The graph in Figure 3.1 shows a graph with five nodes; the neighbors and degree of each node are shown in the following table.

X	Neighbors(X)	degree
a	b, c	2
b	a, d, e	3
c	a, e	2
d	b, e	2
e	b, c, d	3

In a *directed graph*, the edges have a direction. We will usually write $X \rightarrow Y$ when $\langle X, Y \rangle \in E$ in a directed graph. In this case, X is a *predecessor* of Y, and Y is a *successor* of X. For an edge $X \rightarrow Y$, X is the *source* node, and Y is the *target* node. We define PRED(X) as the set of all predecessors of node X, and SUCC(X) as the set of all successors of X. If $X \rightarrow Y$, then $X \in$ PRED(Y) and $Y \in$ SUCC(X).

The *indegree* of a node X is the number of edges of the form $W \rightarrow X$, and the *outdegree* of X is the number of edges $X \rightarrow Y$. A node is a *source node*, or *entry node*, if its indegree is zero; and a *sink node*, or *exit node* if its outdegree is zero. By definition, the outdegree of node X is the cardinality of SUCC(X), and the indegree is the cardinality of PRED(X).

A *path* in a graph from node X_0 to X_k ($k \geq 0$) is a list of nodes $\langle X_0, X_1, \ldots, X_k \rangle$ such that $X_0 \rightarrow X_1$, $X_1 \rightarrow X_2$, ..., $X_{k-1} \rightarrow X_k$. The *length* of a path is k, the number of edges making up the path. A trivial path is made from zero edges (such as $\langle X_0 \rangle$); a nontrivial path has one or more edges. We usually write a path as $X_0 \rightarrow X_1 \rightarrow X_2 \rightarrow \cdots \rightarrow X_k$. A path is *simple* if the nodes $X_0, \ldots, X_k$ are distinct, except that X_0 may be the same as X_k. A nontrivial path is a *cycle* if $X_0 = X_k$, and is a *simple cycle* if it is both a cycle and simple. A length-1 path from a node to itself, $X \rightarrow X$, is a *self-cycle*. A directed graph that has cycles is *cyclic*; otherwise the graph is *acyclic*, and is called a directed acyclic graph, or DAG.

Example 3.2

Name the source and sink nodes and the simple cycles of the directed graph in Figure 3.2.

Solution
This directed graph has two source nodes, a and b, and one sink node, g. There are two simple cycles, comprising $c \rightarrow d \rightarrow f \rightarrow c$, which is equivalent to $d \rightarrow f \rightarrow c \rightarrow d$ or $f \rightarrow c \rightarrow d \rightarrow f$, and $c \rightarrow e \rightarrow f \rightarrow c$, which also has two equivalent simple cycles.

If there is a path from node X to node Y, then we say Y is *reachable* from X, or that X reaches Y. We write $X \stackrel{*}{\rightarrow} Y$ to mean that there is a path from X to Y, though it may be a trivial path if $X = Y$. We write $X \stackrel{+}{\rightarrow} Y$ to mean there is a path from X

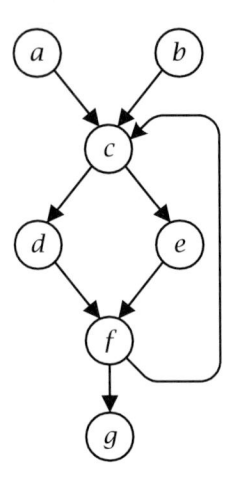

FIGURE 3.2 Sample directed graph.

to Y with length greater than zero. We write $p : X \stackrel{*}{\to} Y$ to mean p is the name of a (possibly trivial) path from X to Y, and $|p|$ is the length of that path.

In general, directed graphs may have many source nodes and sink nodes or none at all. A graph with a single source node that reaches every other node in the graph is called a *single-entry graph*. A graph with a single sink node that is reachable from every other node is a *single-exit graph*.

A *multigraph* is a graph that may have multiple distinct edges between two nodes. In a regular graph, an edge $\langle X, Y \rangle \in E$ is a relation, showing that node X is related by an edge to node Y. In a multigraph, the edge $e_1 = \langle X, Y \rangle \in E$ is an object, which may be distinct from another edge $e_2 = \langle X, Y \rangle \in E$. Figure 3.3 shows a single-entry, single-exit multigraph, with two distinct edges from node c to node e.

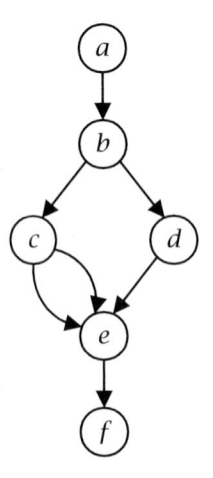

FIGURE 3.3 Sample directed multigraph.

3.2.1 Trees

A *tree* is a DAG with a single source node, called *Root*, and with a unique path from *Root* to every other node. If there is an edge $X \to Y$ in a tree, then X is the *parent* of Y, and Y is a *child* of X. Two nodes with the same parent are *siblings*. Every node (except *Root*) has a unique parent, and thus has indegree of one. If there is a path from X to Y, then X is an *ancestor* of Y, and Y is a *descendant* of X; in addition, if $X \neq Y$, then X is a *proper ancestor* of Y. A *leaf* is a node of the tree with no children.

Levels can be assigned to the nodes of a tree as follows:

- $Level(Root) = 1$;
- $Level(X) = Level(Parent(X)) + 1$ for all $X \neq Root$.

The *height* of a tree is the length of the longest path from *Root* to any leaf. A tree traversal *visits* each node in the tree in some order; visiting a node usually involves some operation on that node. A *breadth-first traversal* of a tree visits all the nodes at level i before visiting any node at level $i+1$, starting at *Root*. A *depth-first traversal* of a tree recursively visits each node and all its descendants before returning to visit any other children of its parent. A simple depth-first traversal program is shown below:

```
(1)    DepthFirst(Root)

(2)    procedure DepthFirst(X)
(3)        for C ∈ Child(X) do
(4)            DepthFirst(C)
(5)        endfor
(6)    end DepthFirst
```

A *preorder* traversal of a tree is a depth-first traversal that visits each node before visiting any of its children. In the procedure DepthFirst, the preorder traversal would visit or operate on each node just before line 3. A preorder numbering starts by numbering *Root* as one, then sequentially numbers each node as it is visited in a preorder traversal. The numbering is not unique; it depends on the order in which the children of each node are visited. If the children of a node are ordered (by any scheme, however arbitrary), the preorder numbering is unique. We assume the children of each node are ordered when the tree is constructed, and the order remains fixed, even if there is no particular reason for the order. By convention, we draw trees with the children ordered in a left-to-right fashion. Given this convention, a preorder numbering visits the children of a node in a left-to-right order.

Example 3.3

Write a depth-first traversal program to assign a preorder number to each node. Show an example tree with numbers assigned.

Solution

A sample solution is shown below:

(1) $N = 0$
(2) LNumber(Root)

(3) procedure LNumber(X)
(4) $N = N + 1$
(5) $NPre(X) = N$
(6)   for $C \in Child(X)$ do
(7)   LNumber(C)
(8)   endfor
(9) end LNumber

Running this algorithm on the tree in Figure 3.4 assigns numbers as shown, where the preorder numbers are to the left of each node, and a is the root node.

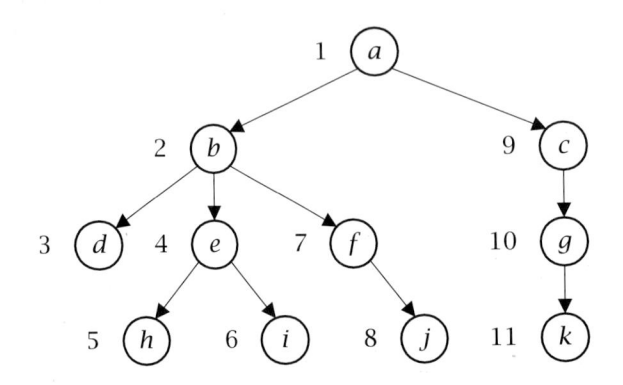

FIGURE 3.4 Sample tree with preorder numbers assigned.

In a preorder numbering, if $NPre(X) < NPre(Y)$, then X is either a proper ancestor of Y in the tree, or X is *to the left* of Y, i.e., a descendant of some left sibling of some ancestor of Y. In contrast, a backward preorder numbering will visit the children in a right-to-left order; if $NPreBack(X) < NPreBack(Y)$, then X is either a proper ancestor of Y in the tree, or is *to the right* of Y, i.e., a descendant of some right sibling of some ancestor of Y. The sample tree with backward preorder numbers is shown in Figure 3.5.

A *postorder* traversal of a tree is a depth-first traversal that visits a node only after visiting all its proper descendants. In the procedure DepthFirst, a postorder

3.2 ▪ Graphs

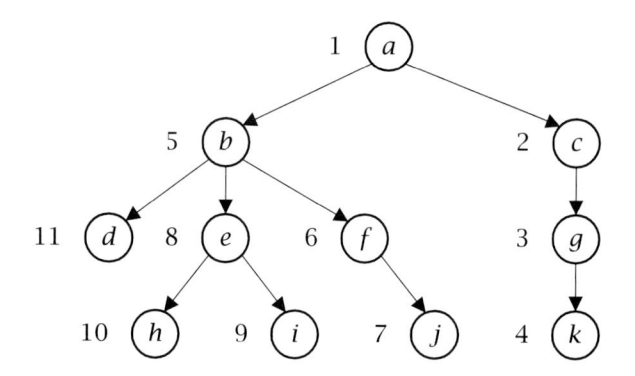

FIGURE 3.5 Sample tree with backward preorder numbers assigned.

traversal would visit or operate on each node just after line 5. A postorder numbering will number the leftmost leaf as one (again using a left-to-right ordering of children), and *Root* will have the largest number. As with preorder numberings, a backward order (right-to-left) can also be used. A reverse numbering visits the nodes in the same order, but assigns numbers to the nodes by counting down from $|V|$ to one, instead of counting up.

Example 3.4

Write a depth-first traversal program to assign a reverse postorder number to each node. Show that this is the same as the backward preorder number.

Solution

A sample reverse postorder numbering algorithm is shown below:

```
(1)    M = |V|
(2)    RPostorder(Root)

(3)    procedure RPostorder(X)
(4)        for C ∈ Child(X) do
(5)            RPostorder(C)
(6)        endfor
(7)        NRPost(X) = M
(8)        M = M − 1
(9)    end RPostorder
```

As with a backward preorder numbering, this algorithm will assign to each node a number that is less than that of its children. Also, each node will have a number less than that of any left sibling; in fact, every descendant of this node will have a number less than that of any descendant of any left sibling. Thus, if *NRPost*(*X*) < *NRPost*(*Y*), then *X* is either a proper ancestor of *Y* in the tree, or is to the right of Y, i.e., a descendant of some right sibling of some ancestor of Y. These are the properties satisfied by the backward preorder numbering. Running this algorithm on the same tree as before assigns the same numbers as shown in Figure 3.5.

▲

We can use the properties of preorder and postorder numbers to determine, in constant time, whether one node is a proper ancestor of another. Just keeping the preorder number at each node is not sufficient; $NPre(X) < NPre(Y)$ can't distinguish whether X is a proper ancestor or just to the left of Y. However, we can keep both the preorder and reverse postorder numbers; whenever

$$(NPre(X) < NPre(Y)) \wedge (NRPost(X) < NRPost(Y))$$

then X must be a proper ancestor of Y in the tree. Another well-known method keeps a count of the number of proper descendants of each node. Then,

$$NPre(X) < NPre(Y) \wedge NPre(X) + Count(X) \geq NPre(Y)$$

indicates that X is a proper ancestor of Y.

3.2.2 The Control Flow Graph

Compilers use directed graphs to represent various data structures in the program, the most important of these graphs is the control flow graph (CFG). The program is broken up into a set of *basic blocks*, each of which is a sequence of (zero or more) instructions with no branch instructions, except perhaps the last instruction, and no branch targets or labels, except perhaps at the first instruction. Each basic block may correspond to a straight-line sequence of statements, a single statement, or even an individual operation. In a CFG, each node represents a basic block, while edges represent potential flow of control between basic blocks. A conditional branch is represented by a node with two or more graph successors.

One characteristic of a CFG that distinguishes it from other directed graph is the presence of a unique source node, called *Entry*, from which all other nodes in the CFG are reachable.

We denote a CFG as the tuple $\langle V, E, Entry \rangle$ such that:

- $\langle V, E \rangle$ is a directed graph (or multigraph);
- $Entry \in V$ is a unique source node; and
- all nodes are reachable from $Entry$: $(\forall v \in V)[Entry \xrightarrow{*} v]$.

A sub-CFG is a subgraph of a CFG with the same properties as a CFG. that is, a sub-CFG has a set of nodes and edges, with a unique entry node, such that all other nodes are reachable from the entry node.

3.2.3 Spanning Trees

Given a CFG $G = \langle V_G, E_G, Entry_G \rangle$, a *spanning tree* is a subgraph T of G with $V_T = V_G$ and $E_T \subseteq E_G$ such that T is a tree with $Root_T = Entry_G$. That is, a spanning tree is a tree rooted at *Entry* that *spans* (contains) all the nodes in the CFG, and where all the edges in the spanning tree are edges in the CFG. Since all the nodes in a CFG are reachable from *Entry*, such a spanning tree can always be constructed.

The spanning tree of a CFG is (in general) not unique. Given a particular spanning tree, the edges of the CFG can be partitioned into four sets:

1. *Tree edges* are edges in the CFG that are also edges in the spanning tree.
2. *Advancing edges*, or *chords*, are edges $X \rightarrow Y$ that are not tree edges but where Y is a proper descendant of X in the spanning tree.
3. *Retreating edges* are edges $X \rightarrow Y$ where Y is an ancestor of X in the spanning tree; note that an edge $X \rightarrow X$ is a retreating edge.
4. *Cross edges* are edges $X \rightarrow Y$ in the CFG such that Y is neither an ancestor nor a descendant of X in the spanning tree.

To build a spanning tree, an algorithm that visits and marks all nodes in the CFG is used. Often, a depth-first spanning tree (or DFST) is used, which is constructed by a depth-first traversal of the CFG. We use the convention that the tree is constructed in a left-to-right fashion (the first child added to the tree is the leftmost child, etc.). By construction, any node Y reachable from X will either be a descendant of X, an ancestor of X (via a retreating edge), or to the left of X in any DFST. In particular, any cross edges $X \rightarrow Y$ in the CFG will go to the left.

Example 3.5

Show an algorithm to build a depth-first spanning tree, distinguishing between tree, advancing, retreating, and cross edges. Give each node a preorder number and a reverse postorder number as the DFST is built.

Solution

The algorithm starts by initializing the preorder and reverse postorder numbers for each node to zero. A recursive procedure is used to construct the DFST, starting at *Entry*. At each node, the procedure looks at each successor to determine whether it has already been added to the tree; this can be checked by testing whether the preorder number has a nonzero value. If not, this edge is a tree edge, and the procedure recurses to that successor. If the successor is already in the tree, then a few more tests determine whether this edge is an advancing, retreating, or cross edge. The complete algorithm is shown in Figure 3.6. The data structures used are as follows:

- $NPre(X)$ is the preorder number assigned to each node as the algorithm builds the depth-first spanning tree, initialized to zero for all nodes.
- $NRPost(X)$ is the reverse postorder number assigned to each node, also initialized to zero for all nodes.
- N is the global counter for assigning preorder numbers, initialized to zero.

- M is the global counter for assigning reverse postorder numbers, initialized to $|V|$, the number of nodes.

Running this algorithm on the CFG in Figure 3.7 might build the DFST as shown in bold. The preorder number, followed by the reverse postorder number, is shown to the left of each node.

(1) $NPre(*) = 0$
(2) $NRPost(*) = 0$
(3) $N = 0$
(4) $M = |V|$
(5) DFST(*Entry*)

(6) procedure DFST(X)
(7) $N = N + 1$
(8) $NPre(X) = N$
(9)   for $Y \in$ SUCC(X) do
(10)   if $NPre(Y) = 0$ then
(11)   DFST(Y)
(12) $X \rightarrow Y$ is a tree edge
(13)   else if $NPre(X) < NPre(Y)$ then
(14) $X \rightarrow Y$ is an advancing edge
(15)   else if $NRPost(X) = 0$ then
(16) $X \rightarrow Y$ is a retreating edge
(17)   else
(18) $X \rightarrow Y$ is a cross edge
(19)   endif
(20)   endfor
(21) $NRPost(X) = M$
(22) $M = M - 1$
(23) end DFST

FIGURE 3.6 Algorithm to construct a DFST from a CFG.

The algorithm in Figure 3.6 will classify a self-cycle $X \rightarrow X$ as a retreating edge. Remember that in general the DFST is not unique; given a particular ordering of successors, however, the DFST will be unique. The reverse postorder numbering of a DFST satisfies a particularly interesting property. The only edges $X \rightarrow Y$ with $NRPost(X) > NRPost(Y)$ are retreating edges in the DFST. This means that if the nodes of the CFG are visited in reverse postorder—that is, in numerical order according to the reverse postorder numbering—then all predecessors of a node will be visited before the node itself, except for retreating edges. This is true because

3.2 • Graphs

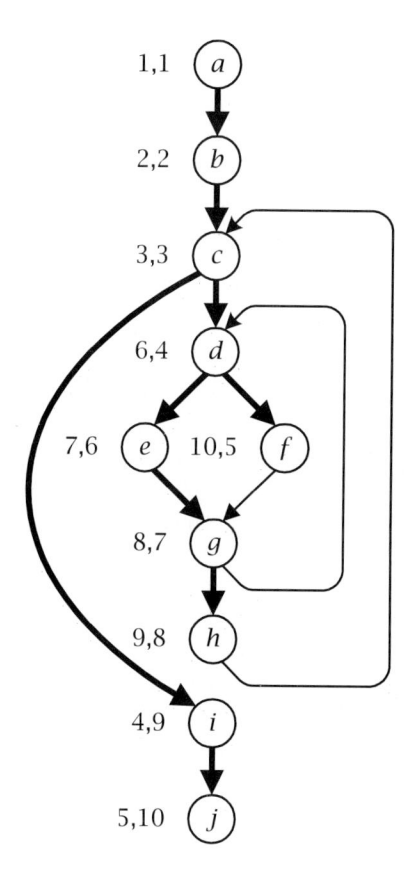

FIGURE 3.7 Depth-first spanning tree of a control flow graph. Tree edges are shown in bold; preorder and reverse postorder numbers, respectively, are shown to the left of each node.

the DFST is constructed left to right, meaning all cross edges go to the left. The reverse postorder numbering will give a larger number to the left subtree of a node, so cross edges go from smaller reverse postorder numbers to larger ones, as do tree edges and advancing edges. For this reason, reverse postorder numbers are often used to order CFG nodes. We will use reverse postorder numbers to refer to nodes in control flow graphs.

The generalization of a spanning tree for any directed graph is a *spanning forest*, which is a subgraph that comprises a set of trees that span the nodes. In a CFG, at least one tree in the spanning forest must be rooted at *Entry*. Since each node by itself is a height-zero tree, the set of nodes with no edges is a degenerate spanning forest. In a general directed graph, a depth-first spanning forest (DFSF) is a spanning forest constructed in a depth-first traversal. Preorder and reverse postorder numbers can be assigned to nodes in the DFSF as in a DFST, and the same properties hold. The construction of a spanning forest partitions the edges of the graph into five sets:

1. *Tree edges*
2. *Advancing edges*
3. *Retreating edges*
4. *Cross edges* $X \to Y$ where X and Y are in the same tree.
5. *Cross-tree edges* $X \to Y$ where Y is in a different tree of the spanning forest.

Using the left-to-right construction convention, if the edge $X \to Y$ is a cross edge in a DFSF, then Y must be to the left of X in the same tree. If the edge $X \to Y$ is a cross-tree edge, then the tree containing Y must be to the left of the tree containing X.

3.2.4 Finding Cycles in Directed Graphs

When compiling a program, we will deal with several directed graphs that abstract different sorts of information about the program. The CFG is one such graph; compilers also deal with data-flow graphs, dependence graphs, call graphs, and so on. It is often useful to detect whether the graph is cyclic or acyclic, and to find the cycles in the graph. Formally, a cycle in the graph is a *strongly connected region*, that is, a set of nodes S such that there is a path $S_1 \xrightarrow{*} S_2$ for any two nodes $S_1, S_2 \in S$. By this definition, every node by itself is a trivial strongly connected region (SCR). The *strongly connected components* (SCCs) are the maximal SCRs (SCRs that are not proper subsets of any other SCR). Strongly connected components will partition the nodes of any directed graph.

Here we describe a fast algorithm for finding the SCCs in any directed graph. The algorithm works by building a depth-first spanning forest of the directed graph. The nodes in an SCC will comprise a subtree of any DFSF. Identifying the SCCs boils down to finding the root and leaves of the subtree corresponding to each SCC.

The SCC algorithm constructs a DFSF recursively and identifies the SCC root nodes in bottom-up order. When it identifies a root node, it effectively prunes that subtree from the DFSF, so the SCC for the parent of the root will not include the subtree. The complete algorithm is shown in Figure 3.8. The data structures used are as follows:

- N is the global counter for assigning preorder numbers, initialized to zero.
- *CountSCC* is the count of strongly connected components found, initialized to zero.
- *Stack* is a push-down (LIFO) stack of nodes, initialized to empty.
- $NPre(X)$ is the preorder number assigned to each node as the algorithm builds a depth-first spanning forest, initialized to zero for each node.

```
            Algorithm SCC:
 (1)    for X ∈ V do
 (2)        NPre(X) = 0
 (3)        InStack(X) = False
 (4)    endfor
 (5)    N = 0
 (6)    CountSCC = 0
 (7)    Stack = ∅
 (8)    for X ∈ V do
 (9)        if NPre(X) = 0 then
(10)            SCCRecurse(X)
(11)        endif
(12)    endfor

(13)    procedure SCCRecurse(X)
(14)        Lowlink(X) = NPre(X) = N = N + 1
(15)        push X onto Stack
(16)        InStack(X) = True
(17)        for Y ∈ SUCC(X) do
(18)            if NPre(Y) = 0 then
(19)                SCCRecurse(Y)
(20)                Lowlink(X) = min(Lowlink(X), Lowlink(Y))
(21)            else if NPre(Y) < NPre(X) and InStack(Y) then
(22)                Lowlink(X) = min(Lowlink(X), NPre(Y))
(23)            endif
(24)        endfor
(25)        if NPre(X) = Lowlink(X) then
(26)            CountSCC = CountSCC + 1
(27)            repeat
(28)                pop W off Stack
(29)                InStack(W) = False
(30)                SCC(W) = CountSCC
(31)            until W = X
(32)        endif
(33)    end SCCRecurse
```

FIGURE 3.8 Algorithm to find strongly connected components.

- *Lowlink(X)* keeps track of whether each node has a path to a spanning forest ancestor.
- *SCC(X)* is the SCC number assigned to each node; two nodes with the same SCC number are in the same strongly connected component.

- *InStack(X)* is a flag to keep track of whether each node is on the stack, and is initialized to *False* for all nodes.

The algorithm hinges on the properties of the depth-first traversal and on the computation of *Lowlink(X)*. *Lowlink(X) < NPre(X)* only when there is some node *W* in the same SCC such that *NPre(W) < NPre(X)* (so *W* is either an ancestor of *X*, or is to the left of *X*) and there is an edge from *X* or one of its spanning tree descendants to *W*. The update of *Lowlink(X)* at line 22 will occur only when the edge $X \to Y$ is a retreating edge or a cross edge. If it is a retreating edge, clearly *X* and *Y* are in the same SCC. If it is a cross edge, and *Y* is still on the stack, then *Y* is in the same SCC as some ancestor of *X*, or else *Y* would have been popped off the stack. In either case, *X* is not the root of an SCC.

After visiting all the successors (and therefore all the DFSF descendants), line 25 will find whether node *x* is the root of a strongly connected component. If it is, the algorithm pops nodes off the stack corresponding to the subtree rooted at node *x*, which comprises the SCC. This algorithm is very fast and practical; it visits each node and each edge only once, and uses only a few temporary data values per node.

Example 3.6

Illustrate algorithm SCC on the directed graph in Figure 3.9.

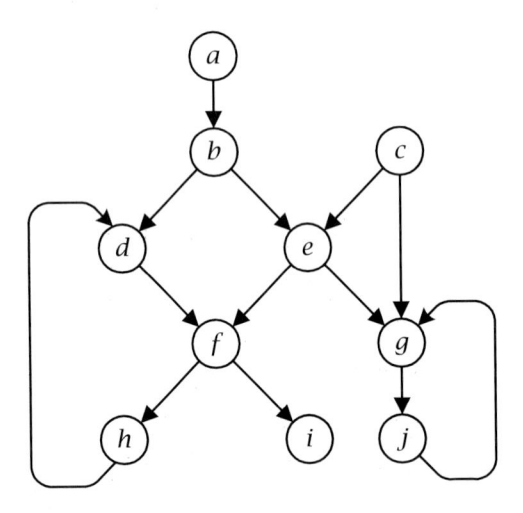

FIGURE 3.9 Sample directed graph.

Solution

Assume that the algorithm starts at node *c*, and always visits the leftmost successor first. Figure 3.10 shows the spanning tree rooted at *c* (in bold) in construction. Each node that has been visited is labeled with its *NPre* and *Lowlink*, respectively;

3.2 ▪ Graphs

node *d* is the current node, and line 21 has just looked at the retreating edge $d \to f$, setting *Lowlink(d)* to 3. The final result is shown in Figure 3.11. The spanning forest comprises two trees, rooted at *c* and *a*, and there are seven strongly connected components. The roots of these SCCs are at nodes *i, f, g, e, c, b*, and *a*, in order of discovery.

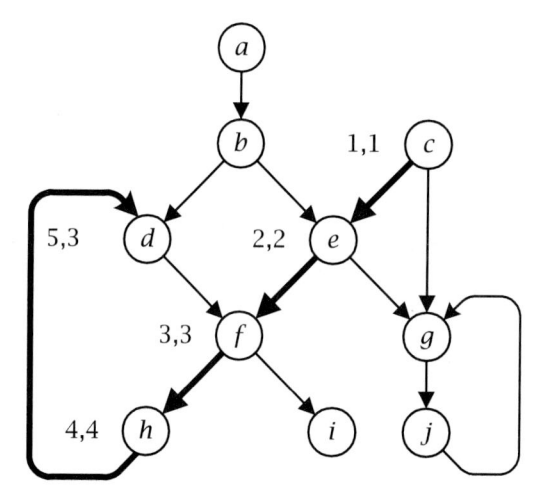

FIGURE 3.10 Algorithm SCC just after looking at edge $d \to f$.

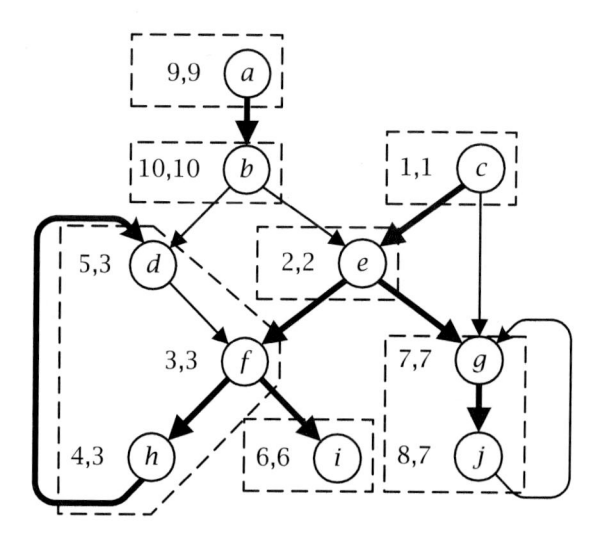

FIGURE 3.11 Final results of algorithm SCC showing SCCs and final values of *NPre, Lowlink*.

When we have identified the SCCs of a directed graph G, we can construct a new graph called the *acyclic condensation* of G. The acyclic condensation of G is a DAG with a node (called an SCC node) for each SCC in G and an edge between two SCC nodes whenever there is an edge between two graph nodes in distinct SCCs in G.

Example 3.7

Show the acyclic condensation of the graph in Figure 3.9.

Solution

The acyclic condensation will have seven nodes, one for each SCC, and eight edges, as shown in Figure 3.12.

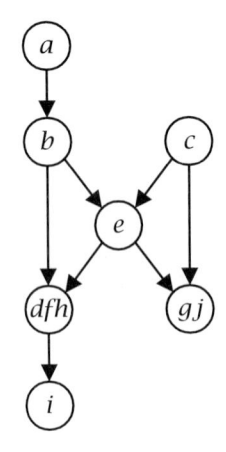

FIGURE 3.12 Acyclic condensation of the sample graph.

3.2.5 Dominators

We say a node X in a CFG *dominates* a node Y if every path from *Entry* to Y includes X; we write this X DOM Y. If X DOM Y, then any path $p : Entry \stackrel{*}{\to} Y$ can be split into two parts: $p_{prefix} : Entry \stackrel{*}{\to} X$ and $p_{suffix} : X \stackrel{*}{\to} Y$. By this definition, every node dominates itself, and *Entry* dominates every node in the CFG, including itself.

We can represent the *DOM* relation by the dominator set $DOM(X)$, which is the set of nodes that dominate X. Note that $DOM(X) \neq \emptyset$, since $X \in DOM(X)$. Alternatively, we can represent this by the inverse set $DOM^{-1}(X)$, which is the set of nodes dominated by X; note that this is also nonempty.

Example 3.8

What are the dominator sets for the CFG in Figure 3.7?

Solution
The dominator set and dominator inverse sets for each node are shown in Figure 3.13.

X	$DOM(X)$	$DOM^{-1}(X)$
a	$\{a\}$	$\{a,b,c,d,e,f,g,h,i,j\}$
b	$\{a,b\}$	$\{b,c,d,e,f,g,h,i,j\}$
c	$\{a,b,c\}$	$\{c,d,e,f,g,h,i,j\}$
d	$\{a,b,c,d\}$	$\{d,e,f,g,h\}$
e	$\{a,b,c,d,e\}$	$\{e\}$
f	$\{a,b,c,d,f\}$	$\{f\}$
g	$\{a,b,c,d,g\}$	$\{g,h\}$
h	$\{a,b,c,d,g,h\}$	$\{h\}$
i	$\{a,b,c,i\}$	$\{i,j\}$
j	$\{a,b,c,i,j\}$	$\{j\}$

FIGURE 3.13 Dominator sets for the CFG in Figure 3.7.

We say a node X in a CFG *strictly dominates* a node Y if X DOM Y and $X \neq Y$; for shorthand, we write this X SDOM Y. The set of nodes that strictly dominate Y is $DOM(Y) - \{Y\}$, and may be empty. We can define an *immediate dominator* of a node Y as the *closest* strict dominator of Y. That is, X is an immediate dominator of Y, written X IDOM Y, iff

$$X \text{ SDOM } Y \wedge (\forall W \mid W \text{ SDOM } Y)[W \text{ DOM } X]$$

We define $SDOM^{-1}(X)$ analogously to $DOM^{-1}(X)$, and we say $X \overline{\text{DOM}} Y$ to mean X does not dominate Y.

A convenient way to represent the *DOM* relation of a CFG is to draw a dominator tree, rooted at *Entry*, with an edge $X \stackrel{IDOM}{\longrightarrow} Y$ in the tree iff X IDOM Y. The *DOM* tree for the CFG in Figure 3.7 is shown in Figure 3.14.

One way to find dominators in a graph takes advantage of the following basic relation:

$$DOM(X) = \{X\} \cup \bigcap_{P \in PRED(X)} DOM(P)$$

That is, the *DOM* set of X includes X and any node that also dominates *all* its predecessors. An iterative algorithm to find dominators is shown in Figure 3.15. It uses a set data structure $DOM(X)$ for each node X to hold the dominators of that node. The algorithm must terminate, since the values assigned to $DOM(X)$ in line 10 are always a subset of the values from the previous iteration of the while loop. When the algorithm terminates, the value of $DOM(X)$ is the set of nodes that dominate X. This algorithm can be implemented efficiently, using bit vectors (with

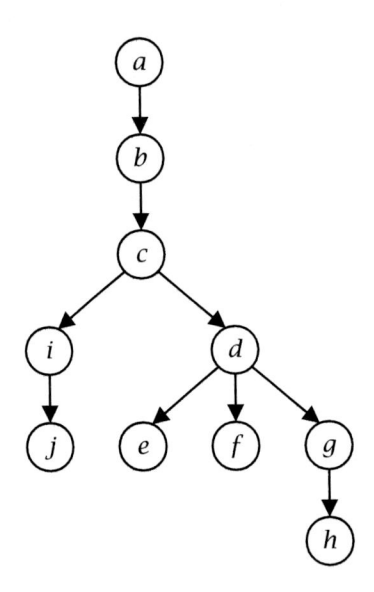

FIGURE 3.14 Dominator tree of sample CFG.

```
        Algorithm DOM
(1)        DOM(Entry) = {Entry}
(2)        for X ∈ V − {Entry} do
(3)           DOM(X) = V
(4)        endfor
(5)        Changed = True
(6)        while Changed do
(7)           Changed = False
(8)           for X ∈ V − {Entry} do
(9)              OldDOM = DOM(X)
(10)             DOM(X) = {X} ∪ ⋂   DOM(P)
                               P∈PRED(X)
(11)             if DOM(X) ≠ OldDOM then
(12)                Changed = True
(13)             endif
(14)          endfor
(15)       endwhile
```

FIGURE 3.15 Algorithm to find dominators in a CFG.

$|V|$ bits, one for each node in the CFG) to represent the *DOM* sets, and logical **and** and **or** for the union and intersection operations.

Example 3.9

Show how algorithm DOM works on the CFG in Figure 3.7.

Solution

The values assigned to the *DOM* set for each node are shown in Figure 3.16. The initial value is V for all nodes except *Entry*, in this case, a. For this CFG, the algorithm converges after just one iteration if the nodes are visited in the order given by the reverse postorder numbers; the `while` loop will iterate one more time to verify convergence, but the values will not change.

node	initial *DOM* set	after iteration 1
a	$\{a\}$	$\{a\}$
b	$\{a,b,c,d,e,f,g,h,i,j\}$	$\{a,b\}$
c	$\{a,b,c,d,e,f,g,h,i,j\}$	$\{a,b,c\}$
d	$\{a,b,c,d,e,f,g,h,i,j\}$	$\{a,b,c,d\}$
e	$\{a,b,c,d,e,f,g,h,i,j\}$	$\{a,b,c,d,e\}$
f	$\{a,b,c,d,e,f,g,h,i,j\}$	$\{a,b,c,d,f\}$
g	$\{a,b,c,d,e,f,g,h,i,j\}$	$\{a,b,c,d,g\}$
h	$\{a,b,c,d,e,f,g,h,i,j\}$	$\{a,b,c,d,g,h\}$
i	$\{a,b,c,d,e,f,g,h,i,j\}$	$\{a,b,c,i\}$
j	$\{a,b,c,d,e,f,g,h,i,j\}$	$\{a,b,c,i,j\}$

FIGURE 3.16 Results of running algorithm DOM.

A *region* is a sub-CFG with a unique *header node* such that the header dominates all nodes in the region. By definition, a region will be a single-entry subgraph of the CFG. Any CFG edge $Y \rightarrow X$ where X *DOM* Y is called a *back edge*. A *natural loop* is a region where the header is the target of a back edge (or several back edges), and all the nodes in the loop can reach the back edge (or one of the back edges). The *body* of a loop is the set of nodes dominated by the header that can reach a back edge to the header.

Example 3.10

Find the natural loops in the CFG in Figure 3.7.

Solution

The edge $h \rightarrow c$ is a back edge, which has header at node c. The body of this loop is the set $\{c,d,e,f,g,h\}$. Another back edge is $g \rightarrow d$, with header at d and loop body $\{d,e,f,g\}$. Because this is a subset of the body of the first loop, this is an inner loop.

One of the properties of natural loops is that two natural loops will either be completely disjoint or properly nested. When there is a single back edge, the source node of that edge is called the *postbody*. Similarly, if there is only one predecessor of the header outside the loop, it is called the *preheader*. It is often convenient for the compiler to have loop header nodes with two predecessors, a preheader and postbody. Compilers often insert artificial preheader and postbody nodes to the CFG, where the preheader collects any loop-entry edges and the postbody collects any back edges.

3.2.6 Dominance Frontier

Two more concepts related to dominators are needed. One is the *dominance frontier*. The dominance frontier of a node X is the set of nodes Z such that X dominates some predecessor of Z, but not all; formally:

$$DF(X) = \{Z \mid (\exists Y, Y' \in \text{PRED}(Z))[X \text{ DOM } Y \land X \overline{\text{DOM}} Y']\}$$

Clearly, if X dominates all predecessors of Z, then X must strictly dominate Z itself, so Z would not be in the dominance frontier of X.

Alternatively, if we define

$$\text{SUCC}(S) = \bigcup_{s \in S} \text{SUCC}(s)$$

then we can define

$$DF(X) = \text{SUCC}(DOM^{-1}(X)) - SDOM^{-1}(X)$$

Example 3.11

Compute the dominance frontiers for the CFG in Figure 3.7.

Solution

We already computed the dominator sets for this CFG. We can compute the dominance frontiers using set differences as shown in Figure 3.17. Note that since, by definition, a node does not strictly dominate itself, it may be in its own dominance frontier, as is the case with nodes c and d in Figure 3.17.

The dominance frontier can be found by a postorder (bottom-up) traversal of the dominator tree. $DF(X)$ can be defined as the union of two computations:

$$DF(X) = DF_{local}(X) \cup \bigcup_{C \in Child(X)} DF_{up}(C)$$

where $Child(X)$ is the set of children in the DOM tree (the nodes *immediately dominated* by X). The set $DF_{local}(X)$ is the set of successors of X in the CFG that are not strictly dominated by X:

$$DF_{local}(X) = \{Y \mid Y \in \text{SUCC}(X) \land X \overline{\text{SDOM}} Y\}$$

X	$DOM^{-1}(X)$	$SUCC(DOM^{-1}(X))$	$SDOM^{-1}(X)$	$DF(X)$
a	$\{a,b,c,\ldots,j\}$	$\{b,c,d,\ldots,j\}$	$\{b,c,d,\ldots,j\}$	$\emptyset$
b	$\{b,c,d,\ldots,j\}$	$\{c,d,f,\ldots,j\}$	$\{c,d,f,\ldots,j\}$	$\emptyset$
c	$\{c,d,f,\ldots,j\}$	$\{c,d,f,\ldots,j\}$	$\{d,e,f,\ldots,j\}$	$\{c\}$
d	$\{d,e,f,g,h\}$	$\{c,d,e,f,g,h\}$	$\{e,f,g,h\}$	$\{c,d\}$
e	$\{e\}$	$\{g\}$	$\{\}$	$\{g\}$
f	$\{f\}$	$\{g\}$	$\{\}$	$\{g\}$
g	$\{g,h\}$	$\{c,d,h\}$	$\{h\}$	$\{c,d\}$
h	$\{h\}$	$\{c\}$	$\{\}$	$\{c\}$
i	$\{i,j\}$	$\{j\}$	$\{j\}$	$\emptyset$
j	$\{j\}$	$\{\}$	$\{\}$	$\emptyset$

FIGURE 3.17 Dominance frontier computation for the CFG in Figure 3.7.

These nodes must be in the dominance frontier of X, since X dominates itself, and therefore dominates a predecessor of Y. The set $DF_{up}(C)$ is the subset of $DF(C)$ that is not strictly dominated by $IDOM(C)$.

$$DF_{up}(C) = \{Y \mid Y \in DF(C) \land IDOM(C) \overline{SDOM} \, Y\}$$

If $Y \in DF(C)$, then C dominates some predecessor of Y but not all predecessors; thus $IDOM(C)$ must dominate that same predecessor of Y. If $IDOM(C)$ does not strictly dominate Y itself, then Y must be in the dominance frontier of $IDOM(C)$.

An algorithm to find dominance frontiers is shown in Figure 3.18. The data structures used are:

1. $DF(X)$ is the set of nodes in the dominance frontier for each node X.
2. $Child(X)$ is the set of dominator tree children of X.

The loop at lines 6-10 adds $DF_{up}(C)$ to $DF(X)$ for dominator children of X, and the loop at lines 12-16 computes $DF_{local}(X)$. Note that some nodes may be added more than once.

3.2.7 Postdominators

The second concept related to dominators is *postdominance*. To use this concept we must refine our definition of a control flow graph. The characteristic that distinguishes a CFG from other directed graphs is the presence of a unique *Entry* node, from which all other nodes are reachable; the dominator relationship is defined in terms of paths from *Entry*. To define postdominance we must also have a unique *Exit* node, which is reachable from all other nodes; formally, we define a single-exit control flow graph as CFG = $\langle V, E, Entry, Exit \rangle$, where V, E, and *Entry* are as before, and $Exit \in V$ is reachable from all other nodes:

$$(\forall X \in V)[X \stackrel{*}{\to} Exit]$$

```
             Algorithm DomFront:
   (1)   DFront(Entry)

   (2)   procedure DFront(X)
   (3)       DF(X) = ∅
   (4)       for C ∈ Child(X) do
   (5)           DFront(C)
   (6)           for Y ∈ DF(C) do
   (7)               if X $\overline{SDOM}$ Y then
   (8)                   DF(X) = DF(X) ∪ {Y}
   (9)               endif
  (10)           endfor
  (11)       endfor
  (12)       for Y ∈ SUCC(X) do
  (13)           if X $\overline{SDOM}$ Y then
  (14)               DF(X) = DF(X) ∪ {Y}
  (15)           endif
  (16)       endfor
```

FIGURE 3.18 Algorithm to find dominance frontier; $Child(X)$ is the set of children in the dominator tree.

We say a vertex Y in a CFG *postdominates* a vertex X if every path from X to *Exit* includes Y; we write this Y PDOM X. If Y PDOM X, then any path $X \xrightarrow{*}$ *Exit* can be split into two parts: $X \xrightarrow{*} Y$ and $Y \xrightarrow{*}$ *Exit*. By this definition, every vertex postdominates itself, and *Exit* postdominates every vertex in the graph (including itself). As with dominance, postdominance can be represented by a tree (rooted at *Exit*).

With a flow graph $G = \langle V_G, E_G, Entry_G, Exit_G \rangle$, we can define the *reverse control flow graph* (RCFG) $G^R = \langle V_G, E_G^R, Exit_G, Entry_G \rangle$, with the same set of vertices, but with an edge $Y \rightarrow X \in E_G^R$ for each edge $X \rightarrow Y \in E_G$. Note that $Entry_G$ and $Exit_G$ switch roles. The dominator relationship in the RCFG is the same as the postdominator relationship in the original CFG.

As with dominators, we define strict postdominance as

$$Y \text{ SPDOM } X \equiv (Y \text{ PDOM } X) \wedge (Y \neq X)$$

The postdominance frontier is the set of vertices

$$PDF(Y) = \{W \mid (\exists X \in SUCC(W))[Y \text{ PDOM } X] \wedge Y \overline{\text{ SPDOM }} X\}$$

The immediate postdominator of a node is defined similar to the immediate dominator.

Example 3.12

Show the postdominator tree for the flow graph in Figure 3.7.

3.3 ■ Control Dependence

Solution

Node *j* is the *Exit* node for this graph. The postdominator tree is shown in Figure 3.19.

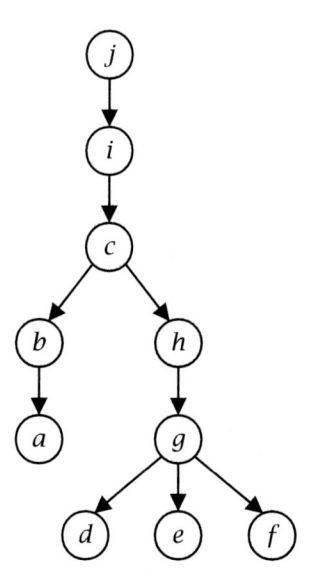

FIGURE 3.19 Postdominator tree of sample CFG.

3.3 Control Dependence

A basic block is a single-entry, single-exit block of code. All of the statements or operations in a basic block execute under the same conditions. That is, if the program flow enters this basic block, it will execute all the operations in the block. Thus, if any operation in the block executes, all the operations will execute (barring exceptions).

Control-dependence relations are a more general method to capture the essential conditions controlling the execution of code in the program. For instance, control dependence captures the fact that in the CFG shown in Figure 3.20, node *b* is executed under exactly the same conditions as node *e*, and nodes *c* and *d* both *depend* somehow on the outcome of (the condition computed in) *b*, even though they are mutually exclusive.

Formally, a CFG node *Y* is *control dependent* on node *X* if:

1. *Y* postdominates some successor of *X*, and
2. *Y* does not postdominate all successors of *X*.

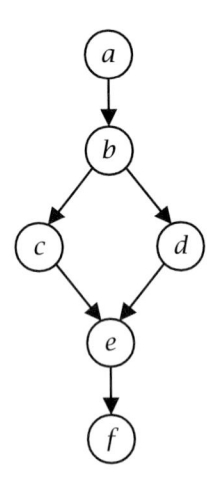

FIGURE 3.20 Nodes *b* and *e* are control dependence-equivalent.

A less formal description is to say that *Y* is control dependent on *X* if:

1. Following one edge out of *X* will eventually always execute *Y*; the only way out, after taking this edge, is through *Y*.
2. Choosing some other edge out of *X* *may* avoid *Y*.

Thus, node *X* can decide whether to definitely execute *Y* (eventually).

It is easy to verify that the conditions for control dependence are the same as for postdominance frontiers. In fact, *Y* is control dependent on *X* iff $X \in PDF(Y)$.

Clearly, nothing can be control dependent on any node that has only a single successor. If *X* has a single successor and *Y* postdominates that successor, *Y* must also postdominate *X*. To compute control dependence, we add an (artificial) edge *Entry* → *Exit*. We refer to this edge as the *slicing edge*. The effect of the slicing edge is that no node will strictly postdominate *Entry* except *Exit* (and no node will strictly dominate *Exit* except *Entry*). The slicing edge makes a node control dependent on *Entry* if the node will always be executed whenever this program or procedure is entered.

Example 3.13

Find the control dependence relations for the sample CFG in Figure 3.21. The postdominator tree (rooted at the *Exit* node, in this case node *h*) is also shown.

Solution

The only predicate nodes (nodes with more than one successor) are *a*, *b*, and *c*. We see that there is control dependence from *a* to *b*, because *b* postdominates a successor of *a* (*b* itself), but does not postdominate *h*, the other successor. There is

3.3 • Control Dependence

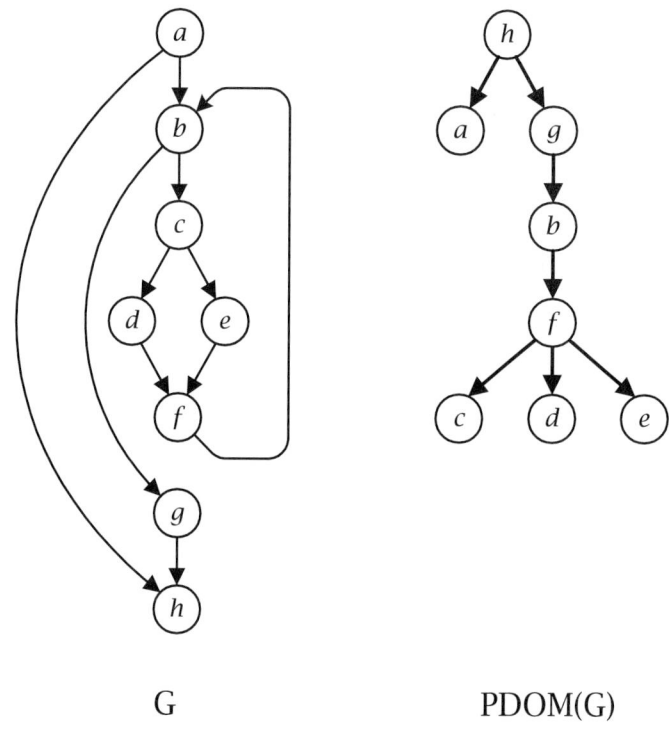

FIGURE 3.21 Sample CFG.

control dependence from *b* to itself because *b* postdominates one of its successors (*c*) but not all of them (not *g*). The complete list of control dependence relations are as follows:

$$a \xrightarrow{CD} b \qquad a \xrightarrow{CD} g$$
$$b \xrightarrow{CD} c \qquad b \xrightarrow{CD} f \qquad b \xrightarrow{CD} b$$
$$c \xrightarrow{CD} d \qquad c \xrightarrow{CD} e$$

Control dependences can be found by using algorithm DomFront to compute postdominance frontiers. We represent the control dependence relationships in a *control dependence graph*, with the same vertices as the CFG and an edge $X \xrightarrow{CD} Y$ whenever *Y* is control dependent on *X*. In general, since the *Exit* node is not control dependent on any other vertex, we will not show the *Exit* vertex in our CD graphs. The sample control dependence graph is shown in Figure 3.22. The nodes that are control dependent upon *Entry* are executed unconditionally. Note that a loop in the flow graph appears in the control dependence graph as a cycle ($b \xrightarrow{CD} b$). Except for the self-cycle at *b*, the graph is a tree. This is not an accident; any CFG that comprises structured conditionals (`if-then-else`) and `while` loops will have a tree (with self-cycles) for the CD graph.

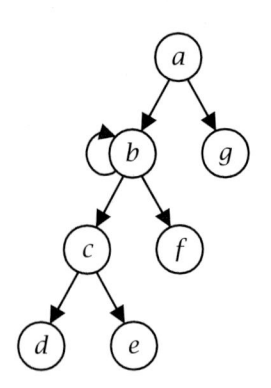

FIGURE 3.22 Control dependence graph.

3.3.1 Labeled Control Dependence Edges

In the previous example, it was not possible to distinguish the $c \xrightarrow{CD} d$ edge from the $c \xrightarrow{CD} e$ edge. In fact, since execution of nodes d and e is mutually exclusive, it is important to distinguish these cases. To handle this, we add labels to the CFG successor edges of conditional nodes, and to the edges of the CD graph. In practice, any labeling can be used, such as *True* and *False* labels for two-way branches, integer labels for multiway `case` statements, and so forth. We will write $X \rightarrow_l Y$ to mean a $X \rightarrow Y$ is a CFG edge with label l. By convention, the slicing edge Entry → Exit edge has a *False* label.

In labeled control dependence, a CFG node Y is control dependent on node X with label l if:

1. Y postdominates some successor S of X,
2. Y does not strictly postdominate X, and
3. $X \rightarrow S$ has label l.

Example 3.14

Show the labeled control dependence graph for the CFG in Figure 3.21.

Solution

First we must show the control flow graph with conditional edges appropriately labeled. This is on the left in Figure 3.23. The control dependence relations are annotated with the label of the first edge on the path causing that dependence relation, on the right in Figure 3.23.

3.3.2 Data Structure for Control Dependence

We can use the postdominator tree and the CFG successor edges to find all control dependence relations. The key observation is that for any control flow graph edge

3.3 ▪ Control Dependence

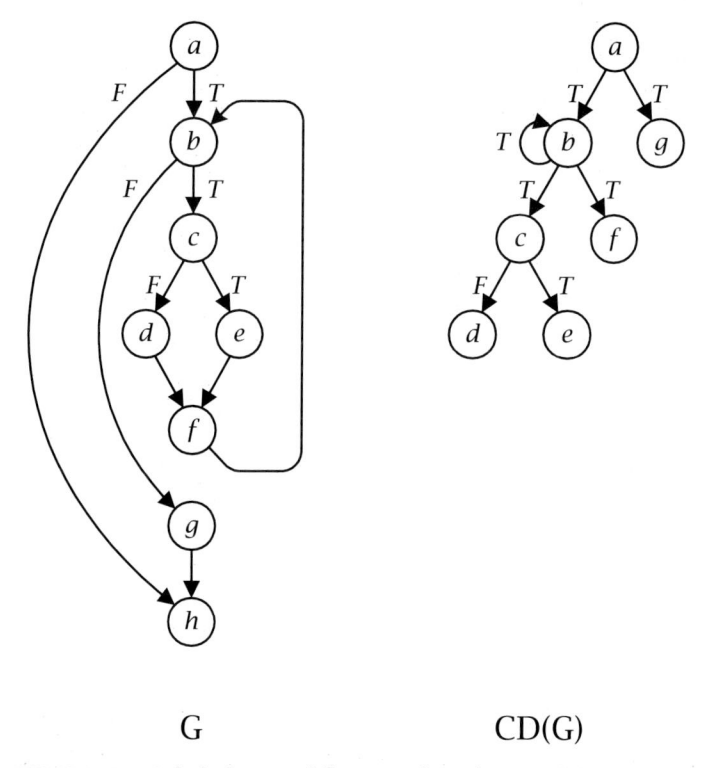

FIGURE 3.23 Labeled control flow graph and control dependence graph.

$X \rightarrow_l Y$, either Y immediately postdominates X ($Y = IPDOM(X)$; i.e., Y is the parent of X in the postdominator tree), or is control dependent on X with label l. Moreover, if Y is control dependent on X, then every node on a PDOM tree path, from Y up to but not including $IPDOM(X)$, is also control dependent on X with this label. These nodes all postdominate Y and cannot strictly postdominate X. Given a control flow graph edge $X \rightarrow_l Y$ and the postdominator tree, procedure CDsucc, shown in Figure 3.24, will find all nodes control dependent on a node X with label l.

```
(1)     procedure CDsucc(X →_l Y)
(2)         if Y ≠ IPDOM(X) then
(3)             Z = Y
(4)             while Z ≠ IPDOM(X) do
(5)                 Z is control dependent on X with label l
(6)                 Z = IPDOM(Z)
(7)             endwhile
(8)         endif
(9)     end CDsucc
```

FIGURE 3.24 Finding control dependence successors.

Example 3.15

Use procedure CDsucc to find the labeled control dependence graph for the CFG in Figure 3.7.

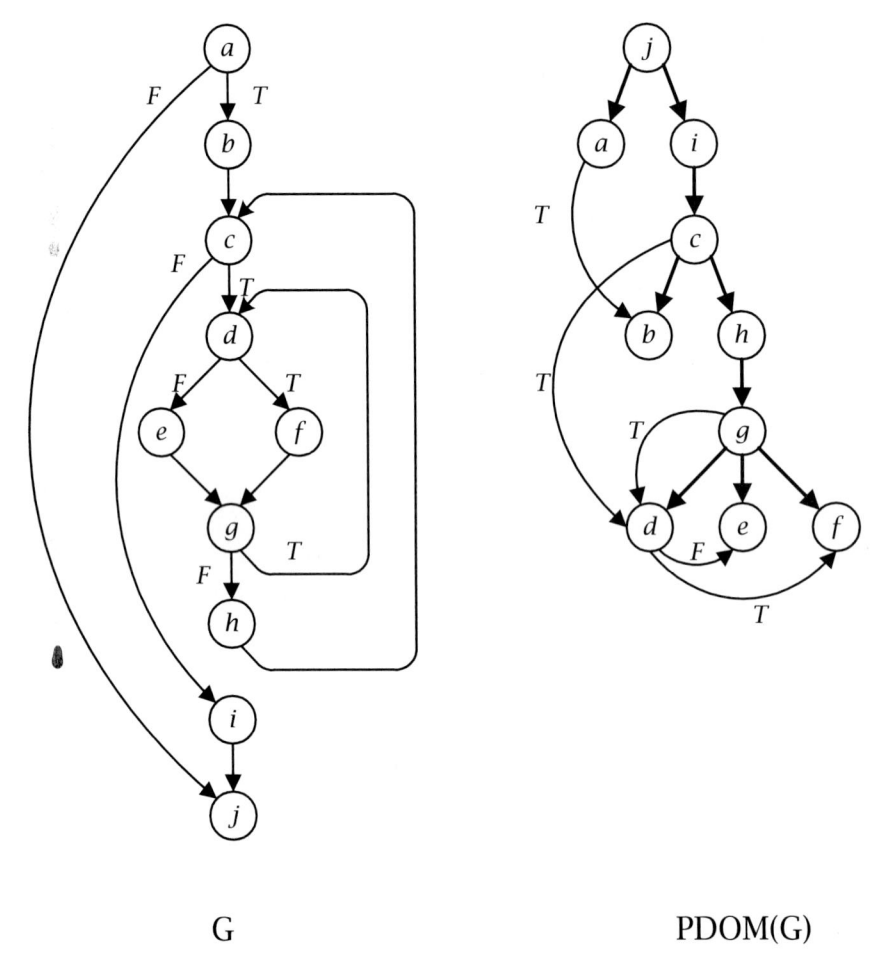

G PDOM(G)

FIGURE 3.25 Sample CFG with edges labeled, and postdominator tree. CFG edges that do not climb the postdominator tree are superimposed onto the tree.

Solution

We first must add the labels to the CFG edges. This is shown in Figure 3.25, along with the postdominator tree. The flow graph edges that cause control dependence—that is, that do not go from a node to its immediate postdominator—are superimposed on the postdominator tree. To find control dependence using procedure CDsucc, we look at each CFG node to find edges that do not climb the PDOM tree. The table below shows the flow graph edges that pass the test at line 2, along with the control dependence edges due to that edge.

CFG edge	CD edges
$a \to_T b$	$a \xrightarrow{CD}_T b$, $a \xrightarrow{CD}_T c$, $a \xrightarrow{CD}_T i$
$c \to_T d$	$c \xrightarrow{CD}_T d$, $c \xrightarrow{CD}_T g$, $c \xrightarrow{CD}_T h$, $c \xrightarrow{CD}_T c$
$g \to_T d$	$g \xrightarrow{CD}_T d$, $g \xrightarrow{CD}_T g$
$d \to_F e$	$d \xrightarrow{CD}_F e$
$d \to_T f$	$d \xrightarrow{CD}_T f$

The control dependence graph itself is shown in Figure 3.26.

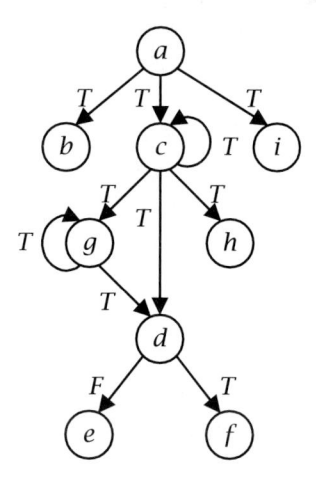

FIGURE 3.26 Control dependence graph.

The control dependence graph for this example is not a simple treelike structure, since the program is not structured using only `if` and `while` constructs. Node d is control dependent on both c and g. This is because d is inside a `repeat` loop (with the exit at the bottom). The body of such a loop is always executed at least once, under the same conditions that the `repeat` expression is evaluated; this is the reason for the $c \xrightarrow{CD} d$ edge. Continued execution of the loop depends on the loop predicate (node g) choosing to iterate, and hence the $g \xrightarrow{CD} d$ edge. Note the two cycles in the control dependence graph corresponding to the two nested loops in the CFG. In particular, note that the control dependence cycles for nested loops are disjoint cycles, and the inner loop cycle is control dependent on the outer loop cycle. For a loop with multiple exits, the control dependence cycle would include all the loop-exit nodes.

3.3.3 Single-Exit Control Flow Graphs

Since control dependence is defined in terms of postdominators, it is only defined for single-exit control flow graphs. A CFG with multiple entry points (such as a Fortran or PL/I program with `Entry` statements) can be easily converted into a single-entry graph by adding a global *Entry* node with an edge to each of the actual entry points. Nodes that are not reachable from the *Entry* node can be removed, since that code can never be executed. For instance, the CFG in Figure 3.27 has two entry points at nodes a and f. To model this with a single-entry flow graph, the compiler can add the global entry node E with edges to a and f. Since node l has no predecessors and is not an entry point, it is unreachable and can be removed. In fact, nodes l through p can all be removed as unreachable.

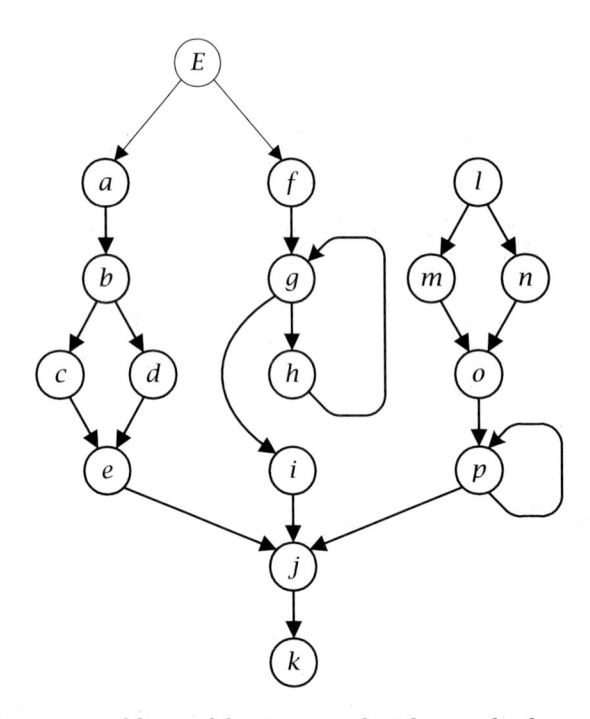

FIGURE 3.27 Adding a false *Entry* node E lets multiple entry programs be modeled with a single entry graph.

Similarly, graphs with multiple exit nodes can be modeled with a single-exit graph by adding a global *Exit* node and edges from each sink vertex to the global *Exit*. However, whereas nodes that are not reachable from *Entry* can be removed, the same is not true for nodes that do not reach *Exit*. This would be the case for a program with an infinite loop, for instance, as in embedded systems; see Figure 3.28. In situations like this, a compiler cannot use control dependence analysis to analyze the whole program. It can divide the program into single-entry, single-exit regions and apply control dependence analysis within each region. Using this technique, the body of the infinite loop shown in Figure 3.28 could be analyzed by treating the header node (*h*) as *Entry* and the source of the back edge (*j*) as *Exit*. An alternative would be to add a (phantom) edge from, say, the entry point of the infinite loop to *Exit*. This false edge would correspond to the decision by the user to turn the power off, and would normally never be taken. In Figure 3.28, the compiler could add an edge $h \to f$, which would allow it to use control dependence to analyze the program.

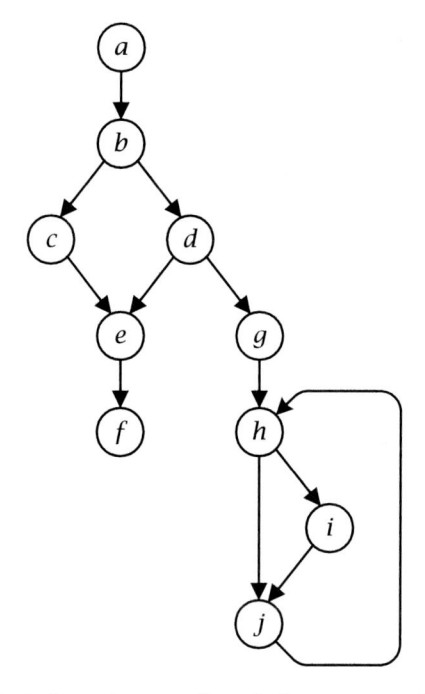

FIGURE 3.28 Infinite loop at $\{h, i, j\}$ does not reach *Exit* at *f*.

3.4 Further Reading

Any general textbook on discrete math will cover basic concepts of sets and logic, such as the books by Stanat and McAllister (1977), Tremblay and Manohar (1975), and Gries and Schneider (1993). Aho et al. (1974) give many graph algorithms that are in common use in compilers. Cormen et al. (1990) describe and analyze many algorithms that are in general use; they give an alternate algorithm for finding strongly connected components for a directed graph. The algorithm to find strongly connected components shown here is due to Tarjan (1972), who proves it correct.

Control flow graphs and dominators have long been used in compilers. Lengauer and Tarjan (1979) describe a fast and efficient algorithm to find the dominator tree of a CFG. Ferrante et al. (1987) define the concept of control dependence in terms of postdominators, and use the control dependence graph to replace the control flow graph; they use an irreflexive definition of postdominance, and a different but equivalent definition of control dependence. Cytron et al. (1991) describe the algorithm for finding dominance frontiers, and show the relationship between the postdominance frontiers and control dependence graph.

Our definition of dominance frontier is slightly different than that used in previous work. Cytron et al. (1990) show a more concise algorithm for finding dominance frontiers and control dependence relations.

EXERCISES

3.1 Write a depth-first tree traversal program to assign levels to nodes in a tree.

3.2 Write a breadth-first tree traversal algorithm.

3.3 Algorithm DFST in Figure 3.6 distinguishes advancing, retreating, and cross edges by comparing the preorder and reverse postorder numbers of the nodes. Show that the test $NPre(X) < NPre(Y)$ at line 13 means that X must be an ancestor of Y. Show that the test $NRPost(X) = 0$ at line 15 means that X must be a descendant of Y.

3.4 Unreachable code is a part of a program that can never be executed because there is no path to it from any point in the program; this may be due to an unreferenced label just after an unconditional branch. How can a depth-first spanning tree algorithm identify unreachable code?

3.5 Use algorithm SCC to find the strongly connected components in the graph shown in Figure 3.29, starting at the *Entry* node. Draw the spanning tree constructed by the algorithm, and identify each SCC in the spanning tree. Draw the acyclic condensation of this graph.

3.6 Prove that the SCCs on a graph are exactly the same as the SCCs on the reverse graph (the graph with the same nodes, but with an edge $Y \rightarrow X$ for every edge $X \rightarrow Y$ in the original graph).

3.7 Modify algorithm SCC to construct the acyclic condensation of a graph, by creating SCC nodes and edges where appropriate. In what order are the SCC nodes created? How could you modify the program to create the SCC nodes in another order?

3.8 Implement algorithm SCC and use it to find strongly connected components on a variety of directed graphs.

3.9 Use the algorithm DOM shown in Figure 3.15 to find dominators of the CFG in Figure 3.29, and draw the dominator tree.

3.10 Given the dominators $DOM(X)$ of a node X, how can the immediate dominator $IDOM(X)$ by found using the depth-first numbers?

3.11 Implement the algorithm in Figure 3.15, and demonstrate how it converges for different control flow graphs. Try visiting the nodes in reverse postorder and see how many iterations are required before the algorithm converges. Try visiting the nodes backwards and see whether the convergence slows down.

3.12 Find the natural loops in Figure 3.29.

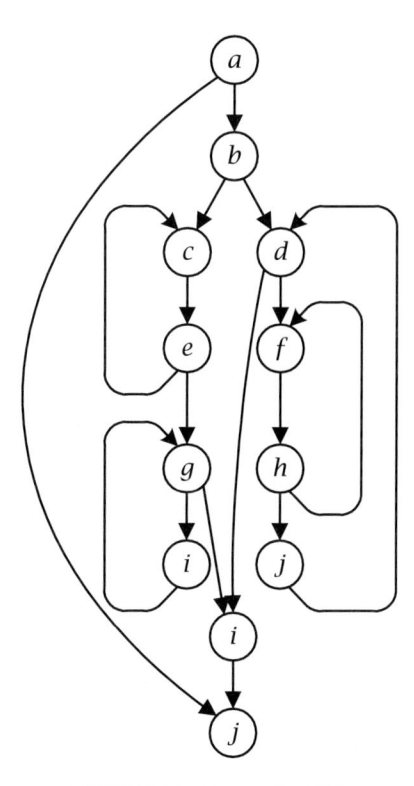

FIGURE 3.29 Example CFG.

3.13 Use algorithm DomFront in Figure 3.18 to compute $DF_{up}(X)$ and $DF_{local}(X)$ for each node X in the CFG in Figure 3.7.

3.14 Repeat the above exercise for the CFG in Figure 3.29.

3.15 Implement algorithm DomFront, and run it on a variety of control flow graphs. In theory, the sum of the cardinality of the dominance frontiers for all nodes in the graph can be within a constant of $|V|^2$. How does the dominance frontier grow in your experiments with larger flow graphs? What control structures make for large dominance frontiers?

3.16 Our definition of dominance frontier is different than that given in the references; a more general definition is that the dominance frontier of a node X is the set of nodes Z such that X dominates a predecessor of Z but does not strictly dominate Z itself. The two definitions are identical in all CFGs; however, there are situations in which our definition will determine an empty dominance frontier set for a node where the more general definition will have a nonempty dominance frontier. Find a graph where this happens. Describe a method the compiler can use to avoid this situation.

3.17 Postdominators can be computed using algorithm DOM of Figure 3.15 on the reverse CFG. Show that visiting the nodes in reverse postorder will visit every node after all its successors, except for retreating edges.

3.18 Prove that $IDOM(X)$ PDOM S for all $S \in SUCC(X)$.

3.19 Show that if Y PDOM S, then for every path $p : S \to X_1 \to X_2 \to \cdots \to X_N \to Y$, Y PDOM X_i for all i.

3.20 The slicing edge was added to compute control dependence. Suppose we did not have this edge. Draw two control flow graphs with the following edges:

G_1:	G_2:
Entry → a	Entry → a
a → b	a → b
b → a	b → a
a → Exit	b → Exit

Find the postdominator trees for G_1 and G_2, without adding the slicing edge. Apply the definition of control dependence and draw the control dependence graphs. What is the difference between $CD(G_1)$ and $CD(G_2)$? Now add the slicing edge and again find the two postdominator trees and draw the control dependence graphs. What is the difference between the two control dependence graphs after adding the slicing edge? What program characteristic is exposed by this difference?

3.21 Use algorithm DomFront in Figure 3.18 to compute the control dependence graph for the CFG in Figure 3.29, and draw the graph. Does the control dependence graph identify the same loop structure as the natural loops?

3.22 Find the natural loops for the CFG in Figure 3.30. Find the control dependence graph for the same CFG. Compare the loop structure found by the definition of natural loops with the one found by control dependence. Why are they different?

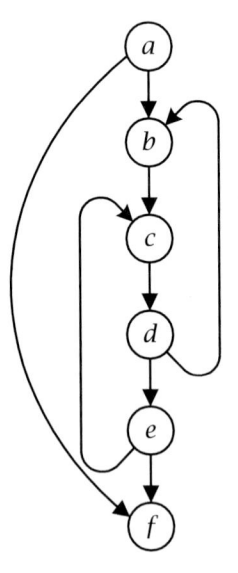

FIGURE 3.30 Control flow graph for exercises.

3.23 Implement algorithm DomFront Figure 3.18 to find control dependence relations, and use it on a variety of control flow graphs.

3.24 Implement procedure CDsucc in Figure 3.24 and use it in a program to compute control dependence relations. Compare its performance to that of algorithm DomFront.

3.25 Nodes in a CFG that have the same control dependence predecessors are called *control equivalent*. Show that if two nodes X and Y in a CFG are control equivalent, then one must postdominate the other.

3.26 Assume that X and Y are control equivalent and that Y PDOM X; show that X DOM Y.

3.27 Show that if X DOM Y and Y PDOM X, then X and Y are control equivalent.

3.28 A subgraph of a CFG with a single entry node X (all nodes in the subgraph are dominated by X) and a single exit node Y (all nodes are postdominated by Y) is called a single-entry, single-exit (SESE) region. Clearly, each node by itself is a trivial SESE region. Show an algorithm that uses $DOM^{-1}(X)$ and $PDOM^{-1}(X)$ for all nodes X to find all SESE regions of a CFG. Implement your algorithm and comment on its effectiveness.

4 REVIEW OF LINEAR ALGEBRA

Several program analysis and transformation techniques can be cast in terms of linear algebra. In subsequent chapters, we will cast data dependence testing between array references as finding integer solutions to a set of integer equations and inequalities; we will also see how to cast loop restructuring optimizations in terms of linear algebra. This chapter introduces the terminology we will use and presents important algorithms that can be used in subsequent chapters.

We denote the set of real numbers by $\mathbb{R}$ and the set of integers by $\mathbb{Z}$. The sign of a real or integer number α is given by $sign(\alpha)$, defined as

$$sign(\alpha) = \begin{cases} 1 & \text{if } \alpha > 0 \\ 0 & \text{if } \alpha = 0 \\ -1 & \text{if } \alpha < 0 \end{cases}$$

There are six possible ordering relations between two real or integer numbers: $<, =, >, \leq, \geq$, and $\neq$. It will be convenient to also have an ordering relation that implies no ordering; we define $\star$ as an ordering relation between two real or integer numbers such that $\alpha \star \beta$ is always true. We first review basic concepts and terminology for real numbers, then concentrate on the more interesting problems in the integer domain.

4.1 Real Vectors and Matrices

An *n*-tuple or *n*-vector of real numbers represents a point in *n*-space, or an element of $\mathbb{R}^n$. We will denote a *vector* by bold lowercase, such as $\mathbf{v}$, or if the vector size is not clear from the context, $\mathbf{v}^n$. The elements of a vector are denoted with subscripts, as shown:

$$\mathbf{v}^n = \begin{pmatrix} v_1 \\ v_2 \\ v_3 \\ \vdots \\ v_n \end{pmatrix},$$

We usually write vectors as a column, but to save space, we may use a rowwise orientation when there is no ambiguity. Scaling a vector by a real number, written $\alpha \mathbf{v}$, means multiplying every element of $\mathbf{v}$ by α. The *zero vector*, $\mathbf{0}$, is the vector of all zeros. The *unit normal vector* $\mathbf{e}_i$ has a one at position i and zeros elsewhere. Let V be a finite set of *n*-vectors $\{\mathbf{v}_1, \mathbf{v}_2, \ldots, \mathbf{v}_m\}$. A *linear combination* of the vectors of V is a vector $\mathbf{x}$ defined by

$$\mathbf{x} = \alpha_1 \mathbf{v}_1 + \alpha_2 \mathbf{v}_2 + \cdots + \alpha_m \mathbf{v}_m$$

where the coefficients $\alpha_1, \alpha_2, \ldots, \alpha_m$ are real numbers. The set V is *linearly dependent* if there is a linear combination that results in the zero vector with one or more of the coefficients being nonzero; otherwise, the set is *linearly independent*.

A nonempty subset S of $\mathbb{R}^n$ is a called a *subspace* of $\mathbb{R}^n$ iff

1. $\mathbf{x}, \mathbf{y} \in S \Longrightarrow \mathbf{x} + \mathbf{y} \in S$
2. $\mathbf{x} \in S \land \alpha \in \mathbb{R} \Longrightarrow \alpha \mathbf{x} \in S$

That is, any linear combination of two elements of S is also in S. Given a set of vectors V, *span* (V) is the subspace spanned by V, which is the subspace of $\mathbb{R}^n$ that can be expressed as a linear combination of the vectors in V. The dimensionality of the subspace, written $dim(V)$, is the number of linearly independent vectors in V. A *basis* for an m-dimensional vector space is a set of m linearly independent vectors such that every point in the vector space can be expressed as a linear combination of the vectors in the basis. The vectors in the basis are called *basis vectors*. A basis for $\mathbb{R}^n$ is:

$$\left\{ \mathbf{e}_1 = \begin{pmatrix} 1 \\ 0 \\ 0 \\ \vdots \\ 0 \end{pmatrix}, \mathbf{e}_2 = \begin{pmatrix} 0 \\ 1 \\ 0 \\ \vdots \\ 0 \end{pmatrix}, \mathbf{e}_3 = \begin{pmatrix} 0 \\ 0 \\ 1 \\ \vdots \\ 0 \end{pmatrix}, \ldots, \mathbf{e}_n = \begin{pmatrix} 0 \\ 0 \\ 0 \\ \vdots \\ 1 \end{pmatrix} \right\}$$

Example 4.1

Find the dimensionality of and a basis for the subspace of $\mathbb{R}^3$ spanned by the three vectors:

$$\mathbf{v}_1 = \begin{pmatrix} 1 \\ 2 \\ 3 \end{pmatrix}, \mathbf{v}_2 = \begin{pmatrix} 0 \\ -1 \\ 1 \end{pmatrix}, \mathbf{v}_3 = \begin{pmatrix} 1 \\ 0 \\ 5 \end{pmatrix}$$

Solution

Vectors $\mathbf{v}_1$ and $\mathbf{v}_2$ are linearly independent, but $\mathbf{v}_3$ can be expressed as a linear combination of the other two: $\mathbf{v}_3 = \mathbf{v}_1 + 2\mathbf{v}_2$. Thus the vector space spanned by these three vectors is only two-dimensional. In this case we can choose any two of the vectors as a basis, or in fact any two linearly independent combinations of the vectors. The subspace spanned by these vectors is thus a plane in three-space. Note that the origin (the vector $\mathbf{0}$) is a member of every subspace spanned by a set of vectors.

Two n-vectors $\mathbf{a}$ and $\mathbf{b}$ are equal if $a_i = b_i$, $1 \leq i \leq n$. We define several ordering relations on vectors. A vector ordering compares each element of two vectors pairwise. We say that $\mathbf{a}$ is less than $\mathbf{b}$, written $\mathbf{a} < \mathbf{b}$, if $a_i < b_i$, $1 \leq i \leq n$; we also say $\mathbf{a} \leq \mathbf{b}$, if $a_i \leq b_i$ $1 \leq i \leq n$, which is not quite the same as saying $\mathbf{a} < \mathbf{b} \vee \mathbf{a} = \mathbf{b}$. We say that $\mathbf{a}$ is *lexicographically less than* $\mathbf{b}$ at level j, or $\mathbf{a} \prec_j \mathbf{b}$, if $a_i = b_i$, $1 \leq i < j$ and $a_j < b_j$. We say that $\mathbf{a}$ is lexicographically less than $\mathbf{b}$, written $\mathbf{a} \prec \mathbf{b}$, if there is a j, $1 \leq j \leq n$, such that $\mathbf{a} \prec_j \mathbf{b}$, and we write $\mathbf{a} \preceq \mathbf{b}$ if $\mathbf{a} \prec \mathbf{b} \vee \mathbf{a} = \mathbf{b}$. Sometimes we will use the notation $\mathbf{a} \prec_\infty \mathbf{b}$ to mean $\mathbf{a} = \mathbf{b}$. A vector $\mathbf{a}$ is *lexicographically positive* if $\mathbf{0} \prec \mathbf{a}$, and *lexicographically nonnegative* if $\mathbf{0} \preceq \mathbf{a}$.

Finally, we define an ordering vector to be a vector of ordering relations. Given an ordering vector $\check{\mathbf{w}}$, we say $\mathbf{a}\,\check{\mathbf{w}}\,\mathbf{b}$ when the relations $a_i\,\check{w}_i\,b_i$ all are true. Thus, $\mathbf{a}\,(\star, \star, \ldots, \star)\,\mathbf{b}$ is always true. Saying $\mathbf{a} < \mathbf{b}$ is the same as saying $\mathbf{a}\,(<, <, \ldots, <)\,\mathbf{b}$. Saying $\mathbf{a} \prec_j \mathbf{b}$ is the same as saying $\mathbf{a}\,\check{\mathbf{w}}\,\mathbf{b}$ where w_i is $=$ for $1 \leq i < j$, w_j is $<$ and w_i is $\star$ for $j < i \leq n$. An ordering vector with only $<$, $=$, and $>$ entries is *simple*.

A more restrictive representation of the ordering vector is to use $sign(\mathbf{a} - \mathbf{b})$, where $sign(\mathbf{v})$ is defined as the vector $(sign(v_1), sign(v_2), \ldots, sign(v_n))$. The vector of signs of the difference is a vector containing zeros, ones, and negative ones, and is equivalent to a simple ordering vector.

Example 4.2

How can the following three vectors be related?

$$\mathbf{a} = \begin{pmatrix} 3 \\ 5 \\ 4 \end{pmatrix}, \quad \mathbf{b} = \begin{pmatrix} 1 \\ 4 \\ 0 \end{pmatrix}, \quad \mathbf{c} = \begin{pmatrix} 3 \\ 9 \\ 3 \end{pmatrix}$$

Solution

Figure 4.1 gives the vector relation, lexicographic relation, and ordering vector relating each pair of vectors. Note that $\mathbf{a}$ is neither greater than nor less than $\mathbf{c}$, but they can be related lexicographically and by an ordering vector.

relation	a, b	b, c	a, c
vector relation	$\mathbf{b} < \mathbf{a}$	$\mathbf{b} < \mathbf{c}$	
lexicographic relation	$\mathbf{b} \prec_1 \mathbf{a}$	$\mathbf{b} \prec_1 \mathbf{c}$	$\mathbf{a} \prec_2 \mathbf{c}$
ordering vector	$\mathbf{b} \begin{pmatrix} < \\ < \\ < \end{pmatrix} \mathbf{a}$	$\mathbf{b} \begin{pmatrix} < \\ < \\ < \end{pmatrix} \mathbf{c}$	$\mathbf{a} \begin{pmatrix} = \\ < \\ > \end{pmatrix} \mathbf{c}$

FIGURE 4.1 Examples of ordering relations for vectors.

4.1.1 Matrices

An $n \times m$ real matrix $\mathbf{A}$ has n rows and m columns of real numbers:

$$\mathbf{A}^{n \times m} = \begin{pmatrix} a_{11} & a_{12} & a_{13} & \cdots & a_{1m} \\ a_{21} & a_{22} & a_{23} & \cdots & a_{2m} \\ a_{31} & a_{32} & a_{33} & \cdots & a_{3m} \\ \vdots & \vdots & \vdots & \ddots & \vdots \\ a_{n1} & a_{n2} & a_{n3} & \cdots & a_{nm} \end{pmatrix}$$

The *transpose* of a matrix, $\mathbf{B} = \mathbf{A}^T$, is the $m \times n$ matrix where $b_{ij} = a_{ji}$. When the number of rows and columns are equal, the matrix is called a *square matrix*. The elements a_{ii} are said to lie on the *diagonal*. A square matrix is a *diagonal matrix* if all elements not on the the diagonal are zero. The elements a_{ij} are below the diagonal if $i > j$, and above the diagonal if $i < j$. A *symmetric matrix* is a square matrix such that $\mathbf{A} = \mathbf{A}^T$; that is, $a_{ij} = a_{ji}$. An *upper trapezoidal* (*lower trapezoidal*) matrix has zeros below (above) the diagonal. A square upper or lower trapezoidal matrix is called *upper triangular* or *lower triangular*, respectively. A strictly lower triangular matrix has zeros on the diagonal as well. We write $(\mathbf{A}|\mathbf{B})$ to mean the matrix comprising the columns of the $\mathbf{A}$ matrix concatenated with the columns of the $\mathbf{B}$ matrix. We write

$$\begin{pmatrix} \mathbf{A} \\ \mathbf{B} \end{pmatrix}$$

to mean the matrix comprising the rows of $\mathbf{A}$ above the rows of $\mathbf{B}$.

An n-vector $\mathbf{v}$ is equivalent to an $n \times 1$ matrix, sometimes called a *column vector*. A $1 \times m$ matrix $\mathbf{V}^{1 \times m}$ is a row vector. The ith column of a matrix A is the column vector:

$$\mathbf{a}_{[i]} = \begin{pmatrix} a_{1i} \\ a_{2i} \\ a_{3i} \\ \vdots \\ a_{ni} \end{pmatrix}$$

The jth row of a matrix is the row vector:

$$\mathbf{A}_{[j]} = (a_{j1}, a_{j2}, \ldots, a_{jm})$$

The dot-product of two vectors, written $\mathbf{x} \cdot \mathbf{y}$, is a real number, defined as:

$$\mathbf{x}^n \cdot \mathbf{y}^n = \sum_{i=1}^{n} x_i y_i$$

The product of two matrices, written $\mathbf{A} \times \mathbf{B}$ or $\mathbf{AB}$, is defined only when the number of columns in $\mathbf{A}$ matches the number of rows in $\mathbf{B}$. The result of multiplying $\mathbf{A}^{n \times m} \times \mathbf{B}^{m \times k}$ is another matrix $\mathbf{C}^{n \times k}$, where c_{ij} is the dot-product of the ith row of

A and the jth column of **B**:

$$c_{ij} = \mathbf{A}_{[i]} \cdot \mathbf{b}_{[j]}$$

Matrix multiplication is associative, but not commutative.

A linear function $f : \mathbb{R}^m \longrightarrow \mathbb{R}^n$ satisfies

$$f(\alpha \mathbf{x} + \beta \mathbf{y}) = \alpha f(\mathbf{x}) + \beta f(\mathbf{y})$$

for $\alpha, \beta \in \mathbb{R}$. Such a function is easily represented by the matrix $\mathbf{F}^{n \times m}$, where the ith column is $\mathbf{f}_{[i]} = f(\mathbf{e}_i)$. The function $f(\mathbf{x})$ is then computed by the matrix-vector product $\mathbf{Fx}$. The identity matrix $\mathbf{I}^{n \times n}$ has ones on the diagonal and zeros elsewhere; the identity matrix represents the identity function: $\mathbf{Ix} = \mathbf{x}$ for all vectors $\mathbf{x}^n$. The zero matrix, $\mathbf{0}^{n \times m}$, has all zero entries, and represents the zero function.

Example 4.3

What is the matrix representation of the linear function $h : \mathbb{R}^3 \longrightarrow \mathbb{R}^2$, defined by $h(\mathbf{x}) = f(g(\mathbf{x}))$, where f and g are represented by the matrices $\mathbf{F}$ and $\mathbf{G}$, respectively, shown below:

$$\mathbf{F} = \begin{pmatrix} 1 & 0 & 1 & 0 \\ 3 & 1 & 9 & 1 \end{pmatrix} \quad \mathbf{G} = \begin{pmatrix} -1 & 1 & 0 \\ 2 & 1 & 0 \\ 0 & 2 & 2 \\ 3 & 3 & 1 \end{pmatrix}$$

Solution

In functional notation, we seek to characterize h as the composition of f and g, $h = f \circ g$. Computing $f(g(\mathbf{x}))$ is the same as computing $\mathbf{F} \times (\mathbf{G} \times \mathbf{x})$. Because matrix multiplication is associative, this can be written $(\mathbf{F} \times \mathbf{G}) \times \mathbf{x}$. Thus, the function h can be represented by the matrix product

$$\mathbf{H} = \mathbf{F} \times \mathbf{G} = \begin{pmatrix} -1 & 3 & 2 \\ 2 & 25 & 19 \end{pmatrix}$$

The *right-inverse* of a matrix $\mathbf{A}$ is the matrix $\mathbf{A}^{-1}$ such that $\mathbf{A}\mathbf{A}^{-1} = \mathbf{I}$. If $\mathbf{A}$ is square, then the right-inverse, if it exists, is unique and also satisfies $\mathbf{A}\mathbf{A}^{-1} = \mathbf{A}^{-1}\mathbf{A} = \mathbf{I}$, and is simply called the *inverse*. A square matrix that has an inverse is called *nonsingular*; otherwise it is *singular*.

The *range* (or *image*) of a matrix, written *range* $\mathbf{A}^{n \times m}$, is the set $\{\mathbf{Ax} \mid \mathbf{x} \in \mathbb{R}^m\}$. This is identical to *span* $\mathbf{A}$, the subspace of $\mathbb{R}^m$ which is spanned by the columns of $\mathbf{A}$. The *null space* (or *kernel*) of a matrix, written *kernel* $\mathbf{A}^{n \times m}$, is the set $\{\mathbf{x}^m \mid \mathbf{Ax} = \mathbf{0}\}$. The null space is a subspace of $\mathbb{R}^m$. The dimensionality of *range* $\mathbf{A}$ is defined to the rank of $\mathbf{A}$, written *rank*($\mathbf{A}$). The *nullity* of $\mathbf{A}$ is the dimensionality of *kernel* $\mathbf{A}$, written *nullity*($\mathbf{A}$). For any matrix $\mathbf{A}^{n \times m}$, *rank*($\mathbf{A}$) + *nullity*($\mathbf{A}$) = n. The rank of

4.1 ▪ Real Vectors and Matrices

a matrix is the number of linearly independent rows of the matrix, which is the same as the number of linearly independent columns. Thus $rank(\mathbf{A}) = rank(\mathbf{A}^T)$; however, $nullity(\mathbf{A})$ and $nullity(\mathbf{A}^T)$ will not be the same if the matrix is not square. If a square matrix $\mathbf{A}^{n \times n}$ has rank n, then it has an inverse (and vice versa).

Example 4.4

Compute the rank and nullity, and describe the range, of the matrix:

$$\mathbf{A} = \begin{pmatrix} 1 & 2 & 1 & 4 \\ 2 & 3 & 0 & 2 \\ 0 & 0 & 1 & 3 \\ 2 & 5 & 1 & 5 \end{pmatrix}$$

Solution

The first three columns of the matrix are linearly independent. This can be verified by looking for solutions to the equation:

$$\alpha_1 \mathbf{a}_{[1]} + \alpha_2 \mathbf{a}_{[2]} + \alpha_3 \mathbf{a}_{[3]} = \mathbf{0}$$

which gives the system of equations

$$\begin{aligned} \alpha_1 + 2\alpha_2 + \alpha_3 &= 0 \\ 2\alpha_1 + 3\alpha_2 &= 0 \\ \alpha_3 &= 0 \\ 2\alpha_1 + 5\alpha_2 + \alpha_3 &= 0 \end{aligned}$$

The only solution to these equations is $\alpha_1 = \alpha_2 = \alpha_3 = 0$. The fourth column of $\mathbf{A}$ is not linearly independent, since $\mathbf{a}_{[4]} = \mathbf{a}_{[1]} + 3\mathbf{a}_{[3]}$. Thus $rank(\mathbf{A}) = 3$ and $nullity(\mathbf{A}) = 4 - 3 = 1$. The range of $\mathbf{A}$ can be simply described by finding a basis; the first three columns clearly span the range and are linearly independent, so they can serve as a basis for the range.

Elementary Row Operations

There are three *elementary row operations* on a matrix $\mathbf{A}$ that produce a new matrix:

1. multiply (scale) each element of the ith row by a factor α,
2. add α times row i to row j,
3. transpose (interchange) rows i and j.

We call these scale, skew, and transpose operations, respectively. Each can be performed by premultiplying $\mathbf{A}$ by a transformation matrix $\mathbf{T}$, which is formed as follows for each operation:

1. For scaling, $\mathbf{T}$ is the same as the identity matrix, except that $t_{ii} = \alpha$.

2. For skewing, $\mathbf{T}$ is the same as the identity matrix except $t_{ij} = \alpha$.
3. For transposition, $\mathbf{T}$ is the same as the identity matrix, except $t_{ii} = 0, t_{ij} = 1, t_{ji} = 1, t_{jj} = 0$.

A sequence of elementary row operations can be applied using a sequence of matrix operations:

$$\mathbf{T}_n \times (\mathbf{T}_{n-1} \times (\cdots (\mathbf{T}_2 \times (\mathbf{T}_1 \times \mathbf{A})) \cdots))$$

Because matrix multiplication is associative, the transformation matrices can be combined into a single transformation matrix, as

$$\mathbf{T} = \mathbf{T}_n \times \mathbf{T}_{n-1} \times \cdots \times \mathbf{T}_2 \times \mathbf{T}_1$$

and then computing $\mathbf{T} \times \mathbf{A}$.

Example 4.5

Apply to the matrix A, below, the following sequence of elementary row operations:

- Multiply the second row by 2.
- Subtract three times the first row from the second.
- Interchange rows 2 and 3.

$$\mathbf{A} = \begin{pmatrix} 1 & 2 & 3 \\ 0 & -2 & 9 \\ 18 & 7 & -3 \end{pmatrix}$$

Solution

The first operation can be performed by computing the matrix product of a scale matrix by $\mathbf{A}$:

$$\mathbf{T}_1 = \begin{pmatrix} 1 & 0 & 0 \\ 0 & 2 & 0 \\ 0 & 0 & 1 \end{pmatrix}, \mathbf{T}_1 \times \mathbf{A} = \mathbf{A}_1 = \begin{pmatrix} 1 & 2 & 3 \\ 0 & -4 & 18 \\ 18 & 7 & -3 \end{pmatrix}$$

The second operation is performed by premultiplying that result by a skew matrix:

$$\mathbf{T}_2 = \begin{pmatrix} 1 & 0 & 0 \\ -3 & 1 & 0 \\ 0 & 0 & 1 \end{pmatrix}, \mathbf{T}_2 \times \mathbf{A}_1 = \mathbf{A}_2 = \begin{pmatrix} 1 & 2 & 3 \\ -3 & -10 & 9 \\ 18 & 7 & -3 \end{pmatrix}$$

The final operation is performed by applying a transposition matrix:

$$\mathbf{T}_3 = \begin{pmatrix} 1 & 0 & 0 \\ 0 & 0 & 1 \\ 0 & 1 & 0 \end{pmatrix}, \mathbf{T}_3 \times \mathbf{A}_2 = \mathbf{A}_3 = \begin{pmatrix} 1 & 2 & 3 \\ 18 & 7 & -3 \\ -3 & -10 & 9 \end{pmatrix}$$

The three elementary operations can be composed into the following transformation matrix:

$$\mathbf{T}_3 \times \mathbf{T}_2 \times \mathbf{T}_1 = \begin{pmatrix} 1 & 0 & 0 \\ 0 & 0 & 1 \\ -3 & 2 & 0 \end{pmatrix}$$

There are also scale, skew, and transposition elementary column operations. These can be performed by postmultiplying the matrix $\mathbf{A}$ by a corresponding transformation matrix.

The row-interchange transformation is a simple transposition of two rows; the product of many transposition matrices is a general *permutation matrix*. A permutation matrix is a square matrix with a single one in each row and column, and zeros elsewhere.

Polyhedra

A subset C of $\mathbb{R}^n$ is *convex* if $\alpha\mathbf{x} + (1 - \alpha)\mathbf{y} \in C$ for all $\mathbf{x}, \mathbf{y} \in C$, and $0 \le \alpha \le 1$. Essentially, for every two vectors $\mathbf{x}$ and $\mathbf{y}$ in C, all vectors "between" $\mathbf{x}$ and $\mathbf{y}$ are also in C. The intersection of two convex sets is another convex set. The *convex hull* of a nonempty set of vectors is the smallest convex set containing all the vectors in the set.

An affine *half-space* of $\mathbb{R}^n$ is the set of vectors $\mathbf{x}$ that satisfy the linear inequality $\mathbf{a} \cdot \mathbf{x} \le \beta$ for some vector $\mathbf{a}$ and real number β; a half-space is a convex set. The intersection of a set of half-spaces is called a *polyhedron*. A polyhedron can be represented by the set of linear inequalities $\mathbf{A}\mathbf{x} \le \mathbf{b}$, for some matrix $\mathbf{A}$ and vector $\mathbf{b}$. A polyhedron in $\mathbb{R}^n$ is *bounded* if there is a vector $\mathbf{v}^n$ such that $-\mathbf{v} \le \mathbf{x} \le \mathbf{v}$ for all vector $\mathbf{x}$ in the polyhedron; a bounded polyhedron is called a *polytope*. The n-dimensional *unit cube* is the polytope such that $0 \le x_i \le 1$ for all elements of $\mathbf{x}$ in the polytope. It can be characterized by the following set of linear inequalities:

$$\begin{pmatrix} -1 & 0 & \cdots & 0 \\ 1 & 0 & \cdots & 0 \\ 0 & -1 & \cdots & 0 \\ 0 & 1 & \cdots & 0 \\ \vdots & \vdots & \ddots & \vdots \\ 0 & 0 & \cdots & -1 \\ 0 & 0 & \cdots & 1 \end{pmatrix} \begin{pmatrix} x_1 \\ x_2 \\ \vdots \\ x_n \end{pmatrix} \le \begin{pmatrix} 0 \\ 1 \\ 0 \\ 1 \\ \vdots \\ 0 \\ 1 \end{pmatrix}$$

A polytope is the convex hull of a finite set of points; the smallest such set is called the *set of vertices* of the polytope. The vertices of the unit cube are all the vectors whose entries are either zero or one.

Determinants

Let $\mathbf{A}^{n \times n}$ be a square matrix and $\mathbf{A}^{[ij]}$ be the matrix formed by deleting the ith row and the jth column. The *determinant* of $\mathbf{A}$ can be computed as

$$\det(\mathbf{A}) = \sum_{j=1}^{n}(-1)^{i+j}a_{ij}\det(\mathbf{A}^{[ij]})$$

for any value of i; the value of $(-1)^{i+j}\det(\mathbf{A}^{[ij]})$ is the *cofactor* of a_{ij}. This computation finds the determinant by expansion of cofactors of the ith row of $\mathbf{A}$. Likewise, the determinant could be computed by expansion of cofactors of column j, for any value of j:

$$\det(\mathbf{A}) = \sum_{i=1}^{n}(-1)^{i+j}a_{ij}\det(\mathbf{A}^{[ij]})$$

A row or column with many zeroes is often chosen to simplify the computation. The determinant of a 2×2 matrix is:

$$\det\begin{pmatrix} a & b \\ c & d \end{pmatrix} = ad - bc$$

Example 4.6

Compute the determinant of the matrix:

$$\mathbf{A} = \begin{pmatrix} 1 & 2 & 4 \\ 2 & 0 & 9 \\ 3 & 0 & 0 \end{pmatrix}$$

Solution

Expanding by the cofactors of the third row, we get:

$$\det(\mathbf{A}) = 3 \cdot \det\begin{pmatrix} 2 & 4 \\ 0 & 9 \end{pmatrix} - 0 \cdot \det\begin{pmatrix} 1 & 4 \\ 2 & 9 \end{pmatrix} + 0 \cdot \det\begin{pmatrix} 1 & 2 \\ 2 & 0 \end{pmatrix}$$

$$= 3(2 \cdot 9 - 4 \cdot 0)$$

$$= 54$$

Alternatively, we could expand by the cofactors of the second column, giving:

$$\det(\mathbf{A}) = -2 \cdot \det\begin{pmatrix} 2 & 9 \\ 3 & 0 \end{pmatrix} + 0 \cdot \det\begin{pmatrix} 1 & 4 \\ 3 & 0 \end{pmatrix} - 0 \cdot \det\begin{pmatrix} 1 & 4 \\ 2 & 9 \end{pmatrix}$$

$$= -2(2 \cdot 0 - 9 \cdot 3)$$

$$= 54$$

Properties of the determinant include:

- If a square matrix has a nonzero determinant, it is nonsingular and has an inverse.
- For any square matrices **A** and **B**, det(**A** × **B**) = det(**A**) · det(**B**).
- The determinant of the identity matrix is 1.
- If $\mathbf{A}^{-1}$ exists, then det(**A**) $\neq$ 0 and det($\mathbf{A}^{-1}$) = 1/ det(**A**).
- The determinant of a diagonal matrix is the product of the diagonals.
- The determinant of an upper or lower triangular matrix is the product of the diagonals.
- The determinant of the three elementary row operation transformation matrices are $T_1 = \alpha$, $T_2 = 1$, and $T_3 = -1$.

When **A** represents a linear transformation from $\mathbb{R}^n \longrightarrow \mathbb{R}^n$, the value of |det(**A**)| is the change in volume induced by the transformation. That is, |det(**A**)| is the volume of the polyhedron produced by transforming the vertices of the unit cube by the transformation **A**.

Matrix Inverse

We can find the inverse of a square nonsingular matrix by a series of elementary row operations. For each column j, we find a row $i \geq j$ with a nonzero element in that column and interchange the ith row with the jth row, so the nonzero entry is on the diagonal. We then scale that row by the inverse of the diagonal element, so the diagonal becomes unity. Finally, we subtract multiples of that row from all other rows to *annihilate* (reduce to zero) all other entries in the jth column. At the end, the matrix is reduced to the identity matrix.

Suppose we have a sequence of elementary row operations to reduce matrix **A** to the identity matrix:

$$\mathbf{T}_n \times (\mathbf{T}_{n-1} \times \cdots \times (\mathbf{T}_2 \times (\mathbf{T}_1 \times \mathbf{A})) \cdots) = \mathbf{I}$$

By reassociation, we have

$$\mathbf{T}_n \times \mathbf{T}_{n-1} \times \cdots \times \mathbf{T}_2 \times \mathbf{T}_1 = \mathbf{A}^{-1}$$

Thus, if we initialize another matrix to the identity matrix, and apply the same sequence of elementary row operations to this matrix as we reduce **A** to the identity matrix, the result will be the inverse of the original matrix. Algorithm Invert, shown in Figure 4.2, performs matrix inversion. Given a matrix $\mathbf{A}^{n \times n}$, it returns a matrix **B** such that $\mathbf{B} = \mathbf{A}^{-1}$; if **A** is singular, it returns its rank in r.

4.2 Integer Matrices and Lattices

We start our discussion of the integer domain by studying the problem of finding the greatest common divisor (gcd) of two integers. Euclid's algorithm to find greatest common divisors computes a sequence of values $g_1 > g_2 > \cdots > g_{n-1} > g_n = 0$

```
        Algorithm Invert:
 (1)    procedure Invert( A ) returns( B, r )
 (2)    initialize B to I
 (3)    r = 0
 (4)    for j = 1 to n do
 (5)        find k ∈ [r + 1 : n] such that a_kj ≠ 0
 (6)        if a_jk = 0 for all k ∈ [r + 1 : n] then
 (7)            A is singular
 (8)        else
 (9)            r = r + 1
(10)            if k ≠ r then
(11)                interchange row A_[r] with row A_[k]
(12)                interchange row B_[r] with row B_[k]
(13)            endif
(14)            if a_rj ≠ 1 then
(15)                c = a_rj
(16)                divide row A_[r] by c
(17)                divide row B_[r] by c
(18)            endif
(19)            for i = 1 to n do
(20)                if i ≠ r and a_ij ≠ 0 then
(21)                    α = a_ij
(22)                    let A_[i] = A_[i] − αA_[r]
(23)                    let B_[i] = B_[i] − αB_[r]
(24)                endif
(25)            endfor
(26)        endif
(27)    endfor
(28)    end Invert
```

FIGURE 4.2 Algorithm to find the inverse of a square $n \times n$ matrix **A**.

that all have the same gcd. The algorithm stops when the sequence reaches zero; the last nonzero value is the gcd. Suppose we want to find the gcd of a and b where $b > 0$, and $c = a \bmod b$. The key observation of Euclid's algorithm is that if $c = 0$, then $\gcd(a,b) = b$, and if $c \neq 0$, then $\gcd(a,b) = \gcd(b,c)$. Clearly, if $c = a \bmod b = 0$, then b divides a as well as itself, and no larger integer has that property. On the other hand, since $c = a \bmod b$, we can express a as $a = bd + c$, or c as $c = a - bd$, for some value of d. Since $\gcd(a,b)$ divides both a and bd, it must divide c. A similar argument shows that $\gcd(b,c)$ must divide a. Since $b > c > 0$, we can repeat the argument until the algorithm terminates, which it must do.

4.2 ▪ Integer Matrices and Lattices

In its simplest form, Euclid's algorithm is as follows:

```
procedure Euclid( a, b, gcd )
g₀ = a
g₁ = abs(b)
for i = 1 to ∞ do
    gᵢ₊₁ = gᵢ₋₁ mod gᵢ
    if gᵢ₊₁ = 0 then gcd = gᵢ; return
endfor
end Euclid
```

In addition to finding the gcd of two numbers, we often want to find values x and y such that $ax + by = \gcd(a, b)$. We can modify Euclid's algorithm to find these values also. We keep values x_i and y_i such that $g_i = ax_i + by_i$. The initial values for x_0, x_1, y_0, y_1 are trivial. When we compute $g_{i+1} = g_{i-1} \bmod g_i$, we also find d such that $g_{i-1} = g_i d + g_{i+1}$. By induction, we want to find x_{i+1} and y_{i+1} to satisfy $ax_{i-1} + by_{i-1} = (ax_i + by_i)d + (ax_{i+1} + by_{i+1})$. We can satisfy this by satisfying the two equations:

$$ax_{i-1} = ax_i d + ax_{i+1}$$
$$by_{i-1} = by_i d + by_{i+1}$$

or, simplifying, by computing:

$$x_{i+1} = x_{i-1} - x_i d$$
$$y_{i+1} = y_{i-1} - y_i d$$

The modified procedure to compute the gcd and factors is:

```
procedure Euclid2( a, b, gcd, x, y )
g₀ = a
x₀ = 1; y₀ = 0
g₁ = abs(b)
x₁ = 0; y₁ = sign(b)
for i = 1 to ∞ do
    gᵢ₊₁ = gᵢ₋₁ mod gᵢ
    d = (gᵢ₋₁ - gᵢ₊₁)/gᵢ
    xᵢ₊₁ = xᵢ₋₁ - xᵢd
    yᵢ₊₁ = yᵢ₋₁ - yᵢd
    if gᵢ₊₁ = 0 then
        gcd = gᵢ; x = xᵢ; y = yᵢ
        return
    endif
endfor
end Euclid2
```

In fact, any value of d can be used in the procedure, as long as g_{i+1} gets a value equal to $g_{i-1} - g_i d$. The usual way to do this is through integer division, letting $d = g_{i-1} \text{ div } g_i$; this may result in a negative answer if we let g_0 be negative. The discussion above will still hold, except we have $|g_1| > |g_2| > |g_3| > \cdots$, and the result may be the negative of the gcd, a problem easily fixed. Two more changes can be made; rather than computing a sequence of values, we want to use a small number of variables. Also, given $ax + by = g$, if we know a, b, g, and either x or y, we can compute the other directly, rather then leaving the computation in the loop. Figure 4.3 shows the final form of the algorithm.

```
Algorithm GCD:
(1)   procedure findgcd( a, b) returns( g, x, y )
(2)       g₀ = a; g₁ = b
(3)       x₀ = 1; x₁ = 0
(4)       y₀ = 0; y₁ = 1
(5)       repeat
(6)           d = g₀ ÷ g₁
(7)           g₂ = g₁ - dg₀
(8)           g₀ = g₁; g₁ = g₂
(9)           x₂ = x₁ - dx₀
(10)          x₀ = x₁; x₁ = x₂
(11)      until g₂ = 0
(12)      g = g₀
(13)      x = x₁
(14)      y = (g - ax)/b
(15)      if g < 0 then
(16)          g = -g
(17)          x = -x
(18)          y = -y
(19)      endif
(20)  end findgcd
```

FIGURE 4.3 Algorithm to find $g = \gcd(a, b)$ and to find one solution to $ax + by = g$.

4.2.1 Integer Matrices

An integer matrix has all integer entries; it follows that the determinant of an integer matrix must be an integer, and the product of two integer matrices is also an integer matrix. Note that the inverse of an integer matrix will, in general, have rational, noninteger entries.

An integer matrix is called *unimodular* if its determinant is ±1. Since it is nonsingular, its inverse exists and in fact the inverse is itself unimodular. A linear transformation characterized by a unimodular matrix preserves the volume of a

4.2 • Integer Matrices and Lattices

polytope under the transformation. A permutation matrix is a unimodular matrix, as is a skew matrix if the off-diagonal element is an integer; clearly, the product of two unimodular matrices is another unimodular matrix. Note that the transformation matrix to scale a row by a factor is not unimodular.

There are three *unimodular row operations* that produce a new matrix:

1. Negate each element of the ith row,
2. add α times row i to row j, for some integer α, and
3. interchange rows i and j.

Each row transformation can be performed by premultiplying the matrix **A** by a unimodular transformation matrix, and the row operations can be composed. There are also corresponding unimodular column operations; unimodular operations preserve the determinant of the matrix under transformation.

Example 4.7

What is the composite unimodular transformation matrix of the following three unimodular column transformations on 3×3 matrices?

1. Interchange columns 1 and 3,
2. add twice the first column to the second, and
3. negate column 1.

Solution

The three individual transformation matrices are:

$$\mathbf{T}_1 = \begin{pmatrix} 0 & 0 & 1 \\ 0 & 1 & 0 \\ 1 & 0 & 0 \end{pmatrix}, \quad \mathbf{T}_2 = \begin{pmatrix} 1 & 2 & 0 \\ 0 & 1 & 0 \\ 0 & 0 & 1 \end{pmatrix}, \quad \mathbf{T}_3 = \begin{pmatrix} -1 & 0 & 0 \\ 0 & 1 & 0 \\ 0 & 0 & 1 \end{pmatrix}$$

Applying the transformations to a matrix **A** corresponds to the sequence of postmultiplications $\mathbf{A} \times \mathbf{T}_1 \times \mathbf{T}_2 \times \mathbf{T}_3$. The composition of these transformation matrices is:

$$\mathbf{T}_1 \times \mathbf{T}_2 \times \mathbf{T}_3 = \begin{pmatrix} 0 & 0 & 1 \\ 0 & 1 & 0 \\ -1 & 2 & 0 \end{pmatrix}$$

4.2.2 Hermite Normal Form

For an integer matrix $\mathbf{H}^{n \times m}$ with rank n, is in *Hermite normal form* (HNF) if it is lower trapezoidal and has positive elements where the diagonal is the largest element in each row. If $\mathbf{A}^{n \times m}$ has rank n, then there is an $m \times m$ unimodular matrix U such that $\mathbf{AU}$ is in HNF; moreover, the HNF of a matrix is unique.

The HNF of a matrix (along with the corresponding unimodular transformation matrix) can be found by a sequence of unimodular column operations to *annihilate* elements of the matrix above the diagonal, then to reduce the elements below the diagonal. Suppose we have a matrix **H**, and we want to annihilate the element h_{ij} above the diagonal. We use the diagonal element h_{ii} and construct a unimodular matrix as follows. Use algorithm GCD to find $g = \gcd(h_{ii}, h_{ij})$ and x, y such that $h_{ii}x + h_{ij}y = g$. Let **T** be an identity matrix except in columns i and j; let $t_{ii} = x$, $t_{ij} = y$, $t_{ji} = -h_{ij}/g$ and $t_{jj} = h_{ii}/g$. **T** looks like the following:

$$\begin{pmatrix} 1 & 0 & \cdots & 0 & \cdots & 0 & \cdots & 0 \\ 0 & 1 & \cdots & 0 & \cdots & 0 & \cdots & 0 \\ \vdots & \vdots & \ddots & \vdots & \ddots & \vdots & \ddots & \vdots \\ 0 & 0 & \cdots & x & \cdots & -h_{ij}/g & \cdots & 0 \\ \vdots & \vdots & \ddots & \vdots & \ddots & \vdots & \ddots & \vdots \\ 0 & 0 & \cdots & y & \cdots & h_{ii}/g & \cdots & 0 \\ \vdots & \vdots & \ddots & \vdots & \ddots & \vdots & \ddots & \vdots \\ 0 & 0 & \cdots & 0 & \cdots & 0 & \cdots & 1 \end{pmatrix}$$

Clearly, this is an integer matrix, and the determinant is equal to $xh_{ii}/g + yh_{ij}/g = g/g = 1$, so the matrix is unimodular. Multiplying **HT** will change only columns i and j by accumulating $x\mathbf{h}_{[i]} + y\mathbf{h}_{[j]}$ and $h_{ii}/g\mathbf{h}_{[j]} - h_{ij}/g\mathbf{h}_{[i]}$ into $\mathbf{h}_{[i]}$ and $\mathbf{h}_{[j]}$, respectively. The elements below the diagonal can be reduced in similar fashion by finding suitable multipliers. Such transformation matrices can be composed in the usual way. Figure 4.4 shows the complete algorithm. It builds the HNF in the matrix **H**, and collects the unimodular transformations in the matrix **U**. After each step in the algorithm, **AU = H**.

Often, we don't need to complete the HNF algorithm; if we want only to make the matrix trapezoidal, we can eliminate lines 6-13 from algorithm Hermite. We call this a Hermite trapezoidal form (HTF) of the matrix; note that it is not unique, but does not need to be for many purposes.

4.2.3 Lattices

A vector with all integer entries is called a *lattice point*; thus a lattice point is a member of $\mathbb{Z}^n$. For an integer matrix $\mathbf{A}^{n \times m}$, we define the set $\mathcal{L}(\mathbf{A})$ to be the subset of $\mathbb{Z}^m$ that can be described by an integer combination of the columns of **A**:

$$\mathcal{L}(\mathbf{A}) = \{\alpha_1 \mathbf{a}_{[1]} + \alpha_2 \mathbf{a}_{[2]} + \cdots + \alpha_m \mathbf{a}_{[3]}\}$$

This is the *lattice* generated by the columns of **A**. Each point in $\mathcal{L}(\mathbf{A})$ can be described as **Ax** for some $\mathbf{x} \in \mathbb{Z}^n$. A *basis set* for a lattice is the set of linearly independent integer vectors that generates the lattice. We say a lattice is *dense* if

4.2 ▪ Integer Matrices and Lattices

```
        Algorithm Hermite:
(1)     procedure Hermite( A ) returns( H, U )
(2)     initialize H^{n×m} to A
(3)     initialize U^{m×m} to I

(4)     for i = 1 to n do
(5)         Reduce( i, i + 1 : n, H, U )
(6)         if h_{ii} < 0 then
(7)             negate h_{[i]}
(8)             negate u_{[i]}
(9)         endif
(10)        for j = 1 to i − 1 do
(11)            α = ⌊h_{ij}/h_{ii}⌋
(12)            let h_{[j]} = h_{[j]} − αh_{[i]}
(13)        endfor
(14)    endfor
(15)    procedure Reduce( row i, columns j : n, H, U )
            /* reduce row i, columns j : n to a single nonzero */
(16)        for k = j to n do
(17)            if h_{ik} ≠ 0 then
(18)                /* annihilate h_{ik} */
(19)                a = h_{ii}; b = h_{ik}
(20)                findgcd( a, b, g, x, y )
(21)                let p = xh_{[i]} + yh_{[k]}
(22)                let q = −(b/g)h_{[i]} + (a/g)h_{[k]}
(23)                h_{[i]} = p; h_{[k]} = q
(24)                let v = xu_{[i]} − (b/g)u_{[k]}
(25)                let w = yu_{[i]} + (a/g)u_{[k]}
(26)                let u_{[i]} = v; u_{[k]} = w
(27)            endif
(28)        endloop
(29)    end Reduce
(30) end Hermite
```

FIGURE 4.4 Algorithm to find the HNF of a matrix **A**.

for all $\mathbf{x}, \mathbf{y}$ in the lattice and $0 \le \alpha \le 1$ where $\mathbf{z} = \alpha\mathbf{x} + (1 − \alpha)\mathbf{y}$ is an integer vector, $\mathbf{z}$ is in the lattice. Otherwise, the lattice is *sparse*.

Applying unimodular column operations to a matrix preserves the lattice generated by the matrix. In fact, postmultiplying an integer matrix by any unimodular matrix preserves the lattice generated by the matrix. In particular, the nonzero columns of the HNF of a matrix are a basis for the lattice generated by that matrix. In fact, the nonzero columns of any HTF of a matrix are a basis for that lattice.

Example 4.8

Find the HNF of the following matrix:

$$\begin{pmatrix} 2 & 6 & 1 \\ 4 & 7 & 7 \\ 0 & 0 & 1 \end{pmatrix}$$

Solution

The sequence of steps is as follows:

$H = \begin{pmatrix} 2 & 6 & 1 \\ 4 & 7 & 7 \\ 0 & 0 & 1 \end{pmatrix}$ annihilate $h_{12} = 6$ $\quad T = \begin{pmatrix} 1 & -3 & 0 \\ 0 & 1 & 0 \\ 0 & 0 & 1 \end{pmatrix}$
$\gcd(2, 6) = 2, (x, y) = (1, 0)$

$H = \begin{pmatrix} 2 & 0 & 1 \\ 4 & -5 & 7 \\ 0 & 0 & 1 \end{pmatrix}$ annihilate $h_{13} = 1$ $\quad T = \begin{pmatrix} 0 & 0 & -1 \\ 0 & 1 & 0 \\ 1 & 0 & 2 \end{pmatrix}$
$\gcd(2, 1) = 1, (x, y) = (0, 1)$

$H = \begin{pmatrix} 1 & 0 & 0 \\ 7 & -5 & 10 \\ 1 & 0 & 2 \end{pmatrix}$ h_{11} is positive $\quad T = \begin{pmatrix} 1 & 0 & 0 \\ 0 & -1 & -2 \\ 0 & 0 & -1 \end{pmatrix}$
annihilate $h_{23} = 10$
$\gcd(-5, 10) = 5, (x, y) = (-1, 0)$

$H = \begin{pmatrix} 1 & 0 & 0 \\ 7 & 5 & 0 \\ 1 & 0 & -2 \end{pmatrix}$ h_{22} is positive $\quad T = \begin{pmatrix} 1 & 0 & 0 \\ -1 & 1 & 0 \\ 0 & 0 & 1 \end{pmatrix}$
reduce $h_{21} = 7$
$\lfloor 7/5 \rfloor = 1$

$H = \begin{pmatrix} 1 & 0 & 0 \\ 2 & 5 & 0 \\ 1 & 0 & -2 \end{pmatrix}$ make h_{33} positive $\quad T = \begin{pmatrix} 1 & 0 & 0 \\ 0 & 1 & 0 \\ 0 & 0 & -1 \end{pmatrix}$

$H = \begin{pmatrix} 1 & 0 & 0 \\ 2 & 5 & 0 \\ -1 & 0 & 2 \end{pmatrix}$ done

4.3 Linear System of Equations

A system of m linear equations in n unknowns

$$\begin{aligned} a_{11}x_1 + a_{12}x_2 + \cdots + a_{1n}x_n &= b_1 \\ a_{21}x_1 + a_{22}x_2 + \cdots + a_{2n}x_n &= b_2 \\ &\vdots \\ a_{m1}x_1 + a_{m2}x_2 + \cdots + a_{mn}x_n &= b_m \end{aligned}$$

4.3 ▪ Linear System of Equations

with unknowns $x_1, x_2, \ldots, x_n$ can be written in the matrix form

$$\mathbf{Ax} = \mathbf{b}$$

where $\mathbf{A}$ is called the coefficient matrix, and $\mathbf{b}$ is the right-hand side.

There is a solution if $\mathbf{b}$ is in *range* $\mathbf{A}$. If *rank*$(\mathbf{A}) \leq m$ then the system of equations always has a solution. Given one solution $\mathbf{x}'$ of the system, all other solutions can be found by adding vectors $\mathbf{y}$ in the null space of $\mathbf{A}$. The solution is unique only if *kernel* $\mathbf{A}$ is empty. When $\mathbf{A}$ is square and nonsingular, the system of linear equations can be solved algebraically by inverting the matrix $\mathbf{A}$ and solving for $\mathbf{x}$:

$$\mathbf{x} = \mathbf{A}^{-1}\mathbf{b}$$

Another method, called *variable elimination*, solves the linear system by eliminating one unknown at a time from the set of equations. One of the equations is rewritten to find one of the unknowns in terms of the others. This equality is substituted for that unknown in the other equations, eliminating that unknown from those equations. The remaining equations can be solved with one fewer unknown.

Example 4.9

Use variable elimination to solve the system of equations:

$$\begin{aligned} 1 \cdot x_1 + 2 \cdot x_2 + 3 \cdot x_3 &= 15 \\ 2 \cdot x_1 + 2 \cdot x_2 + 1 \cdot x_3 &= 29 \\ 0 \cdot x_1 + 8 \cdot x_2 + 1 \cdot x_3 &= 17 \end{aligned}$$

Solution

From the first equation we can determine that $x_1 = 15 - 2 \cdot x_2 - 3 \cdot x_3$ and substitute this into the second two equations to get:

$$\begin{aligned} 1 \cdot x_1 + 2 \cdot x_2 + 3 \cdot x_3 &= 15 \\ -4 \cdot x_2 - 8 \cdot x_3 &= -16 \\ 8 \cdot x_2 + 1 \cdot x_3 &= 14 \end{aligned}$$

We can simplify the second equation and determine that $x_2 = 4 - 2x_3$, then substitute this into the last equation to get:

$$\begin{aligned} 1 \cdot x_1 + 2 \cdot x_2 + 3 \cdot x_3 &= 15 \\ -1 \cdot x_2 - 2 \cdot x_3 &= -4 \\ -15 \cdot x_3 &= -15 \end{aligned}$$

This sequence of steps is the elimination phase; the substitution phase proceeds as follows. From the last equation we get $x_3 = 1$. The second equation reduces to $x_2 = 2$. Substituting these into the first equation gives us $x_1 = 8$.

We can also use matrix methods to solve the linear system, via Gaussian elimination. Given a matrix equation $\mathbf{Ax} = \mathbf{b}$, we want to find a suitable nonsingular matrix **M** to premultiply both the coefficient matrix **A** and the right-hand side **b** so that

$$\mathbf{Ax} = \mathbf{b} \Longrightarrow \mathbf{MAx} = \mathbf{Mb}$$

The goal is to find a matrix **M** that *annihilates* some of the nonzero elements of **A**. Eventually we want a sequence of matrices $\mathbf{M}_1, \mathbf{M}_2, \ldots, \mathbf{M}_k$ such that $\mathbf{M}_k \mathbf{M}_{k-1} \cdots \mathbf{M}_2 \mathbf{M}_1 \mathbf{A}$ is a triangular matrix (if **A** is square). One common method is to use *elementary lower triangular* matrices, which have ones on the diagonal, nonzeros below the diagonal in exactly one column, and zeros everywhere else. To annihilate the nonzeros below the diagonal of the kth column of some coefficient matrix **A** we use the following matrix, assuming $a_{kk} \neq 0$:

$$M = \begin{pmatrix} 1 & 0 & \cdots & 0 & 0 & 0 & \cdots & 0 \\ 0 & 1 & \cdots & 0 & 0 & 0 & \cdots & 0 \\ \vdots & \vdots & \ddots & \vdots & \vdots & \vdots & \ddots & \vdots \\ 0 & 0 & \cdots & 1 & 0 & 0 & \cdots & 0 \\ 0 & 0 & \cdots & 0 & 1 & 0 & \cdots & 0 \\ 0 & 0 & \cdots & 0 & -a_{k,k+1}/a_{kk} & 1 & \cdots & 0 \\ 0 & 0 & \cdots & 0 & -a_{k,k+2}/a_{kk} & 0 & \cdots & 0 \\ 0 & 0 & \cdots & 0 & -a_{k,k+3}/a_{kk} & 0 & \cdots & 0 \\ \vdots & \vdots & \ddots & \vdots & \vdots & \vdots & \ddots & \vdots \\ 0 & 0 & \cdots & 0 & -a_{kn}/a_{kk} & 0 & \cdots & 1 \end{pmatrix}$$

Algorithm GE in Figure 4.5 uses Gaussian elimination to reduce a matrix to upper trapezoidal form, which is returned in **U**; the transformed right-hand side is returned in **c**. Because of the way **U** and **c** are constructed, the solution to $\mathbf{Ux} = \mathbf{c}$ is the same as that to $\mathbf{Ax} = \mathbf{b}$.

```
        Algorithm GE:
(1)     procedure GE( A^{n×m}, b^m ) return ( U^{n×m}, c^m )
(2)     let U = A, c = b
(3)     for k = 1 to m do
(4)        /* annihilate elements below diagonal in column k */
(5)        for j = k + 1 to n do
(6)           α = -u_{jk}/u_{kk}
(7)           let U_{[j]} = U_{[j]} - αU_{[k]}
(8)           let c_j = c_j - αc_k
(9)        endfor
(10)    endfor
(11)    end GE
```

FIGURE 4.5 Algorithm to do Gaussian elimination on a matrix and right-hand side vector.

Example 4.10

Use Gaussian elimination to solve the same system of equations as in Example 4.9.

Solution

In matrix notation, the system of equations is:

$$\begin{pmatrix} 1 & 2 & 3 \\ 3 & 2 & 1 \\ 0 & 8 & 1 \end{pmatrix} \begin{pmatrix} x_1 \\ x_2 \\ x_3 \end{pmatrix} = \begin{pmatrix} 15 \\ 29 \\ 17 \end{pmatrix}$$

The first step is to annihilate the nonzeros below the diagonal in the first column; we use the elementary lower triangular matrix:

$$\begin{pmatrix} 1 & 0 & 0 \\ -3 & 1 & 0 \\ 0 & 0 & 1 \end{pmatrix}$$

This results in the system of equations:

$$\begin{pmatrix} 1 & 2 & 3 \\ 0 & -4 & -8 \\ 0 & 8 & 1 \end{pmatrix} \begin{pmatrix} x_1 \\ x_2 \\ x_3 \end{pmatrix} = \begin{pmatrix} 15 \\ -16 \\ 17 \end{pmatrix}$$

The second step annihilates the nonzeros below the diagonal of the second column, using the elementary lower triangular matrix:

$$\begin{pmatrix} 1 & 0 & 0 \\ 0 & 1 & 0 \\ 0 & 2 & 1 \end{pmatrix}$$

This modifies the system of equations to:

$$\begin{pmatrix} 1 & 2 & 3 \\ 0 & -4 & -8 \\ 0 & 0 & -15 \end{pmatrix} \begin{pmatrix} x_1 \\ x_2 \\ x_3 \end{pmatrix} = \begin{pmatrix} 15 \\ -16 \\ -15 \end{pmatrix}$$

We complete this problem in Example 4.11 by using back substitution to find the final solution.

Two potential problems can arise when using Gaussian elimination. One is that the element on the diagonal is used in the denominator for the elementary lower triangular matrices to annihilate entries in the current column. If that diagonal element is zero, this will not work. If we were eliminating variables, we would choose either to eliminate a different variable, or to use a different equation to eliminate this variable. In matrix notation, this corresponds either to interchanging columns (changing the order of the unknowns) to put a variable with a nonzero coefficient in this column, or to interchanging rows (changing the order of the equations) to put a different coefficient on the diagonal. If there is no nonzero element on or below the diagonal for this column, then this column is linearly dependent on the preceding columns; the unknown corresponding to this column can be eliminated from the system of equations and solved as a function of the earlier unknowns.

The other problem is that real arithmetic in computer systems usually is not exact. Computers use floating point approximations to real numbers, and computations can accumulate roundoff errors in the approximations. In certain circumstances, the roundoff errors can cause serious accuracy problems in a sequence of operations, such as Gaussian elimination. For that reason, a *pivot* step usually precedes each annihilation step, to find an appropriate element to place on the diagonal and preserve numerical accuracy.

If the matrix is square and full rank, the result of Gaussian elimination is an upper triangular matrix. In the modified set of equations, $\mathbf{U}\mathbf{x} = \mathbf{c}$, the last equation is particularly trivial: $u_{nn}x_n = c_n$. This can be solved as $x_n = c_n/u_{nn}$. The next to last equation is also simple: $u_{n,n-1}x_{n-1} + u_{nn}x_n = c_n$. Four of these values are now known, and we can compute $x_{n-1} = (c_n - u_{nn}x_n)/u_{n,n-1}$. This process can be repeated, and is called *back substitution*. Algorithm BackSubstitute, shown in Figure 4.6, gives the full details.

```
         Algorithm BackSubstitute:
(1)      procedure Back( U, c ) returns ( x )
(2)         for i = n downto 1 do
(3)            x_i = (c_i - Σ_{k=i+1}^{n} u_{ik}x_k)/u_{ii}
(4)         endfor
(5)      end Back
```

FIGURE 4.6 Back substitution algorithm for solving triangular system of equations.

Example 4.11

Use back substitution to complete Example 4.10.

Solution

Gaussian elimination left us with the matrix in the form:

$$\begin{pmatrix} 1 & 2 & 3 \\ 0 & -4 & -8 \\ 0 & 0 & -15 \end{pmatrix} \begin{pmatrix} x_1 \\ x_2 \\ x_3 \end{pmatrix} = \begin{pmatrix} 15 \\ -16 \\ -15 \end{pmatrix}$$

Back substitution computes the following values:

$$x_3 = -15/(-15) = 1$$
$$x_2 = (-16 - (-8)(1))/(-4) = 2$$
$$x_1 = (15 - 2(2) - 3(1))/1 = 8$$

When there are more equations than unknowns, or when there are linearly dependent rows in the matrix, there is may be no solution to the system of equations. The Gaussian elimination algorithm will find a linearly dependent row when the row is all zeros. If the corresponding right-hand side element is nonzero, that equation shows up as an inconsistency, meaning there is no solution to the system of equations.

When there are more unknowns than linearly independent equations, there is a subspace of solutions to the equations. For a solution $\mathbf{x}$ to $\mathbf{Ax} = \mathbf{b}$ and any vector $\mathbf{w} \in$ kernel $\mathbf{A}$, $\mathbf{x} + \mathbf{w}$ is also a solution to the equation. In such a case, we can find a single solution and describe the null space of the matrix to characterize all solutions.

Example 4.12

Characterize all solutions to the equation $\mathbf{Ax} = \mathbf{b}$, with the matrix and right-hand side given below:

$$\begin{pmatrix} 2 & 1 & 3 \\ 0 & 1 & 0 \\ 4 & 3 & 6 \end{pmatrix} \begin{pmatrix} x_1 \\ x_2 \\ x_3 \end{pmatrix} = \begin{pmatrix} 1 \\ 2 \\ 4 \end{pmatrix}$$

Solution

Apply Gaussian elimination to annihilate nonzeros below the diagonal in the first column to get:

$$\begin{pmatrix} 2 & 1 & 3 \\ 0 & 1 & 0 \\ 0 & 1 & 0 \end{pmatrix} \begin{pmatrix} x_1 \\ x_2 \\ x_3 \end{pmatrix} = \begin{pmatrix} 1 \\ 2 \\ 2 \end{pmatrix}$$

The second step eliminates nonzeros below the diagonal in the second columns, which gives:

$$\begin{pmatrix} 2 & 1 & 3 \\ 0 & 1 & 0 \\ 0 & 0 & 0 \end{pmatrix} \begin{pmatrix} x_1 \\ x_2 \\ x_3 \end{pmatrix} = \begin{pmatrix} 1 \\ 2 \\ 0 \end{pmatrix}$$

At this point we notice that the third row and its right-hand side are all zero, so we can ignore that equation. Since there are three unknowns and only two linearly independent equations, there will be an infinite number of solutions. Since the rank of the matrix is 2, we can set one of the unknowns arbitrarily; in this example, we choose to set $x_3 = 0$. The back substitution step will then compute $x_2 = 2$ and $x_1 = -1/2$.

To characterize all solutions, we can characterize the null space of the matrix. We do this by looking for solutions to the system of equations $\mathbf{Ax} = \mathbf{0}$. Using the upper triangular matrix from Gaussian elimination, we let the last $n - rank(\mathbf{A})$ unknowns be *independent variables*, and solve for the other variables in terms of the independent variables. In this problem, it means we solve for x_1 and x_2 in terms of x_3. A basis for the null space of $\mathbf{A}$ is computed as:

$$\begin{pmatrix} -3/2 \\ 0 \\ 1 \end{pmatrix}$$

4.4 System of Integer Equations

Many of the problems we will address can be formulated as a system of linear equations, but the coefficients, right-hand sides, and solutions are restricted to being integers. The methods used to solve real linear systems cannot always be used to solve integer systems; for instance, Gaussian elimination uses division, and the result of dividing two integers is not always an integer. In general, the existence of a real solution to a system of equations does not imply that there is an integer solution to the system.

4.4.1 Single Equation

We start with the simple case of a single equation with two unknowns x_1 and x_2, such as

$$a_1 x_1 + a_2 x_2 = b$$

where the coefficients a_1, a_2 and the right-hand side b are known integers, and a_1 and a_2 are not both zero. Suppose one of the coefficients—say, a_1—is equal to one. Then the equation simplifies to:

$$x_1 = b - a_2 x_2$$

For any integer value of x_2, we can compute an integer value of x_1 that solves the equation. We call x_2 the *independent variable*, and x_1 the *dependent variable*.

Example 4.13

Find all solutions to the integer equation $3x_1 - x_2 = -4$.

4.4 • System of Integer Equations

Solution

Since the magnitude of the coefficient for x_2 is one, we let x_2 be the dependent variable and x_1 be the independent variable. We rewrite the equation to find x_2 in terms of x_1:

$$x_2 = 3x_1 + 4$$

For any integer value of x_1, we can find an integer value of x_2 that solves the equation, as shown in the table below:

x_1	...	-2	-1	0	1	2	...
x_2	...	-2	1	4	7	10	...

Suppose neither coefficient has magnitude one. Then there is an integer solution iff $\gcd(a_1, a_2)$ divides b exactly. If the gcd does not divide the right-hand side, there are no integer solutions; if it does, we can divide all the coefficients and the right-hand side by the gcd to get an equivalent integer equation, but with smaller coefficients. If this division reduces one of the coefficients to ± 1, then we are in the same situation as before, and can solve for one variable in terms of the other. If neither coefficient has magnitude one, then given any one integer solution (x'_1, x'_2), all integer solutions (x_1, x_2) can be found by enumerating

$$x_1 = x'_1 - (a_2/g)t$$
$$x_2 = x'_2 + (a_1/g)t$$

where $g = \gcd(a_1, a_2)$ and t can take on any integer value. Here t is the independent variable, and x_1 and x_2 are both dependent variables.

Example 4.14

Find all integer solutions to $18x_1 + 24x_2 = 32$.

Solution

First we find $\gcd(18, 24) = 6$. Since 6 does not divide 32, there are no integer solutions to this equation.

We can use algorithm GCD to find the $g = \gcd(a_1, a_2)$ and a solution (x_1, x_2) to the equation $a_1 x_1 + a_2 x_2 = g$. If g does not divide b in the original equation, there are no integer solutions, as mentioned earlier. If g does divide b, then $(x_1 \cdot b/g, x_2 \cdot b/g)$ gives a sample solution to the original equation.

Example 4.15

Find all integer solutions to $18x_1 + 24x_2 = 30$.

Solution

Again we find $\gcd(18, 24) = 6$. Since 6 does divide 30, we can reduce the integer equation to $3x_1 + 4x_2 = 5$. Neither coefficient has magnitude one, so we look for a single solution to the equation. One solution can be found at $(x_1' = 3, x_2' = -1)$. Thus, all integer solutions to this equation are found when

$$x_1 = 3 - 4t$$
$$x_2 = -1 + 3t$$

Example solutions are given in the following table:

t	-2	-1	0	1	2	3
(x_1, x_2)	$(11, -7)$	$(7, -4)$	$(3, -1)$	$(-1, 2)$	$(-5, 5)$	$(-9, 8)$

4.4.2 Many Unknowns

Given a single equation with many unknowns, such as

$$a_1 x_1 + a_2 x_2 + a_3 x_3 + \cdots + a_n x_n = b \qquad (4.1)$$

there is an integer solution only when the gcd of the coefficients divides the right-hand side:

$$\gcd(a_1, a_2, a_3, \ldots, a_n) | b$$

the gcd of the coefficients divides the right-hand side. Since $\gcd(a_1, a_2, a_3, \ldots, a_n) = \gcd(a_1, \gcd(a_2, \gcd(a_3, \ldots)))$, we can use the two-variable algorithm to find the gcd of the whole vector.

Again, if one of the coefficients has magnitude one, we can rewrite the equation with one dependent and $n - 1$ independent variables. If $a_1 = 1$, we get

$$x_1 = b - a_2 x_2 - a_3 x_3 - \cdots - a_n x_n$$

where x_1 is the dependent variable. For any integer values of the independent variables, we can find a value for the dependent variable that solves the equation. If none of the coefficients has magnitude one, we can divide all the coefficients by the gcd to get a reduced equation, perhaps with a unit coefficient.

In the general case, none of the coefficients is ± 1. We will show two approaches to the problem of finding all solutions to the equation; the first uses variable substitution and the second uses algebraic methods.

Given the integer equation above, let a_k be the coefficient with smallest magnitude. Define a new variable y_k as

$$y_k = \sum_{i=1}^{n} (a_i \text{ div } a_k) x_i \qquad (4.2)$$

4.4 ▪ System of Integer Equations

(where, again, div is integer division). Since $a_k \text{ div } a_k = 1$, we can solve this equation for x_k:

$$x_k = -\sum_{i=1}^{k-1}(a_i \text{ div } a_k)x_i + y_k - \sum_{i=k+1}^{n}(a_i \text{ div } a_k)x_i \qquad (4.3)$$

Substituting this into the original integer equation gives:

$$\sum_{i \neq k}(a_i - a_k(a_i \text{ div } a_k))x_i + a_k y_k = b$$

The magnitude of all the coefficients (except for y_k) after the substitution will be smaller than a_k. In fact, the new coefficients are $a'_i = \text{sign}(a_i) \cdot (|a_i| \mod |a_k|)$. After the substitution, we can divide by the gcd of the coefficients. One of the coefficients may be reduced to ± 1; in that case we can solve for the corresponding variable in terms of the others. Note that this solves for y_k and all the x_i except x_k; we can then use equation 4.3 to get a solution for x_k.

Example 4.16

Find all integer solutions to the equation $6x_1 - 4x_2 + 14x_3 = 98$.

Solution

First, divide all coefficients (and the right-hand side) by their gcd, which in this case is two, to get:

$$3x_1 - 2x_2 + 7x_3 = 49 \qquad (4.4)$$

None of the coefficients has magnitude one, so we find the smallest coefficient ($a_2 = -2$), and define y_2 as:

$$y_2 = -x_1 + x_2 - 3x_3$$

Solving for x_2 gives:

$$x_2 = x_1 + y_2 + 3x_3 \qquad (4.5)$$

Substituting this into equation 4.4 gives:

$$x_1 - 2y_2 + x_3 = 49$$

Now we can choose either x_1 or x_3 as the dependent variable, since both have unit coefficient. Choosing x_1, we get:

$$x_1 = 2y_2 - x_3 + 49$$

Substituting this into equation 4.5, we get:

$$x_2 = 3y_2 + 2x_3 + 49$$

Thus, for any integer values of the independent variables y_2 and x_3, we can find values of the dependent variables x_1 and x_2 to solve the equation.

The variable substitution method is simple to explain and understand. It is also clear that any integer solution to the equation after substitution will generate an integer solution to the original equation. What we need to prove is that every integer solution to the original equation is characterized by an integer solution to the equation after variable substitution. We do this by finding the same solution via algebraic means.

In matrix form, equation 4.1 can be written $\mathbf{A}\mathbf{x} = b$. Suppose we know that there is an integer solution to this equation—we know $g = \gcd(a_1, a_2, \ldots, a_n) \neq 0$—and we show below how to find a unimodular matrix $\mathbf{U}$ such that

$$\mathbf{A}\mathbf{U} = (g, 0, 0, \ldots, 0) \tag{4.6}$$

We will show that we can find all integer solutions to the equation by enumerating $\mathbf{x} = \mathbf{U}\mathbf{t}$, where $\mathbf{t} = (b/g, t_2, t_3, \ldots, t_n)^T$.

1. It is easy to show that any such $\mathbf{x}$ solves the equation. We have

   $$\begin{aligned}\mathbf{A}\mathbf{x} &= \mathbf{A}\mathbf{U}\mathbf{t} \\ &= (g, 0, 0, \ldots, 0)(b/g, t_2, t_3, \ldots, t_n)^T \\ &= b\end{aligned}$$

   where g divides b exactly (or there would be no solution).

2. Now we need to show that all integer solutions to the equation are found by $\mathbf{x} = \mathbf{U}\mathbf{t}$ for integer values of $\mathbf{t}$. We first show that this equation characterizes all real solutions of $\mathbf{x}$, then that all integer solutions of $\mathbf{x}$ require integer values of $\mathbf{t}$.

   - We can certainly find one solution $\hat{\mathbf{x}}$ by setting $t_2, t_3, \ldots, t_n$ all to zero. This will be an integer solution, since the product of the two integer matrices $\mathbf{U}\mathbf{t}$ will be integer. All other real solutions can be found by adding vectors $\mathbf{y}$ in the null space of $\mathbf{A}$. Since $g = \gcd(a_1, a_2, \ldots, a_n)$ and $g \neq 0$, there must be at least one nonzero element of $\mathbf{A}$; therefore $rank(\mathbf{A}) = 1$. This means that $nullity(\mathbf{A}) = n - 1$. Since $\mathbf{U}$ is unimodular, the second through nth columns of $\mathbf{U}$ are linearly independent, and (by equation 4.6) $\mathbf{A}\mathbf{u}_{[i]} = 0$ for $2 \leq i \leq n$. Thus, $\mathbf{u}_{[2]}, \mathbf{u}_{[3]}, \ldots, \mathbf{u}_{[n]}$ form a basis for $kernel\ \mathbf{A}$. Letting $\mathbf{y} = t_2\mathbf{u}_{[2]} + t_3\mathbf{u}_{[3]} + \cdots + t_n\mathbf{u}_{[n]}$, $\mathbf{x} = \hat{\mathbf{x}} + \mathbf{y}$ is a solution to the equation, for any real values of t_i, $2 \leq i \leq n$. This can be rewritten as:

     $$\mathbf{x} = \mathbf{U}\begin{pmatrix} b/g \\ 0 \\ 0 \\ \vdots \\ 0 \end{pmatrix} + \mathbf{U}\begin{pmatrix} 0 \\ t_2 \\ t_3 \\ \vdots \\ t_n \end{pmatrix} = \mathbf{U}\begin{pmatrix} b/g \\ t_2 \\ t_3 \\ \vdots \\ t_n \end{pmatrix} = \mathbf{U}\mathbf{t}$$

- Since **U** is integer and unimodular, its inverse exists and is integer and unimodular. Therefore, for any integer solution **x** we can compute $U^{-1}x = t$. The product of the two integer matrices on the left will give an integer result for **t**. Therefore, all integer solutions to the original equation $Ax = b$ are given by $x = Ut$.

Example 4.17

Find all integer solutions to the equation $6x_1 - 4x_2 + 14x_3 = 98$ (the same as in Example 4.16).

Solution

The matrix form is $(6, -4, 14)x = 98$. We find $\gcd(6, -4, 14) = 2$, which indeed divides 98 exactly. So we find a unimodular matrix **U** that satisfies $(6, -4, 14)U = (2, 0, 0)$. One such solution is:

$$\begin{pmatrix} 1 & 2 & -1 \\ 1 & 3 & 2 \\ 0 & 0 & 1 \end{pmatrix}$$

One solution to the original equation is given by $\hat{x} = U(49, 0, 0)^T$, which is $(49, 49, 0)^T$. All solutions are given by $x = U(49, t_2, t_3)^T$, which gives

$$x_1 = 49 + 2t_2 - t_3$$
$$x_2 = 49 + 3t_2 + 2t_3$$
$$x_3 = t_3$$

where t_2 and t_3 are the independent variables.

It is easy to see that this solution corresponds exactly to the solution shown in Example 4.16, where t_2 is y_2 and t_3 is x_3. In fact, substituting variables corresponds to constructing the unimodular matrix.

Here we show a way to find an appropriate unimodular matrix **U**, corresponding to the way we compute variable substitutions. We start by initializing a $1 \times n$ matrix D_0 to the coefficient matrix **A**, and an $n \times n$ square matrix U_0 to the identity matrix. Note that U_0 is unimodular, and $AU_0 = D_0$. The algorithm proceeds by applying the same unimodular column operations to D_i and U_i. This is effectively the same as postmultiplying both matrices by a unimodular transformation matrix T_i, thus preserving

$$AU_i = D_i$$
$$AU_iT_i = D_iT_i$$
$$AU_{i+1} = D_{i+1}$$

The unimodular column operations are chosen to annihilate or reduce as many nonzero elements in the first (and only) row of $\mathbf{D}_i$. One method to do this is algorithm ReduceRow, shown in Figure 4.7. Each time around the loop at line 6 the algorithm computes $\mathbf{D}_{i+1}$ and $\mathbf{U}_{i+1}$ from $\mathbf{D}_i$ and $\mathbf{U}_i$. Each iteration of the loop corresponds exactly to replacing x_k by $y_k - \sum_{j \neq k}(a_j \operatorname{div} a_k)x_j$ in the equation, where k is chosen to get the smallest nonzero coefficient. Lines 13-14 subtract a multiple of row k from row j (in both $\mathbf{D}$ and $\mathbf{U}$), for all rows with nonzero entries d_{1j}. This continues until the entire $\mathbf{D}$ matrix is annihilated except for one entry. Finally, lines 20-21 swap two columns, moving that nonzero to the first column. As a footnote, the procedure Reduce from algorithm Hermite could also have been used here.

```
        Algorithm ReduceRow:
(1)     procedure Reducerow( A ) return ( D, U )
(2)     U = I
(3)     D = A
(4)     Reduce( 1, 1:n, D, U )

(5)     procedure Reduce( row i, columns j:n, D, U )
                /* reduce row i, columns j:n to a single nonzero */
(6)     repeat
(7)         if D[i,j:n] = 0 then return
(8)         find k ∈ [j:n] such that d_ik has minimum nonzero magnitude
(9)         f = True
(10)        for m = j, j+1, ..., n, m ≠ k do
(11)            q = d_im div d_ik
(12)            if q ≠ 0 then
(13)                d[m] = d[m] − qd[k]
(14)                u[m] = u[m] − qu[k]
(15)                if d_im > 0 then f = False endif
(16)            endif
(17)        endfor
(18)    until f
(19)    if k ≠ 1 then
(20)        d[j] ⇔ d[k]
(21)        u[j] ⇔ u[k]
(22)    endif
(23)    end Reduce
(24)    end Reducerow
```

FIGURE 4.7 Algorithm to reduce coefficient matrix to $\mathbf{D} = (d, 0, 0, \ldots, 0)$, and to find appropriate unimodular matrix $\mathbf{U}$ so that $\mathbf{AU} = \mathbf{D}$.

4.4 • System of Integer Equations

The sequence of steps taken by this algorithm is similar to those to compute the greatest common divisor. The remaining nonzero will be $\gcd(a_1, a_2, \ldots, a_n)$. We showed that the equation $\mathbf{Ax} = b$ can be preconditioned by dividing all coefficients and the right-hand side by $\gcd(a_1, a_2, \ldots, a_n)$. This is not necessary, however, since the reduction algorithm finds the GCD itself. The step to find the minimum magnitude element is not strictly necessary; any nonzero d_{1k} will do. However, since we are trying to annihilate elements, reducing them as fast as possible motivates us to use the smallest element for the modulo operation.

Example 4.18

The integer equation $6x_1 - 4x_2 + 14x_3 = 98$ can be written $\mathbf{Ax} = 98$, where the coefficient matrix is $\mathbf{A} = (6, -4, 14)$. Find a unimodular matrix $\mathbf{U}$ that satisfies $\mathbf{AU} = \mathbf{D}$, $\mathbf{D} = (\gcd(\mathbf{a}), 0, 0)$.

Solution

We initialize the $\mathbf{D}$ matrix to $\mathbf{A}$, and the $\mathbf{U}$ matrix to identity, to get:

$$D_0 = \begin{pmatrix} 6 & -4 & 14 \end{pmatrix}, \quad U_0 = \begin{pmatrix} 1 & 0 & 0 \\ 0 & 1 & 0 \\ 0 & 0 & 1 \end{pmatrix}$$

The element of $\mathbf{D}$ with minimum magnitude is $d_{12} = -4$. We then add one times the second column to the first, and three times the second column to the last, giving:

$$D_1 = \begin{pmatrix} 2 & -4 & 2 \end{pmatrix}, \quad U_1 = \begin{pmatrix} 1 & 0 & 0 \\ 1 & 1 & 3 \\ 0 & 0 & 1 \end{pmatrix}$$

This is equivalent to the step we used in Example 4.16 to define $x_2 = x_1 + y_2 + 3x_3$. Now either the first or last element of $\mathbf{D}$ will suffice; we choose the first. We annihilate d_{12} by adding twice the first column to the second, and annihilate d_{13} by subtracting the first column from the last, giving:

$$D_2 = \begin{pmatrix} 2 & 0 & 0 \end{pmatrix}, \quad U_2 = \begin{pmatrix} 1 & 2 & -1 \\ 1 & 3 & 2 \\ 0 & 0 & 1 \end{pmatrix}$$

This corresponds to defining $x_1 = y_1 + 2y_2 - x_3$, essentially the same as in Example 4.16. The remaining equation $D_2(y_1, y_2, x_3)^T = 98$ is solved when $y_1 = 49$, giving us the same solution as before.

In the last step, we could have chosen to use the last column to annihilate the other two, giving:

$$D_2 = \begin{pmatrix} 0 & 0 & 2 \end{pmatrix}, \quad U_2 = \begin{pmatrix} 1 & 0 & 0 \\ -2 & 7 & 3 \\ -1 & 2 & 1 \end{pmatrix}$$

Interchanging the first and last columns gives the desired result:

$$D_3 = \begin{pmatrix} 2 & 0 & 0 \end{pmatrix}, \quad U_3 = \begin{pmatrix} 0 & 0 & 1 \\ 3 & 7 & -2 \\ 1 & 2 & -1 \end{pmatrix}$$

Note that the resulting unimodular matrix is different, but it serves just as well.

4.4.3 Many Equations

When solving a system of integer equations, we again use a variable substitution method. Simply stated, we can choose one of the equalities from the system, and rewrite it to solve for any variable that has a coefficient of ± 1—say, x_k. If none of the coefficients has unit magnitude, find the x_k with the smallest coefficient, and introduce a new variable y_k such that we can solve for x_k in terms of y_k and the other variables, and such that substituting for x_k will reduce the other coefficients as much as possible. As before, this substitution will make x_k a dependent variable. If after the substitution, the gcd of the coefficients of any equation does not divide the right-hand side, there must be no integer solution to the original equation.

Example 4.19

Find all integer solutions to the system of equations:

$$3x_1 + 2x_2 - x_3 = 9$$
$$2x_1 - 2x_2 + 5x_3 = 7$$

Solution

We can solve the first equation for $x_3 = 3x_1 + 2x_2 - 9$, and substitute this into the second equation to get

$$17x_1 + 8x_2 = 52$$

Since neither coefficient is ± 1, we introduce a new variable $y_2 = 2x_1 + x_2$, solving for $x_2 = y_2 - 2x_1$. Substituting this into the remaining equation, we have

$$x_1 + 8y_2 = 52$$

which lets us solve for $x_1 = 52 - 8y_2$. Substituting into the other equations, we get all three dependent variables in terms of the independent variable y_2:

$$x_1 = -8y_2 + 52$$
$$x_2 = 17y_2 - 104$$
$$x_3 = 10y_2 - 61$$

4.4 ▪ System of Integer Equations

Algebraically, this variable substitution is again equivalent to unimodular column operations on the coefficient matrix. When we had only a single equation, we found a unimodular matrix **U** and a matrix $\mathbf{D} = (g, 0, 0, \ldots, 0)^T$ such that $\mathbf{AU} = \mathbf{D}$. The two matrices were found via unimodular column operations on the coefficient matrix and the identity matrix. Here we will use a similar technique, initializing $\mathbf{U}_0 = \mathbf{I}$ and $\mathbf{D}_0 = \mathbf{A}$, and applying unimodular column operations to reduce $\mathbf{D}_i$ to a special form, called the *column echelon* form. Let r_j be the row containing the first nonzero in column j, where $r_j = \infty$ if the column is entirely zero. A matrix is in column echelon form if

- $r_{j+1} > r_j$ if column j is not entirely zero, and
- column $j+1$ is entirely zero if column j is.

Algorithm ReduceMatrix reduces the coefficient matrix to column echelon form, as shown in Figure 4.8; it uses the same procedure Reduce as shown in Figure 4.7. It is very similar to algorithm Hermite, except the HNF assumes that the matrix has full row rank. Algorithm ReduceMatrix assumes the coefficient matrix has no zero rows.

```
         Algorithm ReduceMatrix:
(1)      procedure Reducemat( A ) return ( D, U )
(2)          U = I
(3)          D = A
(4)          c = 1
(5)          for i = 1 to m do
(6)              Reduce( i, c : n, D, U )
(7)              if d_ic ≠ 0 then c = c + 1 endif
(8)          endfor
(9)      end Reducemat
```

FIGURE 4.8   Algorithm to reduce coefficient matrix to column echelon form.

After reducing **D** to column echelon form, we can easily solve $\mathbf{Dt} = \mathbf{b}$ for integer values of **t**. If there are no integer solutions to this equation, then there are no integer solutions to the original equation $\mathbf{Ax} = \mathbf{b}$. If there is an integer solution, then the sequence:

$$\mathbf{Dt} = \mathbf{b}$$

$$(\mathbf{AU})\mathbf{t} = \mathbf{b}$$

$$\mathbf{A}(\mathbf{Ut}) = \mathbf{b}$$

$$\mathbf{Ax} = \mathbf{b}$$

lets us compute solutions **x** to the original equation. Moreover, because $d_{11} = \gcd(a_{11}, a_{12}, \ldots, a_{1n})$, a proof similar to the one for a single equation shows that all integer solutions **x** to the first equation correspond to integer values of **t**. Thus, all integer solutions to the system of equations are found by $\mathbf{x} = \mathbf{Ut}$. Note that because of the column echelon form of **D**, the solution $\mathbf{Dt} = \mathbf{b}$ will often have zero coefficients for some of the t_i; these will become the independent variables. If we are careful in how we choose to reduce **D** to column echelon form, some of these t_i will correspond exactly to some x_j.

Example 4.20

Find all integer solutions to the system of equations:

$$3x_1 + 2x_2 - x_3 = 9$$
$$2x_1 - 2x_2 + 5x_3 = 7$$

Solution

In matrix form, this system of equations is $\mathbf{Ax} = \mathbf{b}$, or

$$\begin{pmatrix} 3 & 2 & -1 \\ 2 & -2 & 5 \end{pmatrix} \begin{pmatrix} x_1 \\ x_2 \\ x_3 \end{pmatrix} = \begin{pmatrix} 9 \\ 7 \end{pmatrix}$$

We initialize $\mathbf{D} = \mathbf{A}$ and $\mathbf{U} = \mathbf{I}^{3 \times 3}$. The first row is reduced by adding multiples of the third column to the others:

$$\mathbf{D} = \begin{pmatrix} 0 & 0 & -1 \\ 17 & 8 & 5 \end{pmatrix} \quad \mathbf{U} = \begin{pmatrix} 1 & 0 & 0 \\ 0 & 1 & 0 \\ 3 & 2 & 1 \end{pmatrix}$$

Since all but one element in the first row have been reduced to zero, we exchange the third column for the first:

$$\mathbf{D} = \begin{pmatrix} -1 & 0 & 0 \\ 5 & 8 & 17 \end{pmatrix} \quad \mathbf{U} = \begin{pmatrix} 0 & 0 & 1 \\ 0 & 1 & 0 \\ 1 & 2 & 3 \end{pmatrix}$$

The second row of **D** is reduced to eliminate all nonzeros beyond the second column; we start by subtracting twice the second column from the third:

$$\mathbf{D} = \begin{pmatrix} -1 & 0 & 0 \\ 5 & 8 & 1 \end{pmatrix} \quad \mathbf{U} = \begin{pmatrix} 0 & 0 & 1 \\ 0 & 1 & -2 \\ 1 & 2 & -1 \end{pmatrix}$$

Finally we subtract eight times the third column from the second:

$$\mathbf{D} = \begin{pmatrix} -1 & 0 & 0 \\ 5 & 0 & 1 \end{pmatrix} \quad \mathbf{U} = \begin{pmatrix} 0 & -8 & 1 \\ 0 & 17 & -2 \\ 1 & 10 & -1 \end{pmatrix}$$

and interchange the second and third columns to get the final result:

$$\mathbf{D} = \begin{pmatrix} -1 & 0 & 0 \\ 5 & 1 & 0 \end{pmatrix} \quad \mathbf{U} = \begin{pmatrix} 0 & 1 & -8 \\ 0 & -2 & 17 \\ 1 & -1 & 10 \end{pmatrix}$$

We check if there are any integer solutions to $\mathbf{Dt} = \mathbf{b}$:

$$\begin{pmatrix} -1 & 0 & 0 \\ 5 & 1 & 0 \end{pmatrix} \begin{pmatrix} t_1 \\ t_2 \\ t_3 \end{pmatrix} = \begin{pmatrix} 9 \\ 7 \end{pmatrix}$$

Because of the special form of $\mathbf{D}$, this is easy to solve via forward substitution, the obvious analog of back substitution. From the first equation, we find $t_1 = -9$; from the second equation, we have $t_2 = 7 - 5t_1 = 52$. Since t_3 is not bound to any value, it will be an independent variable. All solutions to the equation are given by $\mathbf{x} = \mathbf{Ut}$, or

$$x_1 = -8t_3 + 52$$
$$x_2 = 17t_3 - 104$$
$$x_3 = 10t_3 - 61$$

This is exactly the solution found by direct variable substitution in Example 4.19.

4.5 Systems of Linear Inequalities

Another problem is to determine whether there are any points that satisfy a system of linear inequalities. A linear inequality with n unknowns can be written

$$a_1 x_1 + a_2 x_2 + \cdots + a_n x_n \leq c$$

We choose to write the inequality in this canonical form, so that a system of inequalities can be written in matrix form as $\mathbf{Ax} \leq \mathbf{c}$. In general, some of the inequalities may be $<$ while others may be $\leq$; we restrict our attention to $\leq$ inequalities. A system of linear inequalities describes a polyhedron.

Example 4.21

Determine whether there are any solutions to this system of linear inequalities:

$$x_1 \leq 20$$
$$-x_1 \leq 10$$
$$x_2 \leq 5$$
$$-x_2 \leq 0$$
$$x_1 - x_2 \leq 4$$

Solution

The first two inequalities give x_1 a range between 10 and 20, while the next two give x_2 a range between 0 and 5. The last inequality says that there can be a solution only when $x_1 \leq x_2 + 4$; the largest value that x_2 can take is 5, so the largest value that $x_2 + 4$ can take is 9; since the smallest value that x_1 can have is 10, there is no solution to this system of linear inequalities.

An inequality where x_i appears with a positive coefficient is an *upper bound* for x_i. In the example above, x_1 has two upper bounds, the first and last inequalities. Likewise, an inequality where x_i appears with a negative coefficient is a *lower bound* for x_i. Note that the last inequality in the example is both an upper bound for x_1 and a lower bound for x_2.

Some inequalities have only a single nonzero coefficient; this is the case with the first four inequalities in our example. We call these *simple bounds*. Each gives a constant lower or upper bound for the corresponding variable.

There may also be redundant inequalities. An inequality is redundant if removing the inequality does not change the solution. For instance, if we have $x_1 \leq 10$, then $x_1 \leq 11$ is a redundant bound, since we already have a tighter upper bound for x_1. It is particularly easy to check for redundant simple bounds. If two inequalities have the same coefficients, the one with the larger right-hand side value is redundant (in our standard form).

A variable that has no upper bound or no lower bound is an *unconstrained variable*. When looking for solutions to a system of linear inequalities, any inequality involving an unconstrained variable can be removed. For example, let C be the original system of linear inequalities, and C' by the system after removing any inequalities involving unconstrained variables. If there is a solution to C', then a value for the unconstrained variable can always be found to solve C. Essentially, if some variable x_i is unconstrained, it can always be made small enough (or large enough) to solve any inequalities in which it appears.

Example 4.22

Discover whether there are any solutions to the system of linear inequalities:

$$x_1 \leq 10$$
$$-x_1 \leq 0$$
$$x_1 - x_2 \leq 25$$
$$x_2 + x_3 \leq 15$$

Solution

Since x_3 has no lower bound, the last inequality can be removed. After removing this, x_2 has no upper bound, so the third inequality can also be removed. The remaining inequalities are only simple inequalities involving x_1, for which there is certainly a solution. We can take any value for x_1 in the range from 0 to 10; say, $x_1 = 8$. We can now find a value for x_2 that satisfies the third inequality, any value $x_2 \geq -17$; say $x_2, = 0$. Finally, we can find a value for x_3 that satisfies the last inequality. Thus, there are solutions to this system of inequalities.

4.5.1 Fourier-Motzkin Projection

An algorithmic approach to determining solutions to systems of linear inequalities is Fourier-Motzkin projection (or elimination). In this scheme, the system of inequalities is solved by projecting it onto a reduced number of unknowns, eliminating one unknown. The projection is done by rewriting each lower or upper bound for some unknown x. Then, each lower bound for x is compared to each upper bound to derive a new inequality that does not involve x. All the inequalities involving x are deleted, and the remaining inequalities are in terms of one fewer unknown. This process is continued until a contradiction is reached, or until all the unknowns have been eliminated. If all the unknowns are eliminated without any contradiction, the system of inequalities must have a real solution.

Effectively, Fourier-Motzkin projection finds the shadow, or projection, of an n-dimensional polyhedron along the x_i axis. Figure 4.9 shows graphically the following system of linear inequalities:

$$\begin{pmatrix} 0 & 1 \\ 1 & 1 \\ 1 & -1 \\ -2 & -1 \end{pmatrix} \begin{pmatrix} x_1 \\ x_2 \end{pmatrix} \leq \begin{pmatrix} 6 \\ 9 \\ 5 \\ -7 \end{pmatrix}$$

Projecting along the x_1 direction proceeds by rewriting the inequalities as follows:

$$x_1 \leq 9 - x_2$$
$$x_1 \leq 5 + x_2$$
$$x_1 \geq 7/2 - x_2/2$$

The first inequality is a simple inequality involving only x_2, and so is not considered at this time. Comparing the two upper bounds to the one lower bound gives the bounds on x_2 as:

$$x_2 \leq 11$$
$$x_2 \geq -1$$

Thus, the "shadow" of this region on the x_2 line is $[-1 : 6]$. On the other hand, projecting along the x_2 direction would proceed by rewriting the inequalities as:

$$x_2 \leq 6$$
$$x_2 \leq 9 - x_1$$

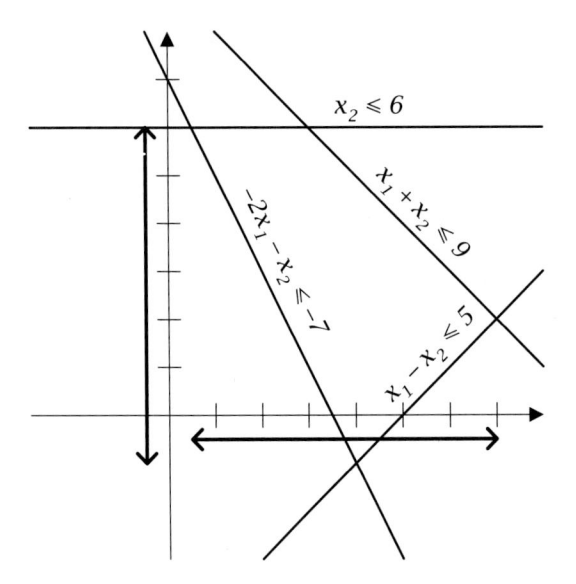

FIGURE 4.9 Example of Fourier-Motzkin projection.

$$x_2 \geq -5 + x_1$$
$$x_2 \geq 7 - 2x_1$$

Comparing the two upper bounds to the two lower bounds gives bounds on x_1 as:

$$x_1 \leq 11$$
$$x_1 \leq 7$$
$$x_1 \geq -2$$
$$x_1 \geq 1/2$$

Thus the "shadow" of this region on the x_1 line is $[1/2 : 7]$.

Figure 4.10 shows the Fourier-Motzkin projection algorithm. Engineering this algorithm to work fast will be important. The work is in adding a new inequality, checking whether it is a simple bound, redundant or inconsistent with the current set of inequalities.

Projection along an unknown does not necessarily reduce the number of inequalities in the system. In the worst case, the number of inequalities may grow exponentially. If there were eight lower bounds and eight upper bounds for some variable, comparing all lower bounds to all upper bounds may give rise to 64 new inequalities. If 32 of these were lower bounds for x_2 and 32 were upper bounds, comparing all of them would result in 1,024 inequalities. In the situations for which we will apply Fourier-Motzkin projection, we usually do not see such growth.

4.5 ▪ Systems of Linear Inequalities

```
        Algorithm FM:
 (1)    procedure Project( A, b )
 (2)    repeat
 (3)        choose an unknown x_j along which to project
 (4)        let L be the set of row indices {i|a_ij < 0}
 (5)        let U be the set of row indices {i|a_ij > 0}
 (6)        if L or U is empty, this is an unconstrained variable
 (7)        for i ∈ L ∪ U do
 (8)            divide row A_[i] and b_i by |a_ij|
 (9)        endfor
(10)        for i ∈ L do
(11)            for k ∈ U do
(12)                add a new inequality A_[i] + A_[k] ≤ b_i + b_k
(13)            endfor
(14)        endfor
(15)        ignore all rows in L and U from further consideration
(16)    until done
(17)    end Project
```

FIGURE 4.10 Algorithm to determine whether there is a solution to a system of linear inequalities $Ax \leq b$.

Example 4.23

Find a solution for the system of inequalities below using Fourier-Motzkin projection:

$$x_1 + x_2 + x_3 \leq 10$$
$$x_1 - x_2 + 2x_3 \leq 20$$
$$2x_1 - x_2 - x_3 \leq -1$$
$$-x_1 + x_2 - x_3 \leq 5$$

Solution
We write this in matrix form as:

$$\begin{pmatrix} 1 & 1 & 1 \\ 1 & -1 & 2 \\ 2 & -1 & -1 \\ -1 & 1 & -1 \end{pmatrix} \begin{pmatrix} x_1 \\ x_2 \\ x_3 \end{pmatrix} \leq \begin{pmatrix} 10 \\ 20 \\ -1 \\ 5 \end{pmatrix}$$

Suppose we choose to eliminate x_3 first. We divide each row by the absolute value of the coefficient for x_3, which changes only the second row:

$$\begin{pmatrix} 1 & 1 & 1 \\ 1/2 & -1/2 & 1 \\ 2 & -1 & -1 \\ -1 & 1 & -1 \end{pmatrix} \begin{pmatrix} x_1 \\ x_2 \\ x_3 \end{pmatrix} \leq \begin{pmatrix} 10 \\ 10 \\ -1 \\ 5 \end{pmatrix}$$

The row index sets are $L = \{3,4\}$ and $U = \{1,2\}$. The new matrix rows are shown below, and all the old rows are deleted:

$$\begin{pmatrix} 3 & 0 & 0 \\ 0 & 2 & 0 \\ 5/2 & -3/2 & 0 \\ 1/2 & 1/2 & 0 \end{pmatrix} \begin{pmatrix} x_1 \\ x_2 \\ x_3 \end{pmatrix} \leq \begin{pmatrix} 9 \\ 15 \\ 9 \\ 15 \end{pmatrix}$$

Now suppose we choose to eliminate x_2; dividing each row by the x_2 coefficient gives us the following:

$$\begin{pmatrix} 3 & 0 & 0 \\ 0 & 1 & 0 \\ 5/3 & -1 & 0 \\ 1 & 1 & 0 \end{pmatrix} \begin{pmatrix} x_1 \\ x_2 \\ x_3 \end{pmatrix} \leq \begin{pmatrix} 9 \\ 15/2 \\ 6 \\ 30 \end{pmatrix}$$

The row index sets are $L = \{3\}$ and $U = \{2,4\}$. The new matrix rows are shown below, with the old first row:

$$\begin{pmatrix} 3 & 0 & 0 \\ 5/3 & 0 & 0 \\ 8/3 & 0 & 0 \end{pmatrix} \begin{pmatrix} x_1 \\ x_2 \\ x_3 \end{pmatrix} \leq \begin{pmatrix} 9 \\ 27/2 \\ 36 \end{pmatrix}$$

Now we have nothing but simple bounds for x_1, which simplify to:

$$x_1 \leq 3$$

$$x_1 \leq 81/10$$

$$x_1 \leq 27/2$$

The tightest bound is 3, so we can choose any value of x_1 less than 3. With $x_1 = 3$, we can choose a value for x_2 between -1 and $7/2$; suppose we choose $x_2 = 0$. The only value of x_3 we can choose to satisfy the inequalities is 7, but we have still found a solution.

A note on this example; when the problem started, there were no unconstrained variables. After the first projection step, however, we could have noticed that x_1 became unconstrained. Deleting all the inequalities containing x_1 would have made x_2 unconstrained; we could have stopped the algorithm at that point and started choosing values to satisfy the inequalities. If we were interested only in whether a solution exists, and not in any particular solution, we could stop as soon as all the variables were unconstrained.

4.5.2 Solution Procedure

The general solution procedure for a system of linear inequalities should check simple cases first:

1. Delete any inequalities with unconstrained variables; if this makes more variables unconstrained, delete them also.
2. Check simple bounds for inconsistencies.
3. Delete redundant inequalities (two inequalities with the same coefficients), keeping only the tighter bound.
4. Check for inconsistent inequalities, that is, two inequalities $\mathbf{A}_{[j]}\mathbf{x} \leq b_j$ and $\mathbf{A}_{[k]}\mathbf{x} \leq b_k$ where $\mathbf{A}_{[j]} = -\mathbf{A}_{[k]}$ and $-b_k > b_j$.
5. Apply Fourier-Motzkin projection to the remaining inequalities. Whenever the projection produces a simple bound for an unknown, save only the tighter of the new bound and the previously computed bound.

When the system of inequalities is being constructed, simple bounds can be identified and handled immediately by keeping a global maximum and minimum for each unknown. Redundant and inconsistent inequalities also can be deleted as the system is constructed.

4.6 Systems of Integer Linear Inequalities

A system of integer linear inequalities is a system of linear inequalities with integer coefficients and integer constants, for which we wish to determine if there are any integer solutions. Applying Fourier-Motzkin projection will tell whether there are real solutions. If there are no real solutions, certainly there are no integer solutions. The existence of a real solution, however, does not necessarily imply that there is an integer solution. Any single integer inequality:

$$a_1 x_1 + a_2 x_2 + \cdots + a_n x_n \leq c$$

can be tightened by dividing by the gcd of the coefficients:

$$\frac{a_1}{g} x_1 + \frac{a_2}{g} x_2 + \cdots + \frac{a_n}{g} x_n \leq \left\lfloor \frac{c}{g} \right\rfloor$$

where $g = \gcd(a_1, a_2, \ldots, a_n)$.

Also, to stay in the integer realm, when eliminating an unknown, we cannot divide by the coefficients. To eliminate x_j using the two inequalities

$$-c_i + \sum_{m \neq j} a_{im} x_m \leq -a_{ij} x_j$$

$$a_{kj} x_j \leq c_k - \sum_{m \neq j} a_{km} x_m$$

where $a_{ij} < 0$ and $a_{kj} > 0$, we must make the coefficients of x_j the same in each; this can be done by multiplying the first inequality by a_{kj} and the second by $-a_{ij}$ to get:

$$-a_{kj}c_i + \sum_{m \neq j} a_{kj}a_{im}x_m \leq -a_{kj}a_{ij}x_j$$
$$-a_{ij}a_{kj}x_j \leq -a_{ij}c_k + \sum_{m \neq j} a_{ij}a_{km}x_m \qquad (4.7)$$

which allows us to eliminate x_j by:

$$-a_{kj}c_i + \sum_{m \neq j} a_{kj}a_{im}x_m \leq \sum_{m \neq j} a_{ij}a_{km}x_m - a_{ij}c_k \qquad (4.8)$$

We can reduce the magnitude of the coefficients, and perhaps get a tighter bound, by taking the gcd of all the coefficients of the new bound. Figure 4.11 shows algorithm FMint, an integer version of Fourier-Motzkin projection. As with the real version, it should be preceded by checking for unconstrained variables and inconsistent simple bounds.

The projection is not exact for the integer problem. There may in fact be an integer solution to equation 4.8 that does not allow an integer solution for x_j in equation 4.7. This can happen if there is no multiple of $a_{1i}a_{2i}$ in the allowable

```
      Algorithm FMint:
 (1)  procedure Projectint( A, b )
 (2)  inexact = False
 (3)  repeat
 (4)      choose a variable x_j along which to project
 (5)      let L be the set of row indices {i|a_ij < 0}
 (6)      let U be the set of row indices {i|a_ij > 0}
 (7)      if L or U is empty, this is an unconstrained variable
 (8)      for i ∈ L ∪ U do
 (9)          g = |gcd(a_i1, a_i2, ...)|
(10)          divide row A_[i] by g
(11)          let b_i = ⌊b_i/g⌋
(12)      endfor
(13)      for i ∈ L do
(14)          for k ∈ U do
(15)              add a new inequality a_kj A_[i] − a_ij A_[k] ≤ a_kj b_i − a_ij b_k
(16)              if |a_kj a_ij| > 1 then inexact = True
(17)          endfor
(18)      endfor
(19)      ignore all rows in L and U from further consideration
(20)  until done
(21)  end Projectint
```

FIGURE 4.11 Algorithm to approximate whether there is an integer solution to a system of integer inequalities $\mathbf{Ax} \leq \mathbf{b}$.

4.6 ▪ Systems of Integer Linear Inequalities

range for the bounds of x_j. The projection is exact if we eliminate only variables that have coefficients with magnitude one. Algorithm FMint sets an *inexact* flag when an inexact projection occurs. The procedure can choose to eliminate the unknown with the most unit coefficients to hopefully improve accuracy.

Example 4.24

Use Fourier-Motzkin projection to see if there are any integer solutions to the set of linear inequalities below:

$$x_1 - 4x_2 \leq 2$$

$$x_1 + 5x_2 \leq 7$$

$$-x_1 \leq -3$$

Solution

In matrix form, these are written:

$$\begin{pmatrix} 1 & -4 \\ 1 & 5 \\ -1 & 0 \end{pmatrix} \begin{pmatrix} x_1 \\ x_2 \end{pmatrix} \leq \begin{pmatrix} 2 \\ 7 \\ -3 \end{pmatrix}$$

Eliminating x_2 by combining five times the first row with four times the second, to get:

$$\begin{pmatrix} 9 & 0 \\ -1 & 0 \end{pmatrix} \begin{pmatrix} x_1 \\ x_2 \end{pmatrix} \leq \begin{pmatrix} 38 \\ -3 \end{pmatrix}$$

This is an inexact projection, but there is no other choice. We can tighten the first bound by dividing by nine and taking the floor on the right-hand side, to get:

$$\begin{pmatrix} 1 & 0 \\ -1 & 0 \end{pmatrix} \begin{pmatrix} x_1 \\ x_2 \end{pmatrix} \leq \begin{pmatrix} 4 \\ -3 \end{pmatrix}$$

The apparent solution space for x_1 is [3 : 4]. However, we had an inexact projection, so the range may not be precise. However, when $x_1 = 3$, the first two original inequalities become:

$$-4x_2 \leq -1$$

$$5x_2 \leq 4$$

which simplify to bounds on x_2 of $1 \leq x_2 \leq 0$, which is a contradiction. Likewise, when $x_1 = 4$, the first two inequalities become:

$$-4x_2 \leq -2$$

$$5x_2 \leq 3$$

which gives the same bounds $1 \leq x_2 \leq 0$. Thus, while Fourier-Motzkin projection determines that there are real solutions to the system, there are in fact no integer solutions.

4.6.1 Dark Shadows

If all the projections are exact (in the integer sense) and algorithm FMint determines that there was a solution, then there must be an integer solution. Whether or not the projections were exact, if FMint determines that there is no solution, there can be no integer solution. However, if FMint says there is a solution but the answer is inexact, it may be interesting to see whether we can prove that there is an integer solution. If we can prove there is, then the inexactness of the projection didn't jeopardize accuracy.

Two methods can be used. In one method, we use the bounds computed by the projection and choose some integer value for each of the unknowns. This is what we did for Example 4.24, choosing values 3 and 4 for x_1. We start by choosing a value for the last unknown that was eliminated, somewhere near the center of the region of values allowed by the bounds. We use that value in the inequalities for the next-to-last unknown eliminated, and choose a value for it. We may be able to find an integer value this way that satisfies all the inequalities, and then we know our solution is exact. If we cannot, we can either backtrack and start over, or give up and assume there is a solution. Naturally, we can't enumerate all values, so backtracking may not be feasible.

The second method is to solve a related set of inequalities such that if the related set has any solution, the original set must have an integer solution. A simplified version of the problem with inexact projection is that we have two bounds:

$$\alpha x \leq c_u$$

$$c_l \leq \beta x$$

To eliminate x, we normalize the bounds to get:

$$\alpha c_l \leq \alpha \beta x \leq \beta c_u$$

If $\alpha c_l \leq \beta c_u$, Fourier-Motzkin projection will determine that there is a solution to the system of inequalities; however, there may be no multiple of $\alpha\beta$ in that range, in which case there is no integer x that satisfies the inequality, which we can express as $\alpha\beta i < \alpha c_l \leq \beta c_u < \alpha\beta(i+1)$, for some integer i. We can tighten these inequalities to $\alpha\beta i + \alpha \leq \alpha c_l \leq \beta c_u \leq \alpha\beta(i+1) - \beta$. Rearranging, we see that the problem arises when $\beta c_u - \alpha c_l \leq \alpha\beta - \alpha - \beta$. Thus, if we add the additional constraint that $\beta c_u - \alpha c_l \geq \alpha\beta - \alpha - \beta + 1$, then we are assured that there must be a multiple of $\alpha\beta$ between the bounds αc_l and βc_u. Adding this constraint will generate a different shadow after eliminating the unknown; we call this the *dark shadow*, and it is a subset of the real shadow. If the dark shadow is nonempty after eliminating all

4.6 ▪ Systems of Integer Linear Inequalities

the unknowns, there must be an integer solution. Note that the dark shadow being empty is not sufficient to determine that there are no integer solutions; the dark shadow is conceptually the region where the polyhedron in $\mathbb{R}^n$ is "thick" enough in the direction specified by the unknown being eliminated. There may be integer solutions that lie outside the dark shadow but inside the real shadow.

Using the dark shadow means doing the Fourier-Motzkin projection twice for each unknown: once to compute the real shadow and once to compute the dark shadow. As long as the projections are exact, they are the same; if the dark shadow becomes empty, only the real shadow is needed.

We compute the dark shadow by changing line 15 in algorithm FMint to

(16) add a new inequality $a_{kj}A_{[i]} - a_{ij}A_{[k]} \leq a_{kj}b_i - a_{ij}b_k + a_{kj}a_{ij} + a_{kj} - a_{ij} - 1$

Example 4.25

Determine whether there are integer solutions to the following set of integer inequalities:

$$2x_2 \leq 3x_1$$
$$3x_2 \geq 2x_1 - 1$$
$$x_2 \leq 2$$

Solution

We rewrite this in standard form as follows:

$$\begin{pmatrix} -3 & 2 \\ 2 & -3 \\ 0 & 1 \end{pmatrix} \begin{pmatrix} x_1 \\ x_2 \end{pmatrix} \leq \begin{pmatrix} 0 \\ 1 \\ 2 \end{pmatrix}$$

We can project along x_1, though it is inexact, to get the following system:

$$\begin{pmatrix} 0 & -5 \\ 0 & 1 \end{pmatrix} \begin{pmatrix} x_1 \\ x_2 \end{pmatrix} \leq \begin{pmatrix} 3 \\ 2 \end{pmatrix}$$

The simple bounds on x_2 reduce to $\lceil -3/5 \rceil \leq x_2 \leq 2$. Since the projection was inexact, we can compute a dark shadow try to determine whether integer solutions must exist. In the projection, $\alpha = 2$ and $\beta = 3$; we now add the "dark" inequality:

$$\begin{pmatrix} 0 & -5 \end{pmatrix} \begin{pmatrix} x_1 \\ x_2 \end{pmatrix} \leq \begin{pmatrix} 3 - 6 + 3 + 2 - 1 \end{pmatrix}$$

The solution space for x_2 now reduces to $\lceil -1/5 \rceil \leq x_2 \leq 2$, which is still $0:2$. Thus, use of the dark shadow determines that there are definitely integer solutions for $0 \leq x_2 \leq 2$.

4.6.2 Solution Procedure

As with systems of linear inequalities, the solution procedure should check simple cases first; a sketch of a solution procedure is shown in Figure 4.12. It uses dark shadows and sample solutions to try to determine exactly whether there is an integer solution to the system of inequalities; if the dark shadow is nonempty, its bounds can be used to find a sample integer solution. If an inexact answer is sufficient, then the dark shadow and sample solution computations can be eliminated.

```
         Algorithm IntegerInequality:
(1)  inexact = False
(2)  darkempty = False
(3)  repeat
(4)     repeat
(5)        delete inequalities with unconstrained variables
(6)     until there are no more unconstrained variables
(7)     check simple bounds for inconsistencies
(8)     delete redundant inequalities
(9)     choose an unknown to eliminate
(10)    if the projection will be inexact then
(11)       inexact = True
(12)    endif
(13)    compute the real projection
(14)    if inexact and not darkempty then
(15)       compute the dark shadow
(16)       if dark shadow is empty then darkempty = True
(17)    endif
(18) until done
(19) if the dark shadow is nonempty then an integer solution exists
(20) if the real shadow is empty then no integer solution exists
(21) for unknown $x_k$ in reverse order of elimination do
(22)    compute bounds for $x_k$ in terms of other chosen values
(23)    if lower bound < upper bound then
(24)       choose a value for $x_k$ between the bounds
(25)    else
(26)       give up
(27)    endif
(28) endfor
(29) use the sample integer solution
```

FIGURE 4.12 Solution procedure for system of integer inequalities.

4.7 Extreme Values of Affine Functions

Where a linear function $f : \mathbb{R}^m \longrightarrow \mathbb{R}^n$ can be represented in matrix notation as $f(\mathbf{x}) = \mathbf{F}\mathbf{x}$, an affine function can be represented as $f(\mathbf{x}) = \mathbf{F}\mathbf{x} + \mathbf{f}_0$; in some sense, an affine function is a linear plus a constant. We want to find the maximum and minimum values that an integer affine function $f : \mathbb{R}^m \longrightarrow \mathbb{R}$ can take for integer valued arguments in a bounded region of $\mathbb{R}^m$, where the bounded region is characterized by a set of linear inequalities. In general, this is equivalent to the integer programming problem. In many cases, the linear inequalities satisfy special properties that make the solution easy to find.

To find the extreme values for this problem, we use the *positive part* r^+ and the *negative part* r^- of a real number, which are defined by:

$$r^+ = \begin{cases} r, & \text{if } r \geq 0 \\ 0, & \text{if } r < 0 \end{cases} \qquad r^- = \begin{cases} 0, & \text{if } r > 0 \\ r, & \text{if } r \leq 0 \end{cases}$$

These values satisfy the following properties:

$$r^+ \geq 0$$
$$r^- \leq 0$$
$$r = r^+ + r^-$$
$$r^- \leq r \leq r^+$$
$$(-r)^- = -(r^+)$$
$$(-r)^+ = -(r^-)$$
$$\text{if } 0 \leq s \leq t, \ r^- t \leq rs \leq r^+ t$$

It is easy to find extreme values for the product ax, for any constant value of a, when x is bound by $l \leq x \leq u$:

$$a^+ l + a^- u \leq ax \leq a^+ u + a^- l.$$

The bounds of $f(x) = 3x$, where x lies in the range $-4 \leq x \leq 10$, must be at the endpoints. Moreover, since $f(x)$ is monotonically increasing, it has its greatest value at the largest value for x, and its smallest value at the lower bound for x. Thus the tightest upper bound is $f(10) = 30$, and the tightest lower bound is $f(-4) = -12$. This is equivalent to computing

$$3^+(-4) + 3^-(10) \leq f(x) \leq 3^+(10) + 3^-(-4)$$
$$3(-4) + 0 \leq f(x) \leq 3(10) + 0$$

Example 4.26

Find extreme values for $f(\mathbf{x}) = 3x_1 - 2x_2 + 3$ for values of $\mathbf{x}$ satisfying

$$1 \leq x_1 \leq 19$$
$$-10 \leq x_2 \leq -3$$

Solution

The extreme values of the affine function will be at two of the vertices of the region satisfying the inequalities. At worst, we need only evaluate $f(\mathbf{x})$ at the four vertices and take the maximum and minimum values. Instead, we can use our inequalities to compute an upper bound as:

$$3x_1 - 2x_2 + 3 \leq 3^+(19) + 3^-(1) + (-2)^+(-3) + (-2)^-(-10) + 3$$
$$\leq 3(19) + 0 + 0 - 2(-10) + 3$$
$$\leq 80$$

The lower bound is computed as:

$$3x_1 - 2x_2 + 3 \geq 3^+(1) + 3^-(19) + (-2)^+(-10) + (-2)^-(-3) + 3$$
$$\geq 3(1) - 0 + 0 - 2(-3) + 3$$
$$\geq 12$$

4.7.1 Nonrectangular Regions

Suppose we are given an integer affine function $f(\mathbf{x}) = \mathbf{Fx} + f_0 = \sum_{i=1}^{m} f_i x_i + f_0$, and a system of at most $2m$ integer inequalities bounding $\mathbb{R}^m$ that can be ordered as:

$$l_{10} \leq x_1 \leq u_{10}$$
$$l_{20} + l_{21}x_1 \leq x_2 \leq u_{20} + u_{21}x_1$$
$$\cdots \quad \cdots \quad \cdots$$
$$l_{i0} + \sum_{j=1}^{i-1} l_{ij}x_j \leq x_i \leq u_{i0} + \sum_{j=1}^{i-1} u_{ij}x_j$$
$$\cdots \quad \cdots \quad \cdots$$

This gives each element x_i a single lower and upper bound, with a unit coefficient for x_i. There may be some freedom in choosing the order of the bounds. An inequality such as $x_2 \leq x_3 + 1$ may be treated as an upper bound for x_2, or as a lower bound for x_3, (but not both). We can model these bounds by strictly lower triangular matrices $\mathbf{L}$ and $\mathbf{U}$ and vectors $\mathbf{ll}$ and $\mathbf{uu}$ such that $(\mathbf{I} - \mathbf{L})\mathbf{x} \geq \mathbf{ll}$ and $(\mathbf{I} - \mathbf{U})\mathbf{x} \geq \mathbf{uu}$.

Let $b_m(\mathbf{x}) = a_m(\mathbf{x}) = f(\mathbf{x})$. By definition, these satisfy $b_m(\mathbf{x}) \leq f(\mathbf{x}) \leq a_m(\mathbf{x})$, bounding f from below and above. Suppose we have a function $b_n(\mathbf{x}_{[1:n]}) = \sum_{i=1}^{n} b_{ni}x_i + b_{n0} \leq f(\mathbf{x})$, for any value of $n \leq m$. We can eliminate x_n by realizing that

$$b_{nn}^+(l_{n0} + \sum_{j=1}^{n-1} l_{nj}x_j) + b_{nn}^-(u_{n0} + \sum_{j=1}^{n-1} u_{nj}x_j) \leq b_{nn}x_n$$

If we let $b_{n-1,j} = b_{nj} + b_{nn}^+ l_{nj} + b_{nn}^- u_{nj}$, for $0 \leq j < n$, then $b_{n-1}(\mathbf{x}_{[1:n-1]}) = \sum_{i=1}^{n-1} b_{n-1,i}x_i + b_{n-1,0}$ satisfies $b_{n-1}(\mathbf{x}_{[1:n-1]}) \leq b_n(\mathbf{x}_{[1:n]}) \leq f(\mathbf{x})$. By letting $n = m, m-1, m-2, \ldots, 1, 0$, we get a sequence of functions that bound f from below, eventually terminating in a single value.

4.7 ▪ Extreme Values of Affine Functions

Similarly, suppose we have a function $a_n(\mathbf{x}_{[1:n]}) = \sum_{i=1}^{n} a_{ni} x_i + a_{n0} \geq f(\mathbf{x})$, for any value of $n \leq m$. We eliminate x_n with the inequality:

$$a_{nn} x_n \leq a_{nn}^+ (u_{n0} + \sum_{j=1}^{n-1} u_{nj} x_j) + a_{nn}^- (l_{n0} + \sum_{j=1}^{n-1} l_{nj} x_j)$$

By letting $a_{n-1,j} = a_{nj} + a_{nn}^+ u_{nj} + a_{nn}^- l_{nj}$, for $0 \leq j < n$, we have $f(\mathbf{x}) \leq a_n(\mathbf{x}_{[1:n]}) \leq a_{n-1}(\mathbf{x}_{[1:n-1]})$. Figure 4.13 shows algorithm Extreme, which computes the extreme lower and upper bounds of a linear function, given the vector of its coefficients (include element f_0), and matrices $\mathbf{L}$ and $\mathbf{U}$ as defined above. In practice, such a procedure must be able to handle cases when bounds are missing, treating them as $+\infty$ or $-\infty$, as appropriate. The extreme value procedure can also be used when there are too many bounds, though some of the bounds may have to be discarded.

```
Algorithm Extreme:
(1)  procedure Extreme( f, L, ll, U, uu ) returns ( low, high )
(2)    b[0:m] = f[0:m]
(3)    a[0:m] = f[0:m]
(4)    for n = m downto 1 do
(5)      a₀ = a₀ + aₙ⁺uuₙ + aₙ⁻llₙ
(6)      b₀ = b₀ + bₙ⁺llₙ + bₙ⁻uuₙ
(7)      for j = 1 to i - 1 do
(8)        aⱼ = aⱼ + aₙ⁺uₙⱼ + aₙ⁻lₙⱼ
(9)        bⱼ = bⱼ + bₙ⁺lₙⱼ + bₙ⁻uₙⱼ
(10)     endfor
(11)   endfor
(12)   high = a₀
(13)   low = b₀
(14) end Extreme
```

FIGURE 4.13 Algorithm to find extreme values of a linear function in bounded region.

We can use the extreme value procedure to try to determine whether there is a solution to a linear equation in a bounded region. Suppose we want to solve $f(\mathbf{x}) = \mathbf{f}\mathbf{x} + f_0 = 0$, where $\mathbf{x}$ is bounded by an appropriate region. If the extreme values of f in the region do not surround zero, there is no real solution $\mathbf{x}$ to the equation in the region.

Note that the computed extreme values may not be "tight"; that is, they may not actually be the values of the function for any point in the region, if the bounds are not themselves tight. Even when the bounds are not tight, the extreme values are valid, though they may not be as good as they could be. Applying Fourier-Motzkin elimination to tighten the bounds may be too expensive in some applications. See the exercises for an example.

Example 4.27

Find extreme values for the function $f(\mathbf{x}) = 2x_1 - 3x_2 - 1$ in the region

$$1 \le x_1 \le 5$$

$$x_1 \le x_2 \le 10 - x_1$$

and see if there is a solution to $f(\mathbf{x}) = 0$ in the region.

Solution

Initially let $b_2(\mathbf{x}) = a_2(\mathbf{x}) = f(\mathbf{x})$. Eliminate x_2 and x_1 in turn, producing the following sequence of bounding functions for the upper bound:

$$f(\mathbf{x}) \le -1 + 2x_1 - 3x_2 = a_2(\mathbf{x})$$

$$f(\mathbf{x}) \le -1 - 1x_1 \qquad\quad = a_1(\mathbf{x})$$

$$f(\mathbf{x}) \le -2 \qquad\qquad\qquad = a_0(\mathbf{x})$$

The sequence of lower bound functions is:

$$f(\mathbf{x}) \ge -1 + 2x_1 - 3x_2 = b_2(\mathbf{x})$$

$$f(\mathbf{x}) \ge -31 + 5x_1 \qquad\quad = b_1(\mathbf{x})$$

$$f(\mathbf{x}) \ge -26 \qquad\qquad\qquad = b_0(\mathbf{x})$$

The lower bound of -26 is the function value at $\mathbf{x} = (1, 9)$, and the upper bound of -1 is the value of $f(1, 1)$. Because 0 does not lie between the two bounds, there is no solution to $f(\mathbf{x})$ in the region given.

4.8 In the Pit

The literature gives two conflicting definitions of a matrix in HNF; the definition we used has positive diagonal elements and positive numbers below the diagonal. The other definition has positive diagonal elements and negative numbers below the diagonal. Either definition may be used, and either is unique. The term HTF is not standard.

When implementing a solver such as those shown here, good engineering will be critical to compiler performance. Depending on how the solver is used, it may be invoked hundreds of times when compiling a single routine.

Integer division (the div operator) is not well defined, either in computer architecture or by programming languages. For positive i and j, integer division $k = i \operatorname{div} j$ satisfies $i = kj + d$, where $d = i \bmod j$, and $k = \lfloor i/j \rfloor$. When i or j is negative, however, these do not hold. A useful programming trick is to only divide positive numbers, scaling when appropriate. Suppose we know that $j > 0$ $i < 0$, and we want to compute $\lfloor i/j \rfloor$. Let $m > 0$ by some large integer, in particular $m > -i$.

Then $\lfloor i/j \rfloor = \lfloor (mj+i)/j - m \rfloor = \lfloor (mj+i)/j \rfloor - m$. Since $m > |i|$ and $j > 0$, we have $mj + i > 0$ and $\lfloor (mj+i)/j \rfloor = (mj+i) \operatorname{div} j$. Choosing m as a large power of two is convenient, so the multiplication mj can be done with shift operators. In the realm of compilers, most of the problems use small integers, so this may be useful.

We defined the positive and negative parts of a number so that $x^- \leq x \leq x^+$. Banerjee first introduced these terms with $x^- \geq 0$, the inverse of the definition we used here. We use our definition to simplify some of the calculations. When reading the references, however, be careful as to which definition of x^- is being used.

4.9 Further Reading

Many of the techniques reviewed here for dealing with integer matrices, as well as more details on integer programming, are discussed in greater detail in the books by Nemhauser and Wolsey (1988) and Schrijver (1986). Banerjee (1993) also discusses these topics in the context of restructuring compilers. General integer programming tries to find a solution that optimizes some cost function in a region bounded by linear inequalities. The problems in which we are interested have no cost function, so we may be able to take advantage of simpler solvers.

Fourier-Motzkin projection is discussed by Williams (1976, 1983), Dantzig and Eaves (1973), and Duffin (1974).

The extreme value method for rectangular regions was used by Banerjee et al. (1979) to solve data dependence problems. Banerjee (1988) extended it to non-rectangular regions, and also describes the algebraic techniques to reduce integer systems of equations. Another method to reduce integer systems of equations was developed by Pugh (1992), who introduces a new operator $(\widehat{\operatorname{mod}})$ that allows the system to reduce more quickly. Pugh also introduced the concept of a dark shadow. His system, called the Omega Test, solves general integer programming problems as well as more complicated Presburger formulas. In the domain studied in this chapter, when the Fourier-Motzkin projection technique is inexact and the dark shadow test fails to find a solution, Pugh's system can splinter the problem into a set of problems, one of which must have an exact solution for the original system to have a solution. Feautrier (1988) describes a scheme called parametric integer programming to solve integer programming problems that arise in the framework of a compiler.

EXERCISES

4.1 Find a basis for the subspace spanned by the following set of vectors:

$$\left\{ \begin{pmatrix} 5 \\ 5 \end{pmatrix}, \begin{pmatrix} 3 \\ 6 \end{pmatrix}, \begin{pmatrix} 1 \\ 9 \end{pmatrix} \right\}$$

The following three exercises use this set of vectors:

$$\left\{ \begin{pmatrix} 5 \\ 5 \\ 0 \end{pmatrix}, \begin{pmatrix} 3 \\ 6 \\ 1 \end{pmatrix}, \begin{pmatrix} 1 \\ 9 \\ 9 \end{pmatrix}, \begin{pmatrix} 18 \\ 0 \\ 1 \end{pmatrix} \right\}$$

4.2 Find a basis for the subspace spanned by the set of vectors.

4.3 Order each pair of vectors using a vector relation, a lexicographic ordering, and an ordering vector.

4.4 Compute the dot product of each pair of vectors.

4.5 Find the convex hull of the vectors.

4.6 Represent the function $f(x_1, x_2, x_3) = 5x_3 - (3x_1 + x_2)/2$ in matrix form; prove that it is a linear function.

Many of the following exercises use these matrices:

$$\mathbf{A} = \begin{pmatrix} 5 & 0 & 4 \\ 5 & 8 & 3 \\ 0 & 9 & 0 \end{pmatrix}, \mathbf{B} = \begin{pmatrix} 5 & 0 & 4 \\ 5 & 9 & 4 \\ 0 & 9 & 0 \end{pmatrix}$$

4.7 Find the inverse of matrix $\mathbf{A}$.

4.8 Use the inverse computed in the previous exercise to solve the system of equations $\mathbf{Ax} = (5, 9, 4)^T$.

4.9 Using elementary row operations, reduce $\mathbf{A}$ to $\mathbf{U}$, an upper triangular matrix.

4.10 Find the determinant of $\mathbf{A}$ and $\mathbf{A}^{-1}$.

4.11 Using elementary lower triangular matrices, reduce $\mathbf{A}$ to $\mathbf{U}$, an upper triangular form. Compute the matrix product $\mathbf{L}$ of the elementary lower triangular matrices. If you did the exercise correctly, $\mathbf{L} \times \mathbf{U} = \mathbf{A}$.

4.12 Find the determinant of $\mathbf{U}$ and $\mathbf{L}$ computed in the previous exercise.

4.13 Prove that the determinant of a triangular matrix is the product of the diagonal elements.

4.14 Find the rank of matrix $\mathbf{B}$.

4.15 Find basis vectors for the range and null space of $\mathbf{B}$.

4.16 Prove that the product of two unimodular matrices is unimodular; Hint: prove that the result is an integer matrix and the determinant is ± 1.

4.17 Implement a program to decompose a matrix into the product of an upper triangular and a lower triangular matrix, at the same time finding whether the matrix is singular or nonsingular and computing its determinant.

4.18 Implement Euclid's algorithm to find greatest common divisors. Determine experimentally how quickly it converges to the gcd depending on the magnitude of the smallest argument.

4.19 The key observation in the proof of Euclid's algorithm is that $g_{i-1} = dg_i + g_{i+1}$ for some value d. The first method we used was $g_{i+1} = g_{i-1} \bmod g_i$, which can be computed as $g_{i+1} = g_{i-1} - g_i \lfloor g_{i-1}/g_i \rfloor$. For instance, $16 \bmod 9 = 7$, and the next iteration will compute

9 mod 7 = 2, and so forth. The values continually get smaller since $0 \le a \bmod b < b$. We can make the algorithm converse more quickly by defining a modified modulo operator, $\widehat{\bmod}$ ("mod-hat"). Let $a \widehat{\bmod} b = a - b\lfloor a/b + 1/2 \rfloor$. This will satisfy the relations $a = bd + a \widehat{\bmod} b$, for some value d, so we can use it in Euclid's algorithm. It also satisfies $\lceil -b/2 \rceil \le a \widehat{\bmod} b \le \lfloor b/2 \rfloor$, so using $\widehat{\bmod}$ will let the value reduce to smaller magnitudes more quickly. For instance, $16 \widehat{\bmod} 9 = -2$, and $9 \widehat{\bmod} -2 = 1$, so that sequence converges in only two iterations.

Improve the convergence of algorithm GCD by using the $\widehat{\bmod}$ operator in your implementation, and compare its convergence with the original algorithm. Be careful how you implement the $\lfloor a/b \rfloor$ operator.

4.20 Prove that the inverse of a unimodular matrix is unimodular.

4.21 Prove that applying unimodular operations to a matrix preserves the lattice generated by the matrix.

4.22 Using unimodular operations, reduce matrix **A** above to Hermite normal form.

4.23 Use the HNF computed for **A** in the previous exercise to solve the integer matrix equation $\mathbf{Ax} = (54, 6, -54)^T$.

4.24 Reduce matrix **B** above to HNF.

4.25 Use the HNF just computed to find a basis for the null space of **B**.

4.26 Find all integer solutions to the following equations:

(a) $3x_1 + 4x_2 = 5$

(b) $12x_1 - 14x_2 + 24x_3 = 5$

(c) $2x_1 - 5x_2 + 24x_3 = 99$

The following two exercises use the following set of inequalities:

$$5x_2 \le 7x_3 + 99$$
$$4x_1 \le 8x_2$$
$$4x_1 \ge x_3$$

4.27 Write this system of inequalities in standard matrix form.

4.28 Use Fourier-Motzkin elimination to determine whether there are any solutions to the system in inequalities.

4.29 Use variable substitution to find dependent and independent variables for the equation $12x_1 - 14x_2 + 24x_3 = 5$. Eliminate the dependent variables in the inequalities above. Determine whether there are any solutions to the new set of inequalities.

4.30 Implement a routine that will reduce a system of integer equalities to dependent and independent variables, using algorithm ReduceMatrix and procedure Reduce from Figure 4.7.

4.31 Modify your procedure from the previous exercise so it will converge faster using the same $\widehat{\bmod}$ trick we introduced for Euclid's algorithm. Replace line 11 of procedure Reduce with:

(11) $q = \lfloor d_{im} \operatorname{div} d_{ik} + 1/2 \rfloor$

Compare the convergence of your procedure. A sample problem is $5x_1 + 9x_2 + 12x_3 = 0$.

4.32 Use algorithm Extreme to find extreme values for the function $f(\mathbf{x}) = 2x_1 + x_2$ in the region:

$$1 \leq x_1 \leq 10$$

$$x_1 \leq x_2 \leq 10 - x_1$$

Find values in the region that actually reach your extreme values.

4.33 In the previous exercise, the problem is that the upper bound for x_1 is not "tight." Devise a procedure using Fourier-Motzkin elimination to tighten a set of linear inequalities.

5 DATA DEPENDENCE

Data dependence relations are used by the compiler to represent the essential ordering constraints among statements or operations in a program. Data dependence relations are less restrictive than using the program flow, and allow the compiler more flexibility in reordering statements for improved performance. This chapter introduces the terminology and notation used to represent data dependence relations, and discusses how dependence relations arise in loops.

In order for the compiler to have the most opportunities to rearrange code, it must analyze the program to find the essential constraints preventing the reordering of operations, statements, or iterations of a loop. Consider the following program:

(1)   A = 0
(2)   B = A
(3)   C = A + D
(4)   D = 2

Here, the compiler must be careful in moving the statements. Moving statement 2 above statement 1 would change the program, since statement 2 would then get some "old" (possibly uninitialized) value for the variable A. Likewise, executing statement 4 before statement 3 would use the wrong value for D in statement 3. However, statements 2 and 3 can be switched without changing the results of the program. We use the concept of data dependence to capture and represent the essential ordering constraints of the program.

One abstraction compilers use to represent this information is a *data dependence graph*. The vertices in the data dependence graph can correspond to statements in the program (source-level statements or intermediate language statements) or to finer-grain or courser-grain blocks of code (such as instructions or basic blocks). The edges in the graph correspond to constraints that prevent reordering the statements. Note that this is a multigraph—two vertices may be connected by several edges. Three types of constraints are usually defined:

- *Flow dependence* occurs when a variable is assigned or defined in one statement and used in a subsequently executed statement.
- *Anti-dependence* occurs when a variable is used in one statement and reassigned in a subsequently executed statement.
- *Output dependence* occurs when a variable is assigned in one statement and reassigned in a subsequently executed statement.

Anti-dependence and output dependence arise from the reuse or reassignment of variables, and are sometimes called *false* dependences. Flow dependence is also called *true* dependence since it is inherent in the computation and cannot be eliminated by renaming variables.

When a statement is flow dependent upon another statement, as statement 2 is flow dependent on statement 1 in the short program above, we write $S_1\ \delta^f\ S_2$; in the dependence graph, the edge is drawn as a plain arrow. Anti-dependence is written $S_2\ \delta^a\ S_4$, and the arrow is drawn with a line crossing through. Output dependence is written $S_1\ \delta^o\ S_4$, and the arrow is drawn with a circle through it. The data dependence graph for the short program above is shown in Figure 5.1. We say that S_2 is data dependent on S_1, written $S_1\ \delta^*\ S_2$, if $S_1\ \delta^f\ S_2$, $S_1\ \delta^a\ S_2$, or $S_1\ \delta^o\ S_2$. In a basic block, or in any program without loops, the data dependence graph will be acyclic; such a dependence graph is sometimes called a *precedence graph*.

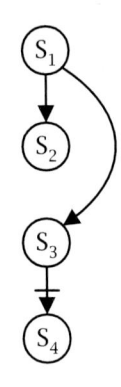

FIGURE 5.1 Data dependence graph for sample program.

Two approaches to defining data dependence relations are addressed-based and value-based dependence. An *address-based* data dependence relation is defined between two references that use the same address. A *value-based* data dependence relation is defined between two references when one reference defines or uses a value, and the other uses or overwrites that value. Value-based data dependence relations are a subset of the address-based data dependence relations. The difference is illustrated by the following program:

(1) A = 0
(2) B = A
(3) A = B + 1
(4) C = A

Statement 2 is flow dependent on statement 1 because it fetches a value from variable A, and the value being used is the one assigned in statement 1. Statement 4 also fetches a value from variable A, but the value used is the one assigned in statement 3. Using the address-based definition of data dependence, there is a flow dependence from statement 1 to statement 4, because of the definition and use of the variable A. Using value-based definition, there is no such dependence; the definition of A in statement 3 "kills" any dependence from previous statements due to variable A (including anti-dependence or output dependence). We will specify which definition we are using when there is an ambiguity.

Address-based dependence relations can be found by comparing the IN and OUT sets of each node in the data dependence graph.

- The IN set of a statement, IN(S), is the set of variables (or, more precisely, the set of memory locations, usually referred to by variable names) that may be read (or fetched) by this statement.
- The OUT set of a statement, OUT(S), is the set of memory locations that may be modified (written or stored) by the statement.

Note that these sets include all memory locations that *may* be fetched or modified; the sets can be conservatively large. Assuming that S_2 is *reachable* from S_1, the following shows how to intersect these sets to test for data dependence:

$OUT(S_1) \cap IN(S_2) \neq \emptyset$	$S_1 \delta^f S_2$	flow dependence
$IN(S_1) \cap OUT(S_2) \neq \emptyset$	$S_1 \delta^a S_2$	anti-dependence
$OUT(S_1) \cap OUT(S_2) \neq \emptyset$	$S_1 \delta^o S_2$	output dependence

We will deal with this in more detail shortly.

What information is gleaned when the intersection of two IN sets is nonempty: $IN(S_1) \cap IN(S_2) \neq \emptyset$? This means that S_1 reads some memory location before S_2 reads that location (or more precisely, *may read* some location). Usually, a compiler does not care about the order in which statements read a value, so no extra constraints are added to the data dependence graph when this happens. Nonetheless, some optimizations can make use of this knowledge; for instance, when optimizing to make more efficient use of a cache or other memory hierarchy, the compiler may want to identify statements that use the same variables and keep them together. Thus this relation is called *input dependence*, and is written $S_1 \delta^I S_2$; usually this is treated as an undirected relation.

5.1 Data Dependence in Loops

In loops, each statement can be executed many times. Dependence can flow from any instance of execution of a statement to any other statement instance, and even to the same statement. Since a compiler can't represent each statement instance individually, some kind of abstraction is needed. The data dependence graph is still constructed with one node for each statement; each node may represent many instances of that statement. Data dependence relations are annotated with information about the relative iterations in which the related instances occur. A data dependence relation between two statement instances in two different iterations of a loop is called *loop carried*, because the dependence relation is carried by the loop from one iteration to another. A data dependence relation between two statement instances in the same iteration of a loop is called *loop independent*, because it does not need the loop to carry the dependence. We say that a dependence relation is *lexically forward* when the source precedes the target lexically; that is, when the source comes before the target without passing through a loop back edge. The dependence is *lexically backward* otherwise. The right-hand side of an assignment is considered to precede the left-hand side; thus an anti-dependence from a statement to itself is considered lexically forward, while a self-flow dependence is lexically backward.

Example 5.1

Find the dependence relations due to the array X in the program below:

```
(1)    for I = 2 to 9 do
(2)        X[I] = Y[I] + Z[I]
(3)        A[I] = X[I-1] + 1
(4)    endfor
```

Solution

To find the data dependence relations in a simple loop, we can unroll the loop and see which statement instances depend on which others:

	I = 2	I = 3	I = 4	...
(2)	X[2]=Y[2]+Z[2]	X[3]=Y[3]+Z[3]	X[4]=Y[4]+Z[4]	
(3)	A[2]=X[1]+1	A[3]=X[2]+1	A[4]=X[3]+1	

It is easy to see that the value assigned to X in each iteration of S_2 is fetched by S_3 in the next iteration of the loop. Since some instance of S_3 depends on some instance of S_2, we write $S_2 \; \delta^f \; S_3$. There are many instances of each statement in the loop, but the data dependence graph contains only one node for each statement, as shown in Figure 5.2. This is a loop-carried, lexically forward flow dependence relation. The (1) annotation in Figure 5.2 will be explained shortly.

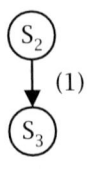

FIGURE 5.2 Data dependence graph for statements in a loop.

5.1.1 Iteration Space

Another concept is the *iteration space* associated with the loop, which contains one point for each iteration of the loop. If any statement in one iteration of the loop depends on any statement in a different iteration of the loop, the dependence would be represented by an edge from the source iteration to the target iteration, creating an *iteration space dependence graph*. Since the compiler can't always determine the number of iterations of a loop, and since space considerations prevent construction of a graph with an arbitrarily large number of vertices, the compiler can't actually build a data structure for the iteration space dependence graph. Instead, each edge in the data dependence graph is annotated with information showing how the dependence relation crosses the iterations in the iteration space. There is a certain amount of information loss in these annotations, which we will discuss shortly.

Example 5.2

Show the iteration space dependence graph for the loop in Example 5.1.

Solution

Since there is only a single loop, the iteration space has only one dimension. The dependence relations go from one iteration to the next, as shown in Figure 5.3.

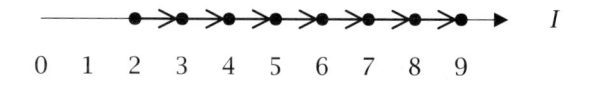

FIGURE 5.3 Iteration space dependence graph.

5.1.2 Iteration Vectors

It is common to compute the vector difference of the source iteration from the target iteration, called the *dependence distance*. In order to discuss vector differences, we must assign a label, which we call an *iteration vector*, to each point in the iteration space, or equivalently, to each iteration of the loop. One obvious way to label the iteration space is to use *index variable iteration vectors*, using the values of the loop index variables as the iteration vector. Each iteration is assigned the iteration vector:

$$\mathbf{i}^{iv} = \begin{pmatrix} I_1 \\ I_2 \\ \vdots \\ I_n \end{pmatrix}$$

where I_k is the value of the loop index variable for the kth nested loop at that iteration.

Another common method is to use a *normalized iteration vector*, where the iterations of each loop are labeled $0, 1, 2, \ldots$; a variation is to label the first iteration 1, then count up from there. In either case, the number of elements in the iteration vector is equal to the number of nested loops. An advantage of using the normalized iteration vector is that the iterations are then a subset of a lattice; we will use this property when generating code for some loop restructuring transformations. Another advantage is that later iterations always have lexicographically larger valued vectors than earlier iterations. In a sequential loop, earlier iterations are executed before later iterations, so iteration $\mathbf{i}_1$ is executed before iteration $\mathbf{i}_2$ if $\mathbf{i}_1 \prec \mathbf{i}_2$. This is not necessarily true using index variable iteration vectors. Also, with normalized iteration vectors, the next iteration in any direction is always just one more than this iteration. For these reasons, we will use normalized iteration vectors for most purposes.

Example 5.3

Show the index variable iteration vectors and normalized iteration vectors for the iterations in the loop below:

```
(1)     for I = 3 to 7 do
(2)         for J = 6 to 2 by -2 do
(3)             A[I,J] = A[I,J+2] + 1
(4)         endfor
(5)     endfor
```

Solution

Since there are two nested loops, the iteration space has two dimensions. The iteration space dependence graph corresponding to index variable iteration vectors is shown in Figure 5.4. Note that the J loop counts down, while the I loop counts up. The same dependence graph with normalized iteration vectors is shown in Figure 5.5. Note that the direction of the arrows with respect to the iteration space axes has changed. There is a clear linear relation between the two types of iteration vectors; if $\mathbf{i}^{iv}$ is the index variable iteration vector and $\mathbf{i}^n$ is the normalized iteration vector, then $i_k^n = (i_k^{iv} - l_k) \div s_k$, where l_k is the lower limit of the kth loop, and s_k is the step (or increment) of that loop.

5.1.3 Dependence Distances

A compiler can compute a *dependence distance* for a data dependence relation by finding the vector difference between the iteration vectors of the source and

5.1 ▪ Data Dependence in Loops

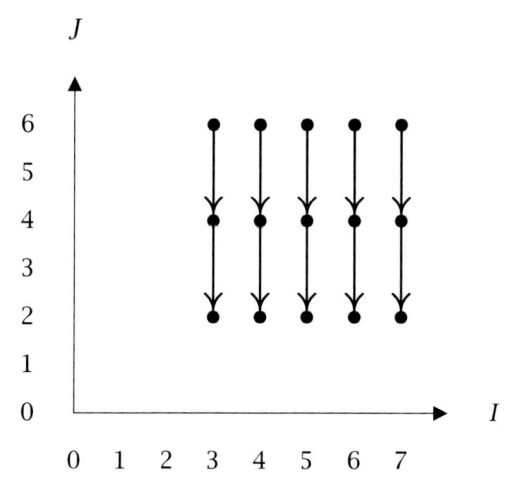

FIGURE 5.4 Iteration space dependence graph with index variable iteration vectors.

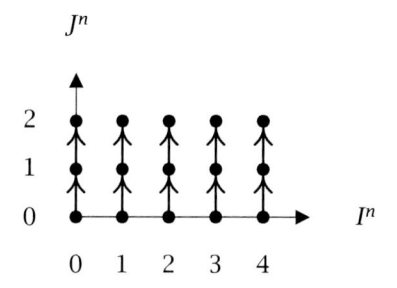

FIGURE 5.5 Iteration space dependence graph with normalized iteration vectors.

target iterations. The dependence distance will itself be a vector **d**, called a *distance vector*, defined as $\mathbf{d} = \mathbf{i}^T - \mathbf{i}^S$, or

$$\mathbf{i}^S + \mathbf{d} = \mathbf{i}^T$$

where $\mathbf{i}^S$ is the source iteration vector for this dependence relation, and $\mathbf{i}^T$ is the target iteration vector. We will write $S_p[\mathbf{i}]$ to mean the instance of statement p with iteration vector $\mathbf{i}$. If there is a dependence from $S_p[\mathbf{i}]$ to $S_q[\mathbf{i} + \mathbf{d}]$, we write $S_p \; \delta^*_{(d)} \; S_q$ to express the dependence relation and show the dependence distance.

Example 5.4

Find the data dependence relations, and compute the dependence, distance for each type of iteration vector for the loop shown in Example 5.3.

Solution

The only data dependence relation occurs when line 3 defines element A[I,J] in one iteration, and then uses that element in the next iteration of the inner loop.

Using the index variable iteration vectors, the dependence relations are shown in the table below.

$$S_3[3,6] \; \delta^f \; S_3[3,4] \quad | \quad S_3[3,4] \; \delta^f \; S_3[3,2]$$
$$S_3[4,6] \; \delta^f \; S_3[4,4] \quad | \quad S_3[4,4] \; \delta^f \; S_3[4,2]$$
$$S_3[5,6] \; \delta^f \; S_3[5,4] \quad | \quad S_3[5,4] \; \delta^f \; S_3[5,2]$$
$$S_3[6,6] \; \delta^f \; S_3[6,4] \quad | \quad S_3[6,4] \; \delta^f \; S_3[6,2]$$
$$S_3[7,6] \; \delta^f \; S_3[7,4] \quad | \quad S_3[7,4] \; \delta^f \; S_3[7,2]$$

In each case, the dependence distance is $\mathbf{d} = (0, -2)$. We can summarize this by noting that the dependence is $S_3[i, j] \; \delta^f \; S_3[i, j-2]$, for appropriate values of i and j.

Using normalized iteration vectors, the dependence distance is $\mathbf{d} = (0, 1)$ (see Figure 5.5), which we would write $S_3 \; \delta^f_{(0,1)} \; S_3$.

5.1.4 Direction Vectors

Another frequently used but less precise annotation for data dependence relations is the ordering vector relating the source and target iteration vectors; this is called a *direction vector*. In the loop shown in Example 5.3, using the normalized iteration vectors, the direction vector is $(=, <)$, since for each source and target iteration $\mathbf{i}^S$ and $\mathbf{i}^T$,

$$i_1^S = i_1^T \quad (5.1)$$
$$i_2^S < i_2^T \quad (5.2)$$

If the compiler can compute a distance vector, it can infer the direction vector. Some optimizations need the sign of the dependence distance, but not its magnitude; for these optimizations, the direction vector is sufficient. Also, some dependence relations do not have a fixed distance, even though they may have a fixed direction. A direction vector with only $<$, $=$, and $>$ is *simple*.

Example 5.5

Find and characterize the data dependence relations in the following loop:

```
(1)     for I = 1 to 10 do
(2)        A[2*I] = B[I] + 1
(3)        C[I] = A[I]
(4)     endfor
```

Compute the dependence distance and direction vectors, if possible.

Solution

There are no dependence relations due to the array B, since it is only read in the loop. The array C is only written; since the same element is never written more than once, there are no output dependence relations for C. However, we must inspect the access patterns for the array A to determine the type of dependence relation. The table on the left in Figure 5.6 shows the element of A that is assigned and used by each iteration of the loop. The dependent relations are shown in the table on the right in Figure 5.6.

iteration vector	I	line 2	line 3	dependence relation	array element
(0)	1	A[2]=	=A[1]	$S_2[0] \; \delta^f \; S_3[1]$	A[2]
(1)	2	A[4]=	=A[2]	$S_2[1] \; \delta^f \; S_3[3]$	A[4]
(2)	3	A[6]=	=A[3]	$S_2[2] \; \delta^f \; S_3[5]$	A[6]
(3)	4	A[8]=	=A[4]	$S_2[3] \; \delta^f \; S_3[7]$	A[8]
(4)	5	A[10]=	=A[5]	$S_2[4] \; \delta^f \; S_3[9]$	A[10]
(5)	6	A[12]=	=A[6]		
(6)	7	A[14]=	=A[7]		
(7)	8	A[16]=	=A[8]		
(8)	9	A[18]=	=A[9]		
(9)	10	A[20]=	=A[10]		

FIGURE 5.6 Definitions and uses of array elements for example loop, and dependence relations showing varying dependence distance.

The dependence distance varies between 1 (from iteration 0 to iteration 1) and 5 (from iteration 4 to iteration 9). Since the distance is not fixed, we will write the dependence distance as $\star$, as in $S_2 \; \delta^f_{(\star)} \; S_3$. However, we can represent this dependence more precisely using a direction vector by writing $S_2 \; \delta^f_{(<)} \; S_3$.

5.1.5 Loop-Carried Dependence Relations

In the example shown in Figure 5.6 we see a flow dependence relation for the array A from line 3 to line 4 with a distance vector of $(0, 0)$, or, equivalently, a direction vector of $(=, =)$. If we focus only on the body of the loop, ignoring the presence if the two loop headers, these two references still have the same data dependence relation; A[I,J] depends on A[I,J] independent of whether I and J are loop index variables, or some other computed value.

The flow dependence relation for B from line 5 to line 6 in Figure 5.7 has a distance vector of $(0, 1)$ and a direction vector of $(=, <)$. If we focus on the body of the loop, again ignoring the two loop headers, there is no dependence relation; B[I,J] is independent of B[I,J+1], since J and J+1 are different values. If we

```
(1)   for I = 1 to N do
(2)     for J = 1 to M do
(3)       A[I,J] = ...
(4)       ... = A[I,J]
(5)       B[I,J+1] = ...
(6)       ... = B[I,J]
(7)       C[I+1,J] = ...
(8)       ... = C[I,J+1]
(9)     endfor
(10)  endfor
```

FIGURE 5.7 Example program showing dependence at different levels.

focus on the inner loop only (still ignoring the I loop), the two references are dependent between different iterations of the inner loop. Thus, this dependence relation is *carried* by the J loop.

Finally, the flow dependence for C from line 7 to line 8 has distance vector $(1, -1)$ and direction vector $(<, >)$. Again, focusing only on the body of the loop, there is no dependence relation for C. If we focus on the inner loop only, the two references are still independent; C[I+1,J] is independent of C[I,J+1] because I and I+1 are different values. Only when we take into account the I loop does the data dependence relation become obvious. This data dependence is *carried* by the outer loop.

We define the *dependence level* as the loop nest level for the loop that carries the data dependence relation. The C dependence is carried by the outer loop, so its level is 1; the B dependence is carried by the inner loop, so its level is 2; the A dependence is *loop independent*, so, by convention, its level is ∞.

There is a simple rule to find the dependence level from the direction vector or distance vector. If the direction vector has all equal entries (all zeros in the distance vector), then the dependence relation must be loop independent. For other dependence relations, the nest level of the outermost loop with a nonequal direction (nonzero distance) *carries* the dependence relation.

Example 5.6

Find the dependence levels for any data dependence relations in the loop shown in Example 5.3.

Solution

The only data dependence relation has distance vector $(0, 1)$, so the dependence level is 2.

5.1.6 More About Iteration Vectors

Two of the advantages of using normalized iteration vectors are that later iterations have larger iteration vector values than earlier iterations, and that adjacent iterations differ by only one in their iteration vectors. Neither of these advantages requires the first iteration to have the iteration vector $(0, 0, \ldots, 0)$. In fact, in some situations we want to relax that requirement. For instance, in the case of triangular or trapezoidal loops, where the iteration space has triangular or trapezoidal shape, we sometimes use iteration vectors such that the value on the first iteration of the inner loop depends on the outer loop. For instance, in the loop below:

```
(1)    for I = 1 to 7 do
(2)        for J = I to 7 do
(3)            A[I+1,J] = A[I,J] + 1
(4)        endfor
(5)    endfor
```

If we use normalized iteration vectors, the iteration space would be as shown in Figure 5.8. Note that the dependence distance vector in this case is $(1, -1)$.

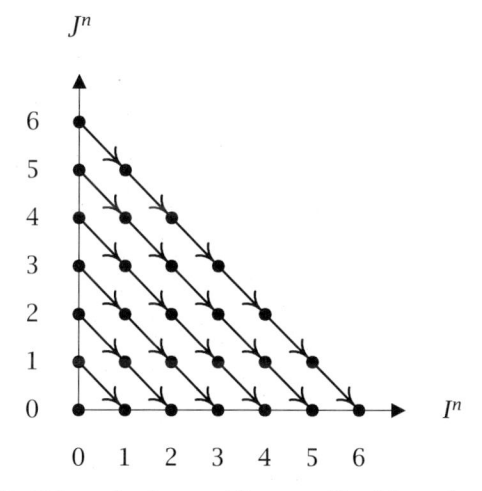

FIGURE 5.8 Triangular loop with normalized iteration vectors.

A more natural way to handle such a loop is to assign iteration vectors to get the same triangular shape that the index variables describe, as shown in Figure 5.9. The dependence distance vector with these iteration vectors is $(1, 0)$. In general, the compiler has quite a bit of freedom in assigning iteration vectors to the iterations. The natural advantages of using normalized iteration vectors do not require strictly normalizing the lower limit of the iteration vectors to zero. When the limits of inner loops depend on the outer loop index, compilers frequently use iteration vectors where the lower limit depends on the outer loop index. *Seminormalized* iteration vectors are assigned such that the distance between successive iterations is one, regardless of whether the lower limit is normalized to zero or some other value. There may even be situations where it is advantageous for the distance between successive iterations to be greater than one; even there, the iteration vectors should be assigned to be a subset of a lattice.

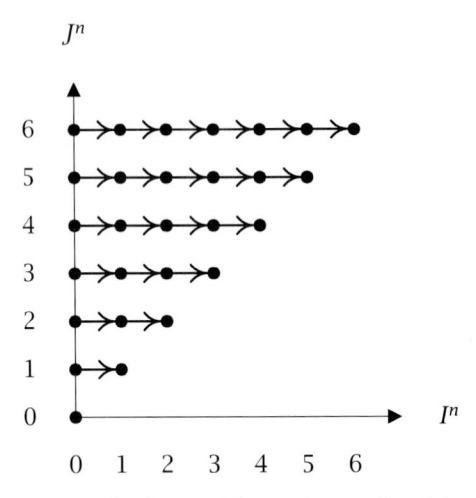

FIGURE 5.9 Triangular loop with seminormalized iteration vectors retains the same triangular shape.

In cases where there are two or more ways to assign iteration vectors, it is difficult to determine from basic principles whether to prefer one way or another. In Chapter 9, we will see how applying transformations changes the iteration vectors, making the initial assignment less important. It is important to remember that changing the iteration vectors can affect the dependence distance vectors.

Example 5.7

Show the iteration space and data dependence distance vector(s) for the following program:

```
(1)    for I = 1 to 8 do
(2)        for J = max(I-3,1) to min(I,5) do
(3)            A[I+1,J+1] = A[I,J] + B[I,J]
(4)        endfor
(5)    endfor
```

Solution

If we normalize the lower limit of the iteration space, the iteration vectors will be as shown in Figure 5.10; the dependence relations in the iteration space are

5.1 ▪ Data Dependence in Loops

also shown. Note that the dependence distance changes at the point where `I-3` becomes greater than one, which is where the `max` function in the loop lower limit crosses over.

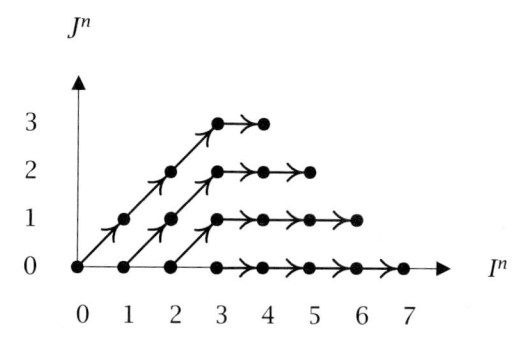

FIGURE 5.10   Strictly normalized iteration space for a loop with complex loop limits.

A more natural iteration vector labeling takes into account the shape of the original iteration space by normalizing only one of the operands of the `max` in the lower limit to zero. Since there are two operands, there are two ways to give such iteration vectors, as shown in Figures 5.11 and 5.12. The choice made in Figure 5.11 normalizes the one to zero, and the dependence direction vector is $(1, 0)$. The choice made in Figure 5.12 normalizes the `I-1` to zero, so the dependence direction vector is $(1, -1)$.

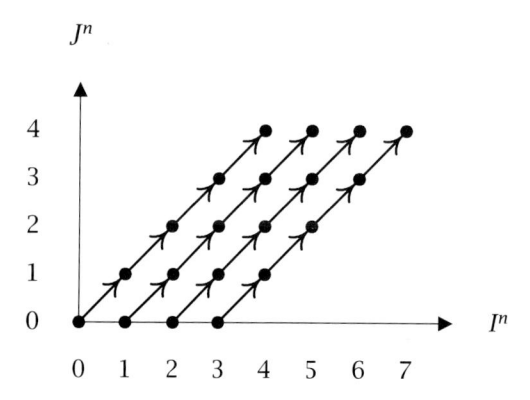

FIGURE 5.11   Seminormalized iteration space for a loop with complex loop limits.

5.1.7 Nontightly Nested Loops

All the examples so far have been of tightly nested loops; that is, there are no statements just before or just after the inner loop. A nontightly nested loop is

J^n

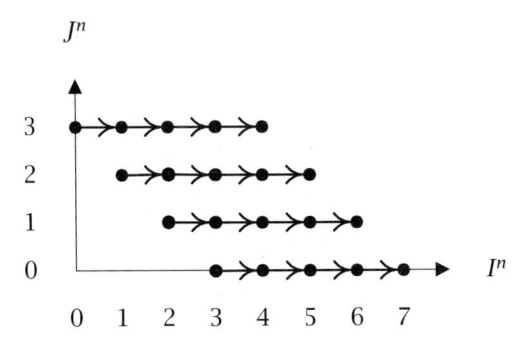

FIGURE 5.12 Another way to choose seminormalized iteration vectors for a loop with complex loop limits.

a nested loop whose outer loop contains additional statements outside the inner loop, perhaps even another, adjacent inner loop. For instance, we can write the back substitution algorithm as a nontightly nested loop, where A is the triangular matrix and B holds the right-hand side values and returns the solution as shown below.

```
(1)     for I = 1 to N do
(2)        B[I] = B[I] / A[I,I]
(3)        for J = I+1 to N do
(4)           B[J] = B[J] - A[I,J]*B[I]
(5)        endfor
(6)     endfor
```

Line 2 is indexed from 1 to N, while line 4 has a triangular iteration space. Thus the iteration space has two components, represented in Figure 5.13 (for N=5) by a box (for the statement at line 2) and a circle (for line 4). Here we use seminormalized iteration vectors (which are equivalent to the index variable iteration vectors).

Note the three dependence relations: Line 4 depends on line 2 (the arcs from the box to the circle in Figure 5.13) because line 2 assigns B[I] and line 4 uses it. There is dependence the other way (the arcs from the circle back to the box) because when J=I+1, line 4 assigns B[I+1], which is used in the next iteration of the outer loop at line 2. Finally, there is dependence from line 4 to itself because the next time around the loop, it uses and reassigns values to B[J].

We must be able to define data dependence distances and directions between the outer loop statements (line 2 in this case) and the inner loop body (line 4) in cases like this. The most general method is to treat the index sets for the different loop bodies independently. Data dependence distances and directions between the two bodies are computed only for the common loops, those that surround both bodies.

5.1 ▪ Data Dependence in Loops

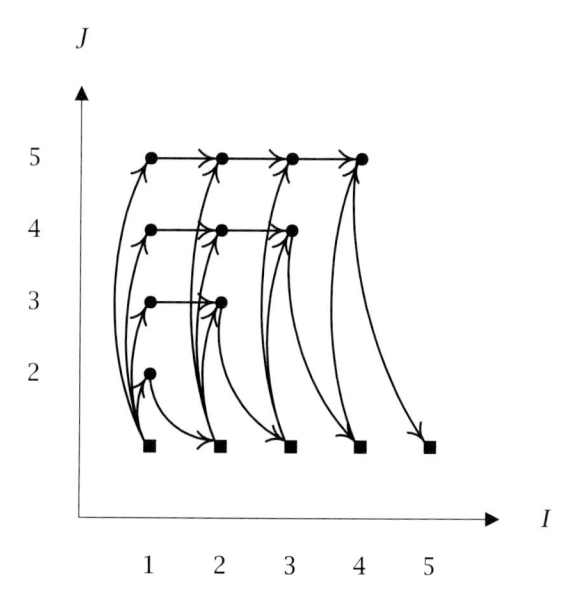

FIGURE 5.13 Iteration space for nontightly nested loop.

In this case, a data dependence distance vector between lines 2 and 4 would have only a single entry, for the `I` loop.

Example 5.8

Show the flow dependence relations and dependence distances for array `B` in the back substitution program. Use the seminormalized iteration vectors shown in Figure 5.13.

Solution

The seminormalized iteration vectors are equivalent to the index variable iteration vectors. Thus, statement $S_2[i]$ fetches and reassigns `B[i]`, while statement $S_4[i, j]$ fetches `B[i]` and `B[j]`, and reassigns `B[j]`.

$S_4[i, j]$ assigns `B[j]`, which is used by $S_4[i + 1, j]$. This results in the dependence relation $S_4 \; \delta^f_{(1,0)} \; S_4$. This pattern is repeated throughout the iteration space of the inner loop.

$S_2[i]$ assigns `B[i]`. This is used by $S_4[i, j]$ for $i \leq j \leq N$. The dependence distance is computed only for the common loop—in this case the outer loop. The distance between i and i is zero, giving us the dependence $S_2 \; \delta^f_{(0)} \; S_4$.

Finally, when $i = j$, $S_4[i, j]$ assigns `B[j]`, which is used by $S_2[i + 1]$. The distance between i and $i + 1$ is one, giving us the dependence relation $S_4 \; \delta^f_{(1)} \; S_2$.

Here we have used value-based dependence; if we use address-based dependence, we get a less precise characterization of the dependence relations.

Code Sinking

In cases where there is only a single inner loop, an alternate approach is to sink the outer loop body into the inner loop by adding a conditional. This can be done by effectively merging the statement(s) above the inner loop with the first iteration of the inner loop, and the statement(s) following the inner loop with its last iteration. A conditional statement protects the execution of the merged statement, so it is executed only once. A variation on this is to add an iteration to the inner loop for the outer loop body; conditional statements are again used to make sure that each statement is executed the proper number of times. In either case, the result is a single iteration space, and distance and direction vectors are well-defined. The details of code sinking are left for Chapter 9.

Example 5.9

Sink the outer loop statement into the inner loop in the back substitution program by adding an iteration to the inner loop. Show the new iteration space, and how the data dependence distance vectors have changed.

Solution

We will add a new iteration to the beginning of the inner loop, so the J loop will start at I instead of at I+1. Conditional statements will be used to ensure the proper execution. The resulting program is:

```
(1)     for I = 1 to N do
(3)        for J = I+1 to N do
(2)           if( J = I ) B[I] = B[I] / A[I,I]
(4)           if( J > I ) B[J] = B[J] - A[I,J]*B[I]
(5)        endfor
(6)     endfor
```

Now the iteration space has only one component for the combined loop body, and all data dependence distance and direction vectors will have two entries. Figure 5.14 shows the iteration space after this process; the nodes with squares represent the merged nodes.

The first of the three dependence relations computed in Example 5.8 is the same: $S_4 \; \delta^f_{(1,0)} \; S_4$.

The second dependence relation, from line 2 to 4, still has zero distance in the outer loop, but now has an inner loop component as well. The definition at iteration (i, i) is used by iterations (i, i), $(i, i + 1)$, and so on. Thus the dependence relation has no fixed distance in the inner loop. The distance is always positive, so we can write $S_2 \; \delta^f_{(=,<)} \; S_4$.

5.2 Data Dependence with Conditionals

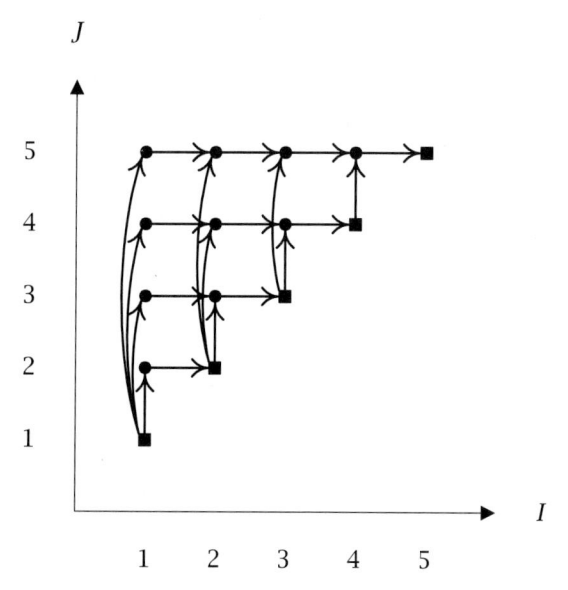

FIGURE 5.14 Iteration space for nontightly nested loop after sinking the nontightly nested statement into the inner loop.

The final dependence relation, from line 4 to 2, now goes from iteration (i, i) to $(i + 1, i + 1)$, producing the dependence relation $S_4 \; \delta^f_{(1,1)} \; S_2$.

5.2 Data Dependence with Conditionals

Our initial definition of data dependence relations described them in terms of assignment and the subsequent use of a variable. This clearly implies that there must be a path from the definition to the use. If there are conditional statements, the compiler cannot determine which path will be executed. It must assume that any path might be taken, and preserve any possible data dependence relation that might occur when the program is running. Data dependence cannot occur between statements that appear in alternate paths of a conditional, since there is no path from one to the other.

Example 5.10

Show the data dependence relations for variable X in the following program:

(1)   X = 1
(2)   Y = 2
(3)   if Y < T then
(4)   X = 2
(5)   else

(6)   Y = X
(7)   endif
(8)   Z = X + Y

Solution

There are definitions of X at lines 1 and 4 and uses of X at lines 6 and 8. There is a flow dependence relation from lines 1 to 6, since if line 6 executes, it will get its value from line 1. Even though line 4 lexically precedes line 6, there can be no dependence between these two lines, since their execution is mutually exclusive.

There are two flow dependence relations for X to line 8: from lines 1 and 4. In fact, line 4 may not execute. If it does, the value used at line 8 will always come from line 4. If it does not, then the value will always come from line 1. However, the compiler must find a conservative approximation to the actual dependence relations, adding all the possible relations that might occur during execution.

Finally, there is an output dependence relation from line 1 to line 4. Again, if line 4 executes, it must follow execution of line 1.

The dependence relations can be summarized as follows:

$$S_1 \; \delta^f \; S_6 \qquad S_1 \; \delta^f \; S_8 \qquad S_1 \; \delta^o \; S_4 \qquad S_4 \; \delta^f \; S_8$$

5.2.1 Conditionals in Loops

In a loop, a conditional may be used to branch around statements in the current iteration. Statements that can't be executed on the same iteration cannot be involved in a loop independent dependence relation. Conditionals will not, in general, affect loop carried dependence relations, since the path taken on a conditional in one iteration does not generally affect the path taken on the next or subsequent iteration.

Example 5.11

Show the data dependence relations in the following loop:

(1)   for I = 2 to 9 do
(2)   if A[I] > 0 then
(3)   A[I] = B[I-1] + 1
(4)   else
(5)   B[I] = A[I] * 2
(6)   endif
(7)   endfor

Solution

Since A[I] is used at line 2 and may be subsequently reassigned in the same iteration at line 3, we have the antidependence relation $S_2 \; \delta^a_{(0)} \; S_3$.

Note that A[I] is assigned in line 3 and is also used at line 5, but since both statements cannot execute in the same iteration, there can be no loop independent dependence.

However, the value assigned to B[I] at line 5 is used on the next iteration at line 3. Despite the conditional, since the compiler cannot determine what path will be taken on what iteration, it must assume that some iteration may take the false path, followed by an iteration that takes the true path. In that case, there will be a loop carried dependence from line 5 to line 3, written $S_5 \; \delta^f_{(1)} \; S_3$.

5.3 Data Dependence in Parallel Loops

All our examples so far have been in terms of sequential loops. Here we look at the three types of parallel looping constructs, and how they affect the computation of data dependence relations.

In general, to find data dependence relations the compiler must determine whether two references to the same variable can ever refer to the same element, and then whether these two references cause a data dependence relation. We say two statements or two loop iterations have a *data access conflict* when they can refer to the same memory location or variable. The rules for the control construct surrounding the data access conflict are used to resolve it into a dependence relation.

For a list of statements, data access conflicts are resolved by completing the first access before initiating the second; thus, an assignment followed by a use is resolved as a flow dependence by first completing the assignment, then fetching that new value. Similarly, a use followed by an assignment is resolved as an anti-dependence by completing the use (of the old value) before starting the assignment. In a sequential loop, data access conflicts between iterations are resolved by completing the access in the earlier iteration first. Using normalized or seminormalized iteration vectors, dependence distances in a sequential loop will always be either zero or positive. In nested sequential loops, dependence distance vectors will be zero or lexicographically positive.

As was mentioned earlier, a compiler usually does not need to preserve the ordering of two fetches of the same variable. Thus, data access conflicts between two variable uses do not usually result in dependence relations.

5.3.1 Forall Loop

A `forall` loop contains one or more assignment statements, and is equivalent to a sequence of array assignments; each statement is executed by computing the right-hand side expression for all values of the index set before any stores are done. The `forall` loop is carefully defined to avoid any dependence relations that would prevent parallel execution. It was originally designed with certain parallel machine models in mind, such as vector execution. Data access conflicts between iterations of a `forall` must be resolved by completing the lexically earliest access first. Note that this does not depend on the iteration in which the conflicts occur, so there can be negative dependence distances.

Example 5.12

Find the data dependence relations for the following loop:

(1)   forall I = 2 to 10 do
(2)   X[I] = X[I-1] + X[I+1]
(3)   endforall

Solution

Each iteration i defines an element X[I] that is used by iterations $i + 1$ and $i - 1$ (except for the boundary conditions). If this were a sequential loop, there would be a flow dependence from X[I] to X[I-1], and an antidependence from X[I+1] to X[I], preserving the data accesses in iteration order. However, the rules for executing a `forall` specify that the right-hand side expression is evaluated for all values of the index variable before any stores are done. Recall that lexical ordering defines the right-hand side of an assignment to precede the left-hand side. Thus, in a single statement of a `forall`, there can be no flow dependence relations, since all the fetches are done before any of the stores. Thus there are two anti-dependence relations, each from the assignment to itself, with distances (1) and (−1).

5.3.2 Dopar Loop

A dopar loop is defined such that each iteration starts with a copy of all variables with the values they had before the loop started; a value computed in one iteration cannot be fetched by any other iteration. Thus, there can only be no flow dependence relations between accesses in different iterations. If there is a data access conflict between two stores, the language model does not define which store takes precedence, so no dependence relation needs to be preserved by the compiler; in fact, it is likely to be an error on the part of the programmer. As mentioned in Chapter 2, a dopar that carries no dependence relations is also called a doall.

5.3 ▪ Data Dependence in Parallel Loops

Example 5.13

Find the data dependence relations for the program below:

(1)   dopar I = 2 to 20 do
(2)   X[I] = Y[I] + 1
(3)   Z[I] = X[I-1] + X[I] + X[I+1]
(4)   enddopar

Solution

The first few iterations produce the execution profile shown in the following table.

i^n	I	2	3
0	2	X[2] = Y[2] + 1	Z[2] = X[1] + X[2] + X[3]
1	3	X[3] = Y[3] + 1	Z[3] = X[2] + X[3] + X[4]
2	4	X[4] = Y[4] + 1	Z[4] = X[3] + X[4] + X[5]
⋮	⋮	⋮	⋮

Since the code within each iteration executes sequentially, the loop independent dependence relations are the same as for sequential code. Thus, there is a loop independent flow dependence relation from line 2 to line 3 due to the definition and use of X[I].

The loop carried dependence relations must use the rules for executing the dopar. For instance, iteration 1 defines X[3], which is used by iterations 0 and 2. In both cases, the value fetched must be the *old* value of X[3], not the value updated by iteration 1. Thus, both iterations have an antidependence relation to iteration 2. The dependence relations can be summarized as shown in the following table.

def	use	dependence	distance
X[I]	X[I-1]	anti-dependence	(−1)
X[I]	X[I]	flow dependence	(0)
X[I]	X[I+1]	anti-dependence	(1)

5.3.3 Dosingle Loop

In a dosingle loop, the single-assignment rule precludes any output dependence relations, since there is no redefinition of any variable. Similarly, there can be no anti-dependence, since each variable is defined only once. Thus, any data access conflicts must be resolved in favor of doing the definition first, followed by the use or fetch; this corresponds to flow dependence.

Example 5.14

Find the data dependence relations for the program below:

(1)   dosingle I = 2 to 20 do
(2)   X[I] = Y[I] + 1
(3)   Z[I] = X[I-1] + X[I] + X[I+1]
(4)   enddosingle

Solution

This is the same program as in Example 5.13, with the dopar replaced by a dosingle. The same execution profile applies; for a dosingle, however, all dependence relations are resolved in favor of flow dependence. The summary of the dependence relations is shown in the following table.

def	use	dependence	distance
X[I]	X[I-1]	flow dependence	(1)
X[I]	X[I]	flow dependence	(0)
X[I]	X[I+1]	flow dependence	(−1)

5.3.4 Other Constructs

The design of coherent parallel language control constructs, especially as extensions to an existing sequential language, is a challenge. When programming a parallel machine, we want to be able to explicitly specify the parallelism in the algorithm. However, there is also a natural desire to be able to execute programs with forall loops on multiprocessors, or dopar loops on vector machines, or all these programs on uniprocessor workstations. Thus we must understand how the various loop constructs affect the computation of data dependence relations. We use the dependence relations to capture all the necessary precedence information; if we are successful, then the compiler can restructure or change the execution order of the loop to optimize for more efficient execution on the target machine.

A common parallel language extension is to define a parallel loop such that different iterations may execute concurrently on different processors, where memory accesses are completed in a sequentially consistent manner. Sequential consistency is preserved if the memory accesses of all processors that are cooperating in the execution of a parallel program appear to be ordered in some sequential order, and all processors appear to see the same sequential order. In its strictest implementation, this requires sequential access to a global memory, which would be a performance bottleneck. In fact, many hardware tricks can be used to give the appearance of sequential consistency while still allowing parallel memory accesses. In such a parallel loop, the resolution between data access conflicts in different iterations is not defined. However, because sequential consistency requires all memory accesses to appear to be ordered, the compiler is also restricted in reordering *any* two memory accesses, even accesses to different variables, unless it can prove that the reordering is not visible to other processors. This is a very difficult problem in general. Since it arises only in the scope of poor programming language designs, we will not explore it further here.

5.3.5 Nested Loops

We have already seen how to resolve data access conflicts in some nested constructs. For instance, in nested sequential loops, if there is a data access conflict between different iterations, it is resolved as a data dependence relation so the dependence distance vector is lexicographically positive.

We can find a data access conflict distance vector (or direction vector) between two iterations that have a conflict. Since the data access conflict relation is unordered, a conflict distance between iterations **i** and **j** can be computed as $\mathbf{d}_{ji} = \mathbf{i} - \mathbf{j}$ or $\mathbf{d}_{ij} = \mathbf{j} - \mathbf{i}$. The rules for resolving data access conflicts into data dependence relations will determine which of these is the dependence distance vector. If it is a dependence from iteration **i** to **j**, we use distance $\mathbf{d}_{ji}$.

As with data dependence relations, a data access conflict is carried by the outermost loop construct with a nonzero data access conflict distance. When resolving data access conflicts into data dependence relations, we look at the outermost loop construct that carries the conflict.

- A data access conflict carried by a sequential `for` loop is resolved so that the dependence distance for that loop is positive (assuming normalized or seminormalized iteration vectors).
- A data access conflict carried by a `dopar` loop is resolved as an anti-dependence between definitions and uses. Between two definitions to the same variable or array element, no ordering is defined, so no dependence ordering needs to be preserved.
- A data access conflict carried by a `dosingle` loop is resolved as a flow dependence between definitions and uses. If there are two definitions to the same variable or array element carried by a `dosingle`, it is an error.
- A data access conflict carried by a `forall` loop is resolved by the rules for the construct inside the `forall`. Usually this is a list of statements, where the rule is to execute the statements in lexical order. However, this rule allows us to write `forall` loops that contain other loops as well.

5.4 Program Dependence Graph

Example 5.10 computed data dependence relations in the presence of conditional control flow. In such cases, the compiler can add the control dependence relations to the same graph as the data dependence relations. With both kinds of edges, this is called a *program dependence graph*, or PDG, comprising two subgraphs: the data dependence subgraph and the control dependence subgraph. Whenever ambiguity might result, we annotate the control dependence edges in the graph with a small *c*. Figure 5.15 shows the program dependence graph for the loop shown in Example 5.10, with one node for each (nontrivial) statement. Note that statements 4 and 6 are both control-dependent on the conditional statement 3, but with opposite labels. A program dependence graph gives a compiler a way to capture both the data and control precedence constraints that prevent it from reordering operations in the program.

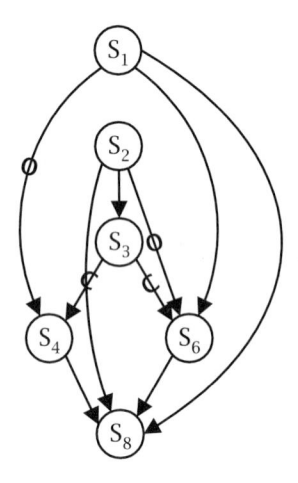

FIGURE 5.15 Program dependence graph.

5.5 In the Pit

Flow dependence, anti-dependence, and output dependence correspond directly to the def-use, use-def, and def-def ordering constraints that are used in instruction scheduling optimizations. Most compilers compute reaching definition information for scalars, which is equivalent to value-based flow dependence.

Some of the literature uses slightly different notation for dependence relations. You may see δ instead of δ^f for flow dependence and $\bar{\delta}$ instead of δ^a for anti-dependence. Banerjee (1993) even uses $\bar{\bar{\delta}}$ for indirect data dependence.

Some descriptions use $(+, -, 0)$ instead of $(<, >, =)$ for direction vectors, with $\pm$ or $0+$ entries for nonsimple directions. Other descriptions use the sign of the distance vector, $sign(\mathbf{d})$, as the direction vector, so the entries are 0, 1, or -1.

When computing data dependence information, the compiler may want to save the information in a dependence graph data structure. The information should include pointers to the source and target of the dependence relation, the type of dependence, and the distance or direction vector. The distance vector is a vector of integers, which may not always be known constants. The compiler may keep a flag for each loop level to show whether the distance is a known constant. Alternatively, the compiler can keep the minimum and maximum distance values.

A convenient representation for direction vectors is a bit vector, with three bits allocated to each loop nest level. In a 32-bit word, a direction vector can be stored for loops nested up to 10 deep. A 64-bit word can hold a direction vector for 21 nested loops, which is probably larger than most compilers will need to optimize. The problem is how to store a direction vector with more than one direction in a single position; for instance, how to store a ($\leq$) direction. This can be done by using two distinct bit vectors, which is precise but takes space and compile time to initialize and search. It can also be done by a simple bitwise **or** of the two bit vectors for the ($<$) and ($=$) directions; this can be imprecise, however. For instance, a bitwise **or** of the three direction vectors:

$$(=, <) \vee (<, <) \vee (<, =) \Rightarrow (\leq, \leq)$$

can't be distinguished from the combination:

$$(=, <) \vee (<, <) \vee (<, =) \vee (=, =) \Rightarrow (\leq, \leq)$$

That is, once the directions are combined, there is no way to tell whether the $(=, =)$ direction is included. This can be a real problem, since the $(=, =)$ direction prevents reordering within a single iteration of the loop.

A second problem is that the combination may include implausible directions, as with:

$$(<, <) \vee (<, =) \vee (<, >) \vee (=, <) \vee (=, =) \Rightarrow (\leq, *)$$

From this combination, it seems as if the program might have dependence with the direction $(=, >)$, which may be implausible.

Both of these problems can be addressed relatively simply. Implausible directions can be ignored within the compiler. Most of the uses of direction vectors are to test for the presence of a dependence with a particular direction; since implausible directions are never tested, their presence will cause no problems.

The problem with the spurious $(=, =)$ direction can be handled by adding one more bit to the direction vector, corresponding to a loop independent dependence relation. If the bit is not set, then there is no loop independent dependence regardless of what is stored in the direction vector. This does not solve all the problems with a bit-vector representation for direction vectors, but is sufficient for many uses. Even if direction vectors are never combined, a bit vector representation is concise and convenient for many operations.

One advantage of direction vectors over distance vectors is that the compiler may be able to include some semantic information, rather than simply ordering information. One suggestion is to allow a special "direction" for reductions. A reduction occurs when a loop accumulates a value into a scalar, such as a sum reduction in the following loop:

```
(1)    for I = 1 to N do
(2)        S = S + A[I]
(3)    endfor
```

For variable S there is a flow dependence with distance one, since the value assigned in one iteration is used in the next iteration. However, mathematically the sum can be accumulated in any order. If the compiler can ignore roundoff error differences between different accumulation orders (see Section 2.3), it should be able to reorder the iterations of the loop with impunity. There is no way to incorporate this information in a dependence distance vector. If we allow a special "reduction" direction, the compiler can encode this case as $S_2 \; \delta^f_{(R)} \; S_2$.

5.6 Further Reading

The concepts of data dependence have been well known for quite some time (Bernstein [1966]); data dependence distance vectors have long been used in the systolic array community to generate regular communication patterns (Karp et al. [1967]). Allen and Kennedy (1987) coined the terms *dependence level*, *loop carried*, and *loop independent dependence*. Kuck et al. (1981) and Allen et al. (1987) show how to use dependence graphs for parallelization and other optimizations.

The distinction between address-based and value-based dependence relations arises frequently. Brandes (1988) uses the term *direct dependence* for value-based dependence; using direct dependences, more aggressive dead code elimination can be done, and variable renaming can be used to eliminate false dependence relations.

EXERCISES

5.1 Find all the data dependence relations, using value-based and address-based definitions, for the following sequence of statements:

```
(1)    B = A * 2
(2)    C = B + 1
(3)    if( C > 0 )then
(4)        B = C + 1
(5)    else
(6)        B = B - 1
(7)    endif
(8)    E = B - D
```

5.2 Find all the data dependence relations in the following loop, including dependence distances:

```
(1)    for I = 3 to N do
(2)        A[I] = (A[I-2] + A[I+2])/2
(3)    endfor
```

5.3 Draw the iteration space of the loop in the previous exercise, including an edge for any loop-carried dependence relation.

5.4 Find all the data dependence relations in the following loop, including dependence distances:

```
(1)    for I = 3 to N by 2 do
(2)        A[I] = (A[I-1] + A[I+1])/2
(3)    endfor
```

5.5 Draw the iteration space of the loop in the previous exercise, including an edge for any loop-carried dependence relation.

5.6 Find all the data dependence relations in the following loop, including dependence distances:

```
(1)    for I = 3 to N by 2 do
(2)        A[I] = (A[I-2] + A[I+2])/2
(3)    endfor
```

5.7 Draw the iteration space of the loop in the previous exercise, including an edge for any loop-carried dependence relation.

5.8 Find all the data dependence relations in the following loop, including dependence distances:

```
(1)    for I = 3 to N by 2 do
(2)        for J = I to N by 2 do
(3)            A[I,J] = (A[I-1,J-1] + A[I+2,J-1])/2
(4)        endfor
(5)    endfor
```

Draw the iteration space of the loop, using for the iterations any iteration vector label you please, and include an edge for any loop-carried dependence relation.

5.9 Find all the data dependence relations for the back substitution loop (including flow, anti-, and output dependence relations). Use both the value-based and address-based definitions.

5.10 Write a doubly nested loop with a dependence relation carried by the inner loop.

5.11 Write a doubly nested loop with an anti-dependence relation with $(1, -2)$ distance vector.

5.12 The last exercise in Chapter 1 shows a loop for Gaussian elimination. Find all the data dependence relations, including distance or direction vectors, for that loop.

5.13 Another way to order the loops for the back substitution algorithm is as follows:

```
(1)    for J = 1 to N do
(2)        for I = 1 to J-1 do
(3)            B[J] = B[J] - A[I,J]*B[I]
(4)        endfor
```

(5)   B[I] = B[I] / A[I,I]
(6)   endfor

Find all the dependence relations in this loop and comment on the differences between these dependence relations and those from the original formulation.

5.14 Show the iteration space for the reordered version of back substitution in the previous exercise, and show all the dependence relations.

5.15 When sinking the body of an outer loop into an inner loop (using conditionals), a problem that must be addressed is handling the situation when the inner loop index is sometimes empty. One way to alleviate this problem is to *peel off* one or more iterations of the outer loop so that the inner loop index set is always nonempty. This can happen when the inner loop limits depend on the outer loop index (triangular inner loop). For the program in exercise 13, the inner loop index set is empty for the first iteration of the outer loop. First, sink the outer loop body into the inner loop without peeling. Then, show the program after peeling off the first iteration of the outer loop, and sinking the outer loop body into the inner loop. Is the inner loop simpler than it was without peeling?

5.16 Devise a general method to determine how many iterations, if any, of the outer loop need to be peeled off to make the inner loop index set always nonempty, given the loop limits of the inner and outer loops.

5.17 Find all the data dependence relations for the following program, replacing the word loop by for, forall, dopar, and dosingle in turn.

(1)   loop I = 2 to 9 do
(2)   P[I] = W[I+1] + 1
(3)   Q[I] = W[I-1] + 1
(4)   R[I] = W[I] + 1
(5)   W[I] = A[I] + B[I]
(6)   X[I] = W[I] + 1
(7)   Y[I] = W[I-1] + 1
(8)   Z[I] = W[I+1] + 1
(9)   endloop

5.18 What does it mean for a dopar loop to contain a for loop? Define how to resolve data access conflicts in this case, and show the dependence relations for the following program:

(1)   dopar I = 2 to 9 do
(2)   for J = 2 to 9 do
(3)   X[I,J] = A[I] + B[J]
(4)   Y[I,J] = X[I-1,J] + X[I,J-1]
(5)   Z[I,J] = X[I+1,J] + X[I,J+1]
(6)   endfor
(7)   enddopar

5.19 What does it mean for a for loop to contain a forall? Define how to resolve data access conflicts in this case, and show the dependence relations for the following program:

```
(1)    for I = 2 to 9 do
(2)        forall J = 2 to 9 do
(3)            X[I,J] = A[I] + B[J]
(4)            Y[I,J] = X[I-1,J] + X[I,J-1]
(5)            Z[I,J] = X[I+1,J] + X[I,J+1]
(6)        endforall
(7)    endfor
```

5.20 Prove that a `forall` loop containing a single assignment statement always computes the same result as a `dopar` containing the same statement, by showing that the two types of loop preserve the same dependence relations for a single statement.

5.21 One of the key transformations of parallelizing compilers is the ability to convert a sequential loop into a parallel one. When can a loop be converted from a sequential loop into a `dopar`? Characterize such a loop by the types of dependence relations that can occur in the sequential loop and that will be preserved by the parallel one.

5.22 When can a parallel `dopar` loop be converted into a sequential `for` loop? Give an example of a `dopar` loop that cannot be trivially converted into a `for` loop.

5.23 Give an example of a `forall` loop that cannot be trivially converted into a `for` loop because the `for` loop will not preserve all the dependence relations.

6 SCALAR ANALYSIS WITH FACTORED USE-DEF CHAINS

Compiler scalar analysis is necessary to support other advanced analysis techniques. In this chapter we introduce factored use-def chains, a sparse representation of use-def chains. We discuss ways to handle arrays and implicit variable references, and give details of three types of analysis based on factored use-def chains: constant propagation, induction variable recognition, and data dependence analysis for scalars.

A compiler often needs to find precise information about the values of variables at various points in the program. For instance, in order to perform precise data dependence analysis in the following program fragment, the compiler must be able to determine that variable K always has the constant value 1 in the array subscript where it is used:

(1)   K = 1
(2)   for I = 2 to N do
(3)   A[I] = A[I-K] + B[I]
(4)   endfor

In this case, the definition of K appears just before the loop, and the value assigned to K is a simple constant. Simple compiler analysis can determine that K has the constant value 1 inside the loop.

   A definition of a variable reaches a use if there is a path in the control flow graph from the definition to the use that does not contain any other definitions of that variable. A compiler can find all the reaching definitions at each use by formulating and solving a data-flow problem. One classical analysis method is to use a bit-vector algorithm, with one bit for each definition. The reaching-definitions solution can be used directly, or it can be used to construct a use-def chain of reaching definitions for each use (or a def-use chain of uses reached by each definition). The use-def chains can then be used for further analysis. For example, we can compute the reaching definitions for the program in Figure 6.1(a). We first label each variable definition and use by a subscript, and shown in Figure 6.1(b).

CHAPTER 6 ▪ *Scalar Analysis with Factored Use-Def Chains*

```
(1)   K = 0                    (1)   K₁ = 0
(2)   if T > K then            (2)   if T₂ > K₃ then
(3)       K = K + 1            (3)       K₅ = K₄ + 1
(4)       M = K * 2            (4)       M₇ = K₆ * 2
(5)   else                     (5)   else
(6)       M = K / 2            (6)       M₉ = K₈ / 2
(7)   endif                    (7)   endif
(8)   K2 = K + 2               (8)   K2₁₁ = K₁₀ + 2
(9)   K3 = K + 3               (9)   K3₁₃ = K₁₂ + 3
(10)  K4 = K + M               (10)  K4₁₆ = K₁₄ + M₁₅

           (a)                            (b)
```

FIGURE 6.1 Reaching definitions example; (a) original and (b) with references labeled.

The reaching definitions after each statement are listed in the following table.

line	reaching defs
1	K_1
2	K_1
3	K_5
4	K_5, M_7
5	K_1
6	K_1, M_9
7	K_1, K_5, M_7, M_9
8	$K_1, K_5, M_7, M_9, K2_{11}$
9	$K_1, K_5, M_7, M_9, K2_{11}, K3_{13}$
10	$K_1, K_5, M_7, M_9, K2_{11}, K3_{13}, K4_{16}$

This analysis finds definitions that reach each point in the program, regardless of whether that variable is used at that point. Use-def chains are direct links from each variable use to the reaching definitions, and can be constructed from the reaching-definitions solution. We represent use-def chains by showing the link from each use to the reaching defs, such as $K_{10 \leadsto 1,5}$ to show that the use K_{10} has use-def links to the definitions K_1 and K_5.

```
(1)   K₁ = 0
(2)   if T₂ > K₃↝1 then
(3)       K₅ = K₄↝1 + 1
(4)       M₇ = K₆↝5 * 2
(5)   else
(6)       M₉ = K₈↝1 / 2
```

(7)   endif
(8) $K2_{11} = K_{10 \leadsto 1,5} + 2$
(9) $K3_{13} = K_{12 \leadsto 1,5} + 3$
(10) $K4_{16} = K_{14 \leadsto 1,5} + M_{15 \leadsto 7,9}$

The use-def chains can be used to recognize that the use K_4 has only one reaching-definition, K_1, and so must have constant value of zero.

One problem with both reaching definitions and use-def chains is that they are not very space efficient. The reaching definitions bit-vectors use d bits at each node in the CFG, where d is the number of definitions in the program. Use-def chains directly link uses to defs, but contain redundant information; in Figure 6.1, three of the uses of K have identical nontrivial use-def chains. Also, use-def chains are typically constructed from reaching-definitions information.

Another problem is that the resulting information is not as precise as we would like for optimization purposes. For instance, suppose the compiler could determine that the conditional in Figure 6.1 was always false. Lines 3 and 4 could then be eliminated as unreachable code. Subsequent analysis would find only one reaching definition of K to lines 8–10, from line 1. Thus the compiler could determine constant values for K2, K3, and K4. If, on the other hand, the compiler determined that the conditional was always true, there would be no dead definitions of K, since the reaching definitions problem was solved before the compiler noticed that line 2 was an invariant branch. To take full advantage of the newly discovered constant conditional test, the compiler would have to solve the reaching-definitions problem and construct the use-def chains from scratch.

Here we introduce a factored form of use-def chains (*factored use-def chains*, or FUD chains), and algorithms to construct them. FUD chains have two important properties. The first is that each use of a variable is reached by a single definition: the use-def chain for any one use is a single link to the unique reaching definition. The second property handles control-flow merge points, when multiple reaching definitions exist in the original program. At merge points, special merge operators called ϕ-terms (Greek *phi*) are inserted into the program when there are multiple reaching definitions. These are essentially pseudo-assignments that factor the multiple incoming reaching definitions, and are used to satisfy the first property for any variable uses after the control-flow merger. The ϕ-term serves as the reaching definition for any uses after the control-flow merge, at which point it factors the reaching definitions. The FUD chain representation is thus more *sparse* than full use-def chains, since the uses after the merge point have only a single FUD chain link, compared to several links at each use.

Example 6.1

Show the FUD chains for variables K and M in the program fragment shown in Figure 6.1.

Solution

The endif at line 7 is a control-flow confluence point with two distinct reaching definitions for K and M. Thus, two ϕ-terms will be added at that line, one for each variable. Using the same reference numbering scheme as shown in Figure 6.1(b), the factored use-def chains for K and M are as shown in Figure 6.2. Each use of

(1) $K_1 = 0$
(2)   if $T_2 > K_{3 \leadsto 1}$ then
(3) $K_5 = K_{4 \leadsto 1} + 1$
(4) $M_7 = K_{6 \leadsto 5} * 2$
(5)   else
(6) $M_9 = K_{8 \leadsto 1} / 2$
(7)   endif
       $\phi(K)_{17 \leadsto 5,1}$
       $\phi(M)_{18 \leadsto 7,9}$
(8) $K2_{11} = K_{10 \leadsto 17} + 2$
(9) $K3_{13} = K_{12 \leadsto 17} + 3$
(10) $K4_{16} = K_{14 \leadsto 17} + M_{15 \leadsto 18}$

FIGURE 6.2   FUD chains solution.

K or M thus has a single reaching definition, while the ϕ-terms have one reaching definition for each control-flow predecessor.

6.1 Constructing Factored Use-Def Chains

Constructing factored use-def chains comprise two phases:

1. Adding the ϕ-terms at control flow merge points for each variable with multiple reaching definitions, and
2. Linking each variable use to the unique reaching definition or ϕ-term.

For straight-line and structured code, this is relatively easy. To handle the general case, we need a more formal approach.

First we need to define exactly where ϕ-terms are needed. If M is a variable in the program, and X_1 and X_2 are nodes in the flow graph that assign M ($X_1 \neq X_2$) satisfying the following four conditions:

1.   Z is a CFG node with two distinct predecessors, Y_1 and Y_2;
2. $p_1 : X_1 \xrightarrow{*} Y_1$ and $p_2 : X_2 \xrightarrow{*} Y_2$ are two paths in the CFG;
3. p_1 and p_2 have no nodes in common; and
4.   there are no definitions of M along either path p_1 or p_2 (except at X_1 and X_2),

then a ϕ-term is needed at vertex Z for variable M. Note that Z may be equal to either X_1 or X_2, but $X_1 \neq X_2$.

In fact, we can relax the fourth condition above; if there is another definition on one of the two paths—say at vertex W on path $p_1 : X_1 \xrightarrow{+} Y_1$—we can use the two paths $p'_1 : W \xrightarrow{+} Y_1$ and $p_2 : X_2 \xrightarrow{+} Y_2$, and a ϕ-term will still be needed at Z.

Example 6.2

Show where ϕ-terms are needed in the control flow graph for the program fragment shown in Figure 6.1.

Solution

The CFG for this program is shown in Figure 6.3, with *Entry* and *Exit* nodes added; in this graph, each node corresponds to a single line of the program. There are assignments to variable K at nodes S_1 and S_3. The two paths $p_1 : S_1 \rightarrow S_2 \rightarrow S_6$ and $p_2 : S_3 \rightarrow S_4$ are paths from nodes containing assignments to two distinct predecessors of S_7. Moreover, the only assignment to K occurs at the first node of each path, and no node appears on both paths. Thus a ϕ-term is needed for K at node S_7.

Similarly, there are assignments to variable M at nodes S_4 and S_6, and trivial paths from these nodes to two distinct predecessors of S_7. Again, a ϕ-term is needed for M at node S_7.

6.1.1 Join Sets

We define the *join* of two distinct vertices in the CFG, $J(X_1, X_2) = \{Z\}$ such that:

- $\exists p_1 : X_1 \xrightarrow{*} Y_1$ and $\exists p_2 : X_2 \xrightarrow{*} Y_2$;
- $Y_1 \rightarrow Z$ and $Y_2 \rightarrow Z$; and
- $p_1 \cap p_2 = \emptyset$,

where the intersection of two paths is defined as the set of nodes that appear on both paths. By convention, $J(X, X) = \emptyset$ for any node X. That is, the join of X_1 and X_2 is the set of vertices Z such that

1. there is a path p_1 from X_1 to a predecessor of Z;
2. there is a path p_2 from X_2 to a different predecessor of Z; and
3. no vertex on the path p_1 appears on the path p_2, and vice versa.

If there are assignments to any variable M at vertices X_1 and X_2, then a ϕ-term for M is needed at all nodes in $J(X_1, X_2)$.

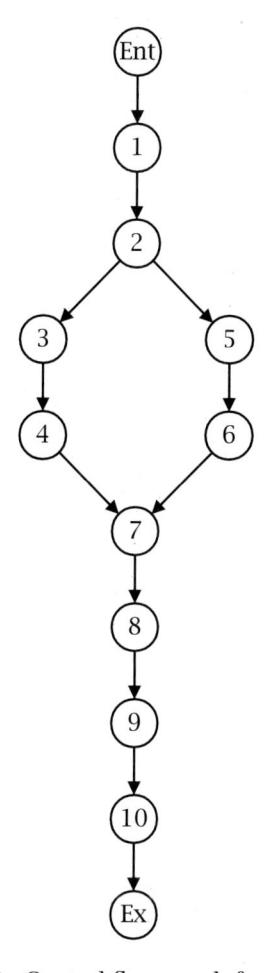

FIGURE 6.3 Control flow graph for example.

Given a set of vertices S, we define the join of that set as the union of the pairwise joins:

$$J(S) = \bigcup_{X_1, X_2 \in S} J(X_1, X_2)$$

Given a set of assignments S for variable M, ϕ-terms will be needed for M at $J(S)$. Of course, this adds some new pseudo-assignments to M, so we may need to iterate this process to find the join of the new assignments with themselves, as well as with the old set of assignments. We define the sequence:

$$J^1(S) = J(S)$$
$$J^2(S) = J(S \cup J^1(S))$$
$$J^i(S) = J(S \cup J^{i-1}(S))$$
$$J^+(S) = limit_{i \to \infty} J^i(S)$$

Since $J^i(S) \subseteq J^{i-1}(S)$, the sets monotonically increase in size; because CFG is a finite graph, the sequence must eventually terminate. The nodes in the *iterated join set*, $J^+(S)$, where S is the original set of assignments to a variable M, are exactly the points in the program where ϕ-terms are needed. These are all the points in the program that two or more distinct definitions can reach.

Example 6.3

For the control flow graph shown in Figure 6.4, find the iterated join set for the set of nodes $\{Entry, S_1, S_5\}$.

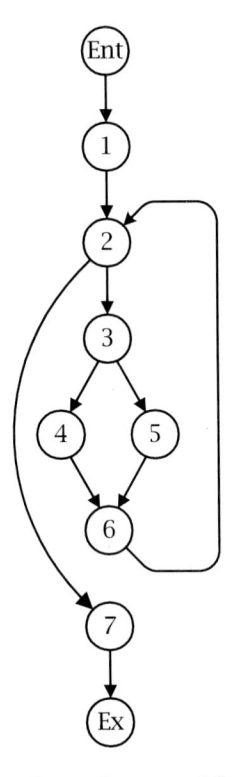

FIGURE 6.4 Example control flow graph.

Solution

Paths S_1 and $S_5 \to S_6$ are two paths to distinct predecessors of S_2 with no nodes in common, so $S_2 \in J(S_1, S_5)$. Additionally, $S_1 \to S_2 \to S_3 \to S_4$ and S_5 are two paths to distinct predecessors of S_6, again with no common nodes, so $S_6 \in J(S_1, S_5)$. The same two nodes are in $J(Entry, S_5)$. No new nodes are added by iteration, so $J(\{Entry, S_1, S_5\}) = \{S_2, S_6\}$.

6.1.2 Equivalence to Iterated Dominance Frontier

Computing the iterated join set directly would be expensive. Fortunately, there is a more efficient way to place ϕ-terms. The definition of the dominance frontier of a node X is

$$DF(X) = \{Z \mid (\exists Y_1, Y_2 \in \text{PRED}(Z))[X \text{ DOM } Y] \wedge [X \overline{\text{DOM}} Y_2]\}$$

As with join sets, given a set of vertices X, we define the dominance frontier of the set as the union of the individual dominance frontiers:

$$DF(S) = \bigcup_{X \in S} DF(X)$$

We define the sequence:

$$DF^1(S) = DF(S)$$
$$DF^2(S) = DF(s \cup DF^1(S))$$
$$DF^i(S) = DF(s \cup DF^{i-1}(S))$$
$$DF^+(S) = \lim_{i \to \infty} DF^i(S)$$

Here we will show that $DF^+(S) = J^+(S)$, if $Entry \in S$. We start by showing that given a path $p : X \stackrel{*}{\to} Y$ and an edge $Y \to Z$, either $Z \in DF^+(X)$ or there is some node $W \in \{X\} \cup DF^+(X)$ such that $W \text{ DOM } Z$. Let W be the last node on the path p in $\{X\} \cup DF^+(X)$. It is easy to show that $W \text{ DOM } Y$; if not, then there is some node W' on the path $W \stackrel{+}{\to} Y$ such that W dominates a predecessor of W' but does not dominate W' itself. In that case, $W' \in DF(W)$, and therefore $W' \in DF^+(X)$, contradicting the choice of W. Therefore, $W \text{ DOM } Y$. If $W \text{ DOM } Z$, we are done; if not, then W dominates a predecessor of Z (namely, Y) but not Z itself, so $Z \in DF(W)$, and therefore $Z \in DF^+(X)$.

Now we show that for any two distinct vertices X_1 and X_2,

$$Z \in J(X_1, X_2) \Longrightarrow Z \in DF^+(X_1) \cup DF^+(X_2)$$

If $Z \in J(X_1, X_2)$, then there are paths $p_1 : X_1 \stackrel{*}{\to} Y_1$ and $p_2 : X_2 \stackrel{*}{\to} Y_2$, with $Y_1 \to Z$ and $Y_2 \to Z$, such that $p_1 \cap p_2 = \emptyset$. Let W_1 be the last node in $\{X_1\} \cup DF^+(X_1)$ on the path p_1, and W_2 be the last node in $\{X_2\} \cup DF^+(X_2)$ on the path p_2. Note that $W_1 \neq W_2$ since the paths p_1 and p_2 are disjoint. We have already shown that either $W_1 \text{ DOM } Z$ or $Z \in DF^+(X_1)$, and either $W_2 \text{ DOM } Z$ or $Z \in DF^+(X_2)$. Thus, $Z \in DF^+(X_1) \cup DF^+(X_2)$ is true unless $W_1 \text{ DOM } Z$ and $W_2 \text{ DOM } Z$. In that case, both W_1 and W_2 appear on all paths from $Entry$ to Z; one of them must appear later than the other. Suppose W_2 appears later than W_1; then any path from W_1 to Z must include W_2, making the paths p_1 and p_2 nondisjoint. Therefore, $Z \in DF^+(X_1) \cup DF^+(X_2)$.

This shows that $J(X_1, X_2) \subseteq DF^+(\{X_1, X_2\})$. Simple extension shows that $J(S) \subseteq DF^+(S)$, for any set of nodes S. Induction on i in the definition of $J^+(S)$ gives us the series of set containments

$$J^{i+1}(S) = J(S \cup J^i(S)) \subseteq J(S \cup DF^+(S)) \subseteq DF^+(S \cup DF^+(S)) = DF^+(S)$$

This shows that $J^+(S) \subseteq DF^+(S)$.

To show containment in the other direction, suppose we have a set S of nodes such that $Entry \in S$. We show that $Z \in DF(S) \Longrightarrow Z \in J(S)$. Given $X \in S$ and $Y \in DF(X)$, we must have a path $p_1 : X \xrightarrow{+} Y$ where all nodes on the path before Y are dominated by X. It follows that there must be another path, $p_2 : Entry \xrightarrow{*} Y$, where none of the nodes on the path before Y are dominated by X. Thus, the paths p_1 and p_2 are disjoint, except at Y; therefore, $Y \in J(Entry, X)$.

Induction on i in the definitions of $J^+(S)$ and $DF^+(S)$ gives us $DF^+(S) \subseteq J^+(S)$. Since we have containment in both directions, $DF^+(S) = J^+(S)$. Thus we can use iterated dominance frontiers to place the ϕ-terms. In fact, for any set of nodes S, $DF^+(S) = J^+(S \cup \{Entry\})$, since $DF(Entry) = \emptyset$.

Example 6.4

Find the iterated dominance frontier of the set of nodes $\{Entry, S_1, S_5\}$ for the control flow graph shown in Figure 6.4.

Solution

The dominance frontiers of the three nodes in the set are:

$$DF(Entry) \quad \emptyset$$
$$DF(S_2) \quad \emptyset$$
$$DF(S_5) \quad \{S_6\}$$

Thus, $DF(\{Entry, S_1, S_5\}) = \{S_6\}$; iterating, we add the dominance frontier of S_6. Thus, $DF^2(\{Entry, S_1, S_5\}) = DF(\{Entry, S_1, S_5\} \cup \{S_6\}) = \{S_6\} \cup \{S_2\}$. Further iteration does not increase the set, so $DF^+(\{Entry, S_1, S_5\}) = \{S_2, S_6\}$.

6.1.3 ϕ-Term Placement Algorithm

To place ϕ-terms the compiler first needs to identify the CFG nodes that have assignments to each variable. In addition, to satisfy the equivalence proof, we consider the *Entry* node to have an assignment to each variable in the program. This corresponds to an initial value, or an undefined value (which may be of use in finding where uninitialized variables are used). We also use the slicing edge *Entry* → *Exit*; this adds a ϕ-term at *Exit* for every variable that is assigned in the program.

6.1 ■ Constructing Factored Use-Def Chains

```
          Algorithm Placement:
 (1)      for X ∈ V do
 (2)          InWork(X) = ⊥
 (3)          Added(X) = ⊥
 (4)      endfor
 (5)      WorkList = ∅
 (6)      for M ∈ Symbols do
 (7)          for X ∈ D(M) do
 (8)              WorkList = WorkList ∪ {X}
 (9)              InWork(X) = M
(10)          endfor
(11)          while WorkList ≠ ∅ do
(12)              remove some node X from WorkList
(13)              for W ∈ DF(X) do
(14)                  if Added(W) ≠ M then
(15)                      add φ-term for M at W
(16)                      Added(W) = M
(17)                      if InWork(W) ≠ M then
(18)                          WorkList = WorkList ∪ {W}
(19)                          InWork(X) = M
(20)                      endif
(21)                  endif
(22)              endfor
(23)          endwhile
(24)      endfor
```

FIGURE 6.5 FUD φ-placement algorithm.

Algorithm Placement places φ-terms for each variable, as shown in Figure 6.5; it assumes that the following data structures are available:

1. $DF(X)$ is the dominance frontier for CFG node X.
2. $D(M)$ is the set of CFG nodes that contain assignments or definitions to variable M.
3. *Symbols* is the set of symbols or variables in the program.

In addition, the algorithm uses the following data structures:

1. *WorkList* is a work list of CFG nodes; each node that contains an assignment or φ-term will be added to the work list.
2. *Added*(X) is used to determine whether a φ-term for the current variable has already been inserted at node X.
3. *InWork*(X) is used to determine whether node X has already been added to *WorkList* for the current variable.

Added(X) and InWork(X) can be implemented as symbol table pointers; they are initialized to some value that corresponds to no symbol. The outer main loop of the algorithm loops through each variable in *Symbols*, the symbol table.

The result of this algorithm is the addition of a ϕ-term for each variable M in $DF^+(D(M))$. Each ϕ-term placed is of the form:

$$\phi(M)_{n \rightsquigarrow \perp, \perp, \ldots}$$

where the ϕ-term has one use-def link for every CFG predecessor of the node in which it is placed. These links will be set by the next step.

Example 6.5

Show the result of algorithm Placement on the control flow graph shown in Figure 6.4, for the set $D(M) = \{Entry, S_1, S_5\}$; remember to add the slicing edge to the CFG.

Solution

The result is shown in Figure 6.6; each ϕ-term has one link, not yet filled in, for each CFG predecessor.

6.1.4 FUD Chaining Algorithm

The second phase links or chains each variable use with its unique reaching definition or pseudo-assignment, and fills in the ϕ-term links.

Algorithm Chain, shown in Figure 6.7, performs this second step. It performs a depth-first traversal of the dominator tree, starting at *Entry*. The algorithm assumes the following data structures or functions are available:

1. *Child(X)* is the set of dominator children of node X.
2. SUCC(X) is the set of CFG successors of X.
3. *WhichPred(X → Y)* is an index telling which predecessor of Y corresponds to the CFG edge from X.

Additionally, the algorithm uses the following data structures:

1. *CurrDef(M)* is a link from the symbol table entry for variable M to the "current" definition of that variable.
2. *Chain(R)* is a link from a use of a variable at reference R to the reaching definition or ϕ-term.
3. ϕ-*Chain(R)[J]* is a vector of links from a ϕ-term at reference R to the reaching definitions along each CFG predecessor.

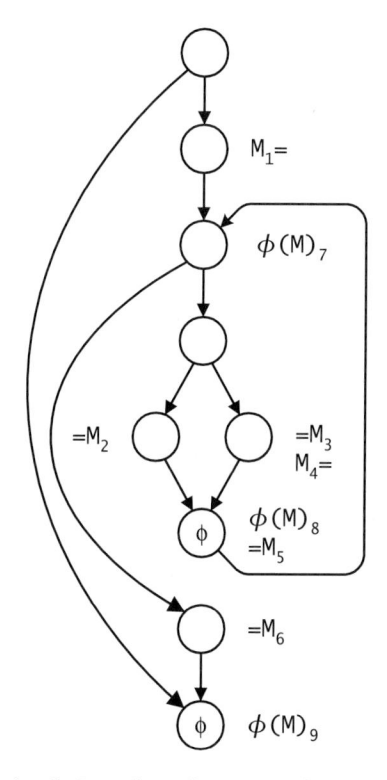

FIGURE 6.6 Result of algorithm Placement if $D(M) = \{Entry, S_1, S_5\}$.

4. *SaveChain(R)* is a temporary placeholder to save the old reaching definition when a new definition or ϕ-term is reached.

SaveChain(R) is used to restore the *CurrDef(M)* links after visiting this subtree of the dominator tree. The initial value for the current definition is empty; after the algorithm, an empty use-def link is either a use of an uninitialized variable, or a use of the initial value of the variable (such as for global variables or formal parameters). The empty link is used to represent the pseudo-assignment at the *Entry* node.

The algorithm works because when any use of variable M in a node X is reached, the definition in *CurrDef(M)* will either be the single reaching definition, if the node containing that definition dominates X, or will be a ϕ-term in a node that dominates X. Recall that from any definition in $D(M)$ to any use in X, there is a node in $X \cup DF^+(X)$ that dominates X.

Example 6.6

Complete Example 6.5 by using algorithm Chain to link each use to the appropriate reaching definition.

```
Algorithm Chain:
(1)  for M ∈ Symbols do
(2)      CurrDef(M) = ⊥
(3)  endfor
(4)  Search(Entry)

(5)  procedure Search(X)
(6)      for each variable use or def or φ-term R ∈ X do
(7)          let M be the variable referenced at R
(8)          if R is a use then
(9)              Chain(R) = CurrDef(M)
(10)         else if R is a def or φ-term then
(11)             SaveChain(R) = CurrDef(M)
(12)             CurrDef(M) = R
(13)         endif
(14)     endfor
(15)     for Y ∈ SUCC(X) do
(16)         J = WhichPred(X → Y)
(17)         for each φ-term R ∈ Y do
(18)             let M be the variable referenced at R
(19)             φ-Chain(R)[J] = CurrDef(M)
(20)         endfor
(21)     endfor
(22)     for Y ∈ Child(X) do
(23)         Search(Y)
(24)     endfor
(25)     for each variable use or def or φ-term R ∈ X in reverse order do
(26)         let M be the variable referenced at R
(27)         if R is a def or a φ-term then
(28)             CurrDef(M) = SaveChain(R)
(29)         endif
(30)     endfor
(31) end Search
```

FIGURE 6.7 FUD chaining algorithm.

Solution

The dominator tree of this CFG is shown in Figure 6.8. Algorithm Chain will proceed as follows:

- *Entry*   contains no definitions
  ϕ-Chain(ϕ_9)[1] ← CurrDef(M) = ⊥
  recurse to *Exit*

6.1 ■ Constructing Factored Use-Def Chains

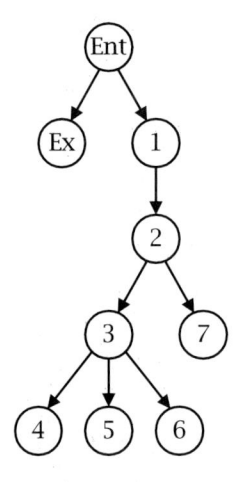

FIGURE 6.8 Dominator tree of example CFG.

- Exit
  $SaveChain(\phi_9) \leftarrow CurrDef(M) = \bot;\ CurrDef(M) \leftarrow \phi_9$
  no dominator tree children
  restore $CurrDef(M) \leftarrow SaveChain(\phi_9) = \bot$
  return to Entry
- Entry recurse to S_1
- S_1
  $SaveChain(M_1) \leftarrow CurrDef(M) = \bot;\ CurrDef(M) \leftarrow M_1$
  $\phi\text{-}Chain(\phi_7)[1] \leftarrow CurrDef(M) = M_1$
  recurse to S_2
- S_2
  $SaveChain(\phi_7) \leftarrow CurrDef(M) = M_1;\ CurrDef(M) \leftarrow \phi_7$
  recurse to S_3
- S_3 no definitions, no uses
  recurse to S_4
- S_4
  $Chain(M_2) \leftarrow CurrDef(M) = \phi_7$
  $\phi\text{-}Chain(\phi_8)[1] \leftarrow CurrDef(M) = \phi_7$
  no dominator tree children, return to S_3
- S_3 recurse to S_5
- S_5
  $Chain(M_3) \leftarrow CurrDef(M) = \phi_7$
  $SaveChain(M_4) \leftarrow CurrDef(M) = \phi_7;\ CurrDef(M) \leftarrow M_4$
  $\phi\text{-}Chain(\phi_8)[2] \leftarrow CurrDef(M) = M_4$
  restore $CurrDef(M) \leftarrow SaveChain(M_4) = \phi_7$
  return to S_3
- S_3 recurse to S_6
- S_6
  $SaveChain(\phi_8) \leftarrow CurrDef(M) = \phi_7;\ CurrDef(M) \leftarrow \phi_8$
  $Chain(M_5) \leftarrow CurrDef(M) = \phi_8$
  $\phi\text{-}Chain(\phi_7)[2] \leftarrow CurrDef(M) = \phi_8$
  restore $CurrDef(M) \leftarrow SaveChain(\phi_8) = \phi_7$
  return to S_3
- S_3 return to S_2

- S_2 recurse to S_7
- S_7 $Chain(M_6) \leftarrow CurrDef(M) = \phi_7$
  $\phi\text{-}Chain(\phi_9)[2] \leftarrow CurrDef(M) = \phi_7$
  return to S_2
- S_2 restore $CurrDef(M) \leftarrow SaveChain(\phi_7) = M_1$
  return to S_1
- S_1 restore $CurrDef(M) \leftarrow SaveChain(M_1) = \bot$
  return to Entry

The final solution, with links shown, is given in Figure 6.9.

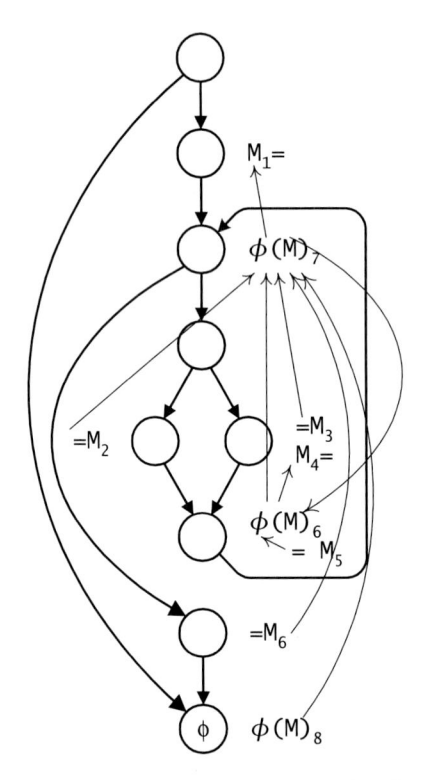

FIGURE 6.9 CFG with FUD chain links shown.

6.2 FUD Chains for Arrays

Factored use-def chains for array variables require special handling. A scalar assignment is a *killing definition* of the scalar; that is, the old value is completely overwritten by the definition. An assignment to an array element changes only one element of the array; the rest of the array is still the same. In data-flow analysis, this is modeled by treating array assignments as *nonkilling definitions* (or

6.2 ▪ FUD Chains for Arrays

preserving definitions) of the array. Prior definitions of the array reach beyond (or "leak through") an array element assignment. Our construction of factored use-def chains can easily keep def-def chains, to represent the nonkilling nature of array element assignments. We do this by adding the following line to algorithm Chain after line 11:

(11a)   if R is a def then *Chain*(R) = *CurrDef*(M)

With this addition, each use of an array element will be chained to a unique reaching array element definition of the same array. However, that definition may or may not define the value for the particular element being used, so it is chained to yet another array element definition, and so on. Thus the compiler can find all the reaching definitions of the array.

Example 6.7

Find the FUD chains for the array A in the program fragment below:

```
(1)   A[1] = 0
(2)   A[2] = 1
(3)   A[3] = 3
(4)   I = 1
(5)   loop
(6)      I = I + 1
(7)      if I > 3 then exit
(8)      A[I] = A[I] + 1
(9)   endloop
(10)  D = A[1] + A[2] + A[3]
```

Solution

Two ϕ-terms for A are needed, at line 5 and at the *Exit* node; we ignore the *Exit* node for this example. We label variable references with subscripts, as before; the FUD chains are shown as:

```
(1)   A₁↝⊥[1] = 0
(2)   A₂↝1[2] = 1
(3)   A₃↝2[3] = 3
(4)   I = 1
(5)   loop
         φ(A)₄↝3,6
(6)      I = I + 1
(7)      if I > 3 then exit
(8)      A₆↝4[I] = A₅↝4[I] + 1
```

(9) endloop
(10) D = $A_{7\leadsto 4}[1]$ + $A_{8\leadsto 4}[2]$ + $A_{9\leadsto 4}[3]$

The link from A_1 would be filled with any reaching definition from earlier in the program, or with $\bot$ if there are none.

6.3 Finding All Reaching Definitions

If a FUD chain links a use to a single killing definition, then the only reaching definition for that use is given by the link. However, the link may be to a ϕ-term, in which case there are two or more reaching definitions. For arrays, there may be many reaching definitions, depending on whether the element assigned is always, sometimes, or never equal to the element being used. Algorithm FollowChain, shown in Figure 6.10, follows the factored use-def links to find all possible reaching definitions of a particular use u. It starts at the link $Chain(u)$ that was filled by algorithm Chain, and uses one temporary location and saves its information in a set:

1. *Marked(d)* keeps track whether a definition d has already been visited for this use; it is initially set to a null value.

```
        Algorithm FollowChain:
(1)  Defs(u) = ∅
(2)  FollowChain( Chain(u), u )

(3)  procedure FollowChain( d, u )
(4)      if Marked(d) = u then return endif
(5)      Marked(d) = u
(6)      if d is a definition for u then
(7)          add d to Defs(u)
(8)      endif
(9)      if d is a φ-term then
(10)         for each link j do
(11)             FollowChain( φ-Chain(d)[j], u )
(12)         endfor
(13)     else if d is a killing definition then
(14)         /* stop here */
(15)     else /* follow def-def link */
(16)         FollowChain( Chain(d), u )
(17)     endif
(18) end FollowChain
```

FIGURE 6.10 Procedure to find all reaching definitions from a use at u.

2. $Defs(u)$ is the set of reaching definitions for use u, initialized to the empty set.

The algorithm requires two tests: one determines whether the definition d can possibly define the location used at use u. This might fail if d defines one element and u uses a different element. The other test determines whether definition d is a killing definition of the location at use u; for scalars, all definitions are killing definitions. For array elements, a definition with the same value in the subscript is a killing definition, as is any assignment that defines the whole array.

Example 6.8

Use algorithm FollowChain to find all reaching definitions for reference A_8[2] in Example 6.7.

Solution

The algorithm follows $Chain(A_8) = \phi(A)_4$. It then recursively follows the first link to $\phi\text{-}Chain(\phi(A))_4[1] = A_3$[3]. Since A[3] cannot be a definition of A[2], it skips this and continues on to $Chain(A_3) = A_2$[2]. Since this reference is a definition of A[2], we add it to $Defs(A_2)$; and since it always defines A[2], the algorithm does not follow its def-def link. Returning to the ϕ-term, the algorithm follows the second link to $\phi\text{-}Chain(\phi(A))_4[2] = A_6$[I]. Since A[I] potentially defines A[2], we add it to $Defs(A_2)$, and follow the def-def link. However, that link merely takes us back to $\phi(A)_4$, which was already visited. Thus, the reaching definitions are $Defs(A_2) = \{A_2[2], A_6[I]\}$.

6.4 Implicit References in FUD Chains

Constructing FUD chains requires the compiler to know the set of variables used and modified by a statement. Some statements have implicit uses or modification, such as through pointer dereferencing, parameter aliasing, or uses or modifications of global variables in external procedures or function calls. To correctly find the reaching definitions of a program, the compiler must deal with implicit as well as explicit references.

6.4.1 Input/Output

Output statements (`write`, `print`, etc.) do not modify any variable and use only the values of explicitly named variables. An exception is for a language that allows the programmer to specify the starting memory address and length of a binary output record. This is used for binary output in some versions for Fortran, for instance. In this instance, the compiler may not be able to determine precisely what variables might be used by the output statement, but it should be able to come up with a conservative overapproximation, based on the storage layout.

From the compiler's point of view, input statements (`read`, etc.) modify their arguments, in much the same way assignments do. In many instances, the input statement will complete only if all the arguments are modified. Two special cases can arise. The first is when the input statement allows the programmer to handle error or end-of-file conditions. When those handlers are invoked, some or all the variables will still have their original values, while others will have been modified by the input statement. The second case is for languages that allow incomplete input, such as Fortran. In list-directed input or namelist-directed input, not all the variables will get new values. In this instance, the compiler must assume that any or all of the variables might not be killed. One conservative method to handle input statements is to treat the statement as a nonkilling definition of each variable on the input list.

Example 6.9

List the variable uses and definitions for the following statements:

(1)   `write A(I+1), B, C, D`
(2)   `read A(I), B, C`

Solution

The `write` statement has uses of the variables A, B, C, and D, as well as I in the subscript expression. The `read` statement has another use of I, a nonkilling definition of the array A (since only a single element is defined), and either killing or nonkilling definitions of B and C, depending on the semantics of the `read` statement.

6.4.2 Procedure Calling

At a procedure call, the compiler must determine what variables are always or sometimes modified or used by the procedure. The effects of the call depend on the argument passing mechanism. Two common mechanisms are pass-by-value and pass-by-reference. The Fortran language essentially passes all arguments by reference; that is, the calling routine passes the address of the actual variable to the subroutine. If the subroutine modifies its formal parameter, that modification is also made to the actual argument. The C language passes all arguments by value; that is, the calling routine passes a copy of the value of the variable to the subroutine. Modifications made to formal parameters by the subroutine are not seen by the calling routine. C programs get around the lack of reference parameters by passing the address of a variable; we will discuss this shortly. One of the additions of the C++ language is a true reference argument. Pascal allows both pass-by-value (the default) and pass-by-reference (`var` parameters); in Pascal, the language does not allow modifications to value parameters. The compiler can model the effects of a procedure call on the arguments by treating each variable in the argument list as (possibly) used, and each variable in a reference argument position as having a nonkilling definition.

In addition to arguments, a procedure call may use or modify global variables. Without additional information, the compiler must assume that all globals may be used and may be modified. Keeping FUD chains for a large number of globals at a procedure call may be somewhat expensive. Of course, the compiler really needs to keep information only for the globals that are used in the routine being compiled, often a small subset of all the globals.

Interprocedural analysis can determine which global variables and formal arguments can never be used or modified by calling that routine. Many languages allow a programmer to declare the subroutine interface that tells which arguments are read and which are modified by calling the subroutine, but it does not usually describe the effects on globals.

There may be global variables that are not visible to the routine being compiled; even local variables can save state from one instance of a subroutine call to another, if the variable is statically allocated, such as a `static` variable in C or a `save` in Fortran. The compiler can model uses and defs to globally static but invisible (to this routine) variables by adding one more symbol to the symbol table; we call this the *phantom global variable*. In the absence of any interprocedural information, each subroutine or function call should be treated as if it had a use and def of the phantom global variable. This models the possibility that values are communicated between subprograms using variables that are not visible to this routine.

Interprocedural analysis or appropriate declarations may allow the compiler to refine these assumptions. For instance, not all reference arguments need to be modified by a call; the compiler may be able to determine exactly which globals are used or modified by call statements. In addition, the compiler may determine that all the use-def effects of the subprogram are visible to this routine, so a use and def of the phantom global variable need not be added to calls to that subprogram.

6.4.3 Aliases

One name may be used in a program to refer to two or more variables. An example that we have already seen is an array; the name of the array is used to refer to many elements of the array. The FUD chain for a use of A(1) would be linked to the most recent definition of the array; this might be an assignment to A(2). In fact, an assignment to A(2) will not define a value for the use of A(1). However, our intermediate representation summarizes all the uses and definitions in a single FUD chain. We can't keep a unique FUD chain for each element, since there can be an unbounded number of elements of the array.

Other aliases arise when two or more names are used to refer to the same variable. The aliases can arise in several ways:

1. Fortran `equivalence` statements allow multiple names to be used for the same location in memory. For example, the declarations:

    (1)   real A
    (2)   integer I
    (3)   equivalence(A, I)

    require variables A and I to share the same memory location. Thus the names A and I are aliases of each other; a definition of one implies a definition of the other. Pascal variant records have the same property. In the C language, the union type is a similar concept, but the language does not guarantee that the union members will share the same memory location, so programs should not depend on union members being aliases.

2. In a language that allows structure assignment, a structure name is an alias for the name of each of its fields. In the program fragment:

    (1)   type newrec = record
    (2)   B, C : integer
    (3)   end
    (4)   var A: newrec
    (5)   A = newrec(1, 0)
    (6)   D = A.B + A.C

    variable A assigned at line 5 is an alias for both A.B and A.C, used in the next line.

3. Formal parameters can be aliased with each other or, for reference formals, with global variables. The Fortran standard allows formals to be aliases of the same locations, but in that case neither alias can be modified by the subroutine, so no problems should occur, though Fortran compilers generally do not check for compliance. Pascal and C++ have no such constraints, however, and many Fortran compilers allow arbitrary argument aliasing. Suppose the parameter passing mechanism uses reference arguments in the following fragment:

    (1)   real A, B
    (2)   call sub1(A, A, B)
    (3)   call sub1(A, B, B)
             ⋮
    (4)   subroutine sub1(X, Y, Z)

```
(5)    real X, Y, Z
(6)    X = Y + Z
(7)    end
```

The formal parameters X and Y are aliases of each other if called from line 2, and the formals Y and Z are aliases if called from line 3. Note that X and Z are never aliases of each other, even though they may each be aliases of Y. When optimizing the subroutine sub1, the compiler may have to assume the worst case. In the absence of any information, the compiler may have to assume that X, Y, and Z are all possible aliases of one another. With interprocedural analysis, the compiler may be able to determine a more optimistic set of aliases.

4. Dereferenced pointers can be aliases of other dereferenced pointers, or of any other visible variable that could have had its address taken. Local analysis may determine which local variables have had their addresses taken and which may be aliases for local pointers, but aliases for global pointers may not be precisely computable. In the presence of pointer dereferencing, a pointer P is treated like any other variable. When dereferencing a pointer (*P in C or P↑ in Pascal), the compiler treats the dereference as another variable, distinct from P. In the following C fragment:

```
(1)    int *P, *Q, I, J;
(2)    P = &I;
(3)    *P = 1;
(4)    J = I;
```

after the assignment at line 2, the "variable" *P is an alias of I. If J has never had its address taken, then *P can never be an alias of J, and vice versa. In the absence of any other information, the compiler will have to assume that *P may also be an alias of *Q.

Aliases can be broadly divided into *static aliases*, like Fortran equivalence statements, and *dynamic aliases*, like dereferenced pointers. Another way to classify them is into *must-aliases* and *may-aliases*. The compiler can determine that static aliases, for instance, must occur. Just after line 2 in the example above, *P must be aliased to variable I. The compiler may not be able to determine the aliases exactly, especially in the presence of conditional branches. In that case, the compiler only has may-alias information: which variables may be aliased with one another. In the general case, finding exact alias information is intractable.

FUD chains cannot represent aliases directly. Instead, we use them to find all reaching definitions for each use. In the presence of aliases, the compiler must be able to identify reaching definitions of the variable used and of any aliases of that variable. Keep in mind that a killing definition of a may-alias for this variable is not a killing definition for this variable. Depending on how aliases are represented, a definition on the FUD chain for a use may be a nonalias for the variable used. We present two ways to handle dynamic aliases using FUD chains. Deciding which to use is more of an engineering issue than a science issue. The tradeoffs are precision, incrementally updating the representation, and the efficiency of finding the reaching definitions.

One Name per Alias Set

The simplest method to handle aliases using FUD chains is to partition the variables into alias equivalence classes. Each partition, or equivalence class, is chained in a single factored use-def chain. This is the method suggested for arrays. One FUD chain is constructed for the entire array; an update of an array element is treated as a nonkilling definition for any element of the array. Note that def-def links must also be constructed.

The same method could be used for structures or records. One FUD chain could be used for the whole structure; an update of a field would be treated like a nonkilling update of the entire structure. A structure assignment would be treated like a killing definition of all fields. As with array references, the ambiguity could then be resolved when following the FUD chains, by noting which reaching definitions are possible definitions of the use in question.

For pointer aliases, this would mean partitioning the names into disjoint sets of names that might be aliased anywhere. In the C language, any formal argument pointer target might be aliased with any other formal argument pointer target. This is especially conservative, but still allows some optimizations.

To construct FUD chains with alias equivalence classes, algorithm Placement would be modified to insert ϕ-terms for each alias equivalence class rather than for each variable, starting at definitions of all variables in the equivalence class. Algorithm Chain would likewise be modified to find the alias equivalence class to which the variable at the current reference belongs.

This method has the distinct disadvantage of creating false aliases. For instance, if a pointer *P could point to either variable A or B, this method would create one alias set for {*P, A, B}, thus making A and B look like aliases of each other. During optimization, when following the FUD chains, the compiler could use an auxiliary structure to determine which definitions on the chain are actual aliases and which are false aliases. This would complicate the analysis and loses some of the advantages of using a sparse FUD chain.

Another disadvantage has to do with how alias information is collected. It is likely that use-def information is needed to find precise alias information. Thus, the FUD chains must initially be constructed with very coarse alias information. It may be difficult to take advantage of improved alias information except by reconstructing the FUD chains. Discovery and refinement of alias information is discussed further in Chapter 8.

Example 6.10

Use alias equivalence classes to construct FUD chains for the following program fragment:

(1) B = 0
(2) A = 0
(3) if phase = full then
(4)   P = &A
(5) else
(6)   P = &B
(7) endif
(8) *P = 1
(9) A = 2
(10) *P = *P + 1
(11) B = 3
(12) print A, B

Solution

Simple analysis of pointer assignments tells us that *P may be an alias of either A or B. Thus, all three variables will be in a single alias equivalence class. We represent the FUD chains by numbering the references and showing the links, as follows:

(1) $B_{1 \rightsquigarrow \bot} = 0$
(2) $A_{2 \rightsquigarrow 1} = 0$
(3) if phase = full then
(4) $P_{3 \rightsquigarrow \bot} = \&A$
(5) else
(6) $P_{4 \rightsquigarrow \bot} = \&B$
(7) endif
    $\phi(P)_{5 \rightsquigarrow 3,4}$
(8) $(*P_{6 \rightsquigarrow 5})_{7 \rightsquigarrow 2} = 1$
(9) $A_{8 \rightsquigarrow 7} = 2$
(10) $(*P_{10 \rightsquigarrow 5})_{11 \rightsquigarrow 8} = (*P_{9 \rightsquigarrow 5})_{10 \rightsquigarrow 8} + 1$
(11) $B_{12 \rightsquigarrow 11} = 3$
(12) print $A_{13 \rightsquigarrow 12}$, $B_{14 \rightsquigarrow 12}$

Note that variable P is distinct from the variable *P, so a definition of *P uses but does not define the value of P. Note also that the value of &A is a constant, equal to the address of A, but neither a use nor a def of A itself. To find the reaching definitions for reference A_{13}, for instance, the compiler would trace the links through

B_{12}, which is not a definition of A; $(*P)_{10}$, which is a possible definition of A; and A_8, which is a killing definition of A.

One FUD Chain for Each Alias

A second way to handle dynamic aliases keeps a FUD chain for each distinct variable that might be aliased. Each use of a variable is linked to the most recent definition of either that variable or an alias. A definition appears on several FUD chains, one for each variable to which it is aliased. This method is not appropriate for array element aliases, for instance, since there would have to be a FUD chain for each element of the array. For structure updates, it may be more feasible; in fact, there may be no need to keep a FUD chain for the structure as a whole, just one for each element. An update of the whole structure is then on the FUD chain for each field of the structure. An update of a single field would appear on the FUD chain for that field only. Thus, each field would have distinct use-def chains, which would merge only at whole structure updates.

An assignment through a pointer would appear on the FUD chains of all its aliases. Subsequent analysis may determine that two variables are actually not aliases; for instance, pointer analysis might determine that a pointer could not point to a particular variable. With this method, the FUD chains can be incrementally updated to eliminate that link.

For this method, algorithm Placement is modified to initialize the *WorkList* for a variable with the set of definitions to that variable or with any alias to that variable. Whereas the previous method added only one ϕ-term for the equivalence class, this method may add a ϕ-term for every variable in an alias set. Algorithm Chain is modified by treating each definition as a though it were a potential definition of every variable with which it is aliased. Each definition must keep several def-def links, one for each alias of the variable.

When following FUD chains, the compiler needs to follow the chains only for the variable in question; if the FUD chains were incrementally updated, the algorithm would immediately get the correct updated value.

Example 6.11

Use multiple def-def links to construct FUD chains for the program fragment in Example 6.10.

Solution

Each definition of A must have a def-def link to the reaching definition for A as well as for *P, since they are aliases, and similarly for B. Each definition of *P will have three links: for itself, and for each of its two aliases, A and B.

(1) $B_{1 \leadsto \perp, *P \leadsto \perp} = 0$
(2) $A_{2 \leadsto \perp, *P \leadsto \perp} = 0$
(3) if phase = full then
(4) $\quad P_{3 \leadsto \perp} = \&A$
(5) else
(6) $\quad P_{4 \leadsto \perp} = \&B$
(7) endif
$\quad \phi(P)_{5 \leadsto 3,4}$
(8) $(*P_{6 \leadsto 5})_{7 \leadsto 2, A \leadsto 2, B \leadsto 1} = 1$
(9) $A_{8 \leadsto 7, *P \leadsto 7} = 2$
(10) $(*P_{10 \leadsto 5})_{11 \leadsto 8, A \leadsto 8, B \leadsto 7} = (*P_{9 \leadsto 5})_{10 \leadsto 8} + 1$
(11) $B_{12 \leadsto 11, *P \leadsto 11} = 3$
(12) print $A_{13 \leadsto 11}$, $B_{14 \leadsto 12}$

To find the reaching definitions for reference A_{13}, the compiler would trace the links through $(*P)_{10}$ (possible definition of A) and A_8 (killing definition of A), skipping over B_{12}.

6.5 Induction Variables Using FUD Chains

Here we introduce an algorithm to detect linear induction variables in a loop with FUD chains. An *induction variable* is any scalar variable for which the value on the next iteration of the loop is some function of loop invariants and of its value on this iteration. The idea is to use a *FUD chain graph*, where the vertices are the individual operations in the program, and the edges point to the operands of each unary or binary operation, or to the reaching definition for each variable use. Within a loop, a basic induction variable will appear as a cycle in the FUD chain graph. Other induction variables will depend on some basic induction variable. Basic induction variables can be identified by looking for cycles in the graph, and inspecting the operations involved in the cycle. For purposes of array subscript analysis, as for data dependence analysis, we want to find the linear induction variables of the program, where the value of the variable on the next iteration of the loop is equal to the value on this iteration of the loop plus or minus a loop invariant value. If a cycle in the FUD chain graph is found where the only arithmetic operations are additions of loop invariant values, and with only one ϕ-term at the loop header, the variable defined in the cycle will be a linear induction variable.

Example 6.12

What are the FUD chains for variable I in the following loop?

```
(1)    I = 0
(2)    loop
(3)       ...(I)...
(4)       I = I + 1
(5)       ...(I)...
(6)    endloop
```

What does the FUD chain graph look like?

Solution

One ϕ-term would be added at the loop header, so the FUD chains would be as shown below.

```
(1)    I₁ = 0
(2)    loop
          φ(I)₂↝1,5
(3)       ...(I₃↝2)...
(4)       I₅ = I₄↝2 + 1
(5)       ...(I₆↝5)...
(6)    endloop
```

The uses of I before the increment at line 4 are reached by the ϕ-term at the loop header, while those after the increment are reached only by the increment. Figure 6.11 shows the part of the FUD graph pertaining to the variable I.

6.5.1 Classifying Cycles

There is a cycle in the graph shown in Figure 6.11. Since the only operations on the cycle are additions, fetches and stores of scalars, and the one ϕ-term at the loop header, this is potentially a basic linear induction variable. The compiler can verify this by checking that any values added during the cycle are in fact loop invariant. In general, there may be more than one addition in the loop; the sum of all the added values is the step for the induction variable. Actually, this defines a family of induction variables (at least two), one for each definition in the cycle. Here, we have two basic linear induction variables, one corresponding to the value of I at the ϕ-term at the loop header, and one for the value of I after the increment. A linear induction variable can be completely defined by its initial value (the value on the first iteration of the loop) and its step. We write this as *initial + step · i*, where *i* is the *basic loop induction variable* with a value starting at zero. In nested loops, the induction step will be associated with the particular loop, and the basic induction variable will be identified with the loop, as we shall see.

A ϕ-term at a loop header is called, naturally enough, a loop-header-ϕ. We assume that a loop-header-ϕ will have exactly two links—one for the back edge and

6.5 ■ Induction Variables Using FUD Chains

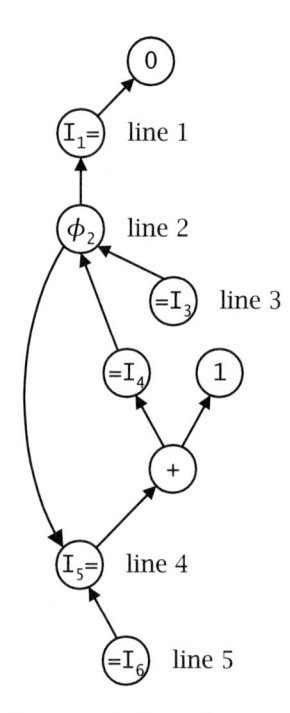

FIGURE 6.11 FUD chain graph for induction variable example.

one for the loop preheader. The compiler can insert loop preheader and post-body nodes when appropriate to satisfy this. In a FUD chain cycle, one of the loop-header-ϕ links will be involved in the cycle, and the other will correspond to the initial value for the induction variable. In Example 6.12, the link from the ϕ-term to I_5 is part of the cycle, and I_1 is the initial value for the induction variable defined at $\phi(I)_2$. Since the only value added along the cycle was the constant 1, the step value is 1. The initial value for this induction variable is also constant. Thus, we can describe the induction variable $\phi(I)_2$ with $0 + i$. At the assignment of I_5, the value 1 is added, so the induction variable I_5 is described by the $1 + i$.

To find additional linear induction variables, the compiler can use a simple algebra for induction variables and loop invariants for addition and multiplication. Each definition or operation will be classified either as a constant, a loop invariant, a linear induction variable, or as complex, which is used for any definition or operation that is not one of the other three types. An addition involving two operations that have been classified as linear induction variables is itself a linear induction variable. Suppose we are adding two operations, one of which has been determined to generate the linear sequence $a + b \cdot i$ and the other generates $c + d \cdot i$. The sum of these two is an operation that takes on the sequence $(a + c) + (b + d) \cdot i$. Similarly, addition or multiplication of a linear induction variable with a constant or loop invariant generates another linear induction variable:

$$(a + b \cdot i) + c = (a + c) + b \cdot i$$
$$(a + b \cdot i)c = (ac) + bc \cdot i$$

The algorithm to find linear induction variables is a modification of algorithm SCC, which was discussed in Chapter 3. The algorithm visits all operations in the loop, following all operand and FUD chain links from each node, looking for cycles. At loop-header-ϕ terms, only the link corresponding to the back edge is followed; the other edge is used only for the initial value. When an SCC is found, it must be classified as a constant, a loop invariant, a linear induction variable, or as complex. One of the features of algorithm SCC is that it visits the nodes in reverse topological order; since we follow operand and FUD chain links from an operation to the sources, this means that when an SCC is identified, all the operands and FUD chain links leading into it will already have been identified and classified.

Algorithm Induct, shown in Figure 6.12, shows the modified algorithm. It assumes that the following information is available:

1. *Loop* is the set of basic blocks comprising the loop being analyzed.
2. *Operations*(X) is the set of operations in basic block X.

The algorithm uses the same intermediate data structures as algorithm SCC:

1. *N* is the global counter for assigning preorder numbers, initialized to zero.
2. *Stack* is a push-down (LIFO) stack of operations, initialized to empty.
3. *NPre*(P) is the preorder number assigned to each operation as the algorithm builds a depth-first spanning forest, initialized to zero for each operation.
4. *Lowlink*(P) keeps track of whether each operation has a path to a spanning forest ancestor.
5. *InStack*(P) is a flag to keep track of whether each operation is on the stack, and is initialized to *False*.

Procedure Check, shown in Figure 6.13, does the recursive call to Procedure Induct Recurse when necessary. When an SCC is identified, the operations are classified; singleton SCCs can be can be classified simply based on the classifications of the operands and FUD chain link or links.

To classify each SCC, the compiler can use rules based on the operation type. For trivial SCCs, the following rules are a sample of what is used:

1. A literal constant is classified as a constant, with the value of that constant.
2. A store operation gets the classification and value of the right-hand side expression.

6.5 ■ Induction Variables Using FUD Chains

```
         Algorithm Induct:
 (1)     for X ∈ Loop do
 (2)         for P ∈ Operations(X) do
 (3)             NPre(X) = 0; InStack(X) = False
 (4)         endfor
 (5)     endfor
 (6)     N = 0
 (7)     Stack = ∅
 (8)     for X ∈ Loop do
 (9)         for P ∈ Operations(X) do
(10)             if NPre(P) = 0 then
(11)                 InductRecurse(P)
(12)             endif
(13)         endfor
(14)     endfor

(15)     procedure InductRecurse(P)
(16)         Lowlink(P) = NPre(P) = N = N + 1
(17)         push P onto Stack; InStack(P) = True
(18)         Check( LeftOp(P), P ); Check( RightOp(P), P )
(19):        if P is a loop-header-φ then
(20)             let j be the link for the back edge
(21)             Check( φ-Chain(P)[j], P )
(22)         else if P is a φ-term then
(23)             for each link j do
(24)                 Check( φ-Chain(P)[j], P )
(25)             endfor
(26)         else
(27)             Check( Chain(P), P )
(28):        endif
(29)         if NPre(P) = Lowlink(P) then
(30)             if P is on top of the stack then
(31)                 classify P as trivial SCC
(32)             else
(33)                 repeat
(34)                     pop W off Stack; InStack(W) = False
(35)                 until W = P
(36)                 classify all operations in the SCC
(37)             endif
(38)         endif
(39)     end InductRecurse
```

FIGURE 6.12 Algorithm to find linear induction variables.

```
(1)    procedure Check( L, P )
(2)        if NPre(L) = 0 then
(3)            InductRecurse(L)
(4)            Lowlink(P) = min(Lowlink(P), Lowlink(L))
(5)        else if NPre(L) < NPre(P) and InStack(L) then
(6)            Lowlink(P) = min(Lowlink(P), NPre(L))
(7)        endif
(8)    end Check
```

FIGURE 6.13 Procedure to build depth-first spanning tree of operations for algorithm Induct.

3. A fetch of a loop-invariant address gets the classification and value of the reaching definition, if that is a killing definition to the same address.
4. Other fetches are classified as complex.
5. Adding or multiplying two constants is a constant, with a value of the sum or product of the values.
6. Adding two linear induction variables is a linear induction variable, with value according to rules for adding induction variables.
7. Adding a complex to anything is another complex.
8. Loop-header-ϕ terms are complex.
9. Other ϕ-terms take the classification and value of the operands, if the classifications and values are exactly the same, and complex otherwise.

Many more rules can be used for other operations; classifying the default case as complex will be safe.

A nontrivial SCC can be classified as a linear induction variable if all the operations are additions of loop-invariant values, fetches and stores of scalars, and the loop-header-ϕ term. Operations in other nontrivial SCCs can be classified as complex. The initial value of a linear induction variable is found by following the FUD chain link from the loop-header-ϕ.

Example 6.13

Find the FUD chain graph and the linear induction variables in the following loop:

```
(1)    I = 3
(2)    M = 0
(3)    loop
(4)        J = 3
(5)        I = I + 1
(6)        L = M + 1
(7)        M = L + 2
```

6.5 ■ Induction Variables Using FUD Chains

(8)   J = I + J
(9)   K = 2 * J
(10)   endloop

Solution

The FUD chains are shown in Figure 6.14, and the FUD chain graph is shown in Figure 6.15. Assume the initial values $J_\perp$, $K_\perp$, and $L_\perp$ are unknown to the compiler.

(1) $I_1 = 3$
(2) $M_2 = 0$
(3)   loop
           $\phi(I)_{3,\rightsquigarrow 1,10}$
           $\phi(J)_{4,\rightsquigarrow \perp,17}$
           $\phi(K)_{5,\rightsquigarrow \perp,19}$
           $\phi(L)_{6,\rightsquigarrow \perp,12}$
           $\phi(M)_{7,\rightsquigarrow 2,14}$
(4) $J_8 = 3$
(5) $I_{10} = I_{9 \rightsquigarrow 3} + 1$
(6) $L_{12} = M_{11 \rightsquigarrow 7} + 1$
(7) $M_{14} = L_{13 \rightsquigarrow 12} + 2$
(8) $J_{17} = I_{15 \rightsquigarrow 10} + J_{16 \rightsquigarrow 8}$
(9) $K_{19} = 2 * J_{18 \rightsquigarrow 17}$
(10)   endloop

FIGURE 6.14 FUD chains for example program.

There is one cycle for variable I in the loop. The only arithmetic operation involved is addition, all the fetches and stores are to scalars, and the only ϕ-term is at the loop header; also, the added value is the constant 1. Therefore, this cycle describes a family of linear induction variables. The initial value for the induction variable I_3 comes from outside the loop at I_1, and the induction sequence can be described by $3 + i$; the induction sequence for I_{10} has an initial value of one more, and is described by $4 + i$.

A second cycle in the FUD chain graph includes the L and M assignments in the loop. Again, the only arithmetic operations in the cycle are additions, the added values are loop invariants (constants here), and the fetches and stores are to scalars, so this defines a family of linear induction variables. The step is the sum of the added values, which is $2 + 1 = 3$. The three induction variables in this cycle are:

M_7	$0 + 3i$
L_{12}	$1 + 3i$
M_{14}	$3 + 3i$

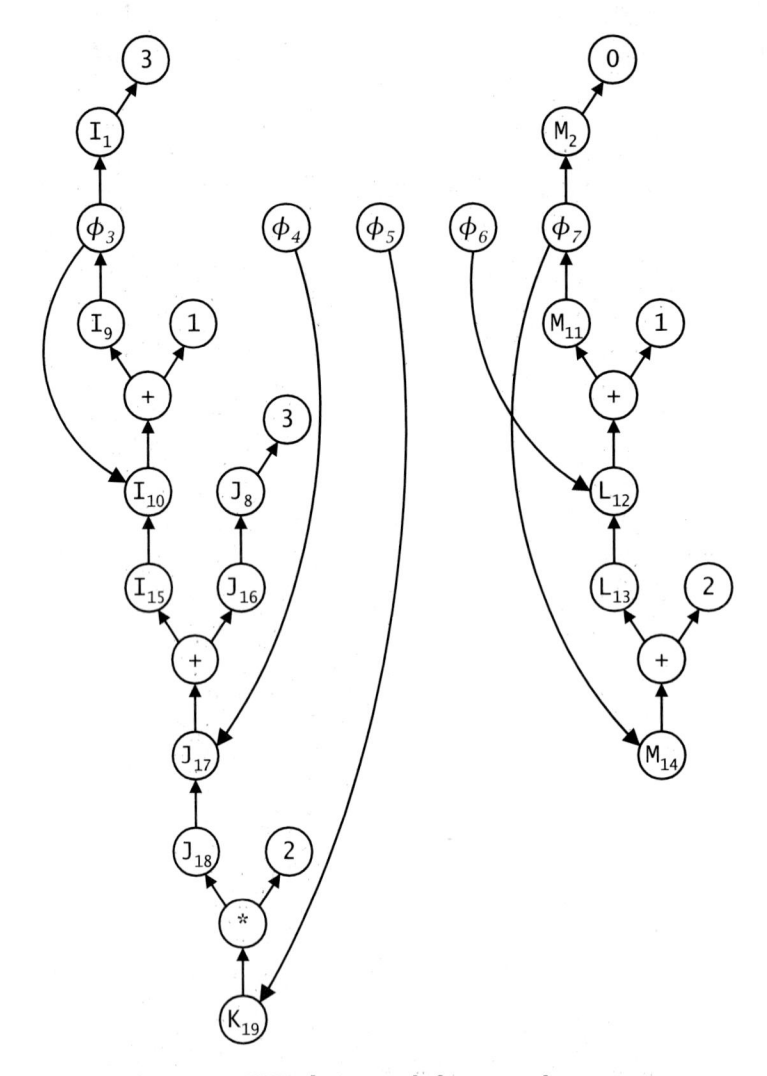

FIGURE 6.15 FUD chain graph for example program.

The other vertices in the FUD chain graph can be visited in topological order, after the basic linear induction variables have been found. This will find the following additional linear induction variables:

$$\begin{array}{c|c} J_{17} & 7+i \\ K_{19} & 14+2i \end{array}$$

Note that J_8 is recognized as having constant value, which is used in the computation of J_{17}.

6.5.2 Wrap-Around Variables

The ϕ-terms J_3, K_3, and L_3 in the previous example are not part of any FUD chain graph cycle, and are not induction variables either. In each case, the ϕ-term link for the back edge is to a definition in the loop that is a linear induction variable. Some programs use constructs that look like this to model a cylindrical data structure using an array, as shown below:

```
(1)     J = N
(2)     I = 1
(3)     loop
(4)         A(I) = ...
(5)         ... = A(J)
(6)         J = I
(7)         I = I + 1
(8)     endloop
```

For most of the loop, the value of variable J is equal to I-1. This corresponds to the "left" neighbor of element I of the array. On the first iteration, however, the left neighbor of the first element of A should be the "last" element of A. The programmer gets this effect by using variable J to point to the left neighbor of the current element, initializing this to start at N, and then reassigning it each iteration of the loop. A loop-header-ϕ for I and J will be added at line 3:

```
(1)     J₁ = N
(2)     I₂ = 1
(3)     loop
            φ(I)₃↝₂,₁₀
            φ(J)₄↝₁,₈
(4)         A(I₅↝₃) = ...
(5)         ... = A(J₆↝₄)
(6)         J₈ = I₇↝₃
(7)         I₁₀ = I₉↝₃ + 1
(8)     endloop
```

The FUD chain graph for these variables is shown in Figure 6.16. The only cycle in the graph involves variable I, which defines the induction variables:

$$\begin{array}{c|c} I_3 & 1+i \\ I_{10} & 2+i \end{array}$$

This also defines the variable J_8 as taking the induction sequence $1+i$; however, this value isn't used within the loop. What we want is to find the value of J_4, which is the ϕ-merge of an induction variable and a value from outside the loop. Many current compilers recognize this pattern, called a *wrap-around variable*. The presence of a wrap-around variable signals to the compiler that the loop can be analyzed and optimized by peeling off its first iteration and optimizing the remaining iterations, for which the value of J can be replaced by I-1. Wrap-around variables can be cascaded, which requires peeling two or more iterations of the loop before finding the linear sequence.

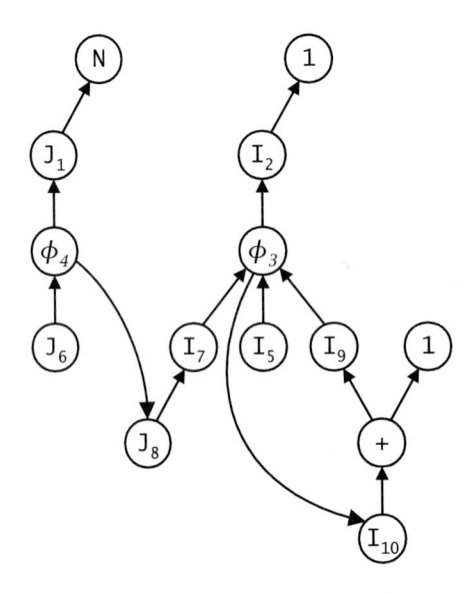

FIGURE 6.16 FUD chain graph.

Wrap-around variables are easily identified by induction variable analysis by looking at trivial SCCs comprising a loop-header-ϕ term. If the back-edge link from the loop-header-ϕ is a linear induction variable, then the ϕ-term is itself a wrap-around variable of level one (meaning that after the first iteration, it takes on a linear sequence of values). If the back-edge link is a wrap-around variable, then the loop-header-ϕ is a wrap-around variable of level one greater.

6.5.3 Trip Counts

Induction variable analysis can also find the *trip count* of the loop, that is, the number of times the loop is executed. We define the trip count (*tc*) of a loop to be the number of times that the back edge is executed; a loop that exits the first time it is executed has a trip count of zero. The header of the loop always executes one more time than the trip count.

When there is a single loop exit test, and that test compares two linear induction variables or a linear induction variable and a constant, the compiler can compute the result directly by finding the smallest integer value of the basic induction vari-

6.5 • Induction Variables Using FUD Chains

able that satisfies the test. For instance, when comparing two induction variables $I_1 < I_2$, where $I_1 = n_1 + s_1 \cdot i$ and $I_2 = n_2 + s_2 \cdot i$, the compiler tries to find the minimum integer value of tc that satisfies the inequality $n_1 + s_1 \cdot tc < n_2 + s_2 \cdot tc$.

When the trip count does not depend on any values computed in the loop, the loop is called a *countable loop*. For a countable loop, the *exit value* of induction variables can also be computed directly. The value of an induction variable described by $init + step \cdot i$ in a countable loop has the value $init + step \times tc$ on the last iteration.

Example 6.14

Find the trip count and exit value of I for the following loop:

(1)   I = 5
(2)   loop
(3)   I = I + 4
(4)   if I > 45 then exit
(5)   endloop

Solution

The FUD chains for this loop will include a ϕ-term at line 2:

(1) I_1 = 5
(2)   loop
           $\phi(I)_{2 \leadsto 1,4}$
(3) $I_4 = I_{3 \leadsto 2} + 4$
(4)   if $I_{5 \leadsto 4}$ > 45 then exit
(5)   endloop

The definitions of I in the loop form a FUD chain cycle; the increment along the cycle is 4, resulting in the induction variables:

I_2	$5 + 4i$
I_4	$9 + 4i$

The exit condition compares the value of I_4 to the constant 45. Thus the trip count is the minimum value of tc that satisfies the inequality $9 + 4 \times tc > 45$. This simplifies to $tc > 9$, for a trip count of 10. Had the exit condition been I >= 45, the trip count would be 9.

The value of I_4 on the last iteration of the loop is $9 + 4 \times 10$, or 49.

6.5.4 Nested Loops

In multiple loops, the initial value of an induction variable for the inner loop may be the value of an induction variable from the outer loop. To handle nested loops, the compiler should first find the linear induction variables for innermost loops. For any countable loop, the exit value of any induction variable that reaches the loop exit should be computed. The induction variables or exit values may be in terms of variables that are assigned in an outer loop.

When finding induction variables for the outer loop, the procedure in algorithm Induct is modified when following FUD chain links, at lines 19-28. If the link is to a definition in the same outer loop, the algorithm should proceed as before. However, if the link is to a definition in an inner loop, and the definition is a linear induction variable with an exit value available, the algorithm should treat this link as if it were a link to the exit value. Since the exit value is in terms of invariants or values computed in the outer loop, the definitions visited will be restricted to being in the outer loop itself. If the link is to an inner loop definition and there is no exit value available, either because the inner loop is not countable or because the definition is not an induction variable, the compiler can treat it as if it were a link to a complex variable, since there is no hope of finding a linear induction sequence in the outer loop.

When an induction variable is found in an inner loop, its initial value will always be a link to some definition in an outer loop. This may be a link to an outer loop induction variable or to a constant value. As a practical matter, the compiler can simplify the expressions it must manipulate if it can find the constant initial values right away, rather than waiting until the outer loop is processed. A simple method is to trace the FUD chains until either the initial value is determined to be constant or a ϕ-term is found. Most of the time, this will find the constant initial values immediately.

Example 6.15

Find the FUD chains for the scalar variables in the loop below; also identify the linear induction variables. What are the final values of I, J, and K?

```
(1)   K = -5
(2)   I = 0
(3)   loop
(4)       I = I + 1
(5)       if I > 100 then exit
(6)       J = 4
(7)       loop
(8)           J = J + 2
(9)           if J > 100 then exit
```

6.5 • Induction Variables Using FUD Chains

(10)　　　　K = K + 3
(11)　　endloop
(12) endloop

Solution

To construct FUD chains, ϕ-terms are needed for I at the outer loop header, and for J and K at both loop headers:

(1)　$K_1 = -5$
(2)　$I_2 = 0$
(3)　loop
　　　　$\phi(I)_{3 \leadsto 2,7}$
　　　　$\phi(J)_{4 \leadsto 1,13}$
　　　　$\phi(K)_{5 \leadsto 1,11}$
(4)　　$I_7 = I_{6 \leadsto 3} + 1$
(5)　　if $I_{8 \leadsto 7} > 100$ then exit
(6)　　$J_9 = 4$
(7)　　loop
　　　　　　$\phi(J)_{10 \leadsto 9,13}$
　　　　　　$\phi(K)_{11 \leadsto 5,16}$
(8)　　　$J_{13} = J_{12 \leadsto 10} + 2$
(9)　　　if $J_{14 \leadsto 13} > 100$ then exit
(10)　　$K_{16} = K_{15 \leadsto 11} + 3$
(11)　　endloop
(12) endloop

Analyzing the inner loop first, the compiler will find two FUD chain cycles; one for J and one for K. These produce the induction variables:

$\phi(J)_{10}$	$J_9 + 2i_2$
J_{13}	$J_9 + 2 + 2i_2$
$\phi(K)_{11}$	$\phi(K)_5 + 3i_2$
K_{16}	$\phi(K)_5 + 3 + 3i_2$

By following the initial value FUD chains, the compiler can immediately see that J_9 is assigned a constant value, so it can replace J_9 by 4 in the induction variable descriptions. The initial value for K is a ϕ-term, so processing is deferred to the outer loop. The trip count for the inner loop can be found by looking at the exit condition $J_{13} > 100$, or $6 + 2i > 100$, giving a trip count of 48. Therefore, the compiler can determine the exit values of the induction variables that reach the loop exit. The value of J_{13} on the last iteration will be $6 + 2 \times 48 = 102$, and the value of $\phi(K)_{11}$ will be $\phi(K)_5 + 3 \times 48$.

In the outer loop, the compiler can identify two more FUD chain cycles, for I and K. When identifying the K SCC, there is a link from $\phi(K)_5$ to $\phi(K)_{11}$, which is defined in the inner loop. This link is thus treated as if it were to a definition with the exit value of $\phi(K)_5 + 3 \times 48$. Thus, the induction variables found are:

$\phi(I)_3$	$I_2 + i_1$
I_7	$I_2 + 1 + i_1$
$\phi(K)_5$	$K_1 + 144 i_1$
$exit(\phi(K)_{11})$	$K_1 + 144 + 144 i_1$

After substituting the constant values for I_2 and K_1, and substituting for K_5 in the inner loop induction variables, all the linear induction variables are:

$\phi(I)_3$	$0 + i_1$
I_7	$1 + i_1$
$\phi(K)_5$	$-5 + 144 i_1$
$exit(\phi(K)_{11}$	$139 + 144 i_1$
$\phi(J)_{10}$	$4 + 2 i_2$
J_{13}	$6 + 2 i_2$
$\phi(K)_{11}$	$-5 + 144 i_1 + 3 i_2$
K_{16}	$-2 + 144 i_1 + 3 i_2$

The outer loop exit condition compares I_7 to 100, giving the trip count 100. The FUD definitions that reach outside the loop are I_7, J_4, and K_5. Thus the exit values for I and K are

I	$1 + 1 \times 100 = 101$
K	$-5 + 144 \times 100 = 14395$

The situation for J is a bit more complex, since the FUD definition that reaches the loop exit is a wrap-around variable, not an induction variable. However, since the trip count is (in this case) a constant known to be greater than zero, the last value of J_4 will be the value of J_{13} on the last iteration of the loop, which we already computed to be 102.

6.6 Constant Propagation with FUD Chains

Here we describe an algorithm using the FUD chains to perform constant propagation. This algorithm takes advantage of conditional branches where the test turns out to have a constant value. The compiler will compute an abstract value for each expression in the program. The abstract value will be either an actual constant, if all the operands are either literal constants or can be shown to have constant value, or one of the special values ⊤ (called *top*) or ⊥ (*bottom*). The initial abstract

6.6 ▪ Constant Propagation with FUD Chains

value for all expressions will be initialized to ⊤; a value of ⊤ means either that the expression has not been evaluated yet, or that it occurs on some unreachable path of the program (the expression has zero values). For instance, a path may be unreachable if some branch turns out to test a condition that always has constant value. An abstract value of ⊥ means the compiler has found that the expression might take on two or more different values, so the expression is treated as not constant. For most operations, we define the abstract value for the result of the operation as follows:

1. the result is ⊥ if any of the operands has abstract value ⊥;
2. it is ⊤ if any of the operands have abstract value ⊤; and
3. it is the appropriate constant value if all the operands are constant.

For example, the abstract value for binary addition given the abstract values of its two operands would be:

+	⊤	c_1	⊥
⊤	⊤	⊤	⊥
c_2	⊤	$c_1 + c_2$	⊥
⊥	⊥	⊥	⊥

We can have special rules for boolean AND and OR, since there are only two possible constant values, as shown in Figure 6.17. Note that this table violates the first two rules for evaluating operations, in that a constant valued result might be computed even if one of the operands has value ⊤ or ⊥. Similarly, multiplication of any abstract value by a constant zero yields the constant zero.

AND	⊤	False	True	⊥
⊤	⊤	False	⊤	⊤
False	False	False	False	False
True	⊤	False	True	⊥
⊥	⊤	False	⊥	⊥
OR	⊤	False	True	⊥
⊤	⊤	⊤	True	⊤
False	⊤	False	True	⊥
True	True	True	True	True
⊥	⊤	⊥	True	⊥

FIGURE 6.17 Abstract values for evaluating AND and OR operations.

For ϕ-terms, the abstract value is $\top$ if all operands have abstract value $\top$; it is a constant if all non-$\top$ operands have the same constant abstract value; and it is $\bot$ otherwise, as shown in the following table:

ϕ-val	$\top$	c_1	$\bot$
$\top$	$\top$	c_1	$\bot$
c_1	c_1	c_1	$\bot$
$c_2 \ne c_1$	c_2	$\bot$	$\bot$
$\bot$	$\bot$	$\bot$	$\bot$

Clever constant propagation analysis will also take advantage of equality tests on conditional branches. For instance, in the following:

(1)   `if I = 1 then`
(2)   `J = I + 2`
(3)   `...J...`
(4)   `endif`
(5)   `...J...I...`

the only way for control to execute line 2 is for variable `I` to have the constant value of 1. Constant propagation should be able to take advantage of this to propagate the value 1 into the assignment to `J` and into all the uses of `I` and `J` within the conditional block. Outside the conditional, however, the value of `I` may or may not have value 1, so no information should be propagated there. This information can be derived by inserting pseudo-definitions between a conditional branch that tests for equality and the target of the branch, assigning the constant value to the variable. In this program, the compiler can add the assignment `I = 1` before line 2. Such an assignment need not be compiled and executed, but is treated as an assertion about the values of variables. We will not discuss this further here.

The constant propagation algorithm is shown in Figure 6.18. It uses the control flow graph and the FUD chain graph, except the FUD chain edges are "turned around"; that is, they go from definitions to uses (def-use chains). Reversing all the edges can be done either at FUD chain construction or afterward, with a single pass through the program. Algorithm ConstantProp assumes the following information is available:

1.   *V* is the set of CFG nodes in the program.
2.   *E* is the set of CFG edges.
3.   *SUCC(v)* is the set of successors of CFG node *v*.
4.   *Count(SUCC(v))* is the number of successors of node *v*.
5.   *Target(s)* is the use for a def-use link *s*.
6.   *Source(s)* is the definition or ϕ-term for a def-use link *s*.

```
        Algorithm ConstantProp:
 (1)    for e ∈ E do Reachable(e) = False endfor
 (2)    for v ∈ V do
 (3)        Reachable(v) = False
 (4)        for x ∈ Expressions(V) do Value(x) = ⊤ endfor
 (5)        for p ∈ Φ(V) do Value(p) = ⊤ endfor
 (6)    endfor
 (7)    for e ∈ SUCC(Entry) do
 (8)        AddCFGEdge( e )
 (9)    endfor
(10)    while CFGWorkList ≠ ∅ ∨ DefUseWorkList ≠ ∅ do
(11)        if CFGWorkList ≠ ∅ then
(12)            remove e from CFGWorkList
(13)            Reachable(e) = True
(14)            v = Target(e)
(15)            for p ∈ Φ(v) do
(16)                Visit-ϕ( p )
(17)            endfor
(18)            if ¬Reachable(v) then
(19)                Reachable(v) = True
(20)                for x ∈ Expressions(v) do
(21)                    VisitExpression( x )
(22)                endfor
(23)            endif
(24)            if Count(SUCC(v)) = 1 then
(25)                AddCFGEdge( SUCC(v) )
(26)            endif
(27)        endif
(28)        if DefUseWorkList ≠ ∅ then
(29)            remove s from DefUseWorkList
(30)            x = Target(s)
(31)            if x is a ϕ-term then
(32)                Visit-ϕ( x )
(33)            else
(34)                VisitExpression( x )
(35)            endif
(36)        endif
(37)    endwhile
```

FIGURE 6.18 Constant propagation with FUD chains.

The algorithm uses the following intermediate data structures:

1. *CFGWorkList* is a work list of CFG edges, initialized to contain the successor(s) of the *Entry* vertex; note that we do not use the slicing edge here.
2. *DefUseWorkList* is a work list of def-use links; it is initially empty.
3. *Reachable(e)* is a flag that determines whether CFG edge *e* has been marked as possibly being reachable, or executable; it is initially false for all edges.
4. *Reachable(v)* for CFG node *v* is a flag that tells whether the algorithm has found that node *v* is reachable; it is initially false for all nodes.
5. *Value(p)* is the abstract value computed for each operation *p*; it is initialized to $\top$.

The result is stored in *Value(p)* for all operations *p*. The algorithm picks edges from either work list until both work lists are empty.

A flow edge is added to *CFGWorkList* the first time the algorithm decides that the edge might be reachable. For unconditional flow edges (nodes with only one successor), this happens at line 24. For conditional edges, this is done in procedure VisitExpression, discussed later. When a flow edge is removed at line 12, the edge is marked as reachable and all the ϕ-terms at the target node are evaluated. If the target CFG node was not previously marked as reachable, this is the first time the node has been visited; it is marked as reachable and any expressions in the node are evaluated.

A def-use link is added to *DefUseWorkList* each time a definition is evaluated to have a different abstract value; this occurs in procedures Visit-ϕ and Visit Expression. When a def-use link is removed at line 29, the target is either a ϕ-term or a variable use in an expression. In either case, the target is reevaluated.

The two Visit procedures are shown in Figure 6.19. When evaluating a ϕ-term, the abstract value is found by ignoring any operand corresponding to an unreachable edge; this is the test at line 4, which prevents unreachable code from affecting the constant propagation result. When the reevaluation results in a different abstract value (line 8), all the def-use links from this ϕ-term are put on *DefUseWorkList*. The first time this happens, the abstract value changes from $\top$ to either some constant value or $\bot$. If one of the operands subsequently changes its value, this expression may change its abstract value from a constant to $\bot$. However, once the abstract value is $\bot$, it never changes again; thus line 8 tests true at most twice for each expression, so the algorithm must terminate.

Each expression is evaluated according to the rules for that expression type. Any expression that is too complex, or requires external functions, user input, or nonscalar memory fetches, can be conservatively evaluated as $\bot$. Again, when the evaluation results in a different abstract value (line 18), any def-use links from this expression are added to *DefUseWorkList*. When an expression that controls a conditional branch is evaluated, the outgoing CFG edges corresponding to the new

```
(1)  procedure Visit-ϕ( p )
(2)      OldValue = Value(p); Value(p) = ⊤
(3)      for n ∈ Operands(p) do
(4)          if Reachable(Edge(n)) then
(5)              Value(p) = ϕ-val(Value(p), Value(Source(n)))
(6)          endif
(7)      endfor
(8)      if Value(p) ≠ OldValue then
(9)          for each def-use link d out of p do
(10)             if Reachable(Target(d)) then
(11)                 add all def-use links d to DefUseWorkList
(12)             endif
(13)         endfor
(14)     endif
(15) end Visit-ϕ

(16) procedure VisitExpression( x )
(17)     OldValue = Value(x); Value(x) = Evaluate(x)
(18)     if Value(x) ≠ OldValue then
(19)         for each def-use link d out of x do
(20)             if Reachable(Target(d)) then
(21)                 add all def-use links d to DefUseWorkList
(22)             endif
(23)         endfor
(24)         if x controls a conditional branch then
(25)             if Value(x) = ⊥ then
(26)                 for s ∈ SUCC(Node(x)) do AddCFGEdge( s ) endfor
(27)             else
(28)                 let s be the edge that value Value(x) would take
(29)                 AddCFGEdge( s )
(30)             endif
(31)         endif
(32)     endif
(33) end VisitExpression

(34) procedure AddCFGEdge( e )
(35)     if ¬(e ∈ CFGWorkList ∨ Reachable(e)) then
(36)         add e to CFGWorkList
(37)     endif
(38) end AddCFGEdge
```

FIGURE 6.19 Procedures used in the constant propagation algorithm.

abstract value are added to the flow graph edge work list; an abstract value of $\bot$ tells the compiler to add all the CFG edges (line 26), while a constant abstract value tells the compiler to choose the one edge that would be taken with that constant abstract value (lines 28–29). The test in procedure AddCFGEdge at line 35 insures that a flow edge is never added to the work list more than once.

To keep *DefUseWorkList* shorter, the algorithm should add def-use links only when the CFG node containing the target is marked as reachable; that is, when at least one of the predecessors of that node is reachable.

Example 6.16

Show the constant propagation algorithm on the following program fragment:

(1) $I_1 = 1$
(2) $J_2 = 2$
(3)   if $I_{3 \leadsto 1} < 2$ then
(4) $J_5 = J_{4 \leadsto 2} + 2$
(5)   else
(6) $J_6 = 99$
(7)   endif
(8) $\phi J_{7 \leadsto 5,6}$
(9) $K_9 = J_{8 \leadsto 7} + 2$

Solution

The control flow graph and def-use links for this fragment are shown in Figure 6.20. Initially, only the *Entry* $\rightarrow B_1$ edge is added to *CFGWorkList*. After visiting B_1, constant values have been found for $I_1 = 1$ and $J_2 = 2$. No def-use links need to be added to *DefUseWorkList*, since the target nodes have yet been marked reachable. However, the branch condition $I < 2$ also has the constant value *True*; thus the flow edge $B_1 \rightarrow B_2$ is added to *CFGWorkList*. After visiting B_2, another constant value has been computed for $J_5 = 4$. Since this node has only one successor, the edge $B_2 \rightarrow B_4$ is added to *CFGWorkList*. Visiting B_4 evaluates the ϕ-term as $J_7 = 4$. Finally, the algorithm evaluates $K_9 = 6$.

Since the assignment to J_6 is not reachable, it can be eliminated as unreachable code. Note that in this example, *DefUseWorkList* was never used, since each time a def-use link was inspected, the target node hadn't yet been marked reachable.

6.7 Data Dependence for Scalars

The last analysis technique we describe that uses FUD chains is a method to compute value-based data dependence relations for scalars assigned in loops, finding the exact data dependence distance and direction. We first focus on computing

6.7 ▪ Data Dependence for Scalars

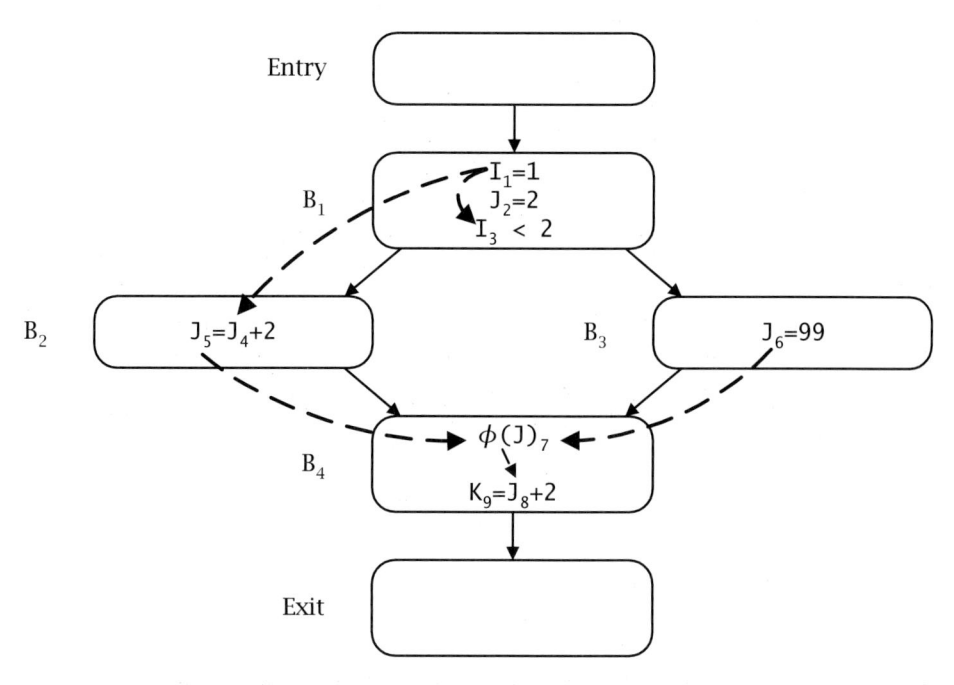

FIGURE 6.20 CFG edges are solid; def-use links are dashed.

[Figure 6.20: Control flow graph with Entry node leading to B_1 containing $I_1=1$, $J_2=2$, $I_3 < 2$; branching to B_2 with $J_5=J_4+2$ and B_3 with $J_6=99$; both merging into B_4 containing $\phi(J)_7$ and $K_9=J_8+2$; then to Exit.]

flow dependence; at the end of this section we discuss how to modify the algorithm for output and anti-dependence.

Algorithm FollowChain follows the FUD chain from a use to determine what definitions reach that use. There is a flow dependence from every real definition (killing or nonkilling) that reaches this use. The only issue is to determine the exact dependence distance or direction. For instance, in the following program:

(1) $T_1 = \ldots$
(2)   loop
          $\phi(T)_{2 \leadsto 1,4}$
(3) $\ldots = T_{3 \leadsto 2} \ldots$
(4) $T_4 = \ldots$
(5) $\ldots = T_{5 \leadsto 4} \ldots$
(6)   endloop

Algorithm FollowChain will find the following reaching definitions for each use:

use	reaching definitions
T_3	T_1, T_4
T_5	T_4

These reaching definitions correspond to three flow dependence relations: $S_1 \; \delta^f \; S_3$, $S_4 \; \delta^f \; S_3$, and $S_4 \; \delta^f \; S_5$. The $S_1 \; \delta^f \; S_3$ dependence has no distance or direction vector associated with it, since S_1 is not in any loops. The dependence distance for $S_4 \; \delta^f \; S_3$ is always exactly 1, since S_4 always assigns a new value to T, so S_3 always gets the value from the previous iteration. With conditional assignments, we may get a nonconstant dependence distance, as we shall see. The dependence distance for $S_4 \; \delta^f \; S_5$ is exactly zero, since S_5 always gets the value assigned to T by S_4 in the current iteration.

In this program, we say the use of T at line 3 is *upward-exposed* from the loop, since it may use a value of T from outside the loop. The use of T at line 5 is not upward-exposed from the loop, since the value it uses is always the one assigned within the loop.

For scalar dependence in a loop, there are four possible situations:

- Data dependence only in the current iteration; dependence distance vector is (0).
- Data dependence only from the one previous iteration; dependence distance vector is (1).
- Data dependence from any previous iteration; dependence direction vector is (<).
- Data dependence from the current or any previous iteration; dependence direction vector is (≤).

Algorithm ScalarDD, shown in Figure 6.21, computes the flow dependence relations to each of a set of uses using FUD chains, handling loop-header-ϕ terms specially. The algorithm is a modification of algorithm FollowChain; as before, we assume that the compiler restructured the CFG so that each loop has a unique preheader and post-body. Each loop-header-ϕ term will have exactly two links, one to the value coming into the loop and one to the value coming around the loop. The algorithm assumes at line 16 that the second link from the loop-header-ϕ term is the link around the loop. The algorithm assumes the following information is available:

1. *Chain(p)* is the FUD chain link for a reference *p*.
2. *ϕ-Chain(p)* is a vector of FUD chain links for a ϕ-term *p*.
3. *Uses* is a set of uses for which the data dependence relations are desired.

The algorithm builds the following intermediate data structures:

1. *Reaching(lh)* is a set of definitions inside a loop that reach the loop-header-ϕ term *lh*, initialized to an empty set; this is constructed using procedure FindReaching, which is shown in Figure 6.22.

6.7 ▪ Data Dependence for Scalars

```
         Algorithm ScalarDD:
(1)      for lh ∈ loop-header-φ do
(2)          Reaching(lh) = ∅
(3)          Self(lh) = False
(4)      endfor
(5)      for u ∈ Uses do
(6)          FindDependence( Chain(u), u )
(7)      endfor

(8)      procedure FindDependence( d, u )
(9)          if Marked(d) = u then return endif
(10)         /* definition d reaches this use */
(11)         Marked(d) = u
(12)         if d is a loop-header-φ then
(13)             let m be the loop
(14)             FindDependence( φ-Chain(d)[1], u )
(15)             if Reaching(d) = ∅ then
(16)                 FindReaching( φ-Chain(d)[2], d )
(17)             endif
(18)             if Self(d) then
(19)                 for c ∈ Reaching(d) do
(20)                     add $S_c\ \delta^f\ S_u$ with (<) direction for loop m
(21)                 endfor
(22)             else
(23)                 for c ∈ Reaching(d) do
(24)                     add $S_c\ \delta^f\ S_u$ with (1) distance for loop m
(25)                 endfor
(26)             endif
(27)         else if d is a φ-term then
(28)             for each link j do
(29)                 FindDependence( φ-Chain(d)[j], u )
(30)             endfor
(31)         else
(32)             add loop independent $S_d\ \delta^f\ S_u$
(33)             if d is a nonkilling definition then
(34)                 FindDependence( Chain(d), u )
(35)             endif
(36)         endif
(37)     end FindDependence
```

FIGURE 6.21 Algorithm for scalar data dependence in loops, with distance.

```
(1)  procedure FindReaching( d, lh )
(2)      if MarkedReaching(d) = lh then return endif
(3)      MarkedReaching(d) = lh
(4)      if d = lh then
(5)          Self(lh) = True
(6)      else if d is a ϕ-term then
(7)          for each link j do
(8)              FindReaching( ϕ-Chain(d)[j], lh )
(9)          endfor
(10)     else
(11)         add d to Reaching(lh)
(12)         if d is a nonkilling definition then
(13)             FindReaching( Chain(d), lh )
(14)         endif
(15)     endif
(16) end FindReaching
```

FIGURE 6.22 Procedure to find all loop definitions that reach a loop-header-ϕ.

2. *Self(lh)* is a flag for each loop-header-ϕ term *lh* that is set when the loop-header-ϕ term reaches itself; that is, when there is a path from the loop header to the back edge without a killing definition of the variable.

3. *Marked(d)* keeps track of whether a definition or ϕ-term *d* has already been visited for this use.

4. *MarkedReaching(d)* is used in procedure FindReaching to keep track of whether definition or ϕ-term *d* has already been visited for this loop header.

Procedure FindReaching is also a modification of algorithm FollowChain, adapted to not follow links outside the current loop.

The output is the construction of scalar data dependence relations with distance or direction vector information. Any real definition reached within the body of the loop before reaching the loop-header-ϕ is the source of a loop independent data dependence; see line 32. The distance vector for a loop independent dependence has all zero entries, where the number of entries is equal to the number of loops that surround both the def and the use; in fact, the distance vector can be length zero. If the loop-header-ϕ term can be reached from a use, then the definitions in *Reaching(lh)* are the sources of loop carried dependence relations to that use, where *lh* is the loop-header-ϕ term. If *Self(lh)* is set, then a definition in the loop might reach a use in any subsequent iteration; in that case, any loop carried dependence has nonconstant distance, as given in line 20. Otherwise, there must be a killing definition of the variable on every path through the loop, and any loop carried dependence has distance one, added in line 24. For loop carried dependence

6.7 • Data Dependence for Scalars

relations, the dependence direction or distance vector has a $<$ or 1 entry for the loop that carries the dependence, with $=$ or 0 entries for outer loops and $\star$ entries for inner loops. The recursive call at line 14 finds dependence from definitions outside the loop or carried by an outer loop.

Example 6.17

What are the dependence relations for the two uses of T in the loop below?

```
(1)    T₁ = ...
(2)    loop
           φ(T)₂~1,5
(3)        if ... then
(4)            T₃ = ...
(5)            ... = T₄~3 ...
(6)        endif
           φ(T)₅~3,2
(7)        ... = T₆~5 ...
(8)    endloop
```

Solution

To find the flow dependence sources for the use T_4, the FUD chain is traced back only to T_3, for the loop independent dependence $S_4\ \delta^f_{(0)}\ S_5$. To find the flow dependence sources for the use at T_6, the FUD chain is followed back to $\phi(T)_5$, then to T_3 and $\phi(T)_2$. From T_3 the algorithm finds the loop independent data dependence $S_4\ \delta^f_{(0)}\ S_7$. When tracing back to $\phi(T)_2$, because it is a loop-header-ϕ term, the algorithm first follows the incoming link to T_1, for which the loop independent dependence $S_1\ \delta^f\ S_7$ from outside the loop is added. Back at $\phi(T)_2$, the algorithm finds the set $Reaching(\phi(T)_2) = \{T_3\}$, and $Self(\phi(T)_2) = True$. Finally, the algorithm adds the loop carried dependence $S_4\ \delta^f_{(<)}\ S_7$. The final dependence relations are shown in the table below:

$$S_4\ \delta^f_{(0)}\ S_5 \qquad S_4\ \delta^f_{(0)}\ S_7$$
$$S_1\ \delta^f\ S_7 \qquad S_4\ \delta^f_{(<)}\ S_7$$

6.7.1 Output Dependence

A trivial change to algorithm ScalarDD will allow it to be used for output dependence relations also. One option for FUD chain construction discussed in Section 6.2 is to add def-def links; that is, a link from each definition to the reaching definition, as if this definition were both a use and a redefinition. If we add def-def links for each definition, then use algorithm ScalarDD starting from *Chain(d)* for a definition *d*, the algorithm will find the output dependence relations to definition *d*.

6.7.2 Anti-Dependence

Finding anti-dependence relations requires a major modification. FUD chains do not contain the proper information to find anti-dependence. What we need is a way to find what uses are redefined by each definition. Another data structure, similar to FUD chains but linked in a different way, can be used for this purpose. This structure, which we call *factored redef-use* (FRUD) chains, links each definition to the closest downward-exposed use that reaches it. FRUD chains are built using the same methods as are used to build FUD chains. Each use is treated in FRUD chains the way a nonkilling definition is treated in FUD chains, and each definition is treated like a use and a killing definition. We use Υ-terms (upsilon-terms) instead of ϕ-terms to collect multiple downward-exposed reaching uses. Algorithm Placement, shown in Figure 6.5, is used (almost unmodified) to place Υ-terms where two or more downward-exposed uses reach, by initializing *WorkList* with the set of CFG nodes in *uses(M)*, nodes containing uses of variable *M*, instead of *D(M)*.

Algorithm FRUD-Chain, shown in Figure 6.23, is a modification of algorithm Chain, with the following corresponding data structures:

FRUD-Chain	Chain
CurrUse(M)	*CurrDef(M)*
Chainuse(R)	*Chain(R)*
SaveChainUse(R)	*SaveChain(R)*
Υ-*Chain(R)*	ϕ-*Chain(R)*

Every use of a variable *M* is linked to the current valueof *CurrUse(M)*, the downward-exposed use reaching *M*, and the value of *CurrUse(M)* is updated. Every definition of *M* is also linked to *CurrUse(M)*; at a killing definition, the value of *CurrUse(M)* is set to $\bot$, meaning that there is no downward-exposed use after the def.

In general, Υ-terms will be placed in different locations than ϕ-terms. There may be definitions of a variable with no uses, required ϕ-terms but no Υ-terms, or vice versa.

Example 6.18

Show the FRUD chains and anti-dependence relations for variable T for the loop in Example 6.20.

Solution

The FRUD placement algorithm will put an Υ-term at the loop header and at the endif. The program text below is a representation of the FRUD chains, where the links are from definitions and uses to downward-exposed uses.

```
        Algorithm FRUD-Chain:
 (1)    for M ∈ Symbols do
 (2)        CurrUse(M) = ⊥
 (3)    endfor
 (4)    Search(Entry)

 (5)    procedure Search(X)
 (6)        for each variable use or def or φ-term R ∈ X do
 (7)            let M be the variable referenced at R
 (8)            if R is a use then
 (9)                Chainuse(R) = CurrUse(M)
(10)                SaveChainUse(R) = CurrUse(M)
(11)                CurrUse(M) = R
(12)            else if R is an ϒ-term then
(13)                SaveChainUse(R) = CurrUse(M)
(14)                CurrUse(M) = R
(15)            else if R is a def then
(16)                Chainuse(R) = CurrUse(M)
(17)                SaveChainUse(R) = CurrUse(M)
(18)                if R is a killing def then
(19)                    CurrUse(M) = ⊥
(20)                endif
(21)            endif
(22)        endfor
(23)        for Y ∈ SUCC(X) do
(24)            J = WhichPred(X → Y)
(25)            for each ϒ-term R ∈ Y do
(26)                let M be the variable referenced at R
(27)                ϒ-Chain(R)[J] = CurrUse(M)
(28)            endfor
(29)        endfor
(30)        for Y ∈ Child(X) do
(31)            Search(Y)
(32)        endfor
(33)        for each variable use or def or ϒ-term R ∈ X in reverse order do
(34)            let M be the variable referenced at R
(35)            CurrUse(M) = SaveChainUse(R)
(36)        endfor
(37)    end Search
```

FIGURE 6.23 FRUD chaining algorithm.

```
(1)     T_1↝⊥ = ...
(2)     loop
            ϒ(T)_{2↝⊥,6}
(3)         if...then
(4)             T_{3↝2} = ...
(5)             ... = T_{4↝⊥} ...
(6)         endif
            ϒ(T)_{5↝4,2}
(7)         ... = T_{6↝5} ...
(8)     endloop
```

To find anti-dependence, algorithm ScalarDD, shown in Figure 6.21, is used, starting from the definitions, tracing back through *Chainuse* and ϒ-*Chain* links to reaching uses. In this case, there are two definitions, T_1 and T_3. In the first case, there are no reaching uses, so there are no anti-dependence relations to that definition. T_3 is reached by any uses that reach $\Upsilon(T)_2$. One of these links is again empty, since there are no uses outside the loop. The other link causes the compiler to find $Reaching(\Upsilon(T)_2)$, the set of uses in the loop that can reach $\Upsilon(T)_2$, and $Self(\Upsilon(T)_2)$, which flags whether $\Upsilon(T)_2$ can reach itself. In this case, the set $Reaching(\Upsilon(T)_2) = \{T_6, T_4\}$, and $Self(\Upsilon) = True$. Thus the algorithm will find the two loop carried anti-dependence relations $S_7 \; \delta^a_{(<)} \; S_4$ and $S_5 \; \delta^a_{(<)} \; S_4$.

6.8 In the Pit

Factored use-def chains are really nothing more than an interpretation of the well-known static single assignment (SSA) form of the program. Our interpretation does not carry the semantic baggage of renaming variables or trying to preserve any single-assignment restrictions.

Experience has shown that the actual number of ϕ-terms is linear in the size of the program, although in the worst case, the number can be nonlinear. Whether FUD chains save space a bit vector representation of reaching definitions depends on how large the data structure is to represent a ϕ-term.

Induction variables detection here is aimed at supporting array dependence analysis by finding the linear sequence of values for each induction variable or even each inductive expression. Standard compiler analysis uses the term *induction variable detection* to find places where strength reduction can be applied, generally replacing a multiplication by an addition. The set of operations that can be strength-reduced is different than the set of linear induction variables as defined in this chapter.

The general formulation of constant propagation uses a meet operation on a lattice of abstract values. Our constant propagation method actually includes constant folding, where the compiler computes expressions whose operands are constants. For integer and logical values, this is generally safe. For floating point values, this may not always produce the same value at compile time as at run time. For instance, in the IEEE floating point standard, zero times another number may not yield zero, if NaNs (not-a-number values) are included in the domain. The IEEE standard also allows the program to dynamically change the rounding mode, which may make compile time constant folding impossible, unless the compiler can determine there is no rounding error.

6.9 Further Reading

The algorithms for finding the FUD chains (equivalent to the static single assignment, or SSA, form) are presented by Cytron et al. (1991). A factored SSA form described by Choi et al. (1994) closely resembles FUD chains.

An alternative sparse data-flow graph representation for program analysis is shown by Johnson and Pingali (1993). The program dependence web (Ballance et al. [1990]) is another representation that encompasses the advantages of several others. One step to build the program dependence web is construction of the gated single assignment form, where ϕ-terms are replaced by gates with a predicate that chooses the appropriate operand; Havlak (1993) discusses how to construct a version of the gated single assignment form.

Wolfe (1992) describes the method presented here for finding induction variables using FUD chains; these advanced methods can also identify and classify a variety of other interesting patterns that are useful for dependence analysis. Note that we are interested in finding induction variables for use in dependence analysis, which is different from finding induction variables for strength reduction.

The constant propagation algorithm shown here was developed by Wegman and Zadeck (1991). An interprocedural constant propagation algorithm is described by Callahan et al. (1986). Handling aliases, such as pointer aliases, in data-flow analyses based on FUD chains or SSA form is discussed by Cytron and Gershbein (1993).

EXERCISES

6.1 With the control flow graph shown in Figure 6.24, find the dominance frontier for each node in the graph.

6.2 Find the iterated dominance frontier for the set of nodes $\{Entry, 1, 3\}$ in the CFG in Figure 6.24.

6.3 Find the join set $J(\{Entry, 1, 3\})$ for the CFG in Figure 6.24.

6.4 Assume there are definitions of variable T as shown in the CFG in Figure 6.24. Find the reaching definitions for each point in the program.

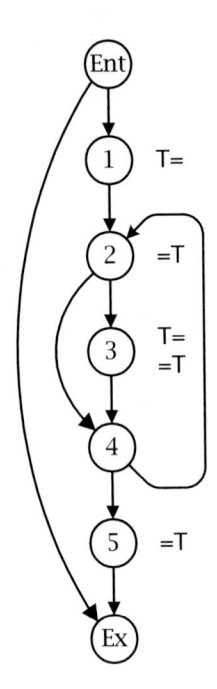

FIGURE 6.24 Control Flow Graph for exercises.

6.5 Place ϕ-terms for variable T in Figure 6.24 and show the FUD chain links.

6.6 Use the FUD chains and algorithm FollowChain to find the reaching definitions for T at each use.

6.7 Use algorithm ScalarDD to find all the flow dependence relations for T in the CFG in Figure 6.24.

6.8 Find the FUD-chains for the scalars I, J, and K in the following loop:

```
(1)   J = 1
(2)   I = 50
(3)   K = 0
(4)   loop
(5)     I = I + 1
(6)     if I < J then exit
(7)     J = J + 2
(8)     K = 2 * J
(9)     if A[I] > 0 then
(10)      K = 2 * I
(11)    endif
(12)  endloop
```

6.9 Use algorithm Induct to identify the linear induction variables in the previous problem. If possible, find the trip count of the loop.

6.10 Place ϕ-operations and find the FUD-chains for the loop nest in the following program. Find the linear induction variables in each loop.

```
(1)   K = 1
(2)   I = 1
(3)   loop
(4)       if I > 100 then exit
(5)       J = 1
(6)       loop
(7)           if J > I then exit
(8)           J = J + 1
(9)           K = K + 1
(10)      endloop
(11)      I = I + 1
(12)  endloop
```

6.11 K is a linear induction variable in the inner loop in the previous problem. What is the behavior of K in the outer loop?

6.12 Show that the iterated Join set $J^+(S)$ for a set of CFG nodes S is equal to $J(S)$; that is, show that iterating adds no new nodes. This can be done by showing that $J(S \cup J(S)) = J(S)$. If $J(S \cup J(S)) \neq J(S)$, then there is some node $c \in J(S)$ ($c = J(a,b)$ where $a, b \in S$) and another node $d \in S \cup J(S)$ such that some $e \in J(c,d)$ is not in $J(S)$.

6.13 Show that algorithm Chain will work with a depth-first traversal of any depth-first spanning tree instead of the dominator tree.

6.14 Some wrap-around variables can be classified as linear induction variables, when the initial value happens to fit the linear sequence properly. Such a case is shown by variable J in the following loop:

```
(1)   J = 1
(2)   I = 2
(3)   loop
(4)       ... = J
(5)       J = I
(6)       I = I + 1
(7)   endloop
```

Insert loop-header-ϕ terms for I and J and show the FUD chains in this loop. Find the cycles in the FUD chain graph. Classify the linear induction variables and find the linear sequence. Determine rules for detecting when a wrap-around variable can fit a linear sequence and be classified as a linear induction variable.

6.15 Find the FUD chains for each example loop below, and find the trip count and exit value for I:

```
(1)   I = 0                       (1)   I = 0
(2)   loop                        (2)   loop
(3)       if I > 100 then exit    (3)       I = I + 1
(4)       I = I + 1               (4)       if I > 100 then exit
(5)   endloop                     (5)   endloop
```

6.16 Find the FUD chains and the linear induction variables for the following loop:

```
(1)   I = 0
(2)   loop
(3)     I = I + 1
(4)     if A(I) > 0 then
(5)       J = 2 * I + 1
(6)       B(J) = ...
(7)     endif
(8)     C(J) = ...
(9)   endloop
```

6.17 When there are multiple exits from the loop, the procedure to find exit values can be applied by looking at the particular exit condition. Determine how to find the exit value for each exit, and apply it to the following loop:

```
(1)    I = 0
(2)    J = 1
(3)    loop
(4)      J = J + 1
(5)      if J > 50 then goto L1
(6)      I = I + 2
(7)      if I > N then goto L2
(8)    endloop
(9)  L1: K = J
(10)     goto L3
(11) L2: L = I
(12) L3: ...
```

6.18 Use algorithm ConstantProp to propagate constants in the following program, after constructing the FUD chains:

```
(1)    I = 1
(2)    J = 2
(3)    K = 0
(4)    M = J
(5)    loop
(6)      L = K
(7)      K = J
(8)      if I = K then
(9)        K = K + 1
(10)     endif
(11)     M = K
(12)     K = L + 1
(13)   endloop
(14)   N = M - I
```

Identify any unreachable code after finding constant predicates.

6.19 Find the FUD chains and scalar flow dependence relations in the following loop:

```
(1)   T = A[N]
(2)   I = 1
(3)   loop
(4)      I = I + 1
(5)      if I >= N then exit
(6)      if I < N then
(7)         U = A[I+1]
(8)      else
(9)         U = A[1]
(10)     endif
(11)     T = (T + U)/2
(12)     A[I] = T
(13)  endloop
```

6.20 Show the def-def links in your FUD chains for the previous exercise. Use them to find scalar output dependence relations.

6.21 Find the FRUD chains and scalar anti-dependence relations in the preceding loop.

7 DATA DEPENDENCE ANALYSIS FOR ARRAYS

Data dependence analysis for arrays determines when two array accesses refer to different array elements, or determines dependence distance when they refer to the same element. This chapter studies how to apply techniques from Chapter 4 to solve the problems that arise when finding dependence relations for arrays.

For scalars, data-flow analysis or the FUD chain–based analysis presented in the previous chapter can find exact data dependence relations along with distance and direction information. For arrays, the compiler must examine the subscript expressions. In the examples shown in Chapter 5, the subscript expressions were trivial. In general, the compiler must formulate a *data dependence system,* and solve it as a system of linear equations and inequalities. This chapter presents a number of solvers, each with different precision and performance characteristics.

We concentrate here on *affine subscript expressions*; that is, subscript expressions that are affine functions of the loop induction variables. These are sometimes called *linear subscripts*, since the expressions are linear combinations of the induction variables. In practice, these are the most common forms of subscripts in loops. Examples of linear and nonlinear subscripts are shown in Figure 7.1.

A[I]	linear
A[I+J-1]	linear
A[I*J]	nonlinear (product of two induction variables)
A[I/J]	nonlinear (ratio of two induction variables)
A[MOD(I,2)+1]	nonlinear (nonlinear function)
A[IP[I]+1]	nonlinear (indexed subscript)
A[10*I-1,2*J]	linear, linear
A[2*I-1,I*J]	linear, nonlinear

FIGURE 7.1 Examples of linear and nonlinear subscript expressions where I and J are linear induction variables.

In the presence of a nonlinear subscript expression, a compiler can either ignore that dimension (equivalent to assuming the worst case), or use a special case solver. There has been some work on handling certain general nonlinear expressions numerically, but they do not appear frequently enough in programs to warrant inclusion in most compilers. Many current compilers do handle certain special cases, such as *indexed subscripts,* A[IP[I]], since they occur frequently in certain applications. The material in this chapter computes address-based dependence relations.

7.1 Building the Dependence System

When a compiler attempts to determine the dependence between two array references with linear subscript expressions, the first step is to form a dependence equation. The loop induction variables are the unknowns in the equation, while the coefficients are compile-time constants. There is one coefficient for each loop induction variable in each subscript expression, plus a constant coefficient.

Generally we will use induction variables corresponding to normalized or seminormalized iteration vectors. Normalized dependence equations are easy to find; the constant part for each subscript function is its value on the first iteration of the loop, and the step for each unknown is the amount by which the value increases for one iteration through the corresponding loop. Also, as shown in Chapter 6, our method for identifying induction variables can also identify linear subscript expressions. When an expression is linear, the coefficients can be read off the induction variable representation. When finding dependence between definitions and uses, we use $i_1^d, i_2^d, \ldots$ for the unknown normalized induction variables at the definition, and $i_1^u, i_2^u, \ldots$ for the unknown at the use. When finding dependence between two definitions, we use $i_1^{d_a}, i_2^{d_a}, \ldots$ and $i_1^{d_b}, i_2^{d_b}, \ldots$ for the unknowns.

Once the dependence equations are found, the compiler looks for solutions. We will express the dependence equations in matrix notation as $\mathbf{Ai} = \mathbf{c}$, where $\mathbf{A}$ is the coefficient matrix, $\mathbf{i}$ is the vector of unknowns, and $\mathbf{c}$ is the constant vector. If there are no solutions to the system of equations, there can be no dependence. The compiler should also consider additional constraints:

1. For dependence to exist, a solution must lie within the limits of the induction variable imposed by the loop limits.
2. For dependence to exist, there must be an integer solution.
3. The compiler will often want to determine a dependence distance or a direction vector.

A system of dependence equations along with these constraints is called a *dependence system*.

Example 7.1

What is the dependence equation for the two references to the array B in the following loop?

```
(1)     for I = 2 to N do
(2)         for J = 1 to I do
(3)             B[I,J] = B[I-1,J] + A[I]*C[J]
(4)         endfor
(5)     endfor
```

Solution

There are two dependence equations; one for each dimension. The two subscript expressions can be classified as linear induction expressions, as follows:

$$B[2+i_1, 1+i_2] = B[1+i_1, 1+i_2] + A[2+i_1]*C[1+i_2]$$

In terms of the normalized iteration vectors, the two dependence equations are:

$$2 + i_1^d = 1 + i_1^u$$
$$1 + i_2^d = 1 + i_2^u$$

There are four unknowns in two equations. We can write this as a single system in matrix notation as:

$$\begin{pmatrix} 1 & -1 & 0 & 0 \\ 0 & 0 & 1 & -1 \end{pmatrix} \begin{pmatrix} i_1^d \\ i_1^u \\ i_2^d \\ i_2^u \end{pmatrix} = \begin{pmatrix} -1 \\ 0 \end{pmatrix}$$

7.1.1 Loop Limit Constraints

As mentioned earlier, the loop limits add constraints to the dependence system that should be taken into account. When using normalized iteration vectors, the lower limit of each induction variable is zero, and the upper limit is one less than the trip count for the loop. In simple countable loops, the trip count is easy to determine from the loop limits. The loop limit constraints appear as inequality constraints on the unknowns.

If the dependence equations are cast in terms of unnormalized index variables, then the lower limits will not be so trivial. In the case of triangular loops, the limit of one index variable may depend on another. As with subscript expressions, most solution methods only handle situations where the limits are a linear combination of outer loop index variables. An entire dependence system can be expressed in matrix notation as a system of linear equalities, **Ai** = **c**, and linear inequalities, **Bi** ≤ **b**. An inequality with a positive coefficient for an unknown is an upper bound for that unknown, while an inequality with a negative coefficient is a lower bound.

When the loop limits are truly nonlinear, such as a function call or an array element, the dependence system may not include a bound for that unknown. The dependence solver will still be conservative. That is, it will compute a potential dependence whenever there really is dependence; but it may also find a potential dependence when the actual loop limits would preclude any such situation. Thus, ignoring the loop limits is always safe.

Example 7.2

Find the dependence system for the two references to the array B in the following loop:

(1)   for I = 2 to 100 do
(2)   for J = 1 to I-1 do
(3)   B[I,J] = B[J,I]
(4)   endfor
(5)   endfor

Solution

The dependence equations for the two references to B are:

$$2 + i_1^d = 1 + i_2^u$$
$$1 + i_2^d = 2 + i_1^u$$

The lower bound of each of the four unknowns is again zero. The trip count for the outer loop is 99, so the upper bounds for i_1^d and i_1^u are 98. The normalized trip count for the inner loop is $1 + i_1$. Thus, the upper bound for the inner loop index variables is $i_2^d \le i_1^d$ and $i_2^u \le i_1^u$. In matrix form, the dependence system is shown in Figure 7.2. The sixth and last inequalities give the upper bounds for i_2^d and i_2^u, respectively, where $i_2^d \le i_1^d$ is written as $-i_1^d + i_2^d \le 0$. This means that the sixth and eighth inequalities can be treated either as upper bounds for i_2^d and i_2^u, as lower bounds for i_1^d and i_1^u, or both.

$$\begin{pmatrix} 1 & 0 & 0 & -1 \\ 0 & -1 & 1 & 0 \end{pmatrix} \begin{pmatrix} i_1^d \\ i_1^u \\ i_2^d \\ i_2^u \end{pmatrix} = \begin{pmatrix} -1 \\ 1 \end{pmatrix}$$

$$\begin{pmatrix} -1 & 0 & 0 & 0 \\ 1 & 0 & 0 & 0 \\ 0 & -1 & 0 & 0 \\ 0 & 1 & 0 & 0 \\ 0 & 0 & -1 & 0 \\ -1 & 0 & 1 & 0 \\ 0 & 0 & 0 & -1 \\ 0 & -1 & 0 & 1 \end{pmatrix} \begin{pmatrix} i_1^d \\ i_1^u \\ i_2^d \\ i_2^u \end{pmatrix} \le \begin{pmatrix} 0 \\ 98 \\ 0 \\ 98 \\ 0 \\ 0 \\ 0 \\ 0 \end{pmatrix}$$

FIGURE 7.2 Dependence system in matrix form.

7.1.2 Symbolic Analysis

User variables may also appear in subscript expressions. A general way to handle them is to treat each user variable as another unknown in the dependence system. When the coefficient for the unknown turns out to be zero, it is effectively eliminated from the dependence system. When the coefficient is nonzero, a dependence system solver may still be able to determine independence. User variables may also appear in loop limits. Those can also be handled by treating the variable as another unknown in the dependence system. In practice, the same unknown may appear in a subscript as well as in an upper limit.

Example 7.3

What is the dependence system for the two references to B below?

(1)   for I = 1 to N-1 do
(2)   for J = 1 to N-I+1 do
(3)   B[I,J] = B[J,N-I]
(4)   endfor
(5)   endfor

Solution

The normalized dependence equations are

$$1 + i_1^d = 1 + i_1^u$$
$$1 + i_2^d = 1 - i_1^u + N$$

The variable N appears in the upper limits of both loops; treating N as another unknown in the system, the dependence system is shown in Figure 7.3.

$$\begin{pmatrix} 0 & 1 & 0 & 0 & -1 \\ -1 & 0 & 1 & 1 & 0 \end{pmatrix} \begin{pmatrix} N \\ i_1^d \\ i_1^u \\ i_2^d \\ i_2^u \end{pmatrix} = \begin{pmatrix} 0 \\ 0 \end{pmatrix}$$

$$\begin{pmatrix} 0 & -1 & 0 & 0 & 0 \\ -1 & 1 & 0 & 0 & 0 \\ 0 & 0 & -1 & 0 & 0 \\ -1 & 0 & 1 & 0 & 0 \\ 0 & 0 & 0 & -1 & 0 \\ -1 & 1 & 0 & 1 & 0 \\ 0 & 0 & 0 & 0 & -1 \\ -1 & 0 & 1 & 0 & 1 \end{pmatrix} \begin{pmatrix} N \\ i_1^d \\ i_1^u \\ i_2^d \\ i_2^u \end{pmatrix} \leq \begin{pmatrix} 0 \\ -2 \\ 0 \\ -2 \\ 0 \\ 0 \\ 0 \\ 0 \end{pmatrix}$$

FIGURE 7.3 Dependence system with unknown variable.

7.1.3 Other Complications

Triangular Lower Limits

As mentioned in Chapter 5, when the lower limit is triangular, we may choose to use seminormalized iteration vectors. In this case, the same iteration space shape must be used for all dependence equations in that loop. Remember that while the existence of an integer solution after such a substitution is the same as before, the actual solutions will be somewhat different. This means that the computed dependence distance or direction can change.

Example 7.4

What is the dependence system for the array B in the example below?

```
(1)   for I = 2 to N do
(2)     for J = I+1 to N+I+1 do
(3)       B[I,J] = B[I-1,J-1] + C[I]
(4)     endfor
(5)   endfor
```

Solution

The normalized form of the example is:

$$B[2 + i_1, 3 + i_1 + i_2] = B[1 + i_1, 2 + i_1 + i_2] + \ldots$$

The normalized dependence equations are:

$$2 + i_1^d = 1 + i_1^u$$
$$3 + i_1^d + i_2^d = 2 + i_1^u + i_2^u$$

with bounds:

$$0 \leq i_1^d \leq N - 2$$
$$0 \leq i_1^u \leq N - 2$$
$$0 \leq i_2^d \leq N - 1$$
$$0 \leq i_2^u \leq N - 1$$

However, the original loop limits for the inner loop are linear in the outer loop index. We can retain the shape of the iteration space by using seminormalized iteration vectors, where the starting value of the inner loop iteration variable increments along with the outer loop. This is the same as subtracting the induction variable $\langle 0, 1 \rangle$ from i_2, wherever it appears in a dependence equation, and adding it to the bounds for i_2. Another explanation is that we are using a new iteration variable for the inner loop, $j_2 = i_2 + i_1$. The dependence equations with the seminormalized iteration variables are:

$$2 + i_1^d = 1 + i_1^u$$
$$3 + j_2^d = 2 + j_2^u$$

with bounds:

$$0 \le i_1^d \le N - 2$$
$$0 \le i_1^u \le N - 2$$
$$i_1^d \le j_2^d \le i_1^d + N - 1$$
$$i_1^u \le j_2^u \le i_1^u + N - 1$$

Multiple Loop Limits

When the lower limit is a maximum of several linear expressions, or the upper limit is a minimum, each limit may induce several bounds on the induction variables. We shall see cases where this happens after certain program transformations. The program below has multiple bounds in both lower and upper inner loop limits:

(1)   for I = 1 to 8 do
(2)   for J = max(I-3,1) to min(I,5) do
(3)   A[I+1,J+1] = A[I,J] + B[I,J]
(4)   endfor
(5)   endfor

Normalizing the 1 bound in the inner loop lower limit gives the normalized form:

(1)   for $0 \le i_1 \le 7$ do
(2)   for $\max(-3 + i_1, 0) \le i_2 \le \min(i_1, 4)$ do
(3) $A[2 + i_1, 2 + i_2] = A[1 + i_1, 1 + i_2] + \ldots$

Thus, the dependence system is shown in Figure 7.4.

Exit in the Middle of a Loop

Another complication that can arise is when the exit is in the middle of the loop. In that case, one statement may execute one time more than the other. The trip count is defined as the number of times the exit test trips, or chooses to stay in the loop. If the exit test is in the middle of the loop, then one reference involved in a data dependence relation might execute one time more than the other reference.

$$\begin{pmatrix} 1 & -1 & 0 & 0 \\ 0 & 0 & 1 & -1 \end{pmatrix} \begin{pmatrix} i_1^d \\ i_1^u \\ i_2^d \\ i_2^u \end{pmatrix} = \begin{pmatrix} -1 \\ -1 \end{pmatrix}$$

$$\begin{pmatrix} -1 & 0 & 0 & 0 \\ 1 & 0 & 0 & 0 \\ 0 & -1 & 0 & 0 \\ 0 & 1 & 0 & 0 \\ 0 & 0 & -1 & 0 \\ 1 & 0 & -1 & 0 \\ 0 & 0 & 1 & 0 \\ -1 & 0 & 1 & 0 \\ 0 & 0 & 0 & -1 \\ 0 & 1 & 0 & -1 \\ 0 & 0 & 0 & 1 \\ 0 & -1 & 0 & 1 \end{pmatrix} \begin{pmatrix} i_1^d \\ i_1^u \\ i_2^d \\ i_2^u \end{pmatrix} \leq \begin{pmatrix} 0 \\ 7 \\ 0 \\ 7 \\ 0 \\ 3 \\ 5 \\ 0 \\ 0 \\ 3 \\ 5 \\ 0 \end{pmatrix}$$

FIGURE 7.4 Dependence system with multiple loop limits.

Example 7.5

What is the dependence system for the two references to the array A in the following loop?

(1)   J = 0
(2)   loop
(3)   J = J + 1
(4)   A[J] = ...
(5)   if J > 10 then exit
(6)   ... = A[J+1]
(7)   endloop

Solution

The value assigned to J at line 3 is $i + 1$, where i is the basic loop induction variable. The trip count is the least value of i satisfying $i + 1 > 10$, which is 10. However, line 4 executes 11 times, since it occurs before the exit test. Therefore, the dependence system is:

$$i^d + 1 = i^u + 2$$
$$0 \leq i^d \leq 11$$
$$0 \leq i^u \leq 10$$

In matrix notation, this is:

$$\begin{pmatrix} 1 & -1 \end{pmatrix} \begin{pmatrix} i^d \\ i^u \end{pmatrix} = \begin{pmatrix} 0 \end{pmatrix}$$

$$\begin{pmatrix} -1 & 0 \\ 1 & 0 \\ 0 & -1 \\ 0 & 1 \end{pmatrix} \begin{pmatrix} i^d \\ i^u \end{pmatrix} \le \begin{pmatrix} 0 \\ 11 \\ 0 \\ 10 \end{pmatrix}$$

Additional Constraints

In addition to the dependence equations and loop limit constraints, a dependence system may include other inequalities, which may arise, for instance, when testing for dependence with a particular direction vector. To test whether there is a flow dependence with a (<) direction in the first loop, for instance, add the constraint $i_1^d < i_1^u$ to the dependence system. Since we are interested only in integer solutions, this can be rewritten as $i_1^d \le i_1^u - 1$ or $i_1^d - i_1^u \le -1$.

Other inequalities restricting the values of user variables may be derived from conditionals in the program. A conditional like if M > 0 then can be used to put a bound on the value of the variable M in the range of the conditional, if M appears in a dependence system. Aggressive compiler analysis will try to find as many constraints as possible to reduce the number of false dependence relations computed.

Example 7.6

What is the dependence system for the two references to A in the following program fragment?

(1)   if M > 0 then
(2)   for I = 1 to 10 do
(3)   A[I] = A[I+M] + B[I]
(4)   endfor
(5)   endif

Solution

There is one dependence equation:

$$i^d + 1 = i^u + M + 1$$

The loop limits give lower and upper bounds on i, and the conditional gives a lower bound for M, as follows:

$$0 \le i^d \le 9$$
$$0 \le i^u \le 9$$
$$1 \le M$$

7.2 Dependence System Solvers

There have been many dependence system solvers developed over the years. In general, the problem can be cast as an integer programming problem; however, exact solvers may be very expensive (exponential or worse). The dependence system solvers used in modern compilers trade off two characteristics:

- efficiency, the speed of the solver itself, and
- precision, reducing the number of "false positives" returned.

All dependence system solvers are conservative; that is, the solver will never return an answer of "no solution" when there is any integer solution to the dependence system. There are really three possible results from a dependence system solver:

- A result of "no solutions" means there are no integer solutions to the dependence system.
- A result of "has solutions" means there definitely are integer solutions to the dependence system; some solvers can also return a method to enumerate the solutions.
- A result of "possible solution" means that the result is inexact; the solver could not prove there was no solution, but neither could it determine that there definitely was a solution.

A false positive is a case where the dependence answers "probably dependent" when there really is no dependence.

Each solver has different characteristics, considering cost, applicability, and how imprecision arises. The simple solver presented earlier has essentially constant execution time, but only works with a single equation involving two unknowns and equal coefficients. The subsequent sections present several more solvers, each varying in complexity and precision.

7.2.1 Single Equation

A single dependence equation $\mathbf{Ai} = c$ can be rewritten

$$\sum_{k=0}^{n} a_k i_k = c$$

where n is the number of unknowns and a_k are the coefficients.

Simple Test

We start by looking at the simplest test, when there is a single loop (two unknowns) and a single dimension with linear subscript expressions. When the subscript expressions are of the form $a \times i + c_1$ at the definition and $a \times i + c_2$ at the use, and have the same coefficient, then the dependence equation simplifies to $ai^d - ai^u = c_2 - c_1$; as shown in Section 4.4.1, there is an integer solution to this equation only if the greatest common divisor of the coefficients divides the right-hand side. In this case, $\gcd(a, a) = a$, so if a does not divide $c_2 - c_1$ evenly, then there is no dependence. This has been called the *strong dependence test*.

If the coefficients are equal and there is an integer solution, then the dependence distance can be found easily. If the computed dependence distance is greater than or equal to the trip count, then again there is no dependence. Although this simple test handles only trivial dependence systems, it is sufficient for many of the problems that arise in practice.

Example 7.7

What is the dependence for the array A in the following loop?

```
(1)    for I = 2 to 10 do
(2)        A[2*I+2] = A[2*I-2] + B[I]
(3)    endfor
```

Solution

Using normalized iteration vectors, the compiler can represent the subscript expressions as:

$$A[6 + 2i] = A[2 + 2i] + B[2 + i]$$

The dependence equation is $6 + 2i^d = 2 + 2i^u$; it can be rewritten as $2i^d - 2i^u = -4$. Since both coefficients have the same magnitude, there can be dependence only when 2 divides the constant term -4. Since it does, the dependence equation reduces to $i^d - i^u = -2$. Now we must determine the actual dependence from the solution of the system of equations. There can either be a flow dependence with distance d^f in the equation $i^d + d^f = i^u$, or anti-dependence with distance d^a in the equation $i^u + d^a = i^d$. From the reduced dependence equation, we see that flow dependence can occur only when $d^f = -2$; since the imperative language used cannot have negative dependence distances, this is an infeasible solution. Anti-dependence can occur when $d^a = 2$, which is feasible, so there is anti-dependence from the use of A to the redefinition of A two iterations later.

GCD Test

The greatest common divisor test applies the result from Section 4.4.2, which states that there is an integer solution to the dependence equation only when $\gcd(a_1, a_2, \ldots, a_n)$ divides c. If not, then there are no integer solutions to the dependence system at all, regardless of the bounds. If the gcd does divide the constant term, then there are integer solutions to the dependence system, but the gcd test does not determine whether the solution satisfies the other constraints.

The gcd test applies to any single dependence equation. Moreover, it is a very inexpensive test; finding the greatest common divisor of two numbers is efficient. In addition, the gcd of a series of numbers can be found as shown in Figure 7.5, where $\gcd(0, x) = x$. In practice, however, the gcd of the coefficients usually turns out to be 1, which divides any constant coefficient, so this test is not very effective.

$$g = |a_1|$$
$$\text{for } i = 2, 3, \ldots, n \text{ while } g \neq 1 \text{ do}$$
$$\quad g = \gcd(g, a_i)$$
$$\text{endfor}$$

FIGURE 7.5 Finding the gcd of a vector of integers.

Note that the gcd test generally tells nothing about the direction vector or dependence distance. However, in the special case where the compiler is testing for a direction vector with one or more directions of (=), the gcd test can sometimes be applied after simplifying the dependence equation.

Example 7.8

Use the gcd test to test for dependence with an equal direction for the outer loop in the following:

```
(1)     for I = 1 to N do
(2)        for J = 2 to 10 do
(3)           A[I+2*J] = ...
(4)           ... = A[I+2*J-1]
(5)        endfor
(6)     endfor
```

Solution

The normalized dependence equation is $5 + i_1^d + 2i_2^d = 4 + i_1^u + 2i_2^u$. This can be rewritten as: $i_1^d - i_1^u + 2i_2^d - 2i_2^u = -1$. We first find $\gcd(1, -1, 2, -2) = 1$, which does divide the constant term. Testing for an equal direction in the outer loop adds the equality $i_1^d = i_1^u$; this simplifies the dependence equation to $2i_2^d - 2i_2^u = -1$. In this case, there are only two nonzero coefficients, and $\gcd(2, -2)$ does not divide

-1. Thus, there are no solutions to this dependence equation, and therefore no dependence with (=) direction in the outer loop.

Extreme Value Test

The extreme value test uses the method shown in Section 4.7 to find the extreme values of the expression in the dependence equation. The dependence equation is

$$\sum_{k=0}^{n} a_k i_k = c$$

where the left-hand side is an affine function of **i**. The region of $\mathbb{R}^n$ under consideration is the one bounded by the loop limit and other constraints. Note that this method can take advantage only of a single lower and upper bound for each unknown, and the unknowns and bounds must be ordered such that each unknown i_k depends only on the values of i_j where $j < k$. When considering auxiliary constraints, such as direction vector constraints, the compiler should use the tightest constraints available, which would usually be the direction vector constraints.

The extreme value method finds a lower and an upper bound for the function being considered. For dependence to exist, the function must be able to take on the value c. If c does not lie between the computed lower and upper bounds, then this test determines that there can be no dependence.

Some of the unknowns may be unbounded. This is particularly true when the dependence system includes user variables that appear in loop limits and are unbounded. In that case, the method may not be able to find a lower or an upper bound for the function; essentially, the lower bound is treated as $-\infty$ or the upper bound as $+\infty$. If neither bound can be computed, then the test cannot determine independence; however, the test can often determine independence even when only one of the bounds can be found.

The extreme value test is efficient but inexact. It determines whether the function (the left-hand side of the dependence equation) can take on a value that allows dependence, but does not enforce the restriction to integer solutions. It also cannot take advantage of more than one lower or upper bound for each unknown. To test for dependence with a direction $i^d < i^u$, the upper bound for i^d is replaced by $i^u - 1$, or the lower bound for i^u is replaced by $i^d + 1$. For rectangular loop limits, since i^d and i^u have the same upper limit, replacing $i^d \leq U$ by $i^d \leq i^u - 1$ still enforces the loop limit, since $i^u - 1 \leq U - 1$. In the presence of triangular loop limits this is not true; if the upper loop limit is $i_2^d \leq i_1^d$, replacing this by $i_2^u - 1$ to test for $i_2^d < i_2^u$ loses the loop limit constraint. In this case, the extreme value test may return a false positive if there is a solution that satisfies both the direction vector constraint and the loop limit constraint, but not both simultaneously. The extreme value test also suffers from the inherent weakness of the method to compute extreme values if the loop limits are not tight.

Example 7.9

Use the extreme value test to determine whether there is dependence for the two references to A in the loop in Example 7.6.

Solution

The normalized dependence equation can be rewritten:

$$-M + i^d - i^u = 0$$

with three unknowns; the bounds on the unknowns are:

$$1 \leq M \leq +\infty$$
$$0 \leq i^d \leq 9$$
$$0 \leq i^u \leq 9$$

Each known bound is simple, so the unknowns can be eliminated in any order.

lower bound	upper bound	step
$-M + i^d - i^u$	$-M + i^d - i^u$	original equation
$-M + i^d - 9$	$-M + i^d - 0$	eliminate i^u
$-M - 9$	$-M + 9$	eliminate i^d
$-\infty$	8	eliminate M

Since zero does lie between $-\infty$ and 8, the extreme value test assumes that there is dependence.

To determine the kind and direction of dependence, direction vector constraints can be applied. First apply the $i^d < i^u$ constraint; in the integer domain this is equivalent to the tighter bound $i^d \leq i^u - 1$. This also gives a tighter lower bound on i^u and a tighter upper bound on i^d, since $0 \leq i^d < i^u \leq 9$. The final set of bounds is:

$$1 \leq M \leq +\infty$$
$$0 \leq i^d \leq \begin{cases} 8 \\ i^u - 1 \ (*) \end{cases}$$
$$\begin{cases} 1 \\ i^d + 1 \ (*) \end{cases} \leq i^u \leq 9$$

Since the extreme value method can use only one bound for each unknown, and the unknowns are eliminated in order, only one of the upper bounds of i^d and the lower bounds of i^u can be used, and only one of the starred bounds can be used. If we eliminate the unknowns in the same order, we get the extreme values shown in the table below.

lower bound	upper bound	step
$-M + i^d - i^u$	$-M + i^d - i^u$	original equation
$-M + i^d - 9$	$-M + i^d - (i^d + 1) = -M - 1$	eliminate i^u
$-M$	$-M - 1$	eliminate i^d
$-\infty$	-2	eliminate M

Since zero does not lie between $-\infty$ and -2, the extreme value test determines that there is no dependence where $i^d < i^u$.

For dependence with the constraint $i^d > i^u$, the bounds on the unknowns are shown below, where the tighter lower bound for i^d is used, with the direction vector constraint as the upper bound for i^u.

$$1 \leq M \leq +\infty$$
$$1 \leq i^d \leq 9$$
$$0 \leq i^u \leq i^d - 1$$

The computation of extreme values proceeds as shown in the table below.

lower bound	upper bound	step
$-M + i^d - i^u$	$-M + i^d - i^u$	original equation
$-M + i^d - (i^d - 1)$	$-M + i^d - 0$	eliminate i^u
$-M + 1$	$-M + 9$	eliminate i^d
$-\infty$	8	eliminate M

Again, since zero lies between $-\infty$ and 8, the extreme value test cannot determine independence.

Finally, to test for dependence with the constraint $i^d = i^u$, the dependence equation is simplified to eliminate one of the unknowns: $-M + i^d - i^u = -M + i^d - i^d = -M$. The bounds on i^d and i^u cannot be tightened, but in this case they do not matter. The extreme values of $-M$ are computed as $-\infty$ and -1. Since zero does not lie between these bounds, dependence with the $i^d = i^u$ constraint cannot exist.

Since the only dependence solution exists when $i^d > i^u$, and this was an imperative sequential loop, the dependence must be an anti-dependence (from the use to the def) with a (<) dependence direction vector.

Two Variable Exact Test

The two variable exact test uses the method discussed in Section 4.4.1 to construct all the integer solutions to a simple dependence equation $ai + bj = c$. If there are no integer solutions, there is no dependence. If there are possible integer solutions, the loop limit and direction vector constraints are placed on the independent variable to determine if there is dependence within those bounds.

Example 7.10

What dependence occurs in the following loop between the two references to X?

```
(1)    for I = 1 to 10 do
(2)        X[I+10] = ...
(3)        ... = X[2*I+1]
(4)    endfor
```

Solution

The normalized dependence equation is $11 + i^d = 3 + 2i^u$, or $i^d - 2i^u = -8$. Letting i^u be the independent variable and i^d the dependent variable, we have $i^d = 2i^u - 8$. We apply the loop limit constraints to place bounds on the range of the independent variable. The loop limits for i^u itself give the bounds $0 \le i^u \le 9$. The loop limits for i^d add the constraints $0 \le 2i^u - 8 \le 9$, which is equivalent to $8 \le 2i^u \le 17$, or $4 \le i^u \le \lfloor 17/2 \rfloor = 8$. The intersection of these ranges includes only $[4:8]$.

Testing for dependence with (=) direction means solving for dependence when $i^d = i^u$, which, by substitution, is $2i^u - 8 = i^u$ or $i^u = 8$. Since this solution lies within the range of dependence computed above, there is dependence with (=) direction; this occurs at the assignment to X[19] at iteration 9 and the use of that element on the same iteration.

Testing for dependence with (<) direction can be done by adding the constraint $i^d < i^u$, or $2i^u - 8 \le i^u - 1$, which simplifies to $i^u \le 7$. Again, the intersection of this with the solution range computed above is nonempty, so there is dependence with (<) direction; for example, X[11] is assigned at iteration 1 and used at iteration 5.

Finally, testing for dependence with a (>) direction adds the constraint $i^d > i^u$, or $2i^u - 8 \ge i^u + 1$, which simplifies to $i^u \ge 9$. Since the intersection of this with the range $[4:8]$ is empty, there is no dependence where $i^d > i^u$.

Direction Vector Hierarchy

Where the simple test can compute a dependence distance, and hence a dependence direction, most of the tests discussed so far do not. The extreme value test and the two variable exact test can use direction vector constraints in the dependence system, but they do not tell how to construct the direction vector. Given a single loop, there are three possible directions of dependence; in two nested loops, there are nine possible directions. In general, there are 3^d possible direction vectors to be tested for a d-nested loop. A structured way to test for dependence is to use a *direction vector hierarchy*.

The direction vector hierarchy has one level for each nest level of the loop. The compiler first tests for dependence with the unrestricted ($\star$) direction; if there is no dependence, it can quit there. If there is dependence, the compiler *refines* the direction of one of the loops to its three components, (<), (=), and (>), and tests each independently. If any of those tests turns out to be independent, the compiler can stop refining that branch. Otherwise, the compiler chooses one branch that still may be dependent, and refines the direction for another loop to its three components. A picture of the direction vector hierarchy for single and double nested loops is shown in Figure 7.6.

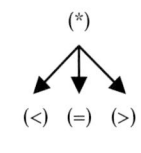

```
              (*)
           ↙  ↓  ↘
         (<) (=) (>)

          One Level
```

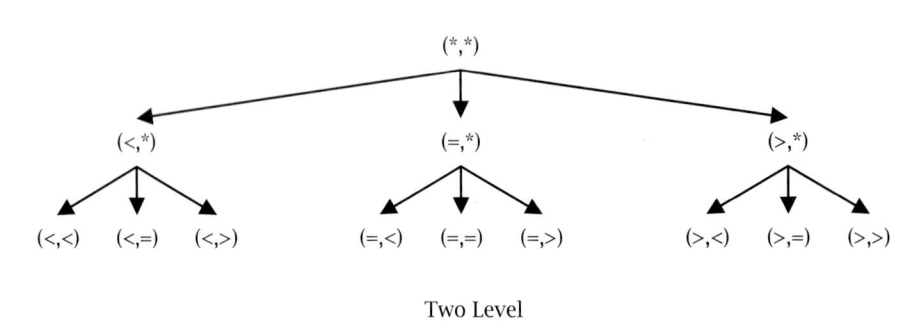

```
                          (*,*)
              ↙            ↓            ↘
           (<,*)         (=,*)         (>,*)
          ↙ ↓ ↘         ↙ ↓ ↘         ↙ ↓ ↘
      (<,<)(<,=)(<,>) (=,<)(=,=)(=,>) (>,<)(>,=)(>,>)

                       Two Level
```

FIGURE 7.6 Direction vector hierarchy for 1 and 2 nested loops.

The goal of the hierarchy is to reduce the number of applications of any single dependence test. This is not always the case, and the effectiveness may depend on the order of refinement.

One minor point is that when refining the levels of a direction vector hierarchy, especially with an inexact test like the extreme value test, there are cases where the test determines dependence at the ($*$) level, but independence for each of the three refined directions: ($<$), ($=$), and ($>$). In this situation, the compiler should (correctly) determine that there is in fact no dependence.

Example 7.11

Use the direction vector hierarchy to compute dependence between the two references to A in the following loop:

(1)   for I = 1 to 10 do
(2)   for J = 1 to 10 do

(3)   A[I*10+J] = ...
(4)   ... = A[I*10+J-1]
(5)   endfor
(6) endfor

Solution
The normalized dependence equation is $11 + 10i_1^d + i_2^d = 10 + 10i_1^u + i_2^u$, or $10i_1^d - 10i_1^u + i_2^d - i_2^u = -1$, where

$$0 \leq i_1^d \leq 9$$
$$0 \leq i_1^u \leq 9$$
$$0 \leq i_2^d \leq 9$$
$$0 \leq i_2^u \leq 9$$

For the $(\star, \star)$ direction, the gcd test gives no information, and the extreme value test computes extreme values of $[-99 : 99]$, which contains -1 and hence allows dependence. For the $(<, \star)$ direction, the extreme value test uses the bounds:

$$0 \leq i_1^d \leq i_1^u - 1$$
$$1 \leq i_1^u \leq 9$$
$$0 \leq i_2^d \leq 9$$
$$0 \leq i_2^u \leq 9$$

The computed extreme values are $[-99 : 9]$, which still contains -1. Similarly, for the $(>, \star)$ direction, the bounds used are:

$$1 \leq i_1^d \leq 9$$
$$0 \leq i_1^u \leq i_1^d - 1$$
$$0 \leq i_2^d \leq 9$$
$$0 \leq i_2^u \leq 9$$

and the extreme values are $[0 : 99]$, which does not admit dependence. Hence, the $(>, \star)$ branch does not need to be expanded. For $(=, \star)$ dependence, the dependence equation is simplified to $i_2^d - i_2^u = -1$, and dependence is still possible. In this case, an exact distance and direction for the second loop can be computed ($i_2^d < i_2^u$), so that level of the hierarchy can be directly computed, instead of testing for the three directions. Figure 7.7 shows the direction vector hierarchy fully expanded, with the extreme values shown and labeled if there is no dependence.

7.2.2 Multiple Equations

When the array has multiple dimensions, dependence must exist in each subscript position simultaneously. Each dimension generates a dependence equation; for

```
                    (*,*)
        10i₁ᵈ − 10i₁ᵘ + i₂ᵈ − i₂ᵘ = −1
                   [−99:99]
```

```
        (*,*)                              (>,*)
      [−99:−1]                             [1:9]
                                         independent
```

```
  (<,<)         (<,=)            (<,>)
 [−99:−11]   10i₁ᵈ − 10i₁ᵘ = −1   [−9:1]
independent    independent
```

```
              (=,*)
           i₂ᵈ − i₂ᵘ = −1
              [−9:9]
```

```
   (=,<)         (=,=)          (=,>)
  [−9:−1]        0 = −1         [1:9]
              independent    independent
```

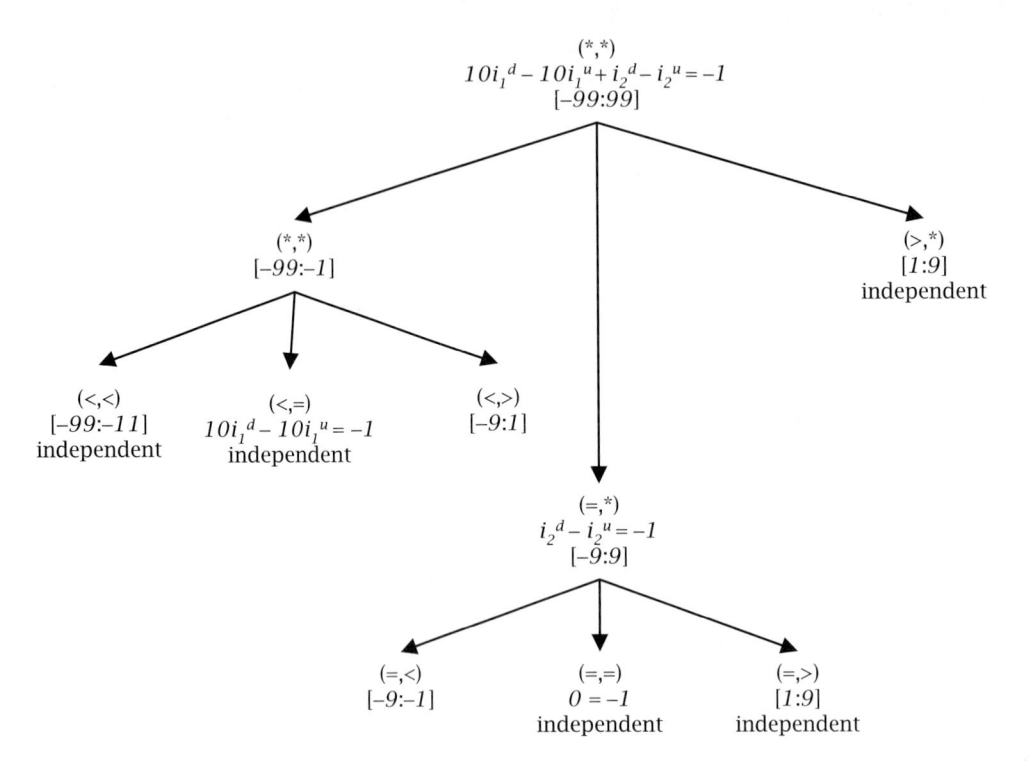

FIGURE 7.7 Direction vector hierarchy for example.

dependence, the solution must satisfy all dependence equations simultaneously. The solvers presented so far only attempt to find solutions for a single dependence equation. For multiple equations, there are two ways to use a single-equation solver. One way is to solve each dependence equation independently, and intersect the solution sets. Another way is to combine the several dependence equations into a single equation such that any solution to the original equation produces a solution to the combined equation. Linear combinations of the equations satisfy this constraint. Note that a solution to a linear combination of two or more equations is not necessarily a simultaneous solution to the original set of equations.

When solving each equation independently, the solution set for each dimension can often be represented as a distance vector or direction vector. Intersecting the distance or direction vector has some of the advantages of solving the equations simultaneously. When the dependence equations for the several dimensions have no unknowns with nonzero coefficients in common, either in the equations or the inequality constraints, then solving the systems separately gives exact simultaneous solutions. The dependence equations in that case are said to be *separable*. When two or more dependence systems include some of the same unknowns, they are called *coupled*.

Example 7.12

Compute dependence for the two references to the array A in the following loop:

```
(1)    for I = 1 to 10 do
(2)        A[I,I] = ...
(3)        ... = A[I,I-1]
(4)    endfor
```

Solution

The normalized dependence equation for the first dimension is $1 + i^d = 1 + i^u$, with a solution when $i^d = i^u$, or with distance (0). The normalized dependence equation for the second dimension is $1 + i^d = 0 + i^u$, with a solution when $i^d + 1 = i^u$, or with distance (1). The intersection of the solution distances for the two dependence equations is empty; thus there are no simultaneous solutions and therefore no dependence.

7.2.3 Linear Combinations

Another approach is to form new equations from combinations of the original dependence equations. Any simultaneous solution to the original dependence equations will be a solution to any linear combination. Unfortunately, the converse is not true, so this is still an inexact method. One obvious combination is to compute the actual offset from the beginning address of the array as it is stored in memory; this is called *linearization,* since it computes the linear offset of the element in memory. Another choice of combination is one that eliminates one or more of the unknowns and produces one or more simpler equations.

Example 7.13

Find the dependence equations for the two references to A in the following loop. Also find two linear combinations of the dependence equations; one corresponding to a linearized equation, and one that eliminates one of the unknowns.

```
(1)    real A[1:30,1:20]
(2)    for I = 1 to 10 do
(3)        for J = 1 to 10 do
(4)            A[I+J+1,J+1] = ...
(5)            ... = A[I+J,J+1]
(6)        endfor
(7)    endfor
```

Solution

The dependence equations are:

$$\text{EQ1:} \quad i_1^d - i_1^u + i_2^d - i_2^u = -1$$
$$\text{EQ2:} \quad i_2^d - i_2^u = 0$$

Using a row-major storage order, element `A[I,J]` is stored at offset $(I-1) * 20 + J - 1 = 20I + J - 21$. The linearized dependence equation is:

$$20\text{EQ1} + \text{EQ2:} -21 \quad 20i_1^d - 20i_1^u + 21i_2^d - 21i_2^u = -21$$

The second dependence equation is trivial, having solution when $i_2^d = i_2^u$, giving dependence distance zero in the second loop. We can eliminate i_2^d and i_2^u from the first equation by taking the linear combination EQ1 − EQ2:

$$\text{EQ1} - \text{EQ2:} \quad i_1^d - i_1^u = -1$$

This is also a trivial equation to solve. Thus, there is flow dependence with distance $d_f = (1,0)$ or anti-dependence with distance $d_a = (-1,0)$. Since d_a is infeasible for a sequential loop, the result must be flow dependence.

▲

7.2.4 Splitting a Dependence Equation

Sometimes a single dependence equation can be split into two or more independent equations. Suppose we have the dependence equation

$$\sum_{k=1}^{n} a_k i_k = c$$

where the terms are sorted by the magnitude of the coefficients (for all k, $|a_{k-1}| \le |a_k|$). If we find a coefficient m such that:

$$g - |c_0| > \max(\textit{maxval}(\sum_{k=1}^{m-1} a_k i_k), -\textit{minval}(\sum_{k=1}^{m-1} a_k i_k)),$$

where $g = \gcd(a_m, a_{m+1}, a_{m+2}, \ldots, a_n)$, c_0 satisfies $c_0 \bmod g = c \bmod g$, and $\textit{maxval}(f(i))$ and $\textit{minval}(f(i))$ are the extreme values of $f(i)$ in the region of the loop limits as found by algorithm Extreme shown in Section 4.7. In that case, the dependence equation can be split into the two parts:

$$(\sum_{k=1}^{m-1} a_k i_k - c_0) + (\sum_{k=m}^{n} a_k i_k - (c - c_0)) = 0,$$

where g is as computed above. In the second parenthesized subexpression, each term is a multiple of g. For the entire expression to be zero, the first subexpression must also be a multiple of g; but the only multiple of g it can take on is zero, since

7.2 ▪ Dependence System Solvers

the range of $\sum_{k=1}^{m-1} a_k i_k$ is restricted. Thus, the only solutions to this equation are those that satisfy the two separate equations:

$$\sum_{k=1}^{m-1} a_k i_k = c_0$$

$$\sum_{k=m}^{n} a_k i_k = c - c_0$$

An obvious choice of c_0 is $\widehat{c \bmod g}$. Splitting a dependence equation can allow the use of a simple dependence test; it can sometimes improve the accuracy of the dependence test, and can improve the speed when using a direction vector hierarchy. Since dependence equation splitting will often be applicable when an array has been linearized manually, splitting is also called *delinearization*.

Example 7.14

What is the dependence equation for the two references to A in the following loop?

```
(1)   for I = 1 to 9 do
(2)       for J = 1 to 10 do
(3)           A[I+J*10] = ...
(4)           ... = A[I+J*10-1]
(5)       endfor
(6)   endfor
```

Solution

The normalized dependence equation is $i_1^d - i_1^u + 10 i_2^d - 10 i_2^u = -1$. Here, $g = 10$, and $c_0 = -1$; the extreme values of $i_1^d - i_1^u + 1$ in the region $0 \le i_1^d, i_1^u \le 8$ are $-7 : 9$. Since $g > \max(7, 9)$, we can split this dependence equation into the two equations:

$$i_1^d - i_1^u = -1$$

$$10 i_2^d - 10 i_2^u = 0$$

From these we can trivially determine that there is a flow dependence with distance vector $(1, 0)$.

Symbolic Equation Splitting

Splitting is particularly important when symbolic coefficients appear. In such a case, the dependence equation is nonlinear and cannot be solved by the usual methods. However, if the symbolic coefficient is used as a loop limit, there is a chance that splitting the dependence equation may simplify it enough to allow elimination of the unknown coefficient. For instance, in the following loop:

```
(1)    for I = 1 to 9 do
(2)        for J = 2 to N do
(3)            A[I*N+J] = ...
(4)            ... = A[I*N+J-1]
(5)        endfor
(6)    endfor
```

the normalized dependence equation is $Ni_1^d - Ni_1^u + i_2^d - i_2^u = -1$. The trip count for the inner loop is $N - 1$, so the extreme values of the subexpression $i_2^d - i_2^u$ are $-(N - 2) : N - 2$. Thus, we can split the dependence equation into two equations:

$$Ni_1^d - Ni_1^u = 0$$
$$i_2^d - i_2^u = -1$$

We can eliminate the unknown symbol by dividing the first equation by N, finding a flow dependence with distance vector $(0, 1)$.

7.3 General Solver

The most general dependence solver in common practice is based on the method discussed in Section 4.4.3 to solve systems of integer equations. This is often called the generalized gcd test; where the gcd test will determine whether one integer equation has any integer solutions, the generalized gcd test will determine whether several integer equations have any simultaneous solutions.

The dependence equations are written in matrix form $\mathbf{Ai} = \mathbf{c}$. The coefficient matrix $\mathbf{A}$ is reduced to a column echelon form matrix $\mathbf{D}$ by a series of unimodular column operations. The equation $\mathbf{Dt} = \mathbf{c}$ is then solved by simple back substitution. If there are no integer solutions to this equation, there are no integer solutions to the original dependence system. If there are, then some of the elements of $\mathbf{t}$ will be solved, while others (those with zero coefficients) will be the independent variables.

By casting the unknowns in terms of the independent variables, dependence distance can sometimes be directly computed. If there is a flow dependence, the distance will be $\mathbf{d}_f = \mathbf{i}^u - \mathbf{i}^d$. If replacing each unknown eliminates all the independent variables for any position in the dependence distance vector, the dependence distance must be constant for that loop.

Example 7.15

Using the generalized gcd method, determine whether the two references shown in Exercise 7.13 might be dependent.

Solution
In matrix form, the dependence equations are:

$$\begin{pmatrix} 1 & -1 & 1 & -1 \\ 0 & 0 & 1 & -1 \end{pmatrix} \begin{pmatrix} i_1^d \\ i_1^u \\ i_2^d \\ i_2^u \end{pmatrix} = \begin{pmatrix} -1 \\ 0 \end{pmatrix}$$

Using unimodular operations, the coefficient matrix can be reduced to the column echelon form below:

$$\mathbf{AU} = \begin{pmatrix} 1 & -1 & 1 & -1 \\ 0 & 0 & 1 & -1 \end{pmatrix} \begin{pmatrix} 1 & -1 & 1 & 0 \\ 0 & 0 & 1 & 0 \\ 0 & 1 & 0 & 1 \\ 0 & 0 & 0 & 1 \end{pmatrix} = \begin{pmatrix} 1 & 0 & 0 & 0 \\ 0 & 1 & 0 & 0 \end{pmatrix} = \mathbf{D}$$

The equation $\mathbf{Dt} = \mathbf{c}$ can be solved by setting $t_1 = -1$ and $t_2 = 0$. All solutions are then found by computing $\mathbf{i} = \mathbf{Ut}$:

$$\begin{pmatrix} 1 & -1 & 1 & 0 \\ 0 & 0 & 1 & 0 \\ 0 & 1 & 0 & 1 \\ 0 & 0 & 0 & 1 \end{pmatrix} \begin{pmatrix} -1 \\ 0 \\ t_3 \\ t_4 \end{pmatrix} = \begin{pmatrix} t_3 - 1 \\ t_3 \\ t_4 \\ t_4 \end{pmatrix} = \begin{pmatrix} i_1^d \\ i_1^u \\ i_2^d \\ i_2^u \end{pmatrix}$$

Since there are integer solutions to the system of equations, the references might be dependent. In fact, if there is a flow dependence, the dependence distance is $d_f = (i_1^u - i_1^d, i_2^u - i_2^d)$; this simplifies to $= (t_3 - (t_3 - 1), t_4 - t_4) = (1, 0)$.

7.3.1 Adding Inequality Constraints

The generalized gcd method effectively reduces the degrees of freedom of the dependence system from n unknowns to $n - r$ independent variables, where r is the rank of the coefficient matrix, and is equal to the number of elements of $\mathbf{t}$ that are solved. The substitution $\mathbf{i} = \mathbf{Ut}$ can be used to recast the inequality constraints from the loop limits and direction vector in terms of the independent variables. This gives a system of integer inequalities that can be attacked by Fourier-Motzkin projection.

As described in Section 4.6, using Fourier-Motzkin projection on a system of integer inequalities is still not exact, in that it may produce a false positive; the order in which the inequalities are eliminated also makes a difference to exactness and performance. The unknowns should be eliminated in the order suggested in Section 4.5.2.

Example 7.16

Determine the dependence relations for the references to A in the following loop:

```
(1)   for I = 1 to 100 do
(2)      for J = 1 to 100 do
(3)         A[3*I+2*J,2*J] = ...
(4)         ... = A[I-J+6,I+J]
(5)      endfor
(6)   endfor
```

Solution

The normalized dependence equations are

$$5 + 3i_1^d + 2i_2^d = 6 + i_1^u - i_2^u$$
$$2 + 2i_2^d = 2 + i_1^u + i_2^u$$

or, in matrix form:

$$\begin{pmatrix} 3 & -1 & 2 & 1 \\ 0 & -1 & 2 & -1 \end{pmatrix} \begin{pmatrix} i_1^d \\ i_1^u \\ i_2^d \\ i_2^u \end{pmatrix} = \begin{pmatrix} 1 \\ 0 \end{pmatrix}$$

This is reduced to column echelon form as follows:

$$\begin{pmatrix} 3 & -1 & 2 & 1 \\ 0 & -1 & 2 & -1 \end{pmatrix} \begin{pmatrix} 0 & 1 & 2 & 0 \\ 0 & 1 & 3 & 2 \\ 0 & 0 & 0 & 1 \\ 1 & -2 & -3 & 0 \end{pmatrix} = \begin{pmatrix} 1 & 0 & 0 & 0 \\ -1 & 1 & 0 & 0 \end{pmatrix} = \mathbf{D}$$

In terms of the free variables, the unknowns are:

$$i_1^d = 2t_3 + 1$$
$$i_1^u = 3t_3 + 2t_2 + 1$$
$$i_2^d = t_4$$
$$i_2^u = -3t_3 - 1$$

Applying the loop limits gives the following constraints:

$$i_1^d \geq 0 \Rightarrow -2t_3 - 1 \leq 0$$
$$-t_3 \leq \lfloor 1/2 \rfloor$$
$$i_1^u \geq 0 \Rightarrow -3t_3 - 2t_2 - 1 \leq 0$$
$$-3t_3 - 2t_2 \leq 1$$
$$i_2^d \geq 0 \Rightarrow -t_4 \leq 0$$
$$i_2^u \geq 0 \Rightarrow 3t_3 + 1 \leq 0$$
$$t_3 \leq \lfloor -1/3 \rfloor$$

Here, the first and last inequalities are simple bounds for t_3; they simplify to $0 \leq t_3 \leq -1$, which is inconsistent. Therefore, there is no dependence in this example.

7.4 Summary of Solvers

Simple and fast solvers can be used when the dependence system is itself simple; to handle the general case, more complex solvers are required. Here we review the various solvers and discuss when each applies. Some tests apply only to a single dependence equation. The simple test applies only when there are two unknowns and the coefficients are equal. Some tests cannot enforce loop limit constraints or direction vector constraints; the gcd and generalized gcd tests can only test for equal directions. The most general test is potentially exponential in cost, though we do not expect to see this behavior in practice. The table shown in Figure 7.8 describes the situations in which each dependence test is applicable.

	number of dependence equations	number of unknowns	loop limit constraints	direction vector constraints	integer constraint
simple test	1	2	yes	yes	yes
two variable exact test	1	2	yes	yes	yes
gcd test	1	many	no	=	yes
extreme value test	1	many	yes	yes	no
linear combinations + other test	many	many			
generalized gcd test	many	many	yes	=	yes
Fourier-Motzkin projection	many	many	yes	yes	no

FIGURE 7.8 Situations in which dependence tests are applicable.

Many early parallelizing compilers used the extreme value test and the gcd test, applied to each subscript dependence equation and to the linearized dependence equation. Recent work has focused on more precise tests, such as the generalized gcd test with Fourier-Motzkin projection.

7.5 Complications

The idea behind a data dependence graph or a program dependence graph is to capture all the relevant ordering information required by the program to allow the compiler to determine when it is legal to reorder operations, statements, or loop iterations. In general, all this science to solve data dependence problems is practical and useful. However, not all problems fall into the nice forms required by these tests.

7.5.1 Storage Association

Some languages (Fortran and C, in particular) have rules about how variables are laid out in memory. While most programs are written so that the dependence analyzer need not know how memory is allocated, there are programs that are manually "optimized" through such tricks as treating an array like a vector and running over array bounds. In programs like these, the dimensions of arrays may not be independent. To be safe, the compiler may need to build a single dependence equation corresponding to the memory locations defined or used at a reference. Using the linearized dependence equation would be safe in this case.

Fortran Equivalence Statements

When two variables appear in a Fortran equivalence statement, the compiler must also determine any dependence between the two variables. The most general way to handle these cases is to linearize both references to compute the offset from the start of the equivalence block, or from the start of any variable in the equivalence block. Often, dependence equation splitting can be applied to the resulting dependence equation.

Example 7.17

Compute the dependence equation for dependence between the references to A and B in the following Fortran loop:

```
real A(10,10),B(10)
equivalence(A(2,4),B(1))
do I = 1, 10
   B(I) = ...
   ... = A(I,I)
enddo
```

Solution

By the rules of Fortran storage association, arrays are laid out in column-major order; that is, element A(1,1) is adjacent in memory to A(2,1). The equivalence statement states that the first element of B must share the same location as the second element in the fourth column of A; in linear memory locations, the first

7.5 ▪ Complications

element of B is at the same memory address as A(2,4), the second element of B is at A(3,4), and so on. Because of the array layout, A(2,4) is offset 31 elements from the start of the array. The linearized address of B(I) is *offset* + *I* − *lower*, where *offset* is 31 and *lower* is one. The linearized address of A(I,J) is *offset* + *I* − *lower*$_1$ + *extent*$_1$(*J* − *lower*$_2$), where *offset* is zero, *lower*$_1$ and *lower*$_2$ are both one, and *extent*$_1$ is 10. Thus the linearized, normalized dependence equation is $31 + i^d = 11 i^u$.

Letting i^d be the dependent variable, we have solutions at $i^d = 11 i^u - 31$ whenever both i^d and i^u lie within the loop limits. The only solution between one and 10 is at $i^u = 3$, $i^d = 2$.

Different Sized Objects

Fortran also allows `equivalence` statements when the types are not the same. For instance, by definition a `complex` variable takes twice as many words to store a number as does a `real` variable. After the following Fortran declarations:

```
real A(100)
complex B(50)
equivalence (A,B)
```

an assignment to one element of B really changes two different elements of A. Constructs such as this are commonly used to conveniently refer to the real and imaginary parts of a complex vector without using the Fortran intrinsic functions REAL and IMAG. A dependence equation based on array elements does not capture the range of possibilities. On a byte-addressable machine, A is (typically) 4 bytes per element, and B is 8 bytes per element. One approach is to reduce everything to the basic addressable units, and find the dependence equation in terms of bytes. This means accounting for all the bytes modified or used by each reference with a false self-loop, and then linearizing.

Example 7.18

What is the dependence between the two references shown in the following Fortran loop:

```
real A(100)
complex B(50)
equivalence (A,B)
do I = 2, 40
    B(I) = ...
    ...= A(2*I-1)
enddo
```

Solution

Since the types of the equivalenced variables do not match and are not the same size, we must go to a lower level to find a coherent dependence equation. Assuming a byte-addressable machine, we can treat the assignment to B(I) as an assignment to each of the eight bytes comprising that element, and the use of A(2*I) as a use of each of its four bytes:

```
do I = 2, 40
    do J = 0,7
        B(J,I) = ...
    enddo
    do J = 0,3
        ...= A(J,2*I-2)
    enddo
enddo
```

Since A and B have the same offset in their joint equivalence block, B(J,I) is $J+8(I-1)$, and A(J,I) is $J+4(I-1)$. Linearizing each reference gives the dependence equation:

$$8 + 8i^d + j^d = 4 + 8i^u + j^u$$

where j^d and j^u represent the self-loop at the def and use points. Within the loop limits, the only dependence can occur when $i_1^d + 1 = i_1^u$, for a flow dependence with distance (1).

Fortran Common Statements

In Fortran, each common block is defined to take up contiguous storage. In a single routine, while arrays are not supposed to be referenced out of bounds, this practice sometimes is used to initialize a block of storage, as in:

```
common/S/ A(1),B,C,D,E,F
    ⋮
do I = 2, 6
    A(I) = 0
enddo
```

In the same way as for equivalence statements, dependence can arise between two references to different names in a common block. The most general way to handle this is to represent the references in terms of the offset from the beginning of the common block.

7.5 ▪ Complications

Structures and Data Types

For most structure or record references, if the reference is to the same element of the structure, the dependence equation can ignore the data structure. If the references are to distinct elements that cannot overlap in memory, there can be no dependence. In the presence of Pascal language variant records or C language union types, the compiler may have to resort to finding the offset of each reference from the base address, perhaps using a self-loop to characterize elements of different sizes.

Example 7.19

What is the dependence equation for the two references in the following C loop?

```
struct{
    float b;
    float c[10];
    struct{
        float f;
        union{
            float h;
            short i;
        }g;
    } e[100];
} a;
for( j = 1; j < 99; ++j ){
    a.e[j].g.h = ...;
    ... = a.e[j-1].g.i;
}
```

Solution

Since the two references are two possibly overlapping elements of the structure, we find their offsets from the base address of a. Assume that a `float` takes four bytes, and a `short` takes two. The offset of field e is 11 words, or 44 bytes, from the start of a. The size of each e structure is eight bytes, and the union type is offset another four bytes from the start of e. Thus, the starting address of a.e[j].g.h (and a.e[j].g.i) is $44 + 8j + 4$. The normalized dependence equation to be solved is $44 + 8(i^d + 1) + 4 + j^d = 44 + 8(i^u) + 4 + j^u$ (where j^d and j^u are the self-loop indices), which simplifies to $56 + 8i^d + j^d = 48 + 8i^u + j^u$. The limits for the self-loops are $0 \leq j^d \leq 3$ and $0 \leq j^u \leq 1$. Within those limits, the only solution occurs when $i^d + 1 = i^u$, which means a flow dependence with distance (1).

7.5.2 Dynamically Allocated Arrays

The new Fortran 90 standard, as well as other high level languages, have dynamically allocated arrays. Dynamically allocated arrays have few hidden aliasing problems; in Fortran 90, they are declared as `Allocatable`, so they must be distinct from any static array or any other dynamically allocated array. The dimensions of a dynamically allocated array must be orthogonal, so linearization is unnecessary. Equivalence statements or other static aliasing problems cannot arise, so dependence analysis for dynamically allocated arrays can proceed as normal.

7.6 Run-Time Dependence Testing

Often the dependence relation cannot be determined at compile time. This may occur when some unknown variable appears in the dependence equation, as in the loop shown in Figure 7.9. Here, the normalized dependence equation is $1 + i^d = 1 + i^u - K$. If K has value zero, this loop has a loop independent anti-dependence relation. If K is greater than zero, it has a loop carried flow dependence relation; if K is less than zero, it has a loop carried anti-dependence relation. Without any information about the value of K, the compiler must assume that any of these conditions may arise, and must optimize accordingly. In subsequent chapters, we will see instances where a compiler may be able to generate more than one version of code for such a loop, depending on the presence or absence of a dependence relation at run-time. To support this type of optimization, the compiler needs to determine when a run-time test can determine whether a dependence relation can be eliminated. In this case, the flow dependence occurs only when $K > 0$, and the anti-dependence is present only when $K \leq 0$. If the compiler can annotate those dependence relations with that information, subsequent optimizations may be able to take advantage of them.

```
(1)    for I = 1 to N do
(2)        A[I] = A[I-K] + B[I]
(3)    endfor
```

FIGURE 7.9 Example loop for run-time dependence testing.

Situations where run-time dependence testing can disambiguate dependence relations are found after applying the generalized gcd test and Fourier-Motzkin elimination. The compiler can apply inequalities that would break the dependence one way or the other; any remaining inequalities involving only independent variables that appear in the definition of unknown variables may be simplified to a test involving those unknown variables.

Example 7.20

Use the generalized gcd test to find a run-time dependence test for the loop shown in Figure 7.9.

Solution

In matrix form, the dependence equation $\mathbf{Ai} = c$ is as follows:

$$\begin{pmatrix} 1 & -1 & 1 \end{pmatrix} \begin{pmatrix} i^d \\ i^u \\ K \end{pmatrix} = 0$$

A unimodular matrix $\mathbf{U}$ that satisfies $\mathbf{AU} = \mathbf{D}$ is:

$$\begin{pmatrix} 1 & -1 & 1 \end{pmatrix} \begin{pmatrix} 1 & 1 & -1 \\ 0 & 1 & 0 \\ 0 & 0 & 1 \end{pmatrix} = \begin{pmatrix} 1 & 0 & 0 \end{pmatrix}$$

Solving $\mathbf{Dt} = c$ results in $t_1 = 0$, while $\mathbf{i} = \mathbf{Ut}$ gives the following definitions:

$$i^d = t_2 - t_3$$
$$i^u = t_2$$
$$K = t_3$$

The dependence distance $i_u - i_d$ includes an independent variable. However, since the distance for flow dependence must be positive, there can be flow dependence only if the inequality $i_u - i_d > 0$ is satisfied. This simplifies to $t_3 > 0$, which can be simplified to $K > 0$. Adding the constraint that the dependence distance must be less than the trip count of the loop, we get $i_u - i_d < N$, or $K < N$. The conjunction of these can be used in a run-time test to find that there is flow dependence only when $0 < K < N$.

7.7 In the Pit

In practice, this simple test (sometimes attributed to Leslie Lamport) is simple, fast, efficient, and applicable to many (if not most) dependence problems; some of the literature calls this the *strong single index test*.

The loop limits used for dependence testing need not be exact; any conservatively large trip count can be used instead. When refining direction vector hierarchies, there is no advantage to refining a direction vector element when the coefficients for the unknowns that correspond to that loop are zero. This merely takes more compile time.

In general, solving a dependence system is related to integer programming, except that all we care about is whether there is an integer solution; there is no objective function that we need to optimize. While more recent work has focused on exact dependence methods, little has been done to justify the extra work in terms of the quality of the generated code. On the other hand, there are certain cases where eliminating a single dependence relation and making one more operation execute in parallel can achieve artificial importance by improving performance on important benchmarks. A good implementation of an expensive dependence test can be faster than a poor implementation of a less expensive test. The methods used in dependence testing are also used in other analysis techniques, such as finding extreme values of affine functions or reducing integer matrices.

Here we focus on dependence distance and direction vectors; other, more precise representations can also be found using modifications of the methods presented here.

7.8 Further Reading

Initial work in array dependence testing was done in the context of systolic array generation for uniform recurrence equations (Karp et al. [1967]). The extreme value test, developed by Banerjee et al. (1979), was one of the first attempts to apply serious mathematics to the problem of dependence between general array references. They also proposed linearization of array subscripts. Banerjee (1988) describes the extensions to triangular loop limits. The direction vector hierarchy is described by Burke and Cytron (1986), as is the idea of a self-loop. Maslov (1992) discusses splitting dependence equations.

Psarris et al. (1991) argue that in practice, the extreme value test is accurate for single dependence equations. Petersen and Padua (1993) describe experiments to evaluate the relative accuracy of various dependence tests, and the importance (or lack thereof) of improving test accuracy.

Kuhn (1980) proposed using Fourier-Motzkin projection for dependence testing, though he did not first consider removing equalities to reduce the number of unknowns. The generalized gcd test was introduced by Banerjee (1988). Maydan et al. (1991) describe a series of techniques to eliminate inequalities in the dependence system (including a loop residue step not presented here) that empirically determine all dependence relations exactly. The Omega test for data dependence is described by Pugh (1992); it includes additional analysis to find an exact solution even when Fourier-Motzkin projection gives inexact integer results.

Nontrivial dependence systems include unknown symbols other than loop induction variables, and have been studied from many points of view. Lu and Chen (1990) point out that unknown loop limits can be treated like additional variables in the dependence system, and that additional constraints can sometimes be found in conditional expressions.

Compiler analysis can compute kill information for scalars precisely, but for array references the analysis is more complex; classical memory-based data dependence analysis is inherently imprecise because it ignores array kills. Maydan et al. (1993) present a data-flow framework for array references, which is similar in concept to, but simpler than, the method presented by Feautrier (1991). Pugh and Wonnacott (1993) describe ways to compute array kills by extending the Omega test to solve more general problems.

EXERCISES

7.1 What is the dependence system for the array A in the following loop?

    (1)   for I = 2 to 10 do
    (2)   A[4*I+2] = A[4*I-3] + B[I]
    (3)   endfor

Find any integer solutions to the dependence system.

7.2 What is the dependence system for the array A in the following loop?

    (1)   for I = 20 to 30 do
    (2)   A[I] = A[I-12] + B[I]
    (3)   endfor

Use the simple test to find solutions.

7.3 Use the gcd test to determine whether there is dependence due to the array A in the following loop:

    (1)   for I = 1 to N do
    (2)   A[4*I] = ...
    (3)   ... = A[6*I-1]
    (4)   endfor

7.4 Use the gcd test to prove there are no dependences in the following loop due to the array A, where K is an unknown integer variable:

    (1)   for I = 1 to N do
    (2)   A[2*I+1] = ...
    (3)   ... = A[2*I+2*K] ...
    (4)   endfor

7.5 Find the dependence system and determine whether there is dependence in the following loop:

    (1)   for I = 1 to 10 do
    (2)   for J = I+1 to 10 do
    (3)   A[I,J] = A[I-9,J]
    (4)   endfor
    (5)   endfor

Use the direction vector hierarchy and the extreme value test.

7.6 Use the generalized gcd test to determine whether the two references to A in the following loop might be dependent.

    (1)   for I = 1 to 10 do
    (2)   for J = 2 to 10 do
    (3)   A[I+1,I+J,J+4] = ...

```
(4)             ... = A[I,I+J-1,J+3]
(5)         endfor
(6)     endfor
```

7.7 Find the dependence systems for the two references to A in the following loop:

```
(1)     for I = 1 to N do
(2)         for J = 1 to I-1 do
(3)             A[I,J] = A[J,I] ...
(4)         endfor
(5)     endfor
```

Use the generalized gcd test and Fourier-Motzkin projection to determine whether there are any data dependence relations in this loop.

7.8 Follow the directions for Exercise 7 for the following loop:

```
(1)     for I = 1 to N do
(2)         for J = 1 to I do
(3)             A[I,J] = A[J,I] ...
(4)         endfor
(5)     endfor
```

7.9 Use the generalized gcd test and Fourier-Motzkin projection to determine whether there are any integer solutions to the dependence equation for the two references to A in the following loop:

```
(1)     for I = 1 to 10 do
(2)         for J = 1 to 10 do
(3)             A[I+J*8+3] = A[I+J*8-6] + ...
(4)         endfor
(5)     endfor
```

Find exact dependence distance, if possible, or use a direction vector hierarchy to find dependence direction.

7.10 Repeat the previous problem, after attempting to split the dependence equation.

7.11 Split the dependence equation for the two references to A in the following loop:

```
(1)     for I = 2 to N do
(2)         for J = 2 to M do
(3)             A[N*I+J+1] = A[N*I+N+J] ...
(4)         endfor
(5)     endfor
```

Find the exact dependence distance.

7.12 What are the data dependence relations for the following loop?

```
(1)    for I = 2 to N-1 do
(2)        if A[I] > 0 then
(3)            B[I] = C[I-1] + 1
(4)        else
(5)            C[I] = B[I] - 1
(6)        endif
(7)    endfor
```

7.13 Implement algorithm ReduceRow and algorithm FMint from Chapter 4. Write a driver routine that accepts a data dependence system and finds whether there are integer solutions, and, if so, finds the dependence distance or direction. Verify your implementation by using your routine to solve the example problems in this chapter.

7.14 Find the dependence relations with exact distances in the following loop:

```
(1)    I = 0
(2)    loop
(3)        I = I + 1
(4)        J = I
(5)        loop
(6)            A[I,J] = A[I-1,J+2]
(7)            J = J + 3
(8)        endloop
(9)    endloop
```

8 OTHER DEPENDENCE PROBLEMS

In order for a dependence graph to represent all the constraints of a program, the compiler must conservatively take into account other aspects of the program. This chapter explores several analysis techniques related to dependence analysis, such as array region summaries, interprocedural analysis, and analysis of pointers and dynamically allocated data structures.

Data dependence analysis for arrays and scalars, along with control dependence analysis, gives the compiler a great deal of information that it can use to restructure and optimize the program. Here we explore additional methods and tools the compiler can use.

When an array is defined in a loop or via an array assignment, the compiler can use region summaries to represent the subarray referenced or modified by the definition. These region summaries can be combined and used to summarize the effects of subroutine calls. Interprocedural analysis itself depends on the construction of the interprocedural call graph, which is usually trivial to solve, but for which there can be various complications. Other interprocedural analysis problems include interprocedural constant propagation and determining whether formal reference arguments are aliased with one another or with global variables. Array region summaries can also be used for array kill analysis, from which the compiler can compute value-based array dependence analysis. Sophisticated linear algebra solution methods can also be used to address the array kill analysis problem, as we shall see. Another important topic is computing dependence for traversals of nonindexed data structures. These are typically implemented as dynamically allocated, pointer-based structures. At the time of this writing, compiler analysis of pointer-based structures is the subject of research, and we present an overview of some of the results. Other important considerations are proper handling of dynamic memory allocation and input/output in general. This chapter discusses each of these topics in order.

8.1 Array Region Analysis

Here we present analysis techniques to summarize the subregion of an array that is affected by a statement or sequence of statements or loops. The goal is to recognize that the region of the arrays defined and used by the following loop are X[1:N] and Y[1:N]:

8.1 ■ Array Region Analysis

```
(1)  for I = 1 to N do
(2)      X[I] = Y[N-I+1] + 1
(3)  endfor
```

There are important decisions to make about the precision of the region representation; the more precise the representation, the more costly it is in terms of the space and time necessary to construct it. For this small loop, all we needed to save were the lower and upper bounds of the region, since every interior element of X and Y was also referenced; this is essentially the simple bounds for the region of the array. Note that precise bounds need to be symbolic, since loop limits are often themselves symbolic. Two additional characteristics that can arise, even for one-dimensional arrays, are a stride and a direction. The stride is used to determine that not every element in the region is referenced, and the direction tells whether the references go up or down the array. We can represent regions with strides by *triplet notation*, where A[1:N:2] represents the region comprising the points A[1], A[3], A[5], ..., up to A[2i+1] such that $2i+1 \leq N$. To show direction, we again use triplet notation, but negate the third element to show a negative direction. Note that this is *not* the same as Fortran 90 triplet notation. Figure 8.1 shows examples of the precision of representations for one dimensional regions; we use the * to represent an unknown lower or upper bound.

```
(1)  for I = 1 to N do
(2)      ...X[I]...
(3)      ...Y[2*I-1]...
(4)      ...Z[N+1-I]...
(5)  endfor
```

constant bounds	X[1:*]	Y[1:*]	Z[1:*]
symbolic bounds	X[1:N]	Y[1:2N-1]	Z[1:N]
triplet	X[1:N:1]	Y[1:2N-1:2]	Z[1:N:1]
triplet + direction	X[1:N:1]	Y[1:2N-1:2]	Z[1:N:-1]

FIGURE 8.1 Array regions in one dimension.

The situation is more difficult for two-dimensional regions. We can represent $A[x_1, x_2]$, giving bounds on x_1 and x_2. If we restrict the representation to simple bounds on x_1 and x_2, then the bounds for each dimension are independent, and the region being described is a rectangle. This is often unsatisfactory, however, since it does not represent diagonal or triangular regions precisely. Allowing general affine bounds can be expensive to represent. An intermediate choice is to restrict the bounds to be *simple pairwise bounds*—that is, $\pm x_1 \leq e$, $\pm x_2 \leq e$ or $\pm x_1 \pm x_2 \leq e$—for expressions e that may allow symbolic variables (depending on the implementation). In each case, there is the choice of whether to save strides and directions and whether to allow symbolic variables in the bounds. Note that for two dimensions, there are only eight simple pairwise bounds.

The simplest representation is to use triplets for each dimension; for Figure 8.2, the array region summaries for the five array references are shown in the following table.

	triplet notation		
A[I,I+1]	A[1:100:1,2:101:1]	B[J,1]	B[2:N:1,1:1:1]
C[I,J+I]	C[1:100:1,3:N+100:1]	D[K,I]	D[1:100:1,1:100:1]
E[2*K,I]	E[2:200:2,1:100:1]		

The simple bounds are the same as the triplet notation without the stride information.

```
(1)   for I = 1 to 100 do
(2)      ...A[I,I+1] ...
(3)      for J = 2 to N do
(4)         ...B[J,1] ...
(5)         ...C[I,J+I] ...
(6)      endfor
(7)      for K = 1 to I do
(8)         ...D[K,I] ...
(9)         ...E[2*K,I] ...
(10)     endfor
(11)  endfor
```

FIGURE 8.2 Two-dimensional array references.

General affine bounds can be found by finding expressions of x_k, representing the array dimension, that equal i_k, the loop induction variables, and then applying the loop limits. If we apply this to the A[I,I+1] reference, we get $x_1 = I$ and $x_2 = x_1 + 1$; from this we can find the affine bounds. This procedure gives the array reference summaries shown in Figure 8.3. Using only simple pairwise bounds, we get eight bounds for each reference. Each bound can be computed by applying algorithm Extreme to the expression in x_1, x_2, $x_1 + x_2$ or $x_1 - x_2$. This gives array reference summaries as shown in Figure 8.4.

8.1.1 Constructing Array Regions

Here we discuss construction of array regions with simple bounds with and without strides. Simple bounds for each subscript expression with strides correspond to triplet notation. We are particularly interested in the regions of arrays that are used, modified, and killed. A region is *used* if its value may be fetched by that statement, it is *modified* if its value may be changed, and it is *killed* if its value is always changed, meaning that the old value cannot be fetched again. The killed region is a subset of the modified subset; the complement of the killed region is the

	affine bounds		
$A[x_1, x_2]$	$-x_1 \leq -1$ $x_1 \leq 100$ $x_1 - x_2 \leq -1$ $-x_1 + x_2 \leq 1$	$B[x_1, x_2]$	$-x_1 \leq -2$ $x_1 \leq N$ $-x_2 \leq -1$ $x_2 \leq 1$
$C[x_1, x_2]$	$-x_1 \leq -1$ $x_1 \leq 100$ $-x_1 + x_2 \leq N$ $x_1 - x_2 \leq -2$	$D[x_1, x_2]$	$-x_1 \leq -1$ $x_1 - x_2 \leq 0$ $-x_2 \leq -1$ $x_2 \leq 100$
$E[x_1, x_2]$	$-x_1 \leq -2$ $x_1 - 2x_2 \leq 0$ $-x_2 \leq -1$ $x_2 \leq 100$		

FIGURE 8.3 Affine bounds for array references.

preserved region. Generally we will find conservative approximations to these regions. We will overestimate the used and modified regions, but will underestimate the killed region. To be precise, we are interested in the *may use*, *may modify*, and *must kill* results. In a control flow graph, a *may* result is true if it may be true on any path through the graph, while a *must* result is true only if it must be true on all paths through the graph. We need to handle the loop back edges and loop exit edges specially in order to capture the behavior of the loop. The following analysis works when the CFG is a DAG when the back edges are removed; such a graph is called a *reducible graph*. We also assume that the compiler has inserted loop preheader and postbody nodes, so the loop header has exactly two predecessors.

Intuitively, the analysis proceeds as follows. For an expression, an array region is used if it appears on the right-hand side. The used region may be an element; for an array assignment, it may be a subarray. We assume the array references can be expressed as affine functions of the basic loop induction variables. We shall also see that calling a subprogram may use large regions of an array. The region should be described symbolically, in terms of user variables and loop induction variables. Similarly, an array region is modified and killed if it appears on the left-hand side of an assignment. Conditional assignments do not kill the left-hand side variables, and we shall see other statements that modify but do not kill their outputs.

A sequence of two statements may use an element of an array region if it may be used by the first statement, or if it may be used by the second statement and is not killed by the first. This finds the upward-exposed uses of the sequence of statements; a conservative approximation is to simply take the union of the used regions for each statement. A sequence of two statements may modify a region if it may be modified by either statement, and the sequence kills a region if it is killed by either statement.

	pairwise bounds	
$A[x_1, x_2]$	$-x_1 \leq -1$ $x_1 \leq 100$ $-x_2 \leq -2$ $x_2 \leq 101$ $x_1 - x_2 \leq -1$ $-x_1 + x_2 \leq 1$ $-x_1 - x_2 \leq -3$ $x_1 + x_2 \leq 201$	$B[x_1, x_2]$ with $-x_1 \leq -2$ $x_1 \leq N$ $-x_2 \leq -1$ $x_2 \leq 1$ $x_1 - x_2 \leq N - 1$ $-x_1 + x_2 \leq -1$ $-x_1 - x_2 \leq -3$ $x_1 + x_2 \leq N + 1$
$C[x_1, x_2]$	$-x_1 \leq -1$ $x_1 \leq 100$ $-x_2 \leq -3$ $x_2 \leq N + 100$ $x_1 - x_2 \leq -2$ $-x_1 + x_2 \leq N$ $-x_1 - x_2 \leq -4$ $x_1 + x_2 \leq N + 200$	$D[x_1, x_2]$ with $-x_1 \leq -1$ $x_1 \leq 100$ $-x_2 \leq -1$ $x_2 \leq 100$ $x_1 - x_2 \leq 0$ $-x_1 + x_2 \leq 99$ $-x_1 - x_2 \leq -2$ $x_1 + x_2 \leq 200$
$E[x_1, x_2]$	$-x_1 \leq -2$ $x_1 \leq 200$ $-x_2 \leq -1$ $x_2 \leq 100$ $x_1 - x_2 \leq 100$ $-x_1 + x_2 \leq 96$ $-x_1 - x_2 \leq -5$ $x_1 + x_2 \leq 300$	

FIGURE 8.4 Pairwise bounds for array references.

At control flow merge points, such as at endif statements, a region may be used or modified if it may be used or modified on either predecessor path. However, it is killed at the merge point only if it is killed at all predecessors. If we think of the array regions as sets, the operations we need to perform are set union, set intersection, and, to precisely represent upward-exposed uses, set difference. The representation we choose for array regions will affect how efficient and precise these operations are.

Using set terminology, the compiler can solve for three sets of array regions at each statement or control flow graph node:

- *MayUse(x)* comprises the array regions that may be used by any execution of the program up to and including statement or node x.
- *MayMod(x)* is the set of array regions that may be modified by any execution up to and including statement or node x.

8.1 ▪ Array Region Analysis

- *Kill(x)* is the set of array regions that are always modified by all executions up to and including statement or node *x*.

The solution proceeds as follows. The compiler analyzes each statement to determine what array region is used, modified, or killed by that statement; this analysis is used to find $MayUse_l(s)$, $MayMod_l(s)$ and $Kill_l(s)$, the local use, mod, and kill sets for statement *s*. The nodes of acyclic control flow graphs are visited in a topological order to find *MayUse*, *MayMod*, and *Kill* by solving the following system of set equations:

$$MayUse(x) = MayUse_l(x) \cup \bigcup_{p \in PRED(x)} MayUse(p)$$

$$MayMod(x) = MayMod_l(x) \cup \bigcup_{p \in PRED(x)} MayMod(p)$$

$$Kill(x) = Kill_l(x) \cup \bigcap_{p \in PRED(x)} Kill(p)$$

where PRED(x) is the set of predecessor statements or nodes of *x*, excluding back edges. When performing set union, depending on the representation, we may choose to summarize two or more references to the same array; summarizing may be less precise but be more efficient. Similarly, when performing set intersection, we may choose to approximate two or more references, which again may trade efficiency for accuracy.

For an innermost loop, we first analyze the body of the loop (which is a DAG) using the systems of equations above, treating PRED(*header*) = ∅. This will find the *MayUse*, *MayMod*, and *Kill* sets for the back edge and for each exit edge, or, more precisely, for the source node of the back and exit edges. We will widen those sets to include the effects of all previous iterations at the back edge, and of all iterations at each exit edge. The widening operation depends on the region representation. The widening for the back edge is necessary only if further analysis of the loop body itself is desired. Widening for the exit edges produces sets *MayUse*(*l*), *MayMod*(*l*), and *Kill*(*l*), which summarize the array regions used, modified, and killed by the execution of that loop. Widening for *MayUse* and *MayMod* should either be exact, or, if not, should err by being too large; that is, it should be large enough to include all elements that may be used or modified. Widening for *Kill* must be conservatively small; that is, it should include only those elements that are definitely modified. Thus, at each node *e* with a loop exit edge, the compiler computes the sets for the entire loop as:

$$MayUse(l) = \mathcal{W}^i_{\supseteq} |_{low(i)}^{high(i)} MayUse(e)$$

$$MayMod(l) = \mathcal{W}^i_{\supseteq} |_{low(i)}^{high(i)} MayMod(e)$$

$$Kill(l) = \mathcal{W}^i_{\subseteq} |_{low(i)}^{high(i)} Kill(e)$$

where

$$\mathcal{W}^i_{\supseteq}\big|^{high(i)}_{low(i)} MayUse(e) \supseteq \bigcup_{i=low(i)}^{high(i)} MayUse(e)$$

and

$$\mathcal{W}^i_{\subseteq}\big|^{high(i)}_{low(i)} Kill(e) \subseteq \bigcup_{i=low(i)}^{high(i)} Kill(e)$$

That is, $\mathcal{W}^i_{\supseteq} MayUse(e)$ is a superset of the union of $MayUse(e)$ for each iteration i of the loop, and $\mathcal{W}^i_{\subseteq} Kill(e)$ is a subset of the union. We say that $\mathcal{W}_{\subseteq}$ is a *conservative* operation, meaning it includes no points that are not in the exact solution, while $\mathcal{W}_{\supseteq}$ is a *liberal* operation, meaning that all points in the exact solution are included.

If we use $\vee$ for conservative union and $\sqcup$ for liberal union, a compiler might implement widening as follows:

$$\mathcal{W}^i_{\supseteq}\big|^{high(i)}_{low(i)} MayUse(l) = \bigsqcup_{i=low(i)}^{high(i)} MayUse(e)$$

$$\mathcal{W}^i_{\subseteq}\big|^{high(i)}_{low(i)} Kill(l) = \bigvee_{i=low(i)}^{high(i)} Kill(e).$$

The precision of the $\mathcal{W}_{\supseteq}$ and $\mathcal{W}_{\subseteq}$ operations depends on the representation and on the particular implementation.

The body of the inner loop is then *collapsed* and replaced by a set of nodes in the outer loop, one for each exit edge; each collapsed node has the preheader as its unique predecessor, and the corresponding exit edge target as its successor. The $MayUse_l$, $MayMod_l$, and $Kill_l$ sets for each collapsed node are the widened sets computed for that exit. Then the next outer loop is processed; because the inner loop has been removed, the body of the outer loop will also be a DAG. Algorithm ArraySummary, shown in Figure 8.5, shows the full procedure. It works on reducible control flow graphs with the following information:

1. *Loops* is the set of loops, ordered from innermost to outermost, along with an additional pseudo-loop corresponding to the body of the procedure.
2. *Nodes(l)* is the set of nodes or statements in loop l.
3. *Exits(l)* is the set of nodes that have exit edges from loop l; for the body of the procedure, this is the *Exit* node.
4. PRED(x) is the set of predecessors of x, except for back edges.

8.1.2 Simple Bounds

If we represent array regions by simple bounds for each dimension, then a single region requires $2d$ bounds, where d is the number of dimensions and each bound

8.1 Array Region Analysis

```
Algorithm ArraySummary:
(1)   for l ∈ Loops from innermost to outermost do
(2)       for x ∈ Nodes(l) do
(3)           find MayUse_l(x), MayMod_l(x), Kill_l(x)
(4)       endfor
(5)       let h be the header of loop l
(6)       MayUse(h) = MayUse_l(h)
(7)       MayMod(h) = MayMod_l(h)
(8)       Kill(h) = Kill_l(h)
(9)       for x ∈ Nodes(l) − {h} in topological order do
```

$$(10) \quad MayUse(x) = MayUse_l(x) \sqcup \bigsqcup_{p \in \text{PRED}(x)} MayUse(p)$$

$$(11) \quad MayMod(x) = MayMod_l(x) \sqcup \bigsqcup_{p \in \text{PRED}(x)} MayMod(p)$$

$$(12) \quad Kill(x) = Kill_l(x) \vee \bigcap_{p \in \text{PRED}(x)} Kill(p)$$

```
(13)      endfor
(14)      let i be the basic induction variable for l
(15)      for e ∈ Exits(l) do
(16)          add a temporary node n
(17)          add a temporary edge from the loop preheader to n
(18)          add a temporary edge from n to the target of the exit from e
```

$$(19) \quad MayUse_l(n) = \mathcal{W}^i_\supseteq MayUse(e)$$
$$(20) \quad MayMod_l(n) = \mathcal{W}^i_\supseteq MayMod(e)$$
$$(21) \quad Kill_l(n) = \mathcal{W}^i_\subseteq Kill(e)$$

```
(22)      endfor
(23)      temporarily eliminate loop l from its outer loop
(24)  endfor
(25)  eliminate all temporary nodes and edges
(26)  replace all temporarily eliminated loops
```

FIGURE 8.5 Array summary analysis.

may itself be a symbolic expression. We express a region by a list of bounds, such as $[l_1 : u_1, l_2 : u_2, \ldots, l_d : u_d]$. Union and intersection can be done on a dimension-by-dimension basis. For each dimension d, the union and intersection of a range is as follows:

$$[l_d^a : u_d^a] \cup [l_d^b : u_d^b] = [\min(l_d^a, l_d^b) : \max(u_d^a, u_d^b)]$$

$$[l_d^a : u_d^a] \cap [l_d^b : u_d^b] = [\max(l_d^a, l_d^b) : \min(u_d^a, u_d^b)]$$

The union and intersection of two regions are defined as taking the intersection and union of the range for each dimension. Note that this is a liberal union, in that the union includes points not in the actual union. While the intersection of two rectangles is another rectangle, the union of two rectangles is not. The intersection and union of two simple regions is shown in Figure 8.6. After intersection, if the lower bound is greater than its upper bound for any dimension, the intersection is empty.

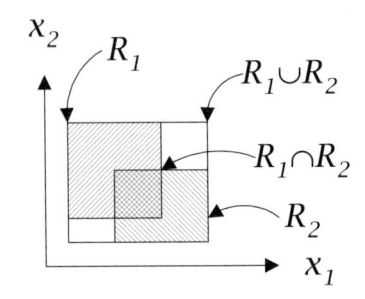

FIGURE 8.6 Intersection and liberal union of two simple regions.

Liberal widening is similar. The lower bound for each dimension is the minimum value taken on by the lower bound expression during the execution of the loop, and the upper bound is the maximum value of the upper bound expression. Algorithm Extreme, discussed in Chapter 4, can find these values, given the loop limits. For conservative widening, the situation is quite a bit different. The result of applying $\mathcal{W}_\subseteq$ will often be smaller than the exact solution because of the precision lost by using only simple bounds. If the loop index variable appears in the bounds of more than one dimension, the region is not rectangular; simple bounds can represent only rectangular regions, so we must handle this case specially, as we discuss shortly. If the loop index variable appears in the bounds of only one dimension—say, dimension k—we can widen the bounds $[l_k : u_k]$ if every point between the widened bounds is visited by the loop; that is, when the conservative union equals the liberal union. For simple bounds, $[l^a : u^a] \vee [l^b : u^b] = [l^a : u^a] \sqcup [l^b : u^b]$ when $u^b \geq l^a - 1$ and $l^b \leq u^a + 1$; this is a density constraint that insures that every integer point between $[\min(l^a, l^b) : \max(u^a, u^b)]$ is in one of the two ranges. For consecutive loop iterations, the compiler should test whether $u_k(i + 1) \geq l_k(i) - 1$ and $l_k(i + 1) \leq u_k(i) + 1$ (where $l_k(i)$ and $u_k(i)$ are the bounds l_k and u_k at iteration i). If these inequalities hold for all values of i in the loop limits, then every point in $[\min_i l_k(i) : \max_i u_k(i)]$ is visited by some iteration of the loop. If the coefficient for i is 1 or -1, then the inequalities hold trivially. If the coefficient has larger magnitude—say, c—but $u_k(i) - l_k(i) \geq |c| - 1$, the inequalities also hold. Remember that algorithm Extreme is not precise when the loop limits are not tight; we must apply tight limits to find $\mathcal{W}_\subseteq$. If the index variable appears in more than one dimension, or the bounds do not satisfy the density constraint, then $\mathcal{W}_\subseteq$ cannot be applied. The only way to find simple bounds is to choose some value that the loop index variable takes on during the execution of the loop, and substitute that value for i within all the simple bounds. Several

8.1 ▪ Array Region Analysis

values might be chosen, but the cost (in terms of compile time and space) will also grow.

When there are two or more references to the same array, the summaries can be combined into a single summary. For *MayUse* and *MayMod*, the summaries can be combined using a liberal union operator; the result may be less precise, but there will be savings in compile time and space. For *Kill*, the summaries must be combined using a conservative union operation.

Example 8.1

Find the simple bounds for the sets *MayUse*, *MayMod*, and *Kill* for the arrays in the following loop:

```
(1)  for I = 1 to 10 do
(2)      A[2*I] = B[2*I] - 10
(3)      if A[2*I] > 0 then
(4)          C[2*I] = 0
(5)          C[2*I+1] = 1
(6)      else
(7)          C[2*I] = 1
(8)          C[2*I+1] = C[2*I+1] - 1
(9)          D[I] = 99
(10)     endif
(11) endfor
```

Solution

We first rewrite the array references in terms of the basic loop induction variable, and find the local $MayUse_l$, $MayMod_l$, and $Kill_l$ sets for each statement, as shown in Figure 8.7. We can visit the statements in topological order (in this example,

statement	$MayUse_l$	$MayMod_l$	$Kill_l$
S_2	$B[2i+2:2i+2]$	$A[2i+2:2i+2]$	$A[2i+2:2i+2]$
S_3	$A[2i+2:2i+2]$		
S_4		$C[2i+2:2i+2]$	$C[2i+2:2i+2]$
S_5		$C[2i+3:2i+3]$	$C[2i+3:2i+3]$
S_7		$C[2i+2:2i+2]$	$C[2i+2:2i+2]$
S_8		$C[2i+3:2i+3]$	$C[2i+3:2i+3]$
S_9		$D[i+1:i+1]$	$D[i+1:i+1]$

FIGURE 8.7 Local *Use*, *Mod*, and *Kill* sets.

lexical order will suffice) to find the complete sets for the body of the loop; the *MayUse* set after each statement is given in the Figure 8.8. The *MayMod* sets are shown in Figure 8.9. Note that for statements S_5 and S_8 we applied conservative union in Figure 8.9 to $C[2i+2:2i+2] \vee C[2i+3:2i+3]$ to get $C[2i+2:2i+3]$.

Finally, the *Kill* sets are shown in Figure 8.10. In this loop, since we know the trip count, we can treat it as if the loop exit is at the bottom; thus the reference sets at the loop exit are the same as after S_{10}. Widening the *MayUse* and *MayMod* sets can be done by applying algorithm Extreme. To find *Kill* for the assignment to A, we see that the conservative union of $A[2i+2:2i+2]$ for two consecutive iterations is not equal to the liberal union; our methods here will result in either finding an empty set for A or finding one or more sets for individual values of *i*. If we find the set for the first and last iteration of the loop, the final result for the loop is in the following table.

MayUse(l)	$A[2:20], B[2:20]$
MayMod(l)	$A[2:20], C[2:21], D[1:10]$
Kill(l)	$A[2:2], A[20:20], C[2:21]$

statement	MayUse
S_2	$B[2i+2:2i+2]$
S_3	$A[2i+2:2i+2], B[2i+2:2i+2]$
S_4	$A[2i+2:2i+2], B[2i+2:2i+2]$
S_5	$A[2i+2:2i+2], B[2i+2:2i+2]$
S_7	$A[2i+2:2i+2], B[2i+2:2i+2]$
S_8	$A[2i+2:2i+2], B[2i+2:2i+2]$
S_9	$A[2i+2:2i+2], B[2i+2:2i+2]$
S_{10}	$A[2i+2:2i+2], B[2i+2:2i+2]$

FIGURE 8.8 *MayUse* sets for each statement.

statement	MayMod
S_2	$A[2i+2:2i+2]$
S_3	$A[2i+2:2i+2]$
S_4	$A[2i+2:2i+2], C[2i+2:2i+2]$
S_5	$A[2i+2:2i+2], C[2i+2:2i+3]$
S_7	$A[2i+2:2i+2], C[2i+2:2i+2]$
S_8	$A[2i+2:2i+2], C[2i+2:2i+3]$
S_9	$A[2i+2:2i+2], C[2i+2:2i+3], D[i+1:i+1]$
S_{10}	$A[2i+2:2i+2], C[2i+2:2i+3], D[i+1:i+1]$

FIGURE 8.9 *MayMod* sets.

statement	Kill
S_2	$A[2i+2 : 2i+2]$
S_3	$A[2i+2 : 2i+2]$
S_4	$A[2i+2 : 2i+2], C[2i+2 : 2i+2]$
S_5	$A[2i+2 : 2i+2], C[2i+2 : 2i+3]$
S_7	$A[2i+2 : 2i+2], C[2i+2 : 2i+2]$
S_8	$A[2i+2 : 2i+2], C[2i+2 : 2i+3]$
S_9	$A[2i+2 : 2i+2], C[2i+2 : 2i+3], D[i+1 : i+1]$
S_{10}	$A[2i+2 : 2i+2], C[2i+2 : 2i+3]$

FIGURE 8.10 *Kill* sets.

8.1.3 Triplet Notation

Using triplet notation allows a more precise representation when the loop index coefficient is not one. As with the simple bounds, we must define the union and intersection operations, as well as how to handle widening. As with simple bounds, we perform union and intersection on a dimension-by-dimension basis. To find the liberal union of $[l^a : u^a : s^a]$ and $[l^b : u^b : s^b]$, the lower and upper limits are computed as for simple bounds. To find the stride, we must find a stride s such that every point in $l^a + is^a$ and $l^b + js^b$ can be represented as $\min(l^a, l^b) + ks$. The largest stride is $s = \gcd(s^a, s^b, l^a - l^b)$. The resulting liberal union is

$$[\min(l^a, l^b) : \max(u^a, u^b) : \gcd(s^a, s^b, l^a - l^b)].$$

The intersection of two triplets is the set of points that is in both regions. This is the set of points such that $l^a + is^a = l^b + js^b$ for values of i and j satisfying the loop limits. This is a simple integer equality in two unknowns, which can be solved using the methods discussed in Chapter 4. If there are any solutions, we can find the smallest and largest values that satisfy this system; the stride of the intersection is the least common multiple of s^a and s^b.

Liberal widening involves finding the least lower bound and greatest upper bound in each dimension; the strides are the greatest common divisor of the given stride and the coefficient of the basic loop induction variable being widened. As with simple bounds, triplets can be conservatively widened precisely only when a single dimension depends on the loop induction variable. For a single triplet $[l(i) : u(i) : s]$, conservative widening of the loop induction variable i is precise when the coefficients of i in $l(i)$ and $u(i)$ are integer multiples of s, and when the density constraint $u^b \geq l^a - s$ and $l^b \leq u^a + s$ is satisfied. The resulting widened triplet is $[\min_i(l(i)) : \max_i(u(i)) : s]$. In the degenerate case when the lower and upper bounds are equal—that is, when the range is a single point $[p(i) : p(i) : \infty]$—the widened triplet is $[\min_i(p(i)) : \max_i(p(i)) : s]$, where s is the coefficient of i.

Example 8.2

Describe the regions of the arrays used and modified in the following loop using triplets:

```
(1)   for I = 2 to 20 by 2 do
(2)       A[I] = B[I] + C[I]
(3)       D[I] = (A[I-1] + A[I+1])/2
(4)       E[2*I] = D[I-2] + D[I+1]
(5)   endfor
```

Solution

In terms of the basic loop induction variable, the local $MayUse_l$, $MayMod_l$, and $Kill_l$ sets for each statement are as shown in Figure 8.11. After visiting the statements in topological order, we have the sets shown in Figure 8.12 for the exit edge at the bottom of the loop.

statement	$MayUse_l$
S_2	$B[2i+2 : 2i+2 : \infty], C[2i+2 : 2i+2 : \infty]$
S_3	$A[2i+1 : 2i+1 : \infty], A[2i+3 : 2i+3 : \infty]$
S_4	$D[2i : 2i : \infty], D[2i+3 : 2i+3 : \infty]$
statement	$MayMod_l$
S_2	$A[2i+2 : 2i+2 : \infty]$
S_3	$D[2i+2 : 2i+2 : \infty]$
S_4	$E[4i+4 : 4i+4 : \infty]$
statement	$Kill_l$
S_2	$A[2i+2 : 2i+2 : \infty]$
S_3	$D[2i+2 : 2i+2 : \infty]$
S_4	$E[4i+4 : 4i+4 : \infty]$

FIGURE 8.11 Local *Use*, *Mod*, and *Kill* sets.

MayUse	MayMod	Kill
$A[2i+1 : 2i+1 : \infty]$	$A[2i+2 : 2i+2 : \infty]$	$A[2i+2 : 2i+2 : \infty]$
$A[2i+3 : 2i+3 : \infty]$	$D[2i+2 : 2i+2 : \infty]$	$D[2i+2 : 2i+2 : \infty]$
$B[2i+2 : 2i+2 : \infty]$	$E[4i+4 : 4i+4 : \infty]$	$E[4i+4 : 4i+4 : \infty]$
$C[2i+2 : 2i+2 : \infty]$		
$D[2i : 2i : \infty]$		
$D[2i+3 : 2i+3 : \infty]$		

FIGURE 8.12 *Use*, *Mod*, and *Kill* sets for the loop exit.

These can be widened to get the following sets for the loop:

MayUse(l)	MayMod(l)	Kill(l)
A[1 : 19 : 2]	A[2 : 20 : 2]	A[2 : 20 : 2]
A[3 : 21 : 2]	D[2 : 20 : 2]	D[2 : 20 : 2]
B[2 : 20 : 2]	E[4 : 40 : 4]	E[4 : 40 : 4]
C[2 : 20 : 2]		
D[0 : 18 : 2]		
D[3 : 21 : 2]		

The two uses of A could have been combined to a single region:

$$A[2i + 1 : 2i + 1 : \infty] \sqcup A[2i + 3 : 2i + 3 : \infty] = A[2i + 1 : 2i + 3 : 2].$$

Widening this would give the single summary A[1 : 21 : 2]. This would not work so well for the two references to D, however. Combining them would give:

$$D[2i : 2i : \infty] \sqcup D[2i + 3 : 2i + 3 : \infty] = D[2i : 2i + 3 : 3]$$

Widening this would give the less precise summary D[0 : 21 : 1].

8.1.4 Array Kill Analysis

Data dependence analysis as presented in Chapter 7 suffers from an important source of imprecision; it does not account for intervening stores to the same location. That is, if there are two statements that assign the same array element and one statement that uses it, dependence analysis will find the flow dependence from both assignments to the use. If one of the assignments always follows the other but precedes the use, then there is really only one dependence relation. This can occur in loops, as shown in Figure 8.13, where there are three assignments to A and one to B. Each assignment to A assigns a different element on every iteration. We can model array references with affine subscript expressions with a *data access matrix* and a *data offset vector* such as $\mathbf{Ai} + \mathbf{a}^0$. When the rank of

```
(1)    for I = 1 to N do
(2)       A[I,1] = C[I] * D[I]
(3)       for J = 1 to M do
(4)          B[J] = A[I,J]
(5)          A[I,J+1] = B[J]
(6)       endfor
(7)    endfor
```

FIGURE 8.13 Program showing difference between value-based and address-based array dependence.

the data access matrix is equal to the number of loops containing the assignment, each loop iteration assigns a different array element. For the B assignment, the data access matrix is (0, 1), with a rank of 1. We say that such a reference has a *self-conflict*.

For this example program, data dependence analysis will find the following flow dependence relations:

$$
\begin{array}{ll}
A & S_2 \; \delta^f_{(0)} \; S_4 \\
A & S_5 \; \delta^f_{(1,0)} \; S_4 \\
B & S_4 \; \delta^f_{(\leq,0)} \; S_5
\end{array}
$$

Value-based dependence analysis will find flow dependence only when there is an assignment at statement S_d with access function $A_d \mathbf{i} + \mathbf{a}_d^0$ and a use at statement S_u with access function $A_u \mathbf{i} + \mathbf{a}_u^0$, such that $A_d \mathbf{i}^d + \mathbf{a}_d^0 = A_u \mathbf{i}^u + \mathbf{a}_u^0$ and $\mathbf{i}^d \leq \mathbf{i}^u$ (or $\mathbf{i}^d \prec \mathbf{i}^u$, as appropriate), with the additional constraint that there are no other assignments at any other statement S_v with access function $A_v \mathbf{i} + \mathbf{a}_v^0$, $A_v \mathbf{i}^v + \mathbf{a}_v^0 = A_u \mathbf{i}^u + \mathbf{a}_u^0$ and $\mathbf{i}^d \leq \mathbf{i}^v \leq \mathbf{i}^u$ (or $\mathbf{i}^d \prec \mathbf{i}^v \prec \mathbf{i}^u$). That is, there is a value-based flow dependence from an assignment to a use only when there is no intervening killing assignment to the same element. This can be posed as an integer programming problem, and methods have been developed to attack it directly; see the references in the Further Reading section.

Here we propose a method for handling certain common cases. We focus on the property that a dependence from an assignment in the same loop iteration is always more recent than an assignment from any previous iteration. This allows compilers to find value-based, loop independent dependence relations.

This analysis uses the *Kill* analysis; when finding loop independent dependence relations for outer loops, it should also include a widening of the *Kill* assignments in the loop for previous iterations of the inner loops. Viewing *Kill* as a set and the elements used as a *MayUse* set, we want to determine whether *MayUse* ⊆ *Kill* for this iteration of the loop. Since we already know how to find unions of these sets, we can test whether *MayUse* ⊔ *Kill* = *Kill*. If so, then any dependence relation must be loop independent.

Algorithm SimpleValueDD, shown in Figure 8.14, finds value-based, loop independent dependence for arrays. It uses the following information:

1. *Loops* is the set of loops, ordered from innermost to outermost, as with algorithm ArraySummary.

2. *MayUse*$_l$(x) and *Kill*$_l$(x) are the local mod and use sets as used in algorithm ArraySummary.

3. PRED(x) is the set of predecessors of x, except for loop back edges and loop exit edges.

Algorithm SimpleValueDD:
(1)   for $l \in$ Loops from innermost to outermost do
(2)   let h be the header of loop l
(3) $Kill(h) = Kill_l(h)$
(4)   for $x \in nodes(l) - \{h\}$ in topological order do
(5) $Kill_b(x) = \bigcap\limits_{p \in PRED(x)} Kill(p)$
(6)   if x is the target of a back edge from node e then
(7)   let j be the loop index for the back edge
(8) $Kill_b(x) = Kill_b(x) \vee \mathcal{W}_{\supseteq}^{j}|_{low(j)}^{j-1} Kill(e)$
(9)   endif
(10)   if x is the target of an exit edge from node e then
(11)   let j be the index for the loop being exited
(12) $Kill_b(x) = Kill_b(x) \vee \mathcal{W}_{\supseteq}^{j}|_{low(j)}^{high(j)} Kill(e)$
(13)   endif
(14) $Kill(x) = Kill_l(x) \vee Kill_b(x)$
(15)   endfor
(16)   for each reference $r \in MayUse_l(x)$ do
(17)   if r appears in an inner loop then
(18)   let j be the index for the inner loop
(19)   find $\mathcal{W}_{\supseteq}^{j}|_{low(j)}^{j} r$
(20)   endif
(21)   if $r \sqcup Kill_b(x) = Kill_b(x)$ then
(22)   there is only loop independent dependence to r
(23)   remove r from $MayUse_l(x)$
(24)   else if r appears in an inner loop
(25)   let j be the index for the inner loop
(26)   replace r by $\mathcal{W}_{\supseteq}^{j}|_{low(j)}^{high(j)} r$
(27)   endif
(28)   endfor
(29) endfor

FIGURE 8.14   Algorithm to find simple loop independent dependence relations.

The algorithm computes the following sets:

1. $Kill_b(x)$ is the set of array references that is modified in this iteration of the loop being tested just before statement or node x.
2. $Kill(x)$ is the set of array references that is modified in this iteration of the loop up to and including statement or node x.

The computation of $Kill_b(x)$ uses previously computed values of $Kill(e)$ for back edges and loop exit edges of inner loops. Those sets are widened to account for all previous iterations of the inner loop for back edges, and to account for all iterations of the inner loop for exit edges. The test for a loop independent dependence relation involves comparing the references in $MayUse_l(x)$ for this statement to the set of elements already modified up to this point. If the reference appears in an inner loop, the reference is widened to account for all the iterations of the inner loop up to the current one. Note that all statements of all inner loops are visited for each outer loop, so the algorithm is not necessarily an efficient one.

Example 8.3

Find the value-based data dependence relations for Figure 8.13. Use simple bounds to represent array regions.

Solution

The initial $MayUse_l$ and $Kill_l$ sets are given in the following table; as usual, we use normalized loop index variables i for the outer loop and j for the inner loop.

	$MayUse_l$	$Kill_l$
S_2	C[i+1:i+1],D[i+1:i+1]	A[i+1:i+1,1:1]
S_4	A[i+1:i+1,j+1:j+1]	B[j+1:j+1]
S_5	B[j+1:j+1]	A[i+1:i+1,j+2:j+2]

For the inner loop, the analysis computes the following sets for $Kill_b$ and $Kill$:

	$Kill_b$	$Kill$
S_4		B[j+1:j+1]
S_5	B[j+1:j+1]	A[i+1:i+1,j+2:j+2],B[j+1:j+1]

Comparing $Kill_b(S_5)$ to $MayUse_l(S_5)$, we find that this must be a loop independent flow dependence relation in the inner loop; in particular, there is no loop carried flow dependence to the reference to B[J].

For the outer loop, we find sets as shown in the following table for the assignments at lines 2 and 4.

	$Kill_b$	$Kill$
S_2		A[i+1:i+1,1:1]
S_4	A[i+1:i+1,1:1]	A[i+1:i+1,2:j+1]
	A[i+1:i+1,2:j+1]	A[i+1:i+1,1:1]
	B[1:j]	B[1:j]
		B[j+1:j+1]

Note how $Kill(S_5)$ was widened and added to $Kill_b(S_4)$. The two summaries for A and B can be combined using conservative union to get the sets shown in the following table.

	$Kill_b$	$Kill$
S_4	$A[i+1:i+1, 1:j+1]$ $B[1:j]$	$A[i+1:i+1, 1:j+1]$ $B[1:j+1]$
S_5	$A[i+1:i+1, 1:j+1]$ $B[1:j+1]$	$A[i+1:i+1, 1:j+2]$ $B[1:j+1]$

Widening $MayUse(S_4)$ gives $A[i+1:i+1, 1:j+1]$; comparing this to $Kill_b(S_4)$ determines that the only flow dependence relations to this use are independent of the outer loop. In particular, this means that there can be no flow dependence relations to this use from before the loop.

8.2 Pointer Analysis

Languages such as C, Pascal, and Fortran 90 include support for pointers, which are often used to implement dynamically allocated linked lists, trees, graphs, and so on. In order to find the dependence relations, the compiler must understand and characterize statements that build and traverse these pointer-based data structures.

Among the languages mentioned above that use pointers, C stands apart in that it allows pointer arithmetic; that is, the programmer can access and change the value of a pointer in certain ways. Pointer arithmetic is particularly difficult to characterize in general, so we first discuss analysis of programs that do not use pointer arithmetic.

8.2.1 Points-To Analysis

Pointers can contain the addresses of static variables such as globals, stack variables like most procedure locals, or dynamic variables. Note that the pointer itself may be a global or procedure local variable, or it may be part of a dynamically allocated structure. Points-to analysis finds a set of pointer targets for each pointer reference. We artificially separate the problem for static or stack pointers from dynamically allocated pointers, since most dynamically allocated pointers will point to other dynamically allocated pointers.

To represent the set of pointer targets, we use a set of possible names:

- Any visible variable whose address has been or might have been taken is a possible pointer target; we call these *named variables*.

- Variables that are not visible to this routine, such as globals not declared in this routine or local variables for a procedure that called this one, can be pointer targets; we represent this by the abstract name *other*.
- Dynamically allocated memory locations might be pointer targets; we represent this by the abstract name *dynamic*. We may use several different names for different dynamically allocated locations, if they can be distinguished.

The compiler can use any number of abstract names rather than *other* and *dynamic*; for instance, if the language is strongly typed, the compiler might use a different abstract name for each variable type. For dynamic allocation, the compiler may use a different abstract name for each dynamic allocation statement. More names can increase the precision of the analysis, but also its cost.

We use C syntax for pointers dereferences, where if p is a pointer variable, then *p is the dereferenced pointer and &a is the address of named variable a. We represent a points-to relationship by a triple (p,q,d), where p is a pointer variable, q is a pointer target, and d quantifies the definiteness of the pointer relationship. The triple (p,q,D) means that pointer p *definitely* points to q, while (p,q,P) means that p *possibly* points to q. We allow multi-level pointers, so *p itself may be another pointer; if (p,q,D), then *p must be the same as q, and **p is the same as *q. An array is given a single abstract name; an array of pointers is handled by summarizing all the pointer relationships of all the elements.

Analysis Procedure

As with array region analysis, we perform points-to analysis by analyzing each statement in the program to see how it affects the relation. A pointer target can be either a definite or possible target; it is a definite target if it is the address of a named variable, or if it is another pointer variable that has a definite points-to target. It is a possible target only if it is a pointer variable with several possible points-to targets. A pointer assignment of a definite target to a definite target generates a definite points-to relationship, killing any previous points-to relationship of the left-hand side. A pointer assignment of a set of possible targets to a definite target generates possible points-to relationships, again killing any previous points-to relationship of the left-hand side. A pointer assignment to a set of possible targets adds a set of possible points-to relationships to each of the possible targets. For instance, the assignment p=&a creates the definite points-to relation (p,a,D); if this is followed by the assignment q=p, another definite points-to relation (q,a,D) is added. If this is followed by the assignment *q=r, where r has the points-to relationships (r,b,P) and (r,c,P), the new relations (a,b,P) and (a,c,P) will be added. Finally, the assignment *a=&d must add points-to relations (b,d,P) and (c,d,P), along with changing any other definite points-to relation for b and c to possible relations.

The analysis looks at each statement and finds a set of definite and possible points-to relations that are valid before and after each statement. If the statement does not modify any pointers, the set of relations that are valid after the statement are the same as those valid before the statement. Otherwise, the assignment can kill points-to relations, change definite relations to possible relations, and create either definite or possible relations.

First we find the left-hand side pointer by "un-dereferencing" the left-hand side expression. That is, if the left-hand side is *r, we look at the points-to relations for r; if the left-hand side is a named variable r, the un-dereferenced expression is &r, for which the points-to relation is (&r,r,d). An assignment modifies the points-to relations as follows:

1. If the left-hand side pointer has a definite points-to target, the assignment kills any points-to relation for that target.
2. If the left-hand side pointer has possible points-to targets, the assignment changes any definite points-to relations to possible points-to relations for all targets.
3. If both the right-hand side expression and the left-hand side pointer have definite pointer targets, add a definite points-to relation from the left-hand side pointer target to the right-hand side expression target.
4. Otherwise, add possible points-to relations from all left-hand side pointer targets to all right-hand side expression targets.

If the statement allocates new memory, the right-hand side should be treated as the variable *dynamic*. If there are no loops, this analysis procedure will find all points-to relations in one pass through the statements of the program in topological order. At control flow merge points, the points-to relations are merged or unioned. Definite points-to relations are changed to possible points-to relations for any name for which there are conflicts. In the case of loops, the analysis will have to repeat until the points-to relations computed before and after each statement no longer change.

Without interprocedural analysis, the initial conditions at the beginning of a procedure will have to assume that any global or formal argument pointers may point to any other global variable, to any nonvisible global variable, represented by *other*, or to dynamically allocated memory, represented by *dynamic*.

Figure 8.15 shows the algorithm to find the points-to relations in a procedure. It uses the following information about the program:

1. *Statements* is the set of statements in the program, visited in reverse post-order traversal of the CFG.
2. PRED(S) is the set of predecessor statements for statement S.
3. *Variables* is the set of pointer variables in the program.

The algorithm uses the *Changed* flag to determine when it has converged to a final solution. It computes $PTin(S)$ and $PTout(S)$ for each statement, the set of points-to

```
        Algorithm PointsTo:
 (1)    repeat
 (2)        Changed = False
 (3)        for S ∈ Statements do
 (4)            oldPTin = PTin(S)
 (5)            PTin(S) = Merge( ⋃        PTout(P))
                              P∈PRED(S)
 (6)            if oldPTin ≠ PTin(S) then
 (7)                Changed = True
 (8)            endif
 (9)            PTout(S) = Process(S, PTin(S))
(10)        endfor
(11)    until not Changed

(12)    function Merge( PT )
(13)        for V ∈ Variables do
(14)            if (V,x,P) ∈ PT or
(15)                (V,x,D) ∈ PT and (V,y,D) ∈ PT then
(16)                /* change all definites to possibles */
(17)                change (V,x,D) to (V,x,P)
(18)            endif
(19)        endfor
(20)        return PT
(21)    end Merge
```

FIGURE 8.15 Algorithm to find points-to relations.

relationships that hold before and after each statement. Procedure Merge is used to change definite points-to relations to possible relations if there is a conflict at a control flow merge point. Procedure Process, shown in Figure 8.16, handles pointer assignments, deleting or change relations in *PTin* and adding new definite or possible relations, as appropriate.

Example 8.4

Use algorithm PointsTo to find the points-to relations for the following program:

```
(1)  p = &a
(2)  if *p > 0 then
(3)      q = p
(4)      r = &q
(5)  else
(6)      q = malloc(4)
```

(7)   r = &p
(8)   endif
(9)   s = q
(10) *r = &c

Solution

Assume that before the first assignment there are no points-to relations. Line 1 is an assignment of a definite pointer target (the address of a named variable) to a definite pointer target (another named variable), so it adds the relation (p,a,D). This relation is used to find a definite pointer target on the right hand side of line 3; thus, that assignment adds the relation (q,a,D). Lines 4,

```
(1)  procedure Process( S, PTin )
(2)     if S is not a pointer assignment then
(3)        return PTin
(4)     endif
(5)     PTout = PTin
(6)     let L be left-hand side pointer of S
(7)     let R be right-hand side expression of S
(8)     if (L,x,D) ∈ PTin then
(9)        for x such that (L,x,d) ∈ PTin do
(10)          remove (*L,x,d) from PTout
(11)       endfor
(12)    else
(13)       for y such that (L,y,P) ∈ PTin do
(14)          for z such that (y,z,D) ∈ PTin do
(15)             change (y,z,D) to (y,z,P) in PTout
(16)          endfor
(17)       endfor
(18)    endif
(19)    if (L,y,D ∈ PTin and (R,z,D) ∈ PTin then
(20)       add (y,z,D) to PTout
(21)    else
(22)       for y such that (L,y,d) ∈ PTin do
(23)          for z such that (R,z,d) ∈ PTin do
(24)             add (y,z,P) to PTout
(25)          endfor
(26)       endfor
(27)    endif
(28) end Process
```

FIGURE 8.16 Procedure used in algorithm PointsTo to process pointer assignments.

6, and 7 all assign addresses of named variables to a named variable. At the endif, the points-to sets after lines 4 and 7 must be merged, which changes some definite pointer relations into possible relations for q and r. Line 9 shows an assignment of possible pointer targets to a definite target, and line 10 shows an assignment to a set of possible targets. The points-to relation computations for each line are shown in Figure 8.17. The notation −(p,*,*) is used to show that any other points-to relations from p are removed before adding the newly generated relations.

line	PTout
PTout(1):	PTin(1) − (p,*,*) + (p,a,D)
PTout(3):	PTout(1) − (q,*,*) + (q,a,D)
PTout(4):	PTout(3) − (r,*,*) + (r,q,D)
PTout(6):	PTout(1) − (q,*,*) + (q,*dynamic*,D)
PTout(7):	PTout(3) − (r,*,*) + (r,p,D)
PTin(9):	Merge(PTout(4), PTout(7))
	= (p,a,D), (q,a,P), (q,*dynamic*,P), (r,q,P), (r,p,P)
PTout(9):	PTin(9) − (s,*,*) + (s,a,P), (s,*dynamic*,P)
PTout(10):	PTout(9) − (p,a,D) + (p,a,P), (p,c,P), (q,c,P)

FIGURE 8.17 Result of running algorithm PointsTo.

Dependence Analysis Using Points-To Relations

To compute dependence using pointers, each assignment through a pointer is considered to be a definition of every variable in the points-to set for that variable. If the pointer has a definite points-to relation, the assignment can be a killing definition, just as if the named variable were used. An expression involving a pointer dereference must be treated as a use of every variable in the points-to set. Recall that the reference **p is a use of p, *p, and **p. With no further information about dynamically allocated pointer targets, every pointer with a dynamic target in its points-to set might cause dependence with every other, creating many spurious references. This can be alleviated somewhat by keeping more abstract dynamic names—perhaps one for each memory allocation statement—but in a loop, a single allocation statement can be executed many times.

Language Hints

Some languages have hints that can improve the precision of points-to analysis. Fortran 90 has a `target` attribute for variables; a variable without the `target` attribute cannot be a pointer target. Thus, pointer dereferences cannot be aliases for named variables without this attribute. C has a `register` attribute; `register` variables cannot have their address taken, and thus cannot be aliases for pointer dereferences. Fortran 90 also has several classes of pointer variables; in particular, a variable declared with the `dynamic` attribute can be assigned only by allocating new space. If a variable has the `dynamic` attribute but not the `target` attribute, it cannot point to the same memory as any other variable, and no other pointer variable can point to its target.

8.2.2 Array Pointers

The new Fortran 90 standard includes pointers of two flavors. For scalar and structured data types, these pointers function more or less like pointers in C or Pascal, with dynamic allocation, support for recursive data structures (linked lists, trees, directed graphs, etc.), and so on. The Fortran 90 standard also includes support for pointers to arrays and subarrays; these are typically implemented by a compiler with *dope vectors*, as mentioned in Chapter 2, which cause very interesting aliasing problems. An array pointer can be assigned via dynamic allocation or via pointer assignment. In the latter case, the array pointer target can be any subarray of some target array. The target array can be either another array pointer target, or a named variable (as long as the variable has the `target` attribute). Note that Fortran 90 subarrays need not be contiguous in memory.

In the following Fortran 90 program, array a is a fixed-size array, while p is a pointer to a dynamically allocated array. Pointer assignments set q and r to point to subarrays of p and a, respectively.

(1) Real, Target :: a(20,20)
(2) Real, Allocatable, Target :: p(:,:)
(3) Real, Pointer :: q(:,:), r(:,:)
(4) Allocate (p(10,10))
(5) q=>p(2:5,3:6)
(6) r=>a(1:5:2,10:20)

Using standard Fortran column-major storage order and assuming four bytes for each `Real` array element, the dope vector for p might look like the following, where *P* is the base address of the newly allocated memory:

address	*P*
lower-1	1
upper-1	10
stride-1	4
lower-2	1
upper-2	10
stride-2	40

After line 5, q points to a subarray of p. Note that q is a 4 × 4 array, but that q(1,1) is aliased with p(2,3). The pointer assignment sets the dope vector for q as follows:

address	*address of* p(2,3)
lower-1	1
upper-1	4
stride-1	4 (= stride-1 of p)
lower-2	1
upper-2	4
stride-2	40 (= stride-2 of p)

Finally, line 6 makes r point to a subarray of a. The subarray that r points to is 3 × 11, but is scattered across array a. The dope vector for r is constructed as follows:

address	*address of* a(1,10)
lower-1	1
upper-1	3
stride-1	8 (= 2× stride-1 of a)
lower-2	1
upper-2	11
stride-2	80 (= stride-2 of a)

Figure 8.18 shows a and p, and the subarrays aliased with q and r.

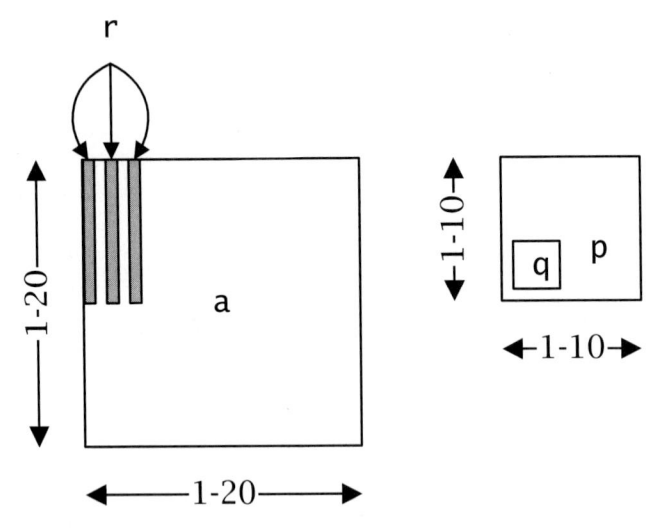

FIGURE 8.18 Array aliasing using pointer assignment.

Simple points-to analysis might keep track of only the target array name; alternatively, the compiler might keep track of as much information about the array target as possible. To find data dependence relations between array pointer references, or between array pointers and target variable references, the compiler needs to determine what pointer assignments can reach each array pointer reference, which is somewhat more precise than points-to analysis, but a similar analysis problem. Dependence analysis is computed conservatively by computing dependence for each reaching pointer assignment.

Example 8.5

Compute data dependence between the references to a and p in the following Fortran 90 loop:

(1) Real, Allocatable, Target :: a(:)
(2) Real, Pointer :: p(:)
(3) Allocate (a(20))
(4) if (upper) then
(5)   p=>a(3:12)
(6) else
(7)   p=>a(1:10)
(8) endif
(9) do i = 1, 10
(10)   a(i+1) = p(i)
(11) enddo

Solution

Simple points-to analysis determines that p points to some subarray of a at line 10. Extended analysis can determine that (p(i),a(i+2),P) and (p(i),a(i),P) are the possible relationships between p and a. Dependence analysis must be performed assuming that either assignment can reach. Using the first relationship, the normalized dependence equation is $2 + i_w = 3 + i_r$, giving an anti-dependence with distance 1. Using the second relationship, the normalized dependence equation is $2 + i_w = 1 + i_r$, resulting in a flow dependence with distance 1. To be conservative, the compiler must assume that it must preserve both the flow dependence and anti-dependence relations.

8.2.3 Dynamic Data Structures

Analyzing programs that construct and traverse dynamic, nonindexed data structures is difficult with current languages. The problem is that while the data structure actually satisfies many useful properties, the implementation using pointers does not convey these properties to the compiler. For instance, in a linked list, the object pointed to by the next link is distinct from the current object, and in fact following a sequence of `next` links will never reach the current object again. A circular list has different properties. In a binary tree, the `left` and `right` links never point to the same object; in fact, the objects reachable by a path that starts with a `left` link are disjoint from the objects reachable by a path that starts with a `right` link.

There are several ways to address this information in the programming language. One way is to add primitives to the language for each actual data structure that the compiler will understand. For instance, the language might include a `tree` type, a `list` type, and so on. The problem is that the language will become large, and the performance of the programs will depend to a great extent on the implementation of each type. A general implementation of each type may include a great deal of functionality that is not always needed.

A second way is to automatically analyze the program to discover the properties of the data structure. To be successful, the compiler must be able to identify all the points in the program where the data structure is constructed and modified, and to discover useful properties of the data structure by the way it is constructed. This has the problem that the data structure may not satisfy all the interesting properties during construction. Also, the actual data structure is unbounded in size; typically, the compiler must use a finite size summary to represent the data structure, frequently resulting in loss of precision.

A third way is to allow the programmer to annotate the program with properties of the data structure, perhaps given as axioms. For instance, axioms about a binary tree might include the following information:

- the left and right links of a node point to distinct objects;
- from two distinct objects, following a left or right link will reach two distinct objects, and
- following a sequence of left and right links will never form a cycle.

Given these axioms, the compiler may be able to prove that two pointer references cannot point to the same object, since one follows the left link from an object and the other follows the right link from the same object. This approach offers a great deal of promise, but needs more research before it is ready for inclusion in production compilers.

8.2.4 Pointer Arithmetic

The C language really has no data structure other than structures and pointers; even arrays are defined in terms of the address arithmetic for the offset from the pointer to the base of the array. Some compilers deal with C array references in the same way they deal with Fortran array references, and continue with array data dependence the same way. For C programs with array accesses written as pointer arithmetic, classical induction variable analysis can be extended to discover the starting point, increment, range, etc., of the pointer itself, which is an induction

8.2 ▪ Pointer Analysis

variable of the loop. For the inner loop, at least, this can be effective in rebuilding the intent of the original program by effectively changing the pointer references back into array references.

Example 8.6

What dependence relations can be computed for the pointer dereferences in the following C loop?

```
(1)   float *ap, *bp;
(2)   float a[100], b[100];
(3)   int i;
(4)   ap = a;
(5)   bp = b;
(6)   for( i = 0; i < 100; ++i ){
(7)       *ap = *bp;
(8)       ++ap;
(9)       ++bp;
(10)  }
```

Solution

Induction variable analysis will find the following linear induction variables:

variable	start	step
i	0	1
ap	&a	4
bp	&b	4

Since a and b are local variables, their memory regions do not overlap. Thus, *ap and *bp do not overlap. Moreover, since ap is an induction variable, there is no loop carried output dependence for the assignment to *ap. More aggressive analysis can even determine that the dereference to *ap is equivalent to a[i] and *bp is equivalent to b[i].

8.2.5 Allocation Dependence

Two dynamic memory allocation statements, such as the Fortran 90 statements allocate p and allocate q look completely independent. However, the order does matter in terms of the memory addresses assigned to p and q. Most programs are written so that the actual addresses allocated by dynamic allocation do not affect the actions of the program. Fortran 90, for instance, has no syntax to allow the program to get to the address of a pointer target, so location independence is assured. C programs, on the other hand, can access, test, and even modify the address contained in pointer variables. When the order of memory allocation is important, the compiler must preserve this order. In that case, the compiler must insert dependence relations between memory allocation statements, corresponding to def-use or flow dependence for the dynamic memory allocation data structures. More commonly, the order of dynamic memory allocation is immaterial; in such cases there is no dependence between the two statements, and they can be reordered at will.

8.3 I/O Dependence

One subtle consideration when looking at all the dependence constraints of a program is that the input/output operations must be ordered as well. Generally, any two reads from the same file must occur in order, and so must any two writes to the same file. However, what look like distinct files at compile time may in fact be connected by the operating system in strange and mysterious ways. For instance, depending on the implementation, two internal file units connected to the same external device may or may not be reading and writing independently. Changing the order of the reads or writes may or may not be legal. Even more interesting are the effects of changing the order in which reads and writes are interleaved. In a batch world, where files are read from (virtual) card readers and written to (virtual) printers, it can hardly matter whether a read that came after a write is moved above the write. However, we live in an interactive world; that write may in fact be the prompt to the user for the data at the read statement. Alternatively, the write may be controlling the device from which the read is being done.

The upshot is that the order of I/O operations in most programs probably can not be changed. This adds the concept of *I/O dependence* to the dependence graph. Any statement that reads from or writes to external devices is dependent on any preceding statement that may do likewise. This dependence must be added in a way that preserves the order of any I/O operations, such as open, close, rewind, status inquiry, etc., in addition to read and write. Since external subroutines may or may not contain I/O, the compiler must assume that subroutines must be called in exactly the order in which the original program calls them, unless it has interprocedural information that I/O does not occur for some routines.

8.4 Procedure Calls

From the point of view of dependence analysis, the effect of calling a procedure is to potentially use and modify any global variable (including global variables that may not be visible to the calling routine) as well as to use all the arguments and potentially modify all the reference arguments. Without analyzing the procedure, the compiler must assume that any or all of these locations might be used or modified. This can add a large number of dependence relations to the program. A procedure call can also change the state of global or static variables that are not even visible from the calling routine. Thus, even procedures with no parameters called from a routine with no visible global variables might be data dependent on some other procedure, since the two procedures can communicate in ways that are not visible at the call site. As just mentioned, procedures may also contain I/O statements. Thus, without precise information about the actions taken by a procedure, the compiler cannot reorder procedure calls. Interprocedural analysis can help with these problems.

Some languages allow a programmer to declare the effects of a procedure call. One common declaration is whether the arguments are read-only or read-write. In Pascal, var arguments are read-write, while others are read-only. Fortran 90 allows declaration of the *intent* of the procedure on each argument, with the options of in, out, or inout, meaning, respectively, read-only, write-only, or read-write. But even these declarations do not tell the compiler whether the procedure includes input or output, or uses or modifications of global variables. Most *intrinsic* functions, built into the language or compiler, use but do not modify their arguments, neither use nor modify global variables, and include no I/O; in general, calling such an intrinsic function has no effect except to return a value that is completely determined by the arguments and that has no effect on the global state of the program. Functions that satisfy these restrictions are called *pure functions*. It is useful when the programmer can declare what user functions also satisfy the constraints of a pure function, such as in High Performance Fortran.

A subroutine does not return values, but we define a *pure subroutine* as one whose only effect is to modify the read-write or write-only arguments, and that does not include any I/O or references to global variables. A pure procedure can include procedure calls, but only to other pure procedures. These restrictions can be checked by the compiler, guaranteeing that a procedure declared to be pure actually satisfies these constraints.

8.5 Interprocedural Analysis

Many compilers now include interprocedural analysis. Some include two or more phases of interprocedural analysis, using the results of the first phase to improve the precision of subsequent phases. For instance, the compiler may try to determine a set of possible pointer targets for formal arguments and global variables, or it may determine whether two formals might be aliases, or it may find what formal arguments or global variables may be modified or killed by a call site. Information about pointer targets or values of formal arguments coming into the procedure can be used to optimize that procedure; we call this *forward interprocedural analysis*, since it carries information from the call site to the called procedure. Information about the effects of a procedure, such as what variables may be modified, can be used to analyze and optimize procedures that call the routine; this is called *backward interprocedural analysis*.

8.5.1 Call Graph Construction

For many programs, constructing the call graph is simple. Each node in the graph represents a procedure. There is an edge from one node to another if one procedure calls another. We use the term *call graph*, even though it is really a multigraph. In the presence of procedure variables or procedure pointers, call graph construction becomes quite a bit more complex. Within a procedure, points-to analysis can determine the set of possible procedures that might be invoked at a call site through a procedure pointer.

However, when procedures are passed as formal arguments, the situation can quickly get much more complex. In Figure 8.19, for instance, there are only four procedures, but the only call graph edge that is immediately obvious is from a to b. Interprocedural analysis is needed to tell that d and c might be bound to formal arguments u and v; this adds a call graph edge from b to c, with a binding of d to the formal arguments w and x. Thus, c can call d, binding b to y and c to z. This results in an edge from d to b, binding c to both u and v. The additional binding for u means that c can be bound to w and x, which means that c can call itself, binding b to w and c to x. This adds an edge from c to b, binding b to u and c to v.

Here we give a simple algorithm to find a conservative overapproximation to the call graph for programs where procedures are passed as arguments. It uses a work list to process actual procedures that are bound to procedure-valued formal arguments. The work list contains three items: a procedure q that is bound to a formal argument, the argument position k to which q is bound, and the procedure p, which is called at the call site. This is written $\langle q, k, p \rangle$, and is read, "q is passed at parameter position k to procedure p." When an entry is removed from the work list, q is added to a set $BoundTo(p, k)$, each call site in p is examined, and one of the following three cases occurs, where f_k is the name of the formal argument at position k:

1. The call site does not invoke f_k, nor does f_k appear as an argument; in this case, the call site is skipped.

2. The call site does not invoke f_k, but f_k does appear as an argument in position m. If the call site invokes an actual procedure a, then the triplet $\langle q, m, a \rangle$ should be added to the work list. If the call site invokes a procedure bound to another formal argument f_j, then for each procedure $a \in BoundTo(p, j)$, the triplet $\langle q, m, a \rangle$ should be added to the work list.

3. The call site invokes f_k. In this case, a new edge $p \to q$ may be added to the call graph. If any actual procedures a appear as arguments at some position m, then $\langle a, m, q \rangle$ should be added to the work list. If a formal argument f_j appears as an argument at some position m, then for any procedures $a \in BoundTo(p, j)$, the triplet $\langle a, m, q \rangle$ should be added to the work list.

In all cases, if the work list already contains that triplet, or if $a \in BoundTo(q, j)$, then the triplet $\langle a, j, q \rangle$ need not be added to the work list.

8.5 ■ Interprocedural Analysis

```
(1)   procedure a
(2)     call b(d,c)
(3)   end
(4)   procedure b(u,v)
(5)     call v(u,u)
(6)   end
(7)   procedure c(w,x)
(8)     call w(b,c)
(9)   end
(10)  procedure d(y,z)
(11)    call y(c,c)
(12)  end
```

FIGURE 8.19 Example program with procedure-valued arguments.

Algorithm CallGraph is shown in two parts. The first part is in Figure 8.20, which shows the initialization routine for the call graph construction algorithm. This routine initializes the *BoundTo* sets for each procedure-valued formal argument, adds call graph edges for calls to procedure constants, and initializes *WorkList* with

```
(1)  procedure InitializeCallGraph
(2)    WorkList = ∅
(3)    for p ∈ Procedures do
(4)      for n = 1 to NumParams(p) do
(5)        if fₙ is procedure-valued then
(6)          BoundTo(p, n) = ∅
(7)        endif
(8)      endfor
(9)      for each call site in p do
(10)       let q be the procedure called
(11)       if q is not a formal argument of p then
(12)         add edge p → q to the call graph
(13)         for n = 1 to NumParams(q) do
(14)           if actual argument n is a procedure constant then
(15)             let a be the actual procedure
(16)             AddWork( a, n, q )
(17)           endif
(18)         endfor
(19)       endif
(20)     endfor
(21)   endfor
(22) end InitializeCallGraph
```

FIGURE 8.20 Procedure to initialize the call graph.

triplets when a procedure constant is passed to a procedure-valued formal argument. Figure 8.21 shows the rest of algorithm CallGraph. The algorithm assumes the following information is available:

1. *Procedures* is the set of procedures in the program.
2. *NumParams(p)* is the number of formal parameters to procedure p.

Additionally, the following data structures are used:

1. *WorkList* is a work list; it may be implemented as a stack, queue or heap.
2. *BoundTo(p, n)* is the set of procedures that are bound to the formal argument position n of procedure p.
3. The call graph is constructed by adding edges $p \rightarrow q$ if procedure p can call procedure q.

The main loop removes one triplet from *WorkList*. Each call site in the called procedure is inspected, as discussed above. If $q \in BoundTo(r, n)$, there is no need to add the triplet $\langle q, n, r \rangle$ to *WorkList*.

Example 8.7

Show how algorithm CallGraph works on the program shown in Figure 8.19.

Solution

The initial call graph has only one edge, a $\rightarrow$ b; *WorkList* is initialized to $\{\langle d, 1, b \rangle, \langle c, 2, b \rangle\}$. The solution procedure is shown in the Figure 8.22, and the final call graph is shown in Figure 8.23.

8.5.2 Interprocedural MOD Information

Here we focus on a backward interprocedural analysis; that is, determining which variables can be modified by a call to a procedure. For each call site, we find a the actual arguments and global variables that might be modified by this call. We solve the problem in two phases. The first phase is to find the reference formal parameters that might be modified. The second phase finds the modified global variables. Here we solve the flow-insensitive (conservative) problem; that is, if there is any path through the procedure on which the variable can be modified, we will say it may be modified by the procedure. A flow-sensitive analysis would find whether the variable is modified on all paths through the procedure.

For each procedure p, we assume the compiler can find the *locally modified* variables of p; that is, those reference arguments of p or variables global to p that are modified by the statements within the procedure or within procedures lexically nested inside p.

8.5 ▪ Interprocedural Analysis

```
        Algorithm CallGraph:
 (1)    InitializeCallGraph
 (2)    while WorkList ≠ ∅ do
 (3)        remove ⟨q, k, p⟩ from WorkList
 (4)        add q to BoundTo(p, k)
 (5)        for each call site in p do
 (6)            if the call site invokes procedure r then
 (7)                for n = 1 to NumParams(r) do
 (8)                    if actual argument n is $f_k$ then
 (9)                        AddWork( q, n, r )
(10)                    endif
(11)                endfor
(12)            else if the call site invokes $f_j \neq f_k$ then
(13)                for r ∈ BoundTo(p, j) do
(14)                    for n = 1 to NumParams(r) do
(15)                        if actual argument n is $f_k$ then
(16)                            AddWork( q, n, r )
(17)                        endif
(18)                    endfor
(19)                endfor
(20)            else if the call site invokes $f_k$ then
(21)                add edge p → q to the call graph
(22)                for n = 1 to NumParams(q) do
(23)                    if actual argument n is $f_k$ then
(24)                        AddWork( q, n, q )
(25)                    else if actual argument n is $f_j \neq f_k$ then
(26)                        for r ∈ BoundTo(p, j) do
(27)                            add ⟨r, n, q⟩ to WorkList
(28)                            AddWork( r, n, q )
(29)                        endfor
(30)                    endif
(31)                endfor
(32)            endif
(33)        endfor
(34)    enddo

(35)    Procedure AddWork( q, k, p )
(36)        if q ∉ BoundTo(p, k) then
(37)            add q to BoundTo(p, k)
(38)            add ⟨q, k, p⟩ to WorkList
(39)        endif
(40)    end AddWork
```

FIGURE 8.21 Algorithm to build the call graph.

⟨d, 1, b⟩	AddWork(d, 1, c)
	AddWork(d, 2, c)
⟨c, 2, b⟩	add edge b → c
⟨d, 1, c⟩	add edge c → d
	AddWork(b, 1, d)
	AddWork(c, 2, d)
⟨d, 2, c⟩	
⟨b, 1, d⟩	add edge d → b
	AddWork(c, 1, b)
⟨c, 2, d⟩	
⟨c, 1, b⟩	AddWork(c, 1, c)
⟨c, 1, c⟩	add edge c → c
	AddWork(b, 1, c)
	AddWork(c, 2, c)
⟨b, 1, c⟩	add edge c → b
	AddWork(b, 1, b)
⟨c, 2, c⟩	
⟨b, 1, b⟩	AddWork(b, 2, c)
⟨b, 2, c⟩	

FIGURE 8.22 Algorithm CallGraph working on the example program.

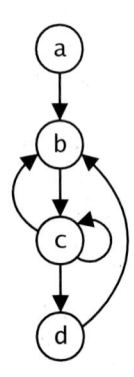

FIGURE 8.23 Final call graph after all analysis.

To solve the first phase for reference parameters, the compiler builds a *binding graph*. The vertices of the binding graph represent formal parameters of the procedures of the program. An edge is added from $p_x.f_i$ to $p_y.f_j$ if procedure p_x calls procedure p_y and passes its formal argument f_i as a reference parameter to f_j. If formal parameter f_j is locally modified by p_y, then f_i may be modified by a call to p_x if p_x calls p_y. Likewise, any variable bound to f_i in a call to p_x may also be modified.

8.5 ■ Interprocedural Analysis

Algorithm FormalMOD, shown in Figure 8.24, solves the first phase by finding strongly connected components in the binding graph. If any argument in the SCC is locally modified, or is bound to some other argument that is then modified, then all arguments in the SCC may be modified by some series of procedure calls. The following information is used:

1. *CallSites* is the set of all call sites in the program.
2. *RefParams(c)* is the set of reference formal parameters for call site c.
3. *Formals* is the set of all formal arguments in the program.
4. *LModified(f)* tells whether the formal argument f is locally modified in the procedure in which it appears (including any modifications in nested procedures).

The data structures used are:

1. Algorithm FormalMOD is a modification to algorithm SCC, and as such uses *Stack*, *NPre(f)*, *InStack(f)*, *Lowlink(f)* and the global counter N.
2. *Modified(f)* tells whether parameter f might be modified by a call to its procedure.

Example 8.8

Build the binding graph for the following program and determine which formal arguments may be modified:

```
(1)   global g1, g2, g3, g4, g5
(2)   procedure main
(3)      local m1, m2, m3
(4)      call r( x, z )
(5)      call p( m2, m3 )
(6)   end
(7)   procedure p( p1, p2 )
(8)      y = 99
(9)      p1 = 98
(10)     q( p2, w )
(11)  end
(12)  procedure q( q1, q2 )
(13)     r( q1, z )
(14)     v = q2*2
(15)  end
(16)  procedure r( r1, r2 )
(17)     r1 = r2 + 1
(18)     q( w, w )
(19)  end
```

```
         Algorithm FormalMOD:
(1)      for c ∈ CallSites do
(2)          for g ∈ RefParams(c) do
(3)              if formal parameter f appears in this position then
(4)                  add edge f → g to the binding graph
(5)              endif
(6)          endfor
(7)      endfor

(8)      for f ∈ Formals do
(9)          NPre(f) = 0; InStack(f) = False
(10)         Modified(f) = LModified(f)
(11)     endfor
(12)     N = 0
(13)     Stack = ∅
(14)     for f ∈ Formals do
(15)         if NPre(f) = 0 then
(16)             BGRecurse(f)
(17)         endif
(18)     endfor

(19)     procedure BGRecurse(f)
(20)         Lowlink(f) = NPre(f) = N = N + 1
(21)         push f onto Stack; InStack(f) = True
(22)         for each g such that f → g do
(23)             if NPre(g) = 0 then
(24)                 BGRecurse(g)
(25)                 Lowlink(f) = min(Lowlink(f), Lowlink(g))
(26)             else if NPre(g) < NPre(f) and InStack(g) then
(27)                 Lowlink(f) = min(Lowlink(f), NPre(g))
(28)             endif
(29)             Modified(f) = Modified(f) ∨ Modified(g)
(30)         endfor
(31)         if NPre(f) = Lowlink(f) then
(32)             repeat
(33)                 pop g off Stack; InStack(g) = False
(34)                 Modified(g) = Modified(f)
(35)             until g = f
(36)         endif
(37)     end BGRecurse
```

FIGURE 8.24 Algorithm to build the binding graph and solve phase 1 of interprocedural MOD problem.

8.5 ■ Interprocedural Analysis

Solution

The binding graph is shown in Figure 8.25. Initially, *Modified* is set for p1 and r1. The *Modified* bit will be propagated to q1 and p2.

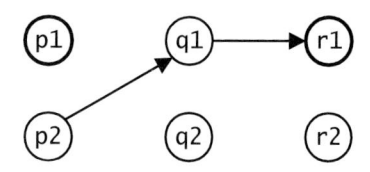

FIGURE 8.25 Binding graph.

Global MOD

The second phase of the interprocedural MOD analysis determines the set of global variables that may be modified by a call to a procedure. A global variable can be modified if the procedure locally modifies it, or if the procedure calls another procedure that locally or indirectly modifies it, or if the procedure passes it as a reference argument to a procedure that modifies that formal parameter. Thus the global MOD problem depends on the solution of the formal parameter MOD problem.

Algorithm GlobalMOD, shown in Figure 8.26, uses the call graph of the program. The nodes represent the procedures, and an edge is added from p to q if procedure p can call procedure q. Each node in the graph is annotated with a set of global variables that are either locally modified in the procedure or are passed as reference arguments to formal parameters that were determined by algorithm FormalMOD to be modified. Again, strongly connected components of the call graph are found; any global variable modified by any procedure in an SCC can be modified by a call to any procedure in the SCC. The following information is used:

1. *Procedures* is the set of all procedures in the program.
2. *InitialGMOD(p)* is the set of global variables that are locally modified in p or are bound to reference formal parameters that might be modified, as determined by algorithm FormalMOD.

The data structures used are:

1. Algorithm GlobalMOD is another modification to algorithm SCC, and so it also uses *Stack*, *NPre(p)*, *InStack(p)*, *Lowlink(p)* and the global counter *N*.
2. *GMOD(p)* is the set of global variables that can be modified by a call to procedure p.

```
Algorithm GlobalMOD:
(1)  for p ∈ Procedures do
(2)      NPre(p) = 0; InStack(p) = False
(3)      GMOD(p) = InitialGMOD(p)
(4)  endfor
(5)  N = 0
(6)  Stack = ∅
(7)  for p ∈ Procedures do
(8)      if NPre(p) = 0 then
(9)          BGRecurse(p)
(10)     endif
(11) endfor

(12) procedure GMODRecurse(p)
(13)     Lowlink(p) = NPre(p) = N = N + 1
(14)     push p onto Stack; InStack(p) = True
(15)     for each q such that p → q do
(16)         if NPre(q) = 0 then
(17)             GMODRecurse(q)
(18)             Lowlink(p) = min(Lowlink(p), Lowlink(q))
(19)         else if NPre(q) < NPre(p) and InStack(q) then
(20)             Lowlink(p) = min(Lowlink(p), NPre(q))
(21)         endif
(22)         GMOD(p) = GMOD(p) ∪ GMOD(q)
(23)     endfor
(24)     if NPre(p) = Lowlink(p) then
(25)         repeat
(26)             pop q off Stack; InStack(q) = False
(27)             GMOD(q) = GMOD(p)
(28)         until q = p
(29)     endif
(30) end GMODRecurse
```

FIGURE 8.26 Algorithm to solve phase 2 of interprocedural MOD problem.

Example 8.9

Complete Example 8.8 using algorithm GlobalMOD.

Solution

Figure 8.27 shows the call graph of the program with the initial and final $GMOD(p)$ sets for each procedure. The final solution of the MOD problem for each procedure is given in the following table.

main	v,w,x,y
p	v,w,y,p1,p2
q	v,w,q1
r	v,w,r1

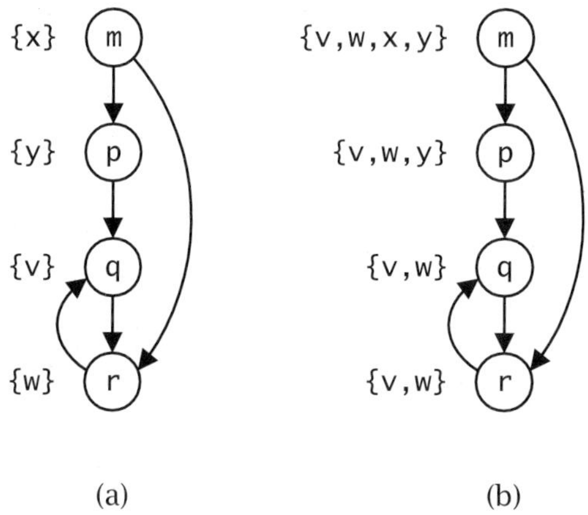

(a) {x} m, {y} p, {v} q, {w} r

(b) {v,w,x,y} m, {v,w,y} p, {v,w} q, {v,w} r

FIGURE 8.27 Call graph with (a) initial and (b) final *GMOD* sets.

Array Region Analysis

Information about whether an array might be modified is very coarse. A compiler can use array region analysis to summarize the effects of the procedure on its arguments and global variables. There can be problems—such as treating a matrix like a vector, and so on—when arguments are reshaped across procedure boundaries. In many cases, the reshaping corresponds to, say, one column of the matrix, and so can often be interpreted correctly by the compiler.

8.5.3 Interprocedural Constant Propagation

Constant propagation within a procedure is very effective. We can extend this analysis across procedure boundaries. The first simple extension is to use the interprocedural MOD analysis to determine which formal arguments are not modified by a call site. In Fortran, for instance, all parameters are passed by reference. This means that without additional information, any variable passed to a procedure call may be changed by the procedure. In the following sequence of Fortran statements:

(1)   n = 100
(2)   ...a[n]
(3)   call sub(a, n)
(4)   ...a[n]

the value of n can be determined to be a constant at line 2, but since the subroutine call might change the value of n, its value at line 4 cannot be determined.

Interprocedural constant propagation can find when formal arguments always have constant values when a procedure is invoked. This is a forward interprocedural analysis, and is in many ways similar to intraprocedural constant propagation. We break the problem into two phases. The first phase uses local analysis of each procedure to determine which actual arguments at each call site are constants or simple functions of formal arguments. The second phase collects this local information to solve the interprocedural constant propagation problem. A third phase would be necessary to propagate the new constant-valued formal parameters into the procedure. Our analysis will allow actual argument expressions that are of the form c or $f + c$, where c is a constant and f is a formal argument. The value of c may be determined to be constant either because it is a literal constant, or because intraprocedural constant propagation found its value to be constant.

We assume the first phase can be done by simple analysis of the program. In fact, this analysis can get quite sophisticated, but experience has shown that simple analysis will get most of the constants values anyway. At each call site, the compiler constructs a *jump function* to represent the value that is passed to each formal parameter by this call site. If procedure p calls procedure q, a jump function $J(q.j)$ for each parameter j of procedure q is generated as one of three cases, and added to a set of jump functions as shown in the following table:

$J(q.j) = c$	Const	if a constant c is passed to $q.j$
$J(q.j) = p.i + c$	Function($p.i$)	the value passed to $q.j$ is $p.i + c$
$J(q.j) = \bot$	NonConst	(bottom) otherwise

The interprocedural analysis phase takes all the jump functions and computes a value for each formal argument. It initializes each value to $\top$, meaning that it has no value yet. First, all $\bot$-valued and constant valued jump functions are processed; any formal parameter that has two different constant values or a nonconstant value passed to it is marked as nonconstant. The other jump functions are processed by initializing a work list with all parameters in the program. As each parameter is removed from the work list, any jump function for which the parameter appears in the expression is evaluated by substituting the abstract value of the parameter. This value is treated as a new constant value for the corresponding parameter. If that parameter gets a new abstract value as a result of this evaluation, it is added to the work list.

Algorithm ICP in Figure 8.28 implements this method; it uses the jump functions as described above, and returns the abstract values for formal parameter f in *Value*(f). *Value*(f) will have a constant value if all call sites to this procedure have the same constant value passed to f and will have $\bot$ otherwise.

Jump function construction for a call site may depend on whether an earlier call site modified one of the formal parameters to this procedure. Therefore, interprocedural constant propagation should follow interprocedural MOD information.

8.5 ▪ Interprocedural Analysis

```
Algorithm ICP:
 (1)  for f ∈ Formals do
 (2)      Value(f) = ⊤
 (3)      add f to WorkList
 (4)  endfor
 (5)  for jump function 'J(f) = ⊥' ∈ NonConst do
 (6)      Value(f) = ⊥
 (7)  endfor
 (8)  for jump function 'J(f) = c' ∈ Const do
 (9)      Value(f) = Meet(Value(f), c)
(10)  endfor
(11)  while WorkList ≠ ∅ do
(12)      remove some parameter f from WorkList
(13)      for jump function 'J(g) = f + c' ∈ Function(f) do
(14)          o = Value(g)
(15)          Value(g) = Meet(Value(g), Value(f) + c)
(16)          if o ≠ Value(g) then
(17)              add g to WorkList
(18)          endif
(19)      endfor
(20)  enddo

(21)  procedure Meet( v, w )
(22)      if v = ⊥ or w = ⊥ then return ⊥ endif
(23)      if v = ⊤ then return w endif
(24)      if w = ⊤ then return v endif
(25)      if v ≠ w then return ⊥ endif
(26)      return v
(27)  end Meet
```

FIGURE 8.28 Algorithm for interprocedural constant propagation.

Example 8.10

Use algorithm ICP to perform interprocedural constant propagation in the following program:

```
(1)  program main
(2)      call p( 10, 20, 30 )
(3)  end
(4)  procedure p( p1, p2, p3 )
(5)      l1 = p1+1
(6)      call q( l1, p2, 40 )
(7)  end
```

```
(8)   procedure q( q1, q2, q3 )
(9)       call r( q3 )
(10)      l2 = q2
(11)      q2 = q2 + 10
(12)      call p( q3-10, l2, q2*2 )
(13)  end
(14)  procedure r( r1 )
(15)      print r1
(16)  end
```

Solution

Local analysis of each procedure will construct appropriate jump functions. In procedure p, symbolic forward substitution would be necessary to determine that l1 has the value of p1+1 to get the best result. In procedure q, variable l2 in the call to p has the value that q2 has when the procedure was entered, even though q2 was modified in the meantime. Also in procedure q, if r1 is a reference parameter, interprocedural MOD information is needed to determine that q3 is in fact not modified by the call to r. In the best case, the jump functions are determined as in the following table.

line	jump function
2	$J(p1) = 10$
2	$J(p2) = 20$
2	$J(p3) = 30$
6	$J(q1) = p1 + 1$
6	$J(q2) = p2 + 0$
6	$J(q3) = 40$
9	$J(r1) = q3 + 0$
12	$J(p1) = q3 - 10$
12	$J(p2) = q2$
12	$J(p3) = \bot$

The last jump function has value $\bot$ because our implementation does not allow for multiplication. After processing the *Const* and *NonConst* jump functions, the values of the parameters are as shown below:

$Value(p1) = 10$	$Value(p2) = 20$	$Value(p3) = \bot$
$Value(q1) = \top$	$Value(q2) = \top$	$Value(q3) = 40$
$Value(r1) = \top$		

As each parameter is removed from *WorkList*, the jump functions in which it appears are evaluated. Only four parameters appear in jump functions in this program; they have the following effects on jump functions.

p1	$Value(q1) = 11$	add q1 to *WorkList*
p2	$Value(q2) = 20$	add q2 to *WorkList*
q2	$Value(p2) = 20$	value didn't change
q3	$Value(r1) = 40$	add r1 to *WorkList*
	$Value(p1) = \bot$	add p1 to *WorkList*
p1	$Value(q1) = \bot$	add q1 to *WorkList*

The final interprocedural constants found are:

$Value(p1) = \bot$	$Value(p2) = 20$	$Value(p3) = \bot$
$Value(q1) = \bot$	$Value(q2) = 20$	$Value(q3) = 40$
$Value(r1) = 40$		

8.6 In the Pit

The array region analysis shown here does not properly take into account the fact that a loop may not even be executed, if the loop limits are symbolic. A more precise representation would be a conditional section, with the condition being that the trip count of the loop were greater than zero.

Call statements can result in a large, complex dependence graph, due to the potential use and redefinition of a large number of global variables in addition to the arguments. In a production compiler, this can be avoided by not using data dependence to optimize regions of the program that contain call statements.

Interprocedural analysis can be very effective in improving the generated code. New object-oriented languages make such analysis harder, since the compiler cannot determine exactly what routines are invoked at a call site; different methods might be invoked for different objects.

Construction of the call graph can be treated as an interprocedural points-to analysis. The problem is simplified since generally there are no arithmetic or other operations allowed on procedure-valued variables; however, the problem is significantly complicated by the fact that, unlike other data-flow problems, the call graph depends on itself. More precise (but more expensive) algorithms to construct call graphs are cited in the references.

The most useful interprocedural analysis is type checking of parameters for correctness. While optimizations have also been shown to be worthwhile, the simplest type checking is highly appreciated by the majority of programmers.

Interprocedural MOD analysis should also take into account aliasing information. If a reference argument p might be aliased at a call site with global variable g, then modifying p also modifies g, and vice versa.

8.7 Further Reading

Pointer analysis is the subject of a great deal of research. Jones and Muchnick (1981) present some of the first work to try to automatically determine the structure of the dynamic data structure from program analysis. The points-to analysis presented here is shown in more detail by Emami et al. (1994). See the short article by Marlowe et al. (1993) for a discussion of two general pointer-aliasing approaches. Realizing that pointers are used to implement complex data structures that may have regular characteristics, Hendren et al. (1992) have developed a language for annotating programs to describe characteristics of the actual data structure that is being constructed and/or traversed with the pointers.

Interprocedural data-flow analysis was studied by Barth (1978). Cooper and Kennedy (1988) show an efficient scheme for addressing the interprocedural MOD problem, from which the solution presented in this chapter is derived.

A fast algorithm to find aliases for formal reference arguments and global variables is described by Cooper and Kennedy (1989). Callahan et al. (1986) developed the interprocedural constant propagation presented here. Grove and Torczon (1993) discuss an implementation of interprocedural constant propagation, with the costs and benefits of more powerful jump function implementations analyzed.

Triolet et al. (1986) show how summarizing the effects of a procedure can be used to parallelize loops containing calls to that procedure. Havlak and Kennedy (1991) describe experience with an implementation of array-region analysis and give a good summary of various related methods.

Constructing the call graph in the presence of procedure parameters when there is no static or dynamic recursion is discussed by Ryder (1979). An extension that allows recursion is presented by Callahan et al. (1987). Hall and Kennedy (1992) show the efficient but less precise method presented here.

EXERCISES

8.1 Find the simple bounds for the liberal union and intersection of the following regions:
  (a) $[1:10]$ and $[2:20]$
  (b) $[1:10, 2:20]$ and $[9:15, 2:20]$
  Draw the regions and show graphically the intersection and union.

8.2 Find the simple bounds for the following regions:
  (a) $\mathcal{W}_{\supseteq}^i[i:i]$, for $0 \leq i \leq 14$
  (b) $\mathcal{W}_{\supseteq}^i[5i:5i+4]$, for $0 \leq i \leq 12$
  (c) $\mathcal{W}_{\supseteq}^i[3i-3:4i+4]$, for $0 \leq i \leq 10$.

8.3 Find the simple bounds for the following regions:
  (a) $\mathcal{W}_{\subseteq}^i[i:i]$, for $0 \leq i \leq 14$
  (b) $\mathcal{W}_{\subseteq}^i[5i:5i+2]$, for $0 \leq i \leq 12$
  (c) $\mathcal{W}_{\subseteq}^i[3i-2:3i]$, for $0 \leq i \leq 10$.

8.4 Find the simple bounds for the *MayUse*, *MayMod*, and *Kill* regions of the arrays in the following loop:

```
(1)   for I = 1 to 20 do
(2)      for J = 1 to 10 do
(3)         A[I,J] = B[J,I+1] + C[I+J]
(4)      endloop
(5)      A[I,I] = 1
(6)   endloop
```

8.5 Find the triplet bounds for the liberal union and intersection of the following regions:
  (a) $[1:10:2]$ and $[2:20:2]$
  (b) $[1:10:3, 2:20:1]$ and $[7:16:3, 2:20:2]$
Draw the regions and show the intersection and union.

8.6 Determine which regions of the array are killed on every iteration of the outer loop below, and identify the flow dependence relations that are loop independent because of this.

```
(1)   for I = 1 to 10 do
(2)      for J = 1 to 10 do
(3)         A[I] = B[I] + 1
(4)         if A[I] > 0 then
(5)            C[J+1] = 0
(6)         else
(7)            C[J] = 9
(8)         endif
(9)         D[I+1] = C[J]
(10)     endfor
(11)     E[I] = D[I+1] - 1
(12)  endfor
```

8.7 Use algorithm PointTo on the following procedure:

```
(1)   r = &p
(2)   *r = malloc(4)
(3)   r = malloc(4)
(4)   *r = malloc(4)
(5)   q = r
```

8.8 Find the dope vectors for the Fortran 90 array allocations and pointer assignments in the program below:

```
(1)   real, allocatable, target :: a(:,:)
(2)   real, pointer, target :: p(:,:),r(:),s(:)
(3)   allocate a(2:20,2:20)
(4)   p => a(2:10,5:9:2)
(5)   r => p(1:5,1)
(6)   s => r(2:3)
```

8.9 Use algorithm CallGraph to find the call graph for the following program:

```
(1)  procedure a
(2)    call b(c,d)
(3)  end
(4)  procedure b(w,x)
(5)    call w(x,1)
(6)    call x(w,2)
(7)  end
(8)  procedure c(y,i)
(9)    call y(c,i+1)
(10) end
(11) procedure d(z,j)
(12)   call z(d,j+1)
(13) end
```

8.10 Show that algorithm CallGraph is conservative by using it to find the call graph for the following program:

```
(1)  procedure a
(2)    call b(c,d)
(3)    call b(e,f)
(4)  end
(5)  procedure b(v,w)
(6)    call v(w)
(7)  end
(8)  procedure c(x)
(9)    call x
(10) end
(11) procedure d
(12)   print "stuff"
(13) end
(14) procedure e(y)
(15)   call y
(16) end
(17) procedure f
(18)   print "and more stuff"
(19) end
```

What edges are added to the call graph by algorithm CallGraph that never occur in the program?

8.11 Algorithm CallGraph assumes that all the procedures in the program are in fact called somewhere in the program. If some procedure is never called, the dynamic bindings from it should not be added either. Modify the algorithm to add nodes to the call graph dynamically, starting from the main procedure.

8.12 The interprocedural constant propagation algorithm finds either a constant value or $\bot$ for each formal parameter. Modify the algorithm to possibly find a range of values $[l : u]$ for each formal parameter.

9 LOOP RESTRUCTURING

Loop restructuring is used to reorder the execution of statements and loop iterations. Restructuring is legal if it preserves the behavior of the program; here we focus on preserving the dependence relations of the program.

When optimizing the performance of programs, the most gains will come from optimizing the regions of the program that require the most time—the repetitive regions of the program. These correspond either to iterative loops or recursive procedures. Here we concentrate on a bag of tricks that we will use to optimize loops. For the most part we will focus on countable loops, where the trip count can be determined without executing the loop, as opposed to `while` loops.

Most presentations of loop restructuring methods focus on the *legality* and *benefits* of performing a transformation or optimization. The benefits of a transformation cannot be determined until the target computer architecture is known; we will discuss the benefits of the transformations for the various architectures in subsequent chapters. Likewise, the legality of a transformation depends on the semantics of the target machine and language. Most machines today comprise one or more sequential processors connected in some fashion; for that reason, we will concentrate on compiling for collections of sequential machines. The compiling strategy would be quite different if the target machine were a dataflow machine.

Our general rule for a legal transformation is simple. If we are successful in capturing all the essential dependence relations of the program in our data dependence and control dependence graphs, then we can apply any transformation as long as the transformed program preserves each dependence relation. On a sequential uniprocessor, a dependence relation is preserved by executing the dependence source before the dependence target. On a multiprocessor, there are several ways to preserve a dependence relation, such as through scheduling or one of various forms of synchronization. While the original program (by definition) satisfies all the dependence relations, that does not mean that the program can always be compiled without transformation. Remember that even a sequential source language (like Fortran 90) may include parallel constructs (such as array assignments, or a `forall` statement). Executing such constructs on a sequential machine requires analysis and perhaps transformation to satisfy all the dependence relations.

The rest of this chapter describes a number of restructuring transformations. Each section gives a motivating example and describes the details of the transformation, how it affects the execution of the loop, and how it affects the dependence relations. Some discussion of what types of dependence relations are preserved or violated will also be included.

9.1 Simple Transformations

We start our discussion with some simple transformations used frequently in the remainder of the chapter.

9.1.1 Statement Reordering

The first transformation presented here is statement reordering. Reordering can be done at any granularity, operation, statement, sequence of statements, and so on. Here we consider reordering at the statement and loop granularity with an acyclic control flow graph; a node in the CFG or dependence graph is either a simple statement or an entire loop. Since the CFG is acyclic, the dependence graph will be acyclic also. Reordering can be recursively applied inside the body of an inner loop, treating each simple statement and inner loop as a node. Recalling that a transformation is legal as long as the dependence relations are preserved, any topological sort of the dependence graph is a legal ordering of the statements.

A compiler can use statement reordering for several purposes. It is used at the operation granularity for instruction scheduling in the back end of a compiler, to amortize pipeline and memory latencies. It can be used to improve data locality, by moving statements or loops that use the same variables closer together. It can also be used to move separate loops closer together, perhaps to allow *loop fusion* or other loop transformations.

The dependence graph must include both data and control dependence relations. If the CFG has no branches, there will be no relevant control dependence relations. If it has branches, a topological sort of the dependence graph will still satisfy the reordering, but generating correct and efficient code may be complex. Each statement under the control of a conditional in the original code must be protected by the conditional in the generated code. It may be easier to treat any control region as a single node, or to use some other method to keep conditional code contiguous, to simplify code generation. If not, a temporary variable must be used to hold the result of the conditional test and then to guard the conditionally executed statements.

Example 9.1

Reorder the statements in the following program fragment so that all uses of the array a are adjacent:

(1)   A(1) = 0
(2)   B(1) = 0
(3)   if C > 0 then
(4)   A(2) = 1
(5)   B(2) = 9
(6)   endif

9.1 • Simple Transformations

```
(7)  for I = 3 to 9 do
(8)      A(I) = A(I-2) + A(I-1)*2
(9)      B(I) = B(I-2)*2 + B(I-1)
(10) endfor
```

Solution

The dependence graph for the example is shown in Figure 9.1. We want to place statements 1 and 4 and the loop at 7 as close together as possible. One way to do that is to reorder the code into the following sequence: 2, 3, 5, 1, 4, 7, as shown in Figure 9.2. This preserves all the dependence relations. Remember that statements 4 and 5 must be protected by the condition under which they originally executed.

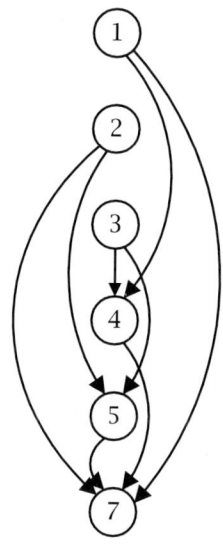

FIGURE 9.1 Dependence graph at the statement/loop level for statement reordering.

```
(2)  B(1) = 0
(3)  Test = C > 0
(5)  if Test then B(2) = 9
(1)  A(1) = 0
(4)  if Test then A(2) = 1
(7)  for I = 3 to 9 do
(8)      A(I) = A(I-2) + A(I-1)*2
(9)      B(I) = B(I-2)*2 + B(I-1)
(10) endfor
```

FIGURE 9.2 Code after reordering.

9.1.2 Unswitching

Unswitching is a simple transformation to remove a loop independent conditional from a loop. Unswitching takes a loop containing a conditional and makes a conditional surrounding one or two loops; the condition being tested must be completely independent of the loop. Unswitching is always legal; the advantage is that it reduces the frequency of execution of the conditional statement by removing the branch from the loop. A disadvantage is that it makes the loop structure more complex; an outer loop containing a single inner loop may be transformed into a loop containing two or more inner loops. This can affect the applicability of other transformations, such as loop interchanging.

Unswitching takes a loop like the following, where the conditional test is independent of the loop:

```
(1)    loop
(2)        statements
(3)        if test then
(4)            then part
(5)        else
(6)            else part
(7)        endif
(8)        more statements
(9)    endloop
```

It transforms the loop into the following code, by copying statements:

```
(3)    if test then
(1)        loop
(2)            statements
(4)            then part
(8)            more statements
(9)        endloop
(5)    else
(1)        loop
(2)            statements
(6)            else part
(8)            more statements
(9)        endloop
(7)    endif
```

Example 9.2

Apply unswitching to the inner loop below:

9.1 ▪ Simple Transformations

```
(1)    for I = 1 to N do
(2)        for J = 2 to N do
(3)            if T[I] > 0 then
(4)                A[I,J] = A[I,J-1]*T[I] + B[J]
(5)            else
(6)                A[I,J] = 0.0
(7)            endif
(8)        endfor
(9)    endfor
```

Solution

Unswitching removes the conditional from the inner loop, as follows:

```
(1)    for I = 1 to N do
(3)        if T[I] > 0 then
(2)            for J = 2 to N do
(4)                A[I,J] = A[I,J-1]*T[I] + B[J]
(8)            endfor
(5)        else
(2)            for J = 2 to N do
(6)                A[I,J] = 0.0
(8)            endfor
(7)        endif
(9)    endfor
```

9.1.3 Loop Peeling

Loop peeling removes the first (or last) iteration of the loop into separate code; this can be generalized into peeling several iterations of the loop. We have already seen this used to handle wrap-around variables. Simple peeling will work if the compiler knows that the trip count is always positive; otherwise, the peeled code will have to be protected by a zero-trip test. We will see peeling used to adjust the trip count of a loop (to enable loop fusion), or to remove a conditional that tests the index variable. Peeling can also be used to remove loop invariant code, by executing that code only on the first iteration.

For countable loops with trip count *tc*, peeling transforms a loop like this one:

```
(1)    compute tc
(2)    for i = 0 to tc-1 do
(3)        body
(4)    endfor
```

into the following code.

```
(1)     compute tc
        if tc > 0 then
            i = 0
            body
(2)         for i = 1 to tc-1 do
(3)             body
(4)         endfor
        endif
```

Example 9.3

Peel off the first iteration of the following loop, saving and reusing the value of the loop invariant code in a temporary variable:

```
(1)     for I = 1 to N do
(2)         A[I] = (X + Y) * B[I]
(3)     endfor
```

Solution

If the value of N is not known, the peeled code will have to be protected by a zero-trip test.

```
(1)     if N >= 1 then
(2)         A[1] = X + Y * B[1]
(1)         for I = 2 to N do
(2)             A[I] = X + Y * B[I]
(3)         endfor
(3)     endif
```

9.1.4 Index Set Splitting

Index set splitting (or *loop splitting*) is the generalization of loop peeling. Splitting divides the index set of a loop into two portions, replicating the body of the loop as appropriate. As with peeling, splitting may be useful to adjust the trip count of a loop, or to remove conditionals that test the index variable itself.

If the trip count is *tc*, index set splitting at iteration *s* transforms a loop like this one:

```
(1)     compute tc
(2)     for i = 0 to tc-1 do
(3)         body
(4)     endfor
```

9.1 ▪ Simple Transformations

into the following code:

```
(1)   compute tc
(2)   for i = 0 to s-1 do
(3)       body
(4)   endfor
(2)   for i = s to tc-1 do
(3)       body
(4)   endfor
```

Example 9.4

Split the following loop to remove the conditional statement:

```
(1)   for I = 1 to 100 do
(2)       A[I] = B[I] + C[I]
(3)       if I > 10 then
(4)           D[I] = A[I] + A[I-10]
(5)       endif
(6)   endfor
```

Solution

In this example, the trip count is known, so a separate zero-trip test is unnecessary. The conditional statement is false until I is equal to 11, and true thereafter. Thus, splitting the loop at 11 will remove the conditional:

```
(1)   for I = 1 to 10 do
(2)       A[I] = B[I] + C[I]
(6)   endfor
(1)   for I = 11 to 100 do
(2)       A[I] = B[I] + C[I]
(4)       D[I] = A[I] + A[I-10]
(6)   endfor
```

9.1.5 Scalar Expansion

When scalars are assigned and later used in the loop, the dependence graph will include flow dependence relations from the assignment to each use, and loop carried anti-dependence relations from each use back to the assignment. These anti-dependence relations will cause problems in other transformations. The anti-dependence relations can often be broken by *expanding*, or *promoting*, the scalar into an array. Here we use scalar expansion only in countable loops when the scalar has no upward-exposed uses; any flow dependence relations in the loop for the scalar are loop independent. In that case, allocating an array with one element for each iteration and replacing each scalar reference in the loop with a reference to the array will satisfy the flow dependence relations. Because each iteration uses a different array element, the anti-dependence and output dependence relations are eliminated. Scalar expansion can be used in nested loops, but the size of the array may be prohibitive.

The correct last value computed in the loop should be assigned to the original scalar after the loop. If the compiler can determine that the value is never used after the loop, this *last value assignment* can be eliminated. When a scalar is assigned conditionally in the loop, last value assignment may not be possible. In such cases, scalar expansion may not be feasible, unless the scalar is dead after the loop.

Example 9.5

Use scalar expansion to remove the scalar anti- and output dependences in the following loop:

```
(1)    for I = 1 to N do
(2)        T = A(I) + B(I)
(3)        C(I) = T + 1/T
(4)    endfor
```

Solution

The scalar dependence relations for this loop include flow dependence relations from line 2 to line 3, and loop carried anti-dependence relations in the other direction; in addition, there is a self-output dependence relations for T for line 2. The anti-dependence and output dependence relations can be broken by scalar expansion. The resulting loop, including a zero-trip test and last value assignment for T, is:

```
       if N >= 1 then
           allocate Tx(1:N)
(1)        for I = 1 to N do
(2)            Tx(I) = A(I) + B(I)
(3)            C(I) = Tx(I) + 1/Tx(I)
(4)        endfor
           T = Tx(N)
       endif
```

9.2 Loop Fusion

When two adjacent countable loops have the same loop limits, they can sometimes be *fused* into a single loop. Originally, loop fusion was developed as a way of reducing the cost of the test and branch code for the loop itself. However, without some theory of data dependence, early descriptions of loop fusion were restricted to cases where the loops were entirely data independent. The recent development of deep memory hierarchies has made it important to take advantage of memory locality. Fusing loops that refer to the same data enhances temporal locality, and can have a significant impact on cache memory and virtual memory performance. Note that loop fusion increases the size of a loop, which can potentially reduce instruction locality. This is usually not noticeable except with the smallest cache memories. Another benefit of loop fusion is that the larger loop body may allow more effective scalar optimizations, such as common subexpression elimination and instruction scheduling.

Fusion takes two adjacent loops like:

```
(1)     for I = ... do
(2)         body1
(3)     endfor
(4)     for I = ... do
(5)         body2
(6)     endfor
```

where the loop limits are compatible, and generates one loop:

```
(1)     for I = ... do
(2)         body1
(5)         body2
(6)     endfor
```

Fusion is legal if all the dependence relations are preserved. Before fusion, all dependence relations must flow from body1 to body2, unless carried by an outer loop. After fusion, the loop can carry dependence relations from body2 to body1; these would be spurious dependence relations, and the fusion would be illegal. The compiler can test for the legality of loop fusion by testing each dependence relation from body1 to body2 to see if it would be violated by fusion. A dependence relation from iteration i of body1 to any iteration $j < i$ of body2 would be violated by fusion.

Example 9.6

Show the result of fusing the following three loops:

```
(1)     for I = 1 to N do
(2)         A[I] = B[I] + 1
```

(3)   endfor
(4)   for I = 1 to N do
(5)   C[I] = A[I] / 2
(6)   endfor
(7)   for I = 1 to N do
(8)   D[I] = 1 / C[I+1]
(9)   endfor

Solution
All three loops have the same loop limits. The result of fusing all three loops is:

(1)   for I = 1 to N do
(2)   A[I] = B[I] + 1
(5)   C[I] = A[I] / 2
(8)   D[I] = 1 / C[I+1]
(9)   endfor

However, fusing the loops does not preserve all the dependence relations. The original program has two data dependence relations between the loops: $S_2 \; \delta^f \; S_5$ and $S_5 \; \delta^f \; S_8$. However, after fusion, the second dependence relation is violated; instead, the fused loop exhibits the loop carried data dependence relation $S_8 \; \delta^a \; S_5$. Fusion has reversed the sense of the dependence relation. Thus, fusion of all three loops is not legal; fusing the first two loops is still legal, so the following is a legal transformation:

(1)   for I = 1 to N do
(2)   A[I] = B[I] + 1
(5)   C[I] = A[I] / 2
(6)   endfor
(7)   for I = 1 to N do
(8)   D[I] = 1 / C[I+1]
(9)   endfor

9.2.1 Array Assignments

Even with many potential benefits, most current compilers do not attempt loop fusion. However, it is very important for generating good code from Fortran 90 array assignments. A sequence of Fortran 90 array assignments, like the following:

(1)   A(1:N) = B(1:N) + 1
(2)   C(1:N) = A(1:N) / 2
(3)   D(1:N) = 1 / C(2:N+1)

9.2 ▪ Loop Fusion

is defined as computing the right hand side expression for all values of the index set, then performing the assignments to the left hand side array, for each statement in order. A simple-minded way to generate sequential loops is to generate a computation loop to iterate over the index set and compute the right hand side expression into a temporary array, followed by a copy loop to copy the values from the temporary array into the left-hand side:

```
          allocate temp(1:N)
          do I = 1, N
(1)          temp(I) = B(I) + 1
          enddo
          do I = 1, N
(1)          A(I) = temp(I)
          enddo
          do I = 1, N
(2)          temp(I) = A(I) / 2
          enddo
          do I = 1, N
(2)          C(I) = temp(I)
          enddo
          do I = 1, N
(3)          temp(I) = 1 / C(I+1)
          enddo
          do I = 1, N
(3)          D(I) = temp(I)
          enddo
```

Compared to the natural and simple way to write this as a sequential loop, this involves a great deal of undesirable overhead. For instance, there are six sequential loops instead of just one. Half of these loops just copy values from the temporary to the left hand side, which is not necessary in simple sequential code. Even allocation of the temporary array is undesirable. The compiler can eliminate the temporary array and the second copy loop if it can fuse the computation loop with the copy loop for each array assignment. The fusion is legal if it preserves all the dependence relations. Between the computation loop and the copy loop, there is a flow dependence due to `temp`, and a potential anti-dependence due to the left hand side array. If the left-hand side array is not used on the right hand side, this fusion is always legal. In this example, the generated code can be simplified to:

```
          do I = 1, N
(1)          A(I) = B(I) + 1
          enddo
          do I = 1, N
```

```
(2)         C(I) = A(I) / 2
        enddo
        do I = 1, N
(3)         D(I) = 1 / C(I+1)
        enddo
```

Finally, if the loops for each array assignment statement can be fused, efficient code can be generated that takes advantage of data locality between array assignments. Between array assignments there can be flow, anti-, and output dependence relations. In our example, there is a flow dependence from line 1 to line 2 for array A, and from line 2 to line 3 for array C. Fusing the loops for the first two assignments will preserve the A dependence as a loop independent dependence relation. Fusing the loops for line 2 and line 3 will violate the flow dependence relation, since the dependence is from the second iteration of the second statement to the first iteration of the third statement; the sequential loop would have an anti-dependence relation from the C(I+1) reference to C(I). After fusing the loops for the various statements, we get:

```
        do I = 1, N
(1)         A(I) = B(I) + 1
(2)         C(I) = A(I) / 2
        enddo
        do I = 1, N
(3)         D(I) = 1 / C(I+1)
        enddo
```

A Fortran 90 array assignment does not define the order in which the index set should be computed. When generating sequential loops, an order must be chosen; in this example, we chose to iterate from the low value to the high, but there is some additional freedom on the part of the compiler.

9.2.2 Complications

Loop fusion requires that the two loops in question be compatible; that is, that they iterate the same number of times, and that they either appear adjacent to each other, or can be reordered to become adjacent. In practice, this limits loop fusion to countable loops that have the same trip count. The names of the induction variables in the loop need not be the same, but the compiler may have to replace references to the original induction variables with equivalent values.

When the trip count is not the same but loop fusion is still desirable, either the loop with more iterations can be split or peeled, or conditional statements can be used to protect the body of the loop with fewer iterations. Each option has disadvantages; splitting or peeling the loop creates more code either outside the loops or in a short (small trip count) loop, whereas adding conditional statements adds the overhead of a test and branch for each iteration.

An additional complication is that the compiler must ensure that scalars assigned in either loop have the correct value after the fused loop; this includes scalars used as loop index variables. If a scalar is assigned in both loops, its value can't have been used between the first and second loop (or else the two loops couldn't have been legally made adjacent), so only the value from the second loop needs to be preserved.

Example 9.7

Fuse the following two loops:

```
(1)    for I = 1 to 99 do
(2)        A[I] = B[I] + 1
(3)    endfor
(4)    for I = 1 to 98 do
(5)        C[I] = A[I+1]*2
(6)    endfor
```

Solution

The two loops are adjacent and both are countable, but the first loop has one more iteration than the second. One option to fusing the loops is to peel off one iteration of the first loop. Peeling the first iteration gives the following situation:

```
(2)    A[1] = B[1] + 1
(1)    for I = 2 to 99 do
(2)        A[I] = B[I] + 1
(3)    endfor
(4)    for I = 1 to 98 do
(5)        C[I] = A[I+1]*2
(6)    endfor
```

Here, the two loops have the same trip count, and can be fused as:

```
(1)    I = 1
(2)    A[I] = B[I] + 1
       for ib = 0 to 97 do
(1)        I = ib+2
(2)        A[I] = B[I] + 1
(4)        I = ib+1
(5)        C[I] = A[I+1]*2
(6)    endfor
```

where `ib` is a compiler-generated basic induction variable. Note that the correct value of I will be generated by this fused loop. The alternative solution is to use conditional statements to protect line 5 so it executes only 98 times instead of 99.

9.2.3 Fusing Parallel Loops

We only consider fusion of loops of the same type (sequential, parallel, etc.); converting one loop type to another to allow fusion is a different transformation. Before loop fusion, the loops are ordered sequentially; all dependence relations between the two loops must be lexically forward, from the earlier loop to the later. If the two loops being fused appear in an outer loop, dependence relations carried and satisfied by the outer loop need not be considered here; it will still carry such dependence relations after any fusion. If there are no dependence relations, then loop fusion is legal. Fusing two vector loops is always legal, since a vector loop preserves all lexically forward dependence relations. Fusing two parallel loops is legal if the resulting flow dependence relations are all loop independent; that is, the source and target iteration of any flow dependence relation must map to the same iteration of the fused loop. Fusing two `doall` loops is legal if all the resulting dependence relations are loop independent. Finally, fusing two sequential loops is legal if no dependence relations are violated.

Canonical data dependence analysis, as presented in Chapter 5, does not compute a dependence distance between iterations of adjacent loops. However, we can use a *cross-loop distance,* which is the difference between the iteration vectors of the two loops involved in a dependence. This can be computed in the same way as canonical dependence distance. If the loop trip counts are the same and simple loop fusion is applied, this will be the distance for the dependence relation after fusion. Loop peeling or other transformations may change the iteration labels of the iterations, and must be accounted for by the compiler.

Example 9.8

Fuse the following two sequential loops, using dependence analysis to test whether fusion is legal:

```
(1)     for I = 1 to 99 do
(2)         A[I] = B[I] + 1
(3)     endfor
(4)     for I = 1 to 99 do
(5)         C[I] = A[I+1]*2
(6)     endfor
```

Solution

This is the same loop as shown in Example 9.7, except that the trip counts are now identical to each other. There is a flow dependence relation from line 2 to line 5, as before. The normalized dependence equation for this relation is:

$$1 + i^d = 2 + i^u$$

Solving for flow dependence distance gives $i^d - 1 = i^u$, or a cross-loop dependence distance of -1. Simply fusing the two sequential loops will result in another sequential loop, which cannot preserve this dependence relation. Later we will use *loop reversal* to address this problem. Right now, we can see that the problem involves a distance of magnitude one. By adjusting the iteration numbers, we can adjust the cross-loop dependence distance. For instance, we can peel one iteration from each loop to produce:

```
(1)    I = 1
(2)    A[I] = B[I] + 1
(1)    for I = 2 to 99 do
(2)        A[I] = B[I] + 1
(3)    endfor
(4)    for I = 1 to 98 do
(5)        C[I] = A[I+1]*2
(6)    endfor
(4)    I = 99
(5)    C[I] = A[I+1]*2
```

After peeling, the trip counts are still identical, and the modified dependence equation is $2 + i^d = 2 + i^u$, which generates a dependence distance of zero. Since a zero distance is preserved by a sequential loop, we can fuse the loops to get:

```
(1)    I = 1
(2)    A[I] = B[I] + 1
       for ib = 0 to 97 do
(1)        I = ib+2
(2)        A[I] = B[I] + 1
(4)        I = ib+1
(5)        C[I] = A[I+1]*2
(6)    endfor
(4)    I = 99
(5)    C[I] = A[I+1]*2
```

9.2.4 Loop Alignment

In Example 9.8, loop fusion is desired, but the second iteration of one loop should be fused with the first iteration of the other loop, and so on. This is a special case of *loop alignment*. Alignment in conjunction with loop fusion chooses which iteration of the second loop should be fused with which iteration of the first loop. In general, the alignment problem can be stated as finding the integer m such that iteration i of the first loop is fused with iteration $i + m$ of the second loop; the alignment parameter m may be positive or negative. Typically, m is chosen to eliminate negative distance dependences, or to reduce the number of loop carried dependence relations in general. Example 9.8 used peeling to implement alignment; with an alignment parameter of m, that many iterations would have to be peeled off one or both loops to align the proper iterations. Another method is to use conditional statements; here, an extra m iterations are added to the loop, and conditional statements are added to skip execution during either the first m or last m iterations.

Example 9.9

Use conditionals to align the two loops given in Example 9.8.

Solution

The solution, shown below, has one loop with 100 iterations. The body of the first loop executes only on the first 99 iterations; the body of the second loop skips the first iteration:

```
        for ib = 0 to 99 do
            if ib < 99 then
(1)             I = ib+1
(2)             A[I] = B[I] + 1
            endif
            if ib > 0 then
(4)             I = ib+2
(5)             C[I] = A[I+1]*2
            endif
(6)     endfor
```

9.2.5 Fusion with Scalars

If scalars are assigned in the loop, the legality rules are a bit more complicated. A scalar assigned in neither loop or assigned and used in only a single loop does not prevent fusion. A scalar that appears in both loops and is assigned in one or both loops might prevent fusion. Recall that an upward-exposed use of a scalar in a loop is one that is not or might not be assigned in that iteration of the loop; that is, the value at the use might come from outside the loop. If there is an upward-exposed use of a scalar in either loop that is assigned anywhere in the other loop to be fused, the fusion is not legal; if the loops are fused, the upward-exposed use might then get its value from the other loop, rather than from where it should. However, a scalar assigned in both loops with no upward-exposed use in either loop does not prevent fusion, as long as the correct last value is assigned. We have been using this rule implicitly for the loop index variable in the previous examples.

For instance, the following two loops cannot be fused, because the second loop has an upward-exposed use of the scalar D, which is assigned in the first loop:

```
(1)     for I = 1 to 100 do
(2)         D = A[I]
(3)         B[I] = D
(4)     endfor
(5)     for J = 1 to 100 do
(6)         C[J] = C[J] + D
(7)     endfor
```

9.3 Loop Fission

A single loop can be broken into two or more smaller loops; this is the inverse of loop fusion, and is called *loop fission* or *loop distribution*. Loop fission has many uses; on a machine with a very small instruction cache, loop fission can be used to break up a large loop that doesn't fit into the cache into smaller loops that do. It can also improve memory locality, by fissioning a loop that refers to many different arrays into several loops, each of which refers to only a few arrays. We will also see cases where we use loop fission before applying other transformations, such as loop interchanging.

When fissioning a loop, the index or induction variables will often be used in both parts of the loop. To avoid problems of deciding where to do induction variable updates, we replace all references to linear induction variables with functions of the basic loop induction variable. Other induction variables can then be removed from the loop, assigning only the last values.

We first consider the simple case of loop fission of a single loop, perhaps nested within or containing other loops. Loop fission starts by constructing a statement-level dependence graph of the body of the loop. As before, dependence relations carried by and satisfied by an outer loop need not be preserved by loop fission of this loop, and are not considered in the dependence graph. Inner loops will be treated as a single node in the graph; dependence relations to or from any statement in the inner loop will be treated as edges to or from the inner loop node. Since induction variables will be replaced, statements that only update induction variables can be left out of the dependence graph.

If there are no cycles in the dependence graph, loop fission can divide the loop into a separate loop around each node (statement or inner loop). The separate loops can be reordered in any topological ordering of the dependence graph.

If there are cycles in the dependence graph, there must be lexically backward loop carried dependence relations. Putting two nodes involved in a dependence cycle into separate loops cannot preserve all the dependence relations in the cycle. Loop fission must find the strongly connected components of the dependence graph, and keep all the nodes in each strongly connected component in a single loop. In fact, if all the nodes in the dependence graph are in a single strongly connected component, loop fission cannot divide the loop at all. When finding strongly connected components for loop fission, the compiler can ignore loop carried anti-dependence and output dependence relations for scalars that will be expanded before fission.

A legal order of the loops after fission can be found by finding the *acyclic condensation* of the dependence graph; each node in the acyclic condensation will correspond to a single loop after fission. Any topological order of the acyclic condensation will satisfy the inter-loop dependence relations, just as in statement reordering.

Example 9.10

Use loop fission to divide the following loop:

```
(1)    for I = 1 to N do
(2)        A[I] = A[I] + B[I-1]
(3)        B[I] = C[I-1]*X + C
(4)        C[I] = 1/B[I]
(5)        D[I] = sqrt(C[I])
(6)    endfor
```

Solution

The dependence graph for this loop is shown in Figure 9.3. Lines 3 and 4 are in the same strongly connected component, and must be kept in the same loop. Thus loop fission can create three separate loops, around the SCCs {2}, {3,4}, and {5}. Due to the dependence relation from line 3 to line 2, the loop containing line 2 must follow the loop containing line 3. The acyclic condensation of the dependence graph given in Figure 9.3 is shown in Figure 9.4. The result of loop fission is:

```
(1)    for ib = 0 to N-1 do
(3)        B[ib+1] = C[ib]*X + C
(4)        C[ib+1] = 1/B[ib+1]
(6)    endfor
```

9.3 ▪ Loop Fission

```
(1)     for ib = 0 to N-1 do
(2)         A[ib+1] = A[ib+1] + B[ib]
(6)     endfor
(1)     for ib = 0 to N-1 do
(5)         D[ib+1] = sqrt(C[ib+1])
(6)     endfor
(1)     I = N + 1
```

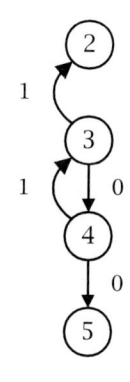

FIGURE 9.3 Dependence graph for loop fission.

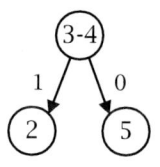

FIGURE 9.4 Acyclic condensation of the sample dependence graph.

9.3.1 Fission with Conditionals

As with statement reordering, loop fission can break up the a block of conditionally executed statements. To apply loop fission, either the entire conditional block must be treated as a unit, or a temporary array must be used to hold the result of the conditional test. The temporary array is used to guard the execution of the conditionally executed statements after fission.

Example 9.11

Apply fission to the following loop:

```
(1)     for I = 1 to N do
(2)         if C[I] > 0 then
```

```
(3)         T = A[I]
(4)         B[I] = T + 1/T
(5)      endif
(6)   endfor
```

Solution

Because there are no upward-exposed uses of T, it can be expanded to eliminate loop carried anti-dependence and output dependence relations. However, T is not assigned on every iteration of the loop. In fact, it may never be assigned in the loop, if the condition is never true. A last value assignment of the Nth value of the expanded array to the scalar T after the loop will not suffice. If the value of T is needed after the loop, the compiler may not be able to expand T. However, if the value of T is not needed after the loop, replacing the conditional and the induction variable and expanding the scalar will produce the loop:

```
         allocate Tx[0:N-1]
         allocate Test[0:N-1]
(1)      for h = 0 to N-1 do
(2)         Test[h] = C[h+1] > 0
(3)         if Test[h] then Tx[h] = A[h+1]
(4)         if Test[h] then B[h+1] = Tx[h] + 1/Tx[h]
(6)      endfor
(1)      I = N + 1
```

Loop fission can then produce the following program:

```
         allocate Tx[0:N-1]
         allocate Test[0:N-1]
(1)      for h = 0 to N-1 do
(2)         Test[h] = C[h+1] > 0
(6)      endfor
(1)      for h = 0 to N-1 do
(3)         if Test[h] then Tx[h] = A[h+1]
(6)      endfor
(1)      for h = 0 to N-1 do
(4)         if Test[h] then B[h+1] = Tx[h] + 1/Tx[h]
(5)         endif
(6)      endfor
(1)      I = N + 1
```

9.3.2 Nested Loops

In nested loops, loop fission can proceed from the inner loop outward. After processing the inner loop, fission on the outer loop should treat each inner loop

9.3 ▪ Loop Fission

as an atomic unit. Remember than when performing loop fission on the inner loop, dependence relations that are carried and satisfied by the outer loop should be ignored.

Example 9.12

Show how nested loop fission is performed on the following loop:

```
(1)    for I = 1 to 100 do
(2)        for J = 1 to 100 do
(3)            A[I,J] = B[I,J] + C[I,J]
(4)            C[I+1,J] = C[I,J] + A[I,J]
(5)            D[I,J] = C[I,J] - 1
(6)        endfor
(7)    endfor
```

Solution

For the inner loop, the relevant dependence relations are shown in Figure 9.5(a); the loop carried dependence relation from line 4 to line 3 is carried by the outer I loop, and so can be safely ignored here. Thus, fission on the inner loop produces:

```
(1)    for I = 1 to 100 do
(2)        for h2 = 0 to 99 do
(3)            A[I,h2+1] = B[I,h2+1] + C[I,h2+1]
(6)        endfor
(2)        for h2 = 0 to 99 do
(4)            C[I+1,h2+1] = C[I,h2+1] + A[I,h2+1]
(6)        endfor
(2)        for h2 = 0 to 99 do
(5)            D[I,h2+1] = C[I,h2+1] - 1
(6)        endfor
(2)        J = 101
(7)    endfor
```

For the outer loop, the relevant dependence relations are shown in Figure 9.5(b). Here the dependence cycle involving lines 3 and 4 appears. Fission of the I loop produces only two loops; the J assignment can be treated as a degenerate induction variable in the I loop, and removed from the loop:

```
(1)    for h1 = 0 to 99 do
(2)        for h2 = 0 to 99 do
(3)            A[h1+1,h2+1] = B[h1+1,h2+1] + C[h1+1,h2+1]
(6)        endfor
```

```
(2)         for h2 = 0 to 99 do
(4)             C[h1+2,h2+1] = C[h1+1,h2+1] + A[h1+1,h2+1]
(6)         endfor
(7)     endfor
(1)     for h1 = 0 to 99 do
(2)         for h2 = 0 to 99 do
(5)             D[h1+1,h2+1] = C[h1+1,h2+1] - 1
(6)         endfor
(7)     endfor
(2)     J = 101
(1)     I = 101
```

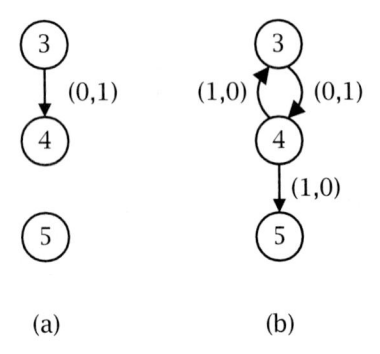

FIGURE 9.5 Data dependence graph for (a) inner loop only and (b) outer loop.

9.3.3 Fission Algorithm

Loop fission need not divide a loop into the smallest units possible. We hinted at this by allowing the compiler to treat a conditional block as a unit, even though replicating the conditional is also feasible. If the compiler should decide to keep two or more statements in the same loop, it should merge the data dependence graph nodes for those two statements. When it does, more cycles in the dependence graph may appear. For instance, suppose there is dependence from line 4 to line 6, and a loop carried dependence from line 6 to line 5. If the compiler decides to keep lines 4 and 5 in the same loop, then merging the data dependence graph nodes for those two lines produces a dependence cycle with line 6, meaning that line 6 would have to be kept in the same loop as lines 4 and 5.

One way to use loop fission to help with data locality is to add input dependence relations to the dependence graph. This adds cycles to the graph for any two statements that refer to the same memory locations. The cycles will keep two statements in the same loop after fission if they use the same data, and separate them if they do not, hopefully improving data locality.

The general method for loop fission proceeds from inner to outer loops. For each loop, a dependence graph is built, treating each inner loop as an atomic unit and ignoring dependence relations carried by outer loops. Loop carried output and anti-dependence relations for scalars that can be expanded can also be ignored. If any two statements are to be kept in the same loop after fission for reasons other than dependence relations, they should be represented by a single node in the dependence graph. The strongly connected components of the final graph are then found, and code generation proceeds by putting each SCC into a separate copy of the loop.

9.3.4 Fission for Parallel Loops

Loop fission can also be applied to `forall` and other parallel loops. Fission for `forall` loops is always legal, since a `forall` loop preserves only lexically forward dependence relations; because of that, there are no dependence cycles. There can be dependence cycles in `dopar` loops, due to anti-dependence relations between different iterations. For `doall` loops, fission is also always legal, since by definition a `doall` carries no dependence relations, and so cannot carry a dependence cycle.

Loop fission is also useful when converting sequential loops into Fortran 90 array assignments or `forall` loops. Remember that any restructuring is legal if the dependence relations are preserved. A `forall` loop or array assignment cannot preserve any lexically backward dependence relation. If a sequential loop has no lexically backward dependence relations, it can be trivially converted into a `forall`. If there are lexically backward dependence relations, statement reordering within the loop body may change them into lexically forward dependence relations. If there are dependence cycles, loop fission can remove the dependence cycle into a separate loop, leaving the rest of the statements in loops that can be converted into `forall`s or into array assignments.

Example 9.13

Convert into array assignments as many statements in the following loop as possible.

```
(1)    for I = 1 to N do
(2)        A[I+1] = A[I+1] + B[I]
(3)        B[I+1] = C[I] + 1
(4)        A[I+1] = A[I] * C[I] + D[I]
(5)    endfor
```

Solution

The dependence graph for this example is shown in Figure 9.6; there are two lexically backward dependence relations; a flow dependence from line 3 to line 2 (for

B), and another from line 4 to itself. Statement reordering could turn the first of these into a lexically forward dependence, but the second dependence creates a cycle. We can apply loop fission, to get:

```
(1)     for h = 0 to N-1 do
(3)         B[h+2] = C[h+1] + 1
(5)     endfor
(1)     for h = 0 to N-1 do
(2)         A[h+2] = A[h+2] + B[h+1]
(5)     endfor
(1)     for h = 0 to N-1 do
(4)         A[h+2] = A[h+1] * C[h+1] + D[h+1]
(5)     endfor
(1)     I = N + 1
```

The first two of these loops have no lexically backward dependence relations, and can be converted into the array assignments:

```
(3)     B[2:N+1] = C[1:N] + 1
(2)     A[2:N+1] = A[2:N+1] + B[1:N]
```

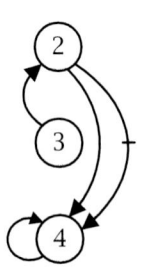

FIGURE 9.6 Data dependence graph for example.

9.4 Loop Reversal

The compiler can decide to run a loop backward; this is called *loop reversal*. Reversal of `forall`, `dopar`, or `dosingle` loops is always legal, since the execution is not defined in terms of the order of the index set. If a sequential loop carries a dependence relation, reversing the loop will reverse the direction of the dependence, violating that dependence relation. Thus, loop reversal is legal only when the loop carries no dependence relations.

In general, loop reversal negates the dependence distance for that loop in any distance vector. One use of loop reversal is to allow loop fusion to proceed where it might otherwise fail. It can be important when compiling array assignments for execution on a sequential machine, since it essentially requires fusion of the right hand side with the left hand side.

Example 9.14

Use loop reversal to improve the loop fusion in Example 9.6.

Solution

Fusion of the original loops ended up with the following two loops:

```
(1)     for I = 1 to N do
(2)         A[I] = B[I] + 1
(5)         C[I] = A[I] / 2
(6)     endfor
(7)     for I = 1 to N do
(8)         D[I] = 1 / C[I+1]
(9)     endfor
```

Since neither loop carries a dependence relation, reversing each loop is legal. Moreover, the cross-loop dependence distance changes from -1 to $+1$ when the two loops are reversed; this means that fusing the two loops after reversal is legal:

```
(1)     for I = N downto 1 do
(2)         A[I] = B[I] + 1
(5)         C[I] = A[I] / 2
(8)         D[I] = 1 / C[I+1]
(9)     endfor
```

9.5 Loop Interchanging

Perhaps the single most important loop restructuring transformation is *loop interchanging*. Interchanging two tightly nested loops switches the inner and outer loop; it was developed initially to help with automatic discovery of parallelism. Converting a sequential nested loop into parallel form would try to find a loop (or loops) that carried no dependence relations. If one loop carried all the dependence relations, that loop would be interchanged to the outermost position, and the rest of the loops would be executed in parallel. For vector machines, a compiler would essentially try to convert a sequential inner loop into a sequence of vector operations, corresponding to array assignments. As we saw earlier, this can be done if there are no dependence cycles. If the inner loop carried a dependence cycle, the compiler would use interchanging to try to move another loop to the innermost position.

More recently, loop interchanging has been used to improve many performance aspects of a program. If the outer loop iterates many times and the inner loop only a few times, there will be significant loop startup overhead for the inner loop. Interchanging these loops means the inner loop startup overhead only occurs a few times. More important, interchanging can change the spatial and sequential memory locality characteristics of the program. If some array reference varies in the inner loop, but is invariant in the outer loop, interchanging the loops makes the reference invariant. Interchanging can also affect spatial locality by changing the stride of array accesses in the inner loop.

9.5.1 Tightly Nested Loops

Two loops are tightly nested when the inner loop is the only code in the outer loop. For countable loops, when the trip count of the inner loop does not depend on the outer loop iteration, interchanging involves merely switching the nesting of the loops. Thus, interchanging the following loops:

```
(1)     for I = ...do
(2)         for J = ...do
(3)             body1
(4)         endfor
(5)     endfor
```

produces this program:

```
(2)     for J = ...do
(1)         for I = ...do
(3)             body1
(4)         endfor
(5)     endfor
```

The only constraints that can prevent interchanging are data dependence relations that might be violated. As before, the interchanged loops must preserve all the original dependence relations. Loop independent dependence relations will still be loop independent after loop interchanging, so they cannot prevent interchanging. A dependence relation that is carried by the inner loop before interchanging must have a zero distance in the outer loop. It will still be carried and satisfied by the same loop after interchanging. A dependence relation that is carried by the outer loop with a zero distance in the inner loop will still be carried and satisfied by the same loop after interchanging. A dependence relation with nonzero distance in both loops is *interchange-sensitive*. Before interchanging, such a dependence is carried by the outer loop; after interchanging, it will be carried by the new outer loop. If the new outer loop resolves the data access conflict in the same way the old outer loop did, the interchange is legal. After interchanging, any dependence relation must be the same, but the distance or direction vector has its entries for the interchanged loops switched.

When interchanging two sequential loops, an interchange-sensitive dependence relation will be preserved if the dependence distance in the inner loop is positive, or the direction is $<$. Since the original outer sequential loop must have carried the interchange-sensitive dependence relation, it must have a positive distance or $<$ direction for that loop. Thus, only dependence relations with a direction vector of $(<, >)$ will be violated by the interchange.

Example 9.15

Determine whether interchanging the following loops is legal:

```
(1)    for J = 2 to M do
(2)        for I = 1 to N do
(3)            A[I,J] = A[I,J-1] + B[I,J]
(4)        endfor
(5)    endfor
```

Solution

There is a single data dependence relation, a flow dependence carried by the outer loop, with direction vector $(1, 0)$. Since it has zero distance in the inner loop, it is not interchange-sensitive. After interchanging, the dependence is carried by the same loop (now in the inner position), so the interchange is legal:

```
(1)    for I = 1 to N do
(2)        for J = 2 to M do
(3)            A[I,J] = A[I,J-1] + B[I,J]
(4)        endfor
(5)    endfor
```

After interchanging, the direction vector's elements are interchanged also, resulting in dependence with direction $(0, 1)$.

9.5.2 Interchanging with Parallel Loops

When interchanging parallel loops, or parallel and sequential loops, the basic rules are the same. Any loop independent dependence relation will be preserved by the interchange. A loop carried dependence with a zero distance in the inner or outer loop will still be carried by the same loop after interchanging, and preserved by that loop. A dependence carried by the outer loop with a nonzero distance in the inner loop must be preserved by the new outer loop in the same way in order for the interchange to be legal. It is not as simple to develop simple direction vector or distance vector rules for interchanging parallel and sequential loops; a dopar loop, as defined in Chapter 2, resolves all loop carried data access conflicts as anti-dependence relations. Sequential loops resolve all loop carried data access conflicts in the order of execution. An anti-dependence relation with positive distance will be resolved in the same way by both loop types.

Example 9.16

Determine whether interchanging the following two loops is legal.

(1)   dopar I = 1 to N do
(2)   for J = 1 to M do
(3)   A[I,J] = (A[I+1,J-1] + A[I-1,J+1])/2
(4)   endfor
(5)   enddopar

Solution

The two data dependence relations are both carried by the outer loop. The rules for resolving data access conflicts carried by a dopar allow only anti-dependence relations. Thus, the two dependence relations are an anti dependence relation with distance vector $(1, -1)$ (for anti-dependence from A[I+1,J-1]) and another with distance vector $(-1, 1)$ (for anti-dependence from A[I-1,J+1]). After interchanging, both dependence relations will be carried by the J loop in the outer position. The data access conflict between A[I,J] and A[I-1,J+1] will still be resolved as an anti-dependence, but the conflict between A[I,J] and A[I+1,J-1] will be resolved as a flow dependence. Since the sense of the dependence is reversed by the transformation, interchanging is illegal.

9.5.3 Multiple Interchanges

Moving a loop to the outermost loop position is sometimes called *outermosting*, and moving a loop to the innermost position is called *innermosting*. Simple direction vector tests for outermosting or innermosting a loop can be found (see the exercises).

Example 9.17

Show whether the following K loop can be interchanged to the outermost position in the following loop nest:

```
(1)     for I = 2 to N do
(2)         for J = 2 to N do
(3)             for K = 2 to N-1 do
(4)                 A[I,J,K] = (A[I-1,J-1,K-1] + A[I-1,J-1,K+1]) / 2
(5)             endfor
(6)         endfor
(7)     endfor
```

Solution

There are two flow dependence relations in the loop:

source	target	distance vector
A[I,J,K]	A[I-1,J-1,K-1]	$(1,1,1)$
A[I,J,K]	A[I-1,J-1,K+1]	$(1,1,-1)$

The K loop can be interchanged with the J loop, since no dependence relation is carried by the J loop to prevent it. The dependence relations after the interchange are:

source	target	distance vector
A[I,J,K]	A[I-1,J-1,K-1]	$(1,1,1)$
A[I,J,K]	A[I-1,J-1,K+1]	$(1,-1,1)$

Interchanging the K loop with the I loop is not legal; it would violate the second dependence.

9.5.4 Loop Limits

When the limits of the inner loop are invariant in the outer loop, the loops can be interchanged without changing the loop limits. When the limits do vary in the outer loop, interchanging can change the limits. Essentially, interchanging two loops is equivalent to transposing the iteration space; the loop limits must be modified to reflect this. To find the new loop limits, we describe a simple method that works when the original lower limits are a maximum of a set of expressions that are affine in the outer loop index variables, the upper limits are a minimum of a set of affine expressions, and the loop increment (step) is one; normalizing or seminormalizing a loop can be used to satisfy these constraints. These are often called triangular or trapezoidal loops, depending on the shape of the iteration space. In such a case, the loop limits can be described by a set of inequalities; after a series of loop interchanges, the new limits are found using Fourier-Motzkin projection. The variables in the inequalities are the loop index variables. Let i_k be the index variable for the loop at nest level k after interchanging. We use algorithm FMint, discussed in Section 4.6, to eliminate the variables in the order $i_n, i_{n-1}, \ldots, i_2$. Finally, we construct the loop limits for i_k from the inequalities that involve $i_1, i_2, \ldots, i_k$, but not $i_{k+1}, \ldots, i_n$.

Noncountable loops (while loops) are more difficult to interchange. In general, since the limits cannot be computed, it is difficult or impossible to determine how to traverse the same iterations after interchanging as before.

Example 9.18

Show the unnormalized iteration space of the following loop before and after interchanging:

```
(1)     for I = 1 to 10 do
(2)         for J = I to 12 do
(3)             A[I,J] = A[I,J + 1
(4)         endfor
(5)     endfor
```

Solution

The lower limit of the J loop varies in the I loop; the original iteration space can be described by the graph shown in Figure 9.7. The limits before interchanging can be described by the following set of inequalities:

$$-I \leq -1$$
$$I \leq 10$$
$$I - J \leq 0$$
$$J \leq 12$$

After interchanging, J is the outer loop; we find the limits for J by eliminating I from any inequalities containing J. We must project the third inequality by substituting the smallest value for I. The third and first inequalities give $-J \leq -1$; together with the fourth inequality, we derive the limits for the outer loop as $1 \leq J \leq 12$. The first through third inequalities then give the limits for the inner loop as $1 \leq I \leq \min(10, J)$. The modified program is:

```
(2)     for J = 1 to 12 do
(1)         for I = 1 to min(10,J) do
(3)             A[I,J] = A[I,J + 1
(4)         endfor
(5)     endfor
```

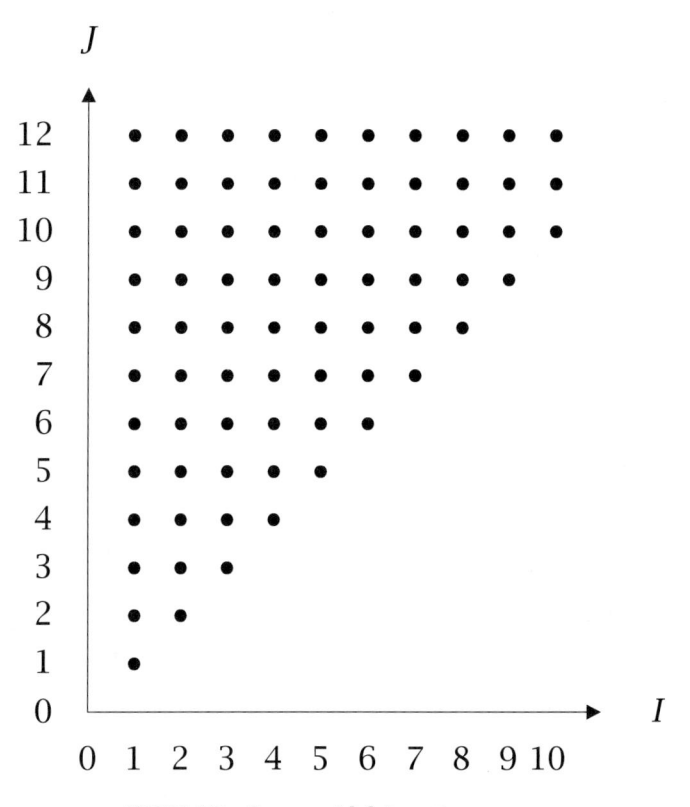

FIGURE 9.7 Trapezoidal iteration space.

9.5.5 Nontightly Nested Loops

There are situations in which the compiler may want to be able to interchange loops that are not tightly nested. Often, loop fission can break up the outer loop, resulting in a tightly nested loop around the inner loop; sometimes, however, this is not possible. As we saw in Chapter 5, the nontightly nested portion of outer loop can be *sunk* into the inner loop by adding conditionals so that it executes at the right time. The portion above the inner loop can either be merged with the first iteration of the inner loop, or prepended to the first iteration by adding a new iteration. Similarly, the portion below the inner loop can be merged with the last iteration, or a new last iteration can be appended. Sinking code into a loop cannot change dependence relations, but it does require adding an entry to direction or distance vectors for dependence relations that involve the code being sunk. For instance, when sinking the `before` statement in the following loop:

```
(1)     for ... do
(2)        before
(3)        for ... do
```

```
(4)         body
(5)     endfor
(6) endfor
```

into the body of the inner loop, as in:

```
(1) for ... do
(3)     for ... do
(2)         if( i₂ = 0 ) before
(4)         body
(5)     endfor
(6) endfor
```

dependence relations involving statement before, which used to have a single distance or direction vector entry, now must have two such entries. A dependence equation from a definition in before to a use in body might involve normalized basic loop induction variables i_1^d, i_1^u, and i_2^u, but cannot involve i_2^d, since statement before wasn't nested in the inner loop, and so can't use its index variable. However, because of the if statement, we know that $i_2^d = 0$, and can use that information to solve the dependence system and find dependence distance or direction information for the inner loop.

There does not seem to be any obvious rule to determine whether to sink code into a loop by merging it into the first (or last) iteration of the inner loop, and by prepending (or appending) a new iteration. When the dependence relations one way or the other become loop independent, that method may be more advantageous.

Example 9.19

Interchange the I and J loops below:

```
(1) for I = 1 to N do
(2)     A[I] = sqrt(A[I])
(3)     for J = I+1 to N do
(4)         A[J] = A[J] / A[I]
(5)     endfor
(6) endfor
```

Solution

There is a dependence cycle preventing loop fission from dividing the outer loop into two parts. The relevant dependence relations are given in the table below.

9.5 ▪ Loop Interchanging

from	to	type	dependence vector
2:A[I]	2:A[I]	flow	(0)
4:A[J]	4:A[I]	flow	(<)
4:A[J]	4:A[I]	anti	(<)
4:A[J]	4:A[I]	output	(<)

We can sink line 2 into the inner loop by prepending an iteration as follows:

```
(1)     for I = 1 to N do
(3)        for J = I to N do
              if J = I then
(2)              A[I] = sqrt(A[I])
              else
(4)              A[J] = A[J] / A[I]
              endif
(5)        endfor
(6)     endfor
```

Dependence relations between lines 2 and 4 must now add a dependence vector element for the J loop. Any dependence from line 2 comes from the first J iteration (by construction); since the first dependence is independent of the I loop, it must be carried by the J loop. The dependence relations from line 4 to line 2 are all similar; each can be characterized by solving the following dependence system, where I_2 and J_2 mean the values of the index variables at line 2, and similarly for I_4 and J_4.

$$
\begin{array}{ll}
J_4 = I_2 & \text{dependence equation} \\
J_2 = I_2 & \text{if statement} \\
J_4 > I_4 & \text{loop limits and if statement} \\
I_2 \geq 1 & \text{loop limits} \\
I_4 \geq 1 & \text{loop limits}
\end{array}
$$

Solving this system determines that $I_4 < I_2$ and $J_4 = J_2$; thus, the dependence relations after sinking are:

from	to	type	dependence vector
2:A[I]	2:A[I]	flow	(0, <)
4:A[J]	4:A[I]	flow	(<, 0)
4:A[J]	4:A[I]	anti	(<, 0)
4:A[J]	4:A[I]	output	(<, 0)

None of these dependence relations prevent interchanging; the resulting loop, after finding appropriate loop limits, is as follows:

```
(3)    for J = 1 to N do
(1)        for I = 1 to J do
               if J = I then
(2)                A[I] = sqrt(A[I])
               else
(4)                A[J] = A[J] / A[I]
               endif
(5)        endfor
(6)    endfor
```

By peeling off the last iteration of the inner loop, this can be converted to the nontightly nested loop:

```
(3)    for J = 1 to N do
(1)        for I = 1 to J-1 do
(4)            A[J] = A[J] / A[I]
(5)        endfor
(2)        A[J] = sqrt(A[J])
(6)    endfor
```

9.5.6 Interactions with Other Loop Transformations

Interchanging can work in conjunction with other transformations. We have already discussed using loop fission for a nontightly nested outer loop to allow interchanging. Loop reversal can also enable interchanging; for instance, nested loops cannot be interchanged if there is a dependence relation with a dependence vector of $(<, >)$. Since reversal negates dependence distances, reversing the inner loop will turn the $(<, >)$ dependence vector into a $(<, <)$ dependence; if there is no $(<, <)$ dependence vector in the original loop, then the reversal will enable interchanging. Another example is to use interchanging to enable loop fusion. As mentioned earlier, interchanging also interacts with unswitching. In Example 9.2, applying unswitching disables interchanging; however, interchanging the loops first disables unswitching.

Example 9.20

Use loop interchanging to enable fusion in the following nested loop:

```
(1)    for I = 1 to N do
(2)        X[I] = 0
```

```
(3)     endfor
(4)     for J = 1 to N do
(5)         for K = 1 to N do
(6)             X[K] = X[K] + A[K,J]*Y[J]
(7)         endfor
(8)     endfor
```

Solution

The I and J loops cannot be fused due to data dependence relations; the original program has a flow dependence from line 2 to line 6, which would be violated by fusion. However, after interchanging the J and K loops, fusion can proceed to produce the loop:

```
(1)     for I = 1 to N do
(2)         X[I] = 0
(4)         for J = 1 to N do
(6)             X[I] = X[I] + A[I,J]*Y[J]
(7)         endfor
(8)     endfor
(5)     K = N + 1
```

9.6 Loop Skewing

In Chapter 5, we mentioned that *normalization,* or using the normalized iteration vectors, can change the shape of the iteration space. In some cases, it can affect the ability to interchange loops. In the following program there are two data dependence relations:

```
(1)     for I = 2 to N do
(2)         for J = I to N do
(3)             A[I,J] = 0.5*(A[I,J-1] + A[I-1,J])
(4)         endfor
(5)     endfor
```

Using unnormalized iteration vectors, the dependence distances are $(0, 1)$ and $(1, 0)$, as shown in Figure 9.8. After interchanging, the loop has the following form:

```
(2)     for J = 2 to N do
(1)         for I = 2 to J do
(3)             A[I,J] = 0.5*(A[I,J-1] + A[I-1,J])
(4)         endfor
(5)     endfor
```

Using normalized iteration vectors, however, the shape of the iteration space changes, as does the dependence distances. As shown in Figure 9.9, the dependence distances are $(0, 1)$ and $(1, -1)$; this latter dependence relation prevents simple loop interchanging.

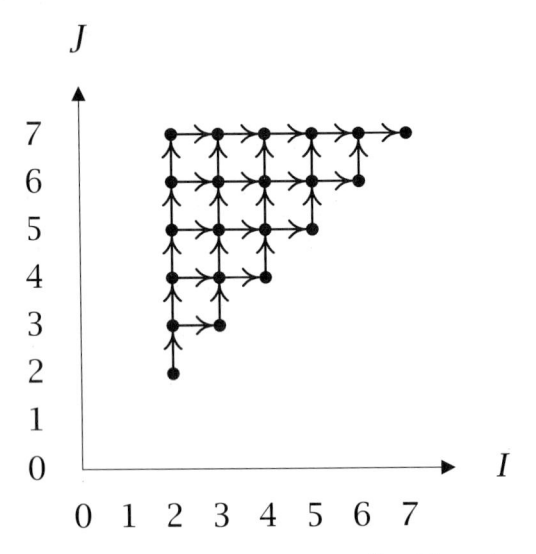

FIGURE 9.8 Iteration space using unnormalized iteration vectors.

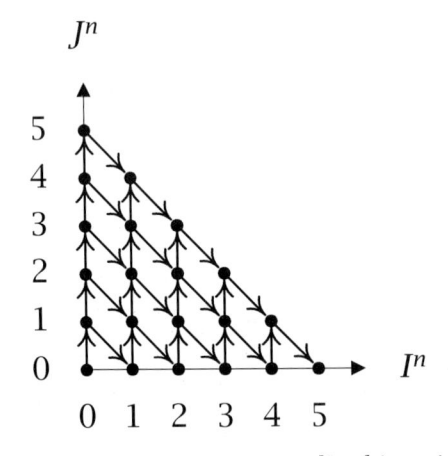

FIGURE 9.9 Iteration space using normalized iteration vectors.

If normalizing can prevent interchanging, then perhaps unnormalizing can enable interchanging. We call this *loop skewing*. Skewing changes the iteration vectors for each iteration by adding the outer loop index value to the inner loop index; thus, iteration (i, j) becomes relabeled as $(i, j + i)$. A dependence relation from iteration (i_1, j_1) to (i_2, j_2) will have distance $(i_1, j_1) - (i_2, j_2) = (d_1, d_2)$. After skewing, the

9.6 ■ Loop Skewing

dependence distance will be changed to $(i_1, j_1 + i_1) - (i_2, j_2 + i_2) = (d_1, d_2 + d_1)$. In general, loops can be skewed by a factor f, changing the iteration label from (i, j) to $(i, j + fi)$; this changes dependence distances from (d_1, d_2) to $(d_1, d_2 + fd_1)$. Note that f can also be negative. Choosing whether to skew and the factor by which to skew is driven by the goal to enable other transformations, or, as we shall see later, to improve parallelism after another interchanging.

Example 9.21

Interchange the following loops using skewing:

```
(1)    for I = 2 to N do
(2)        for J = 2 to M do
(3)            A[I,J] = 0.5*(A[I-1,J-1]+A[I-1,J+1])
(4)        endfor
(5)    endfor
```

Solution

The two dependence relations for A have distances $(1, 1)$ and $(1, -1)$, the second preventing interchanging. Skewing the loops would change the dependence distances to $(1, 2)$ and $(1, 0)$, allowing the interchange. The compiler must now generate correct loop limits and subscript expressions. Before skewing, the loop variables are related to the normalized iteration vector (i^n, j^n) by $I = i^n + 2$ and $J = j^n + 2$. After skewing, the skewed iteration vector (i^s, j^s) is defined by $i^s = i^n$ and $j^s = j^n + i^n$, making $I = i^s + 2$ and $J = j^s - i^s + 2$. The loop limits are defined as:

$$i^s + 2 \geq 2$$
$$i^s + 2 \leq N$$
$$j^s - i^s + 2 \geq 2$$
$$j^s - i^s + 2 \leq M$$

We solve for the limits of j^s (the new outer loop) using algorithm FMint, and then for i^s in terms of j^s, as follows:

$$j^s \geq 2$$
$$j^s \leq N + M - 2$$
$$i^s \leq j^s$$
$$i^s \geq j^s - M + 2$$
$$i^s \geq 0$$
$$i^s \leq N - 2$$

The final form of the loop is:

```
(2)    for jˢ = 2 to N+M-2 do
(1)        for iˢ = max(0,jˢ-M+2) to min(N-2,jˢ) do
(1)            I = iˢ + 2
(2)            J = jˢ - iˢ + 2
(3)            A[I,J] = 0.5*(A[I-1,J-1]+A[I-1,J+1])
(4)        endfor
(5)    endfor
```

9.7 Linear Loop Transformations

Loop interchanging, loop reversal, and loop skewing can all be unified by casting them as linear transformations of the iteration space or the iteration vectors. Such a framework allows a compiler to perform several transformations in one step. As discussed in Chapter 4, a linear transformation can be represented by a transformation matrix. Composition of linear transformations is performed by multiplying the transformation matrices. For any transformation matrix T, a dependence relation from iteration $\mathbf{i}^s$ to $\mathbf{i}^t$ (with distance $\mathbf{d}$) will be transformed into a dependence relation from iteration $T\mathbf{i}^s$ to iteration $T\mathbf{i}^t$ (with distance $T\mathbf{d}$).

Interchanging two loops changes the iteration vector (i, j) to (j, i); this can be modeled by the linear transformation:

$$\begin{pmatrix} 0 & 1 \\ 1 & 0 \end{pmatrix} \begin{pmatrix} i & j \end{pmatrix} = \begin{pmatrix} j & i \end{pmatrix}$$

The transformation matrix in this case is

$$T = \begin{pmatrix} 0 & 1 \\ 1 & 0 \end{pmatrix}$$

Outermosting the inner loop from a nest (i, j, k) can be modeled by interchanging j and k, then i and k. The two steps can be modeled by transformation matrices T_1 and T_2 such that

$$T_1 \begin{pmatrix} i \\ j \\ k \end{pmatrix} = \begin{pmatrix} i \\ k \\ j \end{pmatrix}, \quad T_2 \begin{pmatrix} i \\ k \\ j \end{pmatrix} = \begin{pmatrix} k \\ i \\ j \end{pmatrix}$$

The transformations can then be composed to get $T = T_2 T_1$:

$$T = \begin{pmatrix} 0 & 0 & 1 \\ 1 & 0 & 0 \\ 0 & 1 & 0 \end{pmatrix} = \begin{pmatrix} 0 & 1 & 0 \\ 1 & 0 & 0 \\ 0 & 0 & 1 \end{pmatrix} \begin{pmatrix} 1 & 0 & 0 \\ 0 & 0 & 1 \\ 0 & 1 & 0 \end{pmatrix}$$

Loop reversal can be modeled by negating the index for the loop being reversed. Reversing the inner of two loops and interchanging the loops is modeled by

9.7 ▪ Linear Loop Transformations

composing a reversal transformation matrix $\mathbf{T}_{rev}$ and an interchanging matrix $\mathbf{T}_{int}$:

$$\mathbf{T}_{rev} = \begin{pmatrix} 1 & 0 \\ 0 & -1 \end{pmatrix}, \quad \mathbf{T}_{int} = \begin{pmatrix} 0 & 1 \\ 1 & 0 \end{pmatrix}, \quad \mathbf{T}_{int}\mathbf{T}_{rev} = \begin{pmatrix} 0 & -1 \\ 1 & 0 \end{pmatrix}$$

Finally, loop skewing can be modeled by a transformation matrix $\mathbf{T}_{skew}$, which adds some multiple of the outer loop index to the inner loop index:

$$\mathbf{T}_{skew} = \begin{pmatrix} 1 & 0 \\ f & 1 \end{pmatrix}$$

All these transformations are unimodular; that is, the transformation matrices are unimodular. This means that the integer points of the original iteration space will be mapped onto integer points in the transformed space (because the transformation matrix has integer entries), and the volume of the iteration space is preserved (because the determinant of the transformation is ± 1). Given any unimodular transformation matrix $\mathbf{T}^{n \times n}$, we transform an n-nested loop by applying the transformation matrix. The transformation is legal if it preserves the dependence relations. For sequential loops, this means that the dependence distance vectors must still be lexicographically nonnegative: $\mathbf{0}^n \leq \mathbf{Td}$. The *image* of each iteration $\mathbf{i}$ will be $\mathbf{j} = \mathbf{Ti}$; since $\mathbf{T}$ is square with nonzero determinant, it is nonsingular and has an inverse. We can thus find $\mathbf{T}^{-1}\mathbf{j} = \mathbf{i}$. If the original iteration space loop limits are written as a set of linear inequalities, $\mathbf{Ai} \leq \mathbf{c}$, the limits of the transformed space are found by $\mathbf{AT}^{-1}\mathbf{j} \leq \mathbf{c}$. Applying Fourier-Motzkin projection to these limit inequalities will determine the limits of each loop.

▼
Example 9.22

Apply the linear transformation described by the matrix below:

$$\mathbf{T} = \begin{pmatrix} 0 & 1 & 1 \\ 1 & 1 & 0 \\ 1 & 0 & 0 \end{pmatrix}$$

to the original index set for the following loop:

```
(1)     for I = 1 to N do
(2)         for J = 1 to I+1 do
(3)             for K = J to M do
(4)                 A[I,J,K] = B[I,J] + C[J,K]
(5)             endfor
(6)         endfor
(7)     endfor
```

Solution

The transformed index set is

$$\mathbf{i} = \begin{pmatrix} i_1 \\ i_2 \\ i_3 \end{pmatrix} = \begin{pmatrix} J+K \\ I+J \\ I \end{pmatrix}$$

The inverse of the transformation matrix gives original loop index variables in terms of the transformed variables:

$$\begin{pmatrix} I \\ J \\ K \end{pmatrix} = \begin{pmatrix} 0 & 0 & 1 \\ 0 & 1 & -1 \\ 1 & -1 & 1 \end{pmatrix} \begin{pmatrix} i_1 \\ i_2 \\ i_3 \end{pmatrix} = \begin{pmatrix} i_3 \\ i_2 - i_3 \\ i_1 - i_2 + i_3 \end{pmatrix}$$

The original loop limits can be written as:

$$\begin{pmatrix} -1 & 0 & 0 \\ 1 & 0 & 0 \\ 0 & -1 & 0 \\ -1 & 1 & 0 \\ 0 & 1 & -1 \\ 0 & 0 & 1 \end{pmatrix} \begin{pmatrix} i_1 \\ i_2 \\ i_3 \end{pmatrix} \leq \begin{pmatrix} -1 \\ N \\ -1 \\ 1 \\ 0 \\ M \end{pmatrix}$$

Applying $\mathbf{T}^{-1}$ to this gives:

$$\begin{pmatrix} 0 & 0 & -1 \\ 0 & 0 & 1 \\ 0 & -1 & 1 \\ 0 & 1 & -2 \\ -1 & 2 & -2 \\ 1 & -1 & 1 \end{pmatrix} \begin{pmatrix} j_1 \\ j_2 \\ j_3 \end{pmatrix} \leq \begin{pmatrix} -1 \\ N \\ -1 \\ 1 \\ 0 \\ M \end{pmatrix}$$

Algorithm FMint finds the following bounds:

$$j_1 \geq 2$$
$$j_1 \leq M + N + 1$$
$$j_2 \geq 2$$
$$j_2 \geq 2j_1 - 2M - 1$$
$$j_2 \geq j_1 - M + 1$$
$$j_2 \leq 2N + 1$$
$$j_2 \leq (2N + j_1)/2$$
$$j_3 \geq 1$$
$$j_3 \geq (j_2 - 1)/2$$
$$j_3 \geq (2j_2 - j_1)/2$$

$$j_3 \leq N$$
$$j_3 \geq j_2 - 1$$
$$j_3 \geq M - j_1 + j_2$$

The generated code is:

```
        for j₁ = 2 to M+N+1 do
            for j₂ = max(2,2*j₁-2*M-1,j₁-M+1) to min(2*N+1,N+floor(j₁/2)) do
                for j₃ = max(1,ceil((j₂-1)/2),ceil((2*j₂-j₁)/2)) to
                    min(N,j₂-1,M-j₁+j₂) do
(1)                 I = j₃
(2)                 J = j₂ - j₃
(3)                 K = j₁ - j₂ + j₃
(4)                 A[I,J,K] = B[I,J] + C[J,K]
                endfor
            endfor
        endfor
```

9.7.1 Nonunimodular Transformations

Unimodular transformations preserve the volume of the iteration space; for a dense iteration space, such as a normalized index set, every integer point in the image of the iteration space is the image of an integer point in the original iteration space. In other words, if the original iteration space is dense, so is the transformed space. We can generalize to allow any nonsingular integer linear transformation. In terms of loop transformations, this means allowing the scaling of an index; e.g., transforming iteration i to ki for some integer k. With general linear transformations, there will be integer points in the transformed space that lie within the image of the bounds but do not correspond to loop iterations. The simple case is a single loop with limits $1 \leq i \leq 10$. If we transform this by $j = 2i$, the limits for j are $2 \leq j \leq 20$. But not every integer point in this range corresponds to an integer point in the original range. The problems of generating code for a general integer linear transformation are determining the limits and strides for each loop.

Given a transformation matrix **T**, we showed in Chapter 4 that we can find a unimodular matrix **U** such that **T** = **HU** and **H** is in Hermite normal form. The transformed index set **j** = **Ti** = **HUi**. To find the limits for **j**, we first transform the limits for **i** by applying the unimodular transformation **U**. In other words, we let **k** = **Ui**, and find the limits for **k**, using the procedure already shown; that is, finding $AU^{-1}k \leq c$ and applying the Fourier-Motzkin projection algorithm to get modified bounds $A'k \leq c$.

Since $\mathbf{H}$ must be nonsingular and lower triangular, its inverse is also nonsingular and lower triangular; in fact, its inverse will be a rational matrix (all entries are rational numbers). If we apply the same method for finding the limits for $\mathbf{j}$ by finding $\mathbf{A'H^{-1}j} \le \mathbf{c'}$, we will find the image of the iteration space, but as we showed earlier, it will include points that were not in the original iteration space. Since the Hermite normal form generates the same lattice as the original transformation matrix $\mathbf{T}$, we need to find points within the limits that are in the lattice generated by $\mathbf{H}$, that is, that are of the form $\mathbf{Hk}$ for some value of $\mathbf{k}$. We can do this with the following procedure, using both $\mathbf{H}$ and $\mathbf{H}^{-1}$. Because $\mathbf{H}$ is in HNF, the relationship between the $\mathbf{j}$-lattice and the $\mathbf{k}$-lattice is $\mathbf{j} = \mathbf{Hk}$. Because $\mathbf{H}$ and $\mathbf{H}^{-1}$ are lower triangular, j_m can be expressed as a function of $k_1, k_2, \ldots, k_m$, and vice versa:

$$j_m = \sum_{p=1}^{m} h_{mp} k_p$$

$$k_m = \sum_{p=1}^{m} h_{mp}^{-1} j_p$$

For the outermost loop, this simplifies to $j_1 = h_{11} k_1$, which means that the limits for j_1 are exactly h_{11} times those for k_1, as already computed (recall that $h_{11} > 0$). The stride of the j_1 loop should also be h_{11}, so it visits only $\mathbf{j}$-lattice points that are images of $\mathbf{k}$-lattice points. For any subsequent loop, we have to translate the bounds from the $\mathbf{k}$-lattice to a bound on the $\mathbf{j}$-lattice. Take any one bound on k_m from $\mathbf{A'k} \le \mathbf{c'}$, which we can write as $\mathbf{a} \cdot \mathbf{k} \le c$. Because this is a bound for k_m, $a_{m+1} = a_{m+2} = \cdots = a_n = 0$; we only need to deal with the first m entries in $\mathbf{k}$. We can rewrite this bound as $a_m k_m \le (c - \mathbf{a}_{[1..m-1]} \mathbf{k}_{[1..m-1]})$, or

$$\text{sign}(a_m) k_m \le \lfloor (c - \sum_{p=1}^{m-1} a_p k_p)/|a_m| \rfloor.$$

However, we can replace k_p by $\mathbf{H}^{-1}_{[p]} \mathbf{j}$:

$$\text{sign}(a_m) \mathbf{H}^{-1}_{[m]} \mathbf{j} \le \lfloor (c - \sum_{p=1}^{m-1} a_p \mathbf{H}^{-1}_{[p]} \mathbf{j})/|a_m| \rfloor.$$

Again, because $\mathbf{H}$ is lower triangular, so is $\mathbf{H}^{-1}$, and so the row $\mathbf{H}^{-1}_{[p]}$ has zero entries in columns $p+1$ through n. We can write this as:

$$\text{sign}(a_m) \sum_{q=1}^{m} h_{mq}^{-1} j_q \le \lfloor (c - \sum_{p=1}^{m-1} a_p \sum_{q=1}^{p} h_{pq}^{-1} j_q)/|a_m| \rfloor.$$

Because all we want is a bound on j_m, we find this by rearranging terms:

$$\text{sign}(a_m) h_{mm}^{-1} j_m \le \lfloor (c - \sum_{p=1}^{m-1} a_p \sum_{q=1}^{p} h_{pq}^{-1} j_q)/|a_m| \rfloor - \text{sign}(a_m) \sum_{q=1}^{m-1} h_{mq}^{-1} j_q.$$

9.7 ▪ Linear Loop Transformations

Finally, because $h_{mm}^{-1} = 1/h_{mm} > 0$, we get the following:

$$sign(a_m)j_m \le h_{mm} \lfloor (c - \sum_{p=1}^{m-1} a_p \sum_{q=1}^{p} h_{pq}^{-1} j_q)/|a_m| \rfloor - sign(a_m)h_{mm} \sum_{q=1}^{m-1} h_{mq}^{-1} j_q.$$

Again, the stride of the j_m loop is h_{mm}.

Example 9.23

After applying the linear transformation

$$\mathbf{j} = \begin{pmatrix} 1 & 2 \\ 1 & 0 \end{pmatrix} \mathbf{i}$$

generate code for the following loop:

```
(1)    for i₁ = 1 to 5 do
(2)       for i₂ = 1 to min(i+1,4) do
(3)          A[i₁-2*i₂,i₂] = ...
(4)       endfor
(5)    endfor
```

Solution

First, we decompose $\mathbf{T}$ into $\mathbf{HU}$ where $\mathbf{U}$ is unimodular and $\mathbf{H}$ is in HNF. Algorithm Hermite, discussed in Chapter 4, actually finds $\mathbf{H}$ and $\mathbf{U}^{-1}$ such that $\mathbf{TU}^{-1} = \mathbf{H}$; this is fine since we need $\mathbf{U}^{-1}$ to translate the loop limits for $\mathbf{i}$ into loop limits for $\mathbf{k}$. The results of algorithm Hermite are:

$$\mathbf{H} = \begin{pmatrix} 1 & 0 \\ 1 & 2 \end{pmatrix}, \quad \mathbf{U}^{-1} = \begin{pmatrix} 1 & 2 \\ 0 & -1 \end{pmatrix}$$

The loop limits for $\mathbf{i}$ are expressed in matrix form $\mathbf{Ai} \le \mathbf{c}$ as:

$$\begin{pmatrix} -1 & 0 \\ 1 & 0 \\ 0 & -1 \\ -1 & 1 \\ 0 & 1 \end{pmatrix} \begin{pmatrix} i_1 \\ i_2 \end{pmatrix} \le \begin{pmatrix} -1 \\ 5 \\ -1 \\ 1 \\ 4 \end{pmatrix}$$

We convert these into bounds for $\mathbf{k}$ by finding $\mathbf{A}' = \mathbf{AU}^{-1}$ so that $\mathbf{A}'\mathbf{k} \le \mathbf{c}$:

$$\begin{pmatrix} -1 & 0 \\ 1 & 0 \\ 0 & -1 \\ -1 & 1 \\ 0 & 1 \end{pmatrix} \begin{pmatrix} 1 & 2 \\ 0 & -1 \end{pmatrix} \begin{pmatrix} k_1 \\ k_2 \end{pmatrix} = \begin{pmatrix} -1 & -2 \\ 1 & 2 \\ 0 & 1 \\ -1 & -3 \\ 0 & -1 \end{pmatrix} \begin{pmatrix} k_1 \\ k_2 \end{pmatrix} \le \begin{pmatrix} -1 \\ 5 \\ -1 \\ 1 \\ 4 \end{pmatrix}$$

We project this onto the k_1 axis and find limits $3 \leq k_1 \leq 13$. To get the limits for the **j**-lattice, we use the formulas derived above:

$$\begin{aligned}
(-1 \quad 0) \mathbf{k} &\leq -3 \Rightarrow -j_1 \leq -3 \\
(1 \quad 0) \mathbf{k} &\leq 13 \Rightarrow j_1 \leq 13 \\
(-1 \quad -2) \mathbf{k} &\leq -1 \Rightarrow -j_2 \leq 2\lfloor(j_1-1)/2\rfloor - j_1 \\
(1 \quad 2) \mathbf{k} &\leq 5 \Rightarrow j_2 \leq 2\lfloor(5-j_1)/2\rfloor + j_1 \\
(0 \quad 1) \mathbf{k} &\leq -1 \Rightarrow j_2 \leq j_1 - 2 \\
(1 \quad -3) \mathbf{k} &\leq 1 \Rightarrow -j_2 \leq 2\lfloor(j_1+1)/3\rfloor - j_1 \\
(0 \quad -1) \mathbf{k} &\leq 4 \Rightarrow -j_2 \leq 28 - j_1
\end{aligned}$$

The generated code is shown below:

```
(1)    for j₁ = 2 to 9 do
(2)        for j₂ = max(2*ceil((1-j₁)/2)+j₁,j₁-8,2*ceil((-1-j₁)/3)+j₁) to
                      min(2*floor((5-j-1)/2)+j₁,j₁-2) by 2 do
           i₁ = j₂
           i₂ = (j₁-j₂)/2
(3)        A[i₁-2*i₂,i₂] = ...
(4)        endfor
(5)    endfor
```

9.8 Strip-Mining

Strip-mining decomposes a single loop into two nested loops; the outer loop (the strip loop) steps between strips of consecutive iterations, and the inner loop (the element loop) steps between single iterations within a strip. Strip-mining itself is always legal; we will see how it is used to generate code for vector computers in Chapter 12. It gets its name from the way a steam shovel loads a strip of earth at a time before moving on to the next strip.

To strip-mine the following loop with a strip size of s:

```
(1)    for I = 1 to N do
(2)        A[I] = B[I] + C[I]
(3)    endfor
```

the loop is decomposed into two nested loops; the outer strip loop will have a step size of s (the strip size), and the inner loop limits depend on the outer loop index:

```
(1)    for Is = 1 to N by s do
(1)        for I = Is to min(N,Is+s-1) do
(2)            A[I] = B[I] + C[I]
(3)        endfor
(3)    endfor
```

9.8 ▪ Strip-Mining

In this example, the inner loop executes strips of size s until the last strip, which may be a short strip (if N is not divisible by s). The computation of the inner loop trip count involves a `min` function call inside the strip loop. This can be removed by executing the short strip first, as:

```
         tc = N
         Itc = mod(tc,s)
         if( Itc = 0 ) Itc = s
         If = 1
         loop:
(1)          for I = If to If+Itc-1 do
(2)              A[I] = B[I] + C[I]
(3)          endfor
             tc = tc - Itc
             If = If + Itc
             Itc = s
             if tc > 0 goto loop
```

In this code, the global trip count is computed (simply N in this example), and the size of the first strip is found (either a short strip, if necessary, or a full-size strip, if the trip count is divisible by the strip size). The variable `If` holds the starting point of the element loop, and `Itc` holds its trip count. For subsequent strips, the starting point is moved, and the trip count always the size of a long strip. The outer strip loop iterates as long as there is more work to be done.

Since strip-mining increases the loop nest level, it must also modify the dependence vectors. If the dependence distance d and strip size s for the loop being strip-mined are known, then the dependence distance change to $(d \operatorname{div} s, d \bmod s)$; if $d \bmod s$ is not zero, another dependence relation with distance $(d \operatorname{div} s + 1, -((s - d) \bmod s))$ is also generated. If the exact distance is not known, or the strip size is not a compile-time constant, then the best the compiler can do is to convert the dependence relation into one or two dependence relations with direction vector information, as follows:

old direction	new direction
(<)	$\begin{cases} (<, \star) \\ (=, <) \end{cases}$
(=)	(=, =)
(>)	$\begin{cases} (>, \star) \\ (=, >) \end{cases}$

If the loop being strip-mined is one of a set of nested loops, the dependence vector entries for any other loop are not modified. This scheme lets the compiler treat the strip and element loops just like any other loop; for instance, it might interchange the strip loop outward, or the element loop inward.

Example 9.24

Strip-mine the following loop to a strip size of 5, and show the modified dependence distance and direction vectors.

(1)   for I = 1 to 16 do
(2)   A[I+3] = A[I] + B[I]
(3)   endfor

Solution

The loop contains a loop carried flow dependence relation with dependence distance vector (3). Strip-mining the loop to a strip size of 5 produces the following loop:

(1)   for It = 1 to 16 by 5 do
(1)   for I = It to min(16,It+4) do
(2)   A[I+3] = A[I] + B[I]
(3)   endfor
(3)   endfor

After strip-mining, there are two dependence distance vectors, since 3 mod 5 ≠ 0; these are $(0, 3)$ and $(1, -2)$, as shown in Figure 9.10.

9.9 Loop Tiling

Strip-mining for single-nested loops is well-defined; for nested loops, we use a different formulation, called *loop tiling*. The difference between strip-mining and tiling is that tile boundaries will be parallel to the iteration space axes, not to the iteration space boundaries. This is important for triangular or other convex-shaped iteration spaces. The eventual goal is to interchange the tile loops outward and the element loops inward. The compiler can use tiling to automatically create "blocked" or submatrix versions of many linear algebra algorithms, such as we saw in Chapter 1.

For strip-mining, the beginning of each strip is determined by the strip size s, and the first iteration of the original loop. For tiling, the beginning of each tile is independent of the first iteration of the original loop. Tiling is characterized by the tile size ts, and by a tile offset to ($0 \leq to < ts$); each tile will start at an iteration i such that $i \bmod ts = to$. Each tile iterates from $tn \cdot ts + to$ to $(tn+1) \cdot ts + to - 1$, where

9.9 ▪ Loop Tiling

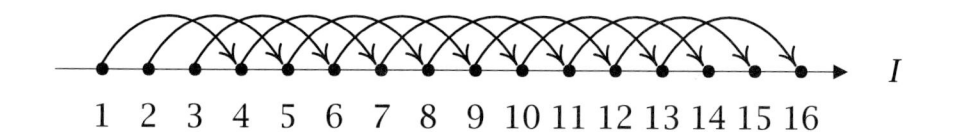

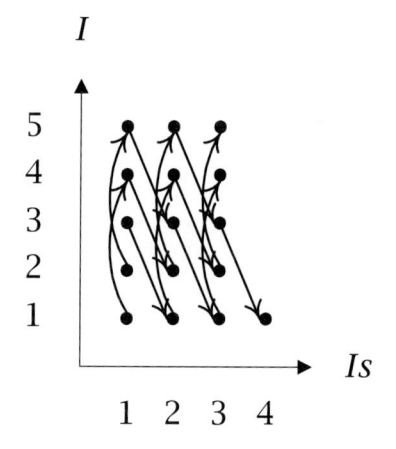

FIGURE 9.10 Dependence distances before and after strip-mining.

tn is the tile number. The compiler must determine the minimum and maximum tile numbers, and must also make sure the element loop does not execute outside its original iteration space. We actually use the tile index $ti = tn \cdot ts + to$ to simplify the code (in most cases). For a loop such as:

    for I = *lo* to *hi* do

the general formula for tiling is:

    for It = floor((*lo-to*)/*ts*)*ts+*to* to floor((*hi-to*)/*ts*)*ts+*to* by *ts* do
        for I = max(*lo*,It) to min(*hi*,It+*ts*-1)

With an offset of zero, the formulas are somewhat simpler; with an offset equal to *lo* mod *ts*, tiling is functionally the same as strip-mining.

The dependence relations are modified by tiling exactly as they are by strip-mining. Determining the legality of interchanging a tile loop with an element loop uses the same rules for loop interchanging that we have already discussed. Once all the tile loops are adjacent and all the element loops are adjacent, normal rules for loop interchanging will apply.

Interchanging an inner tile loop with an outer element loop—where the limits of the tile loop depend on the element loop index—needs special handling because of the floor operations in the tile boundary computations. For instance, to interchange the following two loops, where I is an element loop and Jt is a tile loop:

```
for I = max(l₁,l₂,...) to min(u₁,u₂,...) do
    for Jt = floor((k_l*I+m_l)/ts)*ts+to
            to floor((k_u*I+m_u)/ts)*ts+to by ts do
```

The limits for the `I` loop do not change; the limits for the `Jt` loop must take into account each of the lower and upper limits for `I`. The new lower limit for `Jt` will be the maximum of a set of expressions, where each expression is its old limit with `I` replaced by one of $l_1, l_2, \ldots$ (if k_l is positive), or $u_1, u_2, \ldots$ (if k_l is negative). Similarly, the new upper limit for `Jt` is the minimum of a set of expressions, each equal to its upper limit with `I` replaced by one of $u_1, u_2, \ldots$ (if k_u is positive), or $l_1, l_2, \ldots$ (if k_u is negative).

Example 9.25

Tile each of the following loops with a tile size of 20 and an offset of 5; interchange the tile loops to the outermost position.

```
(1)    for I = 1 to 50 do
(2)        for J = I to 60 do
(3)            A[I,J] = A[I,J] + 1
(4)        endfor
(5)    endfor
```

Solution

Simply applying the formulas produces the following tiled loop:

```
(1)    for It = -15 to 45 by 20 do
(1)        for I = max(1,It) to min(50,It+19) do
(2)            for Jt = floor((I-5)/20)*20+5 to 45 by 20 do
(2)                for J = max(I,Jt) to min(60,Jt+19) do
(3)                    A[I,J] = A[I,J] + 1
(4)                endfor
(4)            endfor
(5)        endfor
(5)    endfor
```

The tiled iteration space is shown in Figure 9.11. To interchange the `Jt` loop with the `I` loop, the compiler must find a new lower limit for `Jt`. It can substitute each lower limit for `I` in the `Jt` lower limit, and take the maximum. The first expression is $\lfloor (1-5)/20 \rfloor \times 20 + 5 = -15$. The second is $\lfloor (It-5)/20 \rfloor \times 20 + 5$; because the tile offset and tile size of `It` are 5 and 20, respectively, we know that `It − 5` is divisible by 20; this expression simplifies to `It − 5 + 5`, or `It`. The resulting program is:

9.9 ▪ Loop Tiling

```
(1)    for It = -15 to 45 by 20 do
(2)      for Jt = max(-15,It) to 45 by 20 do
(1)        for I = max(1,It) to min(50,It+19) do
(2)          for J = max(I,Jt) to min(60,Jt+19) do
(3)            A[I,J] = A[I,J] + 1
(4)          endfor
(4)        endfor
(5)      endfor
(5)    endfor
```

A little more analysis would determine that since It is always greater than -1, the maximum operation is not necessary in the Jt lower limit. Since the only dependence relation for this loop is a loop independent anti-dependence relation, the interchange is legal.

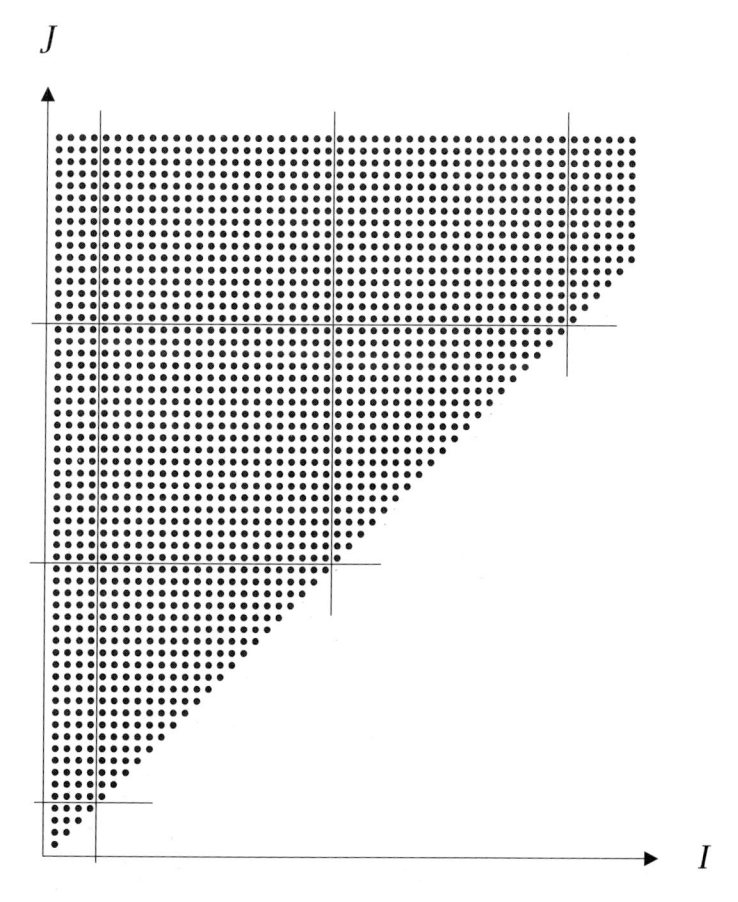

FIGURE 9.11   Tiled triangular iteration space.

9.10 Other Loop Transformations

9.10.1 Circular Loop Skewing

A variation of loop skewing is to skew the inner loop iterations in such a fashion that they wrap around a cylinder; we call this *circular loop skewing*. The shape of the iteration space does not change, but the relative position of the individual iterations does. This is shown in Figure 9.12. In the figure, j^c is the circularly skewed inner loop index; inside each circle is an iteration vector (i^n, j^n). Since the iterations of the inner loop (being circular skewed) are reordered, this transformation is legal as long as the inner loop carries no dependence relations.

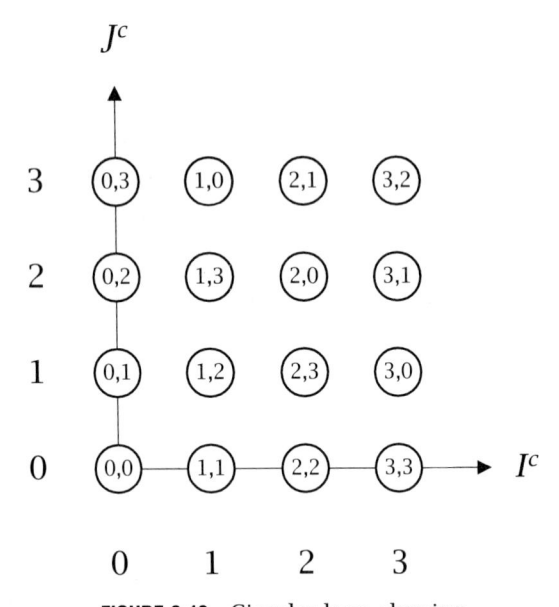

FIGURE 9.12 Circular loop skewing.

The generated code contains modulo operations to determine the iteration to be executed.

We can compare the skewed and circular skewed versions of the following nested loop:

```
(1)     for i^n = 0 to N-1 do
(2)         for j^n = 0 to N-1 do
(3)             A[i^n] = A[i^n] + B[i^n] * C[j^n]
(4)         endfor
(5)     endfor
```

The result of skewing with a factor of -1 is shown below, where i^s and j^s are the skewed index set:

9.10 ▪ Other Loop Transformations

```
(1)     for iˢ = 0 to N-1 do
(1)         iⁿ = iˢ
(2)         for jˢ = -iˢ to N-1-iˢ do
(2)             jⁿ = jˢ + iˢ
(3)             A[iⁿ] = A[iⁿ] + B[iⁿ] * C[jⁿ]
(4)         endfor
(5)     endfor
```

Circular skewing, in contrast, does not change the shape of the iteration space, just the iterations computed at each point:

```
(1)     for iᶜ = 0 to N-1 do
(1)         iⁿ = iᶜ
(2)         for jᶜ = 0 to N-1 do
(2)             jⁿ = mod(jᶜ+iᶜ, N)
(3)             A[iⁿ] = A[iⁿ] + B[iⁿ] * C[jⁿ]
(4)         endfor
(5)     endfor
```

Here, i^c and j^c are iteration numbers after circular skewing; note that the sequence of values assigned to j^n is not a linear progression, though it is piecewise linear.

We can think of circular loop skewing as a combination of skewing and moving a block of iterations in the iteration space. In Figure 9.13, the original iteration space is square; we first skew the loop by a factor of -1, transforming the iteration space into a rhombus. Circular skewing will restore the square iteration space shape by cutting the rhombus into two regions, separated in the figure by a line. Moving the portion of the iteration space below the dotted line to the "empty" region above the diagonal completes the transformation.

9.10.2 Striping

If the strip and element loops are interchanged after strip-mining, we get a transformation called *striping*. Essentially, the outer loop steps through the starting positions of the stripes, and each stripe steps through the iterations with step size equal to the number of stripes. The changes to the dependence relations are essentially the same as for strip-mining, except that the loops are interchanged; note that where strip-mining is always legal, striping may not be. If a loop has a dependence relation with dependence distance (3), striping with five stripes produces a loop with dependence relations that have distance vectors of $(3, 0)$ and $(-2, 1)$. Sequential execution of the resulting loop will not satisfy the negative distance, so striping would not be legal.

Striping with s stripes takes a loop of the following form:

```
(1)     for I = lo to hi do
(2)         body
(3)     endfor
```

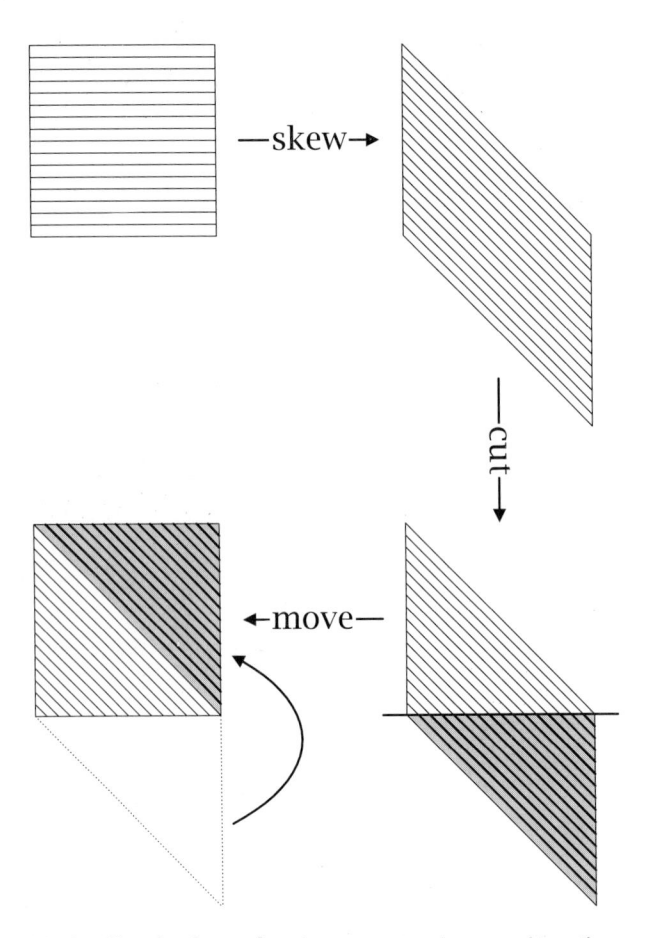

FIGURE 9.13 Circular loop skewing as operations on iteration space.

and changes it into nested loops, as follows:

(1)   for Is = 0 to *s*-1 do
(1)   for I = *lo*+Is to *hi* by *s* do
(2)   body
(3)   endfor
(3)   endfor

9.10.3 Loop Collapsing

Two nested loops that refer to arrays can sometimes be *collapsed* into a single loop with a very long loop length. When the loop limits match the array bounds, and the array layout is such that the memory stride is the same between consecutive inner loop iterations as it is between outer loop iterations, collapsing is possible. Loop collapsing generates fewer loops with longer loop limits, which can be advantageous for some machines. It does require that the array layout be known to the

9.10 ▪ Other Loop Transformations

compiler, which is usually the case for statically allocated arrays. Loop collapsing is usually implemented late in the optimization phase, when regenerating source code is not necessary.

Example 9.26

Collapse the following nested Fortran loop:

(1) Real A(100,100), B(100,100)
(2) do I = 1, 100
(3)   do J = 1, 90
(4)   A(I,J) = B(I,J) + 1
(5)   enddo
(6) enddo

Solution

Because of Fortran column-major array storage, the first dimension is laid out contiguously in memory. As written, the memory stride for the references to A (or B) between consecutive iterations of the inner loop is 100 words. Between the last reference in one iteration of the outer loop and the first reference in the next outer loop iteration, the memory stride is −8,899 words (the memory distance between A(1,90) and A(2,1), for instance). Interchanging the loops, however, gives us:

(3) do J = 1, 90
(2)   do I = 1, 100
(4)   A(I,J) = B(I,J) + 1
(5)   enddo
(6) enddo

Now the memory stride in the inner loop is 1 (the distance from A(1,1) to A(2,1)), and the memory stride between consecutive references across the outer loop is also 1 (the distance from A(1,100) to A(2,1)). Thus, collapsing is feasible, and produces the following program:

(1) Real A(100,100), B(100,100)
(1) Real AC(10000), B(10000)
(1) Equivalence (A,AC),(B,BC)
(3) do IJ = 1, 9000
(4)   AC(IJ) = BC(IJ) + 1
(6) enddo
(2) I = 100
(3) J = 90

Loop Coalescing

When the loop limits do not match the array bounds, or the strides are not constant, nested loops can still be *coalesced* by computing the original index values. The advantage is that coalescing reduces the number and nest level of the loops, although the extra computation within the loop may make it costly unless additional optimizations or parallelism can be found. If the original loop limits are invariant (not triangular or trapezoidal), then coalescing the following nested loop:

```
(1)     for I = loI to hiI do
(2)        for J = loJ to hiJ do
(3)           A[I,J] = B[J,I] + 1
(4)        endfor
(5)     endfor
```

produces a single loop for all iterations, extracting the values of I and J as follows:

$tc_I = hi_I - lo_I + 1$
$tc_J = hi_J - lo_J + 1$
for IJ = 0 to $tc_I * tc_J - 1$ do
```
(1)     I = IJ/tcJ + loI
(2)     J = MOD(IJ,tcJ) + loJ
(3)     A[I,J] = B[J,I] + 1
        endfor
```

9.11 Interprocedural Transformations

From the point of view of a restructuring compiler, a procedure boundary is a barrier to analysis and optimization. If the procedure call appears in a loop and another loop appears in the procedure, the procedure boundary hinders any loop transformations involving those two loops. Several interprocedural transformations have been developed that in themselves do not optimize the program, but that enable other optimizations across procedure boundaries.

9.11.1 Procedure Inlining

Inline expansion or integration of a procedure means copying the text of the procedure in place of the procedure call. This has many advantages, not the least of which is the removal of the overhead associated with the call (managing the call stack and frame pointer, saving and restoring processor registers, etc.), which is important when the subroutine call itself appears in other loops. Additionally, after inlining the procedure, dead code may be eliminated and more opportunities for other optimizations may become obvious. Even more important, inlining allows the optimization of the procedure to be tailored to each call site; if the call appears in a loop, the inlining allows the compiler to attempt loop optimizations (e.g., interchanging) between loops from the calling and called procedures.

Disadvantages of inlining include the fact that now the compiler must optimize the called routine many times, once for each call site. If large routines are inlined, or if small routines are inlined many times, the size of the object code can grow too large. Inlining of small routines, especially run-time library routines, has been shown to be successful and effective. This is especially true in the C language, where the passing of pointer arguments for arrays effectively prevents many optimizations.

There can be unexpected effects at a procedure call that are hard to take advantage of through inlining. For instance, Fortran and C allow arguments to be reshaped across procedure calls; that is, a two-dimensional array may be passed to a procedure that treats the formal argument as a one-dimensional vector. The storage association rules determine how the elements of the actual argument are related to the elements of the formal argument. Fortran also has the rule that a procedure cannot modify a formal argument if it is aliased with another formal argument or with a global variable. If regions of a single array are passed as actual arguments, the called procedure can use this rule to assume that the formal arguments that are modified are distinct from one another. Inlining the procedure will rewrite the formal argument references as references to the original single array. The compiler may have to resort to dependence analysis to determine whether the arguments are distinct.

9.11.2 Loop Embedding and Extraction

Loop embedding (or loop jamming) is the process of taking a loop surrounding a procedure call and embedding or jamming the loop into the procedure. This will generally mean making a special version of the procedure containing that loop, keeping the original version for calls that appear outside of loops. Essentially, procedure inlining expands the body of the procedure at the call site, whereas loop embedding puts the context of the call site into the body of the procedure. As with procedure integration, it allows the use of loop restructuring techniques between loops originating in the calling and called procedures. In addition to adding a control structure to the procedure, loop embedding may require changing the formal argument list to add dimensions to some of the arguments.

The inverse of loop embedding is *loop extraction*. Loop extraction takes a main loop out of a procedure and puts it at the call site. Again, a special version of the procedure may be required. Loop extraction allows transformations involving loops from the call site and in the procedure, but does not allow other optimizations in the procedure. It can be treated as a restricted form of inline expansion.

9.12 In the Pit

Some languages, like SISAL, have neither a parallel nor a sequential interpretation; the evaluation order is determined by the dependences (not the other way around). Compiling such a language for a sequential machine uses different rules for applying transformations. Nonetheless, such compilers use exactly the same sorts of dependence analysis and restructuring transformations described here, that have been used in optimizing Fortran compilers for years.

Generating correct and efficient code after reordering based on dependence graphs has been explored in the literature. When conditional regions are separated into multiple regions, the conditional expression will in general have to be computed once and saved in a temporary variable.

As mentioned in Chapter 5, a reduction direction can be defined and used for operations that accumulate reductions. Because a reduction direction is treated as a loop carried dependence direction, however, the assumption is that the order of accumulation is not important. Loops that carry only reduction direction dependences can be reversed or interchanged without violating the dependence relations.

Using temporary variables to hold conditional test results and replicating the conditional test for each statement essentially converts the control dependence relation into a data dependence relation.

One way to use fission to achieve locality is to use input dependence relations. Another way to achieve a similar effect is to apply loop fission as aggressively as possible, then use loop fusion to put the loops that use the same data back together. The second approach sounds like more work, but can also fuse loops from different source loops.

Loop reversal has a small twist when the loop has a step other than one. Simply exchanging the upper and lower limits and counting down instead of up will not work, since there is no guarantee that the exact upper limit will be reached. Thus, reversing the loop

```
for I = 1 to 10 by 2 do
```

must become

```
for I = 1+((10-1)/2)*2 downto 1 by -2 do
```

where ((10-1)/2) is the trip count computation.

9.13 Further Reading

Some of the transformations presented in this chapter have been well known for some time; see the descriptions by Allen and Cocke (1972) and Loveman (1977).

Automatic loop interchanging was first implemented in the compiler for the TI Advanced Scientific Computer (Cohagan [1973]). A general discussion is presented by Banerjee (1989). Ancourt and Irigoin (1991) discuss using Fourier-Motzkin projection to find loop limits after restructuring (reordering) the loops.

Polychronopoulos (1987) introduces loop coalescing with the goal of simplifying code generation and scheduling for parallel computers. Irigoin and Triolet (1988) introduce the concept of tiling for locality and parallelism.

There have been many attempts to place a number of transformations in a single framework, such as a matrix formulation. Wolf and Lam (1991a) explore unimodular transformations for tightly nested loops. Linear loop transformations have long been used in the systolic array community to map regular algorithms onto a regular processor ensemble (Karp et al. [1967]). The method presented here for code generation for nonunimodular transformations is derived from the work by Li and Pingali (1994).

Interprocedural program transformations can also play an important role in a restructuring compiler. Procedure cloning is well known in the partial evaluation literature, where it is called *polyvariant partial evaluation.* Cooper et al. (1990) discuss cloning in the framework of a programming environment that manages interprocedural issues. Hall et al. (1991) describe interprocedural loop extraction and loop embedding and their use in a programming environment. Cooper et al. (1991) show results of an experiment with procedure inline substitution, including increases in object code size and compile time, and reductions in execution time.

EXERCISES

9.1 In the body of a loop, how can statement reordering be applied? Which dependence relations must be preserved by statement reordering, and which can be ignored?

9.2 Expand the scalar T in the following loop, if possible:

```
(1)    for I = 1 to N do
(2)       if A[I] > 0 then
(3)          T = A[I] + B[I]
(4)       else
(5)          T = D[I] + 1
(6)       endif
(7)       C[I] = T / 2
(8)    endfor
(9)    U = T/2
```

9.3 Expand the scalar T in the following loop, if possible:

```
(1)    for I = 1 to N do
(2)       if A[I] > 0 then
(3)          T = X[I] + B[I]
(4)       endif
```

(5)   C[I] = T / 2
(6)   endfor
(7) U = T/2

9.4 Can the following two loops be fused? Why or why not? If so, what is the result?

(1) for I = 1 to 100 do
(2)   D = A[I]
(3)   B[I] = D
(4) endfor
(5) for J = 1 to 100 do
(6)   if E[J] > 0 then
(7)   D = -E[J]
(8)   endif
(9)   C[J] = C[J] + D
(10) endfor

9.5 Can the following two loops be fused? Why or why not? If so, what is the result?

(1) for I = 1 to 100 do
(2)   D = A[I]
(3)   B[I] = D
(4) endfor
(5) for J = 1 to 100 do
(6)   if E[J] > 0 then
(7)   D = -E[J]
(8)   C[J] = C[J] + D
(9)   endif
(10) endfor

9.6 Write the following array assignments as sequential loops. Fuse to use as few sequential loops as possible.

(1) A[1:N] = B[1:N] + C[2:N+1]
(2) C[1:N] = A[1:N] /2
(3) D[1:N] = B[1:N] + 1

9.7 Find the dependence graph for the following loop. Perform loop fission on the loop in two ways. The first time, treat all the statements in the conditional block as a unit. The second time, save the conditional test result in a temporary variable, and treat each statement in the conditional block individually.

(1) for I = 1 to 100 do
(2)   A[I] = B[I] + C[I]
(3)   if A[I] > 0 then
(4)   C[I] = D[I] + 1
(5)   D[I] = C[I] / E[I]
(6)   endif
(7)   E[I+1] = C[I] + 1
(8) endfor

9.8 Given a loop nest with *n* tightly nested sequential loops, what is the direction vector test for innermosting the loop at nest level *k*? Hint: For a dependence carried at loop nest level *k*, what dependence directions in the inner loops might prevent innermosting the *k* loop?

9.9 Given a loop nest with *n* tightly nested sequential loops, what is the direction vector test for outermosting the loop at nest level *k*?

9.10 Show how to sink line 2 into the inner loop in Example 9.19 by merging the nontightly nested portion into the first iteration of the loop. What are the dependence relations after sinking the code? Since the inner loop does not iterate for the last iteration of the outer loop, the last iteration must be handled in a special manner.

9.11 Use code sinking to make a tightly nested loop from the following example, and interchange the resulting three loops in all possible ways, checking for legality using data dependence analysis. Either use seminormalized or unnormalized dependence vectors:

```
(1)    for K = 1 to N do
(2)        A(K,K) = sqrt(A(K,K))
(3)        for I = K+1 to N do
(4)            A(I,K) = A(I,K)/A(K,K)
(5)            for J = K+1 to I
(6)                A(I,J) = A(I,J) - A(I,K)*A(J,K)
(7)            endfor
(8)        endfor
(9)    endfor
```

9.12 Skew the inner loop with respect to the outer loop to allow the loops to be interchanged; determine the minimum skew factor that allows interchanging.

```
(1)    for I = 1 to N do
(2)        for J = 1 to M do
(3)            A[I+1,J] = A[I,J+2] + A[I,J-1] + A[I,J]
(4)        endfor
(5)    endfor
```

9.13 Show that in a nested sequential loop, if all dependence distance vectors have non-negative elements, the loops can be reordered in any way using loop interchanging. Further, show how to restructure the loops so that the outer loop carries all the loop carried dependence relations.

9.14 After applying the unimodular transformation

$$\begin{pmatrix} 1 & 2 \\ 2 & 3 \end{pmatrix}$$

generate code for the following loop:

```
(1)    for I = 3 to 100 do
(2)        for J = I+1 to 101 do
(3)            A[I,J] = A[I-2,J+1] + 2
(4)        endfor
(5)    endfor
```

Determine whether the transformed program preserves the dependence relations in the loop.

9.15 Generate code for the same loop as in the previous exercise after applying the nonunimodular transformation

$$\begin{pmatrix} 2 & 3 \\ 3 & 2 \end{pmatrix}$$

9.16 Unimodular and linear transformations can be used to translate parallel loops to sequential code. For two nested loops with the data dependence distance vectors $d_1, d_2, \ldots, d_n$, how can the loops be transformed so that sequential execution preserves the dependence relations? Under what circumstances will linear transformations be insufficient?

9.17 Find the dependence relations in the following parallel loop; use linear transformations to change the index set so that the loop can be executed as a sequential loop:

```
(1)    doall I = 2 to N-1
(2)        doall J = 2 to N-1
(3)            A[I,J] = (A[I-1,J] + A[I,J-1] + A[I+1,J] + A[I,J+1])/4
(4)        enddoall
(5)    enddoall
```

9.18 Tile the two loops below; let the tile size for the outer loop be 20 with offset 0, and the tile size for the inner loop be 10 with offset 5. Show the dependence relations before and after tiling. Show the result of interchanging the inner tile loop with the outer element loop.

```
(1)    for I = 1 to 40 do
(2)        for J = 2 to I+10 do
(3)            A[I,J] = (A[I,J-1] + A[I,J] + A[I,J+1])/3
(4)        endfor
(5)    endfor
```

9.19 When collapsing two nested loops with loop independent dependence relations, the resulting loop also has loop independent dependence relations. Under what circumstances can loop collapsing apply with loop carried dependence relations? What will the resulting dependence relations be?

9.20 When coalescing two loops with a dependence relation with distance vector (d_1, d_2), what is the distance vector for the dependence relation in the resulting loop?

10 OPTIMIZING FOR LOCALITY

> *Optimizing for locality in memory hierarchies uses the same technology as optimizing for parallel computers. We show loop restructuring techniques applied to optimizing for uniprocessor caches.*

The first optimization target we discuss is a sequential machine with a memory hierarchy. Almost all general-purpose computer systems, from personal computers to workstations to large systems, have a memory hierarchy comprising three to five levels. At the highest level, closest to the processor, is the register file. Since the registers are managed explicitly by the compiler, they are often considered separate from the rest of the hierarchy; however, we will see some instances, particularly with vector processors, in which registers can be fruitfully treated as part of the hierarchy. The next highest level is cache memory. Some machines have separate caches for instructions and data; here we focus on data references. Many systems have two levels of cache: a small, fast, primary cache close to the processor (often physically located on the processor chip), and a larger, secondary cache.

The next level is the main memory, followed by the disk or another large storage unit for virtual memory management. The goal of the memory hierarchy is to provide applications with the illusion of a large memory at an average cost per bit close to that of the cheapest (largest and slowest) level of the hierarchy, and with an average access time close to the fastest (smallest and most expensive) level of the hierarchy. Usually, a memory hierarchy satisfies the inclusion principle; that is, the memory locations present at a high level in the hierarchy are a subset of the locations at the next level, though the values in the lower levels may not be up to date. A memory access will be satisfied by the highest level of the hierarchy in which that memory location is present. Usually, an access to a memory location will bring that location up to the highest level of the hierarchy; for instance, an access that misses in the cache, but hits in the main memory will allocate and fill a line or block (comprising several consecutive words) in the cache memory. Subsequent references to any location in that cache line will hit in the cache.

In this chapter we study how to optimize nested loops to take advantage of a memory hierarchy. We say an array element is *reused* if it is fetched or stored by more than one reference in the loop, or is used in more than one iteration. The *reuse distance* is the distance in memory locations between two memory references. There are three types of reuse in loops. *Temporal reuse* occurs when two uses refer to the same memory location at different times. *Spatial reuse* occurs between two uses of nearby memory locations. A special case of spatial reuse is *sequential reuse*, which occurs when two uses refer to consecutive memory locations (reuse distance of ±1).

Reuse is a property of the program; it can occur between two references to the same array in the same or different iterations. It is closely related to data dependence; whenever there is a flow or input data dependence relation, there is temporal reuse between the dependent references. Spatial reuse, however, can occur even between data independent references.

When a memory location is still present in the higher levels of the memory hierarchy at the time of reuse, we say the reference to that location exhibits *locality*. There are three types of locality—*temporal locality, spatial locality,* and *sequential locality*—corresponding to the three types of reuse that generated the locality.

Studies have shown that most programs exhibit data locality as well as program locality. We take advantage of program locality by focusing our compiler optimization techniques on the parts of the program that we expect to be executed repeatedly, that is, the loops. Data caches should work transparently to the program; if the program exhibits locality, it will run faster with a cache memory, without any modifications at all. However, compiler optimizations can enhance the locality characteristics of a program, improving the benefits of the memory hierarchy.

This chapter discusses methods that compilers can use to turn a pattern of reuse into locality in the memory hierarchy. For instance, compiler optimizations can improve sequential locality by reordering the loops so that the inner loop steps through the data arrays sequentially in memory; this is often called *stride-1 indexing*. Temporal locality can be improved by reordering the loops and data accesses so that the inner loop has more accesses to loop invariant memory addresses. Tiling also improves temporal locality when the data needed by each tile fits into the higher levels of the memory hierarchy, and there is significant data reuse within each tile.

10.1 Single Reference to Each Array

We first study how to improve the cache performance of a single array reference. A compiler can improve the performance of a loop containing many references by restructuring the loop so as to improve the most individual references.

When one of the loop index variables appears only in the stride-1 dimension of an array, and has a coefficient of 1 or −1, reordering the loops to move that index to the innermost position will make that array reference step sequentially through memory (forward or backward). After a cache line is filled for the first reference in that line, the next iteration of the loop will refer to an adjacent location in the same cache line. In this way, reordering the loops for sequential locality improves cache performance. We assume here that the step for the loop index variable is one; otherwise, the coefficient should be multiplied by the loop increment.

When the memory address is independent of one of the loops, innermosting that loop will make the memory address invariant in the inner loop. The reference will exhibit temporal reuse in the inner loop; an additional benefit is that the compiler may be able to replace the array reference with a reference to a scalar, which could be allocated to a register.

Example 10.1

Reorder the loops below to improve both the sequential and temporal locality of the array references:

(1)   for I = 1 to N do
(2)   for J = 1 to M do
(3)   X[I,J] = Y[I] + Z[J]
(4)   endfor
(5)   endfor

Solution

Assume X is stored in row-major order, so J is the stride-1 index for that reference. The Z[J] reference is also a stride-1 reference in the J loop, but is invariant in the I loop; the Y[I] reference is stride-1 in the I loop, but invariant in J. The given loop order has one loop invariant reference (Y[I]) and two stride-1 references (X[I,J] and Z[J]) in the inner loop. Reordering the loops so that I is the inner loop gives one stride-1 reference (to Y) and one loop invariant reference (to Z). Thus, leaving the loops in the given order should result in better cache performance.

10.1.1 Tiling

In Example 10.1, the entire vector Z is fetched for each iteration of the outer loop. If M is relatively small, the entire vector can fit into the cache. Thus, in addition to the sequential locality for Z, the performance of the loop will benefit from temporal locality across iterations of the I loop, because the reference is invariant in the I loop. If M is relatively large, however, the cache may not be large enough to hold all of Z. In fact, for each iteration of the outer loop, the entire vector Z may have to be fetched from memory again, and overall performance will be somewhat lower. If M varies from small to large values, the loop's performance will vary also, from high performance for small values of M to lower performance with larger values, with a discontinuity in performance where the loop limits cause the vector size to exceed the cache size. To take advantage of such temporal locality, the compiler can tile the two loops, so that the data brought into the cache by the inner loop will not overflow the cache size.

While the examples here are in terms of caches, similar methods may be used to enhance the performance of other levels of the memory hierarchy. For instance, optimizing for temporal locality may be used to reuse values loaded into registers more frequently. Similarly, optimizing for locality at the page level in a virtual memory hierarchy may be important for programs with very large data sets. At any level of the hierarchy, spatial locality is important only if the distance in memory locations is less than the size of an allocation unit, be it a page, cache line, or single register.

Example 10.2

Tile the loops in Example 10.1 to take advantage of sequential and temporal locality for the reference to Z.

Solution

Here we tile both loops with a tile size of B; the order of the element loops is chosen to optimize sequential and spatial locality in the inner loop, as in the previous example. If B is chosen properly, the B elements of Z brought into the cache will be used B times in this tile before moving on to the next tile.

```
(1) for It = 1 to N by B do
(2)     for Jt = 1 to M by B do
(1)         for I = It to min(It+B,N) do
(2)             for J = Jt to min(Jt+B,M) do
(3)                 X[I,J] = Y[I] + Z[J]
(4)             endfor
(5)         endfor
(4)     endfor
(5) endfor
```

The order of the tile loops can be chosen to enhance the locality between tiles; here we choose to step to the next tile along the J direction, to take advantage of sequential locality between tiles for the references to X and Z. Had we chosen the other order for the tile loops, the It tile and I element loops could have been collapsed back into a single loop, reducing loop overhead somewhat. Note that the reference to Y is invariant in the inner element loop, and exhibits sequential locality for the outer element loop.

10.1.2 Quantifying Reuse

We focus on the common case of array references with affine subscript expressions, as we did for data dependence testing in Chapter 7. Each such array reference can be modeled by a coefficient matrix $\mathbf{A}^{d \times n}$ and offset vector $\mathbf{c}$, where the array has

d dimensions and the reference appears in n loops. A reference X[I,J+1] in two loops is represented by X[**Ai** + **c**], where

$$\mathbf{A} = \begin{pmatrix} 1 & 0 \\ 0 & 1 \end{pmatrix}, \quad \mathbf{i} = \begin{pmatrix} \mathtt{I} \\ \mathtt{J} \end{pmatrix}, \quad \mathbf{c} = \begin{pmatrix} 0 \\ 1 \end{pmatrix}$$

A reference X[**Ai** + **c**] exhibits self-temporal reuse with distance **d** when **Ad** = **0**. The set of all solutions to this is the null space of **A**, or *kernel* **A**. If the null space is empty, the reference exhibits no self-temporal reuse. Otherwise, choosing some index from the null space as the inner loop index will allow this reference to exploit temporal locality. We say that a loop k *carries* reuse if there is a vector $\mathbf{d} \in$ kernel **A** such that d_k is the first nonzero element in **d**. Of particular interest are reuse distances that are multiples of $\mathbf{e}_k$, the unit normal vector. Practically speaking, self-temporal reuse occurs when **A** has zero coefficients in the kth column; in other words, the index variable for the kth loop does not appear in the subscripts.

Spatial reuse occurs when references are made to the same element in the stride-1 dimension. If we eliminate the row in **A** for the stride-1 dimension, giving $\mathbf{A}_S$, there may be spatial reuse with distance **d** if $\mathbf{A}_S\mathbf{d} = \mathbf{0}$; as before, the solutions to this are in *kernel* $\mathbf{A}_S$. Spatial reuse occurs for loop k only when $\mathbf{e}_k \in$ kernel $\mathbf{A}_S$ and the coefficient of the index variable for loop k in the subscript expression for the stride-1 dimension is smaller than the size of the cache line. This occurs when the index variable for the kth loop appears only in the stride-1 dimension.

Reuse Factor

We can measure the level of reuse with a *reuse factor*. For a given loop $\mathtt{I}_k$, the reuse factor due to temporal reuse is the trip count of that loop, $\mathtt{N}_k$, if $\mathbf{e}_k \in$ kernel **A**, and one otherwise. If $\mathbf{e}_k \in$ kernel $\mathbf{A}_S$, the reuse factor due to spatial reuse for loop $\mathtt{I}_k$ is $\max(1, l/a_{sk})$, where l is the cache line size, and a_{sk} is the coefficient of the loop index for loop k in the stride-1 dimension s; the spatial reuse factor is one otherwise.

The self-reuse factor R_k for a reference in loop k is equal to the temporal reuse factor if it is greater than one, and equal to the spatial reuse factor otherwise. The cumulative self-reuse R_k^* for a reference in loop k is the product of the self-reuse factors for that reference at loop k and all inner loops containing the reference.

The cumulative self-reuse factor is a measure of how often an array element will be reused inside each loop. We find the cumulative reuse factor for a loop by summing the cumulative self-reuse factors for all references in the loop. Intuitively, we want the loops with high reuse factors to be the innermost loops, since that will exploit the most reuse. At the next level out, the cumulative reuse factor does not depend on the order of the loops; if all the data for two nested loops fits in the cache, then it can exploit reuse across both loops, and the cumulative reuse factor is a measure of the references that will be satisfied in the cache.

Data Footprint

The *data footprint* of a reference is the number of cache lines that will be brought into the cache by a particular loop. If there is no reuse, then the loop will refer to one element in each iteration; moreover, each element will be on a different cache line (or else there would be spatial reuse). Thus, the data footprint will be the product of the loop trip counts times the cache line size; the footprint is directly related to the number of lines that must be brought into the cache. If there is reuse, the footprint will be reduced by the reuse factor; this is not exact, but should be a good first-order approximation. The footprint at level k out of n nested loops is

$$F_k^* = l \prod_{i=k}^{n} \frac{N_k}{R_k}.$$

Data reuse can be exploited as cache locality if the footprint fits into the cache.

Estimates of the footprint and reuse are somewhat coarse, but frequently allow a compiler to select a loop ordering that improves locality. Choosing the loop ordering may require an exhaustive search of all the possible orderings. Simple heuristics can reduce the search to a reasonable number of possibilities.

Example 10.3

Compute the coefficient matrices, reuse factors, and footprints for the array references given in Examples 10.1 and 10.2.

Solution

For Example 10.1, the reuse factors and footprints are given in Figure 10.1, where the cache line size is assumed to be four array elements. At the outer loop, if the data fits into the cache, each element will be fetched from memory to cache only once.

For the tiled loop in Example 10.2, the reuse factors for the element loops are in Figure 10.2. The compiler can choose the tile size B such that the footprint of an entire tile ($B^2/4 + B/2$ cache lines) will fit into the cache.

Degree of Reuse

There can be reuse in a nested loop even when there is no reuse for a single loop index. In such a case, computing the footprint and self-reuse factor as above does not characterize the reuse, but other approximations can be used. The *degree of reuse* for temporal locality at loop nest level k is:

$$R_k^D = \text{dim}(\text{span}\,(\mathbf{e}_k, \mathbf{e}_{k+1}, \ldots, \mathbf{e}_n) \cap \text{kernel}\,\mathbf{A})$$

where *span* $(\mathbf{e}_k, \ldots, \mathbf{e}_n)$ is the portion of the iteration space spanned by the inner loops, from k through n. A higher degree of reuse means there is more reuse in this loop; it is in some sense the order of magnitude of the reuse in the loop.

The *degree of footprint* at loop nest level k is $d - R_k^D$, where d is the dimensionality of the array. As before, the degree of spatial reuse is found by using the reduced

| reference | reuse factors ||||| self-reuse || cumulative || footprint ||
| | temporal || spatial || R_J | R_I | R_J^* | R_I^* | F_J^* | F_I^* |
	J	I	J	I						
X[I,J]	1	1	4	1	4	1	4	4	M/4	NM/4
Y[I]	M	1	1	4	M	4	M	4M	1	N/4
Z[J]	1	N	4	1	4	N	4	4N	M/4	M/4
loop					$M+8$	$N+5$	$M+8$	$4M+4N+4$	$M/2$	$NM/4+N/4+M/4$

Figure 10.1 Reuse factors for Example 10.1.

| reference | reuse factors ||||| self-reuse || cumulative || footprint ||
| | temporal || spatial || R_J | R_I | R_J^* | R_I^* | F_J^* | F_I^* |
	J	I	J	I						
X[I,J]	1	1	4	1	4	1	4	4	B/4	$B^2/4$
Y[I]	B	1	1	4	B	4	B	4B	1	B/4
Z[J]	1	B	4	1	4	B	4	4B	B/4	B/4
loop					$B+8$	$B+5$	$B+8$	$8B+4$	$B/2+1$	$B^2/4+B/2$

Figure 10.2 Reuse factors for Example 10.2.

access matrix $\mathbf{A}_S$. A smaller degree of footprint means that less data needs to be cached for this loop.

For instance, consider the following loop:

(1)   for I = 1 to N do
(2)   for J = 1 to M do
(3)   ... X[I-J] ...
(4)   endfor
(5)   endfor

The null space of the coefficient matrix is $span\,((1,1)^T)$. Since neither $\mathbf{e}_1$ nor $\mathbf{e}_2$ is in the null space, neither loop exhibits simple reuse. However, at the outer loop we can consider any reuse in $span\,(\mathbf{e}_1, \mathbf{e}_2)$. The degree of reuse in the outer loop is the dimensionality of $span\,(\mathbf{e}_1, \mathbf{e}_2) \cap kernel\,\mathbf{A}$, which in this case is one; this means the degree of footprint is also one.

The dimensionality of $span\,(\mathbf{e}_k, \mathbf{e}_{k+1}, \ldots, \mathbf{e}_n) \cap kernel\,\mathbf{A}$ can be found by representing the basis set for $kernel\,\mathbf{A}$ in matrix form. Finding the Hermite normal form of this matrix gives another basis set for the same range. Counting the number of basis vectors with zero elements in positions $1, 2, \ldots, k-1$ gives R_k^D.

Example 10.4

Find the degree of reuse for array A in the following loop at each nest level:

(1)   for I = 1 to N do
(2)   for J = 1 to M do
(3)   for K = 1 to L do
(4)   ... A[I,J+K-1] ...
(5)   endfor
(6)   endfor
(7)   endfor

Solution

In matrix form, this array access is represented as:

$$\begin{pmatrix} 1 & 0 & 0 \\ 0 & 1 & 1 \end{pmatrix} \begin{pmatrix} I \\ J \\ K \end{pmatrix} + \begin{pmatrix} 0 \\ -1 \end{pmatrix}$$

The rank of the data access matrix is 2, and $(0, -1, 1)^T$ is a basis for the $kernel\,\mathbf{A}$. For the inner loop, we find $R_3^D = dim(span\,(\mathbf{e}_3) \cap span\,((0, -1, 1)^T)) = 0$. However, since the only basis vector of $kernel\,\mathbf{A}$ has a zero in position 1, $R_2^D = 1$, and $R_1^D = 1$ also.

10.1.3 Other Considerations

Cache memories are usually implemented with limited associativity; this means that even when there are unused cache lines, some cache lines may be evicted due to a cache line conflict. If the memory layout of the arrays shown in Example 10.2 is such that some tile needs to refer to a region of X, Y, and Z that all map to the same cache set, a two-way associative or direct-mapped cache will not be able to keep all three sets of cache lines resident. Caches are typically mapped by physical address, and a compiler has little influence over this. Compilers can deal with this in either of two ways. The first way is to assume that it will occur infrequently enough to ignore. The second is to watch for situations in which several different arrays need to be cache-resident for best performance. In these situations, insert code to copy one or more of the arrays to other locations that the compiler can ensure will not conflict with the other data. The copy loop is pure overhead; nonetheless, there are situations in which the performance difference is significant enough to warrant such a measure. The array to be copied should be one that has high reuse, so that the overhead of the copy is amortized as much as possible. This can be especially effective if the data layout has little or no spatial reuse, as is the case with array references that have large strides or irregular subscript expressions; copying the data to consecutive locations can significantly reduce the number of cache lines needed in the inner loop.

Faster processors and caches make the main memory look very slow. Caches reduce the average latency when the data references exhibit locality. However, the full latency will be paid for the first access to each cache line, and any reference with no reuse will not benefit from the cache at all. For array references with affine subscript expressions, the next element to be referenced can be computed in this iteration. For processors with *prefetch* instructions, the compiler can insert a prefetch for the data to be used in the next iteration, or even in the second or third subsequent iteration. If the data is prefetched early enough, it will have migrated to the cache by the time the actual fetch is issued. The danger is that the prefetch will evict some another array element that will be needed earlier than the prefetched data. The *prefetch distance* is the number of iterations between the prefetch operation and the actual fetch; it should be large enough to tolerate the expected memory latency, but not so large as to increase the danger of harmful cache line replacements. Prefetch instructions can be inserted only when the data reference pattern is predictable (as with affine array references); they need not be inserted into loops where the reference exhibits locality, since most of those references will be satisfied in the cache anyway. Another way to tolerate the long latency of memory is to use aggressive instruction scheduling.

Finally, when a data reference exhibits no reuse, there is no benefit to using the cache memory. In fact, there can be a performance penalty if filling a cache line for that reference evicts data that does have reuse. Some processors have a special load instruction that will bypass the cache memory and not fill a cache line. The compiler can detect this situation and replace the regular load with a bypass load instruction, potentially improving the locality for the other data references in the loop.

10.2 Multiple References

When a loop has multiple references to the same array, there can be *group reuse*, or reuse between different references. We focus on exploiting reuse between references that have affine subscript expressions with the same data access matrix; these can be written X[$\mathbf{Ai} + \mathbf{c}_1$] and X[$\mathbf{Ai} + \mathbf{c}_2$]. There is temporal reuse between two such references with distance $\mathbf{d}$ if there are iterations $\mathbf{i}_1$ and $\mathbf{i}_2$ such that $\mathbf{Ad} = \mathbf{A}(\mathbf{i}_2 - \mathbf{i}_1) = \mathbf{c}_1 - \mathbf{c}_2$. The set of all such solutions $\{\mathbf{d}\}$ is essentially all the address-based dependence distances between the two references, and is equal to $\mathbf{d} + \mathbf{x}$, where $\mathbf{d}$ is a particular solution and $\mathbf{x} \in$ kernel $\mathbf{A}$. Of particular interest are solutions where $\mathbf{d} \cdot \mathbf{x} = 0$, $\forall \mathbf{x} \in$ kernel $\mathbf{A}$; that is, the null space of $\mathbf{A}$ spans only dimensions where the particular solution has zero values. Here we focus on the reuse between references, characterized by $\mathbf{d}$. If $\mathbf{d} = \mathbf{0}$, then the same location is used by both references in the same iteration. Otherwise, the reuse is carried by the outermost loop with a nonzero entry in $\mathbf{d}$; if this is the kth loop, we look at d_k. The memory location used by the first reference will not be used again until d_k iterations later of the kth loop.

We characterize this by the *group-temporal reuse factor*: if $\mathbf{d} = \mathbf{0}$, the group-temporal reuse factor is ∞ for all loops. Otherwise, let k be the index of the first nonzero entry in $\mathbf{d}$; the group-temporal reuse factor for the kth loop is N_k/d_k and one for all other loops. We sort the references in question such that the reuse distance between adjacent references is lexicographically nonnegative, and compute a group-temporal reuse factor for each reference (except the first) relative to its predecessor in the list.

There may also be spatial reuse between two references with distance $\mathbf{d}$ if $\mathbf{A}_S \mathbf{d} = \mathbf{c}_{S,1} - \mathbf{c}_{S,2}$, where $\mathbf{A}_S$, $\mathbf{c}_{S,1}$, and $\mathbf{c}_{S,2}$ are $\mathbf{A}$, $\mathbf{c}_1$, and $\mathbf{c}_2$ with the row for the stride-1 dimension removed.

In summary, spatial reuse occurs only in the stride-1 dimension, and only when the reuse distance in array elements is less than the cache line size. There can be group-spatial reuse without self-spatial reuse, as between X[4*I] and X[4*I+1]. Since we only consider group reuse between references with the same coefficient matrix, if one reference has self-spatial reuse, they all do. Spatial reuse will improve due to multiple references only when the gcd of the coefficients in the stride-1 dimension is greater than one, and the offset $c_{1,s1} - c_{2,s1}$ (where $s1$ is the index of the stride-1 dimension) is not a multiple of that gcd; otherwise, group spatial reuse is merely a subset of group-temporal or self-spatial reuse.

As before, we concentrate on solutions where $\mathbf{d} \cdot \mathbf{x} = 0$, $\forall \mathbf{x} \in$ kernel $\mathbf{A}_S$. We sort the references so that the reuse distance between adjacent references is lexicographically nonnegative. We compute the *group-spatial reuse factor* between two

10.2 • Multiple References

references as follows, where **d** is the reuse distance: if there is self-spatial reuse for the references, or if $\gcd(a_{s1,1}, a_{s1,2}, \ldots, a_{s1,n})$ divides $c_{1,s1} - c_{2,s1}$, the group-spatial reuse factor is one for all loops. If **d** = **0**, the group-spatial reuse factor is N_k for the innermost loop and one for all other loops. Otherwise, let d_k be the outermost nonzero element in **d**; the group-spatial reuse factor for loop k is N_k/d_k, and one for all other loops.

The total group reuse factor for each reference for each loop is the product of group-temporal and group-spatial reuse factors for that loop. The *cumulative group reuse factor* of a loop is the product of the group reuse factors of that loop and all inner loops containing that reference. When computing a generalized reuse factor or a generalized footprint for a reference, we multiply the cumulative self-reuse factor by the cumulative group reuse factor, or divide the footprint by the cumulative group reuse factor to take into account reuse between references.

Example 10.5

Compute the reuse factors for the references to X in the following loop:

```
(1)     for I = 1 to N do
(2)         for J = 1 to M do
(3)             ...X[I,J]...
(4)             ...X[I+1,J]...
(5)             ...X[I,J]...
(6)             ...X[I,J-1]...
(7)         endfor
(8)     endfor
```

Solution

All four references have the same coefficient matrix (the identity matrix, in this case), so all fall into the same group. The sorted list of references, with reuse distance from the previous entry in the list, is given in the following table:

(4)	X[I+1,J]	
(3)	X[I,J]	(1,0)
(5)	X[I,J]	(0,0)
(7)	X[I,J-1]	(0,1)

There is no self-temporal reuse for any of these references. Assuming row-major storage, they all have self-sequential reuse. In addition, there is group-temporal and group-spatial reuse, but the group-spatial reuse factor will not be computed since all the references have self-spatial reuse. The self-spatial, group-temporal, and cumulative generalized reuse factors for each loop are given in the table below, assuming cache lines that hold four array elements.

		self-spatial		group-temporal		cumulative	
line	reference	J	I	J	I	J	I
4	X[I+1,J]	4	1	1	1	4	4
3	X[I,J]	4	1	1	N	4	4N
5	X[I,J]	4	1	∞	1	∞	∞
7	X[I,J-1]	4	1	M	1	4M	4M

The cumulative reuse factor is the ratio of array elements to cache lines needed to hold the data for that reference, given that the previous references are cached. At the outer loop, this says that if the cache is large enough to hold all the data needed, it will need only $NM/4$ cache lines to hold all the data for reference X[I+1,J], only $M/4$ more cache lines to hold all the additional data for the first X[I,J] reference, no more cache lines to hold the data for the next X[I,J] reference (since it will already be in the cache), and $N/4$ additional cache lines for X[I,J-1].

10.2.1 Reducing the Reuse Distance

When the reuse distance for a given loop is a fixed constant, that distance can be reduced by *striping* the loop, with a stripe factor equal to the reuse distance. If there are several distances to be reduced, the stripe factor should be the gcd of all the distances. Recall that striping is not always legal, so dependence tests are necessary. If the reuse distance is a fixed constant, the compiler can also use alignment to change the reuse distance.

Example 10.6

Use striping to reduce the reuse distance in the following loop:

(1)   for I = 2 to N-1 do
(2)   B[I] = (A[I-1] + A[I+2])/2
(3)   endfor

Solution

The reuse distance between the reference A[I+2] and A[I-1] is three. Since the reuse distance is a fixed constant, we can stripe the loop with a factor of three to get the following program:

(1) for Is = 2 to 4 do
(1)   for I = Is to N-1 by 3 do
(2)   B[I] = (A[I-1] + A[I+2])/2
(3)   endfor
(3) endfor

After striping, the reuse distance is one in the inner loop; this means that a value fetched in one iteration is used in the very next iteration rather than the third subsequent iteration. Note that sequential reuse has deteriorated somewhat in the transformed loop.

10.2.2 Reordering Loops for Locality

As with single references, we compute the degree of reuse between two references as $dim(span\,(\mathbf{e}_k, \ldots, \mathbf{e}_n) \cap \{d + kernel\,\mathbf{A}\})$. The compiler should try to improve the reuse in the inner loops as much as possible. Loop reordering can often be used to move a reuse-carrying loop to an inner position. In particular, when $\mathbf{e}_k \in \{d + kernel\,\mathbf{A}\}$, moving that loop to the inner position enhances temporal locality.

The reduction in memory traffic due to self-temporal locality can be on the order of the trip count of the loop that carries the reuse. The reduction in memory traffic due to self-spatial locality is no more than the length of a cache line. For group locality, the reduction in memory traffic can be at most equal to the number of references that share locality in the loop. However, reordering loops to improve locality for one reference may adversely affect locality for other references. The compiler really needs to look at the entire picture when optimizing a nested loop.

Example 10.7

Use loop ordering to improve temporal locality in the following loop:

```
(1)    for I = 1 to N do
(2)        for J = 2 to M-1 do
(3)            for K = 1 to L do
(4)                A[I,J,K] = (B[I,J-1,K] + B[I,J,K] + B[I,J+1,K]) / 3
(5)            endfor
(6)        endfor
(7)    endfor
```

Solution

Between the three references to B there is reuse with distance in $span\,((0, 1, 0)^T)$. In the inner loop, there is no reuse; in the J loop, there is reuse of degree 1. Moving the J loop to the innermost position (which is legal in this example) will let the inner loop carry the reuse. In this way the reuse can be satisfied in the cache, or even by register assignment across loop iterations.

Sorting Loops by Reuse Factor

The compiler can compute an *innermost reuse factor* for each loop as though that loop were in the innermost position; this would treat the loop as if it did not carry any reuse when the reuse distance has more than one nonzero entry, and the computation for group-spatial locality must treat the loop as innermost. The innermost reuse factor is the reuse that would be carried by the loop if it were reordered to the innermost position. Assuming that the loop limits are of the same order of magnitude, the number of data references in the body of the loop is independent of the loop ordering. Choosing the loop with the highest innermost reuse factor, summing the innermost reuse factors for all the arrays in the loop, will give the most reuse within and across iterations, and thus should produce the code with the fewest cache misses.

There may be situations in which the loop with the best innermost reuse factor cannot be reordered to the innermost position, due to data dependence conditions or unstructured loop limits. In such a case, choosing the loop with the second or third best factor for the innermost loop is the obvious approach. If the loop limits are large enough, getting the innermost loop correct is most important; reuse across the next outer loop will be a second order effect.

10.3 General Tiling

We saw earlier how tiling improves self-locality. Similarly, tiling can improve group locality, by allowing group reuse carried by multiple loops to be satisfied in the cache. Without tiling, a large inner loop will evict the cache lines needed for locality carried by the next outer loop.

There is no benefit in tiling a loop that carries no reuse. If a loop index appears in all the array references, but does not appear in the stride-1 index in any of them, then it will not carry any self-reuse. If there are multiple references to an array, however, then the loop may still carry group-reuse, either spatial or temporal.

Skewing may be required to enable the interchanges used by tiling. If the loops are skewed enough to make all the dependence distances nonnegative, then the loops are *fully permutable*. This may not be strictly necessary, however. When tiling nontightly nested loops, code sinking may be required, as discussed in Chapter 9.

If we are tiling for cache locality, the number of memory references within a tile is independent of the order of the element loops. However, tiling is only a probabilistic optimization, and there are still uncertainties at execution time. The element loops should be reordered to enhance temporal locality as much as possible, which may allow register allocation to resolve some of the data references from values already in registers. Sequential locality in the inner loops is also important for taking immediate advantage of a cache line, in case it is evicted for some uncontrollable reason before the loop is finished with it.

Choosing the ordering of the element loops can be done by studying the innermost reuse factors. The innermost loop should be the loop with the highest reuse factor. The reuse factors of the other loops depends on the loop ordering, if the reuse distance is not zero. The compiler can either try an exhaustive search of all the loop orderings, which is reasonable if the nesting depth is small, or simply sort the loops by innermost reuse factors.

The order of the tile loops should be chosen to enhance reuse between tiles. The inner tile loop should be the one that carries the most reuse of any kind, with the highest innermost reuse factor, since this will mean the most overlap of data between tiles. Assuming that the data set is large enough to warrant tiling, locality across iterations of the next outer tile loop may be unimportant. If any data copying is done to reduce cache conflicts, it may be done at tile boundaries.

Our discussion so far has mostly been in terms of tiling for cache memory locality. In fact, the memory hierarchy can be quite a bit deeper. The processor may have multiple levels of cache, as well as a virtual memory level. If the loops can be tiled for locality at the highest level of cache, they can be tiled again (and again) for locality at the secondary cache level and virtual memory level. In particular, if the primary cache is very small, tiling for primary and secondary cache locality followed by unrolling all the element loops may give the best performance. For very large data sets, tiling or otherwise optimizing for virtual memory performance can make a dramatic difference in performance. This becomes less important as main memories increase in size to the gigabyte range.

10.4 Fission and Fusion for Locality

The amount of data required at the highest level of the memory hierarchy is directly related to the number of arrays in the loop and the loop limits. Tiling addresses the loop limits by using small limits for the element loops. Loop fission can reduce the number of arrays used in each loop by breaking the loop up into a sequence of smaller loops, each of which has disjoint or smaller data requirements. The finest partitioning is to break the loop into regions based on the strongly connected components in the dependence graph.

We want to find larger partitions of the statements in the loop such that each partition is processing a disjoint subset of data. We do this by first ignoring the stride-1 dimension of all arrays when computing the dependence graph. This allows two references that are data independent but exhibit spatial reuse to appear dependent on each other. Also, we add input dependence relations to the graph, and call the resulting graph a *reuse dependence graph*. After applying loop fission to split each reuse dependence cycle into a distinct loop, each resultant loop will process disjoint data. Applying this fission before tiling may allow larger, more efficient tiles, due to the reduced data set required for each tile. It may adversely affect reuse between loops, but that should not be important at the higher levels of the memory hierarchy unless the data set is small, in which case tiling is the wrong approach.

Loop fusion can enhance reuse by combining loops when they use the same data. We have already seen some benefits of fusion with respect to data locality between loops generated from Fortran-90 array assignments.

10.5 In the Pit

Reordering loops to move the stride-1 loop to the innermost position requires the compiler to be able to determine the stride-1 dimension for each array reference. While this is usually simple, for higher level language array constructs—such as dynamically allocated arrays, array pointers, and assumed-shape formal parameters introduced in Fortran 90—the stride-1 dimension need not be in any one position. In fact, none of the dimensions of an array may be stride-1.

At the register level, temporal locality is used by reusing values in registers. Some machines can load a pair of registers with a single instruction; reordering loops for sequential locality between iterations followed by unrolling the inner loop may allow the compiler to use more double-register loads.

10.6 Further Reading

McKellar and Coffman (1969) noted that using a submatrix formulation of matrix operations—essentially, tiling—augmented with the proper data layout will improve memory hierarchy performance; at that time, the memory hierarchy in question was paged virtual memory. The earliest work to use automatic program restructuring to optimize for the memory hierarchy was done by Abu-Sufah et al. (1981). The importance of properly taking advantage of the memory hierarchy is conveyed by the design of the Level-3 BLAS (Dongarra et al. [1990]). Callahan and Porterfield (1990) show that up to half the time of some supercomputer applications can be wasted in processing cache misses. Goodman (1983) shows performance characteristics when the cache memory is used to reduce traffic between the processor and the memory. Lam et al. (1991) discuss many aspects of optimizing for locality, such as choosing the tile size and copying data to reduce cache interference. Temam et al. (1993) give other heuristics for choosing data to copy to separate, conflict-free locations.

Gannon et al. (1988) describe early work on an automatic scheme to manage a memory hierarchy automatically in a parallel programming environment using the concept of a *reference window*, which is the number of loop iterations from when the data element is first referenced until it is no longer needed; minimizing reference windows will improve the performance of the memory hierarchy. Wolf and Lam (1991b) distinguish between reuse and locality, and between self-reuse and group-reuse, and show a scheme to quantify reuse and improve locality. Carr and Kennedy (1992) show the strengths and weaknesses of tiling in a compiler; they show several cases in which tiling fails, and that index-set splitting can address some of these cases.

Gornish et al. (1990) describe a scheme for inserting prefetch operations at the earliest point in the program after which the prefetched data is guaranteed to be used. Callahan et al. (1991) describe a simple but effective method for inserting prefetch operations for algorithms with regular data access patterns.

EXERCISES

10.1 Run the following loop, converted to Fortran, C, or Pascal, on any computer system with a cache memory. Let A, B, and C be single precision or double precision floating point arrays. Vary the size of N from 10 to 10,000, and plot the ratio of execution time t to N^2 against N (N on the horizontal axis, t/N^2 on the vertical axis).

```
(1)     for I = 1 to N do
(2)       for J = 1 to N do
(3)         A[I,J] = B[I,J] + C[I,J]*5.1
(4)       endfor
(5)     endfor
```

Note: Initialize the B and C arrays to nonzero values.

10.2 Repeat the previous exercise after interchanging the loops. How does the execution time compare to the previous results? Which form of the loop has more locality? Note: The data layout depends on the language you use.

10.3 Repeat the previous two exercises with the compiler optimizations on and off. Which has a greater effect on performance: data locality or compiler optimizations?

10.4 Try tiling the loops in the first two exercises and repeat the experiments. Does tiling affect performance? Why or why not?

10.5 Try executing the following matrix multiplication loop with all six loop orderings, where the arrays are single or double precision floating point arrays:

```
(1)     for I = 1 to N do
(2)       for J = 1 to N do
(3)         for K = 1 to N do
(4)           A[I,J] = A[I,J] + B[I,K]*C[K,J]
(5)         endfor
(6)       endfor
(7)     endfor
```

Vary the value of N from 10 to 5,000, and plot t/N^3 against N (where t is the execution time) for each of the six loop orderings.

10.6 Tile the matrix multiplication loop that gives the best performance from the previous exercise for large matrix sizes (over 1,000). Vary the tile size from 50 to 500. Compare the performance of different tile sizes. If you can find the cache size for your machine, see if the performance drops when the amount of data needed in a tile exceeds the cache size.

10.7 Identify and characterize the self-temporal and self-spatial reuse for the original matrix multiplication loop.

10.8 Identify and characterize the self-temporal and self-spatial reuse for the matrix multiplication loop with the best performance. Compute the innermost reuse factor for each loop. Is using the innermost reuse factor to reorder loops a good predictor of performance?

10.9 Write a program to find the self-temporal and self-spatial reuse factors and reuse degrees, given a data access matrix. Test your program on the loops in this chapter and in the previous exercises.

10.10 Sort the array references in the following loop so that the reuse distance is positive:

```
(1)    for I = 2 to N do
(2)      for J = 2 to M do
(3)        A[I,J] = (A[I-1,J]+A[I,J-1]+A[I,J+1]+A[I+1,J])/A[I,I]
(4)      endfor
(5)    endfor
```

Find the group reuse for the references in this loop. What loop ordering gives the most reuse?

11 CONCURRENCY ANALYSIS

Compiling for multiprocessors involves many issues in generating concurrent code. Here we present the master/slave paradigm, and discuss generation of concurrent code from sequential as well as parallel loops.

We start by reviewing the execution model for a multiprocessor, which involves many options and tradeoffs. The most common currently available multiprocessors have uniformly shared memory, with all the memory equally accessible to each processor, and with hardware to preserve memory consistency. The number of processors is typically small—from two to 16—and the program executes in a multiprogramming environment; this means that a parallel program usually cannot depend on having all the processors available to it, since other tasks may be using the other processors. An environment in which all the processors are dedicated to a single job can change some of the tradeoff decisions. We also study how to identify loops that can be executed concurrently on a multiprocessor with minimal synchronization between processors, and how to reduce and manage the synchronization when it is necessary.

11.1 Code for Concurrent Loops

We assume the common situation in which the main part of the program is executed by a single *process* (sometimes called a *task* or *thread*), called the *master*. When a parallel region—a concurrent loop or other parallel code—is reached, the master initiates multiple parallel *workers*, or *slaves*, to execute in the parallel region, as shown in Figure 11.1. When the slaves complete execution of the parallel region, they synchronize using a special construct called a *barrier*; the slaves are then disabled, and the master continues with the sequential code following the parallel region. Figure 11.1 also shows the common situation in which some workers in the parallel region finish before others; the barrier insures that the master will not continue until all the workers are done. Sometimes some workers finish much earlier than others; in severe cases, this load imbalance among the workers can affect the parallel performance of the program.

There are many issues regarding the implementation of slaves. In some operating systems, starting up another worker is a costly, or *heavyweight*, operation. In such a system, the program will typically start up the slaves only once; at the barrier, the slaves will be *parked*, or removed from the operating system scheduling queues, while still retaining the process data structures. When another parallel

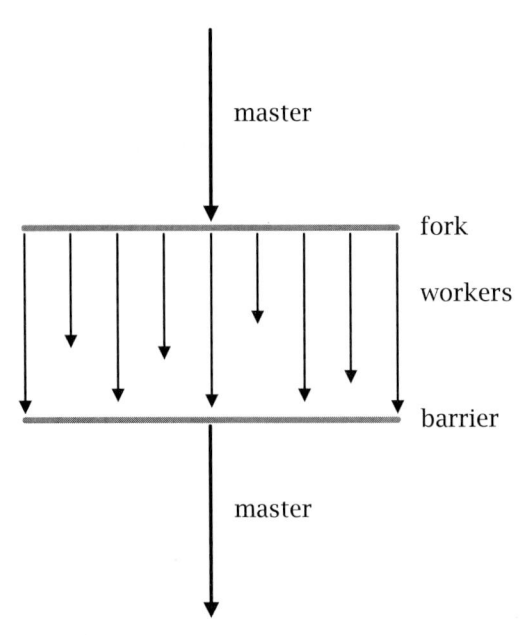

FIGURE 11.1 Master/worker model of multiprocessor parallel computation.

region is reached, the master can quickly and inexpensively reenable the slaves without recreating the workers. In more modern operating systems, starting up multiple workers in a single address space can be done inexpensively. In that case, the system can terminate the workers at the barrier.

Another option is choosing whether the master should participate in the execution of the code in the parallel region. Usually, the master participates just like any slave and shares equally in the work, since there isn't much else for it to do. Another consideration is whether the master is distinguished. In the parallel region, some of the workers (master or slaves) will finish before others. An early finishing slave can either park or terminate itself. However, if the master is distinguished, it must wait at the barrier until all the slaves are done. The manner in which it waits may affect system performance. If the master is not distinguished, then the worker corresponding to the master before the parallel region may just as well park or terminate itself, and let the last slave to finish take on the role of master thereafter.

In a dedicated environment, each worker corresponds to a single processor. When executing on a multiprogramming system, the parallel threads or processes are usually scheduled competitively with any other job in the system. In particular, initiating 10 parallel workers does not mean they will ever all be executing concurrently at any time. In fact, on a heavily loaded computer system, the parallel workers may be scheduled one at a time on the same physical processor, so the parallel program may actually complete no faster than it would on a uniprocessor.

11.1 ■ Code for Concurrent Loops

Task or process management requires cooperation from the operating system. Other policy decisions, discussed below, are the responsibility of the compiler and run-time system.

11.1.1 Scheduling Policies

Any time there is parallel work to be done and parallel workers to do it, there is a question of how to assign the work. For a concurrent loop, each iteration is a unit of work; assigning the iterations to the parallel workers can be done dynamically or statically. Static iteration scheduling, or *prescheduling*, means that each worker is initiated with enough information to characterize all the iterations assigned to it. If there are N iterations to assign to P workers, one common method is to assign $\lceil N/P \rceil$ consecutive iterations to each worker, called *block scheduling*. Another method, called *cyclic scheduling*, assigns every Pth iteration to each worker. These are shown in Figure 11.2.

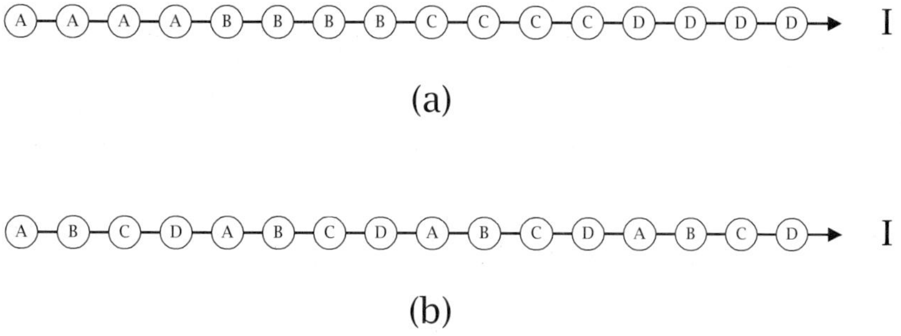

FIGURE 11.2 Prescheduling policies: (a) block scheduling; (b) cyclic scheduling.

In a caching multiprocessor, assigning consecutive iterations to the same processor can improve the cache hit ratio, if consecutive iterations exhibit spatial locality (by referring to consecutive array elements, for instance). On the other hand, if the amount of work in each iteration varies, assigning consecutive iterations may assign an entire low-work region to a single worker; that worker would finish its work early, and, because of the static scheduling policy, could not help with the iterations assigned to other workers. This situation sometimes appears as a concurrent loop containing an inner loop, where the inner loop limit depends on the concurrent loop index; such cases may achieve better load balance by giving each worker every Pth iteration.

In general, static scheduling policies are vulnerable to load imbalance. In particular, when the workers do not correspond to physical processors, some workers may be waiting for the operating system to schedule them when others are already done. Dynamic scheduling, or *self-scheduling*, alleviates load imbalance by assigning small units of work to each worker, and having the workers compete for the next unit of work in a *critical section*. A worker that gets an inexpensive unit of work can compete for more work quickly, while one that gets a costly unit of work will be busy completing its assignment. There is a tradeoff between the overhead of the competition for the next available unit of work and the use of dynamic scheduling to achieve better load balance. Using small units of work, such as a single iteration, has the advantage of potentially giving the best load balance; no one worker will get a huge piece of work. However, it also has the most scheduling overhead, since the critical section must be entered for each iteration. The alternative is to assign *chunks* of iterations, rather than individual iterations, at a time. As the chunk size increases, the scheduling overhead is reduced, but the potential for load imbalance increases. If the chunk size is increased to N/P, this effectively reduces to prescheduling.

Tapering

A variation of chunk self-scheduling is to taper the size of the chunk as the loop nears completion. This tends to alleviate the problem of one processor getting an expensive chunk and being a bottleneck for completion of the parallel loop. Several variants of such a scheme have been proposed; all involve a slightly more expensive critical section to dynamically compute the size of the chunk with the benefit of reduced scheduling overhead, as with chunk scheduling, and good load balance, as with single iteration scheduling. The initial competition to enter the critical section to dynamically get the first iteration or chunk of iterations can be eliminated if the master tells each worker what its first iteration(s) will be.

One tapering method is called *guided self-scheduling*. In this method, the size of the chunk scheduled for a processor is always $1/P$ of the remaining iterations. If we let R_i be the number of iterations remaining after i scheduling operations, and C_i be the chunk size for the ith scheduling operation, we have:

$$R_0 = N$$
$$C_i = \lceil R_{i-1}/P \rceil$$
$$R_i = R_{i-1} - C_i$$

Using guided self-scheduling, if each iteration has the same execution time, but the processors start working at uneven times, all processors will finish within one iteration of each other. Unfortunately, if each iteration has a different execution time, guided self-scheduling tends to schedule a large fraction of the iterations in the first chunk; in fact, the first chunk is N/P. A variation that addresses this concern is to change the formula for C_i to $\lceil R_{i-1}/(2P) \rceil$.

Another tapering scheme is called *factoring*. This scheme resembles guided self-scheduling, except rather than compute the size of one chunk at each scheduling operation, it computes the size of a batch of chunks. Each batch is a fraction of the remaining work, and each chunk is $1/P$ of that batch. Simple factoring chooses a fixed fraction $1/f$, perhaps $f = 2$. If we let C_i be the chunk size for the P chunks after the ith scheduling operation, and R_i be the number of iterations remaining after i scheduling operations, we have:

$$R_0 = N$$
$$C_i = \lceil R_{i-1}/(fP) \rceil$$
$$R_i = R_{i-1} - PC_i$$

Recall that P chunks of size C_i are scheduled in one operation; the batch size is PC_i.

Example 11.1

Compare block scheduling, chunk self-scheduling, guided self-scheduling and factoring when scheduling 100 iterations on 4 processors. Use a chunk size of 10 and a factor $f = 2$.

Solution

The chunk sizes for the different schemes are shown in the following table.

block	25	25	25	25						
chunk	10	10	10	10	10	10	10	10	10	10
guided	25	19	14	11	8	6	5	3	3	2
	1	1	1	1						
factoring	13	13	13	13	6	6	6	6	3	3
	3	3	2	2	2	2	1	1	1	1

Note that guided self-scheduling has 14 scheduling operations, whereas factoring has only 5, since it schedules P chunks at a time.

Master/Slave Code

Figure 11.3 shows an example of code generated for a prescheduled concurrent loop. The master code sets up some shared variables and releases the workers, passing each worker the loop parameters so that it can compute its share of the loop. Note that the master also participates as a worker, so the total number of workers is Workers+1. Each worker will execute the procedure comprising the body of the loop; when done with the loop, each will enter a critical section (protected by a shared lock variable) to decrement the total number of active workers. The last worker will continue executing the code following the loop as the new master. Depending on the operating system and run-time support for parallel programs, the body of the concurrent loop may not have to appear in a separate procedure; however, the effect of starting a concurrent loop is very similar to a procedure call, with allocation of local variables, and so on. The code labeled *update global variables* is discussed shortly.

```
/* Master code for prescheduled concurrent loop */
/* how many workers are there, add one for myself */
Global_Working = Workers+1
Global_Lock = 0 /* critical section lock */
Global_Continuation = label_after_loop
for I = 1 to Workers do
    /* release worker 'I', start at iteration I */
    release_worker( body, I, N, Workers+1 )
endfor
/* participate as worker 'Workers+1' */
call body( Workers+1, N, Workers+1 )
/* Master continues here after concurrent loop */
label_after_loop:
        ⋮
/* Worker code for prescheduled concurrent loop */
procedure body( First, Last, Stride )
for I = First to Last by Stride do
    execute loop for iteration I
endfor
/* enter critical section */
acquire_lock( Global_Lock )
Global_Working = Global_Working - 1
update global variables
if Global_Working > 0 then
    release_lock( Global_Lock )
    park /* wait for next parallel operation */
endif
release_lock( Global_Lock )
goto Global_Continuation
end body
```

FIGURE 11.3 Master and worker code to execute prescheduled concurrent loop.

A self-scheduled concurrent loop has a more complex structure, since the code must dynamically allocate iterations to workers. Figure 11.4 shows an example of code generated for a self-scheduled concurrent loop. The master code is much the same as before, except that it must set up more global variables to support the dynamic iteration assignment. The worker code starts by entering a critical section to get the next iteration that needs to be done, then proceeds to execute that iteration. If a chunking scheme is used, the global iteration counter would

11.1 ■ Code for Concurrent Loops

```
/* Master code for self-scheduled concurrent loop */
/* how many workers are there, add one for myself */
Global_Working = Workers+1
/* initialize global loop parameters */
Global_I = 1 /* starting */
Global_N = N /* last iteration */
Global_Lock = 0 /* critical section lock */
Global_Continuation = label_after_loop
for i = 1 to Workers do
    /* release worker 'i', start at iteration i */
    release_worker( body )
endfor
/* participate as worker 'workers+1' */
call body( )
/* Master continues here after concurrent loop */
label_after_loop:
        ⋮

/* Worker code for self-scheduled concurrent loop */
procedure body( )
loop
    /* enter critical region */
    acquire_lock( Global_Lock )
    /* find next iteration to do */
    I = Global_I
    if I > Global_N then exit
    /* set up for the next processor */
    Global_I = I + 1
    /* leave critical region */
    release_lock( Global_Lock)
    execute loop for iteration I
endloop
/* no more work to do, count myself done */
Global_Working = Global_Working - 1
update global variables
if Global_Working > 0 then
    release_lock( Global_Lock )
    park /* wait for next parallel operation */
endif
release_lock( Global_Lock )
goto Global_Continuation
end body
```

FIGURE 11.4 Master and worker code to execute self-scheduled concurrent loop.

be incremented by the chunk size. Dynamic chunk size computation can also be added to this code in the critical section.

In either style of parallel code, the architecture of the machine and the software protocols will affect the expense of the various operations. Some novel computer architectures allow a master to create a new worker task (in the same address space) with a single instruction. Critical section synchronization may be implemented with a simple test-and-set or swap instruction, if the memory semantics supports efficient sequential consistency, busy-waiting until the lock is free. In a multiprogramming environment, however, busy-waiting may not be effective, since the task that owns the lock may not be currently scheduled. A more robust system might use queues for the critical section, which removes the problems of busy-waiting, but adds its own costs.

11.1.2 Nested Concurrent Loops

Most current multiprocessors do not have a large number of processors, so one level of parallelism is sufficient to keep them busy. For larger parallel machines, it may be necessary to allow nested concurrent loops in order to utilize the machine. Treating the nested loops as a multidimensional iteration space, iterations can be statically or dynamically allocated to each of the various workers, much as with scheduling for a single loop; for instance, the modifications to the worker code to handle nested parallel loops are shown in Figure 11.5.

A more general scheduling scheme uses a queue of *generators*. Each generator is a procedure that returns a descriptor of the next parallel task; the generator keeps some internal state to remember the next parallel task (iteration) to assign, and when to stop. When a parallel iteration is assigned, if it is not the last iteration of the loop, the generator will also push itself back onto the queue.

11.1.3 Private Variables

When executing an iteration of a concurrent loop, the worker may need to allocate a *private* variable. A private variable is one whose value is not available to other workers executing the same parallel code. In the code we used for a concurrent loop, a private variable can be allocated in the worker procedure; this way, the private variable is allocated once per worker, instead of once per iteration of the loop. Private scalars can be allocated to processor registers, in the normal way. Private variables cannot have upward-exposed uses, so there is no initial value problem. The variable used to hold the loop index value will be a private variable, for instance.

11.1.4 Reductions

Reductions in a concurrent loop (reducing a vector of values to a scalar) can be efficiently executed when the reduction is associative and commutative. The most common reduction is accumulating the sum of a vector or an array. This can be done in parallel by allowing each of the workers to accumulate a private partial sum

```
/* Worker code for nested self-scheduled concurrent loop */
procedure body( )
loop
    /* enter critical region */
    acquire_lock( Global_Lock )
    /* find next iteration to do */
    I = Global_I
    J = Global_J
    if J > Global_M then
        J = 1
        I = I + 1
        if I > Global_N then exit
        Global_I = I + 1
    endif
    Global_J = J + 1
    /* leave critical region */
    release_lock( Global_Lock)
    execute loop for iteration I,J
endloop
the rest of the worker is the same
    ⋮
end body
```

FIGURE 11.5 Worker code for nested self-scheduled concurrent loops.

for the iterations assigned to it, and to accumulate the global sum from the partial sums. This reduces the accesses to the global variable holding the final sum. In Figures 11.3 and 11.4, the final accumulation is done where the annotation *update global variables* appears. Note that the order of accumulation depends not only on how the iterations are scheduled to workers, but on the order in which they finish and add their partial sum to the global sum.

11.1.5 Synchronization for Dependence

When the iterations of a concurrent loop are data independent, no synchronization (except for scheduling) is required. When there are data dependence relations between the iterations, synchronization may be required. We explore several types of synchronization here. One simple form of synchronization that we have already seen is a *critical section*. A critical section is a protected region of code such that only one worker or processor can be active in the region at a time. It is typically protected by a critical section lock, which must be acquired before entering the critical section and is released after leaving it. While a compiler may use critical sections to implement parallel code at the low level, it is not usually appropriate for preserving data dependence, since it does not preserve the order of accesses.

A more useful variant is an *ordered critical section*. This is a region of code, protected by a lock, in which only one worker or processor can be active at a time, and that the workers or processors must enter in some predetermined order. We can use an ordered critical section to satisfy loop carried data dependence relations in a concurrent loop. We use the primitives `await` and `advance` to implement the ordered critical section with a shared synchronization counter. An `await` will block or wait until the synchronization counter reaches some value, specified in the `await`; an `advance` atomically increments the synchronization counter. We assume that the `await` will busy-wait; that is, a worker that reaches an `await` will not be able to do any more useful work until the `await` is satisfied.

For any synchronization operation, the architecture must support some form of memory consistency. That is, when one processor executes a `store` followed by an `advance`, and a second processor executes an `await` followed by a `fetch` of the value just stored, the memory model of the architecture must guarantee that the value fetched will be the one just stored. One way to do this is to make the first processor *stall* at the `advance` until all pending stores have completed. Another option is to have two flavors of store instructions: a simple store and a *consistent store*, the latter of which is used for data references involved in dependence relations. In this case, the `advance` operation needs to stall only if there is a consistent store instruction that is not yet complete. Some architectures support a special store instruction that will itself stall the processor until this store and all other pending store operations have completed. Such an instruction can be used to implement an `advance` operation.

An ordered critical section can satisfy any lexically backward loop carried data dependence relation by enclosing both the source and target of the dependence relation in the critical section. Lexically forward loop carried dependence relations can be satisfied by an empty ordered critical section between the source and target; this prevents the worker executing the dependence target from getting ahead of the dependence source. Essentially, the dependence source must be followed by an `advance` and the target must follow an `await`.

If the dependence distance d is a known constant greater than one, the compiler can generate code for iteration i to `await` until iteration $i - d$ has advanced. If the distance is not known, iteration i should `await` until iteration $i - 1$ is complete; while it is safe to wait for any iteration $i - d$ where d is any factor of the actual dependence distance, the only known factor of an unknown distance is one. Note that an `await` with distance one must still precede the `advance`, since the increment operations must occur in order.

Example 11.2

Show how to use an ordered critical section to execute the following loop on a multiprocessor:

11.1 ▪ Code for Concurrent Loops

```
(1)    for I = 2 to n do
(2)        A[I] = B[I] + C[I]
(3)        D[I] = D[I-1] + A[I]
(4)    endfor
```

Solution

There is a loop carried data dependence relation from line 3 to itself; the fetch of D[I-1] must follow the store of D[I] from the previous iteration. Each worker should execute the following code for the body of the loop:

```
fetch C[I] -> r1
fetch B[I] -> r2
add r1+r2 -> r3
store r3 -> A[I]
await(I-1)
fetch D[I-1] -> r4
add r3+r4 -> r5
store r5 -> D[I]
advance
```

This sketch of a solution does not include the computation of the addresses of the array elements, and assumes that the synchronization counter is initialized to the value 1, so iteration 2 can proceed without waiting.

Implementation

Note that no chunk scheduling policy should be used for a concurrent loop with synchronization. It does not make much sense to schedule c consecutive iterations to a single worker if the next worker cannot advance until this one finishes all its iterations. The iterations must be scheduled one at a time, in an order consistent with the dependence distance. Since the compiler can identify the memory accesses that may have interprocessor conflicts, it can flag these or generate special instructions, if necessary.

The synchronization counter may be implemented in a shared register or a special fast memory unit. If the loop is prescheduled, then the dependence distance also determines the worker that will execute the source of a dependence relation. In such a case, the compiler might use one synchronization counter for each worker. The worker keeps track of how far it has advanced; to determine whether a dependence source has completed, the code checks the counter for the worker that was assigned the source iteration.

Another implementation scheme for multiprocessor synchronization is to use a vector of words or bits, one element for each iteration. Each worker sets the appropriate element when it completes the source of each data dependence relation in that iteration, and tests for the completion of the appropriate iteration of the dependence source before starting to execute the dependence target. This has the advantage of not oversynchronizing when the dependence distance is not a known constant, but it uses more memory (for the vector) and has a larger initialization cost. It also allows lexically forward dependences to execute without an ordered critical section.

Example 11.3

Show how to use a synchronization vector to execute the following loop in parallel on a multiprocessor:

```
(1)    for I = 2 to n do
(2)        A[I] = B[I] + C[I]
(3)        D[I] = D[I+1] + A[I]
(4)    endfor
```

Solution

There is a loop carried anti-dependence relation from line 3 to itself; the fetch of D[I+1] must precede the store of D[I] from the next iteration. Each worker should execute the following code for the body of the loop:

```
fetch D[I+1] -> r4
set Sync[I]
fetch C[I] -> r1
fetch B[I] -> r2
add r1+r2 -> r3
store r3 -> A[I]
if I > 2 then wait Sync[I-1] endif
add r3+r4 -> r5
store r5 -> D[I]
```

Here we assume that the Sync vector is initialized to zero, signifying that no iteration has yet completed. The first iteration proceeds without checking by using a conditional. Notice that we moved the fetch of D[I+1] up in the loop, so we could move the set operation as high as possible. This is in the hope that the await operation for the next iteration will not have to wait, even if the iterations do not execute at the same speed.

Busy-Waiting

A common multiprocessor synchronization method is a busy-wait. The processor reaching a critical section will execute a busy-wait loop until the critical section lock is unlocked. The simplest method is to use a single memory location for

11.1 ▪ Code for Concurrent Loops

the critical section lock, where a value of zero means unlocked and a nonzero value means locked. With a `swap` instruction, a processor can wait for the lock by executing the following loop:

```
(1)    mylock = 1
(2)    repeat
(3)        swap(lock,mylock)
(4)    until mylock = 0
```

If `lock` is still locked, then the processor will continue around the loop; as soon as `lock` is unlocked, the processor will lock the value (by swapping the value 1 into it) and will be able to proceed. Unlocking the lock variable is as simple as storing a zero into it. The `swap` instruction must execute *atomically*; that is, if two or more processors try to swap values into the same lock location, the swap operations must execute sequentially (or at least behave as if they executed sequentially).

On current cache-coherent multiprocessors, this busy-wait operation can be effective if there is little contention for the lock. However, if there are several processors actively trying to enter the critical section, the cache behavior will severely affect performance. Since each `swap` instruction is a read-modify-write operation, a processor executing a `swap` must acquire ownership of the cache line holding the lock variable (assuming the common write-exclusive caching protocol). If there are two or more processors trying to grab the lock, that cache line will ping-pong between the processors, even though none of them will actually be able to get the lock. Not only is this unnecessary, but it uses precious bus bandwidth, perhaps even slowing down the one processor that is in the critical section and on which all the others are waiting.

A variation on this is to busy-wait on a shadow read-only copy of the lock. If the shadow copy is unlocked, then the processor will try to execute the expensive `swap` operation; otherwise, it will loop on the read-only copy. Since the cache protocol allows multiple read-only copies of the cache line, each processor can busy-wait on its own copy of the cache line, so it can wait without any bus cycles at all. The busy-wait loop now looks like:

```
(1)    mylock = 1
(2)    repeat
(3)        repeat
(4)        until lock = 0
(5)        swap(lock,mylock)
(6)    until mylock = 0
```

The unlock operation is the same. There is still a potential performance problem when the lock is unlocked. Until that point, each waiting processor is busily testing its own copy of the lock. However, the unlock operation is also a modification operation, so the processor performing the unlock must acquire exclusive ownership of that cache line. Each of the waiting processors will then try to get a read-only copy of that cache line to continue in their busy-wait loop. Since the lock is no longer locked, some number of them will then try the swap operation. Thus, at the time of the unlock operation, there may be a great deal of bus traffic, with the lock being read and modified by many processors, before one of them grabs the lock and the rest enter the busy-wait loop.

A more sophisticated lock uses a queue data structure. The queue keeps the processors in order of arrival, and allows each processor to busy-wait on a different cache line. The data structure uses an array of locks (one per process), a pointer to the last process to enter the queue, and a value to tell the next process the lock value for the last process:

Lock[NPROCS], LastProc, LockValue

Entering the queue requires entering a small critical section, since the lock data structure is being modified. This may seem to be a circular problem; however, a lock protecting a small critical section is probably not highly contested, and either a hardware or the previous software scheme can be used to protect it. The queue lock would be more appropriate for a larger critical section. The critical section to modify the queue lock data structure is itself quite small. The code to enter the queue is four assignments, followed by a busy-wait loop for the previous processor to release its lock:

(1)   local Previous, PrevLockValue

(2)   lock()
(3)   Previous = LastProc
(4)   PrevLockValue = LockValue
(5)   LastProc = myid
(6)   LockValue = Lock[myid]
(7)   unlock()
(8)   repeat
(9)   until Lock[Previous] != PrevLockValue

Releasing the lock means changing the value of Lock[myid]; a simple scheme is to increment it or take the exclusive OR with a nonzero value. The value of Lock[myid] must change, so that if this processor is the next one to enter the queue, it will see that the lock is unlocked.

11.1.6 Procedure Calls

A concurrent loop may contain a procedure call; in such a case, each of the parallel workers needs its own stack frame, so each invocation of the procedure can allocate its local variables on the stack frame of the worker. This is typically called a *cactus stack*, since each worker has its own stack, which is logically connected to the stack of the procedure containing the parallel construct. Since the procedure may be compiled without even knowing that it will be called in a parallel environment, it may contain its own parallel operations. If the system can handle nested parallel constructs, this will work fine. Otherwise, the code must test whether it is already executing in parallel, and, if so, execute sequential code. One option is to generate two versions of every procedure that contains parallel constructs—one with parallelism and one without—and to choose, either at compile time or run time, which version to call.

There may be data dependence relations between different invocations of a procedure being executed in parallel. If the procedure is compiled without the knowledge of the parallel enclosing construct, the data dependence relations must be satisfied by the caller, perhaps enclosing the procedure call in an ordered critical section.

11.1.7 Strength Reduction

Generating code for a concurrent loop prevents some common scalar optimizations, such as strength reduction. Strength reduction typically optimizes the calculation of array addresses. For instance, in the loop shown in Example 11.2, the code generated by an optimizing compiler might use a register to hold the address of each array element, A[I], B[I], C[I], and D[I] (the same pointer could be used for D[I] and D[I-1]). If the word size is four bytes, each pointer would be incremented by four each time around the loop, to point to the next array element.

In the self-scheduled parallel code, however, the compiler can't determine which iteration will be executed next by a particular worker, so it can't determine how much to increment each pointer. In this example, the offset of the element to be fetched is $4i$, which can be calculated with a shift operation, but in the general case an integer multiply may be required, and the advantages of strength reduction can be lost altogether. They can be recovered either by using prescheduling, where the offset for the next iteration can be computed from this iteration, or by using chunk scheduling, which recovers the benefits of strength reduction within each chunk.

11.2 Concurrency from Sequential Loops

One of the main aims of parallelizing compilers is to generate parallel code from sequential programs. Conceptually, this is easy; the iterations of a loop can be executed in parallel with no synchronization if the loop carries no dependence relations. In practice, there are a number of other considerations. Scalars assigned in a loop must be classified and removed, if possible, since any scalar assignment will result in a loop carried output dependence relation, at least. When there are loop carried dependence relations, the compiler has the option of trying to remove them, synchronizing to satisfy them, or using sequential code. Concerns about the granularity of parallelism must also be addressed.

11.2.1 Handling Scalars

Any scalar assigned in a loop will generate one or more loop carried data dependence relations. Many of these can be removed by simple means, such as substituting for induction variables, or *privatization*.

The same rules for scalar expansion are used for privatization; the difference is in implementation. Privatization and induction variable replacement will remove the bulk of the scalar dependence relations in the loop.

Example 11.4

Remove the loop carried data dependence relations in the following loop to generate parallel code:

```
(1)    J = N
(2)    for I = 1 to N do
(3)        T = B[I] + B[J]
(4)        A[I] = T + 1/T
(5)        J = J - 1
(6)    endfor
```

Solution

The two loop carried data dependence relations are due to the scalars T and J. As discussed in Chapter 9, scalar expansion can be used to remove the loop carried dependence relations for T, since there are no upward-exposed uses of T in the loop. A more efficient method is to privatize T, or make T into a private variable for each worker. Effective register allocation will assign the private T to a register, avoiding the memory accesses that scalar expansion would require. J can be recognized as an induction variable, and accesses to J (and I) can be replaced by functions of a basic loop induction variable starting at zero. The generated worker code for each iteration is:

```
executing iteration i
local_T = B[i+1] + B[N-i]
A[i+1] = local_T + 1/local_T
if i = N-1 then
    T = local_T
endif
```

Note the last value assignment for T, which may not be necessary if T is not used after the loop. The last value of J, if necessary, does not depend on anything computed in the loop, and so can be assigned by the master.

Reductions

Some scalar assignments can be recognized as reduction operations; reductions can usually be found using simple pattern recognition. A table of some reduction operations is shown in Figure 11.6. We have already discussed generating parallel code for reductions; the difference here is that converting a sequential reduction into a parallel reduction can change the order of the accumulation of the reduction. The original program would accumulate in a fixed order; the parallel code will accumulate partial sums and combine them in a different order. Due to the finite precision of computer number representation, the roundoff error of the parallel reduction may be different, producing a different answer. We will discuss managing roundoff error differences shortly.

sum	S = S + A[I]
product	T = T * B[I]
max (min)	M = max(M,A[I]) if A[I] > M then M = A[I] endif

max with index	if A[I] > M then
	    M = A[I]
	    IMAX = I
	endif

FIGURE 11.6 Examples of reduction operations.

A reduction can actually span more than one statement; we call this a *coupled reduction*. For instance, the two statements:

```
T = T + A[I]
T = T + B[I]
```

and the two statements

```
S = R + A[I]
R = S + B[I]
```

form coupled reductions. Note that the statements may be separated by other assignments in the loop. Coupled reductions can be computed as with a simple reduction, letting each processor accumulate a partial result.

Array Contraction

If an array is assigned and used in a loop with only loop independent dependence relations, and the array is not used after the loop, the array can be replaced by privatized scalars. This is essentially the inverse of scalar expansion, which we call *array contraction*, and can be particularly useful if loop fusion has removed the need to save all the elements of the array across two loops.

Example 11.5

Use array contraction in the following loop, assuming the arrays A and B are not used after the loop.

```
(1)    for I = 2 to N do
(2)        A[I] = D[I] + 1
(3)        B[I] = A[I] / 2
(4)        C[I] = B[I] + B[I-1]
(5)    endfor
```

Solution

Because the only dependence relations for array A are loop independent, and the array is not used after the loop, it can be contracted by using a scalar variable. Array B has both a loop independent and a loop carried dependence relation, so it cannot be contracted. The result is:

```
(1)    for I = 2 to N do
(2)        Atemp = D[I] + 1
(3)        B[I] = Atemp / 2
(4)        C[I] = B[I] + B[I-1]
(5)    endfor
```

If parallel code were generated for this loop, Atemp would be a private scalar.

11.2.2 Loop Carried Dependence Relations

For most (if not all) scalars assigned in a loop, the previous methods will satisfy the dependence relations. Several methods can be employed to eliminate or satisfy other dependence relations.

Synchronization

Other loop carried dependence relations must be satisfied by adding synchronization, such as an ordered critical section, to the parallel code. The critical section serializes the execution of part of the loop, reducing the potential parallelism. If one-fourth of the code in the loop is in a critical section, then the maximum parallel speedup is four. Careful scheduling of the code in the loop can reduce the size of the critical section. In Example 11.2, the critical section was reduced to three instructions: a load, an add, and a store.

11.2 ▪ Concurrency from Sequential Loops

Since there is often some amount of overhead with synchronization, reducing the amount of synchronization can be important, perhaps even at the expense of reducing the amount of parallelism. To be specific, it may be more effective to have one larger critical section than several smaller ones. The tradeoffs are difficult to generalize, since the relative costs of computation and synchronization differ on each system.

Example 11.6

Generate parallel code for the following loop, using synchronization to satisfy loop carried dependence relations:

```
(1)     for I = 2 to N do
(2)         A = B[I] * 2
(3)         C[I] = C[I+1]*(A+1) + C[I]*D
(4)     endfor
```

Solution

Assume that the value of A is not needed after the loop, so the last value assignment can be left out. There is a loop carried anti-dependence relation from the fetch of C[I+1] to the store of C[I]. This can be satisfied by adding synchronization between the fetch and the store; using await and advance, this looks like:

```
fetch B[I] -> r1
r1 + r1 -> r2    /* r2 holds value of A */
fetch C[I] -> r3
r3 + r4 -> r5    /* assume r4 holds loop invariant value of D */
r2 + 1 -> r2     /* A+1 */
fetch C[I+1] -> r6
await(I-1)
advance
r6*r5 -> r7
r7 + r5 -> r8
store r8 -> C[I]
```

Note that since the dependence was lexically forward, the ordered critical section itself was empty.

Alignment

If there are no dependence cycles, and all the loop carried dependence relations have small, constant dependence distance, the compiler may be able to *align* the loop, changing all loop carried dependence relations into loop independent ones. Alignment here is the same as is used for loop fusion; it is as if we used loop fission to split the loop into individual statements, then used loop fusion with alignment to reconstruct it without loop carried dependence relations. We construct an *alignment graph* for the loop from the dependence graph; the alignment graph has one node per statement and two edges per data dependence edge. One edge corresponds to the dependence edge and is annotated with the dependence distance, and the other is the inverse dependence edge, annotated with the negative dependence distance. If all cycles in the alignment graph have an accumulated distance of zero, then alignment can remove all loop carried dependence relations; the compiler needs only to check the simple cycles. If not, then the compiler may have to choose which dependence relations to synchronize and which to align.

Example 11.7

Build the alignment graph for the following loop and determine whether alignment can remove the loop carried dependence relations.

(1)   for I = 2 to N do
(2)   A[I] = B[I] + C[I]
(3)   D[I] = A[I-1] * 2
(4)   E[I] = A[I-1] + D[I+1]
(5)   endfor

Solution

The alignment graph is shown in Figure 11.7; the three downward edges are dependence edges, and the three upward edges are their inverses. There are two simple cycles with nonzero accumulated distance: 2 → 3 → 4 → 2 and its inverse. Thus, alignment cannot remove all the loop carried dependence relations. However, choosing one dependence relation to synchronize—say, the 3 → 4 edge—removes that edge and its inverse from the alignment graph. The resulting graph is satisfiable, so alignment can remove two of the loop carried dependence relations, and synchronization can be used to satisfy the dependence for D:

(1)   for I = 1 to N do
(2)   if I > 1 then A[I] = B[I] + C[I]
(3)   if I < N then D[I+1] = A[I] * 2
(4)   if I < N then E[I+1] = A[I] + D[I+2]
(5)   endfor

In this example, the remaining dependence relation is an anti-dependence from D[I+2] to D[I+1]. Nothing in the program prevents the compiler from moving the fetch of D[I+2] up in the loop, or even moving that whole statement up in the loop, turning the lexically backward dependence into a lexically forward one, getting more parallelism.

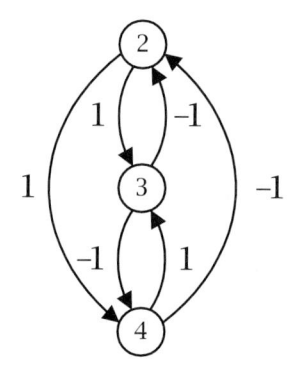

FIGURE 11.7 Alignment graph.

Recurrences

Really aggressive compilers might generate parallel code for *linear recurrence relations*. A first-order linear recurrence looks like:

```
for I = 2 to N do
    X[I] = X[I-1]*A[I] + C[I]
endfor
```

It is *first-order* because the computation of each element X[I] depends only on the value computed one iteration back, in this case X[I-1]; a *second-order* recurrence would use X[I-1] and X[I-2] to compute X[I]. It is a linear recurrence because the expression used to compute X[I] is a linear combination of the recurrent terms; that is, the recurrence is of the form $x_i = \sum_{k=1}^{m} a_{i,k} x_k + c_i$, where m is the order of the recurrence, the $a_{i,k}$ values are called the recurrence *coefficients*, and c_i is the constant term. In this example, all the terms of the recurrence are computed. A *remote-term* recurrence would compute only the last value, as in:

```
for I = 2 to N do
    X = X*A[I] + C[I]
endfor
```

Another interesting form is when the coefficient term is constant (where A is a scalar).

A first-order linear recurrence written simply as $x_i = a_i x_{i-1} + c_i$. Substituting for x_{i-1} in this, we can derive x_i as a function of x_{i-2}, making it independent of x_{i-1}; we can even repeat the substitution, as follows:

$$x_i = a_i x_{i-1} + c_i$$

$$x_i = a_i(a_{i-1} x_{i-2} + c_{i-1}) + c_i$$

$$x_i = (a_i a_{i-1})x_{i-2} + (a_i c_{i-1} + c_i)$$
$$x_i = (a_i a_{i-1})((a_{i-2} a_{i-3})x_{i-4} + (c_{i-3} + c_{i-2})) + (a_i c_{i-1} + c_i)$$
$$x_i = (a_i a_{i-1} a_{i-2} a_{i-3})x_{i-4} + a_i a_{i-1}(a_{i-2} c_{i-3} + c_{i-2}) + (a_i c_{i-1} + c_i)$$

In this way, the recurrence with a dependence distance of one can be changed into a recurrence with any positive distance. The substitution process shown here changes the order of the arithmetic computations, which may change the roundoff error characteristics. Higher order linear recurrences can be substituted like this also by casting the recurrence in matrix algebra.

Another method to parallelize recurrences is to preschedule the iterations onto the workers using block scheduling. Suppose the block size is B, and worker p (out of P total workers) computes iterations $lo(p)$ to $hi(p)$; the worker can find each x_i, $lo(p) \le i \le hi(p)$, as a function of $x_{lo(p)-1}$ as follows:

$$\begin{aligned} b_{lo(p)} &= a_{lo(p)} \\ d_{lo(p)} &= c_{lo(p)} \\ b_i &= b_i b_{i-1} \quad lo(p) < i \le hi(p) \\ d_i &= b_i d_{i-1} + d_i \quad lo(p) < i \le hi(p) \end{aligned}$$

The generated code would have each of the workers compute the local coefficients in parallel, followed by a barrier. Then a smaller recurrence system would be solved, involving the P elements $x_{hi(0)}, x_{hi(1)}, x_{hi(2)}, \ldots x_{hi(P)}$:

$$x_{hi(0)} = b_{hi(0)} x_0 + d_{hi(0)}$$
$$x_{hi(p)} = b_{hi(p)} x_{hi(p-1)} + d_{hi(p)}$$

This recurrence is much smaller than the original system, and can perhaps be solved sequentially. After this computation, the final solutions can be found in parallel as:

$$x_i = b_i x_{lo(p)-1} + d_i, \quad lo(p) \le i \le hi(p)$$

Fission

For lexically forward dependence relations that cannot be removed by other means, splitting the loop across the dependence relation can make two loops, each of which can be executed in parallel with no synchronization. Note that if there are no lexically backward dependence relations, there can be no dependence cycles, so loop fission will always succeed. Fission may be complicated by scalar privatization, however. If a scalar is assigned and used in only one of the loops after fission, it can still be privatized; if the value assigned in one loop is needed in the other, the compiler will have to resort to scalar expansion.

Strip-Mining

Suppose the dependence distance is a known constant $d > 1$, and the loop is strip-mined to a strip size of $s \le d$. If d is divisible by s, the dependence relation is changed to have distance $(d \operatorname{div} s, 0)$; otherwise, it generates two relations with distance (d div s, d mod s) and (d div $s + 1, (d$ mod $s) - s$). In either case, because $s \leq d$, the generated dependence relations are carried by the strip loop. If that is the only loop carried dependence relation, the element loop can be executed in parallel. If there are several loop carried dependence relations with distance greater than one, strip-mining to a strip size equal to the minimum dependence distance will allow the element loop to execute in parallel.

Example 11.8

Show how strip-mining can be used to generate parallel code from the following loop:

```
(1)   for I = 1 to N do
(2)       A[I+8] = A[I] + B[I]
(3)       B[I+5] = C[I] + 1
(4)   endfor
```

Solution

There are two flow dependence relations, with distance 8 (for A) and 5 (for B). Strip-mining to a strip size of 5 generates the following code:

```
(1)   for IS = 1 to N by 5 do
(1)       for I = IS to min(N,IS+4) do
(2)           A[I+8] = A[I] + B[I]
(3)           B[I+5] = C[I] + 1
(4)       endfor
(4)   endfor
```

The dependence relations after strip-mining have distance vectors $(1, 3)$ and $(2, -2)$, for A, and $(1, 0)$, for B. Since all the dependence relations are carried by the strip loop, the element loop can execute in parallel.

Striping

Strip-mining allows some parallel execution, but the overhead of starting the workers and the barrier synchronization may overwhelm the performance improvement due to parallelism. If the dependence distance in the element loop is zero, the compiler can essentially interchange the element and strip loops, and still run the element loop in parallel; the result is just loop striping. This can happen when there is a single loop carried dependence relation in a loop, for instance, or when the greatest common divisor of all the dependence relations is a large integer.

When this technique is used for recurrence relations, as in Example 11.9, it is sometimes called *cycle shrinking*, since the cycle distance (the dependence distance around the dependence cycle) gets smaller. In this case, the original dependence distances were 6 and 9; after striping the loop, the distance in the inner loop is reduced to 2 and 3. When a recurrence relation has a small dependence distance, the substitution technique discussed earlier may be used to increase the dependence distance before applying cycle shrinking.

Example 11.9

Compare strip-mining with striping to parallelize the following loop:

(1)   for I = L to N do
(2)   A[I] = 2*(A[I-9] - A[I-6])/3
(3)   endfor

Solution
There are two dependence relations, with distances 9 and 6. To parallelize with strip-mining, we choose a strip size equal to the minimum distance, which allows parallel execution of the inner loop:

(1)   for IS = L to N by 6 do
(1)   for I = IS to min(N,IS+5) do
(2)   A[I] = 2*(A[I-9] - A[I-6])/3
(3)   endfor
(3)   endfor

To parallelize with striping, we find the gcd of the distances, which in this case is 3; after striping, the outer loop can be executed in parallel:

(1)   for IS = L to L+2 do
(1)   for I = IS to N by 3 do
(2)   A[I] = 2*(A[I-9] - A[I-6])/3
(3)   endfor
(3)   endfor

Strip-mining allows more parallelism (a factor of 6 instead of 3), but striping has much less scheduling overhead.

Multiple Version Loops

There can be cases where the trip count of a loop may be very small at run-time. Even though parallel code can be generated for the loop, it may not be worth the effort for many current systems. In cases where the trip count cannot be computed at compile time, the compiler may generate two versions of the loop—one sequential and one parallel—along with code to choose between them depending on the actual run-time trip count.

While Loops

To execute iterations of `while` loops (noncountable loops) concurrently, the execution strategy cannot schedule more than one iteration at a time, since it can't determine whether more than one iteration will actually be executed. The parallel code to schedule the next iteration must include the computation of the `while` condition, along with any other code in the loop that affects that condition. In terms of dependence relations, any code in the loop upon which the `while` condition directly or indirectly depends must be computed in the scheduling critical section. This may be most or all of the body of the loop, so parallel execution may not achieve much speedup. Some `while` loop structures can be recognized as countable loops, and should be treated as such.

11.3 Concurrency from Parallel Loops

In Chapter 2 we discussed several styles of parallel loops. In fact, generating parallel code from a parallel loop can be as difficult as from a sequential loop. Parallel loops can still carry dependence relations and have dependence cycles. For instance, a `dopar` loop can carry only anti-dependence relations; thus there can be no real dependence cycles, since anti-dependence relations order fetches before definitions, as does the operation ordering within assignments. However, the dependence relation still needs to be preserved, using synchronization, alignment, or some other means. When compiling sequential loops, we know at least one way to generate code for the loop—namely, the sequential code. For a `dopar`, it is not so simple; indeed, there may be no simple sequential code for the loop. One way to compile a `dopar` is to fetch all the values that are sources of loop carried anti-dependence relations ahead of a barrier, and save the values in temporary locations. The fetches themselves can be done in a parallel loop, and the remainder of the `dopar` can execute in parallel after the barrier, using the values from the temporary locations. Thus the anti-dependence relations will be satisfied by the barrier.

Example 11.10

Explain how to generate parallel code for the following loop:

```
(1)    dopar I = 2:N-1
(2)        A[I] = (A[I-1] + A[I+1])/2
(3)    enddopar
```

Solution
The `dopar` resolves the data access conflicts as anti-dependences with dependence distance (1) and (−1). The anti-dependences can be satisfied by performing fetches ahead of a barrier; essentially, the program is transformed as follows:

```
        allocate T1[2:N-1], T2[2:N-1]
(1)     doall I = 2:N-1
(2)         T1[I] = A[I-1]
(2)         T2[I] = A[I+1]
(3)     enddoall
(1)     doall I = 2:N-1
(2)         A[I] = (T1[I-1] + T2[I+1])/2
(3)     enddoall
```

assuming an implicit barrier synchronization at the end of any parallel loop; we use the notation `doall` to signify that neither loop has any loop carried dependence relations after the transformation.

11.3.1 Other Parallel Loops

Generating parallel code from `forall` loops can be done the same way as generating sequential code. A compiler can generate one parallel loop that computes the right hand side expression into a temporary, and a second, parallel loop to assign those values to the left-hand side variable. A barrier between those two loops, and between the code generated for two statements in a `forall`, will satisfy any dependence relations. If there are no loop carried dependence relations, this can be optimized, again similar to the way it was handled in Chapter 9.

Generating concurrency from single assignment code (e.g., a `dosingle`) may be the most challenging of all. All the loop carried dependence relations in a `dosingle` loop are flow dependence relations; unlike `dopar` or `forall` loops, `dosingle` loops can carry dependence cycles, and unlike sequential loops, the distance can be positive or negative. In fact, single assignment programs can be written for which there is no legal execution ordering, such as replacing the `dopar` by a `dosingle` in Example 11.10.

All of the transformations and optimizations already discussed apply for generating concurrent code from parallel loops as well as from sequential loops. The major difference is that the underlying processor executing the final program is itself a sequential processor; all dependence relations will have to be satisfied either by the execution ordering of sequential code or by synchronization between processors.

11.4 Nested Loops

When converting nested loops into parallel code, the compiler has more freedom in choosing what code to generate. A number of options arise; the compiler can try to make an inner loop parallel, for smaller task granularity and less load imbalance between the workers. Alternatively, it can try to make an outer loop parallel, so as to increase the granularity of the parallel tasks and amortize the scheduling overhead. The compiler can also use other transformations to otherwise change the characteristics of the loop.

11.4.1 Synchronization

When a nested loop carries no dependence relations, it can be executed in parallel with no synchronization except for scheduling. Otherwise, executing the loop in parallel requires the compiler to use synchronization to satisfy the dependence relations.

Example 11.11

Show the worker code to execute the following outer loop in parallel:

(1)   for I = 1 to N do
(2)   for J = 1 to M do
(3)   A[I,J] = 0.25*(A[I-1,J] + A[I,J-1] + A[I,J+1] + A[I+1,J])
(4)   endfor
(5)   endfor

Solution

There are four dependence relations, shown in the table below:

type	source	target	distance
flow	A[I,J]	A[I-1,J]	(1,0)
flow	A[I,J]	A[I,J-1]	(0,1)
anti	A[I+1,J]	A[I,J]	(1,0)
anti	A[I,J+1]	A[I,J]	(0,1)

The two inner loop dependences (with distance (0, 1)) will not be affected by parallel execution of the outer loop; the dependence will be satisfied by executing the J loop sequentially on a single processor. The two outer loop dependences need synchronization. For this example we use two bit-matrices for synchronization, named Sync1 and Sync2, with $N \times M$ bits each (one for each iteration of the nested loop). The bit matrices are initialized to zero by the master (or perhaps by another parallel loop). The generated code for the loop body uses Sync1 to ensure that the processor executing iteration *I* does not fetch A[I-1,J] until the store of that value has been completed by the processor executing iteration $I-1$, and uses Sync2 to ensure that the processor executing iteration I does not complete the store of A[I,J] until the old value is fetched by the processor executing iteration $I-1$:

```
for J = 1 to M do
    if I > 1 then wait Sync1[I-1,J] endif
    fetch A[I-1,J] -> r1
    fetch A[I,J-1] -> r2
    fetch A[I,J+1] -> r3
    fetch A[I+1,J] -> r4
    set Sync2[I,J]
    add r1+r2 -> r1
    add r1+r3 -> r1
    add r1+r4 -> r1
    mpy r1*0.25 -> r1
    if I > 1 then wait Sync2[I-1,J] endif
    store r3 -> A[I,J]
    set Sync1[I,J]
endfor
```

Eliminating Synchronization

In this example, Sync1 and Sync2 will synchronize between exactly the same iterations. Since the set for Sync1 follows the set for Sync2, and the wait for Sync1 precedes that for Sync2, we can show that the compiler can safely eliminate the Sync2 synchronization. We use $a \Rightarrow b$ to mean "a must precede b," either because a executes before b on the same processor, or because there is a synchronization to insure that a will precede b. Note that $\Rightarrow$ is transitive. Let $S_1[I,J]$ and $S_2[I,J]$ be the execution of the set operations for iteration $[I,J]$, and $W_1[I,J]$ and $W_2[I,J]$ be the corresponding wait operations. Then $S_2[I,J] \Rightarrow S_1[I,J]$ because of the execution order in a single iteration, $S_1[I,J] \Rightarrow W_1[I+1,J]$ due to synchronization, and $W_1[I+1,J] \Rightarrow W_2[I+1,J]$, again due to execution order. This implies $S_2[I,J] \Rightarrow W_2[I+1,J]$, without the synchronization.

The Sync1 synchronization in this example has the wait preceding the set operation; this is much like a critical section, except that several iterations can be in the critical section of code at one time. For instance, iterations [1,1] and [2,1] cannot be in the critical section simultaneously, since [2,1] depends on [1,1]; however, [1,2] and [2,1] can execute the critical section at the same time. In such a case, where the dependence is lexically backward and the distance is known, the synchronization bit-matrix can be replaced with a vector of synchronization words using `await` and `advance` operations, which might be faster to allocate and initialize:

```
for J = 1 to M do
    if I > 1 then await Sync[J],I-1 endif
    fetch A[I-1,J] -> r1
    fetch A[I,J-1] -> r2
    fetch A[I,J+1] -> r3
    fetch A[I+1,J] -> r4
    add r1+r2 -> r1
    add r1+r3 -> r1
    add r1+r4 -> r1
    mpy r1*0.25 -> r1
    store r3 -> A[I,J]
    advance Sync[J],I
endfor
```

11.4.2 Transformations

Loop interchanging can be used to move the parallel loop to an inner or outer loop nest level. If all the dependence relations have distance zero for this loop, interchanging can move the loop to any nest level, if it is tightly nested and the loop limits allow it. Interchanging can also change the parallel loop; moving a loop with nonzero distance for all dependences to the outer nest level will make that loop carry all the dependence relations. Any of the inner loop(s) can then execute in parallel.

Example 11.12

Use loop interchanging to find parallelism in the following loop:

```
(1)  for I = 2 to N do
(2)      for J = 2 to M do
(3)          A[I,J] = (A[I-1,J-1] + A[I,J-1])/2
(4)      endfor
(5)  endfor
```

Solution

The two dependence relations have distance vectors $(1,1)$ and $(0,1)$; since both loops carry a dependence relation, executing either loop in parallel will require synchronization. Interchanging the loops will make the J loop carry both dependence relations, allowing parallel execution of I.

Linear Transformations

Loop interchanging is just one example of a linear transformation; the compiler can use other linear transformations to improve the parallelism in the loop. If the loop can be transformed such that the outer loop carries all the dependence relations, any of the inner loops can execute in parallel with synchronization. Theoretically, any loop can be so transformed; in practice, unknown dependence distances may make the linear transformation essentially equivalent to sequentializing the loop. Finding an appropriate linear transformation is equivalent to solving an integer programming problem. The goal is to find a linear or unimodular transformation matrix **T** such that all the dependence vectors $\mathbf{d}_1, \mathbf{d}_2, \ldots$, are carried by the outer loop. This means that we want $\mathbf{T}_{[1]}\mathbf{d}_k > 0$ for all dependence vectors $\mathbf{d}_k$, where $\mathbf{T}_{[1]}$ is the first row of **T**; such a matrix generally is not unique. To optimize the execution time we also want to minimize the number of iterations of the outer loop, since this will determine the execution time. If the loop limits are rectangular, the trip count of the outer transformed loop can be easily computed from **T** and the trip counts of the original loop. Let $\mathbf{c} = (c_1, c_2, \ldots)^T$ be a vector where $c_i + 1$ is the trip count of the original loop at nest level i. The trip count of the transformed outer loop will be $\mathbf{T}_{[1]}\mathbf{c} + 1$. Minimizing this objective function should reduce the execution time of the transformed loop, if the inner loops are executed in parallel.

Index Set Partitioning

In a nested loop where both loops carry dependence relations, a mechanism similar to striping or cycle shrinking can be used to divide the index set of the nested loop into independent partitions.

We first form the dependence matrix **D** where each column is a dependence distance vector; if **D** has more rows than columns, it can be augmented with additional zero columns until it is square. We find the Hermite normal form of **D** to be **H** = **DU** for some unimodular matrix **U**. A row with a zero diagonal element is interchanged to the bottom of **H**; this essentially finds a permutation of the rows of **H** such that the first k rows have positive diagonal elements. The diagonal elements of **H** tell how many independent partitions there are of the iteration space. Loop j has h_{jj} independent partitions if $h_{jj} > 0$; if $h_{jj} = 0$, the iterations of loop j can be executed completely independently.

Note that while the HNF of a matrix is unique, allowing row reordering to move zero diagonals essentially finds the HNF of a different matrix, **D'**, which is **D** with the rows reordered, and **D'** is not necessarily unique.

To generate parallel code, the compiler must generate a sequence of parallel loops to iterate through the independent partitions. Then the compiler must generate a sequence of sequential loops that visit the iterations in each partition. Here we assume the loop increments have been normalized to one. The first step is simple; for each diagonal element $h_{jj} > 0$, generate the parallel loop:

```
doall P_j = 0 to h_jj - 1
```

11.4 ▪ Nested Loops

If $h_{jj} = 1$, this could be replaced by the assignment $P_j=0$. For each diagonal element $h_{jj} = 0$, generate the parallel loop:

```
doall P_j = 0 to N_j - 1
```

where N_j is the trip count for the jth loop; if the limits for the jth loop depend on the outer loop indices, it may not be feasible to generate this parallel loop. The loops $P_1\ldots P_n$ iterate through the independent partitions. To visit the iterations in each partition we must find a starting point for each partition in the iteration space of the loop. The outermost serial loop satisfies the dependence relation $I_1 = P_1 + h_{11}q_1$, for some value of q_1. The smallest value q_1 satisfying this, given a lower limit of LO_1, is $q_1 = (LO_1 - P_1)/h_11$. The loop can be computed as:

```
for q₁ = ⌈ (LO₁ - P₁)/h₁₁⌉ to
         ⌊ (HI₁ - P₁)/h₁₁⌋ do
   I₁ = P₁+h₁₁*q₁
endfor
```

The jth loop must satisfy the dependence relation $I_j = P_j + \sum_{k=1}^{j-1} h_{jk}q_k + h_{jj}q_j$, and must also satisfy the loop limits. We find the limits for q_j as follows:

$$\lceil (LO_j - P_j - \sum_{k=1}^{j-1} h_{jk}q_k)/h_{jj} \rceil \leq q_j \leq \lfloor (HI_j - P_j - \sum_{k=1}^{j-1} h_{jk}q_k)/h_{jj} \rfloor$$

Example 11.13
Partition the following loops to uncover parallelism:

```
(1)   for I = 0 to N-1 do
(2)      for J = 3 to M do
(3)         A[I,J] = (A[I-4,J+1]*A[I+4,J+2])/2
(4)      endfor
(5)   endfor
```

Solution
There are two data dependence relations, and the resulting dependence matrix is:

$$\mathbf{D} = \begin{pmatrix} 4 & 4 \\ -1 & 2 \end{pmatrix}$$

The HNF of this matrix is

$$\mathbf{H} = \begin{pmatrix} 4 & 0 \\ -1 & 3 \end{pmatrix}$$

Thus, there are $4 \times 3 = 12$ independent partitions. The generated code is:

```
(1)    doall P₁ = 0 to 3
(2)       doall P₂ = 0 to 2
(1)          for q₁ = ⌈-P₁/4⌉ to ⌊(N - 1 - P₁)/4 do
(1)             I = P₁ + 4*q₁
(2)             for q₂ = ⌈(3 - P₂ + q₁)/3⌉ to ⌊(M - P₂ + q₁)/3 do
(2)                J = P₂ + 3*q₂
(3)                A[I,J] = (A[I-4,J+1]*A[I+4,J+2])/2
(4)             endfor
(5)          endfor
(4)       enddoall
(5)    enddoall
```

11.4.3 Tiling

Just as chunking reduces scheduling frequency for single parallel loops, iteration space tiling can be used for nested parallel loops. A useful paradigm is to schedule each tile as an atomic execution unit. That is, each tile, once initiated, will execute to completion without further synchronization. That means that all dependence relations must be satisfied for the all iterations in the tile before it is initiated. Such a scheme allows each processor to benefit from the advantages of tiling for data locality, and reduces the frequency of scheduling and synchronization. However, as with chunking, it can suffer from load imbalance.

To schedule tiles as atomic units, the loops must be transformed such that there are no dependence cycles between tiles. This can be done if the loops are transformed so there are no negative dependence distance entries for loops to be tiled, meaning the loops are fully permutable.

11.4.4 Optimizing Performance

There are other factors affecting performance besides parallelism; in particular, optimizing for performance of the memory system can be quite important. Modeling the performance of a loop on a multiprocessor is more complex than simply computing the number of iterations of the sequential loops.

For instance, optimizing the memory stride can improve performance. If the parallel loop contains a sequential inner loop that is the stride-1 index for all the arrays, then consecutive iterations of the inner loop will refer to data on the same cache line. This reduces the memory bandwidth required by each processor. On the other hand, if the parallel loop is the stride-1 index, different processors may compete to write to the same cache line; this is called *interprocessor interference*, and it can be quite costly. It can be alleviated somewhat by chunk scheduling, so at least some consecutive iterations are scheduled on the same processor.

Another tradeoff is adding synchronization versus applying transformations to remove the need for synchronization. The transformations have their own overhead; depending on the cost of the synchronization and the number of processors expected to be available to participate, synchronization may be effective. With many processors, however, any sequential part of a parallel loop will hurt performance.

The granularity of the parallel tasks can also affect performance. This gets back to the issue of scheduling policies, prescheduling, self-scheduling, and chunk scheduling. The general strategy of the linear transformation approach is to have a single sequential loop with fully parallel inner loops. It may be more efficient to have a single parallel outer loop, containing nested sequential inner loops. This amortizes the scheduling overhead, since a single iteration of the parallel loop will contain a great deal of work. If the inner loop limits depend on the parallel loop index, then self-scheduling may be necessary to balance the load among the workers, since each iteration of the parallel loop will have a different amount of work.

11.5 Roundoff Error

Except for reassociation, parallel code should produce the same answers as sequential code. Reassociation might occur in an assignment to reduce the size of a critical section. For instance, in the following loop, sequential code might left-associate the expression; parallel code might right-associate it to remove one addition from the critical section.

```
for I = 2 to N do
    A[I] = A[I-1]+B[I]+C[I]
endfor
```

As mentioned in Chapter 2, reassociation of unparenthesized expressions is often allowed by language standards. The different expressions, while computationally and mathematically equivalent, may compute slightly different results due to roundoff error differences. When compiling for parallelism, there may be tradeoffs between preserving the same roundoff errors and increasing parallelism, and the compiler might make different choices than it would for a sequential machine.

More crucial is the situation with reduction operations. Computing a summation in parallel, for instance, may give a different result than sequential code because the summation is accumulated in a different order, so the roundoff error is accumulated slightly differently. In fact, if the loop is self-scheduled, the program may give a different result each time it is executed. This is not always true; some reductions, such as finding the maximum element of a vector, are not subject to roundoff error.

When using advanced techniques to solve recurrence relations, the roundoff error differences can become quite extreme. In particular, each answer may involve more arithmetic operations, and hence more opportunities for roundoff error to accumulate, than are in the original program.

In some instances, the difference in roundoff error may be enough to change the answer significantly. Numerical analysts would point out that such a program may be unstable, and the algorithm should be replaced. Nonetheless, real users sometimes want more predictability in the parallel code; in particular, they often want the roundoff error in the parallel code to be the same as in the sequential code. All parallelizing compilers include a compiler switch to disable all types of reassociation. When the switch is set, reductions must be accumulated sequentially, either by running the loop sequentially or enclosing it in an ordered critical section.

11.6 Exceptions and Debuggers

When an exception is raised in a sequential program, the program is halted and a message is displayed, usually giving the nature of the error and its location in the program. Interactive debuggers may be able to relate the location to the source line and allow other actions by the programmer, such as displaying the values of variables.

In a parallel program, however, halting a running program may require the worker that raises the exception to halt the rest of the workers. Since it takes some time to return control to the program from the operating system after the exception is raised, the other workers may have advanced quite a bit before they can be halted. They may have even raised an exception or two of their own. Displaying the state of the system in a coherent manner is a difficult task, at best.

Debugging optimized code is difficult enough; debugging a program running in parallel is even more difficult. In particular, when the parallel code is generated from a sequential loop, the behavior of the program does not look much like the source program. Iterations do not necessarily execute in order; some variables (induction variables) may be eliminated, while others (privatized scalars) may be replicated. As with any optimized code, the compiler can often inform the debugger about what values are available, and what iterations of what loops are executing at what time. However, presenting this in a clear and useful manner to a user is not simple.

11.7 In the Pit

Scheduling policies may affect the decision to use parallelism. Many multiprocessor operating systems schedule parallel tasks in equal competition with any other process on the system. If there are 10 sequential programs executing on a system with four processors, a fair scheduling policy will give each program 10 percent of the available cycles, or 40 percent of a single processor. However, if one of the programs is a parallel program with 10 tasks, the operating system will competitively these 10 tasks against the nine other programs. The parallel program will get more than half of the available processor cycles, at the expense of the other programs. In some environments, the improved turnaround time in a multiprogrammed environment is an added incentive to use parallelism.

Some systems use extra tags attached to memory words to implement data synchronization. This can be as simple as a full-empty bit, such as in the Denelcor HEP and Monsoon, or as complex as a key word for every data word. Shared data fetches and stores would include extra semantics to test and/or modify the tags, such as setting a word full when stored, or testing the key to see if it had reached a certain value. Data synchronization is very flexible, but is costly in terms of space, since the synchronization bits are allocated to each memory word. The initialization cost is also very high.

Roundoff error differences for reduction operations can sometimes produce surprising results. In one example, the parallel code generated a negative result where the original sequential code generated a positive result. Further inspection found that the result was on the order of 10^{-15}, meaning that the real answer was essentially zero, and the computed answer was nothing but the accumulated roundoff error. Nonetheless, testing the compiler by comparing the two outputs generated a great deal of concern for the compiler writers.

The vendor of one parallel computer system found that generating parallel code for sequential loops, even if the entire loop body had to be enclosed in a single ordered critical section, was still faster than the sequential code, since the loop branch and index calculations could still be overlapped between parallel processors. Of course, the parallel code consumed more resources than the sequential code.

The switch to control reassociation in a parallelizing compiler is sometimes erroneously called a *roundoff switch*; some compilers even allow the user to set the switch `-roundoff=0`, implying that roundoff error will be removed. Of course, the compiler cannot eliminate roundoff error; it can only make the roundoff error match the error of sequential execution.

11.8 Further Reading

Early work on parallelizing compilers is described by Padua et al. (1980). Banerjee (1993, 1994) covers many aspects on parallelization and loop restructuring in a linear algebra framework. See Polychronopoulos (1988b) for a number of parallelization techniques.

One of the first tapering scheduling methods was guided self-scheduling, described by Polychronopoulos and Kuck (1987). The factoring scheduling method is discussed by Hummel et al. (1992), who show it to be experimentally better than simple chunk scheduling or guided self-scheduling; if the coefficient of variance of the execution time for the iterations is known, factoring can be modified to compute a more optimal batch size. Tzen and Ni (1993) describe trapezoidal scheduling, a simpler scheduling algorithm that gets much of the benefit of other tapering schemes, but with a cheaper tapering method.

The cycle-shrinking optimization is due to Polychronopoulos (1988a); he also describes a scheme to strip-mine a loop using dynamically chosen strip sizes such that the iterations in each strip are data independent, allowing the element loop to be executed in parallel.

Several schemes have been proposed to partition iterations so that each partition is independent of the others and can be executed in parallel. Peir and Cytron (1989) show how to partition the loop based on unimodular transformations of the dependence matrix. D'Hollander (1992) uses unimodular transformations on the dependence distance matrix to reduce it to diagonal or triangular form; applying the same transformations to the iteration space relabels the iterations such that independent partitions can be found easily.

Several schemes try to avoid the "one transformation at a time" paradigm. Wolf and Lam (1991a) use unimodular transformations to convert the loop to a fully permutable form, then find coarse-grain (outer loop) or fine-grain (inner loop) parallelism; their method includes tiling for locality.

Hill and Larus (1990) give a short introduction to the problems of caches in multiprocessor systems. Jalby and Meier (1986) first discussed compiling nested loops into tiles for locality in multiprocessor caches.

Hatcher and Quinn (1991) describe generation of parallel code from Dataparallel C, a SIMD-parallel language for a variety of parallel architectures.

Bik and Wijshoff (1993) describe methods to compile operations on sparse matrices, including taking advantage of the sparsity to eliminate unnecessary synchronization.

EXERCISES

11.1 Modify the master code shown in Figure 11.3 to assign the prescheduled iterations in such a fashion that each of the P workers gets an equal number of consecutive iterations, rather than every Pth iteration.

11.2 Modify the worker code in Figure 11.4 to use chunk scheduling, where the chunk size is a parameter of the procedure.

11.3 Modify the sample worker code in Example 11.11 to reduce the size of the code contained in the critical section. This requires reassociation of the addition; comment on the effects on roundoff error.

11.4 Which of the two loops below can be executed in parallel? How can outer-loop parallelism be obtained?

```
(1)     for I = 2 to N-1 do
(2)         for J = 2 to I+1 do
(3)             A[I,J] = B[I,J] + 1
(4)             C[I,J] = A[I-1,J]/2
```

	(5)	endfor
	(6)	endfor

11.5 Use loop fission to find nested loop parallelism in the loop from the previous exercise.

11.6 Use alignment to minimize synchronization for parallel execution of the I loop in the loop from the previous exercise.

11.7 In the following loop, use strip-mining and partitioning to find parallelism.

	(1)	for I = L to N do
	(2)	A[I] = 2*(A[I-9] + A[I+6])/3
	(3)	endfor

11.8 In the previous exercise, which form of the loop has a higher degree of parallelism, the inner loop parallelism of strip-mining or the outer loop parallelism of partitioning? Which has fewer fork and join operations?

11.9 Find the independent partitions for loops with the following dependence matrices:

(a) $\begin{pmatrix} 1 & 2 & 0 \\ -2 & 4 & 4 \end{pmatrix}$

(b) $\begin{pmatrix} 1 & 2 & 0 \\ -2 & 4 & 4 \\ 4 & -1 & 2 \end{pmatrix}$

(c) $\begin{pmatrix} 1 & 2 \\ -2 & 4 \\ 4 & -1 \end{pmatrix}$

12 VECTOR ANALYSIS

> *Compiling for vector machines is the most mature of the parallel compiler technologies. We focus on vector register machines, including generation of vector code and discovery of vector-style parallelism from sequential loops.*

Automatic discovery of vector operations, or *vectorization*, from sequential loops was one of the earliest developments in parallel compilers. Here we present simple methods to discover vector parallelism and ways to optimize for modern vector machines. As before, we start by reviewing the execution model for a vector processor. Current vector processors use vector registers, much as scalar processors have scalar registers. Proper use of the vector registers is important for highest performance. We also review briefly issues for multiprocessor vector machines.

12.1 Vector Code

Vector instructions have two vector operands, or one vector and one scalar operand, and produce a vector result. A vector is usually defined by the starting position, vector length (the number of elements in the vector), and stride between vector elements. Each vector instruction must have some way to specify all three elements of the vector operands and result. Using vector registers simplifies this; the starting position of a vector register is its first element, specified simply by giving the vector register number. The stride of a vector register operand is always one, and does not need to be specified. The vector length is typically stored in a special register, often called VL; the same vector length is used for all vector instructions until the VL register is reset. A vector instruction with a vector length of zero is a no-op.

Even with vector registers, some operands must be loaded from and stored in memory. A vector operand in memory is specified by giving the starting position and stride in scalar registers; if the stride is a small constant, it may be encoded in the instruction.

Vector code for simple operations looks remarkably like its scalar counterparts. We saw examples of this in Chapter 1. When the trip count is unknown at compile time, strip-mining is used to insure that the vector length does not exceed the hardware maximum. Some vector computer systems have a flexible vector register file, which can be treated as a few very long vectors (say, eight vectors of 1,024 elements) or many short vectors (say, 128 vectors of 64 elements) or anything in between. This simplifies life for the vector register allocator in the compiler;

the strip size can be adjusted to take into account the number of vector registers needed. If more registers are needed, the strip size is simply shortened.

12.1.1 Conditionals

Most vector machines have some way to handle conditional code. We assume that the machine has a vector compare instruction, which generates a bit-vector result. For instance, Cray vector machines have a special mask register to hold the bit-vector result of compare instructions; Fujitsu vector machines have a bank of bit-vector registers similar to floating point vector registers. The ratio of 1-bits in a bit vector is the bit vector *density*; a density of 100 percent means that all the bits are on, and a density of 0 percent means all the bits are off.

Some vector machines have conditional vector instructions. That is, each vector operation can take an additional operand, the bit vector register, which disables the operation for elements where the corresponding bit is zero. Typically, the result register is unchanged where the bit vector element is zero, or, in the case of a conditional store, the corresponding memory location is unchanged.

Example 12.1

Show the vector code generated for the following loop:

(1)   forall I = 1 to N do
(2)   A[I] = B[I] + C[I]
(3)   if A[I] > 0 then
(4)   B[I] = B[I] + 1
(5)   endif
(6)   endforall

Use conditional vector instructions.

Solution

The first statement is unconditional, so vector code will be generated as normal. The conditional statement will generate a vector compare instruction, which will store a result into a bit vector or *mask register*. The bit vector will be used for the conditional statements.

```
for I = 1 to N by 64 do
    VL = max(N-I+1,64)
    vfetch B[I],1 -> v1
    vfetch C[I],1 -> v2
    vadd v1+v2 -> v3
    vstore v3 -> A[I],1
    loadi #0 -> r1
```

```
        vcmp v3,r1 -> m1
        loadi #1 -> r2
        vaddc v1+r1 -> v1, m1
        vstorec v1 -> B[I],1, m1
    endfor
```

Note the two conditional vector instructions, `vaddc` and `vstorec`.

Other Options

There are a number of variations in how vector machines handle the specifics of conditional vector code. If there is only a single mask register, it is implicitly an operand to all conditional instructions and the result of all vector compare instructions. If the machine does not have a conditional vector store instruction, the compiler must generate the true path and false path results into the same vector register, so a dense store can be used. In the previous example, the vector add stored its result into `v1`, which already held the appropriate values when the bit vector was zero. Thus, an unconditional store could have been performed, since the proper value would be stored even when the condition was false. If the left hand side of the conditional assignment were a different vector, say `D[I]`, the compiler might have to load `D` into a vector register, conditionally compute the changes, and store the result.

Yet another option is to compute conditional code using sparse vectors. Some machines have an instruction called a *compressed iota*, which produces an index vector result giving the offsets of the 1-bits in the mask register. The index vector can be used in indexed load/store instructions, to load only those vector elements that are needed. The advantage is that the memory and arithmetic operations for the conditional statements are done with short vectors.

12.1.2 Reductions

Some vector computers have intrinsic reduction instructions, such as computing the sum of a vector register. When this is available, the compiler can use the appropriate instruction to accumulate a sum or other reduction, one strip at a time. More often, the compiler will accumulate a vector register of partial results, much like concurrent code would accumulate a partial result for each processor. The vector register is then reduced to a scalar in a sequential loop after the vector loop.

A sequential loop may not be the most efficient way to reduce a vector register to a scalar; another method is to use the following four steps:

1   store the vector register into memory,
2   load the partial sums from memory using a shorter vector length (say, 8),

3 accumulate the short vectors using vector instructions (resulting in eight partial sums), and
4 use a sequence of scalar instructions to add up the resulting partial sums.

Other reductions, such as products, maximum or minimum of a vector, and so on, can be handled in the same way. Finding the a maximum with the index of that maximum may require more hardware support, or may not be feasible.

Example 12.2

Show the vector code (with strip-mining) for the following loop:

```
(1)    forall I = 1 to N do
(2)        A[I] = B[I] + C[I]
(3)        ASUM += A[I]
(4)    endforall
```

Solution

The code below uses vector register v4 as an accumulator for the reduction

```
vsub v4-v4 -> v4
for I = 1 to N by 64 do
    VL = max(N-I+1,64)
    vfetch B[I],1 -> v1
    vfetch C[I],1 -> v2
    vadd v1+v2 -> v3
    vstore v3 -> A[I],1
    vadd v3+v4 -> v4
endfor
for i = 0 to min(N-1,63)
    ASUM = ASUM + v4[i]
endfor
```

The first vector instruction simply clears v4 to all zero. The final sequential loop reduces the vector register accumulator to a single value.

12.2 Vector Code from Sequential Loops

Early vectorizing compilers had a few rules about the types of constructs for which they could generate vector code. Since the 1970s, compilers have used data dependence graphs to find vectorizable loops. Since vector execution preserves lexically forward dependence relations, only sequential loops with acyclic dependence graphs can be vectorized. Statements in a loop with an acyclic dependence graph can be reordered (by topologically sorting the graph) to remove any lexically backward dependence relations. As with parallelizing sequential loops, there are a number of other considerations. For instance, scalars in the loop must be handled again. Loop carried dependence relations are not a problem, but dependence cycles must be handled.

12.2.1 Handling Scalars

As with concurrency analysis, any scalar assigned in a loop will generate one or more data dependence cycles (at least an output dependence cycle for the assignment). We remove induction variable cycles from the loop by substitution, and remove scalar temporaries by scalar expansion. Scalar expansion can proceed after strip-mining, so that the expanded scalar is the size of a vector register, meaning no memory need be allocated for the scalar. Last value assignments must be added, as before, getting the last value from the vector register allocated to the scalar. Scalar reductions can be recognized as for concurrent loops, with vector code generated as described earlier. The vector code does reorder the accumulation, so there are likely to be differences in roundoff error. Coupled reductions can be handled as with simple reductions, accumulating strips of partial reduction results.

Example 12.3

Generate vector code for the following loop:

```
(1)     J = N
(2)     for I = 1 to N do
(3)         T = B[I] + B[J]
(4)         A[I] = T + 1/T
(5)         J = J - 1
(6)     endfor
```

Solution

The scalar T can be expanded to a vector register; J is an induction variable, and references to J can be substituted in the loop.

```
for I = 1 to N by 64 do
    VL = min(N-I+1,64)
    vfetch B[I],1 -> v1
    vfetch B[N-I+1],-1 -> v2
    vadd v1+v2 -> v3
    vdiv 1,v3 -> v4
    vadd v3+v4 -> v5
```

```
        vstore v5 -> A[I],1
    endfor
    T = v3[VL-1]
```

The last value assignment for T will get the last value assigned to the vector register v3 from the last strip.

12.2.2 Dependence Cycles

When the compiler builds a data dependence graph for a loop containing a scalar assignment, the graph will contain a dependence cycle. For most of these cases, the methods shown above will satisfy the dependence relations. For other scalar assignments, or other dependence cycles in general, the compiler must still satisfy the dependence relations. The dependence relations in the cycle can always be satisfied by leaving the loop sequential; that is, by not vectorizing it. To get as much parallelism as possible, however, the compiler can use loop fission to split the dependence cycle off to a separate loop, and vectorize the remainder of the statements. This is sometimes called *partial vectorization*.

Example 12.4

Find as much vector parallelism in the following loop as possible:

```
(1)    for I = 1 to N do
(2)        A[I] = B[I] + C[I]
(3)        D[I+1] = D[I] + A[I]*C[I]
(4)        C[I+1] = C[I+1]*2
(5)    endfor
```

Solution

The dependence graph is shown in Figure 12.1. Array D gives a dependence cycle at line 3. Splitting out the dependence cycle gives the following loops:

```
(1)    for I = 1 to N do
(4)        C[I+1] = C[I+1]*2
(2)        A[I] = B[I] + C[I]
(5)    endfor
(1)    for I = 1 to N do
(3)        D[I+1] = D[I] + A[I]*C[I]
(5)    endfor
```

The first of these two loops can be easily vectorized.

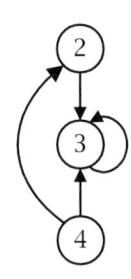

FIGURE 12.1 Data dependence graph for example.

12.2.3 Loop Fission with Temporaries

When applying loop fission, the compiler can ignore dependence relations due to induction variables, reduction variables, and scalar temporaries, since those can be satisfied by induction variable substitution, reduction recognition, and scalar expansion, respectively. When fission splits the assignments and uses of a scalar across two loops, the compiler must replace the scalar even in the sequential code. In particular, when loop fission splits the assignment and use of a scalar temporary across two loops, the scalar may have to be replaced by a dynamically allocated vector in memory; a vector register will not be sufficient. This can be avoided by strip-mining the loop before fission; then the scalar temporary can be replaced by a vector register temporary.

Example 12.5

Find as much vector parallelism as possible in the following loop:

```
(1)   for I = 1 to N do
(2)       A = B[I] + C[I]
(3)       D[I+1] = D[I] + A*C[I]
(4)       C[I+1] = C[I+1]*2
(5)   endfor
```

Solution

The variable A is a scalar temporary. Ignoring the scalar dependence relations for A gives the same dependence graph as shown in Figure 12.1. However, if the compiler applies loop fission as in that example, A will have to be allocated to memory. The real additional cost will be the additional store and load instructions for the expanded scalar. The alternative is to strip-mine the loop, then apply fission to the inner loop, producing the following:

```
(1)   for I = 1 to N by 64 do
(1)       for v = 0 to min(N-I,63) do
```

```
(2)            A[v] = B[I+v] + C[I+v]
(4)            C[I+v+1] = C[I+v+1]*2
(5)         endfor
(1)         for v = 0 to min(N-I,63) do
(3)            D[I+v+1] = D[I+v] + A[v]*C[I+v]
(5)         endfor
(5)      endfor
```

Note that A only needs to be as long as a single strip, and can be held in a vector register, even in the sequential loop.

Loop Fission with Conditionals

When a conditional clause is split by loop fission, the condition itself must be saved in a temporary vector. The control dependence relations for the conditional can essentially be replaced by data dependence relations for purposes of loop fission. For instance, the loop:

```
(1)   for I = 1 to N do
(2)      if A[I] > 0 then
(3)         B[I] = B[I] + 1
(4)         C[I+1] = C[I]*B[I]
(5)      endif
(6)   endfor
```

can be rewritten as follows:

```
(1)   for I = 1 to N do
(2)      T = A[I] > 0
(3)      if T then B[I] = B[I] + 1 endif
(4)      if T then C[I+1] = C[I]*B[I] endif
(6)   endfor
```

Scalar expansion on scalar holding the conditional result allows generation of conditional vector operations.

If the conditional test itself is involved in the dependence cycle, the situation is more interesting. For instance, in the following loop there are control dependence relations from the conditional at line 2 to lines 3 and 5, and data dependence relations from those lines back to the conditional, with dependence distance 1.

```
(1)   for I = 1 to N do
(2)      if A[I] > 0 then
```

(3)   A[I+1] = B[I] + 1
(4)   else
(5)   A[I+1] = A[I+1] / 2
(6)   endif
(7) endfor

The compiler could generate code to find the value of the conditionally assigned variables both when the conditional is true and when it is false.

```
At[2:N+1] = B[1:N] + 1
Af[2:N+1] = A[2:N+1] / 2
```

Then the compiler can generate code to solve a boolean recurrence to compute the value of the bit vector, depending on whether the previous iteration took the True or the False path:

$$cond[1] = A[1] > 0$$
$$cond[i] = (cond[i-1] \land At[i] > 0)$$
$$\qquad \lor (\neg\, cond[i-1] \land Af[i] > 0)$$

Solving such a boolean recurrence requires special hardware, but it is not significantly more complex than current binary adders. Finally, the compiler can generate vector code to assign the appropriate precomputed value to the result vector.

```
where cond(1;N) do
    A[2;N+1] = At[2:N+1]
elsewhere
    A[2;N+1] = Af[2:N+1]
endwhere
```

Since today's computers do not include the hardware to solve this boolean recurrence, this method to vectorize such a data/control dependence cycle is only of academic interest.

12.2.4 Vectorization Despite Cycles

Some loops can be vectorized despite the presence of cycles. This section includes a bag of tricks that the compiler can apply when appropriate.

Anti-Dependence Cycles

When a statement has an anti-dependence relation to itself, it can appear to be in a dependence cycle; this is an artifact of the granularity of the dependence graph. In fact, there can be no anti-dependence cycle from a statement to itself.

Example 12.6

Show the dependence graph for the following loop, and identify any dependence cycles:

```
(1)   for I = 1 to N do
(2)      A[I] = A[I+1] + B[I]
(3)   endfor
```

Solution

There is a loop carried anti-dependence relation from the A[I+1] reference to the store of A[I]. In a statement-level data dependence graph, this appears to be a dependence cycle, as shown on the left in Figure 12.2. However, as shown on the right in that figure, if we look at a finer granularity dependence graph, where each node corresponds to a single operation, there is no dependence cycle. The cycle was an artifact of clumping several operations into a single node at the statement level. Thus, there is no dependence cycle and the loop can be vectorized.

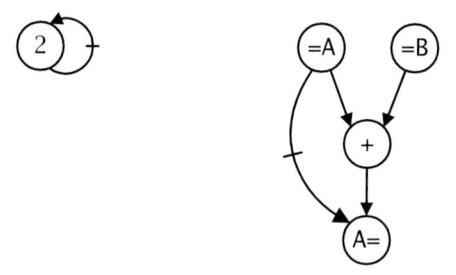

FIGURE 12.2 Statement granularity and operation granularity dependence graphs.

Multiple Statements

At the operation granularity, there is a dependence from the right hand side to the left hand side of a single assignment. Since an anti-dependence relation goes in the same direction, it cannot introduce a cycle. Among multiple statements, anti-dependence relations can cause false dependence cycles. The compiler can resolve some apparent dependence cycles by refining the dependence graph granularity. Topologically sorting the finer granularity graph means reordering the operations, instead of reordering whole statements.

Example 12.7

Show the data dependence graph for the following loop, and show how it can be converted to vector code.

```
(1)    for I = 2 to N do
(2)        A[I] = B[I] + C[I]
(3)        D[I] = (A[I-1] + A[I+1])/2
(4)    endfor
```

Solution

The statement-level data dependence graph has a flow dependence from line 2 to line 3 and an anti-dependence in the reverse direction, for an apparent dependence cycle as shown on the left in Figure 12.3.

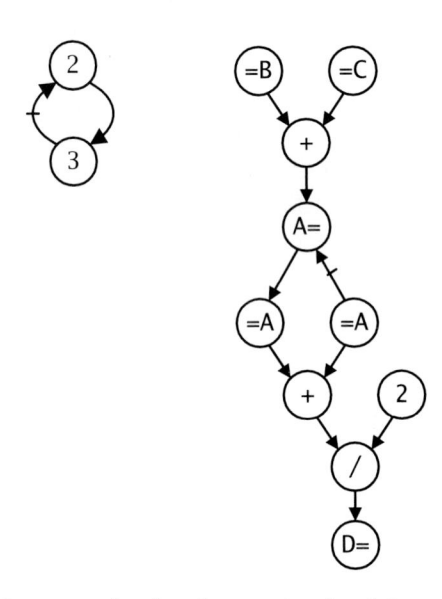

FIGURE 12.3 Statement-level and operation-level dependence graphs.

As shown on the right of Figure 12.3, using a finer granularity dependence graph resolves the dependence cycle. Vector code can be generated as long as the fetch for A[I+1] precedes the store of A[I], to preserve the anti-dependence relation, and the fetch of A[I-1] follows the store of A[I], to preserve the flow dependence relation:

```
for I = 2 to N by 64 do
    VL = min(N-I+2,64)
    vfetch A[I+1],1 -> v5
    vfetch B[I],1 -> v1
    vfetch C[I],1 -> v2
    vadd v1+v2 -> v3
    vstore v3 -> A[I],1
    vfetch A[I-1],1 -> v4
    vadd v4+v5 -> v6
```

12.2 ▪ Vector Code from Sequential Loops

```
        vdiv v6,#2 -> v6
        vstore v6 -> D[I],1
   endfor
```

Partial Expression Vectorization

Even when a true dependence cycle prevents vectorization of any of the statements in the loop, sometimes parts of the expressions can be computed in vector mode. The operation-level dependence graph can identify the subexpressions that can use vector operations. The subexpression results can either be stored into dynamically allocated memory or kept in a vector register. The compiler must determine whether the added complexity and overhead of the partial vectorization is worth the benefit, given that the execution time of the loop will be limited by the speed of the sequential part. This is especially true for machines with deep pipelines, where instruction scheduling can hide some operations in the latency of other instructions.

Example 12.8

Find as much vector parallelism in the following loop as possible:

```
(1)    for I = 2 to N do
(2)        A[I] = B[I] + C[I]
(3)        D[I] = D[I-1] / 2.5 + A[I]*2
(4)    endfor
```

Solution

The statement-level dependence graph is shown on the left in Figure 12.4; since line 2 is not involved in the dependence cycle, it can be executed in vector mode. We can find additional parallelism by looking at the operation-level graph, shown on the right in Figure 12.4.

The multiplication in line 3 is not involved in the dependence cycle, so it can also be split out into the vector part of the loop. The resulting vectorized loop, after accounting for strip-mining and keeping the subexpression in a vector register, is shown below:

```
   for I = 2 to N by 64 do
      VL = min(N-I+2,64)
      vfetch B[I],1 -> v1
      vfetch C[I],1 -> v2
      vadd v1+v2 -> v3
      vstore v3 -> A[I],1
      vmpy v3*#2 -> v4
```

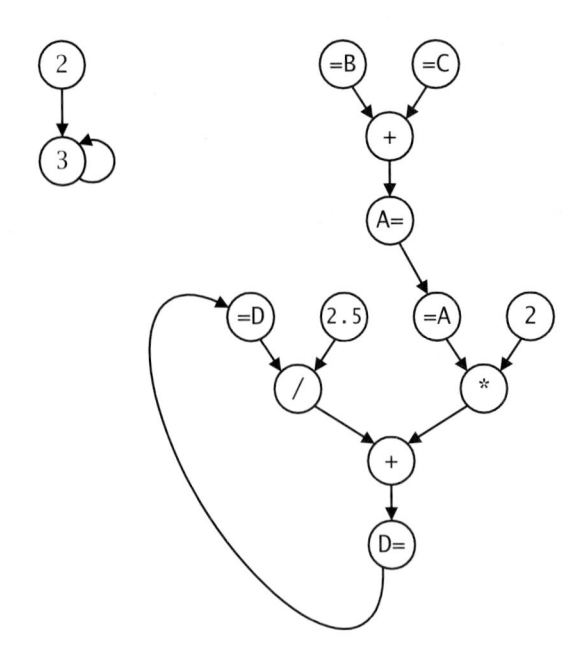

FIGURE 12.4 Statement-level and operation-level dependence graphs.

```
    for i = 0 to VL-1 do
        fetch D[I+i-1] -> r1
        div r1/#2.5 -> r2
        add r2+v4[i] -> r3
        store r3 -> D[I+i]
    endfor
endfor
```

Strip-Mining

As with concurrent code generation, strip-mining can be used to satisfy some dependence relations. Strip-mining a loop to a strip size of s will satisfy all dependence relations with dependence distance s or greater. For vector code, we don't need to satisfy all loop carried dependence relations with strip-mining, only enough of them to break the dependence cycles. To get the most parallelism, we want to find the largest strip size that will still break all the dependence cycles. Again, in general the problem is quite difficult, but in practice we don't see many cases where the dependence distance in a cycle is known to be greater than one, and in those cases the number of edges in the cycle is small.

Index Set Splitting

A few loops have data access conflicts that change direction somewhere in the middle of the index set; this occurs when one data reference is moving forward through an array and the other data reference is moving backward. The forward

12.2 ■ Vector Code from Sequential Loops

reference accesses some array elements that the backward reference will reach later, and vice versa. Thus, the second half of the index set depends on the first half, with the break at the point where the two references cross. By splitting the index set at that point, two vector loops can be generated.

Example 12.9

Generate vector code for the following loop:

```
(1)    for I = 1 to N do
(2)        A[I] = B[I] + C[I]
(3)        D[I] = (A[I] + A[N-I+1]) / 2
(4)    endfor
```

Solution

The forward reference to A[I] in line 2 assigns elements A[1], A[2], ..., that will be fetched by the backward reference A[N-I+1] in later iterations, thus giving a flow dependence relation. However, the backward reference A[N-I+1] will fetch elements A[N], A[N-1], ..., which will be assigned by line 2 in later iterations, thus giving an anti-dependence relation and completing the dependence cycle. The compiler can compute where the two array references cross by setting the two subscript expressions equal, and solving for I:

$$I = N - I + 1$$
$$I = (N+1)/2$$

If N is odd, $(N+1)/2$ is an integer, and there will be a loop independent instance of the dependence relation between these two references at that iteration. All other instances of the dependence relation, whether N is even or odd, will cross the point $(N+1)/2$, so we split the index set at that point:

```
(1)    for I = 1 to (N+1)/2 do
(2)        A[I] = B[I] + C[I]
(3)        D[I] = (A[I] + A[N-I+1]) / 2
(4)    endfor
(1)    for I = (N+1)/2+1 to N do
(2)        A[I] = B[I] + C[I]
(3)        D[I] = (A[I] + A[N-I+1]) / 2
(4)    endfor
```

Both of the resulting loops can now be vectorized.

Run-Time Dependence Testing

Some dependence cycles are caused by unknown user variables in the subscript expressions. Without knowing at least the sign of the variable, the compiler must conservatively assume that it can be either positive or negative, and so the dependence might go in either direction. Modern compilers recognize this situation and generate two versions of the loop, one with dependence one way and one with dependence the other way.

Example 12.10

Vectorize the following loop:

```
(1)    for I = 1 to N do
(2)        A[I] = A[I-K] + B[I]
(3)    endfor
```

Solution

As discussed in Section 7.6, the type of dependence for this example is determined by the sign of K. Here the dependence cycle can be broken by breaking the flow dependence relation with the test $K \leq 0 \vee K \geq N$. If the test succeeds, there is no flow dependence and no dependence cycle; if the test fails, there is a flow dependence cycle, and vector code cannot be generated:

```
       if K <= 0 or K >= N then
(1)        forall I = 1 to N do
(2)            A[I] = A[I-K] + B[I]
(3)        endforall
       else
(1)        for I = 1 to N do
(2)            A[I] = A[I-K] + B[I]
(3)        endfor
       endif
```

Run-time dependence testing like this generates code that works correctly and still gets as much parallelism as possible, even if the sign of K varies at run-time. One way for the compiler to determine whether to make multiple versions of a loop is to find dependence cycles in the normal way, keeping track of any dependence relations that have run-time conditions to break the dependence. If no cycles are found, vectorization can proceed in the normal way. If a cycle is found, the compiler can assert each run-time condition to see if any condition or combination of conditions will break the cycle. In Example 12.10, a dependence cycle comprising a flow dependence with a run-time condition was found. Asserting the condition allowed the compiler to break the cycle, so the compiler can choose to generate two versions of the loop. In some instances, asserting the alternate condition will also break the cycle, allowing both versions of the loop to be vectorized.

Example 12.11

Vectorize the following loop:

```
(1)    for I = 1 to N do
(2)        A[I] = B[I] + C[I]
(3)        D[I] = D[I] + A[I-K]
(4)    endfor
```

Solution

In this case, the dependence cycle involves both a flow and an anti-dependence relation between A[I] and A[I-K]. The flow dependence relation can be broken by the condition $K < 0 \vee K \geq N$, and the anti-dependence relation can be broken by $K \geq 0 \vee -K \geq N$. Asserting the first condition breaks the cycle by breaking the flow dependence relation. Asserting the converse condition, $K \geq 0 \wedge K < N$, breaks the cycle by breaking the anti-dependence relation. Thus, both versions of the loop can be vectorized:

```
        if K < 0 or K >= N then
(1)         forall I = 1 to N do
(3)             D[I] = D[I] + A[I-K]
(2)             A[I] = B[I] + C[I]
(4)         endforall
        else
(1)         forall I = 1 to N do
(2)             A[I] = B[I] + C[I]
(3)             D[I] = D[I] + A[I-K]
(4)         endforall
        endif
```

In the first version, the statements had to be reordered to satisfy the anti-dependence relation.

Ignoring Dependence Cycles

Finally, some dependence cycles can simply be semantically ignored. For instance, a dependence cycle of output dependence relations can be ignored if the value being stored is loop invariant and identical in all the statements. In this case, it doesn't matter what the order of the stores is, since they all have the same value, as in the following loop.

Example 12.12

Show how to vectorize the following loop:

(1)   for I = 1 to N do
(2)   A[IP[I]] = 0.0
(3)   endfor

Solution
There is an output dependence cycle due to the assignment to A[IP[I]], since the compiler cannot generally determine the values of IP[I]. In fact, IP[I] may have the same value for all I, so the loop may be assigning to the same array element over and over again. In general, the order of the stores does matter, so the output dependence relation is significant. However, in this loop the value being assigned is loop invariant. Since it doesn't really matter which zero gets stored last, the loop can be executed in vector mode, assuming the machine has an indexed vector store instruction.

12.3 Vector Code from Forall Loops

When generating vector code from a sequential loop, the compiler must strip-mine the loop to account for the finite vector register length. The strip loop executes sequentially and the element loop executes in vector mode. When generating vector code from a forall loop, or equivalently, from array assignments, strip-mining may not be sufficient, since sequential execution of the strip loop may not satisfy all dependence relations. In Section 9.2 we discussed how to generate a scalar loop from a sequence of array assignments. In order to generate efficient vector code from a forall loop, we must first know that the loop can be scalarized. Although this is counterintuitive, if the vector loop cannot be scalarized, the final vector code must store all intermediate values in temporary arrays in memory, then reload those values to store them into the final result.

In this example, a large temporary array was needed to hold the intermediate result, in order to preserve the dependence relations. When the forall loop can be scalarized, such a temporary array is not needed. Loop transformations, such as loop reversal, can sometimes be used to make the forall loop scalarizable. The key observation is that generating vector code from a vector source is really no easier than generating vector code from sequential loops.

Example 12.13

Generate vector code for the following loop:

```
(1)    forall I = 2 to N-1 do
(2)        forall J = 2 to N-1 do
(3)            A[I,J] = (A[I-1,J] + A[I+1,J]
                        + A[I,J-1] + A[I,J+1])/4
(4)        endforall
(5)    endforall
```

Solution

The vector loop has four anti-dependence relations, with distance vectors $(1, 0)$, $(-1, 0)$, $(0, 1)$, and $(0, -1)$. Since a sequential loop cannot satisfy a dependence with a negative distance, the forall loop cannot be scalarized. Generating vector code must be done by assigning the right hand side expression into a temporary array, then copying that array into the left hand side:

```
       allocate temp[2:N-1,2:N-1]
(1)    for I = 2 to N-1 do
(2)        for J = 2 to N-1 do
(3)            temp[I,J] = (A[I-1,J] + A[I+1,J]
                           + A[I,J-1] + A[I,J+1])/4
(4)        endfor
(5)    endfor
(1)    for I = 2 to N-1 do
(2)        for J = 2 to N-1 do
(3)            A[I,J] = temp[I,J]
(4)        endfor
(5)    endfor
```

Now simple vector code can be generated for the inner loop in each case.

12.4 Nested Loops

Many early vectorizing compilers looked only at the innermost loop, since the target machine supported only one vector index. Converting nested sequential loops into array assignments—for instance, Fortran 77 loops into Fortran 90 array assignments—also corresponds to finding nested vector loops. Finding nested vector parallelism is the same as finding single loop vectorization; as long as the dependence graph is acyclic, all the loops can be vectorized.

Example 12.14

Convert the nested loop below into array assignments using vectorization:

```
(1)    for I = 1 to N do
(2)        for J = 2 to M do
(3)            A[I,J] = B[I,J-1] + C[I,J]
(4)            B[I,J] = B[I,J] * 2
(5)        endfor
(6)    endfor
```

Solution

There is a flow dependence relation from line 4 to line 3 with distance vector $(0, 1)$, but there is no dependence cycle. Thus, both loops can be vectorized and replaced by array assignments. Note that the statements need to be reordered to preserve the flow dependence relation:

```
(4)    B[1:N,2:M] = B[1:N,2:M] * 2
(3)    A[1:N,2:M] = B[1:N,1:M-1] + C[1:N,2:M]
```

There may be additional constraints when converting from loops to array assignments, especially at the source level; for instance, Fortran 90 array assignments must have rectangular index sets (no triangular loops).

12.4.1 Loop Interchanging

When there is a dependence cycle in nested loops, the compiler can use loop fission to split the cycle into separate loops. It can also try executing one or more of the outer loops sequentially; this will satisfy dependence relations carried by those loops, hopefully breaking the cycle. Interchanging the loops can move a dependence-carrying loop to the outermost level, allowing the compiler to break the cycle. Again, the compiler doesn't need to satisfy all loop carried dependence relations by sequentially executing a loop, just enough of them to break the dependence cycles.

Beyond uncovering additional vector parallelism, loop interchanging can be used to find the best loop to run in vector mode. For instance, the memory bandwidth of most vector computers depends on the memory stride; a stride equal to the number of memory banks can reduce bandwidth by a large factor. On the other hand, a stride of one will always give very good performance. Also, short vector operations are not as efficient in amortizing the vector startup time as long vectors. In many nested loops, the compiler can choose which index from a nested loop to run in vector mode. It can choose based on many factors, one of which is whether the inner loop will generate vector code.

In most cases, while the array strides may not be known at compile time, the compiler can use the array layout to identify whether one index has any stride-one accesses. With Fortran 90 array pointers and assumed-shape arguments, the stride for each dimension is not known until run time. Loop limits are also usually unknown until run time. Taking advantage of any such information that is available at compile time is important. The compiler might even generate two (or more) versions of a nested loop, depending on run-time conditions such as the actual loop lengths, or the strides of array accesses.

In general, searching for the best loop transformation is an open problem. Searching among all the ways to reorder the loops can be time consuming for many large programs. One idea is to concentrate on vectorizing the inner loop unless there are problems; for instance, if the inner loop has small limits or array accesses with poor strides, this might be a flag to the compiler to look for a different vector loop.

Outer Loop Vectorization

In a nested loop construct, especially when the loops are not tightly nested, the compiler might be able to generate vector code for an outer loop. The generated code is the same as if the outer loop were strip-mined, and the element loop interchanged to become the inner loop. However, the compiler can perform the analysis and code generation directly, without the intermediate program transformations. The advantage is that the same strip loop is shared over the whole range of the original outer loop, with potential improvements in vector register locality.

Vectorizing the outer loop is legal if all the dependence relations can be satisfied with sequential code while ignoring the dependence vector element for that outer loop. For instance, if there is a dependence distance vector $(1, -1)$, vectorizing the outer loop will not be legal since ignoring the outer loop position gives a distance vector (-1), which cannot be satisfied by sequential code (though loop reversal might make it legal). As mentioned, it is equivalent to strip-mining the outer loop and interchanging the element loop to the inner position. In many cases, as in this example, the memory bandwidth requirements for outer loop vectorization will be much smaller than for simple vectorization, since some of the memory operations can be floated out of the inner sequential loop to the level of the strip loop. One measure of vector performance is the ratio of memory operations to arithmetic operations in the inner loop; since the arithmetic operations are the desired results, and any extra memory operations are in some sense required overhead, this ratio gives the quality of the vectorized code. When loop interchanging improves this ratio, it is sometimes called *supervector performance*, since it is better than simple vector performance.

Example 12.15

Vectorize the I index in the following loop.

```
(1)    for I = 1 to N do
(2)        A[I] = 0
(3)        for J = 1 to N do
(4)            A[I] = A[I] * B[I,J] + C[I]
(5)        endfor
(6)    endfor
```

Solution

One way to vectorize the I index is to apply loop fission and interchanging to make I the innermost loop

```
(1)    for I = 1 to N do
(2)        A[I] = 0
(6)    endfor
(3)    for J = 1 to N do
(1)        for I = 1 to N do
(4)            A[I] = A[I] * B[I,J] + C[I]
(5)        endfor
(6)    endfor
```

This requires initializing the whole vector A, then fetching and storing the whole vector A for each iteration of the J loop. The vector code looks like:

```
for I = 1 to N by 64 do
    VL = min(N-I+2,64)
    vsub v0-v0 -> v1
    vstore v1 -> A[I],1
endfor
for J = 1 to N do
    for I = 1 to N by 64 do
        VL = min(N-I+2,64)
        vfetch A[I],1 -> v1
        vfetch B[I,J],1 -> v2
        vmpy v1*v2 -> v3
        vfetch C[I],1 -> v4
        vadd v3+v4 -> v1
        vstore v1 -> A[I],1
    endfor
endfor
```

There are six vector instructions in the inner loop, four of which are memory loads and stores. An alternative is to vectorize the I loop when it is in the outer position. Then loop fission is not needed, and more efficient vector code can be generated:

```
for I = 1 to N by 64 do
    VL = min(N-I+2,64)
    vsub v0-v0 -> v1
    vfetch C[I],1 -> v4
    for J = 1 to N do
        vfetch B[I,J],1 -> v2
        vmpy v1*v2 -> v3
        vadd v3+v4 -> v1
    endfor
    vstore v1 -> A[I],1
endfor
```

Note that the fetch of C and the store to A are invariant in the J loop, and so can be pulled out of that loop. Now the inner loop has only three vector instructions, only one of which is a memory operation. The memory-to-computation ratio was 4:2 in the simple vector code, and improved to 1:2 by vectorizing the outer loop.

Loop Collapsing

Vector loops are more efficient when the loop limits are large. Loop collapsing can sometimes be used to increase vector length, especially when there is no one single loop long enough to be efficient.

12.5 Roundoff Error, Exceptions, and Debuggers

As with concurrent code, preservation of the dependence relations preserves the behavior of the program. Generating vector code for reduction operations, however, can change the roundoff error accumulation. Also, even with simple vector code, exceptions can be raised in a different order than they would be for the corresponding source code. If any loop transformations are applied, this problem is exacerbated. Few (if any) compilers try to preserve the exception behavior of programs that fail. The problem of debugging is somewhat easier than for multiprocessors, since there is still just a single processor, but it is not the same as debugging the source program. One alternative is to report program position and variable values in terms of the original program, even though the program has changed somewhat. Another is to show the user a modified program, so that it is more obvious what the restructuring the compiler has done and breakpoints and the like can be placed intelligently.

12.6 Multivector Computers

Some current multiprocessor machines have vector processors; these are called multivector computers. Generating code for such a machine usually involves trying to find two levels of parallelism: an outer concurrent loop to spread across the processors, and an inner vector loop within a processor. The issues are no different than they are when considered separately, but together it can become harder for the compiler to determine the most efficient way to restructure a loop. When there is only a single loop, concurrent-vector code can still be generated by strip-mining the loop, then running the strip loop concurrently across the processors.

12.7 In the Pit

The loop below uses a temporary scalar S and another variable T, called a carry-around variable.

```
(1)    T = B[0]
(2)    for I = 1 to N do
(3)        S = B[I]
(4)        C[I] = (S+T)/2
(5)        T = S
(6)    endfor
```

Note that T holds the value of B(I-1). Sophisticated compilers recognize this pattern and will replace both S and T by the appropriate references to the original array B, and thus be able to generate vector code. In this case, T has the value B(I-1) even on the first iteration; when this is not the case, the compiler may have to peel off the first iteration of the loop.

When using loop fission to split out the dependence cycles, the compiler may generate sequential loops from a single source loop. It can be advantageous for several reasons to minimize the number of generated sequential loops. One reason is simply that it reduces the loop overhead, which for some machines can be substantial. Another is that it improves the locality between the statements in the sequential part, if they happen to refer to any common data. Getting the absolute minimal number of sequential loops in general may be difficult, though simple heuristics work well in practice. In some situations, it may be appropriate to generate no more than a single sequential loop, even when that means executing some code sequentially that could have been done in vector mode.

The method of using a fine granularity dependence graph to find vector parallelism has been called *node splitting*, meaning that the node in the statement-level dependence graph is split into two or more nodes to break the cycle.

Linear recurrences can be executed in vector mode using a technique called cyclic reduction, which is similar to executing recurrences using parallel code.

Early Cray Research vector computers had no conditional vector operations; the only way to compute conditional vector code was to compute the True and False results in dense mode, then use a *vector merge* instruction to merge the two results into a single vector register, and store that. The problem with this is that dense computation of code that should be conditional would compute results for index values where the bit vector was zero, which otherwise would not have been computed. In some instances, these computations can produce an exception, which otherwise would not have been raised.

At least one vector machine, the Texas Instruments Advanced Scientific Computer (TI-ASC) had a complex instruction set that could describe three nested vector loops with a single instruction.

12.8 Further Reading

Vectorization was the earliest method of automatically finding parallelism in sequential loops (Schneck [1972]). The Parafrase project at the University of Illinois (Kuck et al. [1980]) and the PFC project at Rice University (Allen and Kennedy [1987]) were two of the earliest projects to use data dependence theory to automatically find vector-style parallelism.

Allen and Kennedy (1992) discuss strip-mining and optimizations to enhance vector register locality. The influence of optimizing for stride on a cached vector machine is described by Erbacci et al. (1989). Tsuda and Kunieda (1990) describe a vectorizing compiler that makes extensive use of indirect addressing after loop coalescing to vectorize nested loops. The scheme presented here for vectorizing loops with conditionals where the condition is in a dependence cycle is taken from Banerjee and Gajski (1984).

EXERCISES

12.1 Is the variable T in the following loop a reduction variable? If not, why not? If so, give the vector code for this loop.

(1) for I = 1 to N do
(2)   A[I] = B[I] + C[I]
(3)   T = T + A[I]
(4)   D[I] = T + 1
(5) endfor

12.2 Is the variable T in the following loop a reduction variable? If not, why not? If so, give the vector code for the loop.

(1) for I = 1 to N do
(2)   A[I] = B[I] + C[I]
(3)   D[I] = D[I] + 1
(4)   T = T * A[I] + D[I]
(5) endfor

12.3 Show how to vectorize the following loop using index set splitting; compute the data dependence relations and find the point where the dependence relation changes.

```
(1)   for I = 1 to N do
(2)      A[I] = A[5]
(3)   endfor
```

12.4 Show how to vectorize the loop in the previous exercise without index set splitting. What property of this loop allows it to simply be vectorized?

12.5 Show how to generate vector code for the following array assignment statements:

```
(1)  A[1:N] = B[1:N] + C[1:N]
(2)  B[1:N] = C[2:N+1] + A[1:N]
```

12.6 Generate vector code for the following array assignments:

```
(1)  A[1:N] = B[1:N] + A[2:N+1]
(2)  B[1:N] = B[0:N-1] + B[2:N+1]
```

12.7 Transform the following loop so that vector code can be generated:

```
(1)   for I = 2 to N-1 do
(2)      for J = 2 to N-1 do
(3)         A[I,J] = 0.25*(A[I-1,J]+A[I,J-1]+A[I,J+1]+A[I+1,J])
(4)      endfor
(5)   endfor
(6)
```

12.8 Draw the data dependence graph for the following loop; use run-time dependence testing to generate vector code.

```
(1)   for I = 2 to N do
(2)      A[I] = B[I] + 1
(3)      B[I+K] = A[I-K] + 2
(4)   endfor
```

12.9 Draw the data dependence graph for the following loop; use loop fission to partially vectorize the loop:

```
(1)   for I = 2 to N do
(2)      A[I] = B[I] + C[I]
(3)      D[I] = A[I]*D[I-1] + E[I]
(4)   endfor
```

12.10 Use loop interchanging to generate vector code without reductions for the following loop:

```
(1)   for I = 1 to N do
(2)      X[I] = B[I] / A[I,I]
```

(3)   for J = 1 to I-1 do
(4)   X[I] = X[I] - A[I,J]*X[J]
(5)   endfor
(6)   endfor

Find the memory-to-computation ratio in the inner loop.

12.11 Use loop interchanging to find the best version of the matrix multiplication loop, where the stride-1 dimension is the last dimension:

(1)   for I = 1 to N do
(2)   for J = 1 to N do
(3)   for K = 1 to N do
(4)   A[I,J] = A[I,J] + B[I,K]*C[K,J]
(5)   endfor
(6)   endfor
(7)   endfor

Find the memory-to-computation ratio in the inner loop.

13 MESSAGE-PASSING MACHINES

SIMD and MIMD message passing machines can be easily designed and built, but are hard to program. We present a scheme for data-parallel applications whereby the programmer writes a single global program, which is partitioned by the compiler to run in parallel on the processor ensemble.

Message-passing machines are a convenient and (recently) popular way to engineer a scalable machine. Each processor of such a machine has fast access to its local memory, but must send messages to remote nodes for data stored elsewhere, with significantly higher latency. The bandwidth of the communication network is usually designed to be sufficient to handle the expected traffic, but optimizing to reduce bandwidth requirements is still important.

Message-passing machines come in two flavors, SIMD and MIMD. A SIMD (single instruction/multiple data) machine has a single instruction stream that controls all the processing elements. A front end decodes and broadcasts the instructions to the processing elements, which execute in parallel in lock-step fashion. A MIMD (multiple instruction/multiple data) machine typically comprises a set of commodity microprocessors, each with memory and a network connection. Both types of machines work best on *data-parallel* applications, which have very large data sets that can be processed in parallel. MIMD machines can also be programmed in a true message-passing style, where each processor is executing a different program.

We focus here on a programming model where the user writes a single global program, and compiles it to run in parallel on the nodes of the processor ensemble. The global data set is actually partitioned and distributed among the processors. For a SIMD machine, the compiler generates a front end program, which controls the processor ensemble directly. For a MIMD machine, the compiler generates a sequential program, a copy of which runs on each processor. When discussing message-passing machines generically, we will speak of the *processor ensemble*, or ensemble. For a SIMD machine in particular, each processor is called a *processing element*, or PE. Each processor on a MIMD machine is called a *node*.

13.1 SIMD Machines

Some of the first large-scale parallel processors were of the SIMD variety. In a SIMD parallel processor, a single instruction stream controls all the PEs, each of which acts on different data. Recent SIMD designs have achieved some commercial success. The economic advantages of SIMD machines are that much of the control logic for fetching and decoding instructions, optimizing branches, and so on, does not need to be replicated for each PE, but can be constructed and optimized once for the whole machine. Only the data path (registers and functional units) needs to be replicated.

Unlike multiprocessors and vector machines, there have not been many successful SIMD designs, so it is hard to make generalizations about how to compile for one. We adhere to a reasonable model of a SIMD machine, and discuss ways to generate and optimize code. Note that automatic parallelization for SIMD machines is not so important an issue. The reason is not that it is simple; rather, the cost of failure is too high. For a multiprocessor, the performance difference between sequential and parallel execution is a factor equal to the number of processors available. If an automatic parallelizing compiler is successful, it can achieve a speedup equal to 12, 16, or however many processors are installed in the machine. Few current multiprocessors have large numbers of processors, so if automatic parallelization fails once in a while, it's not so bad. For a vector processor, the performance difference between sequential and vector execution is a factor ranging between four and 20, depending on the number of pipelines, the pipeline depth, clock speed, and so on. Again, a vectorizing compiler that is successful most of the time is probably adequate.

On the other hand, SIMD machines with hundreds or even thousands of processors are not difficult to construct. Even with custom processors, because of the simplified design of a single PE and the high replication factor, these machines can be built with a high degree of parallelism. The performance difference between sequential and parallel execution is now on the order of hundreds or thousands. A automatic parallelizing compiler that misses one case, even in an infrequently executed part of the program, can cause severe performance degradation because of the large parallelism factor being missed. Thus, these machines are typically programmed using explicitly parallel program constructs, either `forall` loops or, equivalently, array assignments. While the methods we have already seen for vectorization can convert sequential loops to array assignments, current SIMD systems do not depend on compilers to find parallelism. Here, we concentrate on compiling and optimizing parallel program constructs for SIMD machines.

13.1.1 SIMD Code

Generating code for a SIMD data-parallel machine is very much like generating code for a vector machine, except for dealing with the local memories. Our model of a SIMD machine has a single front end which operates as a standard scalar processor, and which controls the processing ensemble, or back end. The front end fetches and decodes the instructions; the scalar instruction subset corresponds to a standard instruction set, with arithmetic, memory, and control instructions. Scalar registers in the front end are used as they would be on any scalar CPU. Parallel instructions are decoded and broadcast to the back end; all the processing elements execute each parallel instruction simultaneously. Each PE has its own private registers and private memory, and can execute any arithmetic and memory operation. There are also instructions for communication between PEs, as we shall see. However, there are no control instructions for the back end; a PE cannot take a branch instruction since it does not fetch and decode instructions at all. Like vector processors, conditional operations are performed by computing a *mask*; PEs that are disabled by the mask will not participate in the current parallel instruction, essentially doing a no-op while the rest of the PEs are computing.

For instance, given two arrays A and B allocated so that elements A[I,J] and B[I,J] are stored at $PE_{I,J}$, the following parallel assignment statement:

```
forall I = 0 to 255 do
    forall J = 0 to 255 do
        A[I,J] = B[I,J] + 1
    endforall
endforall
```

can be executed on a 256×256 ensemble of PEs in one step. Since $PE_{I,J}$ owns the corresponding elements of both A and B, no interprocessor communication is needed at all. Here we make the natural implicit assumption that iteration (I, J) will be computed by $PE_{I,J}$. The parallel code is:

```
PE[0:255,0:255]:
    A = B + 1
```

The PE[0:255,0:255] designator is called the *context*; it tells what PEs are active for the assignment statement. Each PE is allocated a single element of each global array, so the array element appears as a scalar from the viewpoint of the PE.

The front end memory stores scalar values and does all the scalar computation; when a scalar is needed by the PE array, it is broadcast from the front end. Data that is stored on the front end is sometimes called *mono data*, since there is a single copy. The back end memory is distributed such that each PE has a private memory. Large arrays or data structures are partitioned and distributed among the back end memory modules. Data stored in this way is sometimes called *poly data*, since it is allocated across all the PEs. A PE can directly and quickly access its own private memory, but must access remote memory (local to another PE) through the interconnection network. Typically, network accesses are time-consuming, and may involve contention for scarce network bandwidth. In addition to a general interprocessor network, there may be a fixed interconnection network that allows fast communication between network neighbors. If the communication pattern happens to fall along the lines of the fast network, using neighbor communication is much faster than using the general routing network for the same pattern. We concentrate on PE ensembles with one- or two-dimensional communication networks, though larger dimensionalities are also possible.

The communication pattern is determined by the program and the data layout. For instance, the assignment statement:

```
forall I = 0 to 255 do
    forall J = 1 to 255 do
        A[I,J] = B[I,J-1] + 1
    endforall
endforall
```

needs nearest neighbor communication; that is, for $PE_{i,j}$ to compute the value for A[I,J], it must get the value of B[I,J-1] from $PE_{i,j-1}$. Note also that not all PEs participate equally in the assignment; some of the border PEs ($PE_{0,0}\ldots PE_{255,0}$) provide values of B, but do not store any values. There are several ways to generate code for this assignment; all require the assignment to be separated into distinct operations: fetch B, add 1, store to A. The fetch of B[I,J-1] can either be done locally on $PE_{i,j-1}$ or by a remote fetch from $PE_{i,j}$ (if remote fetch is available on the architecture). Since the other operand of the addition is a scalar constant, it will be broadcast from the front end and available to all PEs. For each operation in an assignment like this, the compiler must generate code to let each PE determine whether it is to participate in that operation. One way to generate code for this statement is as follows:

```
PE[0:255,0:254]:
    T = B
    send T right
PE[0:255,1:255]:
    receive T left
    A = T + 1
```

where B and A are the elements of that array stored on the particular PE; note that the context for the two halves of the assignment are different. The front end fetches and decodes the instructions, sets up the context, and broadcasts the operations and addresses or operands to the PE ensemble.

13.2 MIMD Machines

Most new systems of the supercomputer class are multicomputers. The availability of high performance, commodity RISC processors, memory, and network configurations makes it reasonably simple to design and construct large-scale message-passing multicomputer systems. Each node in a multicomputer has one or more processors, local memory, and a network interface. In early systems, the exact network topology was critical; recent designs have been more successful in abstracting the network topology from the software.

In our model, a data-parallel application is executed by generating a *node program*, a copy of which executes on each node, much as the SIMD front end executes one program. However, different nodes may take different paths through the program, depending on the data, unlike on a SIMD machine, where conditional execution is done by enabling and disabling PEs. The model of having a single program execute on multiple nodes is sometimes called SPMD (single program executing with multiple data). We use the term SPDD to denote that there is a single program with distributed data structures (rather than multiple unrelated data structures).

The methods described in this chapter are still the subject of quite a bit of research and development. They have proven useful for certain classes of problems, but have not yet replaced low-level programming for these machines.

13.2.1 SPDD Code

Compiling for the SPDD model generates a single node program, which will be executed by all the active nodes. At the simplest level, the compiler could generate a SIMD program, and have each node play the part of front end as well as of a single PE. Many of the techniques here essentially correspond to that. In particular, each of the nodes will redundantly execute much of the scalar code that would, on a SIMD system, be computed by the front end. While inherently inefficient, redundant execution is faster than transferring results over the communication network. Also, the MIMD nature of a multicomputer allows us to use techniques that would not apply to a SIMD machine.

13.3 Data Layout

An array larger than the processor ensemble must be partitioned across the distributed memories. An array is laid out by first matching array dimensions with ensemble axes. The ensemble can be treated as a one-dimensional vector, or perhaps as having two or three or even more dimensions. A 32×32 processor ensemble can store a 512×512 array with $16 \times 16 = 256$ elements at each processor. There are a number of options for exactly which 256 elements are stored at any processor. For instance, the two ensemble dimensions can be matched with the two array dimensions in either of two ways. Each array dimension is then distributed among the processors of that ensemble dimension by dividing the 512 elements into blocks of K consecutive elements, and distributing one of the $512/K$ blocks to each of the 32 processors, cycling around the processors if there are more than 32 blocks. With a block size of one, the distribution is called *cyclic*, since the array elements are cyclically distributed around the processors. With a block size of $\lceil N/P \rceil$, where N and P are the array dimension size and processor ensemble dimension size, respectively, the distribution is called *block*, since each processor gets only a single block. The general case is *block-cyclic*.

13.3 ▪ Data Layout

In a general distribution, the parameters K and P (block size and number of processors) are used to find the processor index and memory offset of an array element. When allocating ensemble memory, an array is divided into *layers*, where each layer is KP array elements, spread evenly across the P processors. If the array has no more than KP elements, one layer is enough (corresponding to a block distribution). Otherwise, several layers will be allocated in each processor memory. A simple formula will find the layer, processor index, and offset of any array element. Given an array `A[LO:HI]`, we find the address of element `A[k]` by first computing its offset from the first element of the array; in this case, the index offset is $i = k - LO$. The following table shows how to find the layer, processor index, and offset from the first element in that layer where the desired element is stored.

layer	$l = \lfloor i/KP \rfloor$
processor	$p = \lfloor (i \bmod KP)/K \rfloor$
offset	$f = i \bmod K$

Taking advantage of the special case when $K = 1$ (cyclic distribution) and when P and/or K are powers of two (so division and modulo operations can be implemented with shift and mask) will be important for performance.

The number of layers needed is $\lceil N/KP \rceil$, where N is again the number of elements in the array. For multidimensional distributed arrays, the computation for each dimension is done separately. Once the layer, processor index, and offset for each dimension is computed, the local memory address can be found.

When allocating memory for a distributed array using the scheme above, the size of the array is artificially inflated to make the distribution equal across the processors. For instance, distributing 500 elements cyclically on 256 processors is done by essentially extending the array to 512 elements. Each processor will then allocate two elements of the inflated array, at the same memory locations in local memory. When operating on the array, the processors holding "inflated" elements of the array should be disabled by an appropriate context.

The distribution determines the load balance among the processors and the communication patterns. A cyclic distribution often tends to improve load balance, when computation is concentrated on a small part of the array; however, it also tends to increase communication, since element `[I]` and element `[I-1]` will be on different processors. On the other hand, a block distribution tends to have opposite characteristics.

Example 13.1

Show how to find an element of an array `A[2:100]` distributed over eight processors with a block size of five.

Solution

Element k will be found in layer $\lfloor (k-2)/40 \rfloor$, at processor $\lfloor ((k-2) \bmod 40)/5 \rfloor$ with offset $(k-2) \bmod 5$. For instance, A[40] will be in layer 0, on processor 7 at offset 3, and element A[49] is in layer 1, on processor 1 at offset 2. See Figure 13.1 for the data layout. In this case, the inflated locations were placed at the end of the array; they could be at the beginning, or split between the beginning and end.

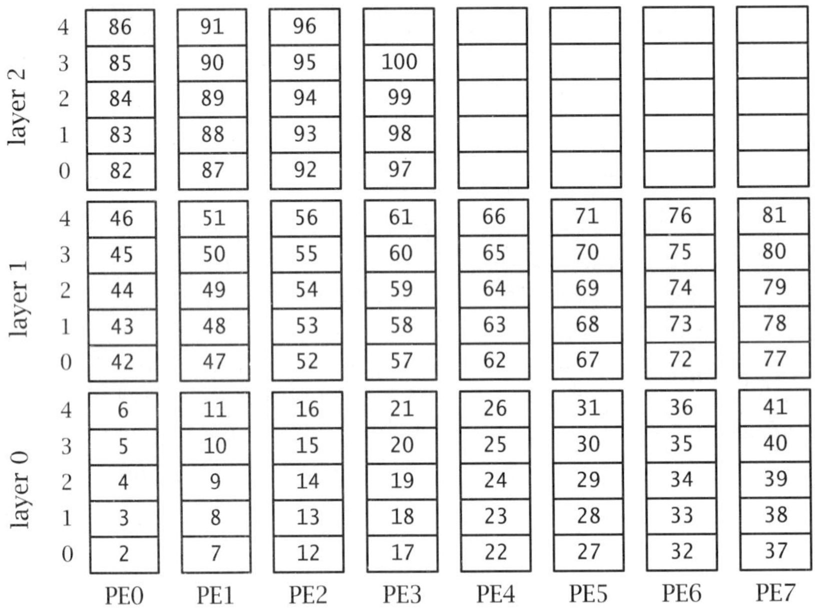

FIGURE 13.1 Simple block-cyclic layout of array A[2:100].

13.3.1 Alignment to Templates

In some languages, such as High Performance Fortran, rather than distributing data directly onto the processor ensemble, an intermediate artificial structure called a *template* is used. A template is a multidimensional object to which data objects are aligned. A distribution is specified for the entire template, which indicates the distribution for all the arrays aligned to it. The template itself takes up no memory at run-time. However, data elements aligned to the same element of a template will be implicitly aligned with one another; that is, will always be allocated to the same processor. The data distribution is thus conceptually broken down into two steps: aligning data to the template, inducing alignments between array elements, and distributing the template onto the processor ensemble.

Suppose we have a two-dimensional template:

```
template T[:,:]
```

13.3 ▪ Data Layout

A simple alignment to this template will give an *axis* alignment; that is, it will tell which array dimension is aligned to which template dimension. Examples of simple alignments are:

    align A[i,j] with T[i,j]
    align B[i,j] with T[j,i]
    align C[i,j,*] with T[i,j]
    align X[i] with T[i,*]
    align Y[i] with T[i,1]

Here, the dimensions of the array A are aligned with dimensions of the template T in order. The dimensions of B are aligned with those of T in reverse order; this means that the elements of B are aligned with the elements of the transpose of A. The array C is three-dimensional; only two of the dimensions are C are aligned with template dimensions. Implicitly, the third dimension of C is *collapsed*; that is, C[i,j,k] will be allocated to the memory of a single processor for all values of k. The single dimension of the vector X, on the other hand, is aligned with the first dimension of the template, and replicated over all elements of the other dimension; eventually, X will be replicated on the processors over which the second dimension of T is distributed. This case is discussed shortly. The vector Y is not replicated; instead, only one copy of Y will appear, and it will be on the processor or processors to which T[:,1] are eventually distributed. To simplify data allocation, memory for nonreplicated data may need to be allocated to each processor, as with inflated arrays, just to keep the memory allocation fixed on each processor.

A slightly more complex alignment allows *offsets* in the alignment specifications:

    align A[i,j] with T[i,j]
    align B[i,j] with T[i+1,j]
    align D[i,j] with T[i,j-2]

The alignment specifications here tell the compiler to make sure that element B[1,1] is allocated to the same processor as elements A[2,1] and D[2,3], since all are aligned to template element T[2,1]. Other more general alignment functions might allow a *scaling factor* or even *skewed alignments*:

    align A[i,j] with T[2*i,3*j-2]
    align B[i,j] with T[i+j-1,j]

The alignment of A is not dense with respect to the template; this means that some processors may not have the same number of elements allocated, or that some processors may not have any elements allocated. The array B uses a skewed alignment; Figure 13.2 shows how these two arrays are aligned with the template T. We do not consider skewed alignments further.

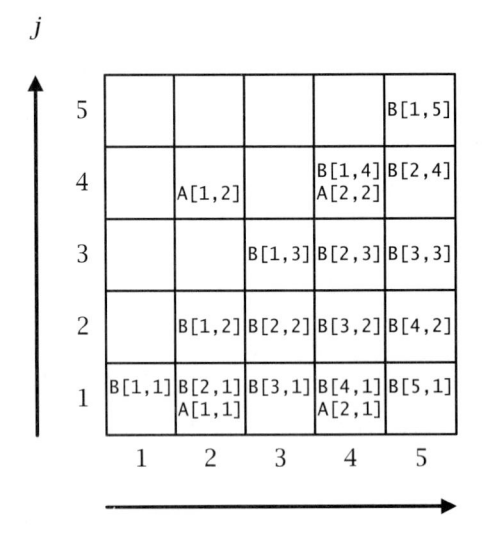

FIGURE 13.2 Partial picture of scaled (A) and skewed (B) alignments to template index T[i,j].

A separate `distribute` statement specifies how the dimensions of the template are distributed across the processor ensemble. We consider general block-cyclic distributions, specified by the keyword `cyclic`, followed by a parameter giving the block size. The specification `cyclic(1)` means a cyclic distribution along that axis. A template dimension may also go undistributed, meaning that all array dimensions aligned to that template dimension are treated as collapsed.

13.3.2 Replication

When data is replicated, there is still only one variable in the program, although its value may be replicated on many processors; this means it is the job of the compiler to ensure that all copies of the variable have the same value. Partial replication may be useful when a vector is aligned with, say, the rows of a distributed matrix. Replicating the vector across each processor row means that a copy of the vector and some of the rows of the matrix will be distributed to each processor row; this should reduce communication due to the vector. It also means that all processors will have to participate in computation, storing values into the replicated vector.

Note that replication is not quite the same as adding a dimension to X and aligning this dimension with the corresponding dimension of the template. When using replication, only one copy of the replicated data needs to be allocated to each processor, regardless of how many or few processors there are in that dimension. Adding a dimension would require one copy of the data for each template element, which will often be quite a bit larger.

Example 13.2

Show the data layout for the vector X below, on a 2×4 processor ensemble:

```
template T[:,:]
real X[1:25]
align X[i] with T[*,i]
distribute T[cyclic(2),cyclic(4)]
```

Solution

The vector X is aligned with the second dimension of the template, and replicated across the first dimension. The first dimension of the template is distributed across the first dimension of the processor ensemble. A solution is shown in Figure 13.3; note that the vector is replicated only once per processor, not once per template index.

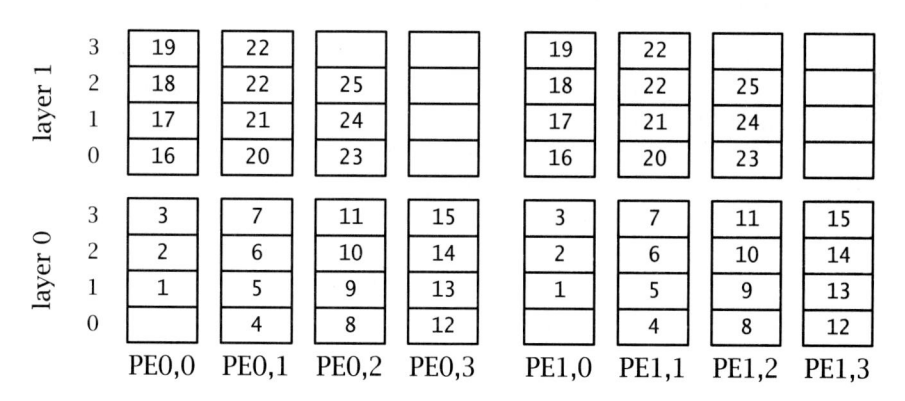

FIGURE 13.3 Data layout for replicated vector.

Moly Variables

On a SIMD machine, scalars are allocated to the front end and broadcast, so they need not be replicated. On a multicomputer, scalars are typically replicated across the whole processor ensemble, so access to the scalar value is immediately available to all processors. Since the scalar is conceptually a single variable, its value must be kept consistent. This can cause additional communication and synchronization. An important optimization will be for the compiler to recognize when a scalar value need not be kept consistent across a multicomputer. A scalar or variable that is allocated to each node of a multicomputer, like a mono variable, but has different values on each node, like a poly variable, is called a *moly* variable.

13.3.3 Distribution of Templates

If all the arrays are aligned to a template, distribution of that template will indicate corresponding distributions of the data. Such a scheme allows a change in one line of the program to change the layout of all or many of the arrays, perhaps to port the program to a different parallel machine. We focus here on general block-cyclic distributions. Earlier we showed a two-dimensional template T. If the processor ensemble is one-dimensional, then only one dimension of the template can be distributed. The choices are which dimension to distribute and what block size to use, where a block size of one is the same as cyclic distribution. With a two-dimensional processor ensemble, both template dimensions can be distributed, each with a different block size. In a real program, there may be two or more different templates. Each template can be distributed independently; the final distribution will generate actual alignments between arrays aligned to different templates, but this may be harder for the compiler to take advantage of.

13.3.4 Local Memory Layout

With a more general alignment and distribution, the compiler must still be able to find the location of any array element. Each distributed template dimension can be mapped independently. The compiler needs to find the number of layers and the layer size for each array in order to allocate local memory, and the layer, processor index, and offset for any array element, given the memory allocation.

For each dimension the compiler must choose an *origin*; that is, the template index that will map to processor 0 at offset 0. The origin t may be chosen as the smallest template index that is aligned to any actual array element. Suppose we have an array dimension, with dimension extents $[l:h]$, that is aligned to this template dimension with a scaling factor a and offset b, and suppose the template dimension is distributed with a block size of K over P processors, as in:

```
A[l:h]
align A[i] with T[a*i+b]
distribute T[cyclic(K)]
```

The array will be aligned with template elements $al + b$ through $ah + b$. The layers and maximum size of a layer are:

$$
\begin{array}{rlcl}
\text{first layer} & L_F & = & \lfloor (al + b - t)/(KP) \rfloor \\
\text{last layer} & L_L & = & \lfloor (ah + b - t)/(KP) \rfloor \\
\text{number of layers} & L & = & \lfloor (a(h-l) + b - t)/KP \rfloor - \lfloor (b-t)/KP \rfloor + 1 \\
\text{maximum layer size} & F & = & \lceil K/a \rceil
\end{array}
$$

We assume a simplified memory allocation where each array is allocated the same number of layers of fixed size (equal to the maximum) on each processor. This

13.3 ■ Data Layout

wastes memory, but simplifies addressing. Effectively, the array A above is changed to have three dimensions, one of which corresponds to the processor index, as in

$$A[L_F:L_L, 0:P-1, 0:F-1]$$

where $L_F : L_L$ are the allocated layers, P is the number of processors, and F is the maximum size of a layer. The layer, processor index, and offset within a layer for element i can be found as follows:

$$\begin{array}{ll} \text{layer} & \lfloor (ai+b-t)/KP \rfloor \\ \text{processor} & \lfloor ((ai+b-t) \bmod KP)/K \rfloor \\ \text{offset} & \lfloor ((ai+b-t) \bmod K)/a \rfloor \end{array}$$

Recall that t is the template origin for this dimension.

Example 13.3

Show the memory allocation of an array B[1:100] aligned as shown below, over eight processors:

```
template T[:]
real B[1:100]
align B[i] with T[2*i+4]
distribute T[cyclic(5)]
```

Solution

Assume that T[1] is the origin. The array B will need layers $\lfloor (2 \cdot 1 + 4 - 1)/40 \rfloor = 0$ through $\lfloor (2 \cdot 100 + 4 - 1)/40 \rfloor = 5$, each with $\lceil 5/2 \rceil = 3$ elements per layer. The first element B[1] is aligned with T[6], which will be at offset 0 on processor 1, and the last element is aligned with T[204], at offset 1 on processor 0. See Figure 13.4 for a picture of the data layout. The distributed array B[1:100] is allocated as a local array lB[0:5,0:2] on each processor.

Template Offset

Henceforth, we will use *template offsets* for array references, defined as the offset from the template origin. For an array aligned to a template as align B[i] with T[a*i+b], an array reference B[i] will be replaced by its corresponding template offset B@[a*i+b-t], where t is again the template origin.

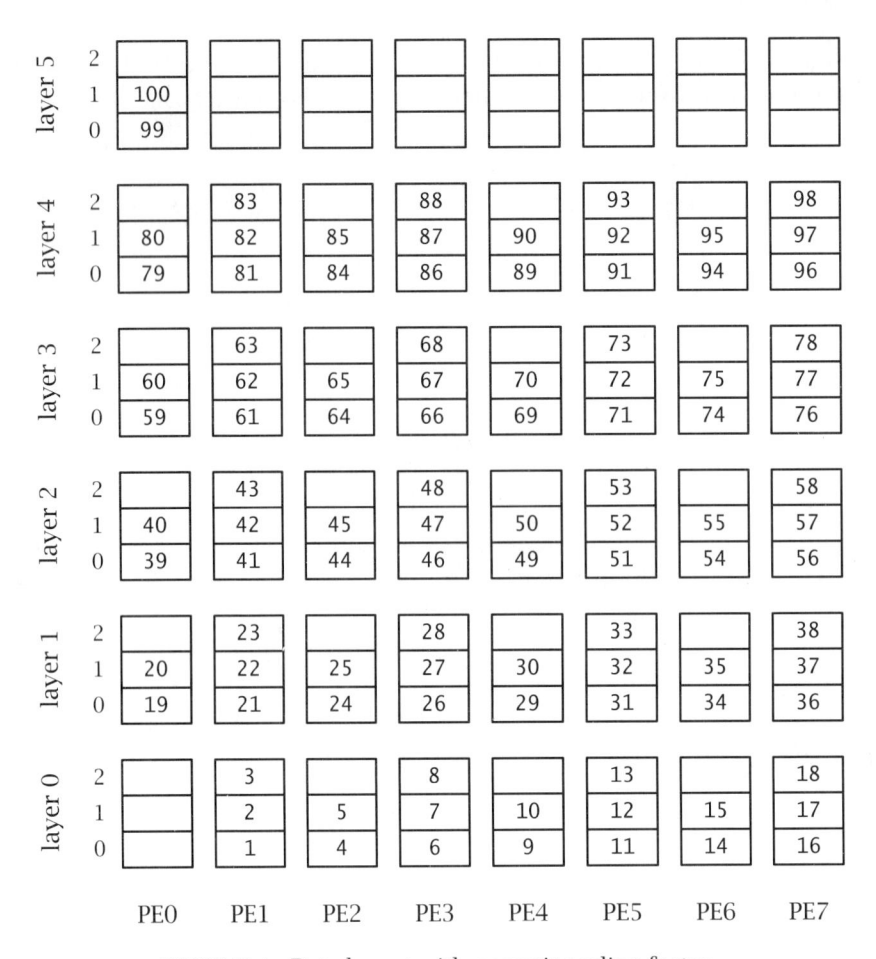

FIGURE 13.4 Data layout with nonunit scaling factor.

Converting from template offsets to layer, processor, and offset indices for a reference B@[i] is simple:

layer	$\lfloor i/KP \rfloor$
processor	$\lfloor (i \bmod KP)/K \rfloor$
offset	$\lfloor (i \bmod K)/a \rfloor$

Note that the scaling factor of the alignment must still be used to find the offset.

Example 13.4

Given array B declared as shown in Example 13.3, rewrite the following assignment using template offsets:

B[5:50:2] = 0.0

13.3 ▪ Data Layout

Solution

The origin is template index 1; in terms of template offsets, the assignment is:

    B@[14:104:4] = 0.0

where the @[] is used to denote template offset indexing. The scaling factor in the alignment is used in the template offset stride. This can also be written as a forall as follows:

    forall I = 14 to 104 by 4 do
        B@[I] = 0.0
    endforall

Element B[5] is B@[14], stored at 1B[0,3] on processor 2.

Collapsed Dimensions

If there are collapsed dimensions, we separate them from the distributed dimensions when using the template offset notation. We will write collapsed dimensions as additional subscripts, such as C@[I][J]. The memory layout is similar to what we have already seen, except that instead of a single element allocated at a particular layer and offset, an entire collapsed dimension will be stored there.

Example 13.5

Describe the allocation for array C as declared below:

(1)   template T[:]
(2)   real C[50,50]
(3)   align with T[i] :: C[*,i+1]
(4)   distribute T[cyclic(4)]

Assume the template origin is element 1 and there are eight processors.

Solution

The second dimension is distributed in blocks of four; each PE will get layers $\lfloor (1 + 1 - 1)/32 \rfloor = 0$ through $\lfloor (50 + 1 - 1)/32 \rfloor = 1$, each with $F = 4$ rows of C, where each row includes 50 elements. The distributed array is declared as 1C[0:1,0:3,1:50], where the first dimension is the column layer, the second is the column offset, and the third corresponds to the collapsed dimension. A reference to C[I,J] is written using template offsets as C@[J+1][I].

Data Allocation Algorithm

A distributed array is one that is allocated on the processor ensemble (as opposed to the front end). Each of the d dimensions has bounds $[l_i : u_i]$, $1 \le i \le d$. A dimension may be collapsed, or it may be aligned with a template dimension. If it is aligned with a template dimension that is not distributed, we treat it as collapsed; otherwise, the alignment and distribution for that dimension have parameters a_i, b_i, K_i, t_i, and P_i:

a_i alignment scaling factor
b_i alignment offset
K_i distribution block size
t_i template origin
P_i number of processors along this dimension

In Example 13.5, the first dimension is collapsed, while the parameters for the second dimension are $a_2 = 1$, $b_2 = 1$, $K_2 = 4$, $t_2 = 1$, and $P_2 = 8$.

Algorithm Bounds, shown in Figure 13.5, finds the bounds for the dimensions of the array to be allocated at each processor. This code can be executed at run-time for arrays that are dynamically allocated to fill in the dope vector information. Note that arrays that are replicated across some processor dimensions use the same algorithm; the only difference is that there will be fewer distributed array dimensions than processor dimensions. Arrays that are allocated to only a subset of processors use the same algorithm. In algorithm Bounds, the dimensions are visited from one to d; we assume that the dimensions can be reordered so that the distributed dimensions appear first, though that is not strictly necessary.

```
         Algorithm Bounds:
(1)      for i = 1 to d do
(2)          if collapsed(i) then
(3)              add dimension bounds l_i : u_i
(4)          else
(5)              L_L = ⌊(a_i l_i + b_i − t_i)/(K_i P_i)⌋
(6)              L_F = ⌊(a_i h_i + b_i − t_i)/(K_i P_i)⌋
(7)              F = ⌈K_i/a_i⌉
(8)              add dimension bounds L_L : L_F, 0 : F − 1
(9)          endif
(10)     endfor
```

FIGURE 13.5 Algorithm to find dimension bounds for allocated distributed array.

13.4 Parallel Code for Array Assignments

Our basic model of a data-parallel operation is an array assignment. To generate code for the processor ensemble, an array assignment must be strip-mined into

13.4 ▪ Parallel Code for Array Assignments

three loops for each index: a processor loop (to be executed in parallel), a layer loop to step between the layers, and an offset loop to step between elements in each layer. In a cyclic distribution, the block size is one, so the offset loop is not needed; similarly, in a block distribution, there is only one layer so the layer loop is unnecessary.

The processor loops are implicit in the generated code. The layer and offset loops are executed sequentially; since originally the array assignment corresponded to `forall` loops, the compiler must correctly convert the `forall`s to sequential loops. We first discuss code generation for dense array assignments (no strides), then sparse assignments.

Example 13.6

Show how to use strip-mining to generate parallel code for the assignment below with eight processors and template origin at 1:

```
(1)       real A[2:100], B[2:100]
(2)       template T[:]
(3)       align A[i] with T[i-1]
(4)       align B[i] with T[i-1]
(5)       distribute T[cyclic(5)]
(6)       A[5:87] = A[5:87] + B[5:87]
```

Solution

We rewrite the array assignment in terms of a `forall` loop with template offset indexing as:

```
forall I = 3 to 85 do
    A@[I] = A@[I] + B@[I]
endforall
```

The data layout for A is the same as that shown in Figure 13.1, and the layout for B matches it. Since all the data in the assignment is aligned, no communication between processors is necessary. The size of a layer is $KP = 5 \times 8 = 40$, so the assignment must go through layers $\lfloor 3/40 \rfloor$ to $\lfloor 85/40 \rfloor$. The layer loops for each index thus will have limits 0 : 2. The offset loops will simply step through all offsets, zero through four, for all layers. The generated parallel code is as follows, where the processor index is [Ip]:

```
for Il = 0 to 2 do
    for Io = 0 to 4 do
        if 3 <= 40*Il+8*Ip+Io <= 85 then
            lA[Il,Io] = lA[Il,Io] + lB[Il,Io]
```

```
            endif
         endfor
      endfor
```

Since there are no loop carried dependence relations in this assignment, conversion to sequential loops is legal. The compiler must change the array references into memory accesses of the local processor address space. The conditional statement determines which processors should be active at each stage (layer and offset) of the computation. Optimizing this conditional will be important.

13.4.1 SIMD Context Computation

For SIMD execution, each operation must execute under the proper context; that is, with the proper PEs enabled. Consider Example 13.6; at the first layer, PE_0 should not participate for offsets 0 through 2, since elements $A[2]$ through $A[4]$ are not changed (refer to Figure 13.1). The context should disable PE_0 for these offsets, then enable it for offsets 3 and 4; at the next layer, however, PE_0 should be enabled for all offsets.

After converting to template offsets, we will denote the *active indices* by the range $\alpha : \beta$. Layer l includes template offsets KPl through $KPl + KP - 1$. We define the *active layers* as the range of layers $l_F : l_L$ that have any active indices. In Example 13.6, the active layers are $0 : 2$; in general, the active layers are the greatest and least solutions to $KPl_F \leq \alpha$ and $KPl_L + KP - 1 \geq \beta$.

For the first and last active layers, some PEs may be inactive at some offsets; indices in any intermediate layers will be fully contained in the range $\alpha : \beta$. In Example 13.6, PE_0 should be inactive at offsets 0 through 2 for layer 0, and PE_4 should be inactive at all offsets for layer 2. To find the appropriate active PEs for offset o at the first active layer l, we need to find values p such that $KPl + Kp + o \geq \alpha$, where $0 \leq o < K$. This has integer solution at $p \geq \lceil (\alpha - KPl - o)/K \rceil$. After the first active layer, $KPl > \alpha$, so the first active processor is $p = 0$. For the first active layer, however, the first active processor at offset o is

$$p_F(o) = \lceil (\alpha - KPl_F - o)/K \rceil.$$

The value of $p_F(o)$ has its greatest solution at $o = 0$; as o increases from 0 to $K - 1$, $p_F(o)$ will either remain unchanged or decrease by exactly one. We can compute the offset where the $p_F(o)$ changes value as $o = \alpha \bmod K$. Thus, for offsets from 0 to $\alpha \bmod K - 1$, $p_F(o) = p_F(0) = \lceil (\alpha - KPl_F)/K \rceil$, and for offsets $o \geq \alpha \bmod K$, $p_F(o) = p_F(0) - 1$.

Similarly, in the last active layer, we want to find the last active processor p at offset o such that $KPl_L + Kp + o \leq \beta$, which simplifies to $p \leq \lfloor (\beta - KPl_L - o)/K \rfloor$. The last active processor at layer l_L and offset o is

$$p_L(o) = \lfloor (\beta - KPl_L - o)/K \rfloor.$$

13.4 ▪ Parallel Code for Array Assignments

This has greatest value at $o = 0$, and will decrease by one when $o = \beta \bmod K$. The context for a dense assignment can be computed by the front end as shown in Figure 13.6.

layer	offset	context lower limit	context upper limit
first	$0 \leq o < \alpha \bmod K$	$\lfloor (\alpha - KPl)/K \rfloor + 1$	$P - 1$
	$\alpha \bmod K \leq o < K - 1$	$\lfloor (\alpha - KPl)/K \rfloor$	$P - 1$
others	$0 \leq o < K - 1$	0	$P - 1$
last	$0 \leq o \leq \beta \bmod K$	0	$\lfloor (\beta - KPl)/K \rfloor$
	$\beta \bmod K < o < K - 1$	0	$\lfloor (\beta - KPl)/K \rfloor - 1$

FIGURE 13.6 Context computation

Procedure Context, shown in Figure 13.7, shows how to emit code to generate the context for a single dimension array assignment. It assumes that the first and last active indices are α to β, that K is the block size, and that P is the number

```
(1)   Procedure Context( α, β )
(2)       emit 'IlFirst = ⌊α/KP⌋'
(3)       emit 'IlLast = ⌊β/KP⌋'
(4)       emit 'IoFx = α mod K'
(5)       emit 'IoLx = β mod K'
(6)       emit 'IpFirst0 = ⌊(α - KP*IlFirst)/K⌋ + 1'
(7)       emit 'IpLast0 = ⌊(β - KP*IlLast)/K⌋'
(8)       emit 'for Il = IlFirst to IlLast do'
(9)       emit 'IpFirst = Merge( Il = IlFirst, IpFirst0, 0 )'
(10)      emit 'IpLast = Merge( Il = IlLast, IpLast0, P-1 )'
(11)      emit 'for Io = 0 to F-1 do'
(12)      emit 'IpFirst = Merge( Il = IlFirst and Io = IoFx,
                IpFirst-1, IpFirst )
(13)      emit 'PE[IpFirst:IpLast]:'
(14)      Generate code for the assignment statement
(15)      for each distributed array do
(16)          emit subscript '[Il,Io]'
(17)      endfor
(18)      emit 'IpLast = Merge( Il = IlLast and Io = IoLx, IpLast-1, IpLast )
(19)      emit 'endloop'
(20)      emit 'endloop'
(21)  end Context
```

FIGURE 13.7 Algorithm to emit code to compute SIMD context for a strip-mined array assignment.

of PEs. The `emit` construct is used to generate code; the procedure emits code to compute the limits for the layer loop and the bounds of active processors. If the arguments are known at compile time, some of these may be computable. Inside the layer loop, two assignments are generated to adjust the first active processor and last active processor; the second of these is generated at the end of the layer loop. The `Merge` function used in the generated code is defined as returning its second argument if the condition in the first argument is true, and returning its last argument otherwise.

Example 13.7

Complete Example 13.6 for SIMD execution by using procedure `Context` to emit code to compute the correct context.

Solution

Since the active indices, block size, and number of PEs are compile-time constants, many of the computations can be made by the compiler. Nonetheless, we show the computations where they would be generated if computed dynamically. Note all the setup code for one line of parallel code.

```
(1)   IlFirst = 0
(2)   IlLast = 2
(3)   IpFirst0 = 1
(4)   IpLast0 = 1
(5)   IoFx = 3
(6)   IoLx = 0
(7)   for Il = IlFirst to IlLast do
(8)       IpFirst = Merge( Il = IlFirst, IpFirst0, 0 )
(9)       IpLast = Merge( Il = IlLast, IpLast0, P-1 )
(10)      for Io = 0 to 4 do
(11)          IpFirst = Merge( Il = IlFirst and Io = IoFx,
                           IpFirst-1, IpFirst )
(12)          PE[IpFirst:IpLast]:
(13)              1A[Il,Io] = 1A[Il,Io] + 1B[Il,Io]
(14)          IpLast = Merge( Il = IlLast and Io = IoLx, IpLast-1, IpLast )
(15)      endfor
(16)  endfor
```

Sparse Contexts

When an array reference has a nonunit stride, or when the alignment has a scaling factor, not every template index is active for the assignment. With a stride of

2, for instance, only every other template element is active; in a cyclic distribution, this means that every other processor participates, while with a block-cyclic distribution with an even block size, the offset loop can skip over the odd offsets.

Consider a reference with active indices from α to β and with stride σ, distributed on P PEs with block size K. As before, we find the active layers by:

$$\begin{aligned} \text{first layer} \quad & l_F = \lfloor \alpha/KP \rfloor \\ \text{last layer} \quad & l_L = \lfloor \beta/KP \rfloor \end{aligned}$$

Within each layer, an offset loop will step through all the offsets. The *active offsets* are those that have one or more active PEs in the current layer, where an active PE is enabled for the operation. At layer l, PE p, and offset o, the corresponding template offset is $KPl + Kp + o$; this PE should be active at this offset only if $KPl + Kp + o = \alpha + \sigma j \leq \beta$, for some nonnegative integer value j. We can rewrite this as $Kp - \sigma j = \alpha - KPl - o$; from Chapter 4, we know that this has an integer solution for p and j only when $g = \gcd(\sigma, K)$ divides $\alpha - KPl - o$. In fact, g must divide KPl, so we only need to check whether g divides $\alpha - o$. Not every offset will participate; if $g > 1$, then only offsets $o \equiv \alpha \pmod{g}$ need to be considered, starting at $\alpha \bmod g$.

At a given offset that satisfies this condition, the active PEs are those with PE index p that satisfy

$$Kp - \sigma j = \alpha - KPl - o. \tag{13.1}$$

Again we apply algorithm GCD from Chapter 4 to find $g = \gcd(K, \sigma)$ and a solution p' and j' to satisfy

$$Kp' - \sigma j' = g. \tag{13.2}$$

All solutions to (13.1) are given by:

$$p = \frac{\alpha - KPl - o}{g} p' + \frac{\sigma}{g} t$$

$$j = \frac{\alpha - KPl - o}{g} j' + \frac{K}{g} t$$

where we have chosen o so that $(\alpha - KPl - o)$ is divisible by g. The PEs that should participate are those that satisfy this and lie between zero and $P-1$. The first such PE has the smallest value t such that $p'(\alpha - KPl - o)/g + t(\sigma/g) \geq 0$, which simplifies to

$$t = \left\lceil \frac{o - \alpha + KPl}{\sigma} p' \right\rceil$$

If σ divides KP, the first active PE at the first active offset will be the same for each layer. Let p_o be the index of the first active PE at offset o; all PEs $[p_o : P-1 : \sigma/g]$ should be active at offset o. Incrementing to the next offset, $o + g$, we want to find the first active PE incrementally. Given our solution p_o, j_o at offset o to

$$KPl + Kp_o + o = \alpha + \sigma j_o, \tag{13.3}$$

the solution at the next offset must be

$$KPl + K(p_o + p_i) + (o + g) = \alpha + \sigma(j_o + j_i), \qquad (13.4)$$

where p_i is the increment in the first active processor at the next active offset. The difference between these two equations is $Kp_i + g = \sigma j_i$, or $Kp_i - \sigma j_i = -g$. This is essentially the same as equation (13.2), which we have already solved. We want the smallest value of $p = p_o + p_i \geq 0$; this will be $p = p_o - p' + t\sigma/g$, for (a different) free variable t. Since $p_o < \sigma/g$, the smallest active PE index at offset $o + g$ will be $(p_o - p') \bmod (\sigma/g)$.

Procedure `SparseContext`, shown in Figure 13.8, shows how to emit code to generate the context for a sparse one-dimension array assignment. It assumes that the first and last active indices are α to β, the stride is σ, K is the block size, and P is the number of PEs. Most of the procedure is similar to procedure `Context`. It uses procedure `Findgcd` from algorithm GCD in Chapter 4, computes both the active processor sets due to the active indices and due to the sparsity, and intersects them. For any computation emitted, if the arguments are known at compile time, the computation should be done by the compiler. The conditional tests optimize the code in certain cases; the conditions should evaluate to false if the expression tested is not a compile-time constant. The division by the scaling factor can be strength-reduced to remove the division operation from the inner loop.

Example 13.8

Use procedure `SparseContext` to generate SIMD code for the following array assignment, assuming A and B are distributed as in Example 13.6.

```
A[12:84:8] = B[12:84:8] * 2
```

Solution
In terms of template offsets, the array assignment is rewritten as:

```
A@[10:82:8] = B@[10:82:8] * 2
```

With all the parameters known, the compiler can compute most of the values at compile time. A compile-time call to `Findgcd` determines that g=3 and pp=-3. Using constant folding, the code can be optimized to the following:

```
for I1 = 0 to 2 do
    IpFirst = Merge( I1=I1First, 2, 0 )
    IpLast = Merge( I1=I1Last, 0, 7 )
    SpFirst = 2
    for Io = 0 to 4 by 1 do
        IpLast = Merge( I1 = 2 and Io > 2, 0, IpLast )
```

13.4 ▪ Parallel Code for Array Assignments

```
(1)   Procedure SparseContext( α, β, σ )
(2)       emit 'IlFirst = ⌊α/(KP)⌋; IlLast = ⌊β/(KP)⌋'
(3)       emit 'Findgcd( K, σ ) returns( g, pp, jj )'
(4)       emit 'IoFirst = α mod g; r = σ/g; ppr = -pp mod r'
(5)       if KP mod σ = 0 then
(6)           emit 't = ⌈(IoFirst-α+KP*IlFirst)*pp/σ⌉'
(7)           emit 'SpFirst0 = (α-KP*IlFirst-IoFirst)*pp/g + r*t'
(8)       endif
(9)       emit 'IoFx = α mod K; IoLx = β mod K'
(10)      emit 'IpFirst0 = ⌊(α-KP*IlFirst)/K⌋ '
(11)      if IoFx > IoFirst then
(12)          emit 'IpFirst0 = IpFirst0 + 1'
(13)      endif
(14)      emit 'IpLast0 = ⌊(β-KP*IlLast)/K⌋'
(15)      emit 'for Il = IlFirst to IlLast do'
(16)      emit 'IpFirst = Merge( Il = IlFirst, IpFirst0, 0 )'
(17)      emit 'IpLast = Merge( Il = IlLast, IpLast0, P-1 )'
(18)      if KP mod σ = 0 then
(19)          emit 'SpFirst = SpFirst0'
(20)      else
(21)          emit 't = ⌈(IoFirst-α+KP*Il)*pp/σ⌉'
(22)          emit 'SpFirst = (α-KP*Il-IoFirst)*pp/g + r*t'
(23)      endif
(24)      emit 'for Io = IoFirst to F-1 by g do'
(25)      if IoFx > IoFirst then
(26)          emit 'IpFirst = Merge( Il=IlFirst and Io>=IoFx,
                        IpFirst0-1, IpFirst )'
(27)      endif
(28)      if IoLx < IoLast then
(29)          emit 'IpLast = Merge( Il=IlLast and Io>IoLx, IpLast0-1, IpLast )'
(30)      endif
(31)      emit 'PE[SpFirst:P-1:r ∩ IpFirst:IpLast]:'
(32)      Generate code for the assignment statement
(33)      for each distributed array with alignment scaling factor a do
(34)          emit subscript '[Il,Io/a]'
(35)      endfor
(36)      if ppr > 0 then emit 'SpFirst = (SpFirst + ppr) mod r' endif
(37)      emit 'endloop; endloop'
(38)  end SparseContext
```

FIGURE 13.8 Algorithm to emit code to compute SIMD context for a strip-mined array assignment.

```
            PE[SpFirst:7:8 ∩ IpFirst:IpLast]
                lA[I1][Io] = lB[I1][Io/2]
            SpFirst = (SpFirst + 3) mod 8
        endfor
    endfor
```

Execution of this code will have only one active processor each time the parallel statement is executed.

Degenerate Cases

To assign a single array element requires setting the context to disable all processors but the one that owns that element. If the left hand side is replicated across some number of PEs, all those that own the element should be enabled. In the following assignment, again using the data layout of Figure 13.1, all processors but one must be disabled:

```
    A[9] = 0
```

In template offsets, this is

```
    A@[7] = 0
```

which can be treated as the array assignment:

```
    A@[7:7] = 0
```

There is only one active layer; in that layer there is only one active offset; at that offset there is only one active processor. The generated code is:

```
    PE[1:1]:
        lA[0][2] = 0
```

For multidimensional distributions, a layer and offset loop will be generated for each distributed index. Sequential loops are used to iterate over nondistributed dimensions. The `forall` loops must be converted into sequential loops using the standard methods.

13.4.2 Multicomputer Code

On a multicomputer, each node could execute a copy of the SIMD front end code for an array assignment; however, since each node can execute independently, each node needs only to iterate through the layers and offsets for which it is active. Thus, for multicomputers, rather than computing the set of active PEs at each

13.4 ▪ Parallel Code for Array Assignments

layer and offset, the problem is to compute the set of active layers and offsets for each PE. This is in some sense the dual problem of that solved for SIMD machines.

For a dense index set $\alpha : \beta$, the first layer for which node p contributes is the smallest value of l such that one of the offsets lies within the index set; thus we want the smallest value of l such that $KPl + Kp + K - 1 \geq \alpha$. Similarly, the last active layer for node p is the largest value of l such that $KPl + Kp \leq \beta$.

At the first and last active layers, not all offsets will necessarily contribute to the computation. The first offset in layer l for node p to contribute to the index set $\alpha : \beta$ is the smallest value of o in the range $[0 : K-1]$ such that $KPl+Kp+o \geq \alpha$. The last active offset is the largest value of $o \in [0 : K-1]$ that satisfies $KPl+Kp+o \leq \beta$. The computation of first and last active layer and offset are shown in the following table:

first layer	$\lceil (\alpha - Kp - K + 1)/KP \rceil$
last layer	$\lfloor (\beta - Kp)/KP \rfloor$
first offset	$\max(0, \alpha - KPl - Kp)$
last offset	$\min(K - 1, \beta - KPl - Kp)$

For dense computations, the first and last offsets will be 0 and $K - 1$ except for the first and last active layers. Thus, the code for executing the parallel loop can be optimized to compute these values only when needed.

Procedure NodeCode, shown in Figure 13.9, shows how to emit the node code for a single dimensional array assignment. As with procedure Context, it assumes

```
(1)  Procedure NodeCode( α, β )
(2)      emit 'IlFirst = ⌈(α-K*p - K + 1)/KP⌉'
(3)      emit 'IlLast = ⌊(β-Kp)/KP⌋'
(4)      emit 'IoFirst0 = max(0,α-KP*IlFirst-K*p)'
(5)      emit 'IoLast0 = min(K-1,β-KP*IlLast-K*p)'
(6)      emit 'for Il = IlFirst to IlLast do'
(7)      emit 'IoFirst = Merge( Il = IlFirst, IoFirst0, 0 )'
(8)      emit 'IoLast = Merge( Il = IlLast, IoLast0, K-1 )'
(9)      emit 'for Io = IoFirst to IoLast do'
(10)     Generate code for the assignment statement
(11)     for each distributed array do
(12)         emit subscript '[Il,Io]'
(13)     endfor
(14)     emit 'endloop'
(15)     emit 'endloop'
(16) end NodeCode
```

FIGURE 13.9 Algorithm to emit node code for array assignment.

that the first and last active indices are α to β, that K is the block size and P is the number of PEs, and that p is the index of this node. In some cases, the compiler can determine that computations using p will compute the same result for all values of p, and can substitute a compile-time value.

Example 13.9
Complete Example 13.6 for multicomputer execution by optimizing the node program.

Solution
In this case, the compiler can determine that since both node zero and node seven will compute the first active layer as zero, all nodes have I1First=0. However, the last active layer is two at node 0 and one at node 8, so each node must compute its own last active layer. The generated code is as follows:

```
I1Last = floor((85-5*p)/40))
IoFirst0 = max(0,3-5*p)
IoLast0 = min(4,85-40*I1Last-5*p)
for I1 = 0 to I1Last do
    IoFirst = Merge(I1=0,I1First0,0)
    IoLast = Merge(I1=I1Last,I1Last0,4)
    for Io = IoFirst to IoLast do
        1A[I1,Io] = 1A[I1,Io] + 1B[I1,Io]
    endfor
endfor
```

Nonunit Strides

When the template offset form has a nonunit stride, we want to find the first active template offset at each layer for each node; the stride $\sigma > 0$ will be the stride within a layer for each node. If the stride is large relative to the block size K (particularly when a cyclic decomposition is used, i.e., $K = 1$), then we want to find not only the active offsets in each layer, but the active layers for each node.

At layer l, node p is active at the first offset o such that $Kpl + Kp + o = \alpha + \sigma j$ with $0 \leq o < K$ and $j \geq 0$. We solve for the value of j for the first offset as follows

$$\alpha + \sigma j - Kp - KPl \geq 0$$

$$j \geq \left\lceil \frac{Kp + KPl - \alpha}{\sigma} \right\rceil$$

The first offset must then satisfy the following equation:

$$0 \geq \alpha + \sigma \left\lceil \frac{Kp + KPl - \alpha}{\sigma} \right\rceil - Kp - KPl \qquad (13.5)$$

13.4 ▪ Parallel Code for Array Assignments

To lie within the limits, the first offset must be:

$$o = \alpha + \max(0, \sigma \left\lceil \frac{Kp + KPl - \alpha}{\sigma} \right\rceil) - Kp - KPl.$$

Since $a + b\lceil -a/b \rceil = a \bmod b$, this simplifies to:

$$o = \max(\alpha - Kp - KPl, (\alpha - Kp - KPl) \bmod \sigma)$$

If σ divides K or KP, the Kp or KPl terms can be pulled out of the modulo operator; for instance, if σ divides K, the first active offset is the same for each node at every layer after the first:

first layer $o = \max(\alpha - Kp - KPl, \alpha \bmod \sigma)$
other layers $o = \alpha \bmod \sigma$

If the stride $\sigma \leq K$, each node will be active at each layer. Let o_1 be the first active offset at layer l computed by equation (13.5). The first active offset for the next layer will be $(o_1 - (KP \bmod \sigma)) \bmod \sigma$, which can be rewritten $(o_1 + ((-KP) \bmod \sigma)) \bmod \sigma$. If KP and σ are known, this can be simplified at compile time.

Procedure SparseNodeCode, shown in Figure 13.10, generates the appropriate node code for sparse array assignments. It is similar to procedure NodeCode, except that it computes a first offset at each layer that is a multiple of the stride away from the starting point.

Example 13.10

Show the node program generated by procedure SparseNodeCode for the following array assignment, with the same alignment and distribution as in Figure 13.1.

```
A[13:87:3] = A[13:87:3] * 2
```

Solution
In terms of template offsets, this is:

```
A@[11:85:3] = A@[11:85:3] * 2
```

The last element to be assigned by this assignment is A@[83], since $83 = 11 + 3 \cdot 24$. The code generated below takes advantage of the fact that K and P are known; for instance, IoInc is computed to have value 2.

```
IlFirst = ceil((7 - 5*p)/40)
IlLast = floor((83 - 5*Ip)/20)
IoFirst0 = 11 - 5*p - 40*IlFirst
IoFirst1 = IoFirst0 mod 3
IoFirst = max( IoFirst0, IoFirst1 )
```

```
IoLast0 = min( 4, 83 - 40*I1Last - K*p )
for I1 = I1First to I1Last do
    for Io = IoFirst to 4 by 3 do
        lA[I1][Io] = lA[I1][Io] * 2
    endfor
    IoFirst1 = mod( IoFirst1+2, 3 )
    IoFirst = IoFirst1
endfor
```

(1) Procedure SparseNodeCode(α, β, σ)
(2)   emit 'I1First = $\lceil(\alpha-K*p - K + 1)/KP\rceil$'
(3)   emit 'I1Last = $\lfloor(\beta-Kp)/KP\rfloor$'
(4)   emit 'IoFirst0 = α - K*p - KP*I1First'
(5)   emit 'IoFirst1 = IoFirst0 mod σ'
(6)   emit 'IoFirst = max(IoFirst0,IoFirst1)'
(7)   emit 'IoInc = (-KP) mod σ'
(8)   emit 'IoLast0 = min(K-1,β-KP*I1Last-K*p)'
(9)   emit 'for I1 = I1First to I1Last do'
(10)   emit 'IoLast = Merge(I1 = I1Last, IoLast0, K-1)'
(11)   emit 'for Io = IoFirst to IoLast by σ do'
(12)   Generate code for the assignment statement
(13)   for each distributed array with alignment scaling factor a do
(14)   emit subscript '[I1,Io/a]'
(15)   endfor
(16)   if IoInc $\neq$ 0 then
(17)   emit 'IoFirst1 = (IoFirst1 + IoInc) mod σ'
(18)   emit 'IoFirst = IoFirst1'
(19)   endif
(20)   emit 'endloop'
(21)   emit 'endloop'
(22) end SparseNodeCode

FIGURE 13.10 Algorithm to emit node code for array assignment with nonunit stride.

Large Strides

If the stride σ is large relative to K—particularly if it is large relatively to KP—we don't want to generate code that iterates through every layer, only to find that there are no active offsets at most of the layers.

One way to find only the active layers is to note that the difference between successive active layers is a repeating pattern, with a period of K or a factor of K. First we find the offsets that might be active at some layer; we saw this for SIMD

13.4 ▪ Parallel Code for Array Assignments

code generation. If σ and KP are relatively prime, then all offsets may be active at some point. Otherwise, only those offsets o such that

$$KPl + Kp + o = \alpha + \sigma j \tag{13.6}$$

for some value of j and l can be active. Thus, there must be an integer solution to

$$KPl - \sigma j = \alpha - Kp - o,$$

meaning that $g = \gcd(\sigma, KP)$ must divide $\alpha - Kp - o$. Only offsets congruent to $\alpha - Kp$ (modulo g) will ever be active. At a given offset o, the first layer active is given by solving for l above. As shown in Chapter 4, we find l' and j' such that $KPl' - \sigma j' = g$. If we choose o so that g divides $\alpha - Kp - o$, all solutions to equation (13.6) are given by

$$\begin{aligned} l &= l' \frac{\alpha - Kp - o}{g} + t\frac{\sigma}{g} \\ j &= j' \frac{\alpha - Kp - o}{g} + t\frac{KP}{g} \end{aligned} \tag{13.7}$$

Solving for $j \geq 0$ gives $t \geq j'(Kp + o - \alpha)/KP$, for a first active layer of

$$l = l' \frac{\alpha - Kp - o}{g} + \frac{\sigma}{g} \left\lceil j' \frac{Kp + o - \alpha}{KP} \right\rceil$$

A method to find the pattern of active layers is to find the first active layer for each potentially active offset. Then the offsets can be sorted based on the active layers; this gives the initial sequence of active layers. By computing the differences between consecutive active layers, we can generate the pattern of active layers, which repeats starting at σ/g layers after the first one. Figure 13.11 shows the code that should be generated by the compiler in the general case when $\sigma > K$; as always, if σ, K, or P are known at compile time, some of the expressions may be computed then. The code constructs a table T that contains the first active layer at each potentially active offset. The table entries are then sorted based on the layer, and relative differences are computed in the T.diff field; the T.next field is the index of the next table entry, linked in a circular list. The generated code for the array assignment then operates like a finite state machine, where t is the state number, computing the next active layer and the offset at that layer.

Example 13.11

Show how the code shown in Figure 13.11 finds the active layers for the following array assignment, where $P = 4$ and $K = 3$:

    A@[0:84:7] = A@[0:84:7] + 1

Solution

Since $\gcd(K, -\sigma) = \gcd(3, -7) = 1$, all offsets are potentially active. A solution to $12l - 7j = 1$ is $l' = 3, j' = 5$; this is used to compute the first active layer at each

```
(1)  Findgcd( KP, -σ ) returns( g, lp, jp )
(2)  n = 0
(3)  for Io = α-K*p mod g to K-1 by g do
(4)      n = n + 1
(5)      T[n].offset = Io
(6)      m = α - K*P - Io
(7)      T[n].layer = (lp*m + σ*⌈ -jp*m/KP ⌉)/g
(8)  endfor
(9)  sort entries of T based on layer field
(10) for t = 1 to n-1 do
(11)     T[t].diff = T[t+1].layer - T[t].layer
(12)     T[t].next = t+1
(13) endfor
(14) T[n].diff = T[1].layer + σ/g - T[n].layer
(15) T[n].next = 1
(16) Il = T[1].layer
(17) Io = T[1].offset
(18) t = 1
(19) while Il*KP + p*K + Io <= β do
(20)     Generate code for the assignment statement
(21)     for each distributed array with alignment scaling factor a do
(22)         emit subscript '[Il,Io/a]'
(23)     endfor
(24)     Il = Il + T[t].diff
(25)     t = T[t].next
(26)     Io = T[t].offset
(27) endwhile
```

FIGURE 13.11 Generated node code when the stride is large.

offset for each node. The following table gives the tuples $\langle l, o \rangle$ showing the first active layer for each offset:

node 0	node 1	node 2	node 3
⟨0,0⟩	⟨5,0⟩	⟨3,0⟩	⟨1,0⟩
⟨4,1⟩	⟨2,1⟩	⟨0,1⟩	⟨5,1⟩
⟨1,2⟩	⟨6,2⟩	⟨4,2⟩	⟨2,2⟩

In the generated code, each node would compute its column in this table. After sorting each column by layer, the result is:

node 0	node 1	node 2	node 3
⟨0,0⟩	⟨2,1⟩	⟨0,1⟩	⟨1,0⟩
⟨1,2⟩	⟨5,0⟩	⟨3,0⟩	⟨2,2⟩
⟨4,1⟩	⟨6,2⟩	⟨4,2⟩	⟨5,1⟩

13.4 ▪ Parallel Code for Array Assignments

The table below shows the offset, difference, and next state fields for the table for each node. These entries in the table are $t : o, d, n$, where t is the state number, o is the offset to use in this state, d is the distance to the layer at the next state, and n is the next state.

	node 0	node 1	node 2	node 3
	1:0,1,2	1:1,3,2	1:1,3,2	1:0,1,2
	2:2,3,3	2:0,1,3	2:0,1,3	2:2,3,3
	3:1,3,1	3:2,3,1	3:2,3,1	3:1,3,1
first layer	0	2	0	1

In this example, each node has the same number of states; in fact, the finite state machines for nodes 0 and 3 (and 1 and 2) are the same, although the starting layers are different.

Active Layers at Each Offset

Another alternative is to use offset and layer loops, as before, but to interchange them; in this scheme, the outer loop iterates through the potential offsets, and the inner loop iterates through the layers active for that offset. As before, only offsets $o \equiv \alpha - Kp \pmod{\gcd(KP, \sigma)}$ are potentially active. Let $g = \gcd(KP, \sigma)$, and l' and j' be solutions to $KPl' - \sigma j' = g$. For each offset o, the first and last active layers are found by solving equation (13.7) for $j \geq 0$ and $alpha + \sigma j \leq \beta$, giving:

$$t \geq j'(Kp + o - \alpha)/KP$$

$$t \leq (g(\beta - \alpha)/\sigma - j'(Kp + o - \alpha)/KP$$

Subsequent layers active at that offset are found by adding $\sigma/\gcd(KP, \sigma)$.

Procedure VerySparse, shown in Figure 13.12, generates the appropriate code for this scheme. The generated code iterates through each potentially active offset and finds all the layers active at that offset.

Example 13.12

Repeat Example 13.11 using offset and layer loops.

Solution

As in Example 13.11, the compiler can perform the call to Findgcd to get $\gcd(K, -\sigma) = \gcd(3, -7) = 1$, and the solution to $12l - 7j = 1$ as $l' = 3, j' = 5$. As before, all offsets may be active at some layer, so the offset loop for each node must visit all offsets. The final program is:

```
for Io = 0 to 2 do
    m = - 3*p - Io
```

```
        I1First = 3*m + 7*ceil( -5*m/12 )
        I1Last = 3*m + 7*floor( (13 - 5*m)/12 )
        for I1 = I1First to I1Last by 7 do
            1A[I1][Io] = 1A[I1][Io] * 2
        endfor
    endfor
```

```
(1)   Procedure VerySparse( α, β, σ )
(2)       emit 'Findgcd( KP, -σ ) returns( g, lp, jp )'
(3)       emit 'for Io = (α-K*p mod g) to K-1 by g do'
(4)       emit 'm = α - K*p - Io'
(5)       emit 'I1First = (lp*m + σ*⌈ -jp*m/KP ⌉)/g'
(6)       emit 'I1Last = (lp*m + σ*⌊ (⌊ (β-α)/σ ⌋*g - jp*m)/KP ⌋)/g'
(7)       emit 'for I1 = I1First to I1Last by σ/g do'
(8)       emit 'Generate code for the assignment statement'
(9)       for each distributed array with alignment scaling factor a do
(10)          emit subscript '[I1,Io/a]'
(11)      endfor
(12)      emit 'endfor'
(13)      emit 'endfor'
(14)  end VerySparse
```

FIGURE 13.12 Algorithm to generate node code for very sparse array assignments.

13.5 Remote Data Access

The examples so far have been pretty trivial; all the data in each assignment was aligned at the same template offset. We naturally decided to compute each element of the expression on the processor that owned the data. In general, one or more of the operands will either be aligned at a different offset in the template, or aligned to a different template, requiring communication. The compiler must first decide on what processor to compute each operator of the expression. Then it needs to insert communication to align the operands to that processor and send the results to the destination. One scheme is to let the owner of the left hand side variable compute the whole expression; this is sometimes called the *owner-computes* rule. Another choice is to let the owner of the most operands do the computation; alternatively, the compiler may choose to break the computation down into subexpressions, computing each subexpression on a different processor. For each expression (or subexpression), the *active indices* are the template offsets at which the computation will be performed.

13.5 ▪ Remote Data Access

The most general solution to remote data access is to use a *remote fetch* capability, where each processor computes the remote processor index and memory address and issues a remote fetch. This requires hardware or software support for remote fetch, which may not be available; also, each element fetched requires two traversals of the network: one for the request and another for the response. An alternative is to invert the access function; if processor i needs element A@[$f(i)$], which is stored at template offset $j = f(i)$ on processor $j_p = f_p(i)$, compute $f^{-1}(j)$, and let processor j_p send the value to processor $f_p^{-1}(j)$. This requires only a single traversal of the network, and thus can be more efficient than remote fetch.

We model computation of expressions that require communication by breaking the array expression into a communication part followed by aligned computation. The communication aligns operands for a subexpression on a single processor. To be general, we break the communication into two parts, a send and a receive, where the send executes on the source and the receive executes on the destination. We use the notation $\Rightarrow$ for a send, and $\Leftarrow$ for a receive. The active indices for a send are those in the source operand, while the active indices for a receive are those in the destination. If the target architecture supports a *remote fetch* operation, the communication can proceed with no active participation on the part of the source processor, and the send part of the communication can be ignored. Alternatively, if the architecture supports a *remote store* operation, the communication can proceed with no active participation on the part of the destination, and the receive part can be ignored. The most common case on current machines is that both the source and destination must participate, with the source processor sending a message and the destination processor receiving the message and storing the data. One potential advantage of using send/receive code is that the transit time can be absorbed by separating the send and receive operations, placing other computation between them. In any case, when the communication is done, the computation then proceeds with all the data available on the same processor.

Example 13.13

Break the assignment below into communication and computation parts, using the owner-computes rule.

    A@[2:50:2] = B@[4:76:3]*(A@[1:49:2]+A@[3:51:2])

Solution

The owner-computes rules states that the owner of the left hand side will compute the expression; thus all operands must be aligned with the active indices $2:50:2$. None of the three operands in the expression is aligned with the left hand side, so all need communication. The assignment can be broken up by adding three temporary communication buffers, T1, T2, and T3, aligned with the active indices, as follows:

```
B@[4:76:3] ⇒ T1@[2:50:2]
T1@[2:50:2] ⇐ B@[4:76:3]
A@[1:49:2] ⇒ T2@[2:50:2]
T2@[2:50:2] ⇐ A@[1:49:2]
A@[3:51:2] ⇒ T3@[2:50:2]
T3@[2:50:2] ⇐ A@[3:51:2]
A@[2:50:2] = T1@[2:50:2]*(T2@[2:50:2]+T3@[2:50:2])
```

13.5.1 Regular Communication

Once the compiler has chosen the active indices for each expression, it needs to align all operands with those indices. We first deal with *affine array accesses*, when the *access function* of the array operand is an affine function of the normalized parallel loop indices. The communication that arises from affine array accesses is called *regular communication*.

We express an affine access function as $\mathbf{j} = \mathbf{Ai} + \mathbf{c}$, where $\mathbf{A}$ is the *data access matrix* and $\mathbf{c}$ is the *data offset vector*, and $\mathbf{j}$ represents the array element, either a source or target location. The target data access matrix $\mathbf{A}_T$ is generally nonsingular, since otherwise some element would be assigned more than once. If the source data access matrix $\mathbf{A}_S$ is also nonsingular, each source element has a single unique target location. The general regular communication can be written:

```
forall i do
    S@[A_S i + c_S] ⇒ T@[A_T i + c_T]
endforall
forall i do
    T@[A_T i + c_T] ⇐ S@[A_S i + c_S]
endforall
```

By changing variables, we can rewrite the send and receive parts in terms of the source and target indices, respectively:

```
forall s do
    S@[s] ⇒ T@[(A_T A_S^{-1})(s − c_S) + c_T]
endforall
forall t do
    T@[t] ⇒ S@[(A_S A_T^{-1})(t − c_T) + c_S]
endforall
```

In each case the compiler can treat $\mathbf{Ai}+\mathbf{c}$ as a nonunimodular transformation of the index set $\mathbf{i}$ (offset by $\mathbf{c}$) to find the bounds for the active source and target indices.

Example 13.14

Show the access function and communication for array B in Example 13.13.

Solution

We rewrite the communication as `forall` loops, as follows:

```
forall i = 0 to 24 do
    B@[3*i+4] ⇒ T1@[2*i+2]
endforall i = 0 to 24 do
    T1@[2*i+2] ⇐ B@[3*i+4]
endforall
```

The access function for B is $(3)i + (4)$, and the access function for the target T1 is $(2)i + (2)$. In this trivial case, it is easy to find the bounds for the source and target template offsets:

```
forall s = 4 to 76 by 3 do
    B@[s] ⇒ T1@[(2/3)*(s-4)+2]
endforall t = 2 to 50 by 2 do
    T1@[t] ⇐ B@[(3/2)*t+1]
endforall
```

The code for each part of the communication can then be generated using the techniques for array assignments.

Multidimensional Data Access Matrix

Similar techniques work for nonsingular multidimensional data access matrices. If the source or target data access function can be represented as $\mathbf{Ai} + \mathbf{c}$, we find a unimodular matrix $\mathbf{U}$ such that $\mathbf{AU} = \mathbf{H}$ where $\mathbf{H}$ is in Hermite normal form. Let $\mathbf{k} = \mathbf{U}^{-1}\mathbf{i}$; given the bounds of the index set $\mathbf{i}$ in matrix form, $\mathbf{Bi} \leq \mathbf{d}$, we use algorithm FMint on the system $\mathbf{BUk} \leq \mathbf{d}$ to find bounds $\mathbf{B'k} \leq \mathbf{d'}$, eliminating the variables in the order $k_n, k_{n-1}, \ldots, k_1$. Let $\mathbf{j} = \mathbf{Hk}$. The rth row of $\mathbf{B'}$ corresponds to a bound for j_m if $\mathbf{b}_{[r,m+1:n]} = \mathbf{0}$; it is a lower bound if $b_{rm} < 0$ and an upper bound if $b_{rm} > 0$. We use this row of $\mathbf{B'}$, along with $\mathbf{H}$ and $\mathbf{H}^{-1}$ to find a bound for j_m as:

$$sign(b_{rm})j_m \leq h_{mm} \left\lfloor \frac{d_m - \sum_{p=1}^{m-1} b'_{rp} \sum_{q=1}^{p} h_{pq}^{-1} j_q}{|b'_{rm}|} \right\rfloor - sign(b'_{rm}) h_{mm} \sum_{q=1}^{m-1} h_{mq}^{-1} j_q$$

This gives bounds on $\mathbf{j} = \mathbf{Ai}$; substituting $\mathbf{s} = \mathbf{j} + \mathbf{c}$ or $\mathbf{t} = \mathbf{j} + \mathbf{c}$ gives bounds for either $\mathbf{s}$ or $\mathbf{t}$, as appropriate. Again, the stride of the mth loop is h_{mm}. Procedure

Communication, shown in Figure 13.13, generates the appropriate limits for the send operation for a loop of the form:

for **i** such that **Bi** ≤ **d** do
    X@[$\mathbf{A}_S\mathbf{i} + \mathbf{c}_S$] ⇒ Y@[$\mathbf{A}_T\mathbf{i} + \mathbf{c}_T$]
endfor

The same procedure will generate the limits for the receive operation by switching the source and target access functions.

```
(1)   Procedure Communication( A_S, c_S, A_T, c_T, B, d )
(2)   Invert( A_S )returns( A_S^-1 )
(3)   Hermite( A_S )returns( H, U )
(4)   Invert( H )returns( H^-1 )
(5)   B' = BU
(6)   Projectint( B', d )
(7)   for r = 1 to rows(B') do
(8)       let b be row r of B'
(9)       find m such that b_m ≠ 0 and b_{m+1:n} = 0
(10)      if b_rm > 0 then
(11)          add ⟨b, d_r⟩ to upper(m)
(12)      else
(13)          add ⟨-b, -d_r⟩ to lower(m)
(14)      endif
(15)  endfor
(16)  for m = 1 to n do
(17)      for each ⟨b, d⟩ in lower(m) do
(18)          emit a lower limit for s_m of Bound( b, d, m, c )
(19)      endfor
(20)      for each ⟨b, d⟩ in upper(m) do
(21)          emit an upper limit for s_m of Bound( b, d, m, c )
(22)      endfor
(23)      emit stride for s_m of h_mm
(24)  endfor
(25)  emit 't = A_T(A_S^-1(s - c_S)) + c_T'

(26)  procedure Bound( b, d, m, c )
(27)      emit 'h_mm ⌈ (d - Σ_{p=1}^{m-1} b_p Σ_{q=1}^{p} h_{pq}^{-1}(s_q - c_q)) / b_m ⌉ - h_mm Σ_{q=1}^{m-1} h_{mq}^{-1}(s_q - c_q)'
(28)  end Bound
(29)  end Communication
```

FIGURE 13.13 Algorithm to generate loop limits for communication operations.

Example 13.15

Use procedure Communication to generate send/receive code for the communication represented by the following parallel loop:

(1)   forall I = 1 to 20 do
(2)   forall J = 2 to 10 do
(3)   A@[I-1,J-1] = B@[I+2*J-1,I+J-1]
(4)   endforall
(5)   endforall

Solution

Since the loop index set already forms a lattice, we need not normalize it further. The data access functions of the communication source and target are:

$$f_S(\mathbf{i}) = \begin{pmatrix} 1 & 2 \\ 1 & 1 \end{pmatrix} \mathbf{i} + \begin{pmatrix} -1 \\ -1 \end{pmatrix}$$

$$f_T(\mathbf{i}) = \begin{pmatrix} 1 & 0 \\ 0 & 1 \end{pmatrix} \mathbf{i} + \begin{pmatrix} -1 \\ -1 \end{pmatrix}$$

We find $\mathbf{H}$ and $\mathbf{U}$ such that $\mathbf{A}_S \mathbf{U} = \mathbf{H}$. Algorithm Hermite gives the following breakdown:

$$\begin{pmatrix} 1 & 2 \\ 1 & 1 \end{pmatrix} \begin{pmatrix} -1 & 2 \\ 1 & -1 \end{pmatrix} = \begin{pmatrix} 1 & 0 \\ 0 & 1 \end{pmatrix}$$

The bounds of the original index set are:

$$\begin{pmatrix} 1 & 0 \\ -1 & 0 \\ 0 & 1 \\ 0 & -1 \end{pmatrix} \begin{pmatrix} i_1 \\ i_2 \end{pmatrix} \leq \begin{pmatrix} 20 \\ -1 \\ 10 \\ -2 \end{pmatrix}$$

Applying $\mathbf{U}$ to the bounds matrix gives $\mathbf{B}'$:

$$\begin{pmatrix} -1 & 2 \\ 1 & -2 \\ 1 & -1 \\ -1 & 1 \end{pmatrix} \begin{pmatrix} k_1 \\ k_2 \end{pmatrix} \leq \begin{pmatrix} 20 \\ -1 \\ 10 \\ -2 \end{pmatrix}$$

Fourier-Motzkin projection along the k_1 axis adds the rows:

$$\begin{pmatrix} 1 & 0 \\ -1 & 0 \end{pmatrix} \begin{pmatrix} k_1 \\ k_2 \end{pmatrix} \leq \begin{pmatrix} 40 \\ -5 \end{pmatrix}$$

The rows are partitioned into lower and upper limits as follows:

$$\text{lower}(1) = \{\langle(1,0), 5\rangle\}$$
$$\text{upper}(1) = \{\langle(1,0), 40\rangle\}$$
$$\text{lower}(2) = \{\langle(-1,2), 1\rangle, \langle(-1,1), -10\rangle\}$$
$$\text{upper}(2) = \{\langle(-1,2), 20\rangle, \langle(-1,1), -2\rangle\}$$

Since **H** is the identity matrix, procedure Bounds generates simple limits for **s**:

```
forall s1 = 4 to 39 do
    forall s2 = max(s1-10,⌈(s1+2)/2⌉) to min(s1-2,⌊(s1+21)/2⌋) do
        B@[s1,s2] ⇒ A@[-s1+2*s1,s1-s2-1]
    endforall
endforall
```

The subscripts for the target array are $\mathbf{A}_T \mathbf{A}_S^{-1}(\mathbf{s} - \mathbf{c})$. For the receive code, since the data access matrix is the identity, the effect is of substituting $\mathbf{t} = \mathbf{i} + \mathbf{c}$ to get:

```
forall t1 = 0 to 19 do
    forall t2 = 1 to 9 do
        A@[t1,t2] ⇐ B@[t1+2*t2+2,t1+t2+1]
    endforall
endforall
```

Bounding Regions

A simpler method to generate code is to find the extreme values of the active indices for the source processors. Algorithm Extreme from Chapter 4 can find conservative bounds for each row of the affine function $\mathbf{Ai} + \mathbf{c}$ and the bounds for **i**. At each point in that range, the code should check that the given index should participate in the communication.

Example 13.16

Repeat Example 13.15 using algorithm Extreme to find bounds for the active indices for the source and target.

Solution

The bounds as found by algorithm Extreme for the source processor are $[4:39, 2:29]$, and for the target processor are $[0:19, 1:9]$. The generated code would test that $\mathbf{A}_T \mathbf{A}_S^{-1}(\mathbf{s} - \mathbf{c})$ is an integer, and lies within the limits:

```
forall s1 = 4 to 39 do
    forall s2 = 2 to 29 do
        t1 = -s1+2*s1
        t2 = s1-s2-1
        if 0 <= t1 and t1 <= 19 and 1 <= t2 and t2 <= 9 then
            B@[s1,s2] ⇒ A@[t1,t2]
        endif
    endforall
```

```
        endforall
        forall t1 = 0 to 19 do
            forall t2 = 1 to 9 do
                s1 = t1+2*t2+2
                s2 = t1+t2+1
                if 4 <= s1 and s1 <= 39 and 2 <= s2 and s2 <= 29 then
                    A@[t1,t2] ⇐ B@[s1,s2]
                endif
            endforall
        endforall
```

Singular Data Access Matrix

When the data access matrix is singular, then each data source may need to be sent to several target locations. We can't simply invert the data access matrix; in fact, we can't even find the HNF. Instead, we make a new access matrix, eliminating the linearly dependent rows and padding the matrix with additional rows so that the result is nonsingular. The extra rows correspond to additional sequential loops that will enumerate the target locations for each source data element. We also need to keep track of the linear dependence between the rows, which we need to find the active processors. We use the new access matrix in the same way as before. Procedure SingularCommunication in Figure 13.14 shows how to generate the appropriate bounds. It uses the routine RemoveRows, which computes linearly dependent rows of the matrix **A**. It returns the rank of **A** in a; a reduced matrix $\mathbf{A}_R$, which is **A** with the linearly dependent rows removed; and a reduced vector $\mathbf{c}_R$, which is **c** with the corresponding entries removed (and padded with zeros). It also returns a matrix **L** that gives the linear relationship between the linearly dependent rows of **A**, and a vector **r** that gives the row in $\mathbf{A}_R$ corresponding to the original row in **A**. Procedure Pad adds rows to $\mathbf{A}_R$ so that the result is nonsingular. The rest of the procedure is similar to procedure Communication. The code generation goes through each variable in **s**, and generates a loop if it corresponds to a linearly independent row in $\mathbf{A}_R$, and an assignment otherwise. It also generates nested sequential loops for the padded rows. The vector **j** is constructed to generate the target for each element.

Procedure RemoveRows, shown in Figure 13.15, is a modified matrix inversion routine; in fact, if the matrix is nonsingular, it returns the inverse of **A** in **B**. Since it destroys the original matrix, it first copies **A** into **M**; each time it interchanges rows of **M** and **B**, it also switches rows of the matrix **A**. In the meantime, x_i keeps track of which original row appears in row i. At the end, all linearly dependent rows of **A** are interchanged to the bottom; only the first r rows of **A** are copied to the reduced matrix **D**. The last $n-r$ rows of **B** are changed to give the linear relation between the original row appearing at that position and the other rows in the matrix. Finally, **x** is inverted, so that w_i gives the position in **D** at which the original row i appears.

(1) Procedure SingularCommunication(A_S, c_S, A_T, c_T, B, d)
(2) RemoveRows(A_S, c_S)returns(a, A_R, L, w)
(3) Pad(a, A_S)returns(A_P)
(4) Invert(A_P)returns(A_P^{-1})
(5) Hermite(A_P)returns(H, U)
(6) Invert(H)returns(H^{-1})
(7) $B' = BU$; Projectint(B')
(8) for $r = 1$ to rows(B') do
(9)   let b be row r of B'
(10)   find m such that $b_m \neq 0$ and $b_{m+1:n} = 0$
(11)   if $b_{rm} > 0$ then add $\langle b, d_r \rangle$ to upper(m) endif
(12)   if $b_{rm} < 0$ then add $\langle -b, -d_r \rangle$ to lower(m) endif
(13) endfor
(14) for $p = 1$ to n do
(15) $m = w_p$
(16)   if $m \leq a$ then
(17)   for each $\langle b, d \rangle$ in lower(p) do
(18)   emit a lower limit for s_p of Bound(b, d, m, c_R)
(19)   endfor
(20)   for each $\langle b, d \rangle$ in upper(p) do
(21)   emit an upper limit for s_p of Bound(b, d, m, c_R)
(22)   endfor
(23)   emit stride for s_p of h_{mm}; let j_m be $s_p - c_p$
(24)   else
(25)   emit '$s_p = L_{[m]}(s - c) + c_p$'
(26)   endif
(27) endfor
(28) for $m = a + 1$ to n do
(29)   for each $\langle b, d \rangle$ in lower(m) do
(30)   emit a lower limit for i_m of Bound(b, d, m, 0)
(31)   endfor
(32)   for each $\langle b, d \rangle$ in upper(m) do
(33)   emit an upper limit for i_m of Bound(b, d, m, 0)
(34)   endfor
(35)   emit stride for i_m of h_{mm}; let j_m be i_m
(36) endfor
(37) emit '$t = A_T(A_P^{-1}j) + c_T$'
(38) end SingularCommunication

FIGURE 13.14 Algorithm to generate loop limits for communication operations with singular data access matrix.

(1) Procedure RemoveRows(A, c)returns(r, D, B, w)
(2)   let **B** = **I**
(3)   let **M** = **A**
(4) $r = 1$
(5)   **x** = $(1, 2, 3, 4, \ldots, n)$
(6)   for $j = 1$ to n do
(7)   find $k \in [r+1:n]$ such that $m_{jk} \neq 0$
(8)   if $m_{jk} \neq 0$ for all $k \in [r+1:n]$ then
(9) $r = r + 1$
(10)   if $k \neq r$ then
(11)   interchange row $\mathbf{M}_{[r]}$ with row $\mathbf{M}_{[k]}$
(12)   interchange row $\mathbf{B}_{[r]}$ with row $\mathbf{B}_{[k]}$
(13)   interchange row $\mathbf{A}_{[r]}$ with row $\mathbf{A}_{[k]}$
(14)   interchange element x_r with element x_k
(15)   endif
(16) $c = m_{rj}$
(17)   divide row $\mathbf{M}_{[r]}$ by c
(18)   divide row $\mathbf{B}_{[r]}$ by c
(19)   for $i = 1$ to n do
(20)   if $i \neq r$ and $m_{ij} \neq 0$ then
(21) $\alpha = m_{ij}$
(22)   let $\mathbf{M}_{[i]} = \mathbf{M}_{[i]} - \alpha \mathbf{M}_{[r]}$
(23)   let $\mathbf{B}_{[i]} = \mathbf{B}_{[i]} - \alpha \mathbf{B}_{[r]}$
(24)   endif
(25)   endfor
(26)   endif
(27)   endfor
(28)   let **D** be $\mathbf{A}_{1:r,1:n}$
(29)   for $i = r+1$ to n do
(30)   negate row $\mathbf{B}_{[i]}$
(31) $m = x_i$
(32) $b_{im} = 0$
(33)   endfor
(34)   for $i = 1$ to n do
(35) $w_{x_i} = i$
(36)   endfor
(37) end RemoveRows

FIGURE 13.15 Modified matrix inversion procedure to remove linearly dependent rows in a matrix and find the linear relation for linearly dependent rows.

Procedure Pad, shown in Figure 13.16, adds $n - r$ rows to the reduced matrix, where each row has a single nonzero entry; that entry is in a column that is otherwise linearly dependent on the other columns, making the resulting matrix nonsingular. Again, since it destroys the working matrix, it copies the input matrix **A** to **B**. The main body of the procedure finds the linearly dependent columns of **B** and interchanges them to the last $n - r$ positions. The vector **x** keeps track of which original column appears in which position of **B**. At the end, a single 1 entry is placed in the linearly dependent columns.

```
(1)   Procedure Pad( r, A )returns( P )
(2)   let P_{1:r,1:n} = A
(3)   let P_{r+1:n,1:n} = 0
(4)   let B = P
(5)   x = (1, 2, 3, ..., n)
(6)   for i = 1 to r do
(7)       find k ∈ [i + 1 : n] such that B_{ik} ≠ 0
(8)       if k ≠ i then
(9)           interchange columns b_{[k]} and b_{[i]}
(10)          interchange elements x_k and x_i
(11)      endif
(12)      c = b_{ii}
(13)      divide column b_{[i]} by c
(14)      for j = i + 1 to n do
(15)          α = b_{ij}
(16)          let b_{[j]} = b_{[j]} − αb_{[i]}
(17)      endfor
(18)  endfor
(19)  for i = r + 1 to n do
(20)      m = x_i
(21)      p_{im} = 1
(22)  endfor
(23)  end Pad
```

FIGURE 13.16 Procedure to pad a rectangular matrix with rows to make it a nonsingular square matrix.

Example 13.17

Use procedure SingularCommunicate to generate code to compute the target locations for each source element of array B in the following assignment:

```
(1)   forall I1 = 1 to 48 do
(2)     forall I2 = 1 to 48 do
(3)       A@[I1+2,I2-1] = B@[I1+1,I1-1]
```

(4)   endforall
(5) endforall

Solution

The assignment is already written in terms of the active indices, using the owner-computes rule. The data access functions are:

$$A_S = \begin{pmatrix} 1 & 0 \\ 1 & 0 \end{pmatrix}, \quad c_S = \begin{pmatrix} 1 \\ -1 \end{pmatrix}, \quad A_T = \begin{pmatrix} 1 & 0 \\ 0 & 1 \end{pmatrix}, \quad c_T = \begin{pmatrix} 2 \\ -1 \end{pmatrix}.$$

Since A_S is singular, each source element will be used at many destinations. Procedure RemoveRows finds the rank of A_S to be 1; the reduced matrix is simply the first row of A_S, and the relation between the rows is given by the second row of $L = (1, 0)$. Procedure Pad adds a second row to A_P:

$$A_P = \begin{pmatrix} 1 & 0 \\ 0 & 1 \end{pmatrix}$$

This is simply the identity matrix, so A_P^{-1}, H, U, and H^{-1} are all equal to I also. The loop limits are represented in matrix form as:

$$\begin{pmatrix} -1 & 0 \\ 1 & 0 \\ 0 & -1 \\ 0 & 1 \end{pmatrix} \begin{pmatrix} i_1 \\ i_2 \end{pmatrix} \le \begin{pmatrix} -1 \\ 48 \\ -1 \\ 48 \end{pmatrix}$$

Computing BU does not change this, and no new limits are found via Fourier-Motzkin projection. Since the second row of A_S was linearly dependent on the first, it will not generate a new loop; s_2 will be computed from the value of s_1. The generated limits for the source elements are:

$$2 \le s_1 \le 49$$
$$s_2 = s_1 - 1$$

An additional sequential loop enumerates the target for each source element; the final generated code is:

```
forall s1 = 2 to 49 do
    s2 = s1-1
    for I1 = 1 to 48 do
        B@[s1,s2] ⇒ A@[s1+1,I1-1]
    endfor
endforall
```

The same algorithm can be used to find the limits for the receive code, generating:

```
forall t1 = 3 to 50 do
    for t2 = 0 to 47 do
```

```
        A@[t1,t2] ⇐ B@[t1-1,t1-3]
    endfor
endforall
```

Collapsed Dimensions

When one or more dimensions of an array are collapsed, communication may mean sending more than one element at a time. The simplest situation occurs when the indices used in the collapsed dimensions are distinct from those used in the distributed dimensions. In such a situation, the communication can simply determine the source and target of each communication from the distributed dimensions, and transfer a set of elements, instead of a single element, from the collapsed dimension(s). If the set of elements is hard to determine, the compiler may choose to transfer a bounding region, which can be simply found by finding the extreme values of the subscript functions in each collapsed dimension, as shown in Chapter 4.

Example 13.18

Show the communication for the following assignment:

```
A@[0:9][0:39] = B@[1:19:2][3:42]
```

Solution

We begin by writing the array assignment as `forall`s, using template offset indexing:

```
forall s = 1 to 19 by 2 do
    forall j = 1 to 40 do
        B@[s][j+3] ⇒ A@[(s-1)/2][j]
    endforall
endforall
forall t = 0 to 9 do
    forall j = 1 to 40 do
        A@[t][j] ⇐ B@[2*t+1][j+3]
    endforall
endforall
```

The second dimension is the collapsed dimension in each array; since only index j is used in the collapsed dimension, and it is not used in any distributed dimension, the problems of determining source/target and the communication set are separable. If using send/receive operations, the active indices for the source are $1:19:2$, and the owner of template offset s should send to template offset $t = (s-1)/2$. The active indices for the target are $0:9$, and the owner of template offset t will receive from template offset $s = 2t + 1$. Each communication comprises most of a column of B, here found as $\min(j+3) : \max(j+3)$, where $1 \leq j \leq 40$. Thus, the source should send elements B@[s][4 : 43], and the target should receive elements A@[t][1 : 40].

Collapsed Dimension Elements

When there is a stride in the collapsed dimension, not every element between the extremes needs to be transferred. If the subscript function in the collapsed dimension s is the affine function

$$f_s(i_1, i_2, \ldots, i_n) = \sum_{k=1}^{n} a_k i_k + a_0$$

where the a_k are zero for any index used in a distributed dimension, the values to be transferred are

$$\min(\sum_{k=1}^{n} a_k i_k + a_0) : \max(\sum_{k=1}^{n} a_k i_k + a_0) : \gcd(a_1, a_2, \ldots, a_n)$$

This may communicate more elements than are actually used, but is the smallest regular set of array elements that includes all the necessary elements.

Even when an index variable is used in both distributed and collapsed dimensions, communication is classified the same way. The active indices for the communication source and target are found separately.

Example 13.19

Show the communication for the following example:

```
(1)  forall t = 1 to N do
(2)     forall j = 1 to N do
(3)        A@[t][j] = B@[t+1][t-1] * 2
(4)     endforall
(5)  endforall
```

Solution

A single value needs to be transferred from row $i_1 + 1$ to row i_1 of the template. We break up the assignment into communication and computation:

```
forall s = 2 to N+1 do
    B@[s][s-2] ⇒ T1@[s-1]
endforall
forall t = 1 to N do
    T1@[t] ⇐ B@[t+1][t-1]
```

```
        endforall
        forall t = 1 to N do
            forall j = 1 to N do
                A@[t][j] = T1@[t] * 2
            endforall
        endforall
```

13.5.2 Communication Optimizations

Since the cost of communication is overhead to the computation, the compiler should reduce this cost as much as possible. One method is to reduce the frequency of communication by floating the communication out of enclosing sequential loops. This may require extra memory to hold the transferred data for the duration of the loop. When the assignment is conditional, the actual conditions may never execute it. Nonetheless, it may be less expensive to float the communication for the assignment out of enclosing loops; if the transferred data is never used, the optimization is a loss, but in the expected case the optimization will reduce the frequency of communication.

Another optimization is to eliminate the intermediate transfer into a communication buffer when the assignment has no computation, as was done implicitly in Example 13.17. This does not reduce the cost of the communication directly, but eliminates the copy operation from the temporary local location into the final result.

Combining Communication

When there are multiple operands being transferred, either in the same assignment or over a sequence of assignments, recognizing commonality between operands may allow the compiler to generate code to transfer one set of elements instead of two or more. In particular, when the data access matrix is the same for two references to the same right hand side array, the only difference is in the offsets (and in any collapsed dimension subscripts). There is overlap in the data to be transferred to a target if the difference in offsets for each dimension is less than the distribution block size for that dimension, and either there are no collapsed dimensions, or the collapsed subscript ranges also overlap. The latter condition may be found with any data dependence test.

Consider the following loop, where the operands are distributed with a block size of 5:

```
(1)     forall I = 1 to 20 do
(2)         A@[I] = B@[2*I] + B@[2*I+2]
(3)     endforall
```

Making the communication operations explicit shows two send and two receive operations, one for each reference to B.

13.5 ■ Remote Data Access

```
B@[2:40:2] ⇒ T1@[1:20]
T1@[1:20] ⇐ B@[2:40:2]
B@[4:42:2] ⇒ T2@[1:20]
T2@[1:20] ⇐ B@[4:42:2]
A@[1:20] = T1@[1:20] + T2@[1:20]
```

In this loop, B@[8] is sent to T1@[4] by the first send/receive pair, and to T2@[3] by the second. Because the block size is 5, both of these elements are on the same processor, P_0. Some elements do need to be sent twice, however, such as B@[10], since T1@[5] and T2@[4] are on different processors. We can address this problem by allocating an oversized communication buffer T on each processor with an overlap between processors. Rather than allocating $T(PKl+Kp : PKl+Kp+K-1)$ to each processor, we allocate $T(PKl + Kp - 1 : PKl + Kp + K)$. This means each processor gets $K + 2$ elements in each layer, with offsets $-1 : K$ (instead of offsets $0 : K - 1$). It also means that some elements are allocated to two processors; for instance, T@[4] and T@[5] would be allocated to both P_0 and P_1. This *overlap region* is shown in Figure 13.17. It does simplify the message code, in that a single set of send/receive messages will satisfy the requirements of both references:

```
B@[2:42:2] ⇒ T@[1:21]
T@[1:21] ⇐ B@[2:42:2]
A@[1:20] = T@[1:20] + T@[2:21]
```

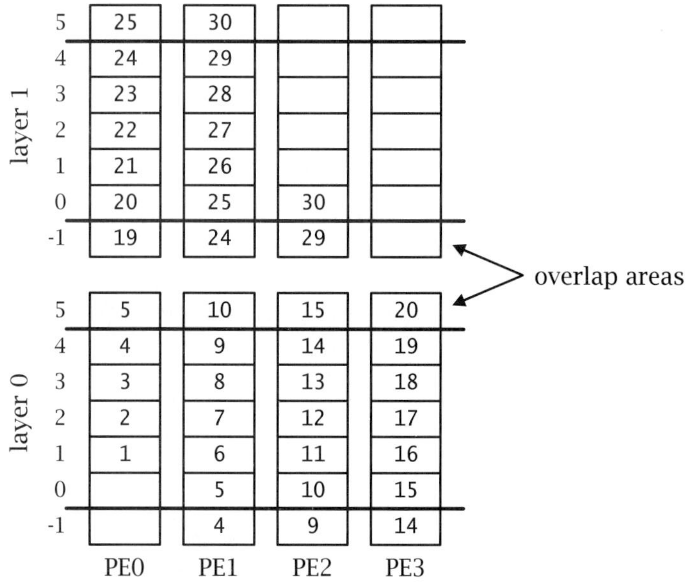

FIGURE 13.17 Data layout of temporary array showing overlap regions.

The generated node code would have to note the overlap area of the target message buffer. See the exercises for more details.

Communication Vectorization

When communication appears in a sequential loop, it may be possible to float the communication out of the loop even when the data being transferred depends on the loop index. This may increase the volume of communication, but reduces the frequency of communication. For systems in which the startup cost of each communication operation is high, this will be an important optimization. This is called *communication vectorization*.

Example 13.20

Show the communication for B in the following loop:

```
(1)     for K = 1 to 10 do
(2)         A@[2:10] = A@[2:10] + B@[4:20:2][K]
(3)     endfor
```

Solution

The simple solution will have a communication operation for each iteration of the K loop:

```
    for K = 1 to 10 do
        B@[4:20:2][K] ⇒ T1@[2:10]
        T1@[2:10] ⇐ B@[4:20:2][K]
        A@[2:10] = A@[2:10] + T1@[2:10]
    endfor
```

However, by increasing the size of the buffer T1 (adding a dimension), we can move the communication out of the K loop, and *vectorize* the communication:

```
    B@[4:20:2][1:10] ⇒ T1@[2:10][1:10]
    T1@[2:10][1:10] ⇐ B@[4:20:2][1:10]
    for K = 1 to 10 do
        A@[2:10] = A@[2:10] + T1@[2:10][K]
    endfor
```

The effect of the vectorization is to send all 10 elements of the row of B in a single communication operation, at the expense of additional memory on the target processor.

Communication and Data Dependence

Communication operations can be moved and floated out of loops as long as data dependence relations are preserved. Our method for adding communication operations separates the communication from the computation. For send and receive operations, there is a dependence relation from the send to the receive that must be preserved. In addition, there is a dependence relation from the receive operation to the computation that uses the communication buffer, and dependence relations to the send operation from any prior computation of that data. Remote fetch or store operations correspond to both the send and receive, for the purposes of dependence analysis. Keep in mind that dependence relations correspond to communication if they cross processor boundaries. Dependences across processors must be satisfied by synchronization or communication.

Example 13.21

Find the dependence relations due to communication in the following loop:

(1) for K = 2 to 10 do
(2)   B@[2:9][K] = (B@[1:8][K-1] + B@[3:10][K+1]) * A@[1:8]
(3) endfor

Solution

The communication statements for this example are as shown below:

```
for K = 2 to 10 do
    B@[1:8][K-1] ⇒ T1@[2:9]
    T1@[2:9] ⇐ B@[1:8][K-1]
    B@[3:10][K-1] ⇒ T2@[2:9]
    T2@[2:9] ⇐ B@[3:10][K+1]
    A@[1:8] ⇒ T3@[2:9]
    T3@[2:9] ⇐ A@[1:8]
    B@[2:9][K] = (T1@[2:9] + T2@[2:9]) * T3@[2:9]
endfor
```

There is a loop carried flow dependence relation from the assignment of B to the T1 communication. This prevents the compiler from floating this communication out of the K loop. There is a loop carried anti-dependence relation from the T2 communication to the assignment of B. This communication can be floated out of the loop if the communication buffer is suitably expanded. The anti-dependence relation must be satisfied by performing the fetch of any remote data before that remote processor proceeds with the assignment. There is no dependence due to A in the loop, so the T3 communication can be moved out of the loop.

Communication and Synchronization

On a SIMD machine, all the processors are synchronized at each instruction. On a multicomputer, on the other hand, the processors may proceed at different rates through the code. Each dependence relation must be satisfied at the dependence target. With send/receive operations, the communication explicitly synchronizes the processors. For a flow dependence, the completion of the receive operation means the data has arrived. For an anti-dependence, the completion of the send means the data has been sent; note that a send in the case of an anti-dependence must know that the data has actually been sent, or that a copy of the data was made to be sent when convenient, so that this processor can proceed to overwrite the array that is the source of the anti-dependence.

With remote fetch operations, the completion of the fetch satisfies a flow dependence relation. However, for anti-dependence, the fetch itself does not signal the remote processor that the data has been fetched and is ready to be overwritten. Conversely, with remote store, the completion of the store satisfies an anti-dependence, but does not signal the remote processor that the data is ready to be read for a flow dependence. In either case, additional synchronization operations are necessary.

In the case of send/receive communication, one processor can get too far ahead of the others, and send too much data to other processors. If the communication is set up to copy data directly into program buffers, there must be acknowledgments that the target buffers are in fact allocated and not being used for anything else. There can also be output dependence relations for program buffers that need to be satisfied by additional synchronization. Another way to avoid this is to allocate system buffer memory for incoming communication, and copy this to program memory when the receive operation is actually executed. This sets up a limited resource, namely the system buffers; if too many incoming messages need to be buffered, the buffer space will be depleted. Deadlock can result if the processor is waiting for a message that cannot arrive because there is no buffer space to receive it.

13.5.3 Communication Patterns

Many communication operations fall into specific patterns. These should be recognized so that efficient code can be generated. Often, optimized communication libraries that take full advantage of the network bandwidth are available for common cases.

With a single dimension template, the patterns that can arise are *shift*, *scale*, and *broadcast*. Examples are shown in Figure 13.18, along with characterization of the data access matrix; all regular one-dimensional communication patterns can be expressed as a composition of these three patterns.

In multidimensional distributions, more complex patterns can appear. In addition to analogs of the one-dimensional patterns along any one dimension, transposes and full broadcasts are common; examples of multidimensional patterns are given in Figure 13.19.

13.5 ▪ Remote Data Access

pattern	example	access matrix
shift	A@[I] = A@[I-1]	identity
scale	A@[I] = A@[2*I]	nonsingular
broadcast	A@[I] = A@[1]	zero

FIGURE 13.18 Examples of single dimension communication patterns.

pattern	example	access matrix
shift	A@[I,J] = A@[I-1,J]	identity
scale	A@[I,J] = A@[2*I,J]	diagonal
multicast	A@[I,J] = A@[1,J]	nonzero, singular
broadcast	A@[I,J] = A@[1,2]	zero
transpose	A@[I,J] = A@[J,I]	transposition

FIGURE 13.19 Examples of multidimensional communication patterns.

For a multicast, such as for C below, it is important to realize that only one copy per processor needs to be kept (not one copy per row of A or B).

```
forall I = 1 to 50 do
   forall J = 1 to 50 do
      A@[I,J] = A@[I,J] + B@[I,J]*C@[I,1]
   endforall
endforall
```

The resulting program should look something like the following:

```
align T1[i] with T[i,*]
C@[1:50,1] ⇒ T1@[1:50]
T1@[1:50] ⇐ C@[1:50,1]
forall I = 1 to 50 do
   forall J = 1 to 50 do
      A@[I,J] = A@[I,J] + B@[I,J]*T1@[I]
   endforall
endforall
```

where the assignment to T1 is really a multicast from the processors with the first column of C to all other processors in the same row.

Another pattern is transposition between a distributed and a collapsed dimension of a matrix. This might occur when row operations are followed by column operations. For example:

```
forall I = 1 to N do
   forall J = 1 to M do
```

```
            A@[I][J] = B@[J][I]
       endforall
    endforall
```

The communication pattern has every processor sending different data to every other processor, an all-to-all communication.

Overlap Regions

The shift pattern is particularly important to recognize. The most common case occurs when element [i] needs to access elements [i-1] and/or [i+1] (or [i±c], where c is a small constant). With a block-cyclic decomposition, only the first and last offset (or the first and last c offsets, in general) for each layer really needs any data from a remote processor. The communication may be able to use a fixed network instead of the general router, if a fixed network is available. Rather than constructing a communication buffer and filling it with mostly local data, the compiler should recognize this situation and communicate only the remote data. This would have the unfortunate effect that some iterations of the offset loop would use only local data while others would use data from the communication buffer. Since conditionals can slow down the computation, an alternative is to unroll the computation loop, separating the computations with local data from those that use the communication buffer. However, this increases the program size.

Another alternative is to allocate an overlap region for the data array, for the -1 and K offsets for each layer. The communication can fill in the overlap entries, and the computation then proceeds with local accesses. In two (or more) dimensions, there may be an overlap region in each dimension. In general, the overlap region represents a *shadow copy* of those elements; the task of keeping the shadow copies coherent with the true value (computed by the owner) is the job of the compiler. Since shadow copies need to be updated only when they will be used, the only real overhead is the extra memory used.

Example 13.22

Show a picture of the data layout for a 16×16 array with an overlap region of size 1 in each dimension. Use this data layout to execute the following assignment:

```
    A@[1:14,1:14] = 0.5*(A@[0:13,1:14] + A@[2:15,1:14])
```

Solution

Conceptually, the array is divided into 4×4 blocks, as shown in Figure 13.20, except that memory is allocated for an overlap region in each processor. Thus, A[2,4] will be allocated to two different processors. Figure 13.21 shows the memory layout for $P_{0,0}$, assuming a 2×2 processor ensemble. The array elements outside the thick square are shadow copies of elements allocated to other processors. For this block

13.5 ▪ Remote Data Access

size, the memory allocated to shadow copies outweighs the actual data assigned to this processor. Note that some of the shadow elements are outside the bounds of the array; they are allocated nonetheless to keep the memory allocation strictly uniform across processors.

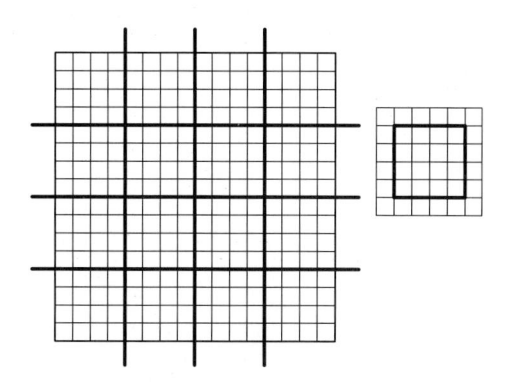

FIGURE 13.20 Two-dimensional block-cyclic distribution of an array; the memory allocated for a single processor with an overlap region is shown to the right.

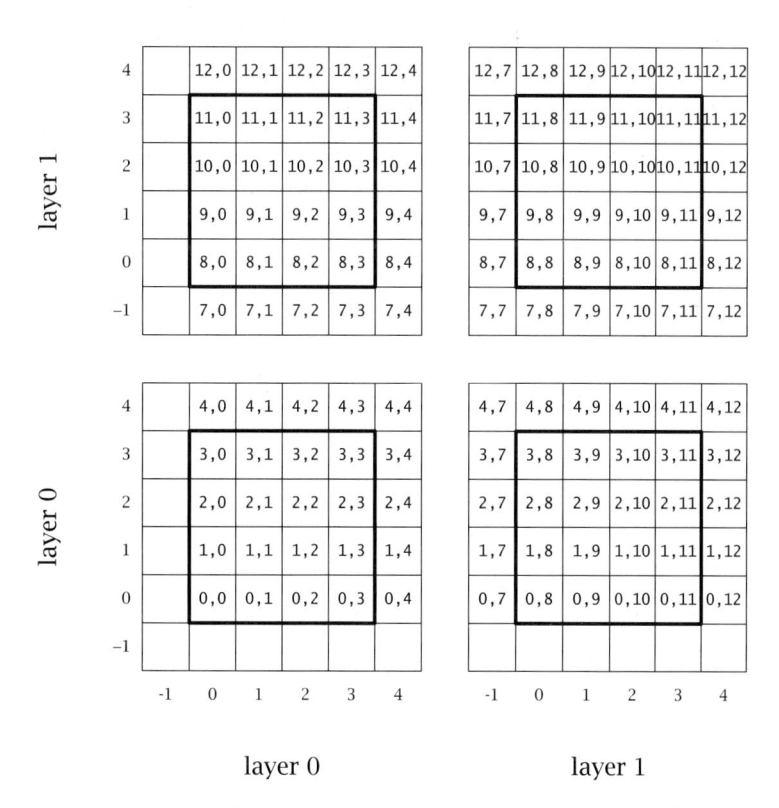

FIGURE 13.21 Data layout on one processor with boundary regions.

The two accesses to A on the right hand side of the assignment are unaligned. However, updating the overlap regions for that dimension allows the assignment to avoid copying any data to a communication buffer. After the update, all elements used in the computation of any element are local to the processor that owns that element.

▲

13.5.4 Irregular Communication

Irregular communication arises when the data access function is not affine. This is often due to index arrays used in subscripts. In such a case, the compiler cannot simply invert the access function, so constructing send/receive operations is difficult or impossible. Remote fetch operations can be used to fetch indexed array elements, but the advantages of using explicit send and receive operations is lost.

However, the compiler can generate code to dynamically construct the inverse map of an irregular access. The program can then use the inverse map to send each element it owns to the processors that need it. The extra code to invert the data access function, called an *inspector*, runs in three phases. First, each processor inspects each irregular data access function to see whether it is nonlocal, and if so, from what processor the data must come. Simultaneously, the processor constructs an alternate data access map (actually an alternate index array); if the data is local to this processor, the alternate map gives the local address of the data element. If the data will be sent from another processor, the alternate map gives the address of the communication buffer element that will hold the data. For each remote access, each processor saves the remote address and local buffer address, to use in the next step.

Second, the processors send messages to each processor from which data is needed. Because all the accesses have been processed, only one message to each processor is necessary, giving the address of each remote element requested and the local buffer address at which to store them. Third, each processor saves the incoming messages to construct a communication schedule.

The execution of the computation, called the *executor*, proceeds in two steps. First, each processor iterates through its communication schedule, sending and receiving messages. After all the communication is done, the processors access the data using the alternate data access map, which will fetch the correct element, whether local or remote.

The advantage of separating the inspector and executor is that even when the communication for the executor cannot be floated out of enclosing loops, the communication pattern, as determined by the inspector, may not change. If the compiler can determine when the data used by the inspector is invariant, it can amortize the cost of the inspector over many iterations through the executor.

13.5 ▪ Remote Data Access

A simple example is shown in the following loop:

(1)   forall I = 1 to 12 do
(2)   Y[I] = Y[I] + A[IP[I]]*X[I]
(3)   endforall

where the four vectors Y, A, IP, and X are all aligned and distributed with a block size of 4 on three processors. Suppose the vector IP has the following values:

i	1	2	3	4	5	6	7	8	9	10	11	12
IP(i)	1	5	9	10	2	4	7	11	10	5	7	11

The code for the inspector and the communication part of the executor can be implemented in a subroutine library. The generated code for the inspector determines what remote data is needed on each processor, and saves this in a *remote data table*. The inspector code also allocates buffer space (local to the processor) for the remote data, and determines where in the buffer the remote data will be stored, as shown in the following table.

target	source	data	buffer
P_0	P_1	A[5]	lT[1]
P_0	P_2	A[9], A[10]	lT[2:3]
P_1	P_0	A[2], A[4]	lT[1:2]
P_1	P_2	A[11]	lT[3]
P_2	P_1	A[5], A[7]	lT[12]

The second phase of the inspector exchanges messages to determine what remote processors need data stored on this processor; this essentially inverts the data access function for remote data. The result is a *remote message table* telling what remote processors need local data, the data to send, and the target location, as shown in the following table.

source	target	data	target buffer
P_0	P_1	A[2], A[4]	lT[1:2]
P_1	P_0	A[5]	lT[1]
P_1	P_2	A[5], A[7]	lT[1:2]
P_2	P_0	A[9], A[10]	lT[2:3]
P_2	P_1	A[11]	lT[3]

The final step is to construct a modified data access function, which will access the local data if it is in fact local, and the target buffer it if is remote. Here, we use pointers as the modified data access function:

i	1	2	3	4	5	6
mIP(i)	A[1]	lT[1]	lT[2]	lT[3]	lT[1]	lT[2]
i	7	8	9	10	11	12
mIP(i)	A[7]	lT[3]	A[10]	lT[1]	lT[2]	A[11]

The code for the executor includes two parts; the first is the code to actually do the communication specified by the remote message table. This may be floated out of inner sequential loops if the data is invariant in those loops. The second part is the actual computation, with the irregular access replaced by the modified data access function:

(1) forall I = 1 to 12 do
(2)   Y[I] = Y[I] + fetch(mIP[I])*X[I]
(3) endforall

13.5.5 Dynamic Alignments

High Performance Fortran, like other languages with distributed data structures, allows the program to dynamically realign and redistribute the arrays throughout the execution. The compiler may need to perform data-flow analysis to find the data layout that is used at each array assignment. This analysis may be interprocedural, to handle formal arguments that inherit the layout of the actual argument. In the best case, the compiler can determine a single data layout for each array section, and can then use the same methods as for static layouts.

In general, however, the layout may be data dependent or truly dynamic. The compiler can either try to generate a generic program that will work with any data layout, or can generate multiple versions of each assignment, one for each actual reaching data layout (as determined by data-flow analysis). A generic program might assume a block-cyclic distribution for each dimension, but is likely to generate far too much communication for any single data layout. Generating multiple versions of each assignment can increase the code size exponentially, if each operand can be redistributed independently. This clearly makes the case that *reaching layouts* data-flow analysis must be as precise as possible. Otherwise, users may feel that programs that use dynamic redistribution suffer unexpected performance penalties.

The most important information found from reaching layouts data-flow analysis is what template dimensions are distributed; whether the distribution is cyclic, block, or block-cyclic; and what array dimension is aligned with each template dimension. Even though block-cyclic distribution is the general case, the potential for optimizations in simple cyclic or block distributions make this determination useful. The actual block size is not so important; two reaching layouts that differ only in the block size may be treated as a single parameterized layout. The generated code will be the same, but the computation of the active layers, processors, and offsets, as well as of the communication sets, will be parameterized by the block size.

13.6 Automatic Data Layout

Parallelization methods can be used to help port sequential programs to message-passing machines, but automatic data layout is still a difficult problem. For short examples, it is clear that the layout should align array elements used in the same computation. For nontrivial cases, the best layout may not be so obvious. A simple automatic layout method is summarized here. This method breaks the problem into two subproblems: axis alignment followed by choice of stride and offset.

Axis alignment chooses which array dimensions to align with which template dimensions (or, equivalently, with which other array dimensions). One method uses an *axis alignment graph* (AAG), which has one node for each dimension of each array. A vector contributes one node, and a matrix two nodes to the AAG. Undirected edges connect nodes that have an alignment preference; when two arrays are used in an array assignment, aligning the corresponding parallel dimensions will give less costly communication, so we connect these edges. The edges can also be weighted, with the weight corresponding to the cost of not aligning these dimensions. Any dimensions that contain no parallel loop index should be marked as sequential. In a sequence of assignments, a dimension may be parallel in some assignments and not in others.

Example 13.23

Construct the AAG for the following example:

(1)   forall I = 1 to N do
(2)   forall J = 1 to M do
(3)   A[I,J] = B[I,J] + C[I]*D[J,I]
(4)   endforall
(5)   endforall

Solution
There are four arrays and seven nodes in the AAG, as shown in Figure 13.22. Edges connect the nodes as shown in the figure, giving the axis alignment preferences; here the edges are not weighted.

Partitioning the AAG

The next step is to partition the nodes of the graph such that the fewest edges are broken (most nodes connected by edges are in the same partition), or the accumulated weight of broken edges is minimized, with the constraint that nodes corre-

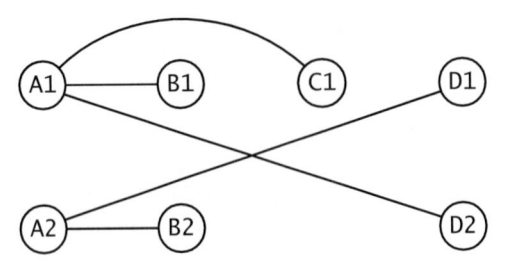

FIGURE 13.22 Axis alignment graph; each node is labeled with the array name and dimension.

sponding to different dimensions of the same array must be in different partitions. The compiler should then choose to distribute the dimensions in the partition that exhibits the most parallelism, i.e., the one with the fewest sequential dimensions.

A variation on this approach is to construct a graph with a node for each dimension of each reference to an array; this allows for realignment or redistribution of arrays between references. Subsequent references to the same array have a preference to be aligned, but need not be. Sophisticated analysis may even allow for multiple copies of an array (between updates) with different alignments or distributions.

Some axis alignment preferences may be ambiguous, as with a diagonal reference:

```
A[I,J] = B[I,I]
```

In this case, node A_1 could be aligned with either B_1 or B_2. Since parallel execution can occur in either case, the cost of breaking each edge is relatively small, assuming A_1 is distributed.

The second step is choosing the relative stride of offset of the array dimension in each partition. These should be chosen to minimize communication; thus, the most common relative stride should prevail. The relative offset should be chosen to remove the most communication.

13.7 Multiple Array Assignments

All our examples so far have been for single array assignments. Generating code for a sequence of assignments can be improved by applying fusion to group the statements together. Fusion may allow the compiler to take advantage of processor registers to hold intermediate values, instead of having to use memory each time. Note that we are fusing the sequential layer and offset loops; it is no help that `forall` loops with conformant limits can always be fused.

Besides the obvious advantages of reducing the amount of loop overhead or context setup code necessary, combining the assignments allows the PEs or nodes to use processor registers to carry values between statements, rather than fetching all values from memory.

Example 13.24

Show SIMD code for the following array assignments on eight PEs, where the block sizes for the two dimensions are $K_1 = 4$ and $K_2 = 8$:

```
A@[0:99,0:99] = A@[0:99,0:99] + 1
B@[0:99,0:99] = A@[0:99,0:99] * 2
```

Solution

For the first dimension, the active layers are zero through six; for the second dimension, they are zero through three. The code for the two statements can be combined into a single set of layer and offset loops, since the limits are conformant and there are no dependences preventing their fusion.

```
for I1 = 0 to 6 do
   Iend = Merge( I1 = 3, 0, 3 )
   for Io = 0 to 3 do
      for J1 = 0 to 3 do
         Jend = Merge( J1 = 3, 0, 3 )
         for Jo = 0 to 7 do
            PE[0:Iend,0:Jend]:
               T = 1A[I1,Io,J1,Jo] + 1
               1A[I1,Io,J1,Jo] = T
               1B[I1,Io,J1,Jo] = T * 2
            Jend = Merge( J1 = 3 and Jo = 3, Jend - 1, Jend )
         endfor
      endfor
      Iend = Merge( I1 = 6 and Io = 3, Iend - 1, Iend )
   endfor
endfor
```

13.8 Other Topics

13.8.1 Conditionals

For SIMD code, conditional operations are done by disabling PEs for which the condition is false. The condition is computed like any other expression. The result is saved in temporary, which is ANDed with the context for any statement under control of the conditional. Multicomputers handle conditional code the same way uniprocessors do, by branching around the conditional operations. Remember that processors that are disabled by the conditional (for SIMD machines) or that branch around the conditional (for multicomputers) may have values that are needed by processors that execute the conditional, and need to participate in communications.

For multicomputers, the only issue with conditional operations is that a processor may be required to participate in communication even if it has no other work to do in that region of code.

13.8.2 Reductions

Reduction operations can be performed by accumulating partial reductions on each processor, then using a logarithmic spanning tree to reduce the P values to a single result. Some parallel machines include a spanning tree in the network for just this reason. For a SIMD machine, when the number of intermediate values is reasonably small, it may be more efficient to do the final reduction to a scalar in the front end, especially when the PEs are much less powerful than the front end. Reductions on multicomputers can be accumulated on a single node and broadcast, or redundantly computed on all nodes.

13.8.3 Pipelining Sequential Loops

When a nested loop has a loop carried dependence in the distributed dimension, but has potential parallelism in a collapsed dimension, naive multicomputer code generation would produce completely sequential execution. For instance, in the following loop, the first dimension is the distributed dimension for both arrays; unfortunately, the index used in the first dimension, I, carries a flow dependence relation, preventing parallel execution.

```
(1)    for I = 2 to N-1 do
(2)        for J = 1 to M do
(3)            A@[I][J] = 0.5*(A@[I-1][J] + B@[I][J])
(4)        endfor
(5)    endfor
```

Naive code generation would produce the following code, assuming an overlap region for A, and leaving out the computation of first and last layers and offsets for each processor:

```
for I1 = I1First to I1Last do
    if I1First+5*Ip+IoFirst != 2 then
        receive( 1A[I1,IoFirst-1][1:M], (Ip-1) mod P )
    endif
    for Io = IoFirst to I1Last do
        for J = 1 to M do
            1A[I1,Io][J] = 0.5*(1A[I1,Io-1][J] + 1B[I1,Io][J])
        endfor
    endfor
```

13.8 ▪ Other Topics

```
            if I1Last+5*Ip+IoLast != N-1 then
                send( 1A[I1,IoLast][1:M], (Ip+1) mod P )
            endif
        endfor
```

This has the unfortunate effect of completely serializing the computation; each processor will completely process one layer, then send a message to the next processor, which will process one layer and send a message to the next processor, and so on. An alternative is to interchange the I and J loops before generating code, but the result is no better:

```
    for J = 1 to M do
        for I1 = I1First to I1Last do
            if I1First+5*Ip+IoFirst != 2 then
                receive( 1A[I1,IoFirst-1][J], (Ip-1) mod P )
            endif
            for Io = IoFirst to I1Last do
                1A[I1,Io][J] = 0.5*(1A[I1,Io-1][J] + 1B[I1,Io][J])
            endfor
            if I1Last+5*Ip+IoLast != N-1 then
                send( 1A[I1,IoLast][J], (Ip+1) mod P )
            endif
        endfor
    endfor
```

For each value of J, the processors sequentially step through the layers, computing one column of A and passing the last value to the next processor.

Pipelining the computation across the processors is an attempt to recover some parallelism despite the dependence in the distributed dimension. Suppose the data is distributed in a block fashion, with only one layer; the alternative code above (with loops interchanged) would overlap between computation of the second column in the first processor with that of the first column in the second processor. This parallelism proceeds as shown in Figure 13.23; the computation

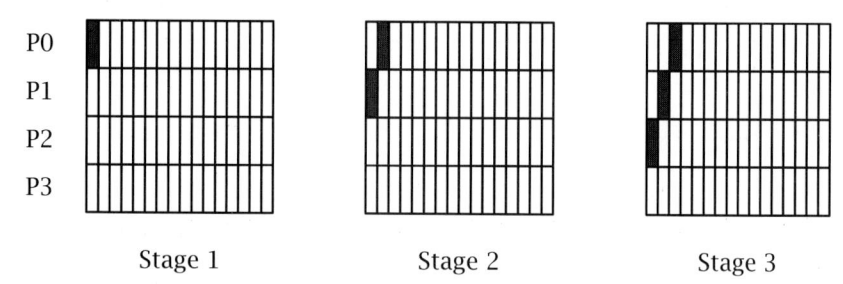

FIGURE 13.23 Pipeline parallelism of a sequential loop across processors.

of the columns is thus pipelined across the processors. The number of messages is quite high, but compared with sequential execution, the performance should be better. The same benefits can be realized in block-cyclic distributions by placing the layer loop outermost, and the offset loop innermost. This pipelines the computation of each column, one layer at a time, across the processors. With a cyclic distribution, the offset loop vanishes and each processor does very little work between messages. We can reduce the number of messages by strip-mining the other loop (in the collapsed dimension), sending one message for each strip; this trades parallelism for less message traffic.

Example 13.25

Show the code to get pipeline parallelism, and compute the number of messages in all.

Solution

The solution is given below:

```
for Il = IlFirst to IlLast do
    for J = 1 to M do
        if IlFirst+5*Ip+IoFirst != 2 then
            receive( lA[Il,IoFirst-1][J], (Ip-1) mod P )
        endif
        for Io = IoFirst to IlLast do
            lA[Il,Io][J] = 0.5*(lA[Il,Io-1][J] + lB[Il,Io][J])
        endfor
        if IlLast+5*Ip+IoLast != N-1 then
            send( lA[Il,IoLast][J], (Ip+1) mod P )
        endif
    endfor
endfor
```

The number of messages for each processor is ML, where L is the number of layers; the total number of messages is PML if we assume the same number of layers for each processor. Strip-mining the J loop and moving the communication out of the element loop will reduce the number of messages by a factor of the strip size.

13.8.4 Multiple Templates

A real program may have two or more templates; while each array will be aligned to only one template, an expression may involve arrays aligned to several different templates. Code generation for such a case proceeds as before, with communication inserted to send values from one template to another. In fact, the templates will be mapped down to the same set of processors, and a little deeper analysis may be able to optimize messages by finding the relative position of different templates. In general, messages from one template to another can be generated by computing the source and destination processors according to the appropriate template.

13.9 In the Pit

The overlap region is sometimes called a boundary region or guard region. The examples in this chapter are written in a style similar to that of the High Performance Fortran language. There are some differences, particularly in that we don't specify the size of a template. We use templates only to align dimensions of data.

The approach described in this chapter is essentially a software scheme to simulate a shared memory. Many computer architects argue that a hardware-oriented approach is more efficient and likely to be more effective in the long run. Such machines are discussed in the next chapter.

The data-parallel algorithms used successfully on this class of machine exhibit the property that all processors proceed at more or less the same rate; for multicomputers, they are called *loosely synchronous algorithms*, since the processors do not execute in lock-step fashion, but do synchronize frequently. In these large-scale machines, peculiar problems can affect the relative progress of different processors. For instance, in a large system cabinet, because heat rises, the processors situated physically near the top of the cabinet may be hotter than others, meaning that the clocks on those boards may be running a little faster than the clocks on other boards. A problem with the loosely synchronous style of computation is that if one processor is slowed down for any reason, it affects the whole computation.

Some of these techniques may be useful for programming a network of workstations as a message-passing machine. The common networks used to connect most workstations cannot support the bandwidth to make this mode of computation fruitful for most programs, but as networks improve, this may be a more desireable migration path for massively parallel computation.

13.10 Further Reading

Much of the early work on automatic compilation for message-passing machines was a result of the Suprenum project in Germany in the 1980s. Zima et al. (1988) describe an interactive software tool called SUPERB for converting sequential programs for parallel execution. Zima and Chapman (1993) give a good overview of compiler technology for message-passing systems.

The owner-computes rule was first described by Rogers and Pingali (1994), who implemented one of the first global compilers for a commercial message-passing machine.

Chatterjee et al. (1993) describe a method using finite-state machines to generate the local addresses of distributed data. The scheme described here was first presented by Gupta et al. (1993).

The design of High Performance Fortran borrowed much from other languages. The `template`, `align`, and `distribute` statements are borrowed from Fortran D, a language and compiler developed at Rice University (Hiranandani et al. [1992]). Vienna Fortran, described by Chapman et al. (1992), is related to High Performance Fortran, but includes some features not yet addressed by that language.

Kung and Subhlok (1991) show the importance of block-cyclic data distributions for matrix operations. The divide operations needed for implementation of block-cyclic distributions can be done with multiplications, as shown by Granlund and Montgomery (1994).

Several optimizations for SIMD machines are summarized by Knobe et al. (1993). Kennedy and Roth (1994) discuss loop fusion and index-set splitting to optimize SIMD context computation.

Automatic data alignment and distribution are subjects of current research. Li and Chen (1991b) describe the axis alignment graph and methods to partition it. Li and Chen (1991a) show a scheme where the data is automatically aligned using an axis alignment graph approach, where collective communication patterns are recognized, and where the choices of which dimensions to distribute and how are made based on the costs of the communication for each pattern. This work is based on a functional language, Crystal, but the techniques can be used in imperative languages. O'Boyle and Hedayat (1992) describe a scheme for automatic data alignment of affine array accesses by finding the Hermite form of the access matrix. Anderson and Lam (1993) try to automatically discover parallelism and an appropriate data layout by distinguishing arrays that can be simply decomposed from those that require communication or reorganization. Gupta and Banerjee (1993) use an axis alignment graph to align arrays, followed by analysis of how to distribute each aligned set of dimensions.

EXERCISES

13.1 For the array layout in Example 13.3, count the number of memory locations "wasted" by the distribution; that is, the memory locations allocated but not used for any array element.

13.2 Given a one-dimensional array with bounds $[l:h]$ aligned with a one-dimensional template with scaling factor a and offset b, where the template originates at t and is distributed with block size K. Find a formula for the memory wasted by the distribution. This is simplified by finding the difference between the number of elements actually needed and the number allocated.

13.3 Convert the array assignment below to template offset indexing:

```
template T[:]
real A[200], B[100]
align A[i] with T[i], B[i] with T[i]
A[9:75] = B[9:75] + 2
```

13.4 Use procedure `Context` to generate SIMD code for the array assignment in the previous exercise, assuming a block size of 10 on four processors.

13.5 Convert the array assignment below to template offset indexing:

```
template T[:]
real A[200], B[100]
align A[i] with T[i], B[i] with T[2*i]
A[1:151:2] = B[1:75] + 2
```

13.6 Use procedure `SparseContext` to generate SIMD code for the array assignment in the previous exercise, assuming a block size of 10 on four processors.

13.7 Use procedures `NodeCode` and `SparseNodeCode` to generate node code for the previous two example loops; generate code for a fixed block size of 10 on four processors, and for a block size of B on P processors.

13.8 Convert the following assignment to template offset indexing:

```
template T[:,:]
real A[100,100], B[100,100]
align A[i,j] with T[i,j], B[i,j] with T[j,i]
A[2:50:2,1:100] = B[1:100,2:50:2] + 5
```

13.9 Generate SIMD code for the array assignment in the previous exercise; note that one index is sparse and the other is dense.

13.10 Generate multicomputer node code for the same array assignment as in the previous exercise.

13.11 Procedure `SparseContext` assumes the layer and offset loops will count up. Since these sequential loops are generated by scalarizing the `forall` loops, they may need to run backward. Generalize procedure `SparseContext` by allowing the loops to run forward or backward.

13.12 For generated multicomputer node code for an array assignment, collapsing the layer and offset loops can improve the efficiency significantly. Under what conditions can these loops be collapsed? Give an example in which collapsing is feasible, and one in which it is not.

13.13 Procedures `Communication` and `SingularCommunication` are essentially the same in most respects. Combine them into a single procedure that handles both singular and nonsingular data access matrices, generating the appropriate code in both cases.

13.14 Rewrite the parallel assignment in Figure 13.24 in terms of template offsets.

13.15 For the loop shown in Figure 13.24, break out the nonaligned operands and insert send and receive communication steps to communication buffers.

13.16 For the result of the preceding exercise, use procedure `SparseNodeCode` to generate code for the assignment.

13.17 For the communication operations inserted by Exercise 15, use procedure `Communication` to generate the loop limits for the send and receive statements.

```
template T[:]
real A[100], B[100]
align A[i] with T[i+1]
align B[i] with T[i]
distribute T[cyclic(8)]
forall I = 1 to N do
    A[2*I+1] = B[2*I+1] - B[2*I] * A[I]
endforall
```

FIGURE 13.24 Sample program.

13.18 For the results of the previous exercise, use procedure `SparseNodeCode` to find the send and receive statements to be executed on each node. The result should be a layer loop and an offset loop for each processor, with a send or receive operation inside.

13.19 A send operation can be optimized if the generated code sends a single message to each target processor, and receives a single message from each source processor, rather than a message for each element. This can sometimes be done by the compiler generating code to strip-mine the offset loop of the send or receive operation according to the target processor of the message destination or source. Determine how to apply procedure `SparseNodeCode` to do this to the result of the previous exercise.

13.20 An option in the previous exercise is to strip-mine the layer loop (instead of the offset loop); when would strip-mining the layer loop for a send operation according to the target processor generate better code (fewer messages) than strip-mining the offset loop?

13.21 Multiple arrays can be sent in a single message if the data access functions (in terms of template offsets) are identical. Show how this might be done in the following example:

```
template T[:]
real A[100], B[200]
align A[i] with T[2*i]
align B[i] with T[i]
A[1:99:2] = B[2:100:2] + A[1:50]
```

13.22 Generate the communication statements for the parallel loop shown in Figure 13.25.

13.23 Optimize the message code in the previous exercise by strip-mining the offset loop according to the target processor, taking advantage of the distribution that the target processor owns offsets 0 : 7 in each layer.

13.24 An important optimization is possible if messages are batched by target processor, as in the previous exercise. Straightforward code generation will send some elements of B to the same target twice. For instance, the processor owning B[3] has to send it to the processors owning A[4] and A[8]. Since the block size is 8, these two elements of A may well be on the same processor, meaning that B[3] gets sent to the same target twice. This situation can be recognized easily because the data access matrices of the two references to B are identical, and the difference in the offsets is less than the block size. By allocating a single oversize message buffer at the target, the source can send

```
template T[:]
real A[100], B[100]
align A[i] with T[i]
align B[i] with T[i]
distribute T[cyclic(8)]
forall I = 1 to N do
    A[2*I] = (B[I-1] + B[I+1])*0.5
endforall
```

FIGURE 13.25 Second sample program.

the union of the two separate messages all at once. Show how this can be done for this example.

13.25 Generalize the method in the previous example for a general data access matrix and an offset vector.

13.26 When converting sequential loops to parallel code for a multicomputer, an important optimization is recognizing when a scalar in the original program can be replaced by a *moly* variable in the generated code; that is, when the value of the scalar on the different processors need not be kept consistent. Determine conditions for converting a left-hand side scalar to a moly variable in a loop that is otherwise parallel.

14 SCALABLE SHARED-MEMORY MACHINES

Scalar shared memory machines are a promising way to build programmable large-scale computer systems, if they deliver to their maximum potential. Locality-sensitive machines need a compiler to optimize for and enhance the locality in the program. Latency-tolerant machines are another category, which use extra parallelism to keep the processors busy while waiting for the memory to respond.

Several scalable shared-memory machines have been designed and built. In a multiprocessor, there is a tradeoff between scalability and memory latency; the common design for small numbers of processors has a single system bus used by all processors to access memory, and a private cache memory at each processor to reduce latency and traffic on the system bus. When multiple caches have a copy of a single memory location, the values are kept coherent by snoopy caches, which watch every bus transaction and thus know if any value they have cached might also appear in any other cache. The number of processors that can be effectively supported is limited by the bus bandwidth, which does not scale as more processors are added. Other interconnection networks improve bandwidth, but increase memory latency and also have problems ensuring cache coherence.

Several architectural approaches have been used to address these problems; we break them into two broad categories, one of which is divided into two subcategories. Machines that depend on cache memories to reduce average latency to memory are *locality-sensitive*; this class includes cache-only memory architecture (COMA) machines. When a program exhibits locality, the caches will work well and the program will run efficiently. If a program has little locality, the caches will be ineffective and the performance will be limited by the speed of memory accesses. We distinguish between locality-sensitive machines with a global cache coherence mechanism and those without. Scalable global cache coherence schemes, such as directory-based caches, are the subject of a great deal of current research and development. Most global cache coherence mechanisms are implemented in hardware, but some work has been done on schemes that use software assistance when the degree of sharing exceeds a certain level. The coherence protocol adds latency to any memory operation that changes cache ownership. To avoid this overhead, which is often unnecessary, machines without global cache coherence depend on compiler analysis and local information to determine when a cached copy of a variable is out of date. The disadvantage of such schemes is the necessity for the compiler to be conservative when generating cache coherence operations.

The other category is *latency-tolerant* machines, which have no cache memories at all; rather than trying to reduce latency to memory, these machines are designed to tolerate the latency by giving the processor something else to do while the memory fetch or store is in progress. The additional work must come from additional parallelism in the application, or from other applications in a multiprogramming environment. Locality in such a machine is of little value.

All of these machines are called NUMA machines, for their nonuniform memory access times to different memory locations.

14.1 Global Cache Coherence

A locality-sensitive machine with a global cache coherence mechanism typically comprises a set of nodes, each with a processor and a private cache memory or even a two-level cache memory. The nodes are connected to one another as well as to a set of memory modules via a network that is often hierarchical. The memories are typically physically distributed among the nodes. In a hierarchical network, the most closely connected nodes are often called a *cluster*; memory local to a cluster may be equally accessible to the processors in the cluster. Such systems may use standard shared-memory multiprocessors as the clusters out of which to construct a larger system. In such a system, the memory may look like a three-level subsystem, with local cache accesses being fastest, local cluster accesses running at essentially memory speed, and remote cluster accesses running at network speed.

A variation of such a machine is the COMA machine. Such a machine has the additional flexibility that main memory addresses are not mapped to fixed physical memory locations. All main memory addresses can be remapped to reside in different memory modules. To find the value given its main memory address, a message may have to traverse each memory module to check whether the address is resident in that module, much as a cache checks for residence of a cache line. For our purposes, we will ignore the cache-like behavior of the main memory of a COMA architecture.

Optimizing for locality is of prime importance for parallel applications on locality-sensitive machines. The tiling techniques developed for locality optimizations will be very useful here in any loop nest. However, tiling can increase locality only within a loop nest that has data reuse. Insertion of prefetch operations can improve the cache hit rate whether there is locality or not. Here we explore techniques to increase locality between loops as well as to reduce cache coherence messages.

14.1.1 Affinity Scheduling

In order to maximize reuse between loop nests, the compiler and run-time system can adjust the scheduling methods to try to get each processor to refer to the same memory locations in different loops. This is called *affinity scheduling*, so-called because the schedule attempts to preserve an affinity for certain memory locations to certain processors.

When a parallel loop is nested in a sequential loop, affinity scheduling will attempt to have each processor refer to the same array elements on each execution of the parallel loop. These elements should still be cached from the last iteration of the outer loop. When two parallel loops appear in sequence and share data, affinity scheduling will apply a schedule to the second loop to match the schedule used in the first loop. Even sequential loop iterations may be scheduled across the processors, to keep data resident in the appropriate processor caches.

The profitability of affinity scheduling can be determined by the compiler using a few simple rules. If two parallel loops access some shared array, indexed by the parallel loop indices, such that the corresponding iterations access the same array elements, then scheduling the corresponding iterations on the same processor will take advantage of the cache locality. The array element reuse can be determined by data dependence analysis, taking into account input dependence. We use the values of loop index variables to denote the corresponding iterations.

For instance, using a dynamic scheduling scheme in the parallel inner loop below may have each processor accessing and assigning different elements of X every time the parallel loop executes.

```
(1)    for I = 1 to N do
(2)        doall J = 1 to M do
(3)            X[J] = X[J] + A[I,J] * B[I]
(4)        enddoall
(5)    endfor
```

However, the compiler can note that there is data dependence carried by the outer sequential loop due to X, and X is subscripted by the parallel loop index. This means the parallel loop is a candidate for affinity scheduling. Using such a scheduling technique, the same processor will execute the same iteration of the parallel loop, and will thus access and assign the same X elements, enhancing cache locality.

The compiler may also restructure loops to improve affinity scheduling. Loop interchanging, skewing, scaling, and alignment can be used to make array accesses in separate loops have the same access function; interchanging and other linear transformations change the data access matrix, while alignment changes the offset vector. The compiler may change one or both of two adjacent parallel loops; for a parallel loop nested within a sequential loop, the compiler may be able to restructure the loop to remove the sequential loop index from the data access function. Loop fission is useful if there are conflicts between alignment for two arrays.

Affinity scheduling is almost the same as making a schedule from an explicit data distribution, as was done for message-passing machines. Although it also implies a static schedule, which does not do a good job of load balancing, it can still be dynamic. One implementation scheme uses the affinity property to find the initial assignment of iterations to processors; if one processor finishes its share early, it can steal work from another processor's iteration share. This can change the cache ownership of data fetched or stored in those stolen iterations, however; the benefits of a dynamic schedule must be balanced against the benefits of decreased data movement when using an affinity schedule.

14.1.2 Reduced Write Sharing

It is not much of a problem when multiple processors share the same read-only data. Each processor will cache a copy of the data, and further reads will hit in the cache. Since the data is read only, there is no coherence traffic.

For read-write data, the iterations should be scheduled onto processors to reduce false sharing. False sharing occurs when two processors access different words on the same cache line; from a coherence point of view, they share the cache line even though they don't share any data. Since cache coherence is typically done on a cache line basis, false sharing of read-write data can cause a great deal of coherence traffic.

Avoiding false sharing may be as simple as avoiding stride-1 accesses in the parallel loop index. More generally, the compiler can often compute the distance (in memory words) between array accesses for consecutive iterations of each loop in a nested loop. If the distance is less than the cache line size, then executing that loop in parallel may schedule two processors to access the same cache line. True read-write sharing will appear as a data dependence relation and must be managed by synchronization, so we only discuss false sharing here.

Example 14.1

Identify potential false sharing in the following loop, assuming the last dimension of the arrays is the stride-1 dimension, and assuming a cache line size of four array elements.

```
(1)    for I = 1 to N do
(2)        for J = 1 to N do
(3)            A[I,J] = B[I,2*J] + C[J,4*I]
(4)        endfor
(5)    endfor
```

Solution

The size of each dimension of the arrays is not specified here, but we can usually assume that the distance in memory words between two consecutive elements in the first dimension is larger than the cache line size. For each array reference, the memory distance between two accesses for each loop is shown in the following table:

	I	J
A[I,J]	> 4	1
B[I,2*J]	> 4	2
C[J,4*I]	4	> 4

Thus we see that executing the J loop in parallel can cause false sharing for accesses to A and B, while executing the J loop in parallel will not.

Complications

The problem can be much more complex than this example shows. For instance, because of the details of array layout, there can still be false sharing at the boundaries of the array, for the last few elements of one row and the first few elements of the next row. Such sharing is very limited, however, and we tend to ignore it since it should have only a small effect on performance.

This example had only one access to each array. We should also find false sharing between different accesses to the same array, if there is more than one. This example also had simple subscript access functions, with distinct loop index variables in each dimension. In general, there can be more complex false sharing patterns, as shown in the following loop:

```
(1)     for I = 1 to N do
(2)       for J = 1 to M do
(3)         A[I+J,4*I+5*J] = ...
(4)       endfor
(5)     endfor
```

For consecutive iterations of the I or J loop the memory stride is certainly larger than the cache line size. If the J loop is executed in parallel, or the I loop is interchanged to the innermost position and executed in parallel, there will be no false sharing between parallel iterations. However, if the parallel loop is outermost in either case, then we should investigate whether there can be any false sharing between any two iterations in the iteration space. For instance, iteration $\langle I, J \rangle = \langle 1, 2 \rangle$ refers to element A[3,14], whereas iteration $\langle 2, 1 \rangle$ refers to element A[3,13]. The memory distance here is only one, with potential false sharing.

To find false sharing in the stride-1 dimension, we can set up a system of equations and inequalities much like a dependence system. For any two references to the same array, we want to determine whether any two iterations can access the elements that are within the cache line size in the stride-1 dimension. Given the two references:

$$A[f_1(\vec{I}), f_2(\vec{I}), \ldots, f_s(\vec{I})]$$
$$A[g_1(\vec{I}), g_2(\vec{I}), \ldots, g_s(\vec{I})]$$

(where the two references may be the same), we want to see whether there are two iterations $\vec{i}$ and $\vec{j}$ such that

$$f_1(\vec{i}) = g_1(\vec{j})$$
$$f_2(\vec{i}) = g_2(\vec{j})$$
$$\vdots \quad \vdots$$
$$f_{s-1}(\vec{i}) = g_{s-1}(\vec{j})$$
$$|f_s(\vec{i}) - g_s(\vec{j})| < c$$

where s is the stride-1 dimension and c is the cache line size. If c is small, this can be solved using the methods shown in Chapter 4 for all $f_s(\vec{i}) - g_s(\vec{j}) = d$ where $-c < d < c$.

14.1.3 Sharing Patterns

Scalable shared-memory systems may implement different coherence protocols. For instance, the obvious strategy for read-only data is to allow copies of the data to reside in multiple processor caches simultaneously. Each copy is marked as read-only and nonexclusive; any attempt to write on such a copy will cause the coherence management system to change the ownership protocols.

For read-write data, two common coherence protocols are write-update and write-exclusive. In the former protocol, an update to a cache line in a shared writable state will cause the updated value to be broadcast to all owners of that line. This may be done by notifying all owners on the sharing list, if a directory scheme is used. In a write-exclusive protocol, an update to a cache line requires exclusive ownership of that line. If the line is cached in a nonexclusive mode, the update will stall until all copies of that line are evicted from other caches. The eviction notices are sent via the same mechanism as write-update notices.

If a system allows software selection of the coherence protocol for writes, the compiler can attempt to choose a protocol to match the reference patterns. For instance, read-write data that is updated frequently but with little sharing between processors should use a write-exclusive protocol. The first write to a cache line will require coherence message traffic to acquire exclusive ownership, but subsequent writes by the same processor to that cache line can be done without any coherence traffic. An example would be an array assigned in a parallel loop and indexed by the parallel loop index variable. Each processor will be assigning different elements; if there is no false sharing, each processor will write to different cache lines, so acquiring exclusive ownership of those cache lines may be beneficial for subsequent stores to that array.

On the other hand, read-write data that has many parallel readers but is updated infrequently should use a write-update protocol. This will cause coherence traffic to update the cached copies only at the infrequent write operations, whereas all the read operations can proceed with local cache copies. This might be the case for synchronization variables or scalar variables used in parallel regions of the code.

14.1.4 Hierarchical Systems

Since a large shared-memory subsystem will be physically large, a common design is to physically distribute the memory modules among the nodes. Thus some of the memory will be local to the processor, while the bulk will be remote. This is similar to the situation in message-passing machines. Such a system may be constructed from workstation units.

In a virtual memory system, the physically local memory can be mapped anywhere in the virtual address space. Moreover, the virtual memory system can make copies of read-only pages, mark dirty pages, and essentially treat the local memory like a software-controlled second-level cache. This gives such a system all the benefits (and headaches) of a COMA architecture. Identifying patterns of memory reuse to the virtual memory manager can help it choose to move copies of read-only pages to the local memory, or try to acquire ownership of read-write pages, to reduce the latency of memory writes.

The nodes of such a system may themselves be multiprocessors. In this case there are two levels of parallelism. Parallelism between nodes should avoid sharing read-write data, which must travel through the network. However, parallelism between processors on a node can share data inexpensively, as long as that data is resident in the local memory. Even if the data is not local, certain multiprocessor cache coherence protocols let one cache satisfy the miss request from another cache on the same bus. This means that certain cache misses can be satisfied without network delays, if any cache on the node has a copy of that cache line. Thus, there is benefit to sharing data between parallel tasks on a single node.

This two-level design may affect the scheduling policy. The compiler may use two-level parallel loops, for instance, where the iterations of the inner parallel loop exhibit more interprocessor data interference than the iterations of the outer parallel loop. The inner parallel loop can be scheduled on the processors of a node, while the outer parallel loop can be scheduled across the nodes. Alternatively, with a single level of parallelism, the compiler may identify clusters, or chunks, of iterations that exhibit data reuse; scheduling the chunks to execute in parallel on the processors of a single node takes advantage of that locality.

14.2 Local Cache Coherence

The problem with global cache coherence mechanisms is that they must be pessimistic in their assumptions about sharing. False sharing causes coherence traffic, even if there is no real data sharing. Also, since global cache coherence is typically implemented in hardware, it adds to the cost of the cache and network. An alternate proposal is to use a cache coherence scheme that relies only on local information. Such a scheme is potentially more scalable, since coherence information need not be propagated globally. Such a machine is very similar to a hardware cache coherent machine, comprising a set of nodes, each with a processor and private cache. The difference is in how the system handles writes and reads of data on different processors.

14.2.1 Cache Policies

On a uniprocessor, cache misses can be classified into three categories (the three Cs):

1. compulsory misses, the first time the cache line is referenced,
2. capacity misses, due to the capacity of the cache, and
3. conflict misses, due to the associativity of the cache.

A compulsory cache miss cannot be avoided; the first time the cache line is referenced, it will be in main memory. The other two types of cache miss occur after a cache line has been loaded and subsequently evicted from the cache. For a multiprocessor, common write-exclusive cache coherence protocols evict lines from this processor's cache when another processor is writing to the cache line. A subsequent reference to that cache line will result in a cache miss due to the eviction, and we call this a coherence miss. This gives four reasons (four Cs) for a cache miss.

A global write-exclusive cache coherence mechanism typically uses hardware to determine when a cache line is shared by more than one cache, and to evict lines from other processor caches when this processor writes to the cache line. An alternative global cache coherence scheme is a write-update scheme, where the new value is broadcast to all processors sharing that cache line.

There are other cache write policies, such as whether a miss on a write will cause that line to be loaded into the local cache (called *write-allocate*) or not (called *write-no-allocate*). In a write-no-allocate cache, a write to a location that is not in the cache will update the main memory value, as well as either updating or evicting copies of that line in other processor caches. A related issue for a write-allocate cache is whether the entire cache line is fetched, or *filled*, for a cache write. If not, then additional cache state bits are needed to mark which words in the cache line are valid; such a cache design is called *write-allocate, no-fill*. Another policy decision is whether the cache is *write-through* or *write-back* (also called *copy-back*). In a write-through cache, a write to a cache line is always propagated through to the main memory. Thus, the main memory location is always up to date; evicting a cache line can be done by simply marking it as invalid. In a write-back cache, a write to a cache line is done only in the cache, and the cache line is marked as *dirty*.

The updated value is propagated only to the main memory when that cache line is evicted. This increases the cost of the eviction, but such a design generally requires less network traffic, since not every write operation is propagated to main memory.

To support these cache policies, each cache line needs additional state bits, such as the following:

- Valid: set if the cache line contains valid data.
- Exclusive: set if the cache line is not shared with other caches.
- Dirty: set if the cache line has been updated locally.
- Filled: one bit per word, if that word in the cache line contains valid data.

14.2.2 Stale Cache Lines

For a local cache coherence mechanism, a write to an address on one processor does not cause a message to be sent to other processors that may have that location present in their local caches. Consider the sequence of parallel loops shown in Figure 14.1, where iteration i is executed on processor $i \bmod P$ for P processors. In the first loop, A[2] is udpated on processor P_2; assuming a write-allocate policy, A[2] is now resident on the cache of P_2. With a write-fill policy, the entire cache line containing A[2] is also loaded, which may include A[1], A[3], and so on. These values are updated by other processors, but without global cache coherence, processor P_2 will not see those updates. In the second loop, processor P_2 fetches the value of A[2]; since it had just updated that value, it will (most likely) still be resident in its cache with the correct value. For the third loop, processor P_2 stores a value into A[3]; given a write-fill cache, that word may have been loaded into the cache at the cache miss for A[2], but the value loaded then was never used. Note that at the same time, processor P_1 is storing a value into A[2]. A global cache coherence mechanism would either update the value of A[2] in the cache of processor P_2, or evict that cache line; with only local information, no

```
(1)   doall I = 1 to N do
(2)     A[I] = B[I] + C[I]
(3)   enddoall
(4)   doall I = 1 to N do
(5)     D[I] = A[I]/C[I] - 1
(6)   enddoall
(7)   doall I = 1 to N do
(8)     A[I+1] = D[I] - 1
(9)   enddoall
(10)  doall I = 1 to N do
(11)    E[I] = A[I]
(12)  enddoall
```

FIGURE 14.1 A sequence of parallel loops.

interprocessor information is communicated. Finally, in the fourth loop, processor P_2 again fetches a value from A[2]. This address is likely to still be cache-resident, but will have the wrong value, since it was updated on another processor. Thus, the value of A[2] on P_2 at this point is *stale*.

14.2.3 Local Cache Coherence Schemes

Several local cache coherence schemes have been proposed. Each of the local cache coherence schemes requires some compiler analysis and support and some hardware support. All divide the execution of the program into *epochs*, where the dividing line between epochs is the boundary between two adjacent parallel loops, or between a parallel loop and a sequential section of code. All processors synchronize at epoch boundaries. In Figure 14.1, for instance, each parallel loop is in a separate epoch. Note that loop fusion may be used to reduce the number of epochs, for instance, fusing the first two loops in Figure 14.1. All the schemes take advantage of the property of a parallel loop that the iterations are data independent. This allows the processors to execute the body of a parallel loop without any coherence problems, since an update in one processor need never be seen by another processor.

Between epoch boundaries, coherence can be insured by having each processor invalidate every cache line that has been updated by any other processor in the epoch that was just completed. Even this may be unnecessarily conservative; in fact, a cache line needs to be invalidated only if (a) it has been updated at some point after it was loaded into the cache, and (b) it will be used in a subsequent epoch by this processor. Local cache coherence schemes use a combination of compiler analysis and hardware support to approximate this. Note that there is some flexibility as to when the invalidation should occur; it can occur any time after the epoch containing the last valid use of that cache line and before the epoch containing the next use, if there is an intervening write to that line.

Simple Invalidation

The simplest scheme is to invalidate the local cache of every processor at the start of every epoch. This requires hardware support to invalidate the entire cache under software control. In a write-through cache, invalidating the cache simply means marking every cache line as invalid, which can certainly be done efficiently. For a write-back cache, there may be data that need to be written back to the main memory. This certainly satisfies the coherence properties; every flow dependence that crosses a processor boundary will be satisfied by storing the data back to main memory, synchronizing at the end of an epoch, and fetching the updated value from main memory in a subsequent epoch. It also requires no compiler analysis and minimal hardware support. The problem with this approach is that it does not take advantage of cache locality between epochs, even for read-only data. This will cause a great deal of unnecessary memory traffic, compared to a global cache coherence scheme.

Selective Invalidation

A modification of the simple invalidation requires the compiler to determine which memory references access shared read-write variables. There must be hardware support for two types of fetch instructions, one of which is used for these shared read-write variables, and each cache line must have an additional state bit, called the *epoch bit*; we assume a write-through cache. Any cache miss will fill the cache line and set the epoch bit; at epoch boundaries, the epoch bit is reset for all cache lines. A shared fetch will hit in the cache only if the cache line is valid and the epoch bit is set. The other type of fetch, used for read-only data and data local to the processor, ignores the epoch bit. A fetch to read-write data will hit in the cache only if it was loaded into the cache in the current epoch; in that sense, this scheme is similar to the simple invalidation scheme. However, this scheme allows the cache to preserve locality for read-only and processor-local data.

Time Stamps

A more desireable scheme will preserve data in the cache as long as it hasn't been written. Another scheme associates *time stamps* with each cache line and a *clock* with each shared array or shared data structure in the program. A clock is a count of the number of epochs in which the array has been updated since the program started. Every processor keeps a copy of the clocks for all shared arrays. Each fetch of a shared array includes the clock for that array; the fetch hits in the cache only if the cache line is valid and the time stamp for the cache line is at least as large as the clock value for the array. On a cache miss, the cache line is loaded and the time stamp set to the clock value for that array. A store to a shared array sets the cache line time stamp one greater than the clock for the array. At the end of an epoch, the time stamp for any array that might have been updated by any processor is incremented. Thus, the time stamp for a cache line is set to what the clock value will be after this epoch. The time stamp strategy can benefit from locality between epochs for read-only as well as for read-write shared data. Compiler analysis must determine what data may have been updated in any epoch, and insert code to increment the clocks for that data. The hardware support includes extra cache logic and some number of extra registers to serve as clocks, as well as more bits on a fetch instruction to specify the clock value. Note that no explicit invalidate instructions are required.

With a dynamic mechanism like the time stamp scheme, processor scheduling can affect the cache performance. If the update and subsequent uses of an array element are all scheduled on the same processor, as with affinity scheduling, they will benefit from cache locality.

14.2.4 Other Schemes

Other schemes have also been proposed. Some suffer from having to explicitly invalidate any data that has been updated by any processor. This may require iterating through all the addresses that may have been updated, which can greatly exceed the size of the cache, or iterating through the entire cache to see if any of that data is resident. Without global information, a local cache coherence mechanism must be conservative with respect to any fetch, insuring that the fetch gets the correct value if it might have been updated by any processor. The disadvantage is that the value may not have been updated, or may not have been cached by this processor, so some of the work may not be strictly necessary. By comparison, a global cache coherence strategy is conservative at write operations, insuring that every other processor either invalidates or updates the value that is being written. The disadvantage is that the other processor may never fetch the value again, so the coherence traffic is again unnecessary. Much more architecture work is needed on local cache coherence schemes before they are generally accepted.

14.3 Latency-Tolerant Machines

A third design for scalable shared-memory systems is to avoid the headaches of caches altogether. Caches are used to reduce average latency for memory accesses and reduce the required memory network bandwidth required. Some machine designers have noted that latency is expensive to improve, whereas it is relatively easy to design high bandwidth networks (though they also may be high latency). A high bandwidth network does not need the bandwidth reduction characteristics of caches; if some way can be found to tolerate the latencies, caches can be done away with altogether. One way to tolerate latencies is to use multithreaded processors. In such a system, the latency of an expensive operation (such as a memory fetch) is tolerated by switching to a parallel thread. The thread switch should be very inexpensive (compared to the memory latency), perhaps a few cycles; some designs can switch threads in a single cycle. When the memory operation responds with the value, the issuing thread again becomes eligible for scheduling the next time a thread switch occurs. Such a processor must be able to keep the state for several threads resident in the processor to support very low-cost thread switching.

Essentially, such a system trades parallelism for memory latency. It uses operations that could be run in parallel to keep the processors busy while they would otherwise be waiting for long-latency memory operations. Thus, a high degree of parallelism is required. Moreover, parallelism is desired at two levels. To utilize multiple processors, the program should spawn large-grain parallel tasks, such as iterations of a parallel outer loop. Depending on whether the number of processors allocated to a particular job is fixed or dynamic, the program can use either static or dynamic scheduling, as can other shared-memory systems.

To utilize a single processor, each large-grain parallel task must be able to spawn many small-grain parallel threads. Each thread takes up state within the processor and takes time to spawn, so the threads should be created on demand, when the processor would otherwise be idle. One scheme would be for each large-grain parallel task to be a *generator* of threads. Each time the generator executes, it spawns another parallel thread. If the generator executes at lower priority than the other parallel threads, then it will be eligible for execution only when all the other threads are waiting for long-latency operations or have completed. In either case, the generator can spawn another thread to keep the processor busy. Such a scheme depends on the multithreading processor supporting at least two priority levels for the resident threads. If not, the program may have to guess how many threads it should spawn in order to keep the processor busy. Since network latency may be nondeterministic, this guess may be inexact.

Aggressive instruction scheduling to fetch data far in advance of when it is needed is another scheme that can be used when latencies are high. There may be hardware assistance for this, either in the form of data fetch queues, so that precious registers are not tied up waiting for data to arrive, or in the form of a separate access processor to initiate the memory fetch operations asynchronously from the execute operations. In loops with regular memory addresses, the access processor can generate addresses and issue memory fetch operations far in advance of when the execute processor needs them, and the two processors proceed in a decoupled fashion. If, however, there is considerable conditional control flow, the results of the execute processor may be needed to feed back to the access processor. This constitutes a loss of decoupling; in that case, the access processor may not get very far ahead of the execute processor, and may not be able to hide the memory latencies.

14.4 Further Reading

Markatos and LeBlanc (1994) show that the potential load imbalance of using affinity scheduling is outweighed by the improved cache locality, even with small numbers of processors, compared to guided self-scheduling, factoring, and other scheduling methods. Appelbe and Lakshmanan (1993) discuss the interaction of loop transformations with affinity scheduling.

Cache memories and the three Cs classification of cache misses are described by Hennessy and Patterson (1990). Compiler-managed cache memories for large-scale multiprocessors have been heavily studied. Cytron et al. (1988) use data-flow analysis to find where to put cache control instructions. Veidenbaum (1986) studies a software-cache coherence scheme with three cache control instructions: invalidate the cache, turn the cache on, and turn the cache off. Cheong and Veidenbaum (1987) evaluate a simple write-through cache that is kept coherent by flushing the cache before and after each parallel loop. This has the unfortunate effect of losing locality between adjacent parallel loops. In a modification to this approach described by Cheong and Veidenbaum (1990b), the software and the cache maintain a version number for each variable; when an access to a variable hits in the cache but that variable has an old version number, the cache value is stale and the cache line must be reloaded. Since the granularity of the version numbers is one per variable, even if that variable is an array, there is still the potential for lots of unnecessary cache traffic. Several of these schemes are summarized by Cheong and

Veidenbaum (1990a). Min and Baer (1990) show through simulations that software-based cache coherence can achieve cache hit rates equivalent to directory-based methods with less network traffic.

Darnell and Kennedy (1993) discuss a hardware-assisted software cache coherence scheme, and show that it can achieve a hit ratio close to a hardware snoopy cache coherence protocol; this paper presents a nice summary of various software cache coherence schemes. Larus (1993) argues that the flexibility of compiler-managed caching can outweigh the performance advantages of hardware-managed caching.

EXERCISES

14.1 Generate a trace of memory addresses (fetches and stores) for a parallel application. Determine the ratio of read-write data to read-only and local-only data.

14.2 Simulate the cache behavior for parallel execution of the following loop, using a global cache coherence scheme:

```
(1)    for I = 1 to 5 do
(2)        doall J = I+1 to 5 do
(3)            A[J] = A[J] + B[I,J] * A[I]
(4)        enddoall
(5)    endfor
```

Vary your cache and scheduling policies. What is the percentage of misses for each of the four categories (the four Cs)? What policies give the best performance for this example?

14.3 Repeat the preceding exercise using a local cache coherence mechanism.

14.4 Restructure the loops below to take advantage of affinity scheduling:

```
(1)    doall I = 1 to 20 do
(2)        A[I] = B[I] + C[I]
(3)    enddoall
(4)    doall I = 1 to 20 do
(5)        D[I] = D[I] + B[20-I]
(6)    enddoall
(7)    doall I = 1 to 10 do
(8)        E[I] = A[2*I]/2
(9)    enddoall
```

14.5 How should scheduling policies be affected by memory strides to improve locality?

GLOSSARY

access conflict *See* data access conflict.

actual argument The actual variable (or expression) passed from the calling routine to the called routine.

acyclic graph A graph with no cycles.

acyclic condensation A DAG constructed from a directed graph with one node for each strongly connected component in the graph, and an edge between two distinct nodes if there is an edge in the original graph between two nodes in the corresponding SCCs.

address-based Data dependence relations that occur when the same memory location is assigned and used, regardless of whether there is an intervening assignment.

adjacent node A node connected by an edge to a given node.

advancing edge A directed graph edge from a node to a spanning tree or spanning forest descendant.

alias A duplicate name for a particular memory location; aliases may arise because of pointers, Fortran equivalence statements, or formal argument association.

ancestor In a tree, a node that appears on a path from the *Root* to a given node.

annihilate Change an element of a matrix or vector to zero.

antecedent In a directed graph, a node that can reach the node in question through a path in the graph.

anti-dependence A data dependence relation from a use to a redefinition or reassignment.

antisymmetric relation A relation R on a set S that satisfies the following property: $sRt \land tRs \implies s = t$. The $\leq$ relation on the set of real numbers is an example of an antisymmetric relation.

array assignment An assignment that defines all the elements of an array or subarray.

asymmetric relation A relation on a set that satisfies the following property: $sRt \implies t\overline{R}s$. The $<$ relation on the set of real numbers is an example of an asymmetric relation.

back edge A CFG edge for which the target dominates the source.

back end The processor ensemble of a SIMD parallel system, controlled by the front end.

backward interprocedural analysis Analysis that finds information about a procedure to be used when optimizing the call site.

barrier A synchronization operation that forces each processor to wait until all active processors have reached the same synchronization point; all processors are then released simultaneously.

basic block A sequence of statements with no branches into or out of the list; a straight-line section of code.

basic induction variable An induction variable that has value zero during the first iteration of a loop, and value one greater on each succeeding iteration.

basis vectors Of a subspace, a set of linearly independent vectors that span the subspace.

block distribution A distribution of the N elements of an array onto P processors such that each processor is allocated N/P consecutive elements of the array.

block-cyclic distribution A distribution of the N elements of an array onto P processors such that the array is divided into blocks of K consecutive elements, and each processor is allocated every Pth block of the array.

broadcast A message that goes to all the active processors.

C A programming language designed for operating systems programming, where the code generated is close to the program written; a high level assembly language for the PDP-11.

cache hit A request from the processor for a memory location that is satisfied by the cache memory.

cache line A number of consecutive main memory words that are loaded into cache memory together, usually aligned at power-of-two address boundaries.

cache memory A fast memory, running at the speed of the processor, that keeps copies of main memory data.

cache miss A request by the processor for a memory location that is not present in the cache memory, and must be satisfied by requesting the location from main memory.

call-by-reference A parameter-passing mechanism where the address of the actual argument is passed to the called routine; an update to the formal argument by the called routine updates the actual argument.

call-by-value A parameter-passing mechanism where the value of the actual argument is copied, and the copy is passed to the called routine; an update to the formal argument by the called routine does not update the actual argument.

call-by-value-result A parameter-passing mechanism where a copy of the value of the actual argument is passed to the called routine, and the value returned from the called routine is copied back to the actual argument; an update to the formal argument by the called routine results in an update to the actual argument, but only when the called routine returns.

call graph A graph with one node for each procedure and an edge connecting the calling routine node to the called routine node for each procedure call.

cardinality The number of elements in a set.

CFG *See* control flow graph.

child A successor of a node in a tree.

chord *See* advancing edge.

chunk scheduling A variation on self-scheduling whereby each processor enters a critical region to find the next chunk of consecutive iterations to execute. *See also* tapered chunk scheduling.

CISC ("sisk") Complex instruction set computer; typically, this means a computer architecture implemented with microcode. *See* RISC.

collapsed dimension An array dimension that is not distributed across the processors of a scalable parallel machine.

collapsing *See* loop collapsing.

column major A storage order for arrays that lays out the leftmost dimension consecutively in memory.

common block A group of global variables in a Fortran program.

conservative union An approximation of the union of two or more sets such that the result is always a subset of the actual union; that is, the members of the conservative union are guaranteed to be members of the actual union.

context The specification of which back-end processor elements are enabled and disabled for a parallel operation in a SIMD machine.

control dependence A relation on the nodes of a control flow graph; we say that node Y is control dependent on node X (written $X \xrightarrow{CD} Y$), if Y postdominates some but not all successors of X.

control dependence graph A graph with the same nodes as a control flow graph, but with an edge $X \xrightarrow{CD} Y$ whenever Y is control dependent on X.

control flow graph (CFG) A graph representing the flow of control of the program, where each vertex represents a basic block, and each edge shows the potential flow of control between basic blocks. For instance, a vertex will have multiple successors for conditional branches. A control flow graph has a unique source node, called *Entry*.

control unit The part of the processor that controls the actions of the data paths, such as the register files and functional units.

correctness preserving optimization An optimization that preserves the observable behavior of programs that execute without exceptions and terminate without optimization.

convex hull The smallest convex set containing all the vectors in a set.

convex set A set $C \subseteq \mathbb{R}^n$ such that $\mathbf{x}, \mathbf{y} \in C \land 0 \leq \alpha \leq 1 \implies \alpha x + (1 - \alpha)y \in C$.

countable loop A loop where the number of iterations can be computed before entering the loop, as in a Fortran do loop or Pascal for loop.

cross edge A CFG edge $X \to Y$ that is not a tree edge, advancing edge, or retreating edge with respect to a given spanning tree, or with respect to a given spanning forest when X and Y are in the same tree of the forest.

cross-tree edge A CFG edge $X \to Y$ that is not a tree edge, advancing edge, or retreating edge with respect to a given spanning forest, and where X and Y are in different trees of the forest.

cycle A nontrivial path from a node to itself.

cyclic distribution A distribution of the N elements of an array onto P processors such that each processor is allocated every Pth element of the array.

cyclic graph A graph that has one or more cycles.

DAG *See* directed acyclic graph.

data access conflict The condition that occurs when two sections of code, such as two loop iterations, access the same memory location.

data dependence A data access conflict where the ordering of the accesses must be preserved.

data dependence graph A graph representing the data dependence relations, with one node for each statement or operation and an edge for each data dependence relation.

data footprint A measure of the number of cache lines allocated for an array reference in a loop.

data hazard A data dependence relation that prevents some optimization.

data path The registers, memories, functional units, and interconnections that store and process data in a computer system, as contrasted to the control signals that determine what data to fetch or store and what operations to perform.

def *See* definition.

definition In an expression or instruction, an appearance of a variable that may assign a new value to the variable. *See also* killing definition.

def-use chain In a compiler, an intermediate data structure that stores all the uses reached by a particular definition.

degree The number of neighbors of a node in an undirected graph.

degree of reuse A measure of reuse in a loop, used when the reuse factor is hard to quantify.

dense lattice A lattice that satisfies the following property: for all $\mathbf{x}, \mathbf{y}$ in the lattice and $0 \leq \alpha \leq 1$, $\mathbf{z} = \alpha \mathbf{x} + (1 - \alpha)\mathbf{y}$ is in the lattice if $\mathbf{z}$ is integral.

dependence level The nest level of the outermost loop that carries the data dependence; i.e., the outermost loop with a nonzero dependence distance.

dependent variable In the solution of a system of equations, the value of a dependent variable is determined by the values of the independent variables.

depth-first spanning forest (DFSF) A spanning forest (set of trees) that is constructed by a depth-first traversal of a directed graph.

depth-first spanning tree (DFST) A spanning tree of a CFG, rooted at *Entry*, that is constructed by a depth-first traversal.

depth-first tree traversal A traversal of the nodes of a tree such that the subtree rooted at each descendant of a node is visited contiguously.

descendant The transitive closure of the child relationship in a tree.

determinant Of a square matrix, the volume of the polytope defined by the convex hull of the vectors produced by transforming the vertices of the unit cube by the matrix.

DFSF *See* depth-first spanning forest.

DFST *See* depth-first spanning tree.

diagonal matrix A matrix with zero elements everywhere except on the diagonal.

diagonal of a matrix The elements of a matrix **A** indexed by the same row and column indices, a_{ii}. The elements a_{ij} with $i < j$ are *above* the diagonal, and with $i > j$ are *below* the diagonal.

dimensionality Of a subspace, the number of linearly independent vectors in the set of vectors that spans the subspace, or the number of vectors in a basis for the subspace.

directed acyclic graph (DAG) A graph that contains no cycles.

directed graph A graph $\langle V, E \rangle$ where $\langle X, Y \rangle \in E \not\Rightarrow \langle Y, X \rangle \in E$.

direction vector An ordering vector between the iteration vectors of the target and source iterations of the dependence relation.

dirty cache line A cache line that has been written by the processor, but whose value has not been propagated to the main memory.

disjoint partition *See* partition of a set.

distance vector A vector of dependence distances, computed as the vector difference between the iteration vectors of the target and source iterations of a dependence relation.

distribution *See* loop fission.

doall A parallel loop that has no data access conflicts between its iterations.

DOM The dominator relation.

dominator A relation on the nodes of a control flow graph; we say *X DOM Y* if *X* appears on all paths from *Entry* to *Y*. Note that every node dominates itself, and *Entry* dominates all nodes in the graph.

dominator back edge *See* back edge.

doall loop A loop that has no loop carried dependence relations.

dopar loop A parallel loop defined such that each iteration starts execution with a copy of the original values of all variables.

dope vector A pointer to an array that includes the base address as well as the allocated bounds and strides of each dimension.

dot product Of two vectors $\mathbf{x}^n$ and $\mathbf{y}^n$, the summation $\sum_{i=1}^{n} x_i y_i$, denoted $\mathbf{x} \cdot \mathbf{y}$.

echelon matrix (column echelon form) A matrix whose first row is either zero or has a single nonzero in the first column, where if the first nonzero in column i appears in row r_i, then the first nonzero in column $i + 1$ appears in row $r_{i+1} > r_i$, and where the last k columns are entire zero for some k.

edge A tuple $\langle X, Y \rangle$ where X and Y are vertices of a graph; this is usually written $X \to Y$.

elementary column operation One of the following three column operations: scaling a column by a real number, transposing two columns, and skewing (adding a multiple of one column to another column).

elementary lower triangular matrix A square matrix with ones on the diagonal, nonzeros below the diagonal in exactly one column, and zeros elsewhere.

elementary row operation One of the following three row operations: scaling a row by a real number, transposing two rows, and skewing (adding a multiple of one row to another row).

empty set A set containing no elements, written $\emptyset$ or $\{\}$.

entry The unique source node for a control flow graph.

equivalence The proposition $P \equiv Q$, read as "P is equivalent to Q," defined as true when both P and Q are true or both are false, and false otherwise.

equivalence relation A relation that is transitive, reflexive, and symmetric.

eviction The action of marking a cache line as invalid or replacing a cache line. Also called invalidation, eviction includes the write-back for dirty cache lines.

exit The unique sink node for a control flow graph, if one exists.

extent The number of elements in a dimension of an array, computed as $upper - lower + 1$.

extreme value The largest value a function can take in a bounded region.

factored redef-use chains An intermediate representation that can be used to find the uses that use values that will be redefined at a definition.

factored use-def chains An intermediate representation of use-def chains such that each use has a single reaching definition, and special ϕ-terms act as pseudo-assignments at points in the program where there are multiple reaching definitions. An implementation of static single assignment form.

FIFO First-in, first-out; the method by which objects are added to and removed from a queue; the first item put on the queue is the first item pulled out of the queue. *See also* LIFO.

fission *See* loop fission.

flow dependence A data dependence relation from a definition or assignment to a use.

for loop A normal sequential loop, where one iteration completes execution before the next iteration starts.

forall loop A loop defined such that each statement in the loop is executed as an array assignment for all iterations before the next statement is executed.

forest A set of zero or more trees.

fork The activation of another parallel task or parallel processor.

formal argument The name of an argument used by the called routine, bound to an actual argument by the subroutine call.

Fortran The first high level programming language with an optimizing compiler; Fortran (*for*mula *tran*slator) has historically been targeted at high performance numeric computing.

forward interprocedural analysis Analysis that finds information at a call site to be used when optimizing the called procedure.

front end The control processor of a SIMD parallel system, controlling the back end.

FRUD chains *See* factored redef-use chains.

FUD chains *See* factored use-def chains.

functional unit A part of a processor that performs some operations on data, such as an integer adder, floating point multiplier, or shift unit.

fusion *See* loop fusion.

Gaussian elimination A method to solve a system of linear equations.

gcd Greatest common divisor.

global analysis Compiler analysis across all the basic blocks of the procedure. *See* local analysis.

graph A tuple $\langle V, E \rangle$ where V is a set of vertices and $E \subseteq V \times V$ is a set of edges; a graph may be directed or undirected.

greatest common divisor The largest positive integer that evenly divides two or more other integers.

group A subset G of $\mathbb{Z}^n$ (or $\mathbb{R}^n$) such that $\mathbf{0}^n \in G$, and $\forall \mathbf{x}, \mathbf{y} \in G, \mathbf{x} \pm \mathbf{y} \in G$.

guard region *See* overlap region.

half-space The subset of $\mathbb{R}^n$ that satisfies $\mathbf{a} \cdot \mathbf{x} \leq b$.

header A CFG node that dominates all the nodes in a region. For a loop, the header is the unique entry point to the loop and the target of all the back edges.

Hermite normal form A lower trapezoidal integer matrix with full row rank and all positive elements, with the diagonal element having the largest magnitude in any row, obtained from a rectangular matrix by a sequence of unimodular column operations.

Hermite trapezoidal form A lower trapezoidal integer matrix with full row rank, obtained from a rectangular matrix by a sequence of unimodular column operations.

HNF *See* Hermite normal form.

HPF High Performance Fortran; a version of Fortran that allows programmers to define data layouts over distributed memory systems.

HTF *See* Hermite trapezoidal form.

identity matrix The matrix with ones on the diagonal and zeros elsewhere, written **I**; for any vector $\mathbf{v}^n$, the product $\mathbf{I}^{n \times n} \mathbf{v}^n = \mathbf{v}^n$.

IDOM The immediate dominator relation.

iff Shorthand for "if and only if."

image of a matrix *See* range of a matrix.

image of a point or vector The result of applying a transformation to that point.

immediate dominator A relation on the nodes of a CFG; we say X IDOM Y if X strictly dominates Y and all other strict dominators of Y also dominate X. The immediate dominator of a node is unique.

immediate postdominator A relation on the nodes of a CFG; we say X IPDOM Y if X strictly postdominates Y and all other strict postdominators of Y also postdominate X. The immediate postdominator of a node is unique.

implication The proposition $P \Longrightarrow Q$, read as "P implies Q," defined as true if P is false or Q is true.

IN set The set of variables used or fetched by a statement.

inclusion principle The property of a memory hierarchy that memory locations present in each level of the hierarchy are a subset of the locations present in the next lower level of the hierarchy.

indegree The number of predecessors of a node in a directed graph.

independent variable In the solution of a system of equations, an independent variable can take any value.

index set splitting Splitting a loop into two loops so that the first loop executes the first part of the index set and the second loop executes the rest.

induction variable A scalar variable assigned in a loop whose value is a function of its value on the previous iteration; the value of a linear induction variable on the next iteration is equal to the value on this iteration plus a constant.

inlining Copying the text of a procedure at a call site, replacing formal arguments with the appropriate actual arguments.

innermosting Interchanging a loop to the innermost position of a set of nested loops.

input dependence A data dependence relation from a use to a reuse of the same variable or array element.

interchanging *See* loop interchanging.

invalidation *See* eviction.

inverse function Of a function f, a function f^{-1} that satisfies $f^{-1}(f(x)) = x$.

inverse matrix Of a square matrix $\mathbf{A}$, a matrix $\mathbf{A}^{-1}$ that satisfies $\mathbf{A} \times \mathbf{A}^{-1} = \mathbf{A}^{-1}\mathbf{A} = \mathbf{I}$, where $\mathbf{I}$ is the identity matrix.

IPDOM The immediate postdominator relation.

iteration vector A vector of integers that corresponds to an iteration of a nested loop.

iteration space The subset of the lattice of integers that correspond to the iterations of a nested loop.

kill *See* killing definition.

killing definition A definition that always assigns a new value to the variable.

lattice A subset of $\mathbb{Z}^n$ that is generated by an integer combination of a set of vectors.

lattice point A vector with all integer entries.

leaf A node in a tree that has no children.

length The number of edges in a path. The length of a trivial path is zero.

lexically backward A data dependence relation from a statement to another statement that precedes it lexically in the program.

lexically forward A data dependence relation from a statement to another statement that follows it lexically in the program.

lexicographic order An ordering relation between vectors. The order $\mathbf{a} \prec_j \mathbf{b}$ means $a_i = b_i, 1 \le i < j$, and $a_j < b_j$; the order $\mathbf{a} \prec \mathbf{b}$ means there is a j ($1 \le j \le n$) such that $\mathbf{a} \prec_j \mathbf{b}$; and the order $\mathbf{a} \preceq \mathbf{b}$ means $\mathbf{a} \prec \mathbf{b} \vee \mathbf{a} = \mathbf{b}$.

lexicographically nonnegative A vector $\mathbf{v}$ such that $0 \preceq \mathbf{v}$; that is, the first nonzero entry in v, if any, is positive.

lexicographically positive A vector $\mathbf{v}$ such that $0 \prec \mathbf{v}$; that is, the first nonzero entry in v is positive.

lexico-positive *See* lexicographically positive.

liberal union A representation of the union of two or more sets such that the result is always a superset of the actual union; that is, the members of the actual union are guaranteed to be members of the liberal union.

LIFO Last-in, first-out; the method by which objects are added to and removed from a stack; the last item pushed on the stack is the first item popped off the stack. *See also* FIFO.

linear combination Of a set of vectors, a combination $\mathbf{x} = \alpha_1\mathbf{v}_1 + \alpha_2\mathbf{v}_2 + \cdots \alpha_m\mathbf{v}_m$, where each α_i is a real number.

linear equation An equation with a linear combination of unknowns on one side and a constant on the other.

linear function A function $f : \mathbb{R}^m \longrightarrow \mathbb{R}^n$ such that $f(\alpha\mathbf{x} + \beta\mathbf{y}) = \alpha f(\mathbf{x}) + \beta f(\mathbf{y})$ for $\alpha, \beta \in \mathbb{R}$.

linear inequality An inequality with a linear combination of unknowns on one side and a constant on the other.

linearly dependent A set of vectors is linearly dependent if there is a linear combination with one or more nonzero coefficients that produces the zero vector.

linearly independent A set of vectors is linearly independent if there is no linear combination with one or more nonzero coefficients that produces the zero vector.

local analysis Compiler analysis within a basic block. *See also* global analysis.

locality A characteristic of most computer programs that once a memory location is accessed, either the same location or a nearby location will be accessed in the near future. Also, locality in some level of a memory hierarchy occurs when a memory reference is satisfied at that level of the hierarchy, exploiting the pattern of reuse.

loop *See* natural loop.

loop carried A data dependence relation from one iteration to another iteration of a loop.

loop coalescing A generalization of loop collapsing where the loop limits need not match the array bounds.

loop collapsing Rewriting two (or more) tightly nested loops as a single loop such that each iteration of the collapsed loop corresponds to an iteration of the original nested loops.

loop distribution *See* loop fission.

loop fission Splitting a loop into two or more separate loops.

loop fusion Combining two or more separate loops into a single loop.

loop independent A data dependence relation of which the source and target are in the same iteration of all containing loops.

loop interchanging A compiler transformation that switches an outer loop and an inner loop.

loop peeling Reducing the trip count of the loop by executing the first or last iteration outside the loop.

loop reordering A compiler transformation that changes the relative nest levels of nested loops; a generalization of loop interchanging.

loop reversal Executing the index set of a loop backward.

loop strip-mining A compiler transformation that converts a loop into two loops: an outer loop to step between strips of iterations, and an inner loop to iterate over the iterations within a strip.

loop tiling A compiler transformation that organizes a set of nested loops to work on small parts of the iteration space, to take advantage of locality.

lowering A phase in a compiler that converts high level constructs, such as loops and data structure references, into low level equivalents, such as conditional branches and address computations.

lower trapezoidal matrix Any matrix with zero elements above the diagonal; that is, $a_{ij} = 0$ whenever $i < j$.

lower triangular matrix A square matrix with zero elements above the diagonal; that is, a square lower trapezoidal matrix.

matrix A two-dimensional array or table of numbers.

matrix product The matrix product of two matrices $\mathbf{A}^{n \times m}$ and $\mathbf{B}^{m \times k}$ is a matrix $\mathbf{C}^{n \times k}$ defined that c_{ij} is the dot product of the ith row of $\mathbf{A}$ and the jth column of $\mathbf{B}$.

memory-based *See* address-based.

memory hierarchy The registers, cache memory, main memory, and backing store (such as disks) that hold programs and data.

MIMD ("mim-dee") Multiple instruction/multiple data computer, typically comprising a set of processors, each of which can execute its own instruction stream. *See also* SIMD.

moly variable A variable stored on a multicomputer with one copy per node, like a mono variable, but where the value need not be kept consistent.

mono variable Data stored on a scalable parallel system such that there is conceptually a single copy with a coherent value.

multigraph A set of nodes and edges that can have multiple distinct edges between the same two nodes; in a graph, edges are relations, whereas in a multigraph, edges are objects.

multiprocessor A computer system architecture with multiple processors sharing a single main memory.

natural loop A set of CFG nodes defined by a header node and one or more back edges; the header node is the target of all the back edges and all the other nodes in the loop can reach a back edge without going through the header node.

neighbor A node connected to a particular node by an edge in a graph.

node (1) An element in a graph; in a control flow graph, nodes (or vertices) are used to represent basic blocks. (2) A processor in a large-scale parallel machine.

nonkilling definition A definition that might not assign a new value to the variable. *See also* killing definition.

nonsingular matrix A square matrix that has an inverse; i.e., a square matrix whose column vectors and row vectors are linearly independent.

nontightly nested loops Two loops nested such that the outer loop contains the inner loop, but also contains statements other than those in the inner loop.

nontrivial path A path in a directed graph with one or more edges; there can be a nontrivial path from a node X to itself, such as $\langle X, X \rangle$, if there is an edge $X \to X$. *See also* trivial path.

no-op An instruction that does nothing—a "no operation" instruction.

normal vector *See* unit normal vector.

normalized iteration vector An iteration vector assignment where the first iteration of each loop has index zero and each subsequent iteration has index one greater.

null space Of an $n \times m$ matrix, the subspace of $\mathbb{R}^m$ that is mapped into the zero vector by applying the matrix.

nullity of a matrix The dimensionality of the null space of the matrix.

ordering vector A vector of ordering relations, used to express ordering between the elements of two vectors.

ordering relation One of the six ordering relations on real numbers: $<$, $=$, $>$, $\leq$, $\geq$, and $\neq$. For convenience, we also define an ordering relation $\star$ that is always true.

origin (1) Of an array, the address at which the element with all zero subscripts would be allocated, whether or not that element is actually part of the array. (2) Of a template, the index that will map to processor zero at offset zero.

OUT set The set of variables defined or assigned by a statement.

outdegree The number of successors of a node in a directed graph.

outermosting Interchanging a loop to the outermost position in a set of nested loops.

output dependence A data dependence relation from a definition or assignment to a redefinition or reassignment.

overlap region The extra local memory allocated on a particular processor of a distributed memory system to hold array elements that are owned by neighboring processors.

parent The unique predecessor of a node in a tree.

partial order A relation that is transitive, reflexive, and antisymmetric.

partition Of a set A, a sequence of sets $A_1, A_2, \ldots, A_n$ such that $\bigcup_i A_i = A$ and $(i \neq j) \implies (A_i \cap A_j = \emptyset)$.

pairwise simple bound A linear inequality where only two unknowns have non-zero coefficients, and those coefficients are ± 1.

path A sequence of nodes connected by edges in a directed graph. For example, we can have a path $\langle X_0, X_1, X_2, \ldots, X_n \rangle$ if there are edges $X_0 \to X_1$, $X_1 \to X_2$, ..., $X_{n-1} \to X_n$; the path may be written $X_0 \to X_1 \to \cdots \to X_n$. The length of the path is n, the number of edges in the path. We use the notation $Q : X_0 \stackrel{*}{\to} X_n$ to mean that Q is a path from X_0 to X_n; Q may be a trivial path. We write $Q : X_0 \stackrel{+}{\to} X_n$ to mean that Q is a nontrivial path from X_0 to X_n.

PDG *See* program dependence graph.

PE *See* processing element.

peeling *See* loop peeling.

perfectly nested loops *See* tightly nested loops.

permutation matrix A square matrix with a single one in each row and column, and zeros elsewhere.

poly variable Data distributed across the memory of a scalable parallel system.

polyhedron The intersection of a set of half spaces; a polyhedron is the set of vectors **x** that satisfy $\mathbf{Ax} \leq \mathbf{b}$, for some matrix **A** and vector **b**.

polytope A bounded polyhedron.

post-body The source of the unique back edge of a natural loop; some compilers insert a post-body artificially to create a unique back edge.

postdominator A relation on the nodes of a control flow graph; we say *Y PDOM X* if *Y* appears on all paths from *X* to *Exit*. Note that *Y* postdominates itself, and *Exit* postdominates all nodes in the CFG.

postorder A depth-first traversal of a tree that visits a node after visiting all its descendants.

precedence graph A data dependence graph or program dependence graph for a program without loops.

PRED The set of predecessors of a node in a directed graph.

predecessor In a directed graph, a node *X* connected to a node *Y* by an edge $X \to Y$.

predicate An expression that controls a conditional branch.

predominator *See* dominator.

preheader The only predecessor of a loop header that is not in the loop; compilers often insert preheaders artificially so there will be a unique nonloop predecessor for the header node.

preorder A depth-first traversal of a tree that visits a node before visiting any of its descendants.

prescheduling A parallel loop scheduling strategy whereby the program tells each processor all the iterations to compute before initiating any computation.

preserving definition *See* nonkilling definition.

processing element A processor in a large-scale parallel machine; sometimes called a node.

processing ensemble The collection of PEs, or nodes, that make up a large-scale parallel machine.

program dependence graph A graph showing control dependence as well as data dependence relations.

proper ancestor In a tree, an ancestor of a node that is distinct from the node; that is, X is a proper ancestor of Y if X is an ancestor of Y and $X \neq Y$.

proper descendant In a tree, a descendant of a node that is distinct from the node; that is, Y is a proper descendant of X if Y is a descendant of X and $X \neq Y$.

proposition A statement that is either true or false, such as "inflation rises" or "$a \in A$."

quantifier A phrase that binds a free variable in a proposition; in the proposition $(\forall i \in \mathbb{Z})[2i \in \mathbb{Z}]$, for example, the phrase $(\forall i \in \mathbb{Z})$ is a quantifier that binds the variable i to be an integer.

range of a matrix The subspace of $\mathbb{R}^n$ spanned by the column vectors of a $n \times m$ matrix.

rank (1) In a programming language, the number of dimensions of an array. (2) In linear algebra, the number of linearly independent rows of a matrix, which is equal to the number of linearly independent columns.

reachable A relation on the nodes of a directed graph; node Y is reachable from node X if there is a path $X \xrightarrow{*} Y$.

reached uses Ot a definition, the set of uses such that there is a path from the definition to the use with no killing definitions of that variable along the path.

reaches A relation on the nodes of a directed graph; node X reaches node Y if there is a path $X \xrightarrow{*} Y$.

reaching definition A definition that has a path to a particular point with no killing definitions along the path.

redefinition A definition that writes a new value to a variable or array element over the value that was previously stored at that location.

reducible CFG A CFG that is a DAG when its back edges are removed.

reduction An operation or loop that computes a scalar value from an array or array expression, such as the sum of a vector.

reflexive relation A relation R on a set S that satisfies the following property: sRs for all $s \in S$. The $\leq$ relation on the set of real numbers is an example of a reflexive relation.

region A region is a subgraph of the CFG with a unique header, such that the header dominates all the nodes in the region.

register file A collection of fast registers in a processor to hold data while operating on it.

relation (from a set S to T) A subset R of the cross product $S \times T$. An element $s \in S$ is related to an element $t \in T$, written sRt, if $\langle s, t \rangle \in R$. A relation from a set S to itself is called a relation on the set S.

reordering *See* loop reordering.

repeat loop A loop with the exit at its bottom; named for the Pascal `repeat-until` construct.

retreating edge A CFG edge $X \rightarrow Y$ from a node to an ancestor in a spanning tree.

reuse A memory location or cache line that is fetched or stored more than once exhibits reuse.

reuse factor A measure of the reuse for an array reference in a loop.

reversal *See* loop reversal.

RISC ("risk") Reduced instruction set computer; typically this means a computer architecture with many general-purpose registers, explicit load and store instructions to access memory, few memory addressing modes, and an instruction set that is designed for efficient pipelining.

root The unique source node of a tree.

row major A storage order for arrays that lays out the rightmost dimension consecutively in memory.

safe optimization *See* correctness preserving optimization.

scalarization A compiler transformation that converts a parallel loop into a sequential loop.

scaling matrix A matrix with ones on the diagonal and zeros off the diagonal, except that one diagonal entry may have any nonzero value.

scaling Of a row or column of a matrix, multiplying each element by a constant value.

SCC *See* strongly connected component.

SCR *See* strongly connected region.

SDOM *See* strict dominator.

self-scheduling A parallel loop scheduling strategy whereby each processor enters a critical section of code that computes the next loop iteration to be executed.

seminormalized iteration vector Any iteration vector assignment where the distance between successive iterations is one.

sequential locality A classification of locality that occurs when a memory location is accessed that is sequentially adjacent to another location that was recently accessed.

set A (possibly empty) collection of objects.

set difference A set operator that finds the elements of one set that are not in a second set; the difference of two sets S and T is the set $S - T$, defined by $S - T = \{s | s \in S \land s \notin T\}$.

set intersection A set operator that finds the elements in both of two sets; the intersection of two sets S and T is the set $S \cap T$, defined by $S \cap T = \{s | s \in S \land s \in T\}$.

set membership An element s is a member of set S, written $s \in S$, if s is in the set S.

set union A set operator that finds the elements in either of two sets; the union of two sets S and T is the set $S \cup T$, defined by $S \cup T = \{s | s \in S \lor s \in T\}$.

sibling In a tree, other children of a node's parent.

SIMD ("sim-dee") Single instruction/multiple data computer system, typically comprising a sequential front-end and a parallel back-end processor element ensemble.

simple bound A linear inequality where only one unknown has a nonzero coefficient.

simple cycle A cycle that is also a simple path.

simple direction vector A direction vector with only <, =, and > entries.

simple path A path whose nodes are all distinct, except perhaps the first and last nodes on the path.

simple ordering vector An ordering vector with only <, =, and > entries.

single entry graph A directed graph with a unique source node, called *Entry*, from which all other nodes are reachable.

single exit graph A directed graph with a unique sink node, called *Exit*, which is reachable from all other nodes.

singular matrix A square matrix that has no inverse; i.e., a square matrix whose column vectors or row vectors are linearly dependent.

sink node A node in a directed graph with no successors. *See* exit.

skew matrix A matrix with ones on the diagonal, a single nonzero value off the diagonal, and zeros elsewhere.

skewing Adding a multiple of one row or column of a matrix to another row or column.

slicing edge An artificial edge in a control flow graph from *Entry* to *Exit*, added for control dependence and dominance frontier computation.

source node (1) In a directed graph, a node with no predecessors. *See* entry. (2) Of an edge $X \rightarrow Y$ in a directed graph, X is the source node.

span Of a set of vectors, the subspace of $\mathbb{R}^n$ that can be expressed as a linear combination of the n-vectors in the set.

spanning forest In a general directed graph, a set of disjoint trees that contains all the nodes in the graph.

spanning tree A tree, rooted at *Entry*, that contains all the nodes in a CFG.

sparse lattice A lattice that is not dense.

spatial locality A classification of locality that occurs when a memory location is accessed that is near another location that was recently accessed.

SPDD ("speedy") Single program/distributed data; a way to program MIMD computer systems so that each processor executes a copy of the same program, but on different parts of a large distributed data set.

SPMD ("spim-dee") Single program/multiple data; a way to program MIMD computer systems so that each processor executes a copy of the same program, but on different data sets.

square matrix A matrix in which the number of rows equals the number of columns.

SSA *See* static single assignment.

stale copy A copy of a memory location in a cache memory subsystem that does not contain the most recently computed value for that location.

static single assignment A compiler intermediate form such that each definition of a variable is renamed so there is a single definition of each name, special ϕ-terms are inserted to act as new definitions, and each use of a variable has a single reaching definition. Factored use-def chains are an implementation of static single assignment form.

strict dominator A relation on the nodes in a CFG; we say X *SDOM* Y if X dominates Y and $X \neq Y$.

strict postdominator A relation on the nodes in a CFG; we say X *SPDOM* Y if X postdominates Y and $X \neq Y$.

strictly lower triangular matrix A square matrix with zero elements on and above the diagonal.

strictly upper triangular matrix A square matrix with zero elements on and below the diagonal.

stride The distance (usually in memory words) between two memory accesses.

strip-mining *See* loop strip-mining.

strongly connected component A maximal strongly connected region (SCR); that is, an SCR that is not a proper subset of any larger SCR.

strongly connected region A subset of the nodes in a directed graph such that each node reaches every other node in the SCR; the nodes in a cycle.

subspace A subset S of $\mathbb{R}^n$ such that any linear combination of two vectors in S is also in S.

SUCC The set of successors of a node in a directed graph; for instance, SUCC(X) is the set of successors of X.

successor In a directed graph, a node Y connected to a node X by an edge $X \rightarrow Y$.

supervector performance Performance that is better than ordinary vector performance, achieved through managing locality in vector registers.

symmetric A relation R on a set S such that $sRt \Longrightarrow tRs$. For example, parallelism on the set of lines in a plane is an example of a symmetric relation.

tapered chunk scheduling A variation on chunk scheduling whereby each processor enters a critical region to find the next chunk of consecutive iterations to execute, and the size of the chunks gets smaller as the loop nears completion.

target node For an edge $X \rightarrow Y$ in a directed graph, Y is the target node.

temporal locality A classification of locality that occurs when the same memory location is accessed more than once in a short period of time.

tightly nested loops Two loops nested such that the outer loop contains the inner loop, but contains no statements other than those in the inner loop.

topological order A traversal order of the nodes in a DAG such that all the predecessors of a node are visited before the node itself.

transitive relation A relation R on a set S such that sRt and tRv implies sRv; the $<$ relation on the set of real numbers is an example of a transitive relation.

transpose Of a matrix $\mathbf{A}$, a matrix $\mathbf{A}^T$ such that $a_{ij}^T = a_{ji}$.

transposition Switching two rows or columns of a matrix.

trapezoidal loop A loop whose iteration space has a trapezoidal shape.

triangular loop A loop whose iteration space has a triangular shape.

tree A directed acyclic graph where each node has a unique predecessor, called its parent, and zero or more successors, called children. The source node for the tree is called the *Root*.

tree edge A CFG edge $X \rightarrow Y$ that is also an edge in a particular spanning tree.

trivial path A path in a directed graph with no edges; i.e., with length equal to zero. For instance, $\langle X \rangle$ is a trivial path from X to itself, but with no edges. *See* nontrivial path.

tuple An ordered pair of objects, written $\langle a, b \rangle$. Two tuples $\langle a, b \rangle$ and $\langle c, d \rangle$ are equal only if $a = c$ and $b = d$. An n-tuple is an ordered list of n objects $\langle a_1, a_2, \ldots, a_n \rangle$.

undirected graph A graph $\langle V, E \rangle$ such that $\langle X, Y \rangle \in E \Longrightarrow \langle Y, X \rangle \in E$.

unimodular column operation One of the following three column operations: negating a column, transposing two columns, and skewing (adding an integer multiple of one column to another column).

unimodular matrix An integer matrix with determinant equal to ± 1.

unimodular row operation One of the following three row operations: negating a row, transposing two rows, and skewing (adding an integer multiple of one row to another row).

unit cube The polytope comprising the vectors **x** where $0 \leq x_i \leq 1$ for all elements x_i; so called because the volume of the unit cube is exactly one.

unit lower triangular matrix A square matrix with zeros above the diagonal and ones on the diagonal.

unit upper triangular matrix A square matrix with zeros below the diagonal and ones on the diagonal.

unit normal vector A vector with a single nonzero element which is equal to one; the unit normal vector $\mathbf{e}_i$ has a one in the ith element and zeros elsewhere.

upper trapezoidal matrix A matrix with zeros below the diagonal; that is, $a_{ij} = 0$ whenever $i > j$.

upper triangular matrix A square matrix with zeros below the diagonal; that is, a square upper trapezoidal matrix.

upward exposed A use of a variable in a basic block such that there is no killing definition of the variable earlier in that block.

use An appearance of a variable in an expression or instruction where the value of the variable is fetched.

use-def chain An intermediate data structure in a compiler that stores all the reaching definitions at each use.

value-based Data dependence relations that occur when the same memory location is assigned and used and there is no intervening assignment.

vector A vector is an n-tuple of real (or integer) numbers, denoted in this text by bold lower case, as **v**.

vector processor A processor with vector instructions; that is, with instructions that can operate on vector data, usually with a vector register file.

vector register file The analog of a register file for vector data, comprising several vector registers; a vector register contains a sequence of elements to make up a vector of data.

vectorization A compiler transformation that converts a sequential loop into vector instructions.

vertex *See* node.

while loop A loop with the exit at the top; typically a loop that is not countable.

zero vector A vector with all zero elements.

ϕ-term (phi) A special term used as a pseudo-definition in factored use-def chains or static single assignment form, inserted in the program at points when two or more definitions reach along different control-flow predecessors.

Υ-term (upsilon) A special term used in factored redef-use chains, inserted in the program at points when two or more downward-exposed uses reach along different control-flow predecessors.

REFERENCES

Abu-Sufah, Walid A., David J. Kuck, and Duncan H. Lawrie (1981). On the Performance Enhancement of Paging Systems Through Program Analysis and Transformations. *IEEE Transactions on Computers*, May, C-30(5):341–356.

Adams, Jeanne C., et al. (1992). *Fortran 90 Handbook.* New York: McGraw-Hill.

Aho, Alfred V., John E. Hopcroft, and Jeffrey D. Ullman (1974). *The Design and Analysis of Computer Algorithms.* Reading, Mass.: Addison-Wesley.

Aho, Alfred V., R. Sethi, and Jeffrey D. Ullman (1986). *Compilers: Principles, Techniques, and Tools.* Reading, Mass.: Addison-Wesley.

Allen, Frances E., and John Cocke (1972). A Catalogue of Optimizing Transformations. In *Design and Optimization of Compilers*, R. Rustin, ed. Englewood Cliffs, N.J.: Prentice-Hall, 1–30.

Allen, Frances E., et al. (1988). An Overview of the PTRAN Analysis System for Multiprocessing. *Journal of Parallel and Distributed Computing*, October, 5(5):617–640.

Allen, J. Randy, David Callahan, and Ken Kennedy (1987). Automatic Decomposition of Scientific Programs for Parallel Execution. In *14th Annual ACM Symposium on Principles of Programming Languages*, held in Munich, Germany, January, 63–76.

Allen, J. Randy, and Ken Kennedy (1987). Automatic Translation of Fortran Programs to Vector Form. *ACM Transactions on Programming Languages and Systems*, October, 9(4):491–542.

——— (1992). Vector Register Allocation. *IEEE Transactions on Computers*, October, 41(10):1290–1317.

Ancourt, Corinne, and François Irigoin (1991). Scanning Polyhedre with DO Loops. In *3rd ACM SIGPLAN Symposium on Principles & Practice of Parallel Programming*, held in Williamsburg, Va., April, 39–50.

Anderson, Jennifer M., and Monica S. Lam (1993). Global Optimizations for Parallelism and Locality on Scalable Parallel Machines. In *ACM SIGPLAN '93 Conference on Programming Language Design and Implementation*, held in Albuquerque, N.M., June, 112–125.

Appelbe, William F., and Balakrishnan Lakshmanan (1993). Optimizing Parallel Programs Using Affinity Regions. In *1993 International Conference on Parallel Processing*, vol. II, held in St. Charles, Ill., August, 246–249.

Backus, John (1981). The History of Fortran I, II and III. In *History of Programming Languages*, Richard L. Wexelblat, ed. New York: Academic Press, 25-74.

Ballance, Robert A., Arthur B. Maccabe, and Karl J. Ottenstein (1990). The Program Dependence Web: A Representation Supporting Control-, Data-, and Demand-Driven Interpretation of Imperative Languages. In *ACM SIGPLAN '90 Conference on Programming Language Design and Implementation*, held in White Plains, N.Y., June, 257-271.

Banerjee, Utpal (1988). *Dependence Analysis for Supercomputing*. Norwell, Mass.: Kluwer Academic Publishers.

——— (1989). A Theory of Loop Permutations. In *Languages and Compilers for Parallel Computing, 1989 Workshop*, held in Urbana, Ill., August, Research Monographs in Parallel and Distributed Computing, Cambridge, Mass.: MIT Press, 54-74.

——— (1993). *Loop Transformations for Restructuring Compilers: The Foundations*. Norwell, Mass.: Kluwer Academic Publishers.

——— (1994). *Loop Parallelization*. Norwell, Mass.: Kluwer Academic Publishers.

Banerjee, Utpal, and Daniel D. Gajski (1984). Fast Execution of Loops with IF Statements. *IEEE Transactions on Computers*, November, C-33(11):1030-1033.

Banerjee, Utpal, et al. (1979). Time and Parallel Processor Bounds for Fortran-Like Loops. *IEEE Transactions on Computers*, September, C-28(9):660-670.

——— (1993). Automatic Program Parallelization. *Proceedings of the IEEE*, February, 81(2):211-243.

Barth, Jeffrey M. (1978). A Practical Interprocedural Data Flow Analysis Algorithm. *Communications of the ACM*, September, 21(9):724-736.

Bernstein, A. J. (1966). Analysis of Programs for Parallel Processing. *IEEE Transactions on Electronic Computers*, October, 15(5).

Bik, Aart J. C., and Harry A. G. Wijshoff (1993). Advanced Compiler Optimizations for Sparse Computations. In *Supercomputing '93*, held in Portland, Ore., November, 430-439.

Brandes, Thomas (1988). The Importance of Direct Dependences for Automatic Parallelization. In *1988 ACM International Conference on Supercomputing*, held in St. Malo, France, June, 407-417.

Burke, Michael, and Ron Cytron (1986). Interprocedural Dependence Analysis and Parallelization. In *ACM SIGPLAN '86 Symposium on Compiler Construction*, held in Palo Alto, Calif., June, 162-175.

Callahan, David, Ken Kennedy, and Allan Porterfield (1991). Software Prefetching. In *4th International Conference on Architectural Support for Program-*

ming Languages and Operating Systems, held in Santa Clara, Calif., April, 40-52.

Callahan, David, and Allan Porterfield (1990). Data Cache Performance of Supercomputer Applications. In *Supercomputing '90*, held in New York City, November, 564-572.

Callahan, David, et al. (1986). Interprocedural Constant Propagation. In *ACM SIGPLAN '86 Symposium on Compiler Construction*, held in Palo Alto, Calif., June, 152-161.

—— (1987). Constructing the Procedure Call Multigraph. *IEEE Transactions on Software Engineering*, April, 16(4):483-487.

Cann, David (1992). Retire Fortran? A Debate Rekindled. *Communications of the ACM*, August, 35(8):81-89.

Carr, Steve, and Ken Kennedy (1992). Compiler Blockability of Numerical Algorithms. In *Supercomputing '92*, held in Minneapolis, Minn., November, 114-124.

Chapman, Barbara M., Piyush Mehrotra, and Hans P. Zima (1992). Programming in Vienna Fortran. *Scientific Programming*, 1(1):31-50.

Chatterjee, Siddhartha, et al. (1993). Generating Local Addresses and Communication Sets for Data-Parallel Programs. In *4th ACM SIGPLAN Symposium on Principles & Practice of Parallel Programming*, held in San Diego, Calif., May, 149-158.

Cheong, Hoichi, and Alexander V. Veidenbaum (1987). The Performance of Software-Managed Multiprocessor Caches on Parallel Numerical Programs. In *Supercomputing: 1st International Conference*, held in Athens, Greece, number 297 in Lecture Notes in Computer Science, Berlin: Springer Verlag, 316-337.

—— (1990a). Compiler-Directed Cache Management in Multiprocessors. *IEEE Computer*, June, 23(6):39-47.

—— (1990b). A Version Control Approach to Cache Coherence. In *1990 ACM International Conference on Supercomputing*, held in Amsterdam, The Netherlands, June, 322-330.

Choi, Jong-Deok, Ron Cytron, and Jeanne Ferrante (1994). On the Efficient Engineering of Ambitious Program Analysis. *IEEE Transactions on Software Engineering*, 20(2).

Cohagan, William L. (1973). Vector Optimization for the ASC. In *Seventh Annual Princeton Conf. on Information Sciences and Systems*, held in Princeton, N.J., March, 169-174.

Cooper, Keith D., Mary W. Hall, and Ken Kennedy (1990). Procedure Cloning. In *1992 International Conference on Computer Languages*, held in Oakland, Calif., March, 96-105.

Cooper, Keith D., Mary W. Hall, and Linda Torczon (1991). An Experiment with Inline Substitution. *Software: Practice & Experience*, June, 21(6):581-601.

Cooper, Keith D., and Ken Kennedy (1988). Interprocedural Side-Effect Analysis in Linear Time. In *ACM SIGPLAN '88 Conference on Programming Language Design and Implementation*, held in White Plains, N.Y., June, 57-66.

—— (1989). Fast Interprocedural Alias Analysis. In *16th Annual ACM Symposium on Principles of Programming Languages*, held in Austin, Tex., January, 49-59.

Cormen, Thomas H., Charles E. Leiserson, and Ronald L. Rivest (1990). *The Design and Analysis of Computer Algorithms.* Cambridge, Mass.: MIT Press.

Cytron, Ron, Jeanne Ferrante, and Vivek Sarkar (1990). Compact Representations for Control Dependence. In *ACM SIGPLAN '90 Conference on Programming Language Design and Implementation*, held in White Plains, N.Y., June, 337-351.

Cytron, Ron, and Reid Gershbein (1993). Efficient Accommodation of May-Alias Information in SSA Form. In *ACM SIGPLAN '93 Conference on Programming Language Design and Implementation*, held in Albuquerque, N.M., June, 36-45.

Cytron, Ron, Steve Karlovsky, and Kevin P. McAuliffe (1988). Automatic Management of Programmable Caches. In *1988 International Conference on Parallel Processing*, held in St. Charles, Ill., August, 229-238.

Cytron, Ron, et al. (1991). Efficiently Computing Static Single Assignment Form and the Control Dependence Graph. *ACM Transactions on Programming Languages and Systems*, October, 13(4):451-490.

Dantzig, George B., and B. Curtis Eaves (1973). Fourier-Motzkin Elimination and Its Dual. *Journal of Combinatorial Theory (A)*, 14:288-297.

Darema, F., et al. (1988). A Single-Program-Multiple-Data Computational Model for EPEX/Fortran. *Parallel Computing*, April, 7(1):11-24.

Darnell, Ervan, and Ken Kennedy (1993). Cache Coherence Using Local Knowledge. In *Supercomputing '93*, held in Portland, Ore., November, 720-729.

D'Hollander, Erik H. (1992). Partitioning and Labeling of Loops by Unimodular Transformations. *IEEE Transactions on Parallel and Distributed Systems*, July, 3(4):465-476.

Dongarra, Jack J., et al. (1990). A set of Level 3 Basic Linear Algebra Subprograms. *ACM Transactions on Mathematical Software*, March, 16(1):1-17.

Duffin, R. J. (1974). On Fourier's Analysis of Linear Inequality Systems. In *Mathematical Programming Study 1.* New York: North Holland, 71-95.

Emami, Maryam, Rakesh Ghiya, and Laurie J. Hendren (1994). Context-Sensitive Interprocedural Points-to Analysis in the Presence of Function Pointers.

In *ACM SIGPLAN '94 Conference on Programming Language Design and Implementation*, held in Orlando, Fla., June, 242-256.

Erbacci, Giovanni, Guiseppe Paruolo, and Giancarlo Tagliavini (1989). Influence of the Stride on the Cache Utilization in the IBM 3090 VF. In *1989 ACM International Conference on Supercomputing*, held in Crete, Greece, June, 443-451.

Feautrier, Paul (1988). Parametric Integer Programming. *Operations Research*, 22(3):243-268.

—— (1991). Dataflow Analysis of Array and Scalar References. *International Journal of Parallel Programming*, 20(1):23-54.

Ferrante, Jeanne, Karl J. Ottenstein, and Joe D. Warren (1987). The Program Dependence Graph and Its Use in Optimization. *ACM Transactions on Programming Languages and Systems*, July, 9(3):319-349.

Fischer, Charles N., and Richard J. LeBlanc, Jr. (1988). *Crafting a Compiler*. Menlo Park, Calif.: Benjamin-Cummings.

Flynn, Michael J. (1972). Some Computer Organizations and Their Effectiveness. *IEEE Transactions on Computers*, September, C-21(9):948-960.

Gannon, Dennis, William Jalby, and Kyle Gallivan (1988). Strategies for Cache and Local Memory Management by Global Program Transformation. *Journal of Parallel and Distributed Computing*, October, 5(5):587-616.

Goodman, James R. (1983). Using Cache Memory to Reduce Processor-Memory Traffic. In *10th International Symposium on Computer Architecture*, held in Stockholm, Sweden, June, 124-131.

Gornish, Edward H., Elana D. Granston, and Alexander V. Veidenbaum (1990). Compiler-Directed Data Prefetching in Multiprocessors with Memory Hierarchies. In *1990 ACM International Conference on Supercomputing*, held in Amsterdam, The Netherlands, June, 354-368.

Granlund, Torbjörn, and Peter L. Montgomery (1994). Division by Invariant Integers Using Multiplication. In *ACM SIGPLAN '94 Conference on Programming Language Design and Implementation*, held in Orlando, Fla., June, 61-72.

Gries, David, and Fred B. Schneider (1993). *A Logical Approach to Discrete Math*. Texts and Monographs in Computer Science. Berlin: Springer Verlag.

Grove, Dan, and Linda Torczon (1993). Interprocedural Constant Propagation: A Study of Jump Function Implementations. In *ACM SIGPLAN '93 Conference on Programming Language Design and Implementation*, held in Albuquerque, N.M., June, 90-99.

Gupta, Manish, and Prithviraj Banerjee (1993). PARADIGM: A Compiler for Automatic Data Distribution on Multicomputers. In *1993 ACM International Conference on Supercomputing*, held in Tokyo, July, 87-96.

Gupta, S. K. S., et al. (1993). On Compiling Array Expressions for Efficient Execution on Distributed-Memory Machines. In *1993 International Conference on Parallel Processing*, vol. II, held in St. Charles, Ill., August, 301–305.

Hall, Mary W., and Ken Kennedy (1992). Efficient Call Graph Analysis. *ACM Letters on Programming Languages and Systems*, September, 1(3):227–242.

Hall, Mary W., Ken Kennedy, and Kathryn S. McKinley (1991). Interprocedural Transformations for Parallel Code Generation. In *Supercomputing '91*, held in Albuquerque, N.M., November, 424–434.

Harbison, Samuel P., and Guy L. Steele, Jr. (1991). *C: A Reference Manual*, third edition. Englewood Cliffs, N.J.: Prentice-Hall.

Hatcher, Philip J., and Michael J. Quinn (1991). *Data-Parallel Programming on MIMD Computers*. Scientific and Engineering Computation Series. Cambridge, Mass.: MIT Press.

Havlak, Paul (1993). Construction of Thinned Gated Single-Assignment Form. In *1993 Workshop on Languages and Compilers for Parallel Computing*, held in Portland, Ore., August, number 768 in Lecture Notes in Computer Science, Berlin: Springer Verlag, 477–499.

Havlak, Paul, and Ken Kennedy (1991). An Implementation of Interprocedural Bounded Regular Section Analysis. *IEEE Transactions on Parallel and Distributed Systems*, July, 2(3):350–360.

Hendren, Laurie J., Joseph Hummel, and Alexandru Nicolau (1992). Abstractions for Recursive Pointer Data Structures: Improving the Analysis and Transformation of Imperative Programs. In *ACM SIGPLAN '92 Conference on Programming Language Design and Implementation*, held in San Francisco, Calif., June, 249–260.

Hennessy, John L., and David A. Patterson (1990). *Computer Architecture: A Quantitative Approach*. Palo Alto, Calif.: Morgan Kaufmann.

Hill, Mark D., and James R. Larus (1990). Cache Considerations for Multiprocessor Programmers. *Communications of the ACM*, August, 33(8):97–102.

Hiranandani, Seema, Ken Kennedy, and Chau-Wen Tseng (1992). Compiling Fortran D for MIMD Distributed Memory Machines. *Communications of the ACM*, August, 35(8):66–88.

Hummel, Susan Flynn, Edith Schonberg, and Lawrence E. Flynn (1992). Factoring: A Method for Scheduling Parallel Loops. *Communications of the ACM*, August, 35(8):90–101.

Hwang, Kai (1993). *Advanced Computer Architecture: Parallelism, Scalability, Programmability*. New York: McGraw-Hill.

Irigoin, François, and Rémi Triolet (1988). Supernode Partitioning. In *15th Annual ACM Symposium on Principles of Programming Languages*, held in San Diego, Calif., January, 319–329.

Jalby, William, and Ulrike Meier (1986). Optimizing Matrix Operations on a Parallel Multiprocessor with a Hierarchical Memory System. In *1986 International Conference on Parallel Processing*, held in St. Charles, Ill., August, 429-432.

Johnson, Richard, and Keshav Pingali (1993). Dependence-Based Program Analysis. In *ACM SIGPLAN '93 Conference on Programming Language Design and Implementation*, held in Albuquerque, N.M., June, 78-89.

Jones, Neil D., and Steven S. Muchnick (1981). Flow Analysis and Optimization of Lisp-like Structures. In *Program Flow Analysis: Theory and Applications*, Steven S. Muchnick and Neil D. Jones, eds. Englewood Cliffs, N.J.: Prentice-Hall, 102-131.

Karp, Richard M., Raymond E. Miller, and Shmuel Winograd (1967). The Organization of Computations for Uniform Recurrence Equations. *Journal of the ACM*, July, 14(3):563-590.

Kennedy, Ken, and Gerald Roth (1994). Context Optimization for SIMD Execution. In *Scalable High Performance Computing Conference*, held in Knoxville, Tenn., November, 445-453.

Knobe, Kathleen, Joan D. Lukas, and Michael Weiss (1993). Optimization Techniques for SIMD Fortran Compilers. *Concurrency: Practice & Experience*, October, 5(7):527-552.

Koelbel, Charles H., et al. (1994). *The High Performance Fortran Handbook*. Cambridge, Mass.: MIT Press.

Kuck, David J., et al. (1980). The Structure of an Advanced Vectorizer for Pipelined Processors. In *Proc. 4th International Computer Software and Applications Conf.*, held in Chicago, October, 709-715.

——— (1981). Dependence Graphs and Compiler Optimizations. In *8th Annual ACM Symposium on Principles of Programming Languages*, January, 207-218.

——— (1984). The Effects of Program Restructuring, Algorithm Change, and Architecture Choice on Program Performance. In *1984 International Conference on Parallel Processing*, held in St. Charles, Ill., August, 129-138.

Kuhn, Robert H. (1980). Optimization and Interconnection Complexity for: Parallel Processors, Single Stage Networks, and Decision Trees. Ph.D. Dissertation UIUCDCS-R-80-1009, University of Illinois, Dept. Computer Science, February (UMI 80-26541).

Kung, H. T., and Jaspal Subhlok (1991). A New Approach for Automatic Parallelization of Blocked Linear Algebra Computations. In *Supercomputing '91*, held in Albuquerque, N.M., November, 122-129.

Lam, Monica S., Edward E. Rothberg, and Michael E. Wolf (1991). The Cache Performance and Optimizations of Blocked Algorithms. In *4th International Conference on Architectural Support for Programming Languages and Operating Systems*, held in Santa Clara, Calif., April, 63-74.

Larus, James R. (1993). Compiling for Shared-Memory and Message-Passing Computers. *ACM Letters on Programming Languages and Systems*, 2:165-180.

Lengauer, Thomas, and Robert E. Tarjan (1979). A Fast Algorithm for Finding Dominators in a Flow Graph. *ACM Transactions on Programming Languages and Systems*, July, 1(1):121-141.

Li, Jingke, and Marina C. Chen (1991a). Compiling Communication-Efficient Programs for Massively Parallel Machines. *IEEE Transactions on Parallel and Distributed Systems*, July, 2(3):361-376.

—— (1991b). The Data Alignment Phase in Compiling Programs for Distributed-Memory Machines. *Journal of Parallel and Distributed Computing*, October, 13(2):213-221.

Li, Jingke, and Michael Wolfe (1994). Defining, Analyzing, and Transforming Program Constructs. *IEEE Parallel & Distributed Technology*, Spring, 2(1):32-39.

Li, Wei, and Keshav Pingali (1994). A Singular Loop Transformation Framework Based on Nonsingular Matrices. *International Journal of Parallel Programming*, April, 22(2):183-205.

Lippman, Stanley B. (1991). *C++ Primer*, second edition. Reading, Mass.: Addison-Wesley.

Loveman, David B. (1977). Program Improvement by Source-to-Source Transformation. *Communications of the ACM*, January, 20(1):121-145.

Lu, Lee-Chung, and Marina C. Chen (1990). Subdomain Dependence Test for Massive Parallelism. In *Supercomputing '90*, held in New York, November, 962-972.

MacDonald, Tom (1991). C for Numerical Computing. *The Journal of Supercomputing*, June, 5(1):31-48.

Markatos, Evangelos P., and Thomas J. LeBlanc (1994). Using Processor Affinity in Loop Scheduling on Shared-Memory Multiprocessors. *IEEE Transactions on Parallel and Distributed Systems*, April, 5(4):379-400.

Marlowe, Thomas J., et al. (1993). Pointer-Induced Aliasing: A Clarification. *Sigplan Notices*, September, 28(9):67-70.

Maslov, Vadim (1992). Delinearization: An Efficient Way to Break Multiloop Dependence Equations. In *ACM SIGPLAN '92 Conference on Programming Language Design and Implementation*, held in San Francisco, Calif., June, 152-161.

Maydan, Dror E., Saman P. Amarasinghe, and Monica S. Lam (1993). Array Data-Flow Analysis and Its Use in Array Privatization. In *20th Annual ACM Symposium on Principles of Programming Languages*, held in Charleston, S.C., January, 2-15.

Maydan, Dror E., John L. Hennessy, and Monica S. Lam (1991). Efficient and Exact Data Dependence Analysis. In *ACM SIGPLAN '91 Conference on Programming Language Design and Implementation*, held in Toronto, Ont., June, 1–14.

McKellar, A. C., and E. G. Coffman, Jr. (1969). Organizing Matrices and Matrix Operations for Paged Memory Systems. *Communications of the ACM*, March, 12(3):153–165.

Metcalf, Michael, and John Reid (1990). *Fortran 90 Explained.* Oxford, England: Oxford University Press.

Min, Sang Lyul, and Jean-Loup Baer (1990). A Performance Comparison of Directory-Based and Timestamp-Based Cache Coherence Schemes. In *1990 International Conference on Parallel Processing*, vol. I, held in St. Charles, Ill., August, 305–311.

Nemhauser, George L., and Laurence A. Wolsey (1988). *Integer and Combinatorial Optimization.* New York: John Wiley & Sons.

O'Boyle, Michael, and G. A. Hedayat (1992). Data Alignment: Transformations to Reduce Communication on Distributed Memory Architectures. In *Scalable High Performance Computing Conference*, held in Williamsburg, Va., April, 366–371.

Padua, David A., David J. Kuck, and Duncan H. Lawrie (1980). High-Speed Multiprocessors and Compilation Techniques. *IEEE Transactions on Computers*, September, C-29(9):763–776.

Peir, Jih-Kwon, and Ron Cytron (1989). Minimum Distance: A Method for Partitioning Recurrences for Multiprocessors. *IEEE Transactions on Computers*, August, 38(8):1203–1211.

Petersen, Paul M., and David A. Padua (1993). Static and Dynamic Evaluation of Data Dependence Analysis. In *1993 ACM International Conference on Supercomputing*, held in Tokyo, July, 107–116.

Polychronopoulos, Constantine D. (1987). Loop Coalescing: A Compiler Transformation for Parallel Machines. In *1987 International Conference on Parallel Processing*, held in St. Charles, Ill., August, 235–242.

——— (1988a). Compiler Optimizations for Enhancing Parallelism and Their Impact on Architecture Design. *IEEE Transactions on Computers*, August, 37(8):991–1004.

——— (1988b). *Parallel Programming and Compilers.* Norwell, Mass.: Kluwer Academic Publishers.

Polychronopoulos, Constantine D., and David J. Kuck (1987). Guided Self-Scheduling: A Practical Scheduling Scheme for Parallel Supercomputers. *IEEE Transactions on Computers*, December, C-36(12):1485–1495.

Psarris, Kleanthis, David Klappholz, and Xiangyun Kong (1991). On the Accuracy of the Banerjee Test. *Journal of Parallel and Distributed Computing*, June, 12(2):152–158.

Pugh, William (1992). A Practical Algorithm for Exact Array Dependence Analysis. *Communications of the ACM*, August, 35(8):102–114.

Pugh, William, and David Wonnacott (1993). An Exact Method for Analysis of Value-Based Array Data Dependences. In *1993 Workshop on Languages and Compilers for Parallel Computing*, held in Portland, Ore., August, number 768 in Lecture Notes in Computer Science, Berlin: Springer Verlag, 546–566.

Rogers, Anne, and Keshav Pingali (1994). Compiling for Distributed Memory Architectures. *IEEE Transactions on Parallel and Distributed Systems*, March, 5(3):281–298.

Ryder, Barbara G. (1979). Constructing the Call Graph of a Program. *IEEE Transactions on Software Engineering*, May, SE-5(3):216–226.

Schneck, Paul B. (1972). Automatic Recognition of Vector and Parallel Operations in a Higher Level Language. *Sigplan Notices*, November, 7(11):45–52.

Schrijver, A. (1986). *Theory of Linear and Integer Programming*. Chichester, England: John Wiley & Sons.

Stanat, Donald F., and David F. McAllister (1977). *Discrete Mathematics in Computer Science*. Englewood Cliffs, N.J.: Prentice-Hall.

Tarjan, Robert E. (1972). Depth-First Search and Linear Graph Algorithms. *SIAM Journal of Computing*, June, 1(2):146–160.

Temam, Olivier, Elana D. Granston, and William Jalby (1993). To Copy or Not to Copy: A Compile-Time Technique for Assessing When Data Copying Should be Used to Eliminate Cache Conflicts. In *Supercomputing '93*, held in Portland, Ore., November, 410–419.

Tremblay, Jean-Paul, and Ram P. Manohar (1975). *Discrete Mathematical Structures with Application to Computer Science*. New York: McGraw-Hill.

Triolet, Rémi, François Irigoin, and Paul Feautrier (1986). Direct Parallelization of Call Statements. In *ACM SIGPLAN '86 Symposium on Compiler Construction*, held in Palo Alto, Calif., June, 175–185.

Tsuda, Takao, and Yoshitoshi Kunieda (1990). V-Pascal: An Automatic Vectorizing Compiler for Pascal with No Language Extensions. *The Journal of Supercomputing*, September, 4(3):251–276.

Tzen, Ten H., and Lionel M. Ni (1993). Trapezoid Self-Scheduling: A Practical Scheduling Scheme for Parallel Compilers. *IEEE Transactions on Parallel and Distributed Systems*, January, 4(1):87–98.

Veidenbaum, Alexander V. (1986). A Compiler-Assisted Cache Coherence Solution for Multiprocessors. In *1986 International Conference on Parallel Processing*, held in St. Charles, Ill., August, 1029–1036.

Wegman, Mark N., and F. Kenneth Zadeck (1991). Constant Propagation with Conditional Branches. *ACM Transactions on Programming Languages and Systems*, April, 13(2):181–210.

REFERENCES

Williams, H. P. (1976). Fourier-Motzkin Elimination Extension to Integer Programming Problems. *Journal of Combinatorial Theory (A)*, 21:118-123.

—— (1983). A Characterisation of All Feasible Solutions to an Integer Program. *Discrete Applied Mathematics*, 5:147-155.

Wolf, Michael E., and Monica S. Lam (1991a). A Loop Transformation Theory and an Algorithm to Maximize Parallelism. *IEEE Transactions on Parallel and Distributed Systems*, October, 2(4):452-471.

—— (1991b). A Data Locality Optimizing Algorithm. In *ACM SIGPLAN '91 Conference on Programming Language Design and Implementation*, held in Toronto, Ont., June, 30-44.

Wolfe, Michael (1989). *Optimizing Supercompilers for Supercomputers.* Research Monographs in Parallel and Distributed Computing. Cambridge, Mass.: MIT Press.

—— (1992). Beyond Induction Variables. In *ACM SIGPLAN '92 Conference on Programming Language Design and Implementation*, held in San Francisco, Calif., June, 162-174.

Zima, Hans P., Heinz-J. Bast, and Michael Gerndt (1988). SUPERB: A Tool for Semi-Automatic MIMD/SIMD Parallelization. *Parallel Computing*, January, 6(1):1-18.

Zima, Hans P., and Barbara M. Chapman (1991). *Supercompilers for Parallel and Vector Computers.* New York: ACM Press.

—— (1993). Compiling for Distributed-Memory Systems. *Proceedings of the IEEE*, February, 81(2):264-287.

AUTHOR INDEX

Abu-Sufah, Walid A. 382
Adams, Jeanne C. 46
Aho, Alfred V. 26, 79
Allen, Frances E. 26, 362
Allen, J. Randy 26, 162, 445
Ancourt, Corinne 363
Anderson, Jennifer M. 510
Appelbe, William F. 526

Backus, John 46
Baer, Jean-Loup 527
Ballance, Robert A. 219
Banerjee, Prithviraj 510
Banerjee, Utpal 26, 133, 160,
      256, 363, 419, 445
Barth, Jeffrey M. 304
Bernstein, A. J. 162
Bik, Aart J. C. 420
Brandes, Thomas 162
Burke, Michael 256

Callahan, David 219, 304, 382
Cann, David 47
Carr, Steve 382
Chapman, Barbara M. .. 26, 509-510
Chatterjee, Siddhartha 509
Chen, Marina C. 256, 510
Cheong, Hoichi 526
Choi, Jong-Deok 219
Cocke, John 362
Coffman, E. G., Jr. 382
Cohagan, William L. 363
Cooper, Keith D. 304, 363
Cormen, Thomas H. 79
Cytron, Ron 80, 219, 256,
      420, 526

Dantzig, George B. 133
Darema, F. 26
Darnell, Ervan 527

D'Hollander, Erik H. 420
Dongarra, Jack J. 382
Duffin, R. J. 133

Eaves, B. Curtis 133
Emami, Maryam 304
Erbacci, Giovanni 445

Feautrier, Paul 133, 256
Ferrante, Jeanne 79
Fischer, Charles N. 26
Flynn, Michael J. 26

Gajski, Daniel D. 445
Gannon, Dennis 382
Gershbein, Reid 219
Goodman, James R. 382
Gornish, Edward H. 382
Granlund, Torbjörn 510
Gries, David 79
Grove, Dan 304
Gupta, Manish 510
Gupta, S. K. S. 509

Hall, Mary W. 304, 363
Harbison, Samuel P. 47
Hatcher, Philip J. 420
Havlak, Paul 219, 304
Hedayat, G. A. 510
Hendren, Laurie J. 304
Hennessy, John L. 526
Hill, Mark D. 420
Hiranandani, Seema 510
Hummel, Susan Flynn 419
Hwang, Kai 26

Irigoin, François 363

Jalby, William 420
Johnson, Richard 219

AUTHOR INDEX

Jones, Neil D. 304

Karp, Richard M. 162, 256, 363
Kennedy, Ken 26, 162, 304, 382, 445, 510, 527
Knobe, Kathleen 510
Koelbel, Charles H. 46
Kuck, David J. 26, 162, 419, 445
Kuhn, Robert H. 256
Kung, H. T. 510
Kunieda, Yoshitoshi 445

Lakshmanan, Balakrishnan 526
Lam, Monica S. .. 363, 382, 420, 510
Larus, James R. 420, 527
LeBlanc, Richard J., Jr. 26
LeBlanc, Thomas J. 526
Lengauer, Thomas 79
Li, Jingke 47, 510
Li, Wei 363
Lippman, Stanley B. 47
Loveman, David B. 362
Lu, Lee-Chung 256

MacDonald, Tom 47
Manohar, Ram P. 79
Markatos, Evangelos P. 526
Marlowe, Thomas J. 304
Maslov, Vadim 256
Maydan, Dror E. 256
McAllister, David F. 79
McKellar, A. C. 382
Meier, Ulrike 420
Metcalf, Michael 46
Min, Sang Lyul 527
Montgomery, Peter L. 510
Muchnick, Steven S. 304

Nemhauser, George L. 133
Ni, Lionel M. 419

O'Boyle, Michael 510

Padua, David A. 256, 419

Patterson, David A. 526
Peir, Jih-Kwon 420
Petersen, Paul M. 256
Pingali, Keshav 219, 363, 509
Polychronopoulos, Constantine D. .. 363, 419-420
Porterfield, Allan 382
Psarris, Kleanthis 256
Pugh, William 133, 256

Quinn, Michael J. 420

Reid, John 46
Rogers, Anne 509
Roth, Gerald 510
Ryder, Barbara G. 304

Schneck, Paul B. 445
Schneider, Fred B. 79
Schrijver, A. 133
Stanat, Donald F. 79
Steele, Guy L., Jr. 47
Subhlok, Jaspal 510

Tarjan, Robert E. 79
Temam, Olivier 382
Torczon, Linda 304
Tremblay, Jean-Paul 79
Triolet, Rémi 304, 363
Tsuda, Takao 445
Tzen, Ten H. 419

Veidenbaum, Alexander V. 526-527

Wegman, Mark N. 219
Wijshoff, Harry A. G. 420
Williams, H. P. 133
Wolf, Michael E. 363, 382, 420
Wolfe, Michael 26, 47, 219
Wolsey, Laurence A. 133
Wonnacott, David 256

Zadeck, F. Kenneth 219
Zima, Hans P. 26, 509

INDEX

access function 480
access matrix
    data 480
active indices 464, 478
active layer 464
active offset 467
active PE 467
acyclic condensation 64, 324
address-based
    data dependence 138
adjacent vertex 50
advance instruction 394
advancing edge 57, 60
affine array access 480
affine function 129
affine subscripts 224
affinity scheduling 515
algorithm BackSubstitute 104
algorithm DOM 65
algorithm DomFront 69, 73
algorithm Extreme 131
algorithm FM 120
algorithm FMint 124, 335, 343, 346, 481
algorithm GCD 96, 107
algorithm GE 102
algorithm Hermite 98, 349
algorithm IntegerInequality 128
algorithm Invert 93
algorithm ReduceMatrix 115
algorithm SCC 60
alias 35
    dynamic 187
    equivalence classes 188
    may 187
    must 187
    static 187
alignment 37, 322, 403, 455

alignment graph 404, 503
alignment template 454
analysis
    points-to 277
ancestor 53
anti-dependence 137
architecture
    cache-only 514–515
    latency-sensitive 514
    latency-tolerant 515
argument
    pass-by-reference 184
    pass-by-value 184
array access
    affine 480
array contraction 402
array inflation 453
array pointer 283
await instruction 394
axis alignment graph 503

back edge 67
back end 449
back substitution 104, 150
barrier 14
basic block 56
basis vectors
    lattice 98
    subspace 85
binding graph 294
block distribution 452
block scheduling 387
block-cyclic distribution 452
body
    loop 67
bound
    lower 118
    simple 118, 261
    upper 118

INDEX

breadth-first traversal 53
broadcast 19, 21
buffer
    communication 480, 493

cache
    hit 5
    line 5
    memory 5
    miss 5
    stale data in 523
cache block 367
cache line 367, 517-519
cache memory 367, 514
cache miss
    capacity 521
    coherence 521
    compulsory 521
    conflict 521
cache policy
    copy-back 521
    write-allocate 521
    write-back 521
    write-exclusive 519, 521
    write-through 521
    write-update 519, 521
cache-only memory architecture ....
    514-515
cactus stack 399
call graph 290
capacity miss 521
cardinality 49
carry-around variable 444
CFG 56
    Entry 56
    Exit 69
    spanning forest 59
    spanning tree 56
child 53
circular loop skewing 356
cluster 515
coalescing 360
cofactor 92

coherence miss 521
collapsed dimension 455
collapsing
    loop 358, 443
column vector 87
COMA 514-515
common blocks 252
communication
    buffer 480, 493
    regular 480
    transit time 479
    vectorization 494
compulsory miss 521
conflict miss 521
conservative union 266
constant propagation
    interprocedural 300
context 450-451, 464
contraction
    array 402
control dependence 71
    graph 73
control equivalent 83
control flow graph 56
    dominator 64
convex hull 91
convex set 91
copy-back cache 521
correctness preserving 23
countable loop 201
coupled
    dependence equations 242
coupled reduction 401, 426
critical section 387, 393
    ordered 394
cross edge 57, 60
cross-loop
    dependence 320
cross-loop distance 320
cross-tree edge 60
cumulative reuse factor 377
cycle shrinking 407, 414
cyclic distribution 452
cyclic scheduling 387

INDEX

DAG 51
data access conflict 155
data access matrix ... 273, 480, 516
data dependence 137, 224
    loop carried 140
    loop independent 140
data distribution 38
data footprint 371
data hazard 24
data offset vector 273, 480
data parallelism 16, 19
definition
    killing 180
    nonkilling 180
def-use chain 166
degree of footprint 372
degree of reuse 372
dense lattice 98–99
dependence
    equation 225
    address-based 138
    anti- 137
    common blocks 252
    control 71, 73
    coupled equations 242
    data 137
    direction vector hierarchy . 239
    distance 141
    equation 225
        separable 242
        splitting 244
    equivalence statement 250
    false 138
    flow 137
    graph 137, 160
        iteration space 141
    input 139
    interchange-sensitive 332

I/O 288
    level 146
    lexically backward 140
    lexically forward 140
    loop carried 146
    loop independent 146
    output 137
    reuse 381
    run-time 436
    system 224–225
    true 138
    value-based 138
dependence cross-loop 320
dependence distance 142
dependence solver
    extreme value test 236
    gcd test 235
    generalized gcd 246
    pointer 277
    simple test 234
    strong 234
    two variable exact test 238
dependent variable 106
depth-first spanning forest ... 59–60
depth-first traversal 53
descendant 53
determinant 92
DFST 57
diagonal matrix 87
directed acyclic graph 51
directed graph 51
direction vector 144, 160
direction vector hierarchy 239
distance
    cross-loop 320
    dependence 141–142
    reuse 367, 376
    vector 143
distribution 323, 458
    block 452
    block-cyclic 452
    collapsed dimension 455

INDEX

cyclic 452
replication 456
template 454
doacross 43
doall 42
dominance frontier 68
dominator 64
back edge 67
dominance frontier 68
immediate 65
post dominator 69
region 67
strict 65
tree 65
dopar 41, 156
dope vector 34, 283, 462
dosingle 43
dot-product 87
dynamic alias 187
dynamically allocated arrays ... 254

echelon form 115
edge 50
advancing 57, 60
cross 57, 60
cross-tree 60
retreating 57, 60
slicing 72
source 51
target 51
tree 57, 60
element loop 350
elementary row operations 89
embedding loops 361
ensemble
processor 448
Entry 51, 56
epoch 523
equivalence classes
alias 188
equivalence statement 250

executor 500
Exit 51, 69, 78
expansion of a scalar 313
extreme value test 236

factor
innermost reuse 379
factored redef-use chains 216
factored use-def chains 168
factoring 388
false dependence 138
false sharing 517
fission 323
loop 440
flow dependence 137
footprint 371
degree 372
forall 41, 155
fork 14
Fortran
High Performance 37
sequence association 35
storage association 35
Fortran 90 pointer 283
Fourier-Motzkin projection 119,
247, 335, 345, 347
for integers 123
front end 449
FRUD chains 216
FUD chain 168
arrays 180, 188
construction 169
graph 191
records 188
structures 188
fully permutable 416
function
access 480
affine 129
intrinsic 289
linear 88
pure 289
fusion 315

Gaussian elimination 101
gcd 93, 107
gcd test 235
generalized cycle shrinking 414
generalized gcd test 246
graph 50
    acyclic 51
    alignment 404
    axis alignment 503
    binding 294
    control dependence 73
    control flow 56
    dependence 137, 160
    directed 51, 56
    dominator 64
    edge 50
    FUD chain 191
    multigraph 52
    node 50
    path 51
    program dependence 160
    reuse dependence 381
    single-entry 52
    single-exit 52, 78
    spanning forest 59
    tree 53
    undirected 50
    vertex 50
    DAG 51
greatest common divisor ... 93, 107
greatest common divisor test ... 235
group reuse 376
group reuse factor 377
group-spatial reuse 376
group-temporal reuse 376
guided self-scheduling 388

half-space 91
header 67
height
    tree 53
Hermite normal form ... 97, 414, 481
Hermite trapezoidal form 98

High Performance Fortran 37
hit
    cache 5
HNF 414, 481
HPF 37

identity matrix 88
image 88
immediate dominator 65
IN set 139
indegree 51
independent variable 106
index set partitioning 414
index set splitting 312, 435
index variable
    iteration vector 141
indices
    active 464, 478
induction variable
    basic 192
inequality
    linear 117
    redundant 118
inflation 453
inlining
    procedure 360
innermost reuse 379
innermost reuse factor 379
innermosting 334
input dependence 139
input/output dependence 288
inspector 500
inspector/executor 500
integration
    procedure 360
interchange-sensitive dependence ... 332
interchanging 331, 344, 413
    loop 440
    trapezoidal loop 335
    triangular loop 335
interprocedural analysis
    backward 289

constant propagation 300
    forward 289
    MOD analysis 292
intrinsic function 289
inverse matrix 88
I/O dependence 288
iteration space 141
    dependence graph 141
iteration vector 141, 147
    index variable 141
    normalized 142, 147
    seminormalized 147

jamming loops 361
join 170
jump function 300

kernel 88
kill 262
killing definition 180

last value assignment 314, 323
latency tolerant 515
lattice 98
    basis vectors 98
    dense 98–99
    point 98
layer
    active 464
leaf 53
level
    of a dependence 146
    of a node in tree 53
lexically backward 140
lexically forward 140
lexicographically less than 86
lexicographically nonnegative ... 86
lexicographically positive 86
liberal union 266
linear combination 84
linear function 88
linear inequality 117
linear recurrences 405

linear subscripts 224
linear transformation 344
linearization 243
locality 16
    sequential 368
    spatial 368
    temporal 368
locality-sensitive 514
loop 67
    coalescing 360
    countable 201
    doacross 43
    doall 42
    dopar 41, 156
    dosingle 43
    forall 41, 155
    postbody 68
    preheader 68
    trapezoidal 147, 335
    triangular 147, 335
    trip count 200, 234
loop alignment 322, 403
loop body 67
loop carried
    dependence 140, 146
loop collapsing 358, 443
loop distribution 323
loop embedding 361
loop extraction 361
loop fission 323, 440
loop fusion 315
loop header 67
loop header ϕ 192
loop independent dependence ......
    140, 146
loop interchanging 6, 12, 331,
    344, 413, 440
    innermosting 334
    outermosting 334
loop jamming 361
loop peeling 164, 200, 311, 318
loop reordering 6
loop reversal 330, 344

loop skewing 342, 344
    circular 356
loop splitting 312, 318
loop striping 357, 378, 407
loop tiling 8, 352, 369, 515
loops
    nontightly nested 150
    tightly nested 150, 332
lower bound 118
lowering 22

matrix 87
    data access 273, 480
    determinant of 92
    diagonal 87
    echelon form of 115
    elementary lower triangular 102
    elementary operations 89
    identity 88
    image of 88
    inverse of 88
    kernel of 88
    nonsingular 88
    null space of 88, 371
    nullity of 88
    permutation 91
    product 87
    range of 88
    rank of 88
    scale 89
    singular 88
    skew 90
    square 87
    symmetric 87
    transpose of 87
    transposition 90
    trapezoidal 87
    triangular 87
    unimodular 96, 345
    unimodular operations 97
    zero 88
may alias 187
memory hierarchy 367

Merge function 466
miss
    cache 5
MOD analysis 292
modify 262
moly variable 457, 513
mono variable 450, 457
multicomputer 19
multigraph 52
multiprocessor 13
multivector computer 443
must alias 187

natural loop 67
negative part 129
neighbor 50
node 50, 448, 451
    adjacent 50
    entry 51
    exit 51
    indegree 51
    neighbor 50
    outdegree 51
    sink 51
    source 51, 56
node program 452
node splitting 444
nonkilling definition 180
nonsingular matrix 88
nontightly nested loops 150
nonuniform memory access 515
normalized iteration vectors ... 142, 147
null space 88, 371
nullity 88
NUMA 515
numbering
    postorder 55
    preorder 53

offset
    active 467
    template 459

ordered critical section 394
origin
        template 458–459
OUT set 139
outdegree 51
outermosting 334
output dependence 137
overlap region 493
owner-computes rule 478

parallel loop
        doacross 43
        doall 42
        dopar 41, 156
        dosingle 43
        forall 41, 155
parameter
        pass-by-reference 184
        pass-by-value 184
parent 53
partial vectorization 427
partitioning 414
pass-by-reference 184
pass-by-value 184
path 51
        cyclic 51
PDG 160
PE 448
        active 467
peeling a loop ... 164, 200, 311, 318
permutation matrix 91
phantom global variable 185

ϕ-term 168
        loop header 192

pipeline parallelism 508
pipelining 508
pointer
        array 283
        dependence 277
        Fortran 90 283
points-to analysis 277

poly variable 450, 457
polyhedron 91
polytope 91
positive part 129
post dominator 69
        strict 70
postbody 68
postorder numbering 55
postorder traversal 54
precedence graph 138
predecessor 51
prefetch 375
preheader 68
preorder numbering 53
preorder traversal 53
prescheduling 387
private variable 392
privatization 400
procedure Extreme 131
procedure Findgcd 96
procedure GE 102
procedure Hermite 98
procedure inlining 360
procedure integration 360
procedure Project 120
procedure Projectint 124
procedure Reducemat 115
processing element 448
processor ensemble 448
program dependence graph 160
promotion of a scalar 313
pure function 289
pure subroutine 289

range 88
rank 88
reachable nodes 51
reaching definitions 166
recurrences 405
reducible graph 263
reduction 392, 401, 424, 426
        coupled 401, 426
redundant inequality 118

region 67
regular communication 480
remote fetch 479
reordering
    statements 308
replication 456
restructuring
    circular loop skewing 356
    linear transformation 344
    loop distribution 323
    loop embedding 361
    loop extraction 361
    loop fission 323
    loop fusion 315
    loop interchanging ... 331, 344, 413
    loop reversal 330, 344
    loop skewing 342, 344
    loop tiling 352, 369, 515
    sinking 337
    strip-mining 350
retreating edge 57, 60
reuse
    degree 372
    group 376
    group-spatial 376
    group-temporal 376
    self-temporal 371
    sequential 368
    spatial 367
    temporal 367
reuse dependence graph 381
reuse distance 367, 376
reuse factor 371, 376
    cumulative 377
    group 377
    innermost 379
reversal 330, 344
root 53
roundoff error 401, 417, 426
row vector 87
row-major 32
run-time dependence 436

safe 23
SAXPY 28
scalar expansion 313, 400, 426
scalar promotion 313
scale
    matrix rows 89
    vector 84
scale matrix 89
SCC 60
scheduling
    affinity 515
    block 387
    cyclic 387
    self 387
SCR 60
self-conflict 274
self-loop 251
self-scheduling 387
    factoring 388
    guided 388
self-temporal reuse 371
seminormalized
    iteration vectors 147
separable
    dependence equation 242
sequence association 35
sequential locality 368
sequential reuse 368
set 49
    cardinality 49
    convex 91
shadow copy 498
sibling 53
SIMD 16
    back end 449
    context 450, 451, 464
    front end 449
simple bound 118, 261
simple bounds 261
simple test 234
single-entry graph 52
single-exit graph 52, 78
singular matrix 88

INDEX

sink node 51
sinking 152, 164, 337
skew
     matrix rows 89
skew matrix 90
skewing 342, 344
slicing edge 72
source 51
source node 51, 56
span 85
spanning forest 59–60
     advancing edge 60
     cross edge 60
     depth-first 59
     retreating edge 60
     tree edge 60
spanning tree 56
     advancing edge 57
     cross edge 57
     depth-first 57
     retreating edge 57
     tree edge 57
spatial locality 368
spatial reuse 367
SPDD 20, 452
splitting 312, 318
     dependence equation 244
SPMD 20, 452
square matrix 87
stale cache line 523
statement reordering 308
static alias 187
storage association 35
strict dominator 65
stride 422
stride-1 dimension 368
stride-1 loop 368
strip loop 350
strip-mining 350
striping 357, 378, 407
strip-mining 11, 18, 21
strong dependence test 234
strongly connected component ... 60

strongly connected region 60
subroutine
     pure 289
subspace 85
     basis vectors 85
successor 51
supervector performance ... 13, 441
symmetric matrix 87
synchronization 385, 393–394
     nested loops 411

target 51
template 37, 454
     offset 459
     origin 458–459
temporal locality 368
temporal reuse 367
thread 525
tightly nested loops 150, 332
tiling 8, 352, 369, 515
time stamps 524
transformations
     peeling 164
     sinking 164
transit time 479
transpose 87
     matrix rows 89
transposition matrix 90
trapezoidal loop 147, 335
trapezoidal matrix 87
tree 53
     ancestor in 53
     child in 53
     descendant in 53
     edge in 57, 60
     height of 53
     leaf in 53
     level in 53
     parent in 53
     root of 53
     sibling in 53
     spanning 56

tree traversal
    breadth-first 53
    depth-first 53
    postorder 54
    preorder 53
triangular loop 147, 335
triangular matrix 87
trip count 200, 234
triplet notation 261
true dependence 138
tuple 49
two variable exact test 238
two-version loops 436

unconstrained variable 118
undirected graph 50
unimodular matrix 96, 345
unimodular row operations 97
unimodular transformation 345
union
    conservative 266
    liberal 266
unit cube 91
unit normal vector 84
unswitching 310, 340
upper bound 118
upward-exposed use 212, 263
use 262
use-def chain 166

value-based
    data dependence 138
variable elimination 101
vector 84
    basis 85, 98
    column 87
    data offset 273, 480
    direction 144, 160

distance 143
dot-product 87
iteration 141
less than 86
lexicographical ordering 86
linear combination 84
linearly dependent 85
linearly independent 85
ordering 86
row 87
span 85
unit normal 84
zero 84
vector conditionals 423
vector processor 8
vector reduction 424
vector stride 422
vectorization 422
    communication 494
    partial 427
vertex 50
    adjacent 50
    indegree 51
    neighbor 50
    outdegree 51
virtual processor 37

widening 265
wrap-around variable 200
write-allocate cache 521
write-back cache 521
write-exclusive cache 519, 521
write-through cache 521
write-update cache 519, 521

zero matrix 88
zero vector 84
zero-trip test 311